Citizenship and Antisemitism in French Colonial Algeria, 1870–1962

Professor Roberts examines the relationship between antisemitism and the practices of citizenship in a colonial context. She focuses on the experience of Algerian Jews and their evolving identity as citizens as they competed with the other populations in the colony, including newly naturalized non-French settlers and Algerian Muslims, for control over the scarce resources of the colonial state. The author argues that this resulted in antisemitic violence and hotly contested debates over the nature of French identity and rights of citizenship. Tracing the ambiguities and tensions that Algerian Jews faced, the book shows that antisemitism was not coherent or stable but changed in response to influences within Algeria, and from metropolitan France, Europe, and the Middle East. Written for a wide audience, this title contributes to several fields including Jewish history, colonial and empire studies, antisemitism within municipal politics, and citizenship, and adds to current debates on transnationalism and globalization.

Sophie B. Roberts is Zantker Assistant Professor of Jewish History and Jewish Studies at the University of Kentucky in Lexington. She received her PhD in History and Jewish Studies from the University of Toronto, Canada, and has previously served as a visiting assistant professor at Stanford University. Proficient in French and Hebrew, she has received several awards and fellowships, including the 2012–2013 Sosland Foundation Fellowship at the Center for Advanced Holocaust Studies at the United States Holocaust Memorial Museum.

Citizenship and Antisemitism in French Colonial Algeria, 1870–1962

Sophie B. Roberts

University of Kentucky

CAMBRIDGE
UNIVERSITY PRESS

CAMBRIDGE
UNIVERSITY PRESS

University Printing House, Cambridge CB2 8BS, United Kingdom

One Liberty Plaza, 20th Floor, New York, NY 10006, USA

477 Williamstown Road, Port Melbourne, VIC 3207, Australia

314–321, 3rd Floor, Plot 3, Splendor Forum, Jasola District Centre, New Delhi – 110025, India

79 Anson Road, #06–04/06, Singapore 079906

Cambridge University Press is part of the University of Cambridge.

It furthers the University's mission by disseminating knowledge in the pursuit of education, learning, and research at the highest international levels of excellence.

www.cambridge.org
Information on this title: www.cambridge.org/9781107188150
DOI: 10.1017/9781316946411

First published 2017

Printed in the United Kingdom by Clays, St Ives plc

A catalogue record for this publication is available from the British Library.

Library of Congress Cataloging-in-Publication Data
Names: Roberts, Sophie B., 1983– author.
Title: Citizenship and antisemitism in French colonial Algeria, 1870–1962 / Sophie B. Roberts.
Description: New York : Cambridge University Press, [2017] | Includes bibliographical references.
Identifiers: LCCN 2017043574 | ISBN 9781107188150
Subjects: LCSH: Jews – Algeria – History – 19th century. | Jews – Algeria – History – 20th century. | Antisemitism – Algeria – History – 19th century. | Antisemitism – Algeria – History – 20th century.
Classification: LCC DS135.A3 R63 2017 | DDC 305.892/406509041–dc23
LC record available at https://lccn.loc.gov/2017043574

ISBN 978-1-107-18815-0 Hardback

Contents

Figures

Preface

This book tackles topics that remind historians that our work is not just to study the past. The central issues of this project are as resonant today as they were in the nineteenth and twentieth centuries. Today the question of national identity, processes of assimilation and integration, and the continued exclusion of certain groups continue to plague all nations, and especially those in Europe. The European Union continues to navigate the complex questions of citizenship and access to it, its translatability, and its relevance in an increasingly complex and entangled world. Antisemitism, which is at the core of this book, still serves political purposes today. France continues to negotiate the complexities of antisemitism and violence in the aftermath of the *Charlie Hebdo* massacre and the attack on the kosher supermarket Hypercacher in Paris in January 2015.

Although Algerian Jews are the central focus of this study, this book considers debates surrounding the meanings of citizenship and the limits imposed upon it by reactionary political antisemitism. Because my subject intersects several topics – Jews in Algeria, antisemitism, citizenship, and municipal government – I draw upon a variety of different archives. Each archive has a particular identity and focus; as a result, multiple archives must be examined in order to triangulate sources. For the core material on the Algerian Jews, I conducted research in a variety of archives in France, Israel, and the United States. I had hoped to go to Algeria to visit their *wilayal* archives, which may contain some further sources on Algerian Jews' political activities; however, there is no clear evidence that relevant sources remain there. Despite the wonderful assistance and support of the directors of the Centre d'Études Maghrébines en Algérie in Oran, my application for a research visa was denied. I am confident, however, that even without being able to access those archives, the story that I tell in the following pages is based on robust evidence and reflects accurately the situation of Algerian Jews' citizenship in the French colonial context. All translations are my own. By using a diverse collection of documents from thirteen archives, I gained access to sources that reflected different interests and perspectives, including those of administrators, journalists, politicians, and Algerian Jews themselves to illustrate the complex experience of Algerian Jewish citizenship. Based on the recent increase in publications on the subject of Algerian Jews, this is an important topic with great resonance for students and scholars of citizenship and national identity today.

The oft-used saying that it "takes a village to raise a child" also holds true for writing a book. This book involved even more than a village – more of an international community of fellow historians, archivists, and kind souls who participated in its development. I am extremely grateful to all the archivists who assisted me during the various research phases of this project: the Alliance Israélite Universelle archives (Paris), the Archives Nationales (Paris), the Central Zionist Archives (Jerusalem), the Centre des Archives d'Outre Mer (Aix-en-Provence), the Centre de la Documentation de l'Historique sur l'Algérie (Aix-en-Provence), Centre de la Documentation Juive Contemporaine (Paris), Hoover Institution Archives, Stanford University (Stanford, CA), Ligue des Droits de l'Homme Archives-BDIC (Nanterre), United States National Archives and Records Administration (College Park, MD), United States Holocaust Memorial Museum and Archives (Washington, DC), YIVO Institute for Jewish Research Library and Archives (New York, NY), and the Yad Vashem Archives (Jerusalem).

I have been truly lucky to have studied with and worked with a wonderful collection of fellow academics and colleagues. My interest in Algerian Jews was first sparked by courses I took with Aron Rodrigue and Steven Zipperstein. Derek Penslar, Eric Jennings, and Doris Bergen shepherded me through the process of developing and conducting a research project, and the sometimes arduous task of writing and revision. They have generously offered their guidance, support, and advice throughout the dissertation and manuscript revision process. In the archives, I worked alongside many kind and generous colleagues, whose collegiality and support helped me enormously. Others have helped me in conversations, by reading parts or all of the manuscript, and through discussions at conferences. A list could never be exhaustive, but I would particularly like to thank Aomar Boum, Joshua Cole, Lien-Hang Nguyen, Karen Petrone, Jeremy Popkin, Aron Rodrigue, Daniel Schroeter, Gretchen Starr-Lebeau, Sarah Abrevaya Stein, Sarah Sussman, and Steve Zipperstein for their intellectual engagement and generosity with their comments, feedback, and stimulation.

I would also like to thank the Center for Advanced Holocaust Studies at the United States Holocaust Memorial Museum in Washington, DC, as well as their staff and archivists who helped me enormously during the revisions of this manuscript, while I was a fellow there. The other fellows there provided me with friendship, coffee, and collegiality as I revised my manuscript. The Taube Center for Jewish Studies at Stanford University sponsored me as I completed final revisions of the manuscript. My colleagues and students at the University of Kentucky offered support and encouragement, even as I spent time away from campus to complete the project. My thanks to my husband, who entered at the end of the project, but whose encouragement and support facilitated the final moments of revisions. Finally, I want to thank my family for everything that they have given me. In particular, I wish to thank my greatest advisor – in history and in life – my father, Richard Roberts. He tirelessly read chapters, drafts, and endless iterations of this book. His advice has made me the scholar and person I am today.

Colonial Algeria

Introduction

In November 1940, a young Algerian Jewish teacher named Edmond wrote a letter to his parents. He described November 11, Armistice Day, a day of celebrating patriotism and veterans, at his school. Just a month earlier, he learned that due to the new antisemitic legislation passed by the collaborationist French government of Vichy, he would no longer be considered a French citizen because he was Jewish. Nor would he be allowed to teach in a French school. Edmond was born a French citizen; his parents were naturalized by the 1870 Crémieux Decree. Edmond had known no other life other than that of a Frenchman, a French citizen. His letter spoke of the deep pain he felt on his last few days teaching his students:

Today is November 11. I watched my little pupils sadly. I spoke to them with my heart, with emotion, of the glorious dead buried on the battlefields. I felt the tears forcing themselves in my eyes, my throat tightened, pressed painfully, by a deep sob. They ignored my secret pain; them: candid, small, pure. My heart bled because I felt how much recent events have impacted me. I thought with despair "but I'm the same, I did not change. These little ones have heard me talk about their country with warmth, with force, with even more conviction than I would want to judge myself, since one cannot judge the sad microcosm that I represent." I do not know if the little students perceived the alteration of my face, as the class breathed in an almost religious silence . . . It causes me so much pain to think that I will leave them soon. I got so used to the little ones. What a joy to instill in these new souls such virtues that will make them later the honest, the good citizen, the ideal towards which I have committed my mind and my heart. I consider myself before God and man as a Frenchman of heart and mind. Nothing will change me. The land of France will never change either. The sky, the sun, her whole face, will always find me moved and grateful for her beauty, her goodness. Because I sense it will remain with me, in the depths of my being, the unfailing mark of the spirit, of reason, of being French. It remains intact, due to the teaching that I received in French schools: My behavior in my external life, as in my internal life, in its most secret meaning, will always be French.[1]

---

[1] Letter from Edmond (no last name recorded) to his parents, Bougie, November 11, 1940, CAOM Alg GGA 6CAB/1. Full information archives appear in the bibliography.

Edmond felt such a deep sense of rupture by the loss of his French citizenship, which was shared by most Algerian Jews. In the seventy years since the 1870 Crémieux Decree, Algerian Jews had become Frenchmen. This was not an easy path. Algerian Jews regularly faced attacks on their new and evolving identities via antisemitism. I found Edmond's letter in a file in the Governor-General's collection in the French colonial archives in a dossier marked "Jews, 1940–1943."[2] The file overflows with letters like Edmond's, often addressed to French government officials, the authors expressing their French identities and begging that they be allowed to maintain their French citizenship.

This book examines the interplay between citizenship and antisemitism in French colonial Algeria. Antisemitism emerged in many different forms in the colony from 1870 to 1962 based on the political, social, and economic exigencies of the time. One of its most salient forms was that located within and around municipal governments, which were the principal arena of civil society in colonial Algeria. Because of antisemitism's ever-changing nature in the colony, it is hard to define. Antisemitism, for the most part, evolved in response to the needs of the time. It was economically oriented during times of economic hardship and politically oriented during electoral periods in particular. It became institutionalized under certain governments, both at the municipal and the national levels. Under antisemitic mayors such as Max Régis of Algiers in the 1890s and Lucien Bellat of Sidi Bel Abbès in the 1930s, antisemitism became institutionalized in municipal government. Under Vichy in World War II, antisemitism became state policy.

In 1870, the Crémieux Decree transformed the Jews of Algeria from colonial subjects into French citizens. Algerian Jews had not agitated aggressively for citizenship in the period leading up to the decree. In the ensuing decades, however, Algerian Jews assimilated to their new status at the behest of their elite and in response to efforts to undermine their rights. Algerian Jewish citizenship became the lightning rod for expressions of political antisemitism by those who resented the Jews' improved status or viewed them as status competitors. Antisemitism in Algeria reflected the particular context of a colonial society and competition for access to power within it. In the colony, citizenship was a precious collection of rights offered only to a small minority of the population. As the principal site of civil society in the colony, competition for the scarce resources of the state took place within municipal governments.

---

[2] "Jews, 1940–1943," CAOM Alg GGA 6CAB/1.

Those who could vote had access to the potential benefits offered by municipal government leadership through systems of patronage. The right to vote, therefore, took on meanings and value beyond civic duty. Because of the centrality of the Crémieux Decree and the citizenship it provided Algerian Jews, this book focuses on the Jews of the three northern departments in the colony, and not the Saharan Jews of the M'Zab, who did not benefit from the Crémieux Decree.

In this book, I argue that Algerian Jews' identity as French citizens developed most powerfully in response to the virulent antisemitism that swept through Algeria in the 1880s and 1890s. During the 1890s, antisemites realized that through control of municipal governments, they could undercut Algerian Jewish citizenship. Thereafter antisemitism became deeply engrained in Algerian colonial society. Antisemitism manifested itself most dramatically concurrently with elections for Algerian municipal government. As Algerian Jews realized the precarious nature of their status, some actively participated in elections and enthusiastically integrated into politics, civil service, and the military. In so doing, Algerian Jews competed with French settlers, and after 1889, with the newly naturalized European immigrants, known at the time as the *néo-naturalisés*, the "newly naturalized." Faced with political competition and episodic violence fueled by demagogic leaders, the Jews of Algeria established associations and political organizations designed to support and defend their interests. Many Algerian Jews served their country with pride and heroism during the Great War only to be confronted under Vichy by state-sponsored institutional antisemitism, which in 1940 led to the abrogation of the Crémieux Decree and the loss of their French citizenship. The abrogation of their citizenship remained in effect for three years. In 1943; Charles de Gaulle finally nullified the abrogation of the Crémieux Decree and Algerian Jews had their status as citizens restored.

Antisemitism both challenged and accelerated the transformation of Algerian Jews into citizens. This antisemitism emerged from an array of sources, including the Muslim and European population. As Algerian Jews entered French civil society as citizens, they were seen as competing for access to the resources of the colonial system, reserved for French and European settlers. Economic and political competition merged with antisemitism in an effort to remove Algerian Jews as competitors. This occasionally evolved into violence, but more often it occurred in a more latent, seemingly indirect discrimination. For example, in 1937, *Le Petit Oranais* newspaper of Oran printed an ad of a 20-year-old man seeking employment. The ad sought employment as an "office job, handyman or otherwise. Wish to be employed by a good National. If Jewish, will abstain."[3] The clear dichotomy of Jew and "good National" illustrates the pervasive nature of antisemitism in the colony.

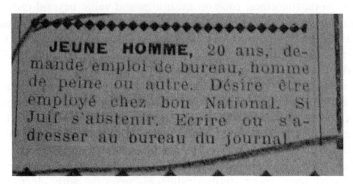

Le Petit Oranais, June 7, 1937

This book traces the intersection of citizenship, antisemitism, municipal politics, and Algerian Jewish identity. It explores responses to various changes and challenges to the status of Jews between the Crémieux Decree in 1870 and the end of the Algerian War in 1962. As Algerian Jews exerted their rights as citizens, particularly by voting in municipal elections and participating in municipal governments, antisemitism developed in step with – or one step ahead of – them. The improvements to the social and political status of Algerian Jews threatened the position of other colonial groups, notably metropolitan French settlers and newly naturalized European immigrants. Frictions developed over competition for access to the state's scarce resources (e.g., municipal government patronage, civil service positions). Non-Jews often articulated these frictions in antisemitic terms. The subsequent limits placed on Jewish integration by antisemites illustrate the complex realities of citizenship in colonial Algeria. Using postcolonial scholar Homi Bhabha's concept of the colonial Other, regardless of how much they might assimilate, Algerian Jews were "the reformed, recognizable Other ... almost the same, but not quite."[4] Jews' status competitors emphasized Jewish difference as a way of questioning their Frenchness. Antisemitism constantly reminded Algerian Jews of the fragility of their claims on citizenship.

---

[3] Chief of Department Security of the Department of Oran to the Prefect of Oran, "Report No. 6780: Demand for employment appeared in the local journal *Le Petit Oranais*," Oran, June 7, 1937, CAOM Alg GGA 3CAB/54.

[4] Homi Bhabha, "Of Mimicry and Man: The Ambivalence of Colonial Discourse," in Frederick Cooper and Ann Laura Stoler, eds., *Tensions of Empire: Colonial Cultures in a Bourgeois World* (Berkeley: University of California Press, 1997), 153.

Citizenship in the colony did not only impact Algerian Jews. As Algerian Jews negotiated the complicated vagaries of their position within the colony, other groups similarly sought to defend their perceived place within the colony. European settlers competed with Jews in political, social, and economic realms. Algerian Muslims called upon the case of Algerian Jews in making their own claims for citizenship within the colony. Jewish and Muslim rights were intrinsically connected in debates on citizenship and identity in the colony. This examination of the intertwined relationship between citizenship and antisemitism in the colonial context is shaped by several questions: What did citizenship in a colonial society mean? What did the granting of citizenship to a group – as opposed to individuals – mean to the Jews both as individuals and collectively? How did these newly created citizens respond to the rights and duties of French citizenship in a colonial society? Finally, how did Jews' citizenship impact their relationship with other groups in the colony, and how did Jews respond to threats to and attacks on their citizenship?

Antisemitism and citizenship have long been linked in studies in Jewish history. Antisemitism is a fluid and changing phenomenon that adapts to the needs or concerns of contemporary society. Those in power used antisemitism to their benefit. This book traces the shifts in the forms of antisemitism based on the activities of those men in power. In particular, it looks at how antisemitism transitioned from the local level, municipal governments, to the national level, in its institutional form under the Vichy government in World War II.

From Subject to Citizen: The Crémieux Decree

The 1870 Crémieux Decree, which made all Algerian Jews into French citizens in the three French departments of Algeria, occupies the center of every study and history of Algerian Jewry. As a watershed, it is crucial to understand the ways in which Algerian Jews and other colonial groups responded to the changes imposed by the mass naturalization. For Algerian Jews, the Crémieux Decree represented the first step in a series of transformations, which would usher in a new, dual identity as both "others" and Frenchmen. Algerian Jewish history, like much of modern Jewish history, is about alterity and assimilation.

Under Islam, Jews were isolated into their status of protected minority, *dhimmis*, but still remained an integral part of North African society, especially within the realm of commerce and in their dealings with North African rulers. Two well-known examples include the Bacri and Busnach families, Jewish merchants whose ties with France ultimately led to the French occupation of Algiers in 1830.[5] Some Algerian Jews celebrated the arrival of the French, who they believed to be their saviors from oppression under Islam.[6]

After welcoming the French to Algiers in 1830, the Algerian Jews' status began to change. By 1842, French courts had jurisdiction over Algerian Jewish affairs, which weakened Jewish communal institutions.[7] French politicians and metropolitan Jews considered how to assimilate Algerian Judaism to that of the metropole. Although assimilation was the ultimate goal, "regeneration" was a more immediate intention among liberal voices in the metropole, tied into the efforts of the *mission civilisatrice* in Algeria. In France, consistories acted as an intermediate representative governing body between the state and different religious groups. Historian Joshua Schreier traces the project of "regenerating" the Jews of Algeria in the early years of colonization in Algeria. He skillfully examines the way in which French-Jewish reformers collaborated with allies in the civil administration to transform the "oppressed victims of despotism" into French citizens. He argues that the "mission to civilize the Jews of Algeria was a multipolar and multidirectional process. Administrators and reformers followed the army into the cities of Algeria, hoping to spread progress and attach the Jewish community to France." Schreier demonstrates the evolution of the colonial mind's interpretation of Jews as "more intelligent, faithful, and redeemable," by deploying the "culturally resonant teleology of Jewish emancipation" in Algeria. The *mission civilisatrice* and the efforts to "regenerate" Algerian Jews gave colonial officials and their representatives access and control over Jewish spaces: the synagogue, the home, and the family.[8]

As early as 1833, Adolphe Crémieux, whose name is attached to the decree that made Algerian Jews French citizens in 1870, began to lobby for French intervention in Algerian Jewish affairs. As a member of the central consistory in Paris, Crémieux wrote to the Minister of the Interior urging him to establish Jewish consistories in the cities of Algeria, which would support France's "political goals" there. Although initially unsuccessful, Crémieux tried again in 1836 and 1839 arguing that establishing Jewish consistories in Algeria would advance colonial interests. Crémieux

---

[5] André N. Chouraqui, *Between East and West: A History of the Jews of North Africa* (New York: Temple Books, 1973), 142.

[6] Richard Ayoun and Bernard Cohen, *Les Juifs d'Algérie: Deux mille ans d'Histoire* (Paris: Éditions Jean-Claude Lattès, 1982), 116.

[7] Andrea L. Smith, "Citizenship in the Colony: Naturalization Law and Legal Assimilation in the 19th Century Algeria," *PoLAR: Political and Legal Anthropology Review*, Vol. 19, No. 1 (1996): 39.

[8] Joshua Schreier, *Arabs of the Jewish Faith: The Civilizing Mission in Colonial Algeria* (New Brunswick: Rutgers University Press, 2010), 2–3, 112.

had hoped that the Algerian consistories would come under the authority of the Central Consistory in Paris (of which he was a part).[9]

Two prominent French-Jewish reformers, Joseph Cohen and Jacques-Isaac Altaras, conducted an investigation into the Algerian Jewish situation in 1842 by order of the Ministry of War. The results, published in 1843 under the title "Report on the Moral and Political State of the Israelites of Algeria, and the Means of Ameliorating It," recommended that the traditional system of Jewish governance be abolished in order for Algerian Jews to become a "pillar" of French domination."[10] On November 9, 1845, Algerian Jewish consistories came under the control of the Ministry of War, with the intention of civilizing a demographically and commercially significant community and strengthening French control in Algeria.[11] In 1862, the French consistory system formally absorbed the local consistories of Algeria, dealing a fatal blow to the older style of Jewish corporatism in Algeria.[12] At that time, there were 23,061 Jews in Algeria: 9,180 in the department of Algiers, 9,414 in Oran, and 6,470 in Constantine.[13] The history of Jews in the French Revolution and their rapid assimilation served as the rationale for the idea of naturalizing Algerian Jews.

The sénatus-consulte of July 14, 1865, was the first major step in incorporating Algerian Jews in the French citizenry, allowing Jews to become citizens on an individual basis.[14] The sénatus-consulte of 1865 was also a major turning point for Algerian Muslims, who were offered the same path to citizenship.[15] Citizenship could be gained in exchange for giving up their personal status, which allowed Jews to be ruled by Jewish law and Muslims to be ruled by Muslim law. By giving up their personal status, Algerian Jews or Muslims could become French citizens, whose lives would be governed by the French civil code. In doing so, the sénatus-consulte established a sharp demarcation between French citizen and

---

[9] Ibid., 45, 53.   [10] Ibid., 44–45, 51.   [11] Ibid., 53–54.

[12] Smith, "Citizenship in the Colony," 40. See also Chouraqui, *Between East and West*, 146.

[13] M. Béquet, *Organisation du Culte Israélite en Algérie, Rapport au Conseil de Gouvernement par M. Béquet, Conseiller-Rapporteur* (Algiers: Imprimerie de Gouvernement, 1888), 9, AN F/ 19/11143.

[14] Michel Ansky, *Les Juifs d'Algérie: Du Décret Crémieux à la Libération* (Paris: Éditions du Centre, 1950), 28, 34–35.

[15] See, for example, Sarah Abrevaya Stein, *Saharan Jews and the Fate of French Algeria* (Chicago: The University of Chicago Press, 2014), xi–xiii; Ethan Katz, *Jews and Muslims in the Shadow of Marianne: Conflicting Identities and Republican Culture in France* (PhD dissertation, University of Wisconsin, 2009), 28–30; Schreier, *Arabs of the Jewish Faith*, 156, 173; Laure Blévis, *Sociologie d'un droit colonial. Citoyenneté et nationalité en Algéria (1865–1947): Une exception républicaine* (PhD dissertation, Institut d'Études Politiques, Aix-en-Provence, 2004), 75–79; Mahfoud Kaddache, *La vie politique à Alger de 1919 à 1939* (Algiers: ENAG Éditions, 2009), 20.

French national. By its logic, the 1865 law stated that "the native is French," but if he maintains his personal status, he is not a citizen. This created a distinction between French nationality (one could be of French nationality even if they maintained their personal status) and French citizenship (one had to be ruled by the French civil code). Sociologist Laure Blévis suggests that the sénatus-consulte set up the principles of "colonial compromise" and created in Algeria a divide between "citizens" who were subjected to the civil code, and "natives" who were French but juridically inferior. This distinction remained until 1947.[16] Very few Jews and Muslims took advantage of this offer, in part because many considered it apostasy. Between 1865 and 1870 in Oran, there were 200 requests (of which 113 were from Jews originally from Morocco or Tunisia) out of 14,000 Jews. In Constantine, only 40 Jews out of 8,000 requested citizenship. By 1878, only 435 Muslims out of more than three million had become French citizens via the sénatus-consulte.[17]

The Jewish Central Consistory, which had religious control over the Jews in the colony, viewed these measures at integrating Algerian Jews as problematic and incomplete. As Schreier shows, Algerian Jews rejected the intrusion of the French consistorial system into their lives, synagogues, and homes. Few of them considered the consistory an emancipatory institution, but rather as a foreign influence that was taking power away from local institutions and authorities. Algerian Jews rejected the appointment of French rabbis to lead their communities. They even couched their complaints in republican terms, demanding that they be allowed to vote for their own religious leaders and to be guaranteed their religious freedom.[18] The 1862 jurisdiction of French courts over Algerian Jews led to further "disorganization." French judicial officials who were largely ignorant of the principles of Jewish personal status and Talmudic law failed to properly adjudicate Jewish affairs.[19] The consistory contended that the only solution to this problem was to naturalize the Jews en masse and remove all confusion regarding their personal status.

As the Jewish Central Consistory, located in Paris, took an interest in their situation, Algerian Jews also took action. At the end of December 1869, the Constantine Jewish consistory submitted a petition to the Central Consistory demanding collective naturalization for the Jews of

---

[16] Blévis, *Sociologie d'un droit colonial*, 38.
[17] Ibid., 75, 79, 81. According to Schreier, only 142 out of 33,000 Jews were naturalized. Schreier, *Arabs of the Jewish Faith*, 173.
[18] Schreier, *Arabs of the Jewish Faith*, 84.
[19] Consistoire Central des Israélites de France, "Note sur le projet de loi relatif à la naturalisation des Israélites de l'Algérie," (1871), AN F/19/11144.

Algeria.[20] In March 1870, members of the Oran Jewish consistory participated in a meeting with the Prefect of Oran on the issue of collective naturalization. On this occasion, the Prefect asked the consistory leadership two questions: would Algerian Jews react favorably to naturalization and should the French administration give the Jews a year in which to decide if they would like to refuse such naturalization and make a declaration to this effect? To the former, the consistory leadership unanimously agreed that Jews would welcome naturalization. On the second issue, they were divided on whether Jews should be given such an option.[21] Members of the Oran consistory wrote to the National Defense Government in September 1870 to offer their support and express their thanks for the work of the government on behalf of Algerian Jews and their rights.[22] Although the Jewish consistory was supposedly representative, most of its leaders were highly assimilated and did not reflect the opinions of Algerian Jews as a whole.

In response to lobbying from the Algerian and Parisian consistories, French politicians took up the issue of naturalizing Algerian Jews. In March 1870, Émile Ollivier, then Minister of Justice, presented a law draft to the Conseil d'État (State Council). The law in question collectively naturalized the Jews of Algeria. Ollivier passed to Adolphe Crémieux responsibility for revising the law. Crémieux also served as president of the Alliance Israélite Universelle and had a reputation for fighting for the rights of Jews in the Maghreb and Mashreq.[23] On July 19, 1870, Crémieux presented to the Legislative Chamber his revised law for the naturalization of Algerian Jews.[24]

Under the National Defense Government, which operated from 1870 to 1871 in the midst of the Franco-Prussian War, Crémieux became Minister of Justice on September 4, 1870. Among his other responsibilities, Crémieux prepared a Constitution for Algeria. On October 24, 1870, he submitted nine decrees to the Government council, which ratified them. These decrees established a civil regime ending the era of military control of Algeria, enforced trial by jury, and naturalized Algerian

---

[20] Members of the Constantine Consistory, J. Stora, Ab. Cahen, Temime, Narboni, "No. 63," Constantine, January 28, 1870, CC Icc 39.

[21] Meeting of Oran Consistory, March 27, 1870, CC Icc 40. "Opting-out" of French mass naturalizations in the late nineteenth century was common.

[22] Karoubi, Charleville, Members of the Oran Consistory to the Members of the National Defense Government, Oran, September 16, 1870, AN F/19/11031.

[23] One Algerian Jew, B. Baruch, a military interpreter in Mostaganem, wrote Crémieux of his fear that Jews faced increased persecution in North Africa as a result of newspaper articles that negatively portrayed Jews and Jewish activities. B. Baruch to M. Adolphe Crémieux, Mostaganem, May 6, 1870 AIU Algérie IIC8.

[24] Chouraqui, Between East and West, 149.

Jews en masse, giving them the status of French citizens.[25] However, in exchange for citizenship, Algerian Jews would no longer maintain their personal status; they would be ruled by the French civil code. The Crémieux Decree represented part of a larger project of the National Defense Government to assimilate Algeria to the metropole.[26] The Crémieux Decree was also significant because it separated Jews from their previous classification as "natives" in order to integrate them as "citizens" without any evidence of cultural assimilation or acceptance by the French colonial population or the colonial administration. The new decree did not cancel out the sénatus-consulte of 1865, which remained in effect. The Crémieux Decree reasserted the central definition established by the 1865 law, which distinguished between French citizenship and French nationality and all concomitant rights and privileges.[27]

Immediately following its promulgation, the Crémieux Decree faced a series of attacks and efforts to abrogate it. Some accused it of being illegal or outside the jurisdiction of the Government of the National Defense. Others blamed the decree for the Muslim Revolt led by Mokrani in 1871.[28] In 1871, Charles du Bouzet, former Prefect of Oran and then Special Commissioner in Algeria, was one of the first to publicly demand the abrogation of the Crémieux Decree on the basis that it caused Muslim unrest. He argued that Algerian Jews spoke Arabic, dressed and acted in an "Oriental" manner, and were decidedly un-French. He called them "Arabs of the Jewish faith," who were "strangers to the tradition of the French nationality ... and civilization."[29]

The Central Consistory of Paris quickly responded to this accusation. Its leaders pointed to the fact that four months had passed between the promulgation of the Crémieux Decree in October and the start of the revolt in March 1871.[30] Some Jews joined Algerian militias in putting down the revolt. The consistory argued that this was proof of Algerian Jewish patriotism and devotion to France. The Central Consistory's 1871

---

[25] Ansky, *Les Juifs d'Algérie*, 38. See also "Décret qui déclare Français les Israélites indigènes de l'Algérie du 24 Octobre 1870," Tours, October 24, 1870, AN F/19/11145.

[26] Jacques Cohen, *Les Israélites de l'Algérie et le Décret Crémieux* (Paris: Libraire nouvelle de Droit et de Jurisprudence, 1900), 222.

[27] Blévis, *Sociologie d'un droit colonial*, 84.

[28] Elizabeth Friedman, *Colonialism and After: An Algerian Jewish Community* (Massachusetts: Bergin and Garvey Publishers, Inc., 1988), 10.

[29] Pierre Birnbaum, "French Jews and the 'Regeneration' of Algerian Jewry," *Studies in Contemporary Jewry: Jews and the State: Dangerous Alliances and the Perils of Privilege*, Vol. 19 (2003): 94. See also Schreier, *Arabs of the Jewish Faith*, 8. Schreier uses de Bouzet's accusation as the title of his book.

[30] Vice President of the Central Consistory to M. Leopold Javal, July 30, 1871, ACC 2E-Boîte 2.

publication on the subject included a copy of a declaration made by Algerian Muslim religious leaders and notables, signed on June 20, 1871, contending that the Crémieux Decree did not anger or excite Muslims, because "it is rational. On the contrary, all sensible people appreciate and approve of it." The consistory leadership concluded that should the petitions for abrogation be successful, Algerian Jews would be thrust into a problematic status. They would be "without nationality, without country, without public rights, without legal administrative and judicial guarantees for the safeguarding of their rights. They are on French territory, but would not be French citizens."[31] Algerian Muslims faced precisely that situation as subjects in the colony, which eventually led to their resentment of Algerian Jews' status.[32] The complicated statuses of Jews and Muslims in the colony after the Crémieux Decree illustrates the intrinsic relationship between Jewish and Muslim rights in colonial discourse and policy. Under Vichy, in 1940, Jews were put into an even worse situation than the consistorial leadership had feared: they no longer had access to the communal institutions so necessary for noncitizens' personal status, which will be examined in depth in Chapter 6.

Crémieux dismissed Du Bouzet's attempt to link the decree to Muslim revolt. "But you know that Muslims want to remain fully Muslim. They want their laws, their courts, their civil status, their personal status, their religious habits ... What promise of the French to the Arabs has the decree violated?"[33] By emphasizing Muslim unwillingness to abandon the rights of their personal status in contrast to the Jews' presumed enthusiasm for French citizenship, Crémieux sought to distance the two groups in the colonial mind. Crémieux described the decree as a gift from France, which removed archaic and despotic Jewish traditional laws, replacing them with the modern and civilized French world.[34] Crémieux added, "I do not deny that the privilege to give the title of French citizens to thirty thousand of my coreligionists was one of the greatest joys of my life."[35]

---

[31] Consistoire Central des Israélites de France, "Note sur le projet de loi relatif à la naturalisation des Israélites de l'Algérie," (1871), AN F/19/11144.

[32] Vice President of the Central Consistory to Leopold Javal, July 30, 1871, ACC 2^E-Boîte 2. The Vice President wrote in a letter that Jews be able to refuse citizenship.

[33] Adolphe Crémieux, *Réfutation de la pétition de M. Du Bouzet* (Paris: Imprimerie Schiller, 1871), 24, AIU 8JBr 1778.

[34] Ibid., 30.

[35] Ibid., 20–21. Crémieux's defense of the decree was one of several. See also C. Taupiac, *Les Israélites Indigènes: Réponse à la Pétition de M. Du Bouzet, ancien Préfet d'Oran, Ancien Commissaire extraordinaire de la République par C. Taupiac, Avocat* (Constantine: Chez L. Marle Librairie, 1871), AIU 8UBr1271.

Crémieux's joy reflected that of the French-Jewish reformers engaged in the project of civilizing, regenerating, and integrating Algerian Jews into the French body politic. It did not, however, represent the reactions of many Algerian Jews, who did not necessarily embrace their new status. In fact, some went so far as to resist the requirement of French civil law by refusing civil marriage. At the exhortation of their leaders and elites, who had petitioned for such naturalization and held great sway over their community, Algerian Jews eventually accepted their new citizenship.[36] In December 1871, the Jewish consistory of Oran noted "very satisfactory" participation in the elections of municipal and general councils. In the department of Oran, 1,440 Jews were registered on electoral lists and 1,179 voted in the past municipal and general council elections, resulting in the election of twenty-two Jews to these councils. The most significant difference between citizen and noncitizen is the right to vote, which became a powerful expression of citizenship among Algerian Jews.[37]

This massive entrée of Jews onto the political scene led to increased competition in elections and greater competition between groups of citizens, especially following the 1889 naturalization of the non-French European immigrants to the colony. The 1889 law established a principle of double *jus soli*, the legal concept of nationality based on birth on the land, which integrated the large population of non-French Europeans in the colony. It did not, however, extend to Algerian Muslims, who still only had access to naturalization through the 1865 sénatus-consulte. In fact, the legally inferior status of Muslims worsened after 1881 with the establishment of the *code de l'indigénat*, a special series of infractions and penalties that only applied to "natives." This code was exported to other French colonies, cementing Algeria's reputation as a testing ground for colonial politics.[38]

By 1891, Algerian Jews were adapting to their new identity and status as citizens. In celebration of his installation as Chief Rabbi, Rabbi Moses Weil gave a sermon in which he contended that no Algerian Jew would allow someone to protest "the signature of our great and glorious Crémieux, placed next to that of the immortal Gambetta, at the bottom of the decree of October 24, 1870 ... on both sides of the Mediterranean,

---

[36] Friedman, *Colonialism and After*, 10, 12.

[37] Consistory of Oran to the Central Consistoire of Paris, "Résultat au point de vue israélite, des derniers élections du Conseil général et du Conseil municipaux de la Province," Oran, December 12, 1871, ACC Icc 40. See also Blévis, *Sociologie d'un droit colonial*, 102.

[38] Blévis, *Sociologie d'un droit colonial*, 93, 112–113. See also Gregory Mann, "What was the Indigénat? The 'Empire of Law' in French West Africa," *The Journal of African History*, Vol. 50, No. 3 (2009): 331–353.

the Jews owe everything to France."[39] Over the next seventy years, Algerian Jews entered politics, joined municipal governments, entered professions, joined the military, and actively defended their rights as citizens and their patriotism. Under Vichy, Algerian Jews recognized the fragility of their citizenship, as expressed in Edmond's letter, and fought for their re-inclusion into the French body politic. At the end of the Algerian War in 1962, Algerian Jews faced a situation that demanded that they choose between the two sides of their identity: Algerian and French. Most chose France.

Three Aspects of Analysis

The book engages a series of historiographical discussions to analyze the history of Algerian Jewish citizenship and the relationship between citizenship and antisemitism in colonial Algeria: citizenship, antisemitism, and municipal government. Precisely because they occupied a complex web of identities, policies, and colonial politics and because Algeria was simultaneously part of the metropole and a colony, Algerian Jews present a unique lens through which to study the colonial politics of difference and the meanings and realities of colonial citizenship. These factors shaped the identity of Algerian Jews, which constantly developed in response to the challenges posed to Algerian Jews' citizenship by antisemitism, particularly within municipal governments.

Many studies of Algerian Jews focus on the evolution of this "Algerian Jewish identity." Algerian Jewish identity was shaped by the binaries of citizen–subject, colonizer–colonized, and included–excluded. However, as Frederick Cooper and Rogers Brubaker argue, the concept of "identity" itself is deeply flawed. It means a great deal and means very little at the same time (and occasionally means nothing at all), and often serves a reflexive category of description. Cooper and Brubaker instead recommend the use of "categories of practice," which are the spaces and experiences used and understood by "ordinary social actors," and include terms such as "ethnicity," "citizenship," "class," and "religious community."[40] Precisely because it is "multiple, fragmented, and fluid" analyzing Algerian Jewish identity is challenging. There was no single "Algerian Jewish identity" – rather, there were multiple identities, which depended on other "categories of practice," such as class, political

---

[39] Consistory of Algiers, *Installation de M. Moïse Weil, Grand Rabbin, 16 Avril 1891, 8 nissan 5651* (Algiers: Imprimerie Franck et Sodal, 1891), AIU 8JBr878, 7–10.

[40] Frederick Cooper and Rogers Brubaker, "Identity," in Frederick Cooper, *Colonialism in Question: Theory, Knowledge, History* (Berkeley: University of California Press, 2005), 59, 62.

affiliation and activity, and interpretations of citizenship. This book argues that Algerian Jewish identity was *processual, fluctuating,* and *multiple* and evolved alongside the practice of and challenges to Algerian Jewish citizenship.[41] I emphasize citizenship as a category of practice, which served to define the politics of exclusion and inclusion in French colonial Algeria and the Jews' role within it.

The experience of Algerian Jews as French citizens served as a kind of litmus test for the success or failure of the French colonial assimilationist program. Although perhaps reluctant at first, Algerian Jews gradually assimilated to their new statuses. Their integration into civil society increased competition between citizen groups and generated resentment among those excluded. This political competition and inequality spawned reactionary antisemitism and fueled violence against Jews. The Jews' status competitors invoked antisemitism to restrict Algerian Jewish integration into civil society and to reduce their supposed competition. Certain Algerian Muslims who were especially active in their efforts to gain political rights, and who eventually sought independence from French colonial rule, were particularly frustrated by the disparity in rights in the colony. Algerian Muslims faced a long and complicated road to receive any form of rights in the colony. The seemingly arbitrary, preferential treatment of Algerian Jews over Muslims greatly frustrated Algerian Muslim leaders. While this book focuses on Algerian Jews and their relationship with citizenship, this story cannot be told without discussing the concomitant lack of parity for Algerian Muslims in the colony and the ways in which the colonial mind perceived the two groups.

Citizenship and the Politics of Difference

Citizenship has long held the interest of historians, political scientists, and anthropologists. In recent years, it has once again become a focus of research as boundaries and borders between citizens and noncitizens and between states sometimes blur, and other times grow sharper in relief. In an era of transnationalism, especially within the European Union, issues of overlapping identities and citizenships emerge in political and philosophical debates.[42] In his 2008 study of French nationality, Patrick Weil argues that concepts of nationality and citizenship are shaped by the contemporary circumstances and contexts.[43] In his 2014 book on

---

[41] Ibid., 64–65.

[42] Birte Siim and Judith Squires, eds., *Contesting Citizenship* (London: Routledge, 2008), 10.

[43] Patrick Weil, *How to Be French: Nationality in the Making since 1789* (Durham: Duke University Press, 2008), 7. Central to the debates on citizenship is the conflict between

citizenship and empire, Frederick Cooper describes the relationship between the state and individuals that occurs via citizenship, which is itself a process of inclusion and a definition of exclusion.[44]

Jewish citizenship is especially complex because it encompasses many internal debates and differences, which Pierre Birnbaum and Ira Katznelson aptly label the multiple "Paths of Emancipation."[45] The Crémieux Decree and the citizenship it bestowed upon Jews meant much more than just the incorporation of a previously marginal and subordinate group into the nation; extending citizenship represented the expansion of the *mission civilisatrice* and the selective development of approaches to assimilation in the colonial context. Joshua Schreier's *Arabs of the Jewish Faith* and Lisa Moses Leff's *Sacred Bonds of Solidarity* depict the metropolitan Jewish lobby's efforts in promoting Algerian Jewish citizenship and convincing the colonial mind of the utility of incorporating Algerian Jews into French civil society.[46] Their successes meant the expansion of the concept of the civilizing mission, which operated in large part in the realm of education. Citizenship was theoretically the end result, or reward, of a process of assimilation.[47] The Crémieux Decree set in motion debates and legislation that increased access to citizenship and naturalization to those deemed assimilable, as evidenced by the 1889 decree that naturalized large numbers of European immigrants in the colony and the metropole.[48]

To appropriate the phrase Claude Lévi-Strauss made famous: in terms of citizenship, Jews have always been "good to think with."[49] Ultimately, "difference" is good to think within the context of citizenship and colonial politics of difference. This becomes clear in the debates on the "Jewish Question" during the French Enlightenment and in the debates surrounding the French 1791 emancipation decree, which gave French

legislation based on principles of *jus soli*, principle of residence, and *jus sanguinis*, principle of descent.

[44] Frederick Cooper, *Citizenship between Empire and Nation: Remaking France and French Africa, 1945–1960* (Princeton: Princeton University Press, 2014), 4–5.

[45] Pierre Birnbaum and Ira Katznelson, *Paths of Emancipation: Jews, States, and Citizenship* (Princeton: Princeton University Press, 1995).

[46] Schreier, *Arabs of the Jewish Faith*, 10; Lisa Moses Leff, *Sacred Bonds of Solidarity: The Rise of Jewish Internationalism in Nineteenth-Century France* (Stanford: Stanford University Press, 2006), 13, 119, 154–156.

[47] Rebecca Rogers, *A Frenchwoman's Imperial Story: Madame Luce in Nineteenth Century Algeria* (Stanford: Stanford University Press, 2013), 66–67.

[48] Jonathan K. Gosnell, *The Politics of Frenchness in Colonial Algeria, 1930–1954* (Rochester: University of Rochester Press, 2002), 141, argues that "notions of French identity in colonial Algeria were slippery–tied to official means of recognition (citizenship)–yet also linked to perceptions based on ethnic, cultural, socioeconomic, and gender constraints."

[49] Claude Lévi-Strauss, *Totemism* (Boston: Beacon Press, 1963), 89.

Jews citizenship.[50] Whereas Jews in France played the crucial role as the "other" in debate about the meaning of citizenship, Jews in Algeria represented a double "other": not only Jewish but also colonial natives who could be used to test the efficacy of assimilation methods, and more precisely the possibility of assimilation through citizenship. In this way, Algerian Jews were "good to think with" for French politicians and colonial administrators. Algerian Jews' engagement with citizenship reveals complex patterns of responses to colonialism and French civilization.

Methods of accessing citizenship in modern states reflect the increasing power of the state over the makeup of its citizens through governmentality and surveillance.[51] By allowing certain groups access to citizenship while excluding others, governments monitor and make legible the expansion of civil society. Sociologist T.H. Marshall emphasizes the tripartite nature of citizenship: political, civil, and social.[52] Underlying Marshall's concept of citizenship is the relationship between rights (abilities of citizens to lay claims on the state) and duties (the state's abilities to lay claims on individuals). Citizenship serves as a means for the state to define groups based on their particular rights and to improve its surveillance of those groups, a form of governmentality.[53] This allows the state to establish politics of difference, defining who is included or excluded based on citizenship status and access to naturalization. Cooper describes citizenship as a relationship: "it defines inclusion – in a formal sense of membership in a polity and a more subjective sense of belonging – and therefore it also defines exclusion."[54] In this same vein, sociologist Charles Tilly defines citizenship as a relational tie between the citizen and the state, made up of "transactions" between the two.[55] Through such transactions certain aspects of identity, such as religion, become subsumed by the category of citizen.[56] Philosopher Etienne Balibar calls this transactional nature of citizenship a "relationship of force" between the state and the

---

[50] Ronald Schechter, *Obstinate Hebrews: Representations of Jews in France, 1715–1815* (Berkeley: University of California Press, 2003), 36.

[51] Michel Foucault, "Governmentality," in Graham Burchell, Colin Gordon, and Peter Miller, eds., *The Foucault Effect: Studies in Governmentality* (Chicago: The University of Chicago Press, 1991), 102–103.

[52] Steven G. Ellis, Gudmundur Hálfdanarson, Ann Katherine Isaacs, eds., *Citizenship in Historical Perspective* (Pisa: Pisa University Press, 2006), 3.

[53] Andreas Fahrmeir, *Citizenship: The Rise and Fall of a Modern Concept* (New Haven: Yale University Press, 2007), 2.

[54] Cooper, *Citizenship between Empire and Nation*, 4.

[55] Charles Tilly, ed., *Citizenship, Identity and Social History* (Cambridge: Cambridge University Press, 1996), 5, 8.

[56] Tilly, *Citizenship, Identity, and Social History*, 10–11.

citizen.[57] Citizenship is therefore a process by which the state creates a boundary between citizens and subjects.[58]

Citizenship legislation in France reflects these relational forces. France's *jus soli*, defining citizenship on the basis of the place of birth, is at the center of several debates. Scholars have argued that France's assimilationist approach and desire to incorporate immigrants into the nation through generational assimilation exemplify *jus soli*.[59] Colonial expansion and the *mission civilisatrice* as well as the assimilationist flavor of citizenship legislation in the 1880s were central to this practice.[60] Others describe France as a "melting pot," which sought to incorporate and mold immigrants to the nation's requirements of Frenchness. This model emphasizes the importance of surveillance and force in the integration of foreigners and immigrants into civil society.[61] These categories of citizens and noncitizens continued into the late nineteenth century and became increasingly racialized and differentiated based on country of origin.

The strategic needs of populating the new settler colony like Algeria in its early years was the impetus for adapting citizenship legislation. While initially, French colonial officials sought to restrict the emigration of poor migrants, the needs of the *travaux publics*, public works programs, as well as emerging industries and settler farms, required workers. The French colonial officials sought out European emigrants from France and the wider Mediterranean to provide the workforce.[62] Emigration rules shifted in the 1830s and 1840s as the French built the colony, but new settlers were not made French citizens. The colonial authorities of the July Monarchy still distinguished among three different categories of colonists: the *colon-ouvrier*, the *colon-laboureur*, and the *colon sérieux*. Only the latter had the capabilities (of intellect and wealth) to properly develop the land, which made him a "good" colonist.[63]

Changing naturalization legislation in France and Algeria, and the 1889 law in particular, increased access to citizenship for immigrants. The law of 1889 created a hierarchy of immigrants based on their

---

[57] Ellis, *Citizenship in Historical Perspective*, 2; Rogers Brubaker, *Citizenship and Nationhood in France and Germany* (Cambridge: Harvard University Press, 1992), xi.

[58] Gideon Calder, Phillip Cole, and Jonathan Seglow, eds., *Citizenship Acquisition and National Belonging: Migration, Membership and the Liberal Democratic State* (London: Palgrave Macmillan, 2010), 3, 6.

[59] Brubaker, *Citizenship and Nationhood*, 51.   [60] Ibid., 11.

[61] Gérard Noiriel, *The French Melting Pot: Immigration, Citizenship, and National Identity* (Minneapolis: University of Minnesota Press, 1996), 45.

[62] Jennifer E. Sessions, *By Sword and Plow: France and the Conquest of Algeria* (Ithaca: Cornell University Press, 2011), 232–233, 272–273.

[63] Sessions, *By Sword and Plow*, 288–289.

perceived capacity for socialization and proper integration into the nation. In particular, this law increased the proportion of French citizens in Algeria by naturalizing the masses of European immigrants.[64] According to the 1889 law, children born on French territory to a parent who himself was born on French territory were citizens based on a double *jus soli*, and children born on French soil to foreigner parents could become citizens at the age of majority.[65]

These debates reflect the complexity of the meanings of citizenship in the context of modern France and its empire. The varied and changing paths of access to citizenship illustrate the fact that citizenship as a concept is dynamic, nuanced, and multifaceted. In theory, all citizens should be equal, but in reality they are not. The changes to citizenship brought about during the French Revolution created distinctions *among* citizens: between *active* and *passive* citizens. According to the 1791 laws in France, an active citizen was someone who had property and voting rights. The qualifications of active citizenship also included being male, able to speak and read French, to have been a resident of France for more than a year, and who paid a certain sum in taxes. This restricted citizenship to a particular group and class. Passive citizens had no voting privileges. They were protected by law but had no rights or say in the role and acts of the government. This included all those who did not qualify to be active citizens, including many Jews, as well as women.[66] This distinction between active and passive citizen continued in the French empire as well, but there were certain groups, such as Algerian Muslims, who were not considered passive citizens. They fell under a particular class of French nationals, but not subjects. This category will be discussed in further detail in later chapters.

Iris Marion Young develops a concept of *differentiated* citizenship as a way of encompassing this diversity.[67] Although Cooper and Brubaker are critical of the overuse and misuse of "identity" as a category of analysis, they argue that the inclusion of "identity" restrains "citizen" from becoming a hegemonic, and ultimately meaningless, term that fails to account for the heterogeneity of citizens.[68] Jürgen Habermas maintains, however, that citizens develop a shared identity through the praxis of their rights.[69]

---

[64] Weil, *How to Be French*, 182–183, 207.
[65] Ibid., 52. Weil emphasizes the role of education, while Bertrand Taithe contends that war and internal conflicts required a strong citizenry to build armies. Bertrand Taithe, *Citizenship and Wars: France in Turmoil, 1870–1871* (London: Routledge, 2001), 1.
[66] Cooper, *Citizenship between Empire and Nation*, 14; Noah Schusterman, *The French Revolution: Faith, Desire and Politics* (New York: Routledge Press, 2014), 47.
[67] Ronald Beiner, ed., *Theorizing Citizenship* (Albany: State University of New York Press, 1995), 176.
[68] Cooper, *Colonialism in Question*, 75.   [69] Beiner, *Theorizing Citizenship*, 258.

At the very least, the praxis of rights articulates the identity of the citizen. However, under conditions of scarcity of the state's resources praxis leads to competition between groups of citizens. Municipal governments in colonial Algeria served as the site where the meanings and identities of citizens were forged.

Most studies of citizenship and its meanings focus on European and postcolonial states.[70] Issues of citizenship, however, are especially relevant to colonialism because citizenship was a primary method of inclusion/exclusion.[71] Moreover, the definition of "citizen" in the colonial context was different than that in the metropole. For example, not all legislation promulgated in the metropole extended to Algeria, even after it was considered an integral part of France. Even within colonial systems, there was disagreement regarding meanings of citizen and noncitizen status.[72] Partha Chatterjee highlights that difference between colony and metropole in the legislation of those differences in status.[73] Cooper elaborates Chatterjee's concept of the "rule of difference" as a way to understand colonialism. He asserts that colonial institutions established difference between various groups.[74] Homi Bhabha's use of the concept of mimicry exposes the importance of assimilability, or at least the appearance thereof, in the colonial politics of difference.[75]

French colonial administrators applied a politics of difference to Algeria. Algeria became a "testing ground" for debates on and developing concepts of citizenship.[76] The debates regarding citizenship in the colony reflected broader debates circulating in the French empire regarding politics of inclusion and exclusion more generally. Jean-Loup Amselle's concept of "affirmative exclusion" encapsulates the choices of whom to

---

[70] On British debates on the concept of colonial citizenship, see Daniel Gorman, *Imperial Citizenship: Empire and the Question of Belonging* (Manchester: Manchester University Press, 2006).

[71] Brubaker, *Citizenship and Nationhood*, 23.

[72] See Christopher Joon-Hai Lee, "The 'Native' Undefined: Colonial Categories, Anglo-African Status and the Politics of Kinship in British Central Africa, 1929–38," in *Journal of African History*, Vol. 46 (2005).

[73] Partha Chatterjee, *The Nation and Its Fragments: Colonial and Postcolonial Histories* (Princeton: Princeton University Press, 1993), 24.

[74] Cooper, *Colonialism in Question*, 23.

[75] Bhabha, "Of Mimicry and Men," 158–159. The Japanese in Korea provide a useful parallel to the French in Algeria. The Japanese conducted similar efforts at assimilation among the Koreans while also emphasizing the distance and difference between the colonizers and the colonized. The central difference between Algerian and Japanese settlers is that the latter did not have citizenship rights, could not vote, and municipal government did not have the same significance. See Jun Uchida, *Brokers of Empire: Japanese Settler Colonialism in Korea, 1876–1945* (Cambridge: Harvard University Press, 2011), 66.

[76] Taithe, *Citizenship and Wars*, 83.

include into and exclude from the masses of citizens in Algeria.[77] Despite efforts to promote "isonomy" (equality of law) sociologist Laure Blévis argues that the complexities of colonial law and the debates surrounding legislation in Algeria differentiated not only between citizen and subject, but between nationality and citizenship.[78] In the minds of French legislators for the colony, law meant the French civil code. Those who clung to their personal status and Muslim law were therefore outside of the realm of isonomy. It allowed the French colonial mind to distinguish between different colonial groups and enabled the French to exclude Algerian Muslims from accessing citizenship in the colony. The only way Algerian Muslims could find entry into the citizenry of France was via the sénatus-consulte of 1865, which required them to forfeit their personal status. By contrast, Algerian Jews entered the community of citizens through the 1870 Crémieux Decree, which required them to be ruled by French civil law. The principle of isonomy also disqualified Algerian Muslims from demanding citizenship on the basis of *jus soli*, as they were not ruled by the law of the land.[79] In this way, colonial law in Algeria both affirmed the republican concepts of French citizenship in Algeria, while simultaneously legislating a particular politics of difference.

Decisions regarding increasing access to citizenship were shaped by ideas regarding race and difference, which in turn were shaped by events. The Franco-Prussian War made the Crémieux Decree possible as a way of shoring up France's defenses.[80] The Crémieux Decree, I argue, was more about the strategic needs of the colonial regime than about Jews. French politicians believed that by assimilating Algerian Jews as citizens, they would enhance the colony's security by bringing to its French population 35,000 new citizens.[81] In contrast, French colonial administrators were convinced that Algerian Muslims were unassimilable or, at the least, unwilling to give up their personal status.[82] Colonial officials thought that some Jews, especially those of the Southern Territories, the M'Zab region, were also unassimilable, thus creating a further politics of difference among Algerian Jews.[83]

As Jews assimilated, they created a gulf between themselves and their former neighbors, Muslims. The differences in their status led to sporadic cases of low-level violence between the two groups, particularly during

---

[77] Jean-Loup Amselle, *Affirmative Exclusion: Cultural Pluralism and the Rule of Custom in France* (Ithaca: Cornell University Press, 2003), xii.

[78] Blévis, *Sociologie d'un droit colonial*, 281–282.   [79] Ibid., 4, 281–282.

[80] Taithe, *Citizenship and Wars*, 88, 92. Amselle, *Affirmative Exclusion*, 62, 104. See also Weil, *How to Be French*, 216. See also Fahrmeir, *Citizenship*, 63–64.

[81] Weil, *How to Be French*, 211; Schreier, *Arabs of the Jewish Faith*, 1.

[82] Weil, *How to Be French*, 53; Blévis, *Sociologie d'un droit colonial*, 2, 143.

[83] Stein, *Saharan Jews*, xiv.

the interwar period when issues of disparate rights among colonial groups came to the fore. Tunisian Albert Memmi criticizes the Jews of North Africa for their assimilation and eventual rejection of their fellow "colonized" Muslims. The Jew "turned his back on the east," Memmi writes, choosing French over Arabic and adopting French customs.[84] The transition from subject to citizen and the assimilation required by it also created a kind of social death – a separation from one's former identity. The concept of social death is one used primarily in the discussion of antisemitism here; however, it is also relevant to discussions of rights and access to citizenship. Algerian Muslims similarly experienced social death by their lack of access to rights and, as a result, their lack of "personhood." However, for Algerian Jews, the process described by Memmi is one of cleaving, separating themselves from their former neighbors and former identities to become French.

Historian and memoirist Benjamin Stora considered the Crémieux Decree to be first of three exiles experienced by Algerian Jews in his *Les Trois Exils*. "The collective naturalization of the Jews of Algeria created a considerable upheaval in the world of their community, who lived, if not in harmony, at least alongside the Muslim population. After this separation, overnight, they changed sides and stood in solidarity with the invader."[85] Stora's critiques of Algerian Jews' assimilation is more nuanced, but he similarly implies a choice made by Algerian Jews, if not in accepting citizenship, than at least in their subsequent actions.

Historians Emily Benichou Gottreich and Daniel Schroeter explain that Europe chose the Jews rather than the Jews choosing to "identify" with Europe. Algerian Jews became French through the assimilation and citizenship imposed on them.[86] The Jews of Algeria thus benefited from the colonial politics of difference. Through the praxis of their citizenship, Algerian Jews assimilated to such an extent that in 1962, as they faced the realities of Algerian independence, they chose France over their *terre natale*, joining nearly one million *pieds-noirs* in immigrating to France.[87]

The colonial politics of difference and the interstitial developments of access to citizenship reflect the complicated realities of the definition of "citizen." Like their metropolitan coreligionists in the French

---

[84] Albert Memmi, *The Colonizer and the Colonized* (Boston: Beacon Press, 1967), xiv.

[85] Stora, *Les Trois Exils*, 14, 54.

[86] Emily Benichou Gottreich and Daniel J. Schroeter, eds., *Jewish Culture and Society in North Africa* (Bloomington: Indiana University Press, 2011), 11.

[87] Sarah Sussman, "Jews from Algeria and French Jewish Identity" in Hafid Gafaïti, Patricia M.E. Lorcin, and David G. Troyansky, eds., *Transnational Spaces and Identities in the Francophone World* (Lincoln: University of Nebraska Press, 2009), 218. Although Jews may not have considered themselves *pieds-noirs*, they became part of that group in the eyes of administrators, journalists, and, ultimately, historians.

Enlightenment, Jews in Algeria proved to be "good to think with" on the topic of citizenship in the nineteenth century. The concomitant lack of naturalization for Algerian Muslims, and the 1889 legislation that opened up citizenship to the European immigrants in Algeria, demonstrated the degree to which colonial administrators depended on affirmative exclusion to form a strategic citizenry. In the colony, all citizens were not created equal. Antisemitism made exercising their rights as citizens nearly impossible for some Jews, who were removed from electoral lists or harassed when they attempted to vote. The Algerian Jewish experience, as well as the antisemitism that they faced as citizens, exposes the fractures and contradictions of colonial citizenship.

Antisemitism/Social Death

A core element of the social and civic lives of inhabitants of French colonial Algeria was the existence of hierarchies and complex power dynamics that separated those who ruled and those who were ruled, citizens and subjects, French and Algerian, assimilated and unassimilable. In French colonial Algeria, the politics of difference ruled all. Those who had access to power, or sought access to power, emphasized difference by underlining the deficient qualities of another group. In the case of colonial Algeria, the non-French European immigrants in particular sought to exclude Algerian Jews because they were status competitors. This is one example among many. In order to assert one's rights for inclusion, many groups endeavored to show that competitors were internal others. This process of "othering" was common in the colony, and was especially directed at Algerian Jews and Algerian Muslims in different ways and at different times.

Orlando Patterson pushes the concept of othering further. In his book *Slavery and Social Death: A Comparative Study*, Patterson explores the evolution of social death as a way of understanding the condition of slaves. Slavery "institutionalized marginality," while also dehumanizing the slave and thus embedding him within dynamics of power and violence and entrenching him as an internal other. The slave represented the "defeated enemy."[88] The slave exists only within the context of the relationship with his master – a relationship of contrasts. "The essence of slavery is that the slave, in his social death, lives on the margin between community and chaos, life and death, the sacred and the secular."[89] This

---

[88] Orlando Patterson, *Slavery and Social Death: A Comparative Study* (Cambridge: Harvard University Press, 1982), 39, 46.
[89] Ibid, 51.

marginality is at the core of Patterson's definition of social death. I will assert that we can apply this concept of social death, which is often used in studies of the Holocaust and genocide, to the case of colonialism and situation of Jews and Muslims in French colonial Algeria.

In her study of German Jews in the late 1930s and the impact of antisemitic legislation, historian Marion Kaplan employs the concept of social death to describe the process of "dehumanizing" German Jews. Employing Patterson's approach, Kaplan defines social death as "their subjection, their excommunication from the 'legitimate social or moral community,' and their relegation to a perpetual state of dishonor."[90] Kaplan argues that social death was the prerequisite for the later deportation and genocide of Jews. Doris Bergen builds upon Kaplan's usage in her article on the social death and international isolation of German Jews, stating that the term can analyze "how official discrimination and persecution systematically cut Jews in Germany off from the majority non-Jewish population."[91] Kaplan and Bergen emphasize the significance of officially implemented discriminatory practices, as well as the general support of the greater population as necessary elements of social death.

The marginalization and discrimination that Algerian Jews and Muslims experienced in the colony can be considered a form of social death. In the Algerian context, as in the cases of slavery and the Holocaust, particular groups were selected for systematic discrimination, often sanctioned, if not implemented by officials. They were "othered," discriminated against for their supposed beliefs, race, or other qualities and were systematically degraded in society. Algerian Muslims in the colony certainly fit this description of social death, and in certain circumstances, such as May 1945 when the French army and civil forces massacred Algerian Muslims, social death evolved into actual death. Algerian Jews experienced social death particularly in times of heightened antisemitism, such as during the 1890s and under the antisemitic Vichy government. In both of these cases, legal discrimination impacted Algerian Jews' daily life, in the former case on the municipal level, while in the latter it was more institutional. In both the cases of the Algerian Muslims and the Algerian Jews, social death in the form of legal and social discrimination significantly limited their civic participation, for those who have access to it. This process of social death and the responses of the two impacted groups to it will be traced throughout this book.

---

[90] Marion A. Kaplan, *Between Dignity and Despair: Jewish Life in Nazi Germany* (New York: Oxford University Press, 1998), 5, 229.

[91] Doris L. Bergen, "Social Death and International Isolation: Jews in Nazi Germany, 1933–1939," in L. Ruth Klein, ed., *Nazi Germany, Canadian Responses: Confronting Antisemitism in the Shadow of War* (Montreal: McGill-Queen's University Press, 2012), 4.

While this book examines the experiences of Algerian Jews and Muslims in their pursuit to gain and maintain rights in the colony, it focuses in particular on the case of Jews and their condition as citizens who had to constantly combat attacks on their rights via antisemitism. Antisemitism was particularly potent and political in the colony. In the late nineteenth century and throughout the twentieth, antisemitism in Algeria blended different forms of anti-Jewish sentiment. Although tinged with religious elements, Algerian antisemitism was ultimately politically oriented, focusing on the naturalization of Algerian Jews en masse as a result of the Crémieux Decree in 1870. Frustration over Jewish citizenship, concerns over political and social competition, and status anxieties produced new forms of antisemitism that circulated among French *colons*, newly naturalized non-French European immigrants, and Algerian Muslims, who remained French subjects even as Algerian Jews became members of the French polity.[92]

The Frenchmen in the colony, including administrators, were anxious that the native Jews of the colony had rights nearly equal to theirs.[93] The status anxieties of other citizens in the colony – the *néos*, as the European immigrants who were naturalized in 1889 were known – centered on the Jew as their main competitor in local politics and the economy. *Néos* were often of working or lower-middle-class origins and competed with Jews for jobs, political offices, and patronage. In the process, the *néos* melded their religious beliefs about Jews with political anxieties to concoct a religiopolitical antisemitism.

Algeria had a special colonial status. Part of it consisted of three French departments established in 1848, which operated like those of the metropole; it also had zones of indirect rule and a military zone in the M'Zab region.[94] Algeria's particular status – at once an integral piece of the

[92] Mark Cohen, "Islam and the Jews: Myth, Counter-Myth, History," in Shlomo Deshen and Walter P. Zenner, eds., *Jews among Muslims: Communities in the Precolonial Middle East* (New York: New York University Press, 1996), 55. See also Robert S. Wistrich, *A Lethal Obsession: Antisemitism from Antiquity to the Global Jihad* (New York: Random House, 2010), 46. On the issue of separation of groups in cities, see Isabelle Grangaud's excellent study of Constantine: Isabelle Grangaud, *La Ville Imprenable: Une histoire sociale de Constantine au 18e siècle* (Paris: Éditions de l'École des Hautes Études en Sciences Sociales, 2002), 31–32.

[93] Despite these rights, Jews were excluded from purchasing lands for colonial expansion (*terres domaniales*). The Comité Algérien des Études Sociales, a Jewish defense organization, fought against this discrimination in the 1910s and early 1920s. This is examined in Chapter 3.

[94] Stein, *Saharan Jews and the Fate of French Algeria*, 46, 51, 60. Algeria had three types of political territories: civil territories, where the majority of Europeans lived; mixed communes, which included a small, but powerful European community and a large Muslim majority; and military territories. John Ruedy, *Modern Algeria: The Origins and Development of a Nation* (Bloomington: Indiana University Press, 1992), 73.

French metropole but also a colony in which Jews formed a significant part of the electorate – made it a fertile ground and active conduit for metropolitan antisemitism. In the colony, unlike the metropole, certain anti-Jewish excesses were acceptable. Edouard Drumont, an infamous metropolitan journalist and politician, capitalized on the receptivity of Europeans in the colony to develop his politics of antisemitism. Drumont was elected as a representative of Algeria in Parliament in 1898.[95]

The study of antisemitism is extremely complex – even the use of the hyphen in the term has been debated.[96] Antisemitism is often used to discuss the general attitude against Jews, often political and racial in orientation. Anti-Judaism is often used in relation to the religious aspects of anti-Jewish behavior. However, historian David Nirenberg uses Karl Marx's writing on the "Jewish question" to analyze the concepts of Jewishness and Judaism. Nirenberg suggests that the term "anti-Judaism" can be used more broadly than in a religious context. Marx's "Judaism" encompasses not only the religion of the Jews but also a set of ideas and concepts of the Jews as a group and Judaism as their religion. Nirenberg writes that anti-Judaism is more all-encompassing than the concept of antisemitism, which has limitations in its historical and conceptual scope.[97] While Nirenberg makes a convincing argument for the use of anti-Judaism, it nonetheless privileges religious connotations. As a result, I use the term "antisemitism," in part because of its historical, political, and social connotations discussed in this book.

Antisemitism can be categorized by three different, but overlapping, forms: religious antisemitism, usually applied to antiquity and medieval anti-Judaism; political or institutional antisemitism used to discriminate and exclude; and racial antisemitism embodied by, but not restricted to, National Socialist doctrine. Political antisemitism often overlaps with and includes economic antisemitism, which emphasizes economic competition as the primary source of conflict between Jews and non-Jews. For the purposes of this project, political antisemitism in its modern form encapsulates racial, economic, and political antisemitism. I refer to this as modern or political antisemitism. These three forms of antisemitism represent the evolution and development of anti-Jewish sentiment as a consequence of changes to social, political, and economic conditions, the

[95] Frederick Busi called Drumont the "Pope of Antisemitism." Frederick Busi, *The Pope of Antisemitism: The Career and Legacy of Edouard-Adolphe Drumont* (Michigan: The University Press of America, 1986).

[96] Shmuel Almog, "What's in a Hyphen?" in *SICSA Report: The Newsletter of the Vidal Sassoon International Center for the Study of Antisemitism*, No. 2 (Summer, 1989), 1–2.

[97] David Nirenberg, *Anti-Judaism: The Western Tradition* (New York: W.W. Norton & Company, 2013), 3–4. Nirenberg argues that anti-Judaism as a concept is "a powerful theoretical framework for making sense of the world." Nirenberg, *Anti-Judaism*, 464.

growth of the nation-state, and developing ideas in science and pseudoscience. Studies of antisemitism rarely escape the specter of the Holocaust or, in the case of more recent books, the threat of "Islamofascism" and jihadism.[98]

For the purposes of this study, I am particularly interested in the evolution of political antisemitism, which developed in the second half of the nineteenth century. Nineteenth-century antisemitism had a racial element to it, although it primarily responded to the evolving political role of Jews in European civil society. The political implications of Jews' entrée into society stimulated modern antisemitism. Antisemitism transformed alongside modernization and its accompanying social change.[99] In the nineteenth century, Frenchmen used "the Jew" to negotiate and deliberate the meanings of citizenship and the role of the citizen in the nation.[100] Modern antisemitism has been linked with the political successes of the Jews of the Republic, specifically those Jews who integrated into the administration.

Those espousing modern antisemitism included those who believed that they were the victims of the rapid economic developments of the late nineteenth century, which encompassed increased social mobility and an emphasis on individual success and social improvement. Those who expected to remain on the top of the social hierarchy were frustrated to find that others, such as Jews, continued to rise in social ranks.[101] Small artisans, shopkeepers, and entrepreneurs found themselves being squeezed by bigger stores and bigger banks, depriving them of clients and capital. To these self-conceived victims, Jews unfairly benefited from the opportunities afforded to them through citizenship and assimilation, most evidently in the economic sphere. Many historians emphasize the economic aspect of late nineteenth- and early twentieth-century antisemitism, although Peter Pulzer argued that antisemitism was not just an "epiphenomenon of economic depression."[102] Pulzer and other historians, including Pierre Birnbaum, believe that others, such as Hannah Arendt, overemphasize the economic elements of antisemitism, whereas

---

[98] Hannah Arendt, *The Origins of Totalitarianism* (New York: Meridian Books, Inc., 1958). Wistrich, *A Lethal Obsession*, 6. On Islamic antisemitism, see, for example, Andrew G. Bostom, *The Legacy of Islamic Antisemitism: From Sacred Texts to Solemn History* (Amherst: Prometheus Books, 2008).

[99] Robert S. Wistrich, *Antisemitism: The Longest Hatred* (London: Thames Methuen, 1991), 43, 53.

[100] See, for example, Julie Kalman, *Rethinking Antisemitism in Nineteenth-Century France* (New York: Cambridge University Press, 2010), 1, 8.

[101] Peter Pulzer, *The Rise of Political Anti-Semitism in Germany and Austria* (Cambridge: Harvard University Press, 1988), 42.

[102] Pulzer, *The Rise of Political Antisemitism*, xix–xx.

for them it was a primarily political movement especially evident in collective action.[103] Nirenberg argues that Marx's approach to the "Jewish question" reflected the tensions borne of emancipation and emerging capitalist society.[104] Marx wrote that the solution to the broader "Jewish question" was the *emancipation of society from Judaism.*[105] In this case, Marx's concept of Judaism is shaped by his distrust of capitalism and his association of capitalism with Judaism.

Hannah Arendt builds upon Marxian approaches to Judaism and capitalism by asserting that antisemitism was born alongside the development of the nation-state in the nineteenth century, which afforded Jews rights as citizens.[106] In Germany, Austria, and France in the 1870s, antisemitic political parties emerged, capitalizing on status anxieties and accusations of Jewish involvement in the financial and political scandals. In late nineteenth-century France, antisemitism became a major ideological force capable of gaining the wide support of public opinion, especially in the wake of the Dreyfus Affair.[107] Arendt's negative view of "bourgeois capitalism" was the source of her argument for Jewish responsibility for antisemitism, and she draws a direct line from Dreyfus to Vichy in the evolution of antisemitism.[108] This problematic trajectory elides intermediary developments, such as the unprecedented antisemitism organized in response to the election of Léon Blum in 1936. Furthermore, the Vichy government's activities represented the first time that antisemitism became the official policy of a modern French government.

While the economic dimensions of antisemitism are significant, this book focuses on the political uses of antisemitism. Antisemitism represented a powerful political tool that offered inclusion to those on the fringes of a group. Citing Proust's *Swann's Way*, Léon Poliakov writes that being anti-Dreyfus at the time of the Dreyfus Affair was a signifier of Frenchness in many circles.[109] In the midst of the Dreyfus Affair, in

---

[103] Pierre Birnbaum, *Anti-Semitism in France: A Political History from Léon Blum to the Present* (Oxford: Blackwell, 1988), 2, 7.

[104] Marx had argued that the "Jewish question" was about the relationship of political and human emancipation rather than political and religious emancipation. Nirenberg, *Anti-Judaism*, 434.

[105] Nirenberg, *Anti-Judaism*, 437. Marxian analysis of "Judaism" forms part of modern antisemitism studies. See, for example, David Shapira, *Les Antisémitismes français: De la Révolution à nos jours* (Paris: Éditions Le Bord de l'Eau, 2011), 12–13.

[106] Arendt, *The Origins of Totalitarianism*, 11, 13.   [107] Ibid., 35–38, 42.

[108] Nirenberg, *Anti-Judaism*, 463.

[109] Léon Poliakov, *The History of Antisemitism, Volume Four: Suicidal Europe, 1870–1933* (New York: The Vanguard Press, Inc., 1985), 56. The Dreyfus Affair also reminded Jews in the metropole of the fragility of their citizenship and status. See Michael R. Marrus, *The Politics of Assimilation: A Study of the French Jewish Community at the Time of the Dreyfus Affair* (Oxford: Clarendon Press, 1971), 196.

January 1898, following the publication of Zola's *J'accuse*, violence broke out throughout the metropole and Algeria. Under the leadership of Max Régis, the son of Italian immigrants and future Algiers mayor, violence in the colony was more severe than that of the metropole.[110] In the aftermath of the 1898 violence, voters elected nineteen antisemitic members to Parliament. Among those nineteen were four from Algeria, including Edouard Drumont. According to Arendt, the election of an unprecedented number of antisemitic deputies "was the earliest instance of the success of antisemitism as a catalytic agent for all other political issues."[111] In the aftermath of the Dreyfus Affair, an internal "Franco-French war" occurred in which antisemites led a campaign to eliminate Jewish functionaries and deputies from the Third Republic leadership.[112]

Jean-Paul Sartre identifies antisemitism as a social phenomenon. According to Sartre, people define themselves in opposition to the Jew, and it is through that comparison that antisemites realize their own rights.[113] The Manichean dialectic of Sartre's argument focuses on the antisemite's thesis that Jews represent evil and the cause of all problems in society, while the antisemite views himself, in contrast, as good.[114] In order to remove Jews as their status competitors, antisemites impeded Jewish assimilation. "The true opponent of assimilation," Sartre argues, "is not the Jew but the antisemite."[115] Sartre thus illustrates the intractable nature of the social and political aspects of modern antisemitism.

Michael Marrus diagrams the varying intensity and character of the social and political aspects of antisemitism as a series of concentric rings. The outermost ring represents the widest realm of anti-Jewish sentiment as a form of discrimination and disparagement. The second band is made up of stronger anti-Jewish feelings, which are "defensive and hostile" and emerge from economic and political problems. The third ring, at the core, is that of anti-Jewish fanaticism, which can influence the other two rings.[116] In periods of national trauma or political and economic uncertainty, the central ring reverberates to the outer rings, impacting the wider public that uses the Jew as the target of its anxieties.[117] In 1898, the activities of

---

[110] Arendt, *The Origins of Totalitarianism*, 111–112.   [111] Ibid., 46.
[112] Pierre Birnbaum, *The Jews of the Republic: A Political History of State Jews in France from Gambetta to Vichy* (Stanford: Stanford University Press, 1996), 136, 312.
[113] Jean-Paul Sartre, *Anti-Semite and Jew* (New York: Grove Press, Inc., 1948), 28.
[114] Sartre, *Anti-Semite and Jew*, 40. See also Phyllis Lassner and Lara Trubowitz, *Antisemitism and Philosemitism in the Twentieth and Twenty-first Centuries: Representing Jews, Jewishness, and Jewish Culture* (Newark: University of Delaware Press, 2008), 48.
[115] Sartre, *Anti-Semite and Jew*, 79, 143.
[116] Michael R. Marrus, "The Theory and Practice of Anti-Semitism," *Commentary*, Vol. 74, No. 2 (August 1982): 39.
[117] Marrus, "Theory and Practice of Anti-Semitism," 42.

the center ring influenced the outer rings, leading to attacks on Jews. In other periods of unrest, such as 1934 in Constantine, similar reverberations led to violence.[118]

The overlap between antisemitism and colonialism has not been adequately examined. In Germany, the two movements had a symbiotic, yet contradictory, relationship. To a certain degree colonialism helped to racialize antisemitism. These concurrent movements fed one another in Germany, in that as the African Other became racialized in the colony, so did the Jewish Other in the metropole.[119] The development of racial concepts of differences in the era of colonialism served the antisemitic cause in that it helped to further differentiate the Jewish Other. In some cases, as in that of Algeria, the combination of colonial racism and antisemitism made for a very potent brew that incited masses of antisemites in the colony. Antisemitism was endemic in social gatherings in the colony, such as "antisemitic banquets" or groups of antisemites enjoying anti-Jewish anisette or cigarettes at a café.[120] French colonial Algeria's role as a crucible for French antisemitism has never been examined in a substantive manner. This is the first examination of the role of citizenship and antisemitism in municipal governments in particular, and in French Algeria more generally.

Algeria represented a crossroads for various forms of antisemitism. Algerian antisemitism was significantly influenced by that of the metropole, but it was also transnational in that it incorporated the antisemitism of European settlers from Italy, Spain, and Malta, as well as Muslim antisemitism. Although antisemitism flourished in municipal governments in Algeria, institutional antisemitism reached its peak under Vichy.[121] The efforts of Algerian administrators and European settlers influenced Vichy's decision to abrogate the Jews' citizenship in 1940.[122] Seventy years after the promulgation of the Crémieux Decree, antisemites finally succeeded in undoing it. Its abrogation created a deep sense of rupture for Algerian Jews who, as a result, were separated from France and from Algerian civil society. They experienced a profound sense of social death.

---

[118] Recent works by historians have examined the significance of antisemitism in the events of Constantine 1934. See, for example, Katz, *Jews and Muslims in the Shadow of Marianne*, 122–123; Joshua Cole, "Constantine before the Riots of August 1934: Civil Status, Anti-Semitism, and the Politics of Assimilation in Interwar French Algeria," *The Journal of North African Studies*, Vol. 17, No. 5 (December 2012): 839–841.

[119] Christian S. Davis, *Colonialism, Antisemitism, and Germans of Jewish Descent in Imperial Germany* (Ann Arbor: The University of Michigan Press, 2012), 3–4, 82.

[120] Birnbaum, *Anti-Semitism in France*, 280.

[121] Henri Msellati, *Les Juifs d'Algérie sous le régime de Vichy* (Paris: L'Harmattan, 1999), 47.

[122] Jacques Cantier, *L'Algérie Sous le Régime de Vichy* (Paris: Éditions Odile Jacob, 2002), 72.

Although the abrogation of the Crémieux Decree by Vichy represented the ultimate rupture of Algerian Jewish identity, periodic explosions of antisemitism created tears in the fabric of their identities. Groups of citizens competed for access to the scarce resources of the state offered in municipal government. Antisemitism burgeoned under the auspices of municipal government. Antisemites used the power of the municipal governments to institute antisemitic policies aimed at diminishing the electoral power of Jews.

Municipal Government

Civil society in colonial settings existed only in a truncated form as a result of the barriers placed on access to citizenship. Mahmood Mamdani describes the colonial system as the model of the "bifurcated state," in which civil society existed for citizens and rural despotism for subjects.[123] Algeria was a "bifurcated state" in some ways; citizens exercised power over a handful of municipalities, while the colony as a whole existed under the jurisdiction of the French military and later the governor-general. In the colonial system, the governor-general acted as the metropole's governing representative in the colony. He was not elected and he reported to the Minister of the Interior. Within the colony, the governor-general operated in a top-down fashion, in that he directed the activities of the prefects and Sub-Prefects of the departments. Over time, municipal governments expanded and military control shrank, leaving municipal government as the locus of significant settler power.

In the early stages of the colony, Alexis de Tocqueville commented in his series of writings on Algeria on the significance of municipal administration in the colony as a way of giving citizen-colonists a sense of control and power. Writing in October 1841 in his "Essay on Algeria," De Tocqueville critiques the lack of settler influence on government. He noted that there was a municipal council in Algiers and the members were appointed by the colonial government. De Tocqueville found this situation a significant issue in the development of the colony:

At this time, there is not a colonist in Algeria who knows whether the community he lives in has revenues, what these revenues are, and how they are spent. There is not one who participates in the most distant and indirect way in the policing of his village . . . all these great affairs are settled in Paris. This is prodigiously absurd.[124]

---

[123] Mahmood Mamdani, *Citizen and Subject: Contemporary Africa and the Legacy of Late Colonialism* (Princeton: Princeton University Press, 1996), 16–17.

[124] Alexis de Tocqueville, *Writings on Empire and Slavery*, trans. Jennifer Pitts (Baltimore: The Johns Hopkins University Press, 2001), 98.

Even in the early stages of the colony, De Tocqueville recognized the importance of municipal governments in allowing colonists access to power over and governance of local affairs.

De Tocqueville emphasized the urgency of establishing municipal power structures. He acknowledged that the heterogeneous nature of the settler population would complicate elections of representative municipal councils. "Give back to these bodies, from whom you have nothing to fear, as they come from you and are dependent on you, the responsibility of making use of the municipality's resources." De Tocqueville continued that the municipal councils would not threaten the colonial authority's control but allow colonists a sense of autonomy in local affairs. "An active municipal power is at the same time more necessary and less dangerous there than elsewhere: more necessary because a social life that does not yet exist must be created there; less dangerous because there is no need to fear that municipal liberty will degenerate into political license."[125] De Tocqueville's comments on the necessities of settler self-government in Algeria reflect the complexities of establishing a colonial authority while also allowing colonists a sense of control over their daily lives.

In his 1847 "First Report on Algeria," De Tocqueville continued to assess the challenges posed by the power structures of the Algerian colony. He argued that the governor-general's "principal mission is to rule the country, govern its inhabitants, take care of peace and war, provide for the army's needs, and oversee the distribution of the European and indigenous populations on the land."[126] The governor-general could not adequately govern local affairs of the settlers. De Tocqueville urged the creation of municipal governments, which would have control of local finances to properly administer the functions of the city. "The village, unrepresented by anyone in particular, without a single director of its finances, often located far from the power that governs it, hardly ever obtains in time or in sufficient quantity the funds necessary for its needs."[127] Municipal governments would eventually become influential centers of local power, and sites of extreme competition over who controlled them.

France's Second Republic in 1848 declared Algeria an extension of French territory and transformed the provinces of the colony into departments, such as those in the metropole. The Republic allowed French citizens in the colony to have some control over their own government by electing municipal councils and choosing their own mayors.[128] The

---

[125] Ibid., 113.   [126] Ibid., 153.   [127] Ibid., 165.
[128] Maurice Viollette, *L'Algérie Vivra-t-Elle? Notes d'un ancien gouverneur général* (Paris: Librairie Félix Alcan, 1931), 277–278.

ordinance of September 28, 1847, and the decree of July 3, 1848, extended the form of French municipal government to civil territories in Algeria.[129]

Municipal government eventually provided its voters and its leaders with a great deal of expendable power and influence on the local level in the form of machine politics. The republican concept of "municipalism" argued for democratic self-government of the local sphere within the larger framework of the centralized government.[130] The municipal government had control over many important services and institutions, such as the police, street cleaning, garbage collection, modern urban infrastructure, electricity, communications, and even casinos. In the same manner as municipal governments in the United States and elsewhere, bosses promised their constituents benefits in exchange for their votes. The boss and the voters therefore developed a patron–client relationship in which the voter became indebted to the boss, only receiving the benefits of patronage if he voted along party lines.[131] Fearing the loss of the benefits, the voter continues to lend his support in order to maintain that patronage relationship. This form of patronage democracy was endemic throughout the western world in the late nineteenth and early twentieth centuries.

The patronage democracy aimed at spreading the spoils of municipal government from the top down. Although the voters received certain benefits, the boss and his immediate supporters had access to significant wealth and power through the patronage system.[132] Public jobs often paid

---

[129] Charles-Robert Ageron, *Les Algériens Musulmans et la France, 1871–1919, Tôme Premier* (Paris: Presses Universitaires de France, 1968), 135. See also Ageron, *Histoire de l'Algérie Contemporaine*, 49. Algerian Muslims were guaranteed six positions on the municipal councils, which was an important concession toward French assimilation program at the time.

[130] Henning Tewes and Jonathan Wright, eds., *Liberalism, Anti-Semitism, and Democracy: Essays in Honour of Peter Pulzer* (Oxford: Oxford University Press, 2001), 160.

[131] Bruce M. Stave and Sondra Astor Stave, eds., *Urban Bosses, Machines, and Progressive Reformers* (Malabar: Robert E. Krieger Publishing Company, 1984), 7.

[132] Politicians such as Boss Tweed in New York and the infamous Tammany Hall emblematized this form of government. Terrence J. McDonald, ed., *Plunkitt of Tammany Hall* (Boston: St. Martin's, 1994), 5. There are few parallel studies in the European context. Most studies of European political corruption are based in Europe, rather than in colonial contexts, and focus on later periods. See, for example, Frédéric Monier, Olivier Dard, and Jens Ivo Engels, *Patronage et corruption politiques dans l'Europe contemporaine, Volume 2: Les coulisses du politique à l'époque contemporaine XIXe–XXe siècles* (Paris: Armand Colin, 2014). For an Ottoman comparison, see Nora Lafi, *Municipalités méditerranéennes: Les réformes urbaines ottomans au miroir d'une histoire comparée (Moyen-Orient, Maghreb, Europe méridionale)* (Berlin: Klaus Schwartz Verlag, 2005). Dider Guignard studies abuses of power in colonial Algeria, particularly in the 1890s. Guignard, *L'abus de pouvoir dans l'Algérie coloniale (1880–1914). Visibilité et singularité* (Paris: Presses Universitaires de Paris Ouest, 2010).

significantly more than private employment.[133] By offering rewards and perks to those who voted their way, bosses and their assistants ensured future electoral victories. These rewards ranged from small loans or gifts of cash, food, and alcohol, from minor gifts to help poor families to the larger benefits such as jobs or contracts. Municipal leaders threw parties and events for their constituents.[134] In Algeria, such festivities often included free-flowing alcohol, which led to skirmishes between European voters and their perceived status competitors.

Bosses and their machines filled a crucial gap in providing services to their constituents who did not benefit fully from national or colonial governmental institutions. In particular, in the face of significant immigration, new immigrants did not necessarily know how to navigate the complicated bureaucracies of the colonial government. Municipal governments were able to woo these new potential citizens with necessary supplements and support. In this way, the political machine and the efforts of the boss filled the gap for those not directly accessing or benefiting from the central government.[135] In the case of colonial Algeria, the *néos* (the recently naturalized non-French Europeans) felt ignored by the French colonial government in contrast to the Jews, whom they felt were the undeserving beneficiaries of citizenship and its attendant rights and benefits. As a result, the *néos* were eager recipients of the patronage offered by the local boss and easily mobilized against the Jews. By attending to the individualized needs of his constituents, the boss won elections locally.[136]

Furthermore, unlike the general government, which was run by French bureaucrats, the municipal government could be under the control of naturalized European settlers.[137] The *néo* believed that his needs would be better served by electing a fellow European settler. As European settlers were more invested in local rather than national metropolitan government, municipal governments grew in local prestige and power. Although French citizens in the colony elected deputies to the National Assembly, the immediate benefits of such elections were intangible. By contrast, electing a municipal government leader could result in immediate results and remuneration.

---

[133] Jessica Trounstine, *Political Monopolies in American Cities: The Rise and Fall of Bosses and Reformers* (Chicago: The University of Chicago Press, 2008). 12.

[134] McDonald, *Plunkitt of Tammany Hall*, 6.

[135] Jerome Krase and Charles LaCerra, *Ethnicity and Machine Politics* (Lanham: University Press of America, 1991), 5–6.

[136] Krase and LaCerra, *Ethnicity and Machine Politics*, 11.

[137] David Prochaska, *Making Algeria French: Colonialism in Bône, 1870–1920* (Cambridge: Cambridge University Press, 1990), 180.

Patronage was endemic in Algerian municipal politics.[138] Voters could be forced to use their vote in certain ways by threatening them with the loss of a particular benefit or reward – a job or a loan. In the same way, the possibility of reward encouraged many voters to cast their ballot in favor of the boss.[139] This desire for power and the power of patronage led to the use of illegal activities to ensure successful elections. Bosses used tactics such as ballot-stuffing, fraudulent ballots, and hiring voters, known as repeaters, to vote multiple times a day, as well as other strategies to encourage voters and discourage those who supported the competition using force.[140] The intensity of competition during electoral periods indicates the extent to which municipal governments acted as the locus of local power within the colony.

In colonial Algeria, municipal government was the forum for exerting citizenship rights. It also polarized those who had a voice – citizens, whether Frenchmen, néos, or Jews – and those who did not, namely Algerian Muslims, who had only a limited degree of involvement. Municipal governments were thus the crucibles of hotly contested competition for the scarce resources and rewards that the state offered its citizens. Charles-Robert Ageron describes the role of elector in the colony as a "title of nobility in this new feudality."[141] When Jews became citizens, they increased the competition for lucrative positions of power and thus encouraged antisemitism.

Municipal councils existed only in civil communes in Algeria, known as communes de plein exercice, which Claude Collot describes as "instruments of European domination."[142] In 1869, 12,000 square kilometers were under the jurisdiction of ninety-six civil communes. That number increased in 1881 to 17,000 square kilometers under the jurisdiction of 196 communes de plein exercice. In these communes, Europeans dominated the municipal councils. In 1884, Muslims were granted a very small electoral college, through which they could choose the Muslim council members. In the communes de pleine exercice, where Europeans were the majority, Europeans were guaranteed two-third of the seats on municipal councils, with the final third set aside for Muslims.[143]

---

[138] Ibid., 192. Prochaska argues that patronage shaped municipal politics throughout the colony.

[139] Alexander B. Callow, Jr, ed., The City Boss in America: An Interpretive Reader (New York: Oxford University Press, 1976), 55.

[140] McDonald, Plunkitt of Tammany Hall, 7.

[141] Ageron, Histoire de l'Algérie contemporaine, 47.

[142] Claude Collot, Les Institutions de l'Algérie durant la période coloniale (1830–1962) (Paris: Édition du CNRS, 1987), 93.

[143] Ruedy, Modern Algeria, 74. See also Azzedine Haddour, Colonial Myths: History and Narrative (Manchester: Manchester University Press, 2000), 4.

Algerian Muslims comprised a separate electoral college for their designated positions on the municipal council.[144] This ratio ensured that European councilors would always be in the majority, and thus hold the power of the municipal council. For example, due to the Municipal Law of April 4, 1884, the municipal council of Algiers had thirty-six French citizens as municipal councilors; twelve councilors were Algerian Muslims. Jews and non-French naturalized citizens were considered French councilors.[145] The mixed communes varied in size but served as an intermediate sphere of interaction between the European stronghold in *communes de plein exercice* and the Muslim-majority military territories.[146] At the same time, Muslim representation on the municipal councils was reduced from one-third to one-fourth, and they lost the right to vote for mayors. In the 1880s, approximately 38,000 Algerians out of 3,300,000 met the criteria to be municipal electors. By 1920, the number increased to 50,000.[147]

Following the Crémieux Decree of 1870, Jews joined the same electoral pool as Europeans. This change increased the pool of electors for European positions on the municipal council and escalated competition for such posts. We can trace the beginning of the political mobilization of antisemitism in Algeria to this situation. The pervasive nature of the competition for power on municipal councils was reflected in the efforts of certain antisemitic groups in municipal governments to remove Jews as competitors by eliminating them from electoral lists. This was the case in Sidi Bel Abbès in 1937–1938. The mayor of Sidi Bel Abbès and his electoral commission endeavored to remove over 300 Jewish voters from the voter lists in the municipality. In addition, the commission also removed many young Jews from the military draft lists, eliminating their ability to serve in the military – one of the duties associated with French citizenship.[148]

The metropolitan government instituted two other layers of colonial government beyond the municipal government: general councils and the financial delegations. General councils, established to serve as an

---

[144] Jean-Claude Vatin, *L'Algérie Politique: Histoire et Société* (Paris: Presses de la Fondation Nationale des Sciences Politiques, 1983), 116–117.

[145] Kaddache, *La vie politique à Alger de 1919 à 1939*, 22.

[146] Ruedy, *Modern Algeria*, 88. The average mixed commune covered 1,136 kilometers and included a population of 294 Europeans and 20,348 Algerian Muslims. By 1920, 3,000,000 out of 4,500,000 Muslims in Algeria lived in mixed communes.

[147] Ibid., 87. In order to be municipal electors, Algerian Muslims had to be male, at least 25 years old, and be a resident of the commune for a minimum of two years. Muslim electors also had to own or lease land, be retired from or active in civil service, or had received a decoration for military service.

[148] Blévis, *Sociologie d'un droit colonial*, 338, 346.

administrative bridge between municipal councils and the colonial government, existed from 1858. By the decrees of June 11, August 10, 1870, 1871, and July 31, 1875, general councils were made up of French citizens elected as councilors, and Algerian Muslims, who were known as assessors, who were appointed by the Minister of the Interior. Before 1870, the general councils consisted of thirty council members, of which twenty would be French citizens (twenty-one in the department of Algiers), eight Muslims (seven in Algiers), and one foreigner or Jew.[149] Following the Crémieux Decree, Jews became part of the competition for the election of the twenty French general council members.[150] The French councilors were elected by their districts. Algerian Muslims could vote for their representatives only after 1908. Algerian Muslim representatives were never more than a quarter of the general council, which ensured that they remained the minority votes.[151]

The third layer of colonial government was the *Délégations financières*, a colony-wide representative body with authority over the budget for the colony, established by decrees of 1898 and 1900. The Financial Delegations gave advice regarding taxes and other fiscal issues. There were three delegations within the Financial Delegations: the first included French citizens/colonists; the second, European taxpayers who were not considered colonists; the third delegation was made up of Algerian Muslims. The two European delegations had twenty-four members each (eight representatives per department), and the Muslim delegation had twenty-one representatives, of which six were Kabyles. The Financial Delegations therefore had sixty-nine members, of whom forty-eight were European. Initially, the European delegates were directly elected while of the twenty-one Muslim delegates, fifteen were elected and six were named by the governor-general. The decree of December 20, 1922, allowed Algerian Muslims to elect their own delegates. The Muslim delegates were appointed or elected by a small Muslim electorate of 5,000 members.[152]

---

[149] Charles-Robert Ageron, *De l'Algérie "Française" à l'Algérie Algérienne* (Paris: Éditions Bouchève, 2005), 131. See also Collot, *Les Institutions de l'Algérie*, 52–53; Kaddache, *La vie politique à Alger*, 22.

[150] Ruedy, *Modern Algeria*, 88–89. The Muslim members of the general council were appointed by the Gov-Gen. Most were members of municipal councils or were chosen from ranks of native civil servants.

[151] Kaddache, *La vie politique à Alger*, 22–23.

[152] Ruedy, *Modern Algeria*, 86–87. See also Kaddache, *La vie politique à Alger*, 23. The Muslim members generally met separately from the rest of the assembly and had very limited impact on the actions of the *Délégation financière*. In his 1931 book, Viollette described the *Délégation financière*, observing, "We are thus very far from universal suffrage." See Viollette, *L'Algérie Vivra-t-Elle?*, 298.

Despite the critical importance of municipal governments and the other governmental structures of the colony in the history of Algeria, the literature on them is surprisingly sparse. One of the few studies on the institutions in colonial Algeria is Claude Collot's idealized administrative outline of the different colonial structures.[153] Jean-Claude Vatin offers another approach and argues that, for the most part, Algerian historiography emphasizes the colonial project at the expense of telling the story of the Algerians.[154] Mahfoud Kaddache also emphasizes the experience of Algerian Muslims in the French colonial politics of Algiers, de-centering the role of the French voters.[155] Jacques Bouveresse explores in depth the goals and failings of the Financial Delegations in Algeria, especially its inherently unequal nature.[156] All of these studies, however, are limited in their analysis of the role of Jewish voters, the competition that occurred between different voting groups, and the role of antisemitism in municipal governments in particular.

As Algeria represented an extension of the metropole, scholarship on French municipal governments illuminates the Algerian case. In his analysis of the growing importance of municipal governments and their control over the politics of French cities, William B. Cohen argues that over the course of the nineteenth century, municipal governments endeavored to make government more representative and democratic.[157] Cohen describes the growing influence of municipal governments on their constituencies through the process of "municipalization." Through municipalization, municipal councils took over services previously privately controlled.[158] Cohen contends that patronage strengthened the role of the mayor, who had the power to appoint members to local councils. It fueled high levels of participation in the electoral process, as the possibility of reward encouraged citizens to vote for certain candidates.[159] In Algeria, efforts by municipal employees to prevent certain voters, often Jews, from participating in elections contributed to the success of particular candidates.

Literature on other French colonies also illuminates the importance of municipal governments in the French empire. G. Wesley Johnson focuses on municipal government as a sphere of power for colonial citizenship in French West Africa. Using the unique case of the Four Communes of

---

[153] Collot, *Les Institutions de l'Algérie*, 6–7.   [154] Vatin, *L'Algérie Politique*, 26–27.
[155] Kaddache, *La vie politique à Alger*, 19–20.
[156] Jacques Bouveresse, *Un parlement colonial? Les Délégations financières algériennes (1898–1945)* (Mont-Saint-Aignen: Publications des universités de Rouen et du Habre, 2008).
[157] William B. Cohen, *Urban Government and the Rise of the French City: Five Municipalities in the Nineteenth Century* (New York: St. Martin's Press, 1998), 33.
[158] Ibid., 67.   [159] Ibid., 71.

Senegal as the locus of his study, Johnson examined the role played by the *originaires* – the African residents of Gorée and St. Louis who in 1848 were granted rights of French citizenship – in the municipal government and the development of emerging African politics.[160] Similar to the municipal governments in Algeria, the elections of municipal council members in Senegal pitted various colonial citizen groups – Frenchmen, *métis*, and urban Africans – against one another as they competed for the limited seats on the council.[161] Until 1914, French and *métis* businessmen dominated most municipal councils and sought to reduce competition for their powerful positions by denigrating their African competitors.[162]

Like the Algerian Jews, the case of the *originaires* in the Four Communes reflected hopes for the assimilationist program. In order to be eligible to participate in elections and to be elected to a municipal government, the candidate had to know how to read and write French.[163] Like the situation in Algeria, the citizenship given to the African *originaires* sought to cement French control in the region, without threatening the authority of the French population in the colony. However, African *originaires* eventually gained control of municipal politics from Frenchmen and *métis*.

Few studies on colonial Algeria emphasize the importance of municipal politics. Charles-Robert Ageron analyzes municipal government primarily as a lens through which to understand the place of Algerian Muslim politics in the colony.[164] John Ruedy's *Modern Algeria* analyzes the organization and significance of the municipal government as the crucible of local politics, but disregards the role of Algerian Jews in electoral contests as being the center of the antisemitic backlash in the colony.[165] Mahfoud Kaddache includes Jews in his analysis of the political conditions of Algiers; however, he focuses primarily on Muslim voters' evolving rights and role in politics.[166]

---

[160] G. Wesley Johnson, *The Emergence of Black Politics in Senegal: The Struggle for Power in the Four Communes, 1900–1920* (Stanford: Stanford University Press, 1971), 38.

[161] Ibid., 81, 84.

[162] Ibid., 46–47. See also Hilary Jones, *The Métis of Senegal: Urban Life and Politics in French West Africa* (Bloomington: Indiana University Press, 2013).

[163] Johnson, *Emergence of Black Politics*, 45.

[164] Ageron's assessment of municipal government was peripheral to his discussion of the role of Muslim municipal council members and their lack of rights in voting for the mayor and his assistants. Ageron, *Histoire de l'Algérie Contemporaine*, 49. See also Ageron, *Les Algériens Musulmans et la France*, 135.

[165] Ruedy outlines the role of the municipal government as appeasing *colon* frustrations regarding the autonomy of the colony and providing them with a greater sense of control of their local politics. Ruedy, *Modern Algeria*, 86–87, 110.

[166] Kaddache, *La vie politique à Alger*.

One of the best analyses of the patronage system inherent in colonial Algerian municipal governments is David Prochaska's study of Jérôme Bertagna's "bossism" in Bône's municipal government. Prochaska uses Bertagna's activities to demonstrate the stronghold that European settlers had on the municipal governments in the colony and their competition with Algerian Jews. Following the 1889 legislation that naturalized the new non-French European immigrants, particularly those from Spain, Malta, and Italy, the ranks of European voters swelled, further cementing the power of the settlers in municipal government.[167] Prochaska's central argument is that patronage and the promise of reward during elections were the salient features of municipal politics in the colony.[168] Antisemitism was a powerful political tool used during elections of municipal governments. Antisemites accused Jews of voting as a bloc, following the directions of their rabbis and the Jewish consistory. Mobilizing antisemitism was a way of blocking the Jewish vote.[169]

The politics of municipal government served as the crucible of status anxieties and competition in the colony. The praxis of citizenship by Algerian Jews acted as the catalyst that resulted in the explosion of antisemitism in the 1890s, and the recurring waves of antisemitism connected to elections in the 1920s and 1930s. The intense contests in municipal elections as well as the promise of subsequent rewards and patronage established Algerian Jews as the enemy of the European settlers and the *néos* and their central competitor for power and authority in the colony. Whether the competition was real or imagined was insignificant in comparison to the power of the status anxieties it caused.

Algerian Jewish Historiography: Identity, Citizenship, and Liminality

In *Le monolingualisme de l'autre*, Jacques Derrida wrote of the trauma of losing his French citizenship in colonial Algeria under Vichy in 1940 at the age of 10. He writes, "an identity is never given, received or attained, no, it only endures the interminable process, fantastically indefinitely, of identification."[170] As Cooper and Brubaker have shown, identity is a complex and occasionally meaningless term. But for Derrida and other Algerian Jews like him, like Edmond the school teacher, citizenship and identity were inextricably intertwined.

---

[167] Prochaska, *Making Algeria French*, 184.   [168] Ibid., 192.   [169] Ibid., 202, 204.
[170] Jacques Derrida, *Le monolingualisme de l'autre; ou la prothèse d'origine* (Paris: Éditions Galilée, 1996), 53.

In her homage to Jacques Derrida, Hélène Cixous uses Derrida's term "circumcision" to depict their shared experience as Algerian Jews. In her rendition, the word conveys various episodes of cleaving: separation from previous identities and adherence to new ones. For Cixous, 1870 and the Crémieux Decree represent one date in a series of "passovers, transfers, expulsions, naturalizations, de-citizenships, exinclusions, blacklistings, doors slammed in your face, dates of wars, of colonization, incorporation, assimilation, assimulation, indigene/ni/zations that constitute the archives of what [Derrida] calls 'my nostalgeria' and that I call my 'algeriance.' "[171] Derrida's "nostalgeria" and Cixous' "algeriance" reflect the nostalgic tinging of the often exclusionary experiences of Algerian Jews' retelling of their past.

Cixous further likens the liminal position of Algerian Jews to the acrobatics of trapeze artists, vaulting between statuses: reaching for the new, the French, while being forced to let go of traditions that linked them to their Muslim neighbors. "Spangled in French but sporting kippas ... out they swung, having to let go of the bar of their old culture, left it far behind them ... swimming across the abyss arms reaching out for the other trapeze, the much-desired French, but there's France, hostile, snatching it back. The Jewish trapezists cling to the void."[172] They were, as Homi Bhabha said, "almost, but not quite" accepted by the French, but also distanced from their native Algerian past.

The concept of liminality features prominently in many texts by Algerian Jews, as well as those who have studied them as a group. Anthropologist Victor Turner developed the concept of "liminality" in his studies of rites of passage in Central Africa, building upon the work of fellow anthropologist Arnold Van Gennep. Liminality, according to Turner, represents an "interstructural situation," a period of marginality of being "between and betwixt" two states or phases. Turner considers a state to include status, such as legal status.[173] As Algerian Jews traversed the in-betweenness of shifting from subject to citizen, and from citizen to subject under Vichy, and ultimately back to citizen, they regularly existed in a liminal state, not quite one or the other. In describing rites of passage, Victor Turner described the liminal period as "one of ambiguity and paradox, a confusion of all the customary categories."[174] Similar to Turner's liminality is J.S. Fontaine's concept of personhood. Fontaine's

---

[171] Hélène Cixous, *Portrait of Jacques Derrida as a Young Jewish Saint* (New York: Columbia University Press, 2004), 5.
[172] Ibid., 115.
[173] Victor Tuner, *The Forest of Symbols: Aspects of Ndembu Ritual* (Ithaca: Cornell University Press, 1967), 93.
[174] Ibid., 97.

approach to personhood emphasizes the gradual accretion of rights and privileges as a marker of personhood.[175] For Algerian Jews, the shifts between subject and citizen were often threatened, challenged, or questioned internally and externally. Algerian Jews were forced to deal with recurrent liminal states as they shifted from subject to citizen and back again.

One of the trends of the early literature on Algerian Jews was that they were written by Algerian Jews, who were impacted by a sense of "nostalgérie," nostalgia felt for Algeria by emigrants.[176] Even the widely published historian Benjamin Stora has submitted to the pull of that nostalgia and "returned" to his homeland. At the start of his 2006 book, Stora describes returning to Khenchela, his *ville natale*, to search for remnants of his family's past. The graves of his ancestors, now in ruins, inspired in Stora a "morose meditation." For Stora, this project was deeply personal. "After studying for so long the history of Algeria, why not research a project on its Jewish population, beginning with the history of my own family?"[177]

Similarly, André Chouraqui dedicated his well-known study of the Jews of North Africa, *Between East and West*, to his parents and his grandfather, Saadia Chouraqui, "who erected a synagogue at Aïn-Témouchent, which now stands deserted."[178] In the *Architecture of Memory*, anthropologist Joëlle Bahloul turns her gaze onto herself and her family in her examination of the role of memory and the shaping of identity in what she called a "Jewish-Muslim household" of Dar-Refayil.[179] The ghosts of the past, as well as the traumatic rupture of leaving Algeria in the wake of the Algerian War, shape the profound "nostalgérie" of many scholars on Algerian Jewry.[180]

For most authors there are three salient benchmarks in Algerian Jewish history: the first is the Crémieux Decree of 1870, by which Algerian Jews became French citizens en masse. The second is the abrogation of the

---

[175] J. S. Fontaine, "Person and Individual: Some Anthropological Reflections," in Michael Carrithers, Steven Collins, and Steven Lukes, eds., *The Category of the Person: Anthropology: Philosophy, History* (Cambridge: Cambridge University Press, 1985), 132.

[176] The term is used widely among Algerian Jews who chose to leave Algeria for France in the context of the Algerian War. "Nostalgérie" applies to the period of French control in Algeria.

[177] Stora, *Les Trois Exils*, 17–18.   [178] Chouraqui, *Between East and West*, dedication.

[179] Joëlle Bahloul, *The Architecture of Memory: A Jewish-Muslim Household in Colonial Algeria, 1937–1962* (Cambridge: Cambridge University Press, 1996), 5. Such examples reveal the crucial role of the emic–etic distinction in the study of Algerian Jews. On the emic–etic dichotomy, see Marvin Harris, "History and Significance of the Emic/Etic Distinction," *Annual Review of Anthropology*, Vol. 5 (1976): 329–350.

[180] Joëlle Allouche-Benayoun and Doris Bensimon, *Les Juifs d'Algérie: Mémoires et Identités Plurielles* (Paris: Éditions Stavit, 1998), 10.

Crémieux Decree in 1940 under Vichy. The third, the Algerian War from 1954 to 1962, looms large over every text by these authors, even if it lies outside the scope of their studies. Over the course of these three events, Algerian Jews were forced to choose between the multiple aspects of their identities. In the midst of the Algerian War, most Jews chose France over independent Algeria. For many, that experience was one of rupture leading to an exile.

Once Algerian Jews became French citizens under the Crémieux Decree, they became the quintessential internal outsiders of the French colonial regime, at once French citizens but simultaneously shaped by their "indigenous" customs and practices. Through attendance at French public schools and the "willingness" to adopt French as their language, Algerian Jews assimilated to their French identities through a simultaneous process of "separation and rapprochement."[181] The imposition of the consistorial system on the Algerian colony assimilated Algerian Judaism to metropolitan Judaism.[182] Despite the assimilatory efforts of Algerian and metropolitan Jews, antisemitism in the colony reminded Jews that in spite of their status as citizens, they were still outsiders in the colon-dominated society. Even when they settled in metropolitan France following the Algerian War, Algerian Jews remained isolated, as internal outsider, not even accepted by Europeans from the colony.[183]

Many of the available works on the Algerian Jewish history are accounts conducted by authors who are personally acquainted with their subject matter. Richard Ayoun, Robert Attal, Joëlle Allouche-Benayoun, Doris Bensimon, Bahloul, Chouraqui, Stora, and Shmuel Trigano, among others, are of Algerian Jewish origin. Their works are colored by their nostalgia for their lives in Algeria. Also connected with this body of works is the large number of memoirs written by Algerian Jews in recent years.[184] These memoirs, inflected by looking backward at a lost homeland, tend to

[181] Jean Jacques Deldyck, Le Processus d'Acculturation des Juifs d'Algérie (Paris: L'Harmattan, 2000), 75.

[182] Shmuel Trigano, ed., L'Identité des Juifs d'Algérie: Une Expérience originale de la Modernité (Paris: Éditions du Nadir, 2003), 74.

[183] Friedman, Colonialism and After, 126. See also Sarah Sussman, Changing Lands, Changing Identities. The Migration of Algerian Jewry to France, 1954–1967, Unpublished Doctoral Dissertation, Stanford University, 2002. The Jews of the southern M'Zab region, conquered after the Crémieux Decree, were even more outside the French system. See Sarah Abrevaya Stein, "Dividing South from North: French Colonialism, Jews, and the Algerian Sahara," in The Journal of North African Studies, Vol. 17, No. 5 (2012). See also Stein, Saharan Jews and the Fate of French Algeria, 115, 119. See also Katz, Jews and Muslims in the Shadow of Marianne, 137–138, 234.

[184] See, for example, Josy Adida-Goldberg, Les Deux Pères (Paris: Orizons, 2008); André Akoun, Né à Oran: Autobiographie en troisième personne (Paris: Éditions Bouchene, 2004); Claudine Favret, Les Tribulations d'une Famille d'Alger (Saint-Cyr-sur-Loire: Éditions Alan Sutton, 2003).

glorify the French colonial period and the assimilation process undergone by Algerian Jews.[185] By negating the positive aspects of Algerian Jewry under Islam, authors depict the French occupation of Algeria and the Crémieux Decree as a significant improvement.

There is a growing literature on the subject of Algerian Jews written recently by non-Algerian Jews as well as non-Jewish scholars. Sarah Stein, Joshua Schreier, and Ethan Katz are but a few of the recent historians who have written about Algerian Jews from an academic perspective. These studies contextualize Algerian Jews in wider historical perspectives. One of the first was David Prochaska's 1990 examination of Bône. Prochaska examines the role of Jews in the Bône community, particularly following the Crémieux Decree, and assessed their subsequent participation in municipal politics. He emphasizes the role of Algerian Jews as important intermediaries for the French colonial regime because of their continued connections and ability to communicate with their Muslim counterparts, with whom they shared many customs and traditions.[186] These similarities between Jews and Muslims motivated metropolitan Jews to undertake an internal colonization of Algerian Jewry alongside the French colonization of Algeria in order to "elevate and civilize" their Algerian brethren.[187]

In a similar manner, demographer Kamel Kateb focuses his study on the positions of Algerian Muslims and Europeans in the colony. Kateb observes that Europeans were the engine of antisemitism in the colony and, for the most part, Algerian Muslims were neither antisemitic nor overtly opposed to the Crémieux Decree.[188] Laure Blévis approaches the issues of access to rights in the French colony from a legal-sociological perspective, examining the position of both Jews and Muslims as legal actors in the colonial context.[189] Ethan Katz studies the shifting relationships between Algerian Jews and Muslims in the twentieth century, particularly in France. Katz focuses on the quotidian interactions of the

---

[185] While some studies describe the coexistence between Jews and Muslims, many of these emic works adhere to what Mark Cohen called a "neo-lachrymose" approach, which emphasizes conflict and friction between Jews and Muslims. Mark R. Cohen, *Under Crescent and Cross: The Jews in the Middle Ages* (Princeton: Princeton University Press, 1994), 4. See also Mark R. Cohen, "The *Neo-Lachrymose* Conception of Jewish-Arab History," *Tikkun*, Vol. 6 (May–June 1991): 55–60. See also Ayoun and Cohen, *Les Juifs d'Algérie*, 68–69; Richard Attal, *Regards sur les Juifs d'Algérie* (Paris: L'Harmattan, 1996), 21; Chouraqui, *Between East and West*, 43.

[186] For more information on Jewish Mediterranean trade networks, see Sarah A. Stein, *Plumes: Ostrich Feathers, Jews, and a Lost World of Jewish Commerce* (New Haven: Yale University Press, 2008).

[187] Prochaska, *Making Algeria French*, 138–139.

[188] Kamel Kateb, *Européens, "Indigènes," et Juifs en Algérie (1830–1962): Représentations et Réalités des Populations* (Paris: Éditions de l'Institut National d'Études Démographiques, 2001), 191–192.

[189] Blévis, *Sociologie d'un droit colonial*.

two groups and how those exchanges evolved, especially in periods of conflict, starting in World War I and continuing through the Algerian War. At the core of the complicated relationship between Algerian Jews and Muslims was the issue of access to rights and their unequal status in the colony.[190]

Joshua Schreier emphasizes the role of Algerian Jews as "natural" intermediaries for the French colonial administration, especially in the early period of colonialism. Because the colonial administration needed intermediaries, it encouraged reformers, including metropolitan Jews, to promote a separate policy for Jews in the colony, which sought to "elevate" them. In large part, the needs of the state as well as the "culturally resonant teleology of Jewish emancipation" informed the decision to "regenerate" Algerian Jews.[191] From the 1840s, Jews in Algeria were thus subject to different legislation than their Muslim counterparts, concluding with the Crémieux Decree.[192] Some Algerian Jews resisted the "civilizing" mission forced upon them by French administrators and metropolitan French Jews, particularly when they felt that the state was infringing upon their personal rights, and when they sought to control Jewish institutions, such as the synagogue, education, and domestic life.[193] Schreier's work complicates the classic portrayal of Algerian Jews as supporting the concurrent assimilation of Algerian Jews to French citizenry and of Algerian Judaism to French Judaism.

The Algerian Jews' path to assimilation and emerging identity as a transnational group was rocky and fraught with conflict, both internal and external. This study builds on this previous work and complicates the history of Algerian Jews' citizenship by positioning Algerian Jews in French colonial society after the Crémieux Decree and examining their relations with various groups in the colony as well as the extreme competition between groups in the colony as they sought control over local government. It emphasizes the interaction of citizenship, antisemitism, and municipal government on the development of Algerian Jewish identity as French citizens.

This book is organized chronologically to illustrate the changes and developments in Algerian Jews' practice of their citizenship, the growing competition between groups in the colony for the scarce resources of

---

[190] Katz, *Jews and Muslims in the Shadow of Marianne*, 9–12.
[191] Schreier, *Arabs of the Jewish Faith*, 2.
[192] Joshua Schreier, " 'They Swore upon the Tombs Never to Make Peace with Us': Algerian Jews and French Colonialism, 1845–1848," in Patricia M.E. Lorcin, ed., *Algeria and France, 1800–2000: Identity, Memory, Nostalgia* (Syracuse: Syracuse University Press, 2006), 102–103.
[193] Schreier, "Algerian Jews and French Colonialism," 93–94, 116, 153–154.

state, and the evolution of political antisemitism. The first chapter deals with the growing antisemitism from European immigrants in Algeria, known as the *néos*, in the 1890s. This competition emerged following the 1889 decree that naturalized many non-French Europeans in Algeria. Many *néos* viewed Algerian Jews as status competitors. Antisemitism grew concurrently with events in the metropole, eventually surpassing that of the metropole in its extremity. The Dreyfus Affair galvanized antisemitism, leading to the 1898 riots in the metropole and the colony, which are the focus of Chapter 2. Chapter 2 also deals with the growing success of the *néos* in Algerian politics, emblematized by the antisemitic mayor of Algiers, Max Régis. In the years immediately following 1898, political antisemitism had its most successful era in Algeria, including the election of four antisemitic deputies to the national assembly. Antisemites found credibility by joining their cause with efforts for Algerian autonomy.

Chapter 3 focuses on the Jewish response to the threats posed to their citizenship by antisemites. In the early twentieth century, and especially following their patriotic efforts of World War I, Algerian Jews defended their rights as French citizens against the ever-present tide of antisemitic criticisms. Jewish defense efforts became linked to the influence of the Alliance Israélite Universelle, which began its work in Algeria in 1900. Defense emphasized assimilation, the major goal of the Alliance and its leaders. Algerian Jewish leaders argued that Jews could best fight antisemitism by disproving antisemitic contentions of Jewish backwardness or corporatism. The Comité Algérien d'Études Sociales, one of the most important defense organizations, used Jewish patriotism in World War I as evidence of Jewish assimilation.

Chapter 4 examines the efforts of Algerian Muslims to gain rights in the colony. It explores daily violent encounters between Jews and Muslims. Relationships between Jews and Muslims deteriorated as Muslim demand for political rights accelerated. Algerian Muslims pointed to service in World War I, in the same manner as Algerian Jews, as the basis for their claims. Algerian Muslim nationalism developed as resentment of the Jews' superior status grew. In August 1934, Jews in Constantine faced a pogrom of an unparalleled scale in Algeria. French colonial administrators, municipal government officials, and police were suspiciously absent over the course of the violence carried out by Algerian Muslims. For Algerian Jews, the Constantine pogrom indicated the frustrations of certain Algerian Muslim leaders, particularly the *évolués*, who believed that Algerian Muslims deserved greater rights.

Chapter 5 follows the efforts of the Popular Front to enhance the political status of Algerian Muslims. Jewish rights proved inextricable from Muslim rights in debates on colonial citizenship in the interwar period. Antisemites believed that they could destroy Algerian Jewish citizenship while preventing the growth of Muslim rights. As Algerian Jews assimilated, affiliating themselves ever more with the French and voting in large numbers in elections, they found that there were indeed limits to their citizenship. Antisemitic politicians and leaders of municipal governments used their power and influence to remove Jewish voters from electoral lists. Algerian Jews called upon international organizations to help them defend their rights against attacks by antisemites. Although they achieved some success, they would soon find out just how pervasive state antisemitism could be in France.

Chapter 6 deals with the most intense and significant rupture experienced by Algerian Jews. Under Vichy, Algerian Jews had their citizenship revoked. According to the 1942 census of Algerian Jews, there were 116,884 Jews in the colony: 34,742 Jews in the department of Algiers, 50,413 in Oran, 25,614 in Constantine, and 6,115 in the southern territories.[194] After seventy years of assimilation and participation in French civil society, Algerian Jews were reduced to subjects in even worse conditions than Algerian Muslims. The abrogation of the Crémieux Decree under Vichy not only demonstrated the power of anti-semitism in the metropole and the colony but also indicated the degree to which Algerian Jews had assimilated and how much their identities had been reshaped over the course of their seventy years as citizens. Following the abrogation, Algerian Jews fought to regain their citizenship, on an individual basis through appeals to Vichy on the grounds of past demonstrations of patriotism and commitment to France, and on a collective level through lobbying the Vichy government as well as coordinating with worldwide Jewish organizations, and military. The plight of Algerian Jews drew important philosophers and academics, among them Hannah Arendt and Henry Torrès, to their cause. Algerian Jews played an important role in the Allied landings in 1942 and helped to topple Vichy rule in Algeria. Antisemitism proved to be a formidable foe, as the Crémieux Decree remained abrogated even after the fall of Vichy in North Africa. It was not until 1943 that Algerian Jews would once again become citizens when Charles de Gaulle finally reinstated the Crémieux Decree.

The final chapter traces the postwar frustrations of Algerian Jews, especially in the aftermath of the battle to reinstate the Crémieux Decree. It focuses on the final test of Algerian Jewish identities: the Algerian War. It also examines the challenges Algerian Muslims faced as they fought to gain rights, especially the extreme violence of Sétif and

---

[194] Service des Questions Juives, *Recensement des Juifs par Nationalité au 15 Juin 1942*, CDJC-LXXXIV-75.

Guelma in May 1945. This chapter traces the final battles fought by Algerian Muslims to gain French rights even as independence became a possibility. Over the course of the war, Algerian Jews attempted to remain on the periphery of the conflict, even as the violence hit close to home. Ultimately, Algerian Jews had to make a choice as to whether their future would be in France or in an independent Algeria. Most reluctantly chose France.

1   Competing for Rights and Identity
Citizenship and Antisemitism in Fin-de-siècle Algeria

In fin-de-siècle Algeria, the colonists endured economic upheavals and political and electoral anxiety.[1] French settlers feared attacks by the Muslim majority and the *peril étranger*, the foreign threat posed by the growing numbers of non-French Europeans who made the colony their home. The enfranchisement of Algeria's native Jews also concerned the French settlers who saw their limited hold on the colony further diminished. In this climate of general insecurity, settlers' anxieties about enfranchised Algerian Jews coalesced in the form of virulent antisemitism. Antisemitism served as a weapon to be used by politicians and opportunists who sought to gain power, prestige, and wealth by controlling municipal governments, the most important site of local power in the colony. The *colons*' "status anxieties" fueled antisemitism.[2] Status anxiety, also called status inconsistency by sociologists, is a result of restricting access to a certain class, status, or community. Studies have shown that concerns regarding status, especially among those who see their status as declining, can lead to extremism.[3] Status anxieties unified French settlers and newly naturalized Europeans under the common cause of restricting the intrusion and perceived threat of Algerian Jews into politics and the economy.

Charles-Robert Ageron argued that in this climate of fear and uncertainty an "abortive" revolution emerged in the 1890s in Algeria, in which *colons* sought to separate the colony from the metropole under the guise of antisemitism.[4] Although Ageron's analysis is well founded, it is also important to examine the competition between various groups of citizens in the colony for the limited resources of state, which could be accessed primarily through municipal government. Antisemitism was not just

---

[1] Ageron, *Les Algériens musulmans et la France 1871–1919*, 546, 552.

[2] Richard Hofstadter used this term in his *Age of Reform* (1955). See also Callow, Jr், ed., *The City Boss in America*, 175.

[3] Gary B. Rush, "Status Consistency and Right-Wing Extremism," *American Sociological Review*, Vol. 32, No. 1 (February 1967): 88–92.

[4] Charles-Robert Ageron, *Modern Algeria: A History from 1830 to the Present* (Trenton: Africa World Press, Inc, 1991), 63.

a cover for separatist impulses, but an entrenched reality in key Algerian cities. Through the processes of naturalization in the colony different groups of citizens in the colony – French of metropolitan origin, known as *français d'origine*, Jews naturalized by the Crémieux Decree in 1870, and the newly naturalized immigrants from Europe in 1889, known as *néos* – articulated their identities by denigrating other groups of citizens as they competed for control over municipal governments.

This chapter analyzes the way in which the *néos* used Jews as a foil to prove themselves as Frenchmen and to assert that they were even "more French than the French."[5] The expansion and diversification of the colonial citizenry during the 1890s led to increased competition for the scarce resources of municipal governments and the colonial state. I argue that antisemitism in Algeria was not a cover for a separatist revolution; rather it was an organic movement, fed by the metropole, but nourished by local conflicts, frustrations, and biases for stratification and self-segregation among the various colonial groups. Antisemitism was a means by which the *néos* sought to integrate themselves more fully into Algerian society. Not all of the newly naturalized French citizens found antisemitism appealing, but some antisemites secured power in municipal governments by harnessing and capitalizing on the anxiety of *néos* and French *colons*.

Citizenship and *le péril étranger*

Following the arrival of the French in Algeria, the colonial project soon met significant hurdles, the most immediate being the question of how to establish and secure a settler society within the majority Muslim colony.[6] In addition to the French settlers, immigrants from Spain, Italy, and Malta settled in the colony, following agricultural, political, and economic crises in their home countries. These Europeans imagined Algeria as a land of opportunity. Although many originally came to Algeria with the expectation of returning home, they later formed the masses of pied-noirs filled with "*nostalgérie*" in 1962.[7] The 1889 legislation that facilitated immigrants' access to naturalization increased the numbers of French in the colony in order to decrease the risk of

---

[5] Andrea L. Smith, *Colonial Memory and Postcolonial Europe: Maltese Settlers in Algeria and France* (Bloomington: Indiana University Press, 2006), 110.

[6] See, for example, Caroline Elkins and Susan Pederson, eds., *Settler Colonialism in the Twentieth Century: Projects, Practices, and Legacies* (New York: Routledge, 2005).

[7] Sheila Crane identifies author Henri de Monthelant as the coiner of the term *nostalgérie* in her article "Architecture at the Ends of Empire: Urban Reflections between Algiers and Marseille" in Gayan Prakash and Kevin M. Kruse, eds., *The Spaces of the Modern City: Imaginaries, Politics, and Everyday Life* (Princeton: Princeton University Press, 2008), 128.

a potential revolution by the Muslim majority. The assimilationist trend in France during the 1880s widened the definition of citizenship, and as a result incorporated immigrants into the mass of citizens.[8] Dissimilar in their origins, these *néos* did not assimilate fully, but rather remained separate and distinct groups in the colony.

The Maltese in Algeria reflect the complicated experience of the *néos*, caught between integration and the desire to return home. The Maltese came to Algeria in the late nineteenth century following a series of droughts, famine, and epidemics.[9] By the 1870s, Algeria had become the "Eldorado" for Maltese emigrants, chosen over other destinations such as Tripoli, Egypt, Tunisia, and Greece.[10] Most Maltese immigrants in Algeria worked in agriculture; others served as government translators because they spoke an Arabic dialect.[11] In fact, the similarities between the Maltese immigrants and the Algerian Muslims led *colons* to lump the two groups together, much to the chagrin of the Maltese. As fervent Catholics and new colonists, the Maltese feared being associated with Muslims, who were seen by the French as inherently unassimilable.[12]

In contrast to the popular theory of a melting pot, or *le creuset algérien*, the experience of the *néos* was heavily racialized and hierarchic. The *français d'origine* were at the top, as administrators, and owners of factories, businesses, and estates, followed by naturalized Spanish and Italian migrants, then the Maltese, and at the bottom the naturalized Jews, just above the Algerian Muslims.[13] Italian and Spanish immigrants distanced themselves from the Maltese, so as not to be associated with them or be seen as a "pale copy of the Arab."[14] Following the naturalization *en masse* of immigrants in 1889, the Maltese integrated into the ranks of the *néo-français*. By the early twentieth century, the Maltese immigrants began intermarrying, arguing for a common "Latin heritage" and blurring distinctions between groups of *néos*.[15] It is important to note, however, that even the term "Latin," which was meant to identify a shared past, was highly racialized.

Spanish immigrants made up the most significant non-French European group in the colony, and as such were considered the representatives of the *péril étranger*.[16] Spanish immigrants came to Algeria to escape the political turmoil in Spain, including the federalist uprisings in

---

[8] Brubaker, *Citizenship and Nationhood*, 107.
[9] Marc Donato, *L'Émigration des Maltais en Algérie au XIXème Siècle* (Montpellier: Éditions Africa Nostra, 1985), 37.
[10] Ibid., 53; Marc Donato, *Elisa, La Maltaise: Histoire des Maltais d'Algérie, 1830–1962* (Nice: Éditions Jacques Gandini, 2002), 37.
[11] Donato, *L'Émigration des Maltais*, 159.   [12] Ibid., 84–85.
[13] The Maltese continued to be associated with Arabs even sixty years following their arrival. Smith, *Colonial Memory*, 21, 94.
[14] Donato, *L'Émigration des Maltais*, 171.   [15] Ibid., 176.   [16] Ibid., 127.

1868 and 1869.[17] Following the overthrow of Queen Isabella II in 1868, the Carlist uprising in 1873 brought many political refugees to Algeria.[18] By 1860, 114,320 Spanish immigrants made Algeria their new home, and their numbers increased further between 1870 and 1890, the "Golden Age" of Spanish migration to Algeria.[19] Most of the new arrivals settled in the department of Oran, which had the largest Spanish population in North Africa.[20] In 1891, 4,000 Italians, 67,000 French (of French metropolitan origin), 20,000 naturalized Jews, and 102,453 Spaniards lived in Oran.[21] Spanish immigrants worked in agriculture, as manual laborers, and as small-scale farmers.[22]

Spanish immigrants increased the French *colons'* general sense of insecurity in the colony. The fear of the *péril étranger*, particularly following the 1889 naturalization law, caused many *colons* to hope for a return to *jus sanguinis* over *jus soli*.[23] However, the new immigrants also represented a significant new political constituency and politicians, particularly those in the radical party at the time, appealed to the antisemitism of Spanish *néos* as a means to gain political power.[24]

Italians in Algeria also proved to be a politically significant group in the colony, although numerically smaller than the Spanish. The earliest Italians arrived soon after the occupation of Algeria in 1830 to work as fishermen. Between the unification of Italy in 1861 and 1866, 5,000 Italian immigrants arrived in Algeria.[25] The height of Italian immigration to Algeria occurred between 1880 and 1890, due to the agricultural crisis in Italy.[26] Most immigrants came from southern Italy and Sicily and by 1889, Italian immigrants numbered 50,000.[27] Max Régis, perhaps the most famous son of Italian immigrants, is the subject of the next chapter.

[17] Jean-Jacques Jordi, *Espagnol en Oranie: Histoire d'Une Migration, 1830–1914* (Calvisson: Éditions Jacques Gandini, 1996), 123.

[18] M. Barthelemy-Saint-Hilaire, minister of foreign affairs, to His Excellency M. le Duc de Fernan-Nunez, Spanish ambassador to Paris, July 23, 1881, in *Affaires Étrangères: Documents Diplomatiques. Affaires de Saida (1881-1882)* (Paris: Imprimerie Nationale, 1883), CAOM FM F/80/1683. See also Jordi, *Espagnol en Oranie*, 127.

[19] Jordi, *Espagnol en Oranie*, 9.

[20] Ibid., 26. See also Brubaker's discussion of the differences between France and Germany naturalization legislation in *Citizenship and Nationhood*.

[21] Jordi, *Espagnol en Oranie*, 10.   [22] Ibid., 183, 193.

[23] Ibid., 156. See also Patrick Weil, "The History and Memory of Discrimination in the Domain of French Nationality: The Case of the Jews and Algerian Muslims," *HAGAR, International Social Science Review*, Vol. 6, No. 1 (2005): 52–53.

[24] Jordi, *Espagnol en Oranie*, 161.

[25] Gérard Crespo, *Les Italiens en Algérie, 1830–1960: Histoire et Sociologie d'une Migration* (Calvission: Éditions Jacques Gandini, 1994), 38, 41.

[26] Ibid., 13.

[27] Kamel Kateb, *Européens, "Indigènes" et Juifs en Algérie (1830–1962): Représentations et réalités des populations* (Paris: Éditions de l'Institut National d'Études Démographiques, 2001), 28; Crespo, *Les Italiens en Algérie*, 11.

Many Italians settled in the department of Constantine.[28] Because maritime activity was an integral element in the Algerian economy, Italians found a niche in occupations relating to the fish market.[29] In 1930, fishermen in Algeria were still known as "Napolitains" even though the fishermen were not necessarily of Italian origin.[30] Italians also concentrated in the fields of stonework, masonry, ironworks, locksmiths, mechanics, wheelwrights, and in building the colony's infrastructure.[31] Even before the 1889 naturalization law, some Italians showed a desire to become French. Italian children learned French, but rarely gave up their native language.[32]

Some Italian *néos* intermarried with French settlers, producing a new generation of *Algériens*, like the fictional Cagayous of the 1890s.[33] Despite the numbers of mixed marriages, Italians, Spanish, and Maltese were still positioned well below the French in the colonial hierarchy. French *colons* deemed these immigrants assimilable due to their shared "Latin" roots, although they often maintained ties to their homelands through language and traditions.

By contrast, French politicians and administrators believed that the native Jewish population could prove useful intermediaries in the colony, in part because they lacked competing national allegiances. In the 1860s, some Jews in Algeria began to demand more access to rights, petitioning Napoleon III during his visit to the colony in 1865. This led to the sénatus-consulte (senate declaration) of July 14, 1865, that allowed Jews (also Muslims and new immigrants) access to a naturalization process. As discussed in the introduction, this naturalization process was complicated and required abandoning one's personal status, which meant giving up the right to be ruled by one's religious law.[34] Approximately 2,000 Muslims requested naturalizations during the eighty years during which the sénatus-consulte remained in effect.[35]

---

[28] Crespo, *Les Italiens en Algérie*, 20. Régis hailed from Sétif, and even following his move to Algiers, Régis' elderly mother remained in the family homestead. Ledger Ligue Antisémite 1899 (surveillance), August 4, 1899, AN F/7/12882.

[29] Crespo, *Les Italiens en Algérie*, 57, 69.   [30] Ibid., 75.   [31] Ibid., 81–84.

[32] Ibid., 135, 144.

[33] According to Crespo, there was more intermarriage between French and Italians than any other immigrant group. Crespo, *Les Italiens en Algérie*, 102. According to Ageron, however, marriages between French and Spanish immigrants were more numerous, based on the belief that such unions produced "a strong race, really Algerian." Ageron, *Les Algériens Musulmans et la France*, 577.

[34] "Interpellation Samary, Chambre des Députés, Séance du 19 février 1898," AN F/19/11145. See also Catherine Coquery-Vidrovitch, "Nationalité et Citoyenneté en Afrique Occidentale Français: Originaires et Citoyens dans le Sénégal Colonial," *The Journal of African History*, Vol. 42 (2001).

[35] Ruedy, *Modern Algeria*, 75–76.

Although often associated with Jews, the sénatus-consulte provided a pathway to citizenship for the growing numbers of non-French immigrants.[36] Upon proving three years of residency, a non-French immigrant could apply for citizenship through the sénatus-consulte. Between 1865 and 1914, 36,869 individual naturalizations on the basis of the sénatus occurred.[37] By contrast, the 1870 Crémieux Decree and 1889 law automatically naturalized Algerian Jews and the sons of immigrants. These laws, for the most part, removed the element of choice from naturalization as opting out was a complicated procedure.

The 1889 law naturalized the children of European immigrants at the age of twenty-one unless they specifically refused the naturalization.[38] David Prochaska identifies this step as an integral action in creating the *pied-noir* community, which he describes as a "heady new Mediterranean stew," and Richard Ayoun calls a mosaic.[39] In 1896, Algeria consisted of 318,137 *français d'origine* and naturalized Frenchmen, 48,763 naturalized Algerian Jews, and 211,580 foreign (European) immigrants. The non-French European immigrants constituted 36.6 percent of the total European/naturalized population.[40]

The images of the stew and of the mosaic imply the integration of the different elements in a coherent manner. Although these groups did at times coexist, they also competed for power. Especially after 1889, there were, however, attempts to create a cohesive French colonial Algerian identity. Historian Patricia Lorcin describes the French effort to discover a Roman or Latin heritage in Algeria. As part of this project, the European population in the colony took on the identity of the "Latins of Africa."[41] These "Latins" were the forebears of a new "handsome, hardworking, ardent race," which at the turn of the century became the "Algerians."[42]

---

[36] Kateb, *Européens, "Indigènes," et Juifs en Algérie*, 29. See also Michael Brett, "Legislating for Inequality in Algeria: The Sénatus-consulte of 14 July 1865," *Bulletin of the School of Oriental and African Studies, University of London*, Vol. 41, No. 3 (1988): 455.

[37] Kateb, *Européens, "Indigènes," et Juifs en Algérie*, 188.

[38] Prochaska, *Making Algeria French*, 153. See also Weil, "The History and Memory of Discrimination," 52–53. Blévis emphasizes the exclusionary aspects of the 1889 law with regard to Algerian Muslims, *Sociologie d'un droit colonial*, 93, 333.

[39] Prochaska, *Making Algeria French*, 155. Richard Ayoun describes the impact of the 1889 law as creating a mosaic in the colony.

[40] Kateb, *Européens, "Indigènes," et Juifs en Algérie*, 187.

[41] Patricia M.E. Lorcin, "Rome and France in Africa: Recovering Colonial Algeria's Latin Past," *French Historical Studies*, Vol. 25, No. 2 (Spring 2002): 311–312.

[42] Ibid., 319; David Prochaska, "History as Literature, Literature as History: Cagayous of Algiers," *The American Historical Review*, Vol. 101, No. 3 (June 1996): 706. Geneviève Dermenjian described the way in which the various groups remained separate and lived in distinct neighborhoods. Geneviève Dermenjian, *Juifs et Européens d'Algérie: L'Antisémitisme Oranais (1892–1905)* (Jerusalem: Institut Ben-Zvi, 1983), 21. Max Régis' older brother, Alfred, and sister, Claudine, rejected French citizenship and

The term "Latin" is highly racialized, in part because it aimed at excluding other groups, such as Jews and Muslims in the colony. Such exclusion often fused with antisemitism.

The law of June 26, 1889, automatically naturalized immigrants on the basis of certain criteria: first, children born to a non-French father, who himself was born on French soil, would be naturalized unless they formally rejected French citizenship upon reaching age twenty-one; second, children themselves born in Algeria, to a father who was not born on French soil, could become citizens as long as they could prove that they had lived on French soil until age twenty-one. Many of these new citizens maintained strong ties to their native cultures, languages, and customs, thus causing the *français d'origine* to question their allegiance to France. In 1899, the governor-general estimated that of 384,000 French, 135,000 came from France, 140,000 were born in Algeria, and 109,000 were naturalized.[43] Although they could technically refuse French citizenship within one year of being naturalized, few did.[44]

The 1889 law nearly immediately doubled the number of young electors in the colony. In the 1890s, some politicians of the *parti français* indulged in xenophobia that reflected the growing concern over the masses of new voters, including Jews and the *néo-français*, also known as citizens of *fraîche date*.[45] Although initially wary of the new citizens, politicians recognized that many of the new French citizens sought to prove themselves to be truly French in contrast to the most questionable French citizens in their eyes, the Jews. The 1889 law "counterbalanced" the Crémieux Decree.[46]

In the 1890s, Auguste Robinet immortalized the *néo* in his fictional character Cagayous, the son of a Spanish immigrant and French *colon*. Cagayous was immensely popular among *néos* who related to his background and exploits. Initially published as a serial in settlers' newspapers and eventually printed in book form, the *Cagayous* series appeared between 1894 and 1920. Cagayous came to represent the evolving identity of the *néos* in the colony, encompassing traits of Maltese, Spanish, and

remained Italian citizens. Richard Ayoun, "Max Régis: Un Antijuif au tournant du XXe Siècle," *Revue d'histoire de la Shoah*, Vol. 173 (October–December 2001): 142, 144.
[43] Ageron, *Les Algériens Musulmans et la France*, 578. How Algerian Jews factor into these calculations is unclear. In some ways, the 1889 naturalization law had larger repercussions for Algeria than the Crémieux Decree because of the larger number of new settlers naturalized by the law. Ayoun, "Max Régis," 141.
[44] Weil, "The History and Memory of Discrimination," 52–53.
[45] The famous cry of the antisemitic parties in the late 1890s "*À bas les Juifs*" (down with the Jews) began as "*À bas les Juifs et les étrangers*" (down with the Jews and foreigners) and "*La France aux Français*" (France for the French). Ageron, *Les Algériens Musulmans et la France*, 579.
[46] Lorcin, "Rome and France," 312.

Italian immigrants, and specifically the lower classes. As such, Cagayous spoke *pataouète*, a French dialect that incorporated Mediterranean languages and Arabic.[47]

In the *Cagayous* series, Robinet found inspiration in the turn of the century debates on the making of a new Algerian people.[48] When asked if he and his comrades were French, Cagayous famously replied: "We are Algerians!" This declaration demonstrates the evolution of the collective identity of the *néos*, while simultaneously excluding Algerian Muslims and Jews from the ranks of "Algerians."[49] In *Cagayous Antijuif*, Cagayous exclaims to his assorted friends "me, if I'm not naturally French, I am Algerian."[50] For Cagayous, complete assimilation to French identity was impossible; however, becoming an Algerian was a way of maintaining his cultural traditions while also finding acceptance among the French of Algeria.

Like Robinet, author Louis Bertrand depicted French Algeria as part of a "Latin Mediterranean," which orbited around France as its spiritual center.[51] Bertrand sought to create a sense of place and history for the Mediterranean and French settlers in the colony, where he "rediscovered" the remains of a shared Latin-Mediterranean culture, while simultaneously rejecting Arab/Berber claims on the land.[52] By alluding to a shared Roman/Latin ancestry, he used the past to establish a claim on the present in Algeria and to unite the heterogeneous masses of the *néos* and French *colons* under a single flag of *Algériens*.[53]

Upon establishing their new identity in the colony after the 1889 naturalization, the *néos* vociferously demonstrated it by taking on a common enemy, the Jews, during the *crise antijuive* of the 1890s. Antisemitism became entrenched in electoral politics in Algeria, because Jews were accused of voting as a bloc. The Opportunist and Radical Republican parties in Algeria competed in close elections. In the late nineteenth century, the Radical Party was the far-left political party, whose influence developed after the Franco-Prussian War. The Opportunists were more moderate. After the Crémieux Decree, Jews generally voted for Opportunists, but they composed only 9 percent of all electors in Algeria in 1899. Their influence was often exaggerated by

---

[47] Robinet used the pseudonym "Musette." Prochaska, "History as Literature," 674–675, 686–687.
[48] Peter Dunwoodie, *Writing French Algeria* (Oxford: Oxford University Press, 1998), 142.
[49] Prochaska, "History as Literature," 706. Furthermore, the identity of the "Algerians" is closely connected to the separatist movement, because they were making explicit the difference between French and Algerian.
[50] Musette, *Cagayous Antijuif* (Alger: Imprimerie Ernest Mallebay, 1898), 18.
[51] Dunwoodie, *Writing French Algeria*, 84. [52] Ibid., 88, 100.
[53] Ibid., 84, 88, 92; Lorcin, "Rome and France," 323.

politicians. Even before the *crise antijuive*, Radical Republicans used the Jews' voting tendencies as anticapitalist rhetoric that appealed to the *néos*.[54] Some Spanish, Italian, and Maltese *néos* were easily influenced by portrayals of Jews as moneylenders sapping the strength of the hard-working artisans, laborers, and small business-owning *néos*.[55] Cagayous expressed his deep antisemitic sentiments in *Cagayous Antijuif*: "there are those who have the courage to say 'Down with the Jews!,' we will kick them [the Jews] into the sea ..."[56] The *néos'* desire to prove themselves as Algerians – and as Frenchmen – coincided with economic crises that fed the rabid antisemitism of fin-de-siècle Algeria.[57]

In the early 1890s, continuing worldwide depression exhausted econo-mies in metropoles and colonies and led to decreasing demand and prices. A series of agricultural crises between 1893 and 1897 eroded settler agriculture and commerce in the colony. Newly arrived settlers to Algeria were rarely prepared for the climate in Algeria, where rainfall was irregular, and faced periodic droughts and plagues. Amid these difficulties, however, advances in mechanization and dry farming improved the production of wheat. In addition, with the phylloxera epi-demic in France, many viticulturists fled to Algeria to renew their lives as *vignerons* in a new place. The growth of the wine industry in Algeria rested on access to credit; many settlers became indebted to the banks. The economy in Algeria became increasingly based on viticulture.[58] After diplomatic ties broke between France and Italy in 1893, which closed the French market to Italian wines, the Algerian wine industry blossomed.[59]

The wine crisis of 1893–1894 in the metropole caused significant problems for the wine industry in Algeria as well, leading to oversupply of wine in the mid- and late 1890s, during which wine sold at cost or below. In Algeria, many, from petty traders to the agricultural laborers,

---

[54] Prochaska, *Making Algeria French*, 202. See also Leo Loubere, *Radicalism in Mediterranean France: Its Rise and Decline, 1848–1914* (Albany: State University of New York Press, 1974).

[55] Prochaska, "History as Literature," 695.   [56] Musette, *Cagayous Antijuif*, 28–29.

[57] Geneviève Dermenjian, *La Crise antijuive Oranaise (1895–1905): L'antisémitisme dans l'Algérie coloniale* (Paris: Éditions L'Harmattan, 1986), 7; Charles-Robert Ageron, *Politiques Coloniales au Maghreb* (Paris: Presses Universitaires de France, 1972), 1895; Jordi, *Espagnol en Oranie*, 165; Crespo, *Les Italiens en Algérie*, 114.

[58] Ageron, *Politiques Coloniales au Maghreb*, 155; James Sampson, "Cooperation and Conflicts: Institutional Innovation in France's Wine Markets, 1870–1911," *The Business History Review*, Vol. 79, No. 3 (Autumn, 2005): 541. See also Owen White's work in progress on wine production in Algeria.

[59] Jean Graniage, "North Africa," in J.D. Fage and Roland Oliver, eds., *The Cambridge History of Africa, Volume 6, 1870–1905* (Cambridge: Cambridge University Press, 1985), 163. See also George Gale, *Dying on the Vine: How Phylloxera Transformed Wine* (Berkeley: University of California Press, 2011), 58.

suffered as a result of the wine slump.[60] Frustrated European Algerians blamed the metropole for its lack of support in the time of crises.[61] It was within this context of economic decline and failed support from the metropole that antisemitism emerged as a powerful political force, including the mass-scale violence of May 1897 in Oran. Although some Jews suffered economically as a result of the *mévente* (slump), few were allowed to own the land necessary to participate in viticulture. As a result, they were mostly spared from the economic depression that followed. For the impacted settlers, the Jews became even clearer economic competitors.

Times of economic crisis often provide fodder for strong discontentment with government and, as a result, scapegoating. Hannah Arendt and Zeev Sternhell have identified the importance of political and economic crises as precursors for totalitarian politics and fascism, respectively. Arendt links the power of the "mob" and its economic frustrations as a necessary prerequisite for totalitarianism.[62] Sternhell analyzes the evolution of France's fascist movements and indicates the significance of "total" crisis in the evolution of fascism. Sternhell adds that antisemitism was a powerful "instrument of unification" of people and emphasizes its political utility.[63] Ageron connects the 1894–1896 economic crisis to the evolution and organization of the new *algérieniste* separatist movement.[64] Indeed, the significant economic downturn in the colony created frustration and resentment among colonists toward the metropole, which had not adequately supported them through the crisis. In this time of discontent, antisemitism flourished in the colony especially during the municipal election cycle of 1898.

Multiple Antisemitisms and Electoral Politics in Fin-de-Siècle France and Algeria

Antisemitism intensified in the metropole and in Algeria in the 1890s. In May 1892, the French antisemitic newspaper *La Libre Parole* published a series on how Jews were invading the French army and were using corrupt means to receive the best assignments without having the requisite skills. These articles preceded the public outrage that followed the November 1894 treason accusation of Alfred Dreyfus. The Dreyfus

---

[60] Pierre Nora, *Les Français d'Algérie* (Paris: René Julliard, 1961), 102.
[61] Pierre Hebey, *Alger 1898: La Grande vague antijuive* (Paris: NiL Éditions, 1996), 74.
[62] Arendt, *Origins of Totalitarianism*, 36, 107, 311, 352.
[63] Zeev Sternhell, *Neither Right Nor Left: Fascist Ideology in France*, trans. David Maisel (Princeton: Princeton University Press, 1986), 1, 14, 44–45.
[64] Ageron, *Les Algériens musulmans et la France*, 574–575.

Affair provided an outlet for the latent antisemitism in both the metropole and the colony and led to violence throughout France and Algeria in 1898. In Algeria, newspaper readers kept current on all of the proceedings of the Dreyfus Affair. Antisemites used the affair as proof of the Jews' lack of patriotism and the threat they posed to the safety of the *mère patrie* and to the French people. Throughout the colony and in the metropole, the war cry of the antisemites rang out: "*À bas les Juifs!*"[65]

Modern antisemitism emerged from multiple sources: from the development of the nation-state and its attendant politics, and from nascent right-wing political movements, like the aggressively nationalistic Boulangists.[66] During a Chamber of Deputies session on November 11, 1898, Deputy Thomson described the antisemitic movement in Algeria as the "new incarnation of Boulangisme."[67] Modern antisemitism incorporated various political and social trends of the era: social radicalism, Social Darwinism, and traditional, religious antisemitism. Antisemites mixed nationalistic sentiment with economic frustrations and religion. The economic frustrations of the lower classes became a source of power for modern antisemites. Antisemites portrayed the Jew as unwilling to do manual labor to earn his income, instead exploiting the working classes and the peasantry, who were idealized as honest, hard-workers.[68] Antisemitism, therefore, became a sign of nationalism and appealed to those seeking inclusion, like the *néos*.[69]

Antisemitism in Algeria surpassed that of fin-de-siècle France as the premiere example of nineteenth-century antisemitism. On both sides of the Mediterranean, antisemitism fused with nationalism, with the Jew

---

[65] Steven Uran, "La réception de l'Affaire en Algérie," in Michel Drouin, ed., *L'Affaire Dreyfus de A à Z* (Paris: Flammarion, 1994), 527. See also James P. Daughton, "A Colonial Affair?: Dreyfus and the French Empire," *Historical Reflections/Réflexions Historiques* Vol. 31, No. 3 (2005): 469–483.

[66] Hannah Arendt identifies politics and the development of the nation-state even more than economics as the major factors in the evolution of what she terms "modern antisemitism" during the last third of the nineteenth century in Germany, Austria, and France. The Dreyfus Affair was emblematic of the ideological and political aspects of nineteenth-century antisemitism. Arendt, *Origins of Totalitarianism*, 28, 35, 42, 45. By contrast, Zeev Sternhell identifies the origin of modern antisemitism in France in the Boulangist movement. Zeev Sternhell, "The Roots of Popular Antisemitism in the Third Republic," in Frances Malino and Bernard Wasserstein, eds., *The Jews in Modern France* (Hanover: University Press of New England, 1985), 103.

[67] "Compte Rendu: Chambre des Deputés," November 11, 1898, CAOM FM F/80/1686. See also "Réunion antisémite de la Salle Wagram," Paris, March 4, 1898, AN F/7/12453.

[68] Sternhell, "The Roots of Popular Antisemitism," 109, 112, 115.

[69] Arendt describes the mob as being the amalgamation of the *déclassés* of all classes, frustrated with the society from which they feel excluded, who develop a hero-worship for their leaders. Arendt, *Origins of Totalitarianism*, 10, 107, 112. See also Gavin I. Langmuir, *Toward a Definition of Antisemitism* (Berkeley: University of California Press, 1990), 332.

serving as the symbol of the "anti-nation." This combination found enormous success in Algeria. The political nature of antisemitic concerns was significantly more fraught in Algeria than in the metropole because of the comparatively large percentage of votes made up of naturalized Algerian Jews – albeit still a small number. Antisemitism in the metropole was largely political in nature, but not explicitly electoral.[70] By contrast, Algerian antisemitism was primarily based on electoral concerns, real or imagined.[71] Prochaska describes the Crémieux Decree as a ticking time bomb that would explode during the Dreyfus Affair.[72] In a 1900 brochure printed in Algiers, "Le Juif Algérien et la question antisémite en Algérie," Gustave des Illiers identified aspects of the Algerian Jew that fomented antisemitic attitudes in the colony. He wrote that the Crémieux Decree required Jews to exercise rights for which they were "entirely unprepared."[73] Des Illiers described the Jews as incapable of having political convictions and voting according to the directions of the consistory leadership.[74]

In his analysis of the colonial city of Bône, now Annaba, Prochaska describes Algerian antisemitism as having a distinctly electoral fous. Prochaska also notes its strong racial element, which was associated with severe status anxiety. The *français d'origine* were also concerned with the fact that Algeria was becoming a "dumping ground" for immigrants. They feared being overrun not only by Algerian Muslims but also by non-French settlers who represented a "foreign peril" to the Frenchness of the colony. The *néos* also experienced heightened anxiety even after 1889, because of their low economic status.[75] The *petits blancs* ultimately viewed the Jews as their main source of competition in the colony and were drawn to the rhetoric of antisemitic politicians in the colony.

The anti-Jewish crisis in Algeria was part of what Ageron calls an "abortive Algerian revolution," but its significance was also independent of the revolutionary goals of some colons.[76] The antisemitism of the

---

[70] Political antisemitism encompassed what I call "electoral antisemitism," which was specific to political campaigns.

[71] Carol Iancu, "Du Nouveau sur les Troubles Antijuifs en Algérie à la Fin du XIXème Siècle" in Centre Nationale de la Recherche Scientifique, *Les Relations entre Juifs et Musulmans en Afrique du Nord, XIXe-XXe Siècles: Actes du colloque international de l'Institut d'Histoire des Pays d'Outre Mer* (Paris: Éditions du Centre Nationale de la Recherche Scientifique, 1980), 173. Sternhell points to the electoral successes of anti-semitic politicians, especially the numbers of antisemitic deputies in Algiers, and the election of Max Régis as mayor. Sternhell, *Neither Right Nor Left*, 46–47.

[72] Prochaska, *Making Algeria French*, 138.

[73] Gustave des Illiers, *Le Juif algérien et la question antisemite en Algérie* (Alger: Imprimerie Pascal Crescenzo, 1900), 27.

[74] Ibid., 27–28.   [75] Prochaska, *Making Algeria French*, 204.

[76] Ageron, *Modern Algeria*, 63.

1890s emerged from the status anxieties of *colons* and *néos*, subsequently fueling the *néos'* desire to be accepted as Frenchmen and to remove Jews as status competitors. Algerian antisemitism was a prime example of nineteenth-century antisemitism, designed to purify the nation, or the colony in this case. In his 1886 tome, Edouard Drumont, a leading French antisemite, correctly predicted that Algeria "would begin the French antisemitic campaign."[77]

Developing Algerian Antisemitism

Antisemitism in the colony developed as a series of waves that predated the violence of 1898. The first wave occurred immediately following the Crémieux Decree. In 1871, Deputy Charles du Bouzet attempted to abrogate the decree by claiming that it had instigated the Arab Revolt of 1871. The Jewish community in France, together with Adolphe Crémieux, immediately refuted du Bouzet's accusation.[78] Du Bouzet's effort failed, but it stimulated the formation of antisemitic leagues in the colony. The first antisemitic league formed in Miliana in 1871 with the goal of combating Jewish voters.[79] In 1884, Fernand Grégoire founded *La Ligue socialiste antijuive*, which attracted colonists. The third antisemitic league was one of the most significant and focused on the economic and social boycotting of Jews. Founded in 1892, its organization coincided with the establishment of Edouard Drumont's *La Libre Parole*. Between 1894 and 1896, more militant antisemitic leagues organized in the major cities of the colony: Algiers, Oran, and Constantine, as well as in smaller towns.[80] In a June 1895 report, the Minister of Justice described the growth of antisemitic leagues in Algiers, Sétif, and Constantine, all of which had a distinctly electoral character. The central goal of the Algiers league, founded in 1892, was the abrogation of the Crémieux Decree. The organizations mobilized themselves in opposition to politicians who had Jewish support. The League of Constantine, like that of Sétif, focused on combating the electoral power of Opportunist Deputy Thomson, who had Jewish support.[81]

---

[77] Edouard Drumont, *La France Juive: Essai d'histoire contemporaine, tome deuxième* (Paris: C. Marpon & E. Flammarion, 1886), 47.
[78] Letter M. Le Vice-President Consistoire Centrale à M. Léopold Javal, July 30, 1871, ACC 2^E-Boite 2; Adolphe Crémieux, *Refutation de la pétition de M. Du Bouzet* (Paris: Imprimerie Schiller, 1871), 13–14.
[79] Uran, "La réception de l'Affaire en Algérie," 521.
[80] Iancu, "Du nouveau sur les troubles antijuifs," 178; Friedman, *Colonialism and After*, 19.
[81] Minister of Justice to the Minister of the Interior, "Report No. 1306.A.95," June 1895, AN F/7/12460.

The establishment of these antisemitic leagues illustrates the politicization of antisemitism in Algeria in the 1880s and 1890s, which developed in response to the alleged electoral power of Jews.[82] In 1881, the Opportunist party emerged, splitting off from the Republicans. The Opportunist party wooed the Jewish vote through its moderate program, and achieved victory.[83] As a result of the role that Jewish electors played in the 1881 elections, violence broke out in the colony, particularly in Oran.[84] Oran was particularly significant for its thriving Jewish community, led by Simon Kanoui, and was known for its recently built, large synagogue.[85] In the political imagination of the defeated parties, Jews emerged as a politically powerful group, ultimately changing the landscape of politics and elections.

One of the first major episodes of antisemitic violence in the colony occurred between June 29 and July 2, 1884.[86] This outburst resulted from the exclusion of Jewish electors from a party thrown by a local municipal political leader.[87] Jewish shops and homes were pillaged. This episode also reflects the growing interplay between antisemitism and municipal politics. In 1884, David de Moise Stora, the Treasurer of the Alliance Israélite Universelle in Algiers, likened the situation of Jews in Algiers to victims of pogroms in Russia, emphasizing the intensity of the violence. Stora complained that "persecution should not exist in civilized countries, especially in the French setting."[88] Algerian Jews would regularly invoke the supposedly civilized nature of France in their requests for intervention in times of antisemitism.

Voting in the colony was the right of citizens. However, it also meant participation in a form of commerce of democracy – earning something in

---

[82] Zosa Szajkowski, "Socialists and Radicals in the Development of Antisemitism in Algeria (1884–1900)," *Jewish Social Studies*, Vol. 10, No. 3 (July 1948): 259.

[83] David Prochaska, "The Political Culture of Settler Colonialism in Algeria: Politics in Bône (1870–1920)," *Revue de l'Occident musulman et de la Méditerranée*, No. 48–49 (1988): 296; Ibid., 260–261.

[84] Jordi, *Espagnol en Oranie*, 160; Harvey Goldberg, "Jean Jaurès and the Jewish Question: The Evolution of a Position," *Jewish Social Studies*, Vol. 20, No. 2 (April 1958): 79.

[85] Valérie Assan, "Les synagogues dans l'Algérie coloniale du XIXe siècle," *Archives juives, revue d'histoire des Juifs de France*, Vol. 37, No. 1 (2004): 78–79.

[86] Ageron, *Les Algériens musulmans et la France*, 585; Szajkowski, "Socialists and Radicals," 265–266. Kanoui references the antisemitic violence in 1884 in his letter to the Members of the Central Jewish Consistory, Paris, Algiers, April 24, 1892, ACC I^cc 38.

[87] Dermenjian, *La Crise antijuive Oranaise*, 55–56.

[88] Letter David de Moise Stora to the Treasurer of the Alliance Israelite Universelle, Paris, July 4, 1884, AIU Algérie IC2. On the 1881–1884 pogroms in Russia, see John Doyle Klier, *Russians, Jews, and the Pogroms of 1881–1882* (Cambridge: Cambridge University Press, 2011). Connecting Algerian Jews to that of Russian Jews appears to have been used to make a point to include the situation of Algerian Jews into that of world Jewry.

exchange for one's vote via the patronage system inherent in Algerian municipal politics, which I discuss in the following chapter. Local elections were the key site in which Algerian Jews' citizenship was asserted and contested. Voting in Algeria was a form of "speculation," particularly among Frenchmen.[89] Vote buying was endemic among all groups in the colony.[90] Antisemites contended that Jewish votes could be bought in a Jewish-owned store. Algerian council members established war chests with which to buy votes and candidates organized *punchs* and *aperitifs* for prospective voters. Hundreds of voters attended these events, eating and enjoying "numerous drinks" on the candidate's tab. Patronage also included other examples of the commercial exchange of votes, including offering temporary jobs or welfare subsidies.[91] Because of these activities and others, the patronage of the "political machine" controlled settler politics in Algeria.[92]

Although all citizens in the colony participated in this system of exchange of votes and benefits, antisemites and other political groups singled out Jews for corrupt voting practices. Upon joining the antisemitic camp, socialists and radicals argued that due to their immoral voting activities, Jews committed a crime against universal suffrage and were undeserving of the Crémieux Decree.[93] Socialist antisemites asserted that in France Jews held significant monetary power, but lacked the numerical strength to have any true electoral power. In Algeria, they argued, Jews had both money and numbers.[94]

Antisemites described Jews as "docile and without political formation," and accused them of blindly following the directions of their consistorial leaders. Known as the "Rothschild of Oran" and Oran's "great elector," Simon Kanoui emblematized such claims.[95] As president of the Oran consistory, Kanoui also directed its welfare funds.[96] He therefore established his own patronage-fueled system within the consistorial system. For antisemites, Kanoui's activities represented the vote-trafficking endemic in the colony.[97] In his 1886 *La France Juive*, Edouard Drumont called Kanoui a "potentate" who controlled the entire department. Within Kanoui's kingdom, the prefect was his "humble slave," as were other government officials. Jews in Constantine also participated in vote-

[89] Szajkowski, "Socialists and Radicals," 261.
[90] Prochaska, *Making Algeria French*, 176.
[91] Ibid., 187. See also McDonald, *Plunkitt of Tammany Hall*, 5.
[92] Prochaska, *Making Algeria French*, 188, 192.
[93] Szajkowski, "Socialists and Radicals," 262.
[94] Goldberg, "Jean Jaurès and the Jewish Question," 81.
[95] Ageron, *Les Algériens musulmans et la France*, 584.
[96] Iancu, "Du Nouveau sur les Troubles Antijuifs," 174.
[97] Dermenjian, *La Crise antijuive Oranaise*, 50.

trafficking. According to Drumont, the Jews in Constantine received on average two or three francs for their votes.[98]

In his 1900 analysis of the Algerian Jewish "political question," Gustave des Illiers identified the lack of Jewish political convictions as the central problem of Jewish corruption. Compounded with their innate commercial nature, he argued, Jews viewed their political rights as citizens as economic opportunity.[99] Rabbis and consistory leadership played the role of electoral advisors. Des Illiers further contended that the corrupt electoral habits of Algerian Jews infected other groups and were therefore responsible for the widespread electoral commerce. "Following the example of the Jews, Europeans, French of origin [de race] or naturalized of fresh date, sell their votes. The shameful haggling, hypocritical maneuvers, unspeakable calumnies have become standard practice during the electoral period."[100] Des Illiers reiterated Drumont's accusation at Jews: "You are French in name and not in heart."[101]

The Dreyfus Affair added fuel to antisemitism in the colony and the metropole by providing "proof" of Jewish treason. In 1895, Oran Prefect de Malherbe suggested to the mayor of Oran that it would be wise to restrict the nominations of Jews to positions within municipal services. He also noted that there were many French applicants, reflecting the growing antisemitism among colonial officials.[102] A short time later, vice president of the Constantine consistory, Abraham Stora, updated the Central Consistory members in Paris on the state of antisemitism in Algeria. Stora requested advice from Chief Rabbi Zadoc Kahn on how to "stave off the consequences of this campaign of hate and defamation, which causes fear for Jews in Algeria in general." He was particularly concerned for Jews in Constantine, where electoral antisemitism was especially strong.[103]

Antisemitism morphed based on the needs of the time. Socialism and electoral antisemitism merged in the mid-1890s alongside the Dreyfus Affair. Jean Jaurès, at the time a socialist deputy, traveled to Algeria in April 1895 to participate in the Algerian Workers Socialist Party Third Congress. There Jaurès discovered the growing intensity of the separatist movement and the power of antisemitism as an "electoral

[98] Drumont, La France Juive, tome deuxième, 34. See also the antisemitic report on the causes of the 1898 riots, Deputy Paul Samary "Interpellation Samary, Chambre des Députés, Séance du 19 février 1898," AN F/19/11145.
[99] Des Illiers, Le Juif Algérien, 27, 32. [100] Ibid., 28–30.
[101] Drumont, La France Juive, tome deuxième, 48.
[102] Prefect de Malherbe of Oran to the Mayor of Oran, "No. 1084," Oran, February 25, 1895, CAOM FM F/80/1685.
[103] Vice President of the Constantine Consistory Ab. Stora to the President and Members of the Central Consistory, Constantine, April 30, 1895, ACC I^cc 39.

platform."[104] In the beginning of May 1895, Jean Jaurès published a series of articles on the Jews of Algeria in the newspaper *La Dépêche de Toulouse*. Jaurès focused on the significant economic troubles in the colony, resulting from the agricultural crises, including the *mévente*. Jaurès portrayed the French, Arabs, and *néos* as the victims of Jewish activity. "In cities, the whole of the French population is exasperated with the Jews because by usury, by tireless commercial activity, and by abuse of political influence, they [Jews] hoard little by little the fortune, trade, profitable jobs, administrative functions, public power."[105] Jews in Algeria were more powerful, and less assimilated, than their coreligionists in France, so much so that "by its votes, the Jewish quarter determines the election."[106] According to Jaurès, the Arab and the Frenchman (either of French origin or a *néo*) could be united under the socialist – and anti-semitic – flag.[107]

In his next article on May 8, 1895, Jaurès described how the antisemitic movement in Algeria had diverged sharply from the metropole and appeared to be taking on a "revolutionary spirit."[108] Unlike most writers of the time, Jaurès took stock of rising antisemitism among Algerian Muslims. "For twenty-five years, since the Crémieux Decree, since the development of an opportunistic Republic, the Arabs watched with stupor and contempt the official control of the Algerian Jew over Algeria."[109] Jaurès depicted the "political hegemony" exercised by Jews – their capitalist regime – as the source of the Algerian Muslims' and Europeans' suffering from material and intellectual misery. He warned that without France's intervention, German and British forces, who were already distributing anti-French propaganda, would succeed in overthrowing the French in Algeria.[110]

An 1896 report on antisemitism in Algeria, directed to the attention of the Central Consistory, argued that Jews were the favorite scapegoat in

---

[104] Ageron, *Politiques Coloniales au Maghreb*, 153–154.

[105] Jean Jaurès, "La Politique: La Question Juive en Algérie," *La Dépêche de Toulouse*, May 1, 1895, CAOM FM F/80/1686.

[106] Because of the highly contested nature of Algerian elections, the Jewish question led to the development of a growing antisemitic movement. Jaurès, "La Politique: La Question juive en Algérie," May 1, 1895, CAOM FM F/80/1686.

[107] Ibid.

[108] Jean Jaurès, "La Politique: Choses algériennes," *La Dépêche de Toulouse*, May 8, 1895, CAOM FM F/80/1686.

[109] Jaurès, "La Politique: Choses algériennes," May 8, 1895, CAOM FM F/80/1686.

[110] Ibid. See Robert S. Wistrich, "Socialism and Antisemitism in Austria Before 1914," *Jewish Social Studies*, Vol. 37, No. 3/4 (Summer–Autumn, 1975): 327. See also Robert S. Wistrich, *From Ambivalence to Betrayal: The Left, The Jews, and Israel* (Lincoln: University of Nebraska Press, 2012), 44, and Harvey Goldberg, *The Life of Jean Jaures* (Madison: University of Wisconsin Press, 1962), 209.

the colony. Jews were "the common enemy, the universal scourge," unifying antisemites under the goal of abrogating the Crémieux Decree.[111] The report's author noted that antisemites found support among Algerian Muslims, whom he described as possessing an excitable character, primitive instincts, and being "half-savages."[112] Although Jews and Muslims had coexisted in Algeria for centuries, the report suggested that Arabs were particularly susceptible to incitements to violence, pillage, and theft.[113]

At the end of 1895 and the beginning of 1896, antisemites in Algeria attempted to revise electoral lists to remove as many Jewish voters as possible and thus reduce competition in elections.[114] The logic behind the purge of electors alleged that the October 7, 1871 decree imposed regulations on the nationalizations of the Crémieux Decree. In order to be an official elector, Jews were required to renounce their indigenous status before a Justice of the Peace in front of seven witnesses within 20 days of the promulgation of the 1871 decree. This regulation afforded antisemites an opportunity to enforce a little known and rarely implemented regulation to achieve their goals of decreasing Jewish electoral competition.[115] According to an April 24, 1896, edition of *La Gazette des Tribunaux* on the electoral rights of Algerian Jews, Jewish voters who were unable to prove their indigenous quality were removed from electoral lists.[116] In 1896, antisemites succeeded in disenfranchising 900 out of 1,100 Jewish voters in Constantine.[117] This tactic would be resurrected in 1937 in Sidi Bel Abbès.

The 1896 report to the Central Consistory concluded that following the revision of the electoral lists, "the Jews are no longer men, they are pariahs, inferior beings, positioned by them [antisemites] and by the authority itself [government] outside the law and humanity, everything is permitted against them."[118] The report's author suggested that without

[111] "Mémoire à Messieurs les Membres du Consistoire Centrale de France," by R.L. probably 1896, CC2E-Boîte 2.

[112] Jewish representations of Muslims are an important area of conflict, which requires further research.

[113] "Mémoire à Messieurs les Membres du Consistoire Centrale de France," ACC 2E-Boîte 2.

[114] Dermenjian, *La Crise antijuive Oranaise*, 67.

[115] "Mémoire à Messieurs les Membres du Consistoire Centrale de France," ACC 2E-Boîte 2. Antisemites used the same logic for the elimination of Jewish electors from voter lists occurred again in Sidi Bel Abbès in 1937.

[116] "Droit Électorale des Israélites en Algérie," April 24, 1896, *La Gazette des Tribunaux*, AN F/19/11145.

[117] Friedman, *Colonialism and After*, 19.

[118] "Mémoire à Messieurs les Membres du Consistoire Centrale de France," ACC 2E-Boîte 2.

electoral power, Jews were in an even more precarious position in the colony than ever before. The disenfranchisement of Jewish voters throughout Algeria paved the way for greater antisemitic electoral successes, winning a series of electoral victories in 1896 and 1897. Antisemites took over municipal councils in Constantine in 1896 and in Oran in 1897. These local successes led to the major parliamentary victories in 1898, including Drumont's election as deputy alongside three other antisemitic deputies.[119] These developments demonstrated the potential power of antisemitism in municipal politics.

Antisemitism, Violence, and Elections in 1890s Algeria

In the wake of their recent electoral successes, Algerian antisemites intensified their burgeoning movement and turned to violence. Although the 1897 violence between Jews and antisemites in Oran is one of the first major violent preludes to the 1898 riots in Algiers, there were earlier cases of antisemitic violence. Antisemites attacked Jews in Constantine in late April and in May 1896 at the time of the municipal elections. The timing of the violence and the elections indicates the inseparable nature of politics and antisemitism in the colony during this time period.

The violence began as a result of ritual murder accusations made by the republican newspaper *Silhouette* on April 26 and 28, 1896. Jewish leaders in Constantine requested the Prefect's assistance in protecting Jewish voters and maintaining calm.[120] In a letter on April 21, 1896, Abraham le Guenseur Attali, president of the Constantine Consistory, described the worsening conditions of Jews in Constantine and his fear that the situation would deteriorate further in the coming electoral period.[121]

On May 17, 1896, Attali described the anti-Jewish violence on the eve of the elections on May 3 in Constantine. As a result of the machinations of the antisemitic press in Constantine, Europeans, along with some Muslim supporters, attacked the Jewish community. According to Attali, the events that occurred around the municipal elections "exceeded our most pessimistic expectations."[122] The police appeared to be complicit with the antisemitic agitators. Attali illustrated the link between the

[119] Prochaska, *Making Algeria French*, 202–203.
[120] The accusation stated that Jews killed children whose blood they used for *galettes* (wafers). Telegram Gov-Gen to the Prefect of Constantine, May 21, 1896, CAOM Alg Const B/3/248. *Galettes* may refer to matzos, given the timing of the incident.
[121] President Abraham le Guenseur Attali (Constantine) to the Central Consistory (Paris), April 21, 1896, ACC 2E-Boîte 2.
[122] Attali to Central Consistory (Paris), May 17, 1896, ACC 2E-Boîte 2.

violence and the election. "It is difficult to imagine the cruel anguish we experienced in the midst of these hostile elements . . . to terrorize Jewish voters and prevent them from voting."[123] Those Jewish voters who decided to brave the voting stations, in spite of the dangers, suffered attacks. Attali depicted groups of "Arabs" patrolling the streets and attacking Jewish voters. Even after calm returned, the antisemitic press continued to incite attacks on Jews, which Attali termed "calls to civil war against our fellow Jews." With the newly elected antisemitic municipal council, Attali feared that the violence would escalate.[124]

This episode is significant for several reasons. First, the fact that the violence coincided with the elections indicates the link in the 1890s between antisemitism and elections and the practice of citizenship more generally. Jews faced disenfranchisement at the hands of antisemitic agitators and violence should they attempt to practice their right to vote.[125] Furthermore, the power of the antisemitic press was evident in the events of 1896 and later in Oran in 1897 and Algiers in 1898. Historian Geneviève Dermenjian describes the antisemitic party in Algeria as "the scandal party," because it leaked rumors about Jews, like ritual murder accusations, to incite both European and Algerian Muslim hostility toward Jews.[126]

Attali carefully noted that the non-Muslim agitators were "European," not explicitly French; the semantic choice infers that the antisemitic Europeans were likely *néos*, although it is impossible to be certain based on this report. The term "European" had racialized connotations and served as a way of excluding Jews and Muslims when referring to groups in Algeria at the time. These *néos* perhaps sought to demonstrate their Frenchness by participating in antisemitic violence against their status competitors, the Jews. However, according to Attali, some Algerian Muslims were the central actors of the violence. Attali wrote, "In the streets of the city, groups of Arabs, vagabonds, attack the Jews that they recognize."[127] He was especially distressed because Jews and Muslims in Algeria were formerly neighbors.

Official French documents did not mention the attacks on Jewish voters in Constantine; as a result, one must rely on Jewish communication between the local and Central consistories. The reasons for Algerian Muslims' involvement are unclear. Were they paid by European

---

[123] Ibid.   [124] Ibid.
[125] This episode is reminiscent of the violence and barriers black voters faced in the South by American *petits blancs*. See, for example, Steven F. Lawson, *Black Ballots: Voting Rights in the South, 1944–1969* (New York: Columbia University Press, 1976).
[126] Dermenjian, *La Crise antijuive oranaise*, 137.
[127] Attali to the Central Consistory (Paris), May 17, 1896, ACC 2E-Boîte 2.

antisemites who wished to keep their hands clean, or were they resentful of the political rights of Jews, rights from which Muslims were excluded? Dermenjian argues that Algerian Muslims were indeed paid to act as agitators. These agitators may not have been representative of Muslims in Algeria more generally. However, Arab-Jewish violence in the Maghreb was not limited to Algeria. In Tunis on March 27, 1897, Arabs took over the souks, beating Jews and attacking Jewish shops. The violence continued until the authorities intervened. There is, however, no obvious link between these tensions in Tunis and Constantine.[128]

Following the 1896 violence in Constantine, Oran became the epicenter of antisemitic agitation in Algeria. The conflict in Oran pitted antisemites, many of whom were *néos* of Spanish origin, against Jews.[129] The May 1897 looting, destruction of synagogues, and violence marked the beginning of the dramatic antisemitic period in Algeria that extended into the next year.[130] Unlike previous episodes of antisemitic violence, all groups participated in the violence in Oran.[131]

Although their motivations varied, antisemitic *néos* and *français d'origine* found common ground alongside some Algerian Muslims in a general distrust of their Jewish neighbors. Despite earlier misgivings, in the late 1890s French antisemites found the *néos* essential for the success of antisemitism in the colony.[132] In the anthem of the Algiers antisemitic party, the *Marseillaise antijuive* of the Bab-el-Oued, the French call upon the Spanish to join them in removing "the Jew" and "disinfecting" Algeria. The Bab-el-Oued was the French-Spanish quarter of Algiers. "Stand, you French, and you brave Spaniards, we have had enough of being subjected to the yoke of *youdis* [derogatory term for Jew]; at our threats of action, they laugh; it is necessary to sweep them away, and disinfect Algeria."[133] The use of the concept of disinfection anticipates the language used later by the Nazis in the Holocaust, but it also reflects a primary concern of the French colonial administration: disease

---

[128] Report Tunis, March 27, 1897, AN F/7/12460.

[129] Jordi, *Espagnol en Oranie*, 167, 174; Dermenjian, *La Crise antijuive Oranaise*, 43.

[130] Ageron argued that the May 1897 violence signaled the onset of the abortive revolution of the *Algériens*, citing Max Régis' term for their program: *notre révolution*. Ageron, *Politiques coloniales au Maghreb*, 161.

[131] Dermenjian, *La Crise antijuive Oranaise*, 87; Emmanuel Sivan, "Stéréotypes antijuifs dans la mentalité pied-noir," in *Les Relations entre Juifs et Musulmans en Afrique du Nord*, 168.

[132] Sivan, "Stéréotypes antijuifs," 166.

[133] Quoted in Sivan, "Stéréotypes antijuifs," 167.

and making uncivilized territories habitable. In order to make colonies a home for colonists, diseases and tropical illnesses had to be eradicated to pave the way for civilization.[134] The antisemites adopted this language of colonialism, and of Pasteur, to make their message more appealing to French colonists.

The antisemitic violence of May 1897 was the most widespread to date in the colony, originating in Mostaganem and radiating throughout the department of Oran. For some néos, participation in the antisemitic attacks served as proof that they were "more French than the French."[135] The violence of 1897 also promoted Algerian Jewish defense, in terms of not only physical self-defense but also the protection of their identity as French citizens. It is also important to note that, coincidentally, antisemitic rumors spread in the metropole in the aftermath of the Charity Bazaar fire in Paris on May 4, 1897. Although the two events are likely unrelated, antisemites surely capitalized on the growing anxiety and paranoia of the public at the time.[136]

The 1897 conflict in Oran began on May 16 when the Joyeux Club Cycle Oranais took part in a bicycle tour of Mostaganem and reflects the intersection of antisemitism and municipal politics. Paul Irr, an antisemitic municipal council member and "one of the most violent antisemites in Oran," served as the leader of the Joyeux Club's delegation, which consisted nearly entirely of Spanish immigrants and other néos.[137] Irr supposedly chose Mostaganem because of its population of approximately 700 Jews. At the end of the first day of the tour, the Joyeux Club, along with their Mostaganem colleagues, adjourned to the Hôtel de France where they enjoyed a dinner on the terrace. During dessert, the young cyclists sang antisemitic songs and Irr made a speech. Among the pedestrians along the sidewalk in front of the hotel were several Jews who took offense to the raucous singing and insults, but did not respond. Following dinner, the already drunk cyclists relocated to the Café Massoulier, the biggest café in Mostaganem.[138]

---

[134] On the subject of health and medicine in the colonies, see Eric T. Jennings, *Curing the Colonizers: Hydrotherapy, Climatology, and French Colonial Spas* (Durham: Duke University Press, 2006). See also Sokhieng Au, *Mixed Medicines: Health and Culture in French Colonial Cambodia* (Chicago: Chicago University Press, 2011).

[135] Smith, *Colonial Memory*, 110; Jordi, *Espagnol en Oranie*, 163.

[136] Michel Winock, *Nationalism, Anti-Semitism, and Fascism in France* (Stanford: Stanford University Press, 1998), 59, 73–74. The subject of the links between antisemitism in the metropole and the colony is the focus of Chapter 2.

[137] "Mémoire sur les troubles de l'Oranie," May 31, 1897, CAOM FM F/80/1685. The provenance of this report is unclear, but it is an official document, perhaps requested by officials and conducted by a third party. It is clear that the author of the report is not antisemitic. See also Jordi, *Espagnol en Oranie*, 169.

[138] "Mémoire sur les troubles de l'Oranie," May 31, 1897, CAOM FM F/80/1685.

A 19-year-old Jewish man, named Serfaty, accompanied by six Catholic friends, entered the café because he heard that Irr had insulted Jews. That Serfaty arrived with Catholic friends reveals that although antisemitism was on the rise, there was still some positive interaction among the various groups in the colony. After confronting Irr, Serfaty stated that "if someone were to yell 'down with the Jews' I would respond 'Vive les Juifs!' " Anticipating a conflict, the café's proprietor asked Serfaty's group to leave and the police forcibly removed three of Serfaty's friends. Serfaty and three other friends remained in the café, drinking beer and keeping Irr in their sights. Frustrated with the continued provocation, Irr demanded why the proprietor could not remove a Jew from the premises. Serfaty responded, "I am the only Jew here and am ready to fight you, where you want, and when you want." Irr's fellow cyclists attempted to calm him, and eventually left the café at 10 or 11 pm.[139]

After leaving, the cyclists found themselves in front of the theater of Mostaganem, where they shouted, "Down with the Jews!" several times. Not far behind, Serfaty and several other young people followed. "You Oranais, you have come here to cause problems and to teach people in our country to do the same," said Serfaty. A fight broke out between Serfaty and Irr, which escalated into a larger brawl between the two groups. After Irr made more antisemitic insults, Serfaty pulled out a knife and stabbed him in the chest. The police arrested Serfaty and four other Jews. The next day, May 17, the news of the attempted murder of Irr and of the critical condition of two young cyclists, one of them a naturalized Spanish immigrant, spread throughout Mostaganem. Newspapers proclaimed Irr a martyr. Jews locked themselves in their homes for fear of retaliation.[140]

On the evening of May 17, antisemitic Arabs, Spaniards, and Frenchmen descended upon the Jewish quarter of Mostaganem. Shouting "death to the Jews," the demonstrators threw stones, breaking shop windows and looting the contents. Eventually the rioters arrived at the synagogue, breaking down the doors, destroying the interior, taking rugs, demolishing pews, and stealing silver and gold, as well as money destined for the poor. According to a report, "Arab" and "Spanish" demonstrators defamed the Torah and Bibles.[141]

---

[139] This report states that the cycling delegation went to a café, whereas other reports and Dermenjian's analysis state that the delegation went to a brothel. See "Mémoire sur les troubles de l'Oranie," CAOM FM F/80/1685; Dermenjian, *La Crise antijuive Oranaise*, 74–75.

[140] "Mémoire sur les troubles de l'Oranie," CAOM FM F/80/1685.

[141] According to the report, they "*s'accroupissent et couvrent d'immondices le Tabernacles, la Tribune et jusqu'aux accessoires qui servent aux inhumations.*" (Translation: they crouched and covered with filth the Tabernacles, the Tribune, and the accessories used for burials.) "Mémoire sur les troubles de l'Oranie," CAOM FM F/80/1685.

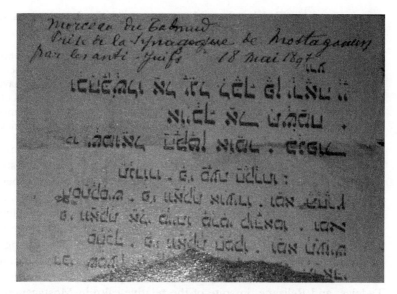

Figure 1.1 A piece of the *Pirkei Avot* text, mistakenly identified as Talmud, taken by the *anti-Juifs* from the synagogue of Mostaganem, May 18, 1897 Source: CAOM FM/80/1683

Finally, the rioters took pieces of the holy books as they left. On these fragments they wrote, "Taken from the Synagogue of Mostaganem by the anti-Juifs, May 18, 1897."[142] On the morning of May 18, the army finally intervened. Despite the army's presence, a group of Arabs attacked the Jewish quarter, armed with clubs, and pillaged as they went. Women accompanied them, filling baskets with stolen objects. It is impossible to glean from the report whether this later looting was opportunistic or antisemitic. Regardless, it was traumatic for the Jewish community. Eventually the Prefect arrived and stopped the looting.[143]

Various telegrams sent to newspapers and individuals during the days of looting and violence offered different versions of the violence. For example, a telegram to the *Petit Parisien* on May 17 stated that during their evening walk, the cyclists were attacked by a band of Jews armed with clubs and knives.[144] In a telegram on May 18, the governor-general expressed his concern for future disturbances, given that the population was greatly agitated. Similar violence and troubles occurred in the

---

[142] Ibid.   [143] Ibid.
[144] Valette to *Petit Parisien*, "Telegram 64559," Oran, May 17, 1897, CAOM FM F/80/1865.

commune of Ain Tedeles, near Mostaganem.[145] The Jewish Consistory published a poster aimed at conciliation:

The Jewish community of Mostaganem completely disavows all those who are guilty of the terrible events which occurred and which it deplores; justice will punish them with all the rigor of the laws. We strongly proclaim that we have no solidarity with the guilty. There has always been a perfect entente with all of the inhabitants of Mostaganem, whatever their religion, and the Jewish community hopes that this isolated event is not of the nature to break this public harmony.[146]

A few hours after the publication, unknown culprits defaced the posters. This effort at reconciliation and dialogue was flatly rejected by the street.

On May 19, President Kanoui, Chief Rabbi Netter, and members of the consistory of Oran wrote of their increasing concern. "Serious anti-semitic troubles exploded in Mostaganem and lasted three days. Jewish shops pillaged, dwellings violated. The rioters twice attacked the communal synagogue .... There is fear of trouble in Oran following the excitation by the malicious press, seditious placards were posted tonight on walls in Oran."[147] On May 20, violence spread to Inkermann, Ain Tedeles, and Relizane, in spite of the relative calm in Mostaganem.[148] Kanoui and Netter informed the Minister of the Interior that "Jewish persons and goods are no longer secure in the city and in the department." They entreated the minister to defend the Jews in Algeria, concluding, "we have faith in your justice and that of France."[149] Kanoui and Netter's concern for the safety of Jews in Oran proved warranted. On May 20, two of the cyclists, Irr and Bonnet, departed Mostaganem for Oran following a farewell reception.[150] Their departure took the form of a parade, filled with shouts of "Vive la France." Even the Prefect was in attendance, further suggesting the administration's support for the antisemites and their recent activities.[151]

---

[145] Gov-Gen to the Minister of the Interior (Paris), "Telegram 65582," Algiers, May 18, 1897, CAOM FM F/80/1865.

[146] Saint-André to *Petit Journal* (Paris), "Telegram 65570," Mostaganem, May 18, 1897, CAOM FM F/80/1865.

[147] Consistory of Oran to the Central Consistory (Paris), "Telegram 65946," Oran, May 19, 1897, CAOM FM F/80/1865.

[148] In Inkermann, a group broke into and ransacked the synagogue. Saint-André to *Petit Journal* (Paris), "Telegram 66455," Mostaganem, May 20, 1897, CAOM FM F/80/1865.

[149] Kanoui and Netter to the Minister of the Interior (Paris), "Telegram 66576," Oran, May 21, 1897, CAOM FM F/80/1865.

[150] Irr alone received forty bouquets at the farewell ceremony attended by 3,000 people. "Mémoire sur les troubles de l'Oranie," CAOM FM F/80/1685.

[151] Saint-André to *Petit Journal* (Paris), "Telegram 66455," May 20, 1897, CAOM FM F/80/1865.

In Oran, the leadership of the *Joyeux Club Cycle Oranais* published a declaration that the club "had not provoked anyone" and printed the results of a study that "proved" that the cyclists were ambushed by a premeditated Jewish attack. This declaration further incensed the already tense antisemitic atmosphere in Oran. On the day of Irr and Bonnet's return, the antisemitic gymnastic club *L'Oranaise* organized a meeting during which participants generated a list of Jewish shops. The list was then given to young "Spanish" men whose main objective was "to defend the rights of the French of France (*français de France*)," and under whose orders were groups of "Arabs" armed with clubs. According to the report, these Arabs received 0.50 francs for the night and were organized by an Arab member of the *L'Oranaise* and employee of the Prefecture. From this we can infer that the "Arab" participants were not necessarily motivated by antisemitism but by economic need. Another municipal employee, Police Commandant Peffau, was an influential member of *L'Oranaise* club. He also served as a municipal council member and as vice president of the *Ligue antijuive* in Oran, illustrating the intimate relationship between municipal government and antisemitism.[152]

Under the leadership of the young Spanish men, a fight broke out between Jews and antisemites in Oran at the Place d'Armes on the evening of May 20. Jews immediately returned to their homes fearing further violence. The rioters broke into and pillaged all the stores on the list, as well as the *Concorde*, the primarily Jewish gymnastic club, and stole their tricolored flag, a symbolic affront to the organization's patriotism. The report on the "Troubles of Oran" noted that the police remained "indifferent to the pillage."[153]

However, on May 21, the police posted notices informing Spaniards that if they were to participate in future violence, they would be expelled from Algeria. As the army attempted to restore the order, Arabs dressed as Europeans continued to pillage. It is unclear whether these individuals were paid or acting on their own volition or whose idea it was to portray themselves as Europeans. On May 22, Jews continued to be attacked on the streets, including Jewish students leaving school. Commandant Peffau directed the municipal police to arrest any Jews who demonstrated a "provocative attitude," indicating Peffau's antisemitism and the role of the municipal police in antisemitic acts. The nonmunicipal police eventually arrested sixty rioters, among them numerous Spaniards dressed as Arabs.[154]

---

[152] "Mémoire sur les troubles de l'Oranie," CAOM FM F/80/1685. See also Dermenjian, *La Crise antijuive Oranaise*, 84.
[153] "Mémoire sur les troubles de l'Oranie," CAOM FM F/80/1685.   [154] Ibid.

Antisemitic violence occurred throughout the department of Oran. On May 20, rioters ransacked the Inkermann synagogue and 400 Arabs invaded Ain Tedeles in hopes of looting Jewish shops.[155] In Perregaux, rioters attacked the synagogue. On May 21, rioters in Ain Temouchent attacked and pillaged Jewish shops, beat Jews unconscious, and threw the Torah into the river.[156] Similar events also occurred in Fortassa, Er Rahel, Rio Salado, and Hammam bou Hadjar. In Noisy les Bains, Arabs attacked a Jewish shop, as well as that of a French merchant, blurring the distinctions between Jews and Frenchmen. French colons worried that the intensity of Arab demonstrators could devolve into an insurrection. Although mostly concentrated in the department of Oran, the violence reached Constantine. On May 22, Arabs and Europeans attacked Jews in Constantine. The antisemitic municipal council of Constantine voted to block Jewish primary school students from receiving school supplies, halted the distribution of aid to Jews, and refused to admit Jewish patients to the hospital.[157]

On May 23, the governor-general released a circular to all colonial administrators requesting Muslim religious leaders to encourage calm among their followers. He also suspended all travel allowances for Arabs in the department of Oran.[158] The governor-general also entreated Kanoui and Rabbi Netter to urge their coreligionists not to retaliate.[159] Although both Muslim and Jewish leaders emphasized the importance of calm, all sectors of the population remained agitated. The widespread nature of the violence, the lack of police control, and the complicity of antisemitic municipal officials indicated that antisemitism was a dangerously potent force in the colony and could potentially extend beyond the Jewish community and negatively impact the security of Frenchmen.

Antisemites, Jewish "Assassins," Police, and *Néos*: Assigning Blame for the Violence

In the months leading up to the violence in Oran, the municipal councils were complicit in antisemitic acts. For example, on March 14, 1897, the newly elected antisemitic municipal council of Oran voted to fire all

---

[155] Monbrun to *Temps*, Paris, "Telegram 67092," Oran, May 22, 1897, CAOM FM F/80/1685.

[156] Jewish Consistory delegate to the Minister of the Interior, Paris, "Telegram 67126," Ain Temouchent, May 22, 1897, CAOM FM F/80/1685.

[157] "Mémoire sur les troubles de l'Oranie," CAOM FM F/80/1685.

[158] Gov-Gen to Chief of Service, Indigenous Affaires, "Telegram 38623," Alger, Paris, May 23, 1897, CAOM FM F/80/1685.

[159] Gov-Gen to Kanoui, President of the Consistory and Netter, Chief Rabbi of Oran, "Telegram 38247," Paris, May 21, 1897, CAOM FM F/80/1685.

Jewish police officers, refused to award scholarships to Jewish applicants, systematically eliminated all Jewish teachers at the girls' school, removed all Jews in municipal services, and refused them admittance to all municipal celebrations. Although the rioters involved in the May 1897 violence were primarily Arabs and Spaniards, they received orders from French antisemites. Antisemites told Arab participants that the administration encouraged their involvement and that they would be paid 6,000 francs for killing a Jew. The Grand Mufti Si Ben Zakour Ben Mortefa Ben Kaddour did not believe that the Arabs' participation in the violence was spontaneous. Rather, the Mufti suspected that antisemites encouraged them. The May 31, 1897, report identified the antisemites as the main instigators: "thanks to them, thanks to their fierce and constant excitations, a simple brawl could escalate into riots."[160] Many of these antisemitic leaders also held municipal positions.

Newspapers, specifically antisemitic ones, published vastly different assessments of responsibility for the Oran violence. According to an article entitled "Les Troubles d'Algérie" written by A. de Boisandré, on May 22 in Drumont's *La Libre Parole*, a group of Jewish bandits armed with knives ambushed the "peaceful" cyclists.[161] The May 23 article "Les Consequences" in *L'Autorité* also placed blame on the Jews. Moreover, the author held Jews responsible for the entire antisemitic movement, due to their constant audacity to "molest the French and the Arabs." In particular, the Crémieux Decree was the root of all problems in Algeria, as "it inserted into Algeria the seeds of hatred, discord, and ruin from which will result the desolation of the most beautiful of our colonies." The author concluded that the "Algerian populations" would have to deal with the Jewish problem on their own, without the support of the administration.[162] This emphasis on the "Algerians" connects the antisemitism of the late 1890s to a purported revolution against the French administration by the *Algériens*. Although there was a separatist element to such arguments, it was not the driving force behind the movement. Rather, economics, politics, and specifically the fears of the power of Jewish voting and the concomitant status anxieties fueled antisemitism in the colony.[163]

[160] "Mémoire sur les troubles de l'Oranie," CAOM FM F/80/1685.
[161] A. de Boisandré, "Les Troubles d'Algérie," *La Libre Parole*, May 22, 1897, AN F/19/11146.
[162] P. de L., "Les Conséquences," *L'Autorité*, May 23, 1897, AN F/19/11146.
[163] In the May 26 article "Solidarité Juive" in *La Libre Parole*, de Boisandré criticized Deputies Thomson and Etienne, elected in large part due to Algerian Jewish votes, for suggesting that Ottoman successes in Thessaly during the 1897 Greco-Turkish War inspired Algerian Muslims. A. de Boisandré, "Solidarité Juive," *La Libre Parole*, May 26, 1897, AN F/19/11146. Gov-Gen Jules Cambon noted that Muslims in Algeria read

Chief Rabbi of France Zadoc Kahn weighed in on the issue of responsibility in an open letter published in a French newspaper. He suggested that a simple fight between Jews and Frenchmen could not have exploded into such disastrous proportions without outside intervention. Kahn wondered how it was possible that following "a fight, certainly deplorable like all fights, which broke out between a few excited excursionists and young Jews, harmless people were attacked, shops looted, synagogues demolished, and sacred books that are revered by Christianity as well as Judaism destroyed ..." Kahn criticized "French and Christian" newspapers for encouraging such violence.[164] Responding to Kahn's article, the antisemitic De Boisandré countered that the true "innocent victims" of the violence were not the Jews, but the settlers and the Arabs, who were "exploited, pressured, stolen from, and murdered" by Jews. He concluded that the metropolitan Jews would come to the aid of the Algerian Jews, despite their guilt, which hints at accusations of Jewish international allegiances.[165]

Jean Drault, a close colleague of Drumont's and journalist for *La Libre Parole*, wrote of the growing antisemitism in Constantine during the same period. Drault described the Jew as the "internal enemy, more dangerous than the others, because they are always prepared ... to sell France and the French." He recounted a meeting of antisemites in Constantine, led by the politician Rejou, and attended by the council member Émile Morinaud.[166] At the meeting, Rejou delivered a speech in which he stated that "treason is in the Jewish soul, as honesty, devotion, and duty is in the French soul. From Judas until Dreyfus, the list is too long of Jews who have sold, betrayed, and delivered their benefactors. It will be the honor of the young generations of Algerians to free the colony of the hateful Jewish domination." In the colony, patriotism was obdurately linked to antisemitism. The Jew was the unifying enemy among antisemites, especially during electoral periods.[167]

newspapers published in Tunis and Cairo and they were encouraged by Turkish successes in challenging French authority. Gov-Gen Jules Cambon to the Minister of the Interior, "No. 1946 Re: Échos des événements d'Orient en Algérie," Algiers, July 2, 1897, CAOM FM F/80/1685. See also Administrator of Mixed Commune of Mascara to the Sub-Prefect of the Arrondissement of Mascara, "No. 2602 Re: Situation Politique; au sujet d'une article du journal *Le Petit Fanal Oranais*," Mascara, June 14, 1897, CAOM FM F/80/1685.

[164] Zadoc Kahn, letter dated May 25, 1897 published in *La Verité*, May 27, 1897, AN F/19/11146.

[165] De Boisandré not only accused metropolitan Jews of solidarity with the Algerian Jews, he also linked the "nation," presumably France, with the "Jewish race," a well-used claim of the anti-Dreyfusards. A. de Boisandré, "Solidarité Juive," *La Libre Parole*, May 26, 1897, AN F/19/11146.

[166] Morinaud would later be involved in antisemitic violence in Constantine in 1934.

[167] The meeting concluded with shouts of "Vive la France! Vive l'Algérie! Vive la Patrie! À bas les Juifs!" Jean Drault, "À Constantine," *La Libre Parole*, June 1, 1897, AN F/7/12842.

Articles such as these indicate a strong level of support in the metropole for antisemitism in Algeria. The use of anti-Dreyfusard language also reveals the assimilation of the violence in Algeria into the rhetoric of metropolitan antisemitism. This trend indicates cooperation and connection between the two antisemitic movements as well as the powerful role of the press.[168] Governor-General Cambon believed that antisemitic newspapers were directly involved in inciting the events in Oran. Citing legislation from August 11, 1848, that made incitement of one class of citizens against another punishable by law, Cambon suggested that the law be applied to the antisemitic events in Algeria.[169] Despite Cambon's proposal, newspapers continued to foment antisemitic feeling among the literate population, especially during electoral periods.[170] The antisemitic political party was known as the *parti du scandale*, and the press participated in its success through the publication of rumors and false information leaked by antisemites aimed at discrediting political opponents supported by Jewish voters.[171]

Similarly culpable in the events of May 1897 were the police and Commandant Peffau. Described as a "soldier of fortune" and an opportunist, Peffau became an antisemite as the antisemitic party gained power. Elected as a municipal council member in Oran in March 1897, Peffau became adjunct to the police and, through that position, played a significant role in the May 1897 violence in Oran.[172] On June 13, the governor-general requested the Prefect of Oran's opinion on Peffau's behavior in the disturbances in May as well as his involvement in firing Jewish teachers at the girls' school of Oran. Peffau's involvement in the latter appeared to be an abuse of his powers. The governor-general wrote that Peffau had committed an "intrusion into a service that does not belong to him. This usurpation constitutes an act serious enough to justify an administrative action and the dismissal of Deputy Peffau."[173] Peffau's activities illustrate the way in which antisemitic politicians often overreached their roles in order to please their antisemitic constituents.

In June, the court in Oran analyzed Peffau's responsibility during the May 1897 violence. M. Lantieri, the Procurer of the Republic,

---

[168] Another article, published in *Le Peuple Français* on June 4, entitled "La Question Juive en Algérie," identified the Jews as the aggressors in the violence and blamed the police for protecting the Jewish instigators. The author blamed the crisis on the Justice of the Peace in Inkermann, who was a Jew. "La Question Juive en Algérie," *Le Peuple Français*, June 4, 1897, AN F/19/11146.

[169] Gov-Gen Cambon, gov-gen Cambon the Minister of the Interior, "Troubles du département d'Oran poursuite à exercer contre les journaux," June 10, 1897, CAOM FM F/80/1685.

[170] Dermenjian, *Juifs et Européens d'Algérie*, 126.   [171] Ibid., 137.   [172] Ibid., 114–115.

[173] Gov-Gen to Prefect of Oran, "Telegram 43254," Paris, June 13, 1897, CAOM FM F/80/1685.

criticized the police for their failure to act and cited the strong antisemitism of the municipality as one of the main reasons for the lack of police response. The latest municipal elections in Oran, which took place in March, resulted in the election of a virulent antisemitic municipal council. The police officers of the municipality therefore found themselves in a "delicate situation" and could not act freely for fear of retribution from the council if they protected Jewish victims. In one specific case, the police arrested an individual who was in the midst of attempting to demolish the doors to a shop (presumably Jewish-owned). The following day the man was released "on the order of Monsieur Peffau," without further consequences.[174] Furthermore, within the patronage system, the police officers' jobs depended upon remaining in the good graces of the municipal council. This meant operating along party lines, even if they themselves were not antisemitic.

The Central Commissioner Ponticelli defended his fellow commissioners' actions. Ponticelli wrote that the commissioners were warned before the violence that they were required to take all necessary actions to prevent violence. "So if a few cadets and police officers demonstrated sluggishness and lack of energy, they ignored the recommendations made to them, or they were afraid of compromising their situation by doing all their duty."[175] Ponticelli's letter echoes Lantieri's argument that police officers feared they could lose the patronage of the antisemitic municipal council if they acted in defense of Jews. On July 17, Governor-General Cambon gave his verdict: "these are law enforcement officers responsible for ensuring the safety of citizens, who, in the presence of serious disorders, provided authorities only an insufficient effort."[176] As a result, Cambon reassigned several police officers to other positions.

Oran's municipal council was not deterred by official accusations against it and continued its antisemitic activities. On May 25, the municipal council voted to regulate the religious washing, transport, and burial of Jewish cadavers under the guise of public hygiene. The mayor of Oran defended the regulations arguing that the tradition of washing the dead was "merely subject to certain precautions that hygiene and public health

---

[174] Procureur de la République Lantieri, "Cours d'Assise et Tribunal de Première Instance d'Oran, Parquet," Oran, June 20, 1897, CAOM FM F/80/1685.

[175] "Copie de la Protestation des Commissaires de Police d'Oran," Algiers, June 24, 1897, CAOM FM F/80/1685.

[176] Gov-Gen Cambon to the Minister of the Interior, "RE: Troubles antisémitiques; au sujet de l'attitude au cours des troubles des commissaires de police de la ville d'Oran," Algiers, July 17, 1897, CAOM FM F/80/1685. See also Gov-Gen Cambon to the Minister of the Interior, "RE: Au sujet de la police municipale d'Oran," Algiers, August 13, 1897, CAOM FM F/80/1680, which details the resistance to Cambon's decision by the municipal council of Oran.

require."[177] Kanoui responded that the new statutes were in fact antisemitic actions cloaked in the guise of hygiene and public health.[178] Governor-General Cambon sided with the municipal council on the issue; given the recent troubles in Oran, he believed it was not the moment to "agitate religious passions."[179] This episode represents another example of how municipal governments continued to use their power to promote and enforce antisemitism.

In the hands of antisemites, municipal governments implemented policies that reduced the electoral power of Jews and infringed upon their civil rights. Antisemites couched their hatred in administrative actions, such as the actions taken by Peffau or the restrictions on Jewish burial practices.[180] Political antisemitism played upon the status anxieties and frustrations of different groups in the colony to encourage extreme violence, facilitated by a difficult economic environment and the complicity of municipal governments.[181] May 1897 was a defining dress rehearsal for the violence that would take place in January 1898 in Algiers, led by the most famous Algerian antisemite, Max Régis. The case of May 1897 and the advances of antisemitic politics in the preceding years demonstrate how municipal councils had become the locus of antisemitic power aimed at eliminating Jews as electors and status competitors by all means necessary, even violence.

---

[177] Mayor of Oran to Prefect, "No. 3822, Re: Cimitière Israélite, Salubrité Publique," Oran, June 11, 1897, CAOM FM F/80/1685.

[178] Kanoui, president of the Consistory of Oran to the Prefect of Oran, "No. 928," Oran, June 8, 1897, CAOM FM F/80/1685.

[179] Gov-Gen Cambon to the Minister of the Interior, "No. 3201, Re: Administration Communale, Ville d'Oran, Inhumation des Israélites," Algiers, June 30, 1897, CAOM FM F/80/1685.

[180] Dermenjian describes the Spanish immigrants as the "shock troops" of the antisemites, who responded to the call to action against Jews based on religious and economic antisemitism. Dermenjian, *Juifs et Européens d'Algérie*, 40.

[181] Ibid., 43, 79.

2   Watering the Tree of Liberties with Jewish Blood
Max Régis, Néos, and the Explosion of Antisemitism in Algeria, 1898

In February 1898, Max Régis, the future mayor of Algiers, participated in a meeting of the Paris chapter of the *Ligue antisémitique française*. He was there to be honored for his leadership of the January 1898 wave of violence in Algiers. After describing his role, Régis urged his fellow anti-semites to remove the Jew from France by any and all means necessary, especially violence. "We will water the tree of our liberties with the blood of Jews," he proclaimed.[1] Régis' attendance at the Paris meeting demonstrated the developing networks among antisemites across the Mediterranean, as well as metropolitan antisemites' admiration for their more aggressive Algerian counterparts. Régis' rise to power illustrated the increasingly critical role that *néos* played in Algerian municipal politics and antisemitism over the course of the 1890s.

This chapter analyzes the connections between colony and metropole in the evolution of antisemitism in France and Algeria during the late nineteenth and early twentieth centuries.[2] It assesses the differences between the antisemitism of Algeria and that of the metropole and the way in which the Dreyfus Affair impacted both movements. There are two central aspects of this examination: the first is the role played by the *néo-naturalisés*, the newly naturalized Europeans in Algeria who contributed to the self-consciousness of "the new race" of European "Algerians" in the colony. Their numerical strength encouraged the antisemitic and

---

[1] "*Nous arroserons de sang juif, l'arbre de nos libertés,*" Commissioner of Police M. Martin, "Au sujet d'une Réunion de la 'Ligue antisémite' à la Salle Chaynes," Paris, February 23, 1898, AN F/7/16001/1.
[2] Despite the similarities in their goals, there were some basic differences between Algerian (European) and metropolitan antisemites. Antisemites in Algeria defined themselves anti-*juifs*, so as to distinguish between Jews and Muslims. Algerian antisemites often attempted to lure Algerian Muslims into their ranks. Metropolitan antisemites maintained the title anti-*sémites*. For the purposes of studying the antisemitic movement as a movement across the Mediterranean, I will generally use the terms "antisemites" and "antisemitism" for Algeria as well as the metropole. I will use the terms "antijuive" or "antijuif" when referencing the writings and self-expression of Algerian antisemites.

municipal leaders of the period, as long as they could harness that force for their own purposes. Régis himself benefited from the strategic legislation of 1889 that naturalized the significant non-French European population in Algeria. The second core theme is the way in which antisemites capitalized on their control over municipal governments to institute antisemitic policies and reward their ranks of antisemites.

The year 1898 cannot be understood without the context of the Dreyfus Affair and the concurrent widespread and popular antisemitism. The resulting concern over the perceived threat posed by the assimilation and integration of Jewish populations in France, and more recently in Algeria, led to significant status anxiety. In 1898, Jews in France had been citizens for over a century. In Algeria, however, Jewish citizenship was relatively new and still very much contested. This population of recently naturalized Jews is one of the most significant factors that explain the intensity of violence of the Algiers riots in comparison to those in metropolitan France.

Antisemitism in Algeria was comparatively so powerful because the Jews, as newly naturalized citizens, controlled an important number of votes and thus threatened the French *colons'*, and especially the *néos'*, control over municipal governments. This electoral power caused severe status anxiety among the lower-class Europeans in the colony, making them more receptive to political antisemitism. The recent cases of antisemitic violence in the colony, such as 1897 in Oran, had preconditioned Algerian antisemites to the acceptability – if not necessity – of violence in defeating the perceived political, social, and economic power of their Jewish status competitors. Those most affected by this status anxiety, the *néos*, considered Régis to be their representative. They supported his activities and leadership of the riots in Algiers, coalescing into a significant political force that reemerged in the 1920s and 1930s as the *Union Latine*.

In the history of antisemitism in France and Algeria, 1898 constituted a watershed. The 1898 wave of riots united disparate groups under the banner of antisemitism.[3] Following the 1870 Crémieux Decree, networks developed among antisemitic leaders in France and in Algeria. For metropolitan antisemites, Algeria served as a testing ground for antisemitism and antisemitic violence. French administrators and politicians, however, feared that the extremism of antisemitism in the colony posed a significant threat to the metropole. Albert Memmi describes colonial antisemitic politics as "a permanent danger, a pocket of venom always at risk of

---

[3] Pierre Birnbaum, *The Antisemitic Moment: A Tour of France in 1898* (New York: Hill and Wang, 2004), 4.

poisoning the metropolitan organism."[4] While extreme violence might have been acceptable in the colony, it constituted a danger in the metropole.

Max Régis and his supporters believed that antisemitic violence could be an important avenue for political success in the colony. He was right. For a period between 1897 and 1902, the French antisemitic leadership fawned over Régis and celebrated his activities in Algeria.[5] By the end of 1902, however, the metropolitan antisemites began to distance themselves from Régis because of his extravagance, erratic behavior, and political extremism.[6] At this time, the unity among antisemites began to fracture.

Studies of *la crise antijuive* and of late nineteenth-century Algeria tend to separate Algeria from the metropole. Historian Charles-Robert Ageron analyzes the violence by focusing on the growing separatist movement in Algeria, led in part by Régis, at the expense of examining the other causes of the violence in 1898 and the political and ideological linkages between Algeria and the metropole.[7] This chapter adds complexity to Ageron's assessment of the violence, highlighting its origins beyond "anti-metropolitanism," and focusing on the important role played by the *néos* in municipal elections and antisemitism. The competition between *néos* and Jews and the development of antisemitism in the early 1890s intensified in 1898 due to a series of lingering economic crises, the concurrent "credit crisis" in the colony, and the Dreyfus Affair.[8] This chapter emphasizes the power of the local, specifically the power of antisemitism in municipal politics.

Ageron describes the antisemitism of the late 1890s in Algeria as "a psychological transference and passionate resentment against the Metropole."[9] Antisemitism in Algeria was highly complex. However, the competition between Jews and *néos* for the rights and benefits of citizenship and control of municipal governments was at its core. Although Max Régis and many others in Algeria were involved in an autonomist movement, to depict the violence of 1898 as part of that failed revolution is to ignore the very significant local and political role of antisemitism in the mentality of the *néos* and French in Algeria. By emphasizing the "revolution" in Algeria, Ageron distances the colony

---

[4] Albert Memmi, *Portrait du Colonisé, Portrait du Colonisateur* (Paris: Gallimard, 1985), 83–84.
[5] "Ledger Ligue Antisémitique, 1902 (premier)," AN F/7/12883.   [6] Ibid.
[7] Ageron, *Les Algériens Musulmans et la France*, 608.
[8] Ageron, *Les Algériens Musulmans*, 593; Ageron, *Modern Algeria*, 63. Michael Marrus wrote that the riots in Algeria "got completely out of hand," and were "little short of a pogrom." Marrus, *The Politics of Assimilation*, 163, 235.
[9] Ageron, *Les Algériens Musulmans*, 594, 596. See also Ageron, *Algériens*, 584.

from the metropole and overlooks the local political aspects of the anti-semitic violence. In contrast, by employing the concept of "political antisemitism" and the use of Jews as political scapegoats, I show that Algerian antisemites were motivated by similar and contingent political and economic frustrations of lower-class whites on both sides of the Mediterranean.[10]

The purpose of this chapter is to reconnect colony to metropole and show that the evolution of the antisemitic crisis in Algeria was not only nourished by events in the metropole, such as the Dreyfus Affair, but also fed by the ambitions of antisemites in France. Studies of the wave of antisemitic riots of 1898 commonly exclude Algeria. Stephen Wilson depicts the 1898 riots in Algiers as separate from those of the metropole.[11] In his study of "the antisemitic moment" of 1898, Pierre Birnbaum only mentions Algeria by suggesting that the French could not imagine that riots and violence like those in Oran in May 1897 could be replicated in the metropole.[12] Richard Ayoun suggests that Algerian antisemitism focused largely on economics whereas metropolitan antise-mites maintained a religious, clerical element.[13] Pierre Hebey acknowl-edges the coincidental nature of the developments of the Dreyfus Affair in 1898 and the riots. He argues, however, that Algerian antisemitism differed from that of the metropole and that the Jews of Algeria suffered far more than their metropolitan counterparts.[14] Carol Iancu emphasizes the unique quality of Algerian antisemitism and its development as an ideology distinct from that of the metropole.[15]

The Algerian riots of 1898 need to be understood as part of the same phenomenon that erupted across the metropole and must be examined in a common context. The 1898 riots and the events of the previous year created connections between antisemites in the colony and the metro-pole. At the same time, however, the local conditions, such as the political power of municipal governments and local leaders, must be carefully examined. The Algerian and metropolitan antisemites differed not because of their focus on economics, but because of their emphasis on

---

[10] Birnbaum, *Anti-Semitism in France*, 5.

[11] Stephen Wilson, "The Antisemitic Riots of 1898 in France," *The Historical Journal*, Vol. 16, No. 4 (December 1973).

[12] Birnbaum, *The Antisemitic Moment*, 8; "Mèmoire sur les Troubles de l'Oranie," May 1897, CAOM FM F/80/1685. The complete absence of any mention of Algeria separates the colony from the metropole.

[13] Richard Ayoun, "Max Régis: Un Antijuif au tournant du XXe Siècle," *Revue d'histoire de la Shoah*, Vol. 173 (October–December 2001): 137.

[14] Hebey, *Alger 1898*, 10, 12.

[15] Carol Iancu, "The Jews of France and Algeria at the Time of the Dreyfus Affair," *Studia Hebraica*, Vol. 7 (2007): 53; Lizabeth Zack, "French and Algerian Identity Formation in 1890s Algiers," *French Colonial History*, Vol. 2, No. 1 (2002): 115–143.

the electoral power of Jews in competition for municipal government. Additionally, the *néos* of Algeria played a significant and unique role in this competition. The *néos* used antisemitism as a platform for expressing their new and evolving identities in the colony as the *Algériens*, the Europeans of Algeria. It is therefore crucial to situate Algerian antisemitism in its local context: the competition for control of municipal governments.

"Cigarettes antijuives," a sign of the linkages between Algerian and metropolitan antisemites. Source: CAOM FM F/80/1687

The Evolution of Antisemitism in Fin-de-Siècle France and Algeria: The Impact of the Dreyfus Affair

The Dreyfus Affair occurred amid the rapid growth of antisemitism in both France and Algeria in the late nineteenth century. Some scholars describe the affair as a public event, during which antisemitism became popular.[16] Hannah Arendt argues that the combination of resentment of Jews and Jewish successes alongside frustrations with the parliament and the nation-state exacerbated the conditions of the Dreyfus Affair.[17]

[16] Stephen Wilson, *Ideology and Experience: Antisemitism in France at the Time of the Dreyfus Affair* (Rutherford: Fairleigh Dickinson University Press, 1982), xvi.
[17] Arendt, *The Origins of Totalitarianism*, 45, 92.

Others depict the Dreyfus Affair as the first in a series of events in which nationalists strove to "close" nationalism, excluding some – the Jews – while including others.[18] The Dreyfus Affair thus reflected several trends in fin-de-siècle France: the treatment of Jews as pariahs and political scapegoats, the growth of a mass of frustrated lower-class Europeans as a result of industrialization and economic crises, and the growing power of antisemitism as a political platform.

For Arendt, the treatment of Captain Alfred Dreyfus represented the failure of French Jewish assimilation. Jewish families long sought to insert their sons in the highest military strata, commonly controlled by the French aristocracy.[19] Dreyfus' arrest and conviction emerged out of the antisemitism of the officer corps and the religiously inspired conception of Jews as "Judas," the eternal traitor. The affair tapped into the latent antisemitism in France and Algeria, which intensified at the onset of the affair.[20] The antisemitic press, such as Edouard Drumont's *La Libre Parole*, played a powerful role in galvanizing popular antisemitic sentiment.[21] Known as the "pope of antisemitism," Drumont exploited it at an unprecedented scale.[22] Drumont's fear of crypto-Jews, those who

---

[18] Winock, *Nationalism, Anti-Semitism, and Fascism*, 115–116.

[19] Arendt, *Origins of Totalitarianism*, 103. See also Birnbaum, *Anti-Semitism in France*, 13.

[20] Wilson, *Ideology and Experience*, 4–5. A significant number of studies link the Dreyfus Affair to violence in Algeria. Few probe the differences. See, for example, the following: Ruth Harris, *Dreyfus: Politics, Emotion, and the Scandal of the Century* (New York: Metropolitan Press, 2010) and Louis Begley, *Why the Dreyfus Affair Matters* (New Haven: Yale University Press, 2009) and Paula Hyman, *From Dreyfus to Vichy: The Remaking of French Jewry* (New York: Columbia University Press, 1979). Hyman assesses the many new works on Dreyfus in "New Perspectives on the Dreyfus Affair," *Historical Reflections*, Vol. 31, No. 3 (Fall, 2005). See also Nancy Fitch, "Mass Culture, Mass Parliamentary Politics, and Modern Anti-Semitism: The Dreyfus Affair in Rural France." *The American Historical Review*, Vol. 97, No. 1 (1992): 55–95; Michael Burns, *Dreyfus: A Family Affair, 1789–1945* (New York: HarperCollins Publishers, 1991) and *Rural Society and French Politics: Boulangism and the Dreyfus Affair, 1886–1900* (Princeton: Princeton University Press, 1984); Christopher Forth, *The Dreyfus Affair and the Crisis of French Manhood* (Baltimore: The Johns Hopkins University Press, 2004); Jean-Denis Bredin, *The Affair: The Case of Alfred Dreyfus*, trans. Jeffrey Mehlman (New York: George Braziller, 1986); Duclert and Perrine Simon-Nahum, eds., *L'Affaire Dreyfus: Les événements fondateurs* (Paris: Hachette Book Group, 2009); Piers Paul Read, *The Dreyfus Affair: The Scandal That Tore France in Two* (London: Bloomsbury Publishing, 2012).

[21] Arendt, *Origins of Totalitarianism*, 96; Wilson, *Ideology and Experience*, 4. See also Carol Iancu, "Du Nouveau sur les Troubles Antijuifs en Algérie à la Fin du XIXème Siècle" in Centre Nationale de la Recherche Scientifique, *Les Relations entre Juifs et Musulmans en Afrique du Nord, XIXe-XXe Siècles: Actes du colloque international de l'Institut d'Histoire des Pays d'Outre Mer* (Paris: Éditions du Centre Nationale de la Recherche Scientifique, 1980), 175.

[22] Busi, *The Pope of Antisemitism*, 4. See also Frederick Busi, "*La Libre Parole* de Drumont et Les Affaires Dreyfus," in Michel Drouin, ed., *L'Affaire Dreyfus de A à Z* (Paris: Flammarion, 1994), 397, 399.

had superficially assimilated enough to not be easily identifiable, but remained Jewish, was a major theme of his book *La France Juive*.[23] Dreyfus confirmed his suspicions and Drumont used *La Libre Parole* to inflame public opinion throughout the affair.[24] Drumont stated, "French people don't think any more . . . they let their newspaper do their thinking for them."[25] The French-reading public was receptive to Drumont's theories and inflammatory articles; many were generally amenable to antisemitism during that period. His publications laid the foundation for his later political career as an antisemitic deputy in Algeria.

The Dreyfus Affair must also be understood within the context of the growing antisemitic crisis in the colony and the circuits of antisemitism that linked colony and metropole. The two crises cannot be viewed as one and the same. It is important not to look at the Algerian antisemitic crisis through the lens of the Dreyfus Affair. Rather, one must examine the Dreyfus Affair through the lens of Algerian antisemitism and understand it as the Algerian and metropolitan antisemites did: as an opportunity.[26]

The first notice of the affair appeared in Drumont's *La Libre Parole*, in an article entitled "High Treason: Arrest of the Jewish officer A. Dreyfus," published on October 29, 1894.[27] Although the early years of the Affair caused a heightened paranoia of a Jewish threat in the nation, a "paranoid nationalism," it was not until 1898 that fear transformed into violence.[28] After 1894, political parties and organizations emerged in response to the affair.[29] These political parties and organizations fed off the economic troubles of the period, particularly in Algeria. It was within this climate that the Dreyfus Affair struck a chord among Algerian antisemites who were eager to remove Algerian Jews as status, economic, and political competitors.[30]

In Algiers in the late 1890s a new leader of the Algerian antisemites emerged: a young law student at the University of Algiers named Max

---

[23] Busi, *The Pope of Antisemitism*, 64. Drumont gives a list of physical characteristics with which to identify a Jew, who sought to assimilate. Edouard Drumont, *La France Juive: Essai d'Histoire Contemporaine, Tome Deuxième* (Paris: C. Marpon & E. Flammarion, 1886), 34.

[24] Busi, *The Pope of Antisemitism*, 140.

[25] Drumont, as cited in Wilson, *Ideology and Experience*, 87.

[26] Dermenjian, *La Crise antijuive Oranaise*, 94. See also Uran, "La réception de l'Affaire en Algérie," 521. Carol Iancu describes the two events as a "coincidence," rather than the same event. Iancu, "The Jews of France and Algeria," 64.

[27] Wilson, *Ideology and Experience*, 9.

[28] Winock, *Nationalism, Anti-Semitism, and Fascism in France*, 116.

[29] Wilson, *Ideology and Experience*, 11, 53. See also Bertrand Joly, "La Ligue antisémitique de Jules Guérin," in Michel Drouin, ed., *L'Affaire Dreyfus de A à Z* (Paris: Flammarion, 1994), 409.

[30] Uran, "La réception de l'Affaire en Algérie," 522–523.

Régis, born Massimiliano Milano. Régis' father was an Italian merchant who moved with his wife to Algeria in 1864. Régis' father lived in Algeria twenty-four years before he became naturalized in 1888. Even after his naturalization, he maintained solid ties to Italy.[31] He was among the many other immigrants from Italy, Spain, Malta, and Portugal who moved to Algeria due to political and economic turmoil in their home countries to engage in new and emerging markets in the French colony. Many of these immigrants did not discover the fortunes that initially drew them to Algeria, and they targeted their economic and political frustrations on their perceived and most accessible economic rival, the Jews.[32]

Régis' main political supporters were the *néos*. Régis' own family reflected the ambiguities of *néo* identity. His older brother joined the Italian army, and his sister married an Italian national. Both maintained their Italian nationalities.[33] However, Max and his younger brother Louis (a medical student at the University of Algiers) identified themselves as fully French and their political activities initially found resonance among the French settler class.[34] In a popular book among settlers, *Cagayous Antijuif*, the main character reads Régis' antisemitic newspaper, *L'Antijuif*, and claims to know its editor.[35] Régis' *néo* identity, which initially brought him popularity, eventually led some French to question his allegiance. As the sun set on Régis' short-lived career as an antisemitic agitator, French *colons* accused him of being an Italian spy.

Before his fall from grace, Régis created hope for cooperation between *néos* and French *colons* within the antisemitic arena. Despite his early successes, the French *colons* were skeptical of the *néos*' allegiances. A surveillance report from 1901 illustrates the divisions between *français d'origine* and the *néos*, even among antisemites. At a meeting of antisemites at a café in Algiers, Régis gave a speech in which he invoked the image of the "blood of our fathers that dyed the tricolor flag." An audience member interrupted, stating, "Our fathers for those of us who are French, yes, but not your father," thus emphasizing Régis' *néo* status.[36] Another critique of Régis' French identity and allegiance

---

[31] Ayoun, "Max Régis," 144. See also Uran, "La réception de l'Affaire en Algérie," 524–525.

[32] Jacques Berque describes the simultaneous tension between assimilation and particularism that marked the development of the new Algerians, a movement personified by Régis. Jacques Berque, *French North Africa: The Maghrib Between Two World Wars*, trans. Jean Stewart (New York: Frederick A. Praeger, Inc., 1967), 208–209.

[33] Ayoun, "Max Régis," 144.

[34] Louis never achieved the same celebrity as Max, but served faithfully as Max's assistant and defender.

[35] Musette, *Cagayous Antijuif*, 18, 10.

[36] Ledger Ligue Antisémitique, 1901 (one of two), January 15, 1901, AN F/7/12882.

appeared in the newspaper *Lanterne Algérienne* on June 30, 1898. A *français d'origine* critiqued Régis: "You are French by a legal act, but you have no French character ... All your family traditions are Italian and not French, and you have the audacity to come raise your voice ... I can say in good conscience that your place is in the shade rather than sunlight."[37] In a contemporary pamphlet, Henri Lazeau wrote that Régis changed his name in an attempt to blur his Italian roots.[38] These criticisms indicate that Frenchmen were wary of Régis' intentions and his potential influence over other *néos*. Much like the Jews, *néos* would always be considered not quite French by the *français d'origine*.

Max and Louis Régis began their political activities in 1897 when a Jew, Professor Levy, received a chair in the Law Faculty at the University of Algiers, where the brothers were students.[39] Max Régis led his fellow students in opposition of the appointment. Those who joined Régis were likely *néos* as well and viewed Jews as competitors within the academic and professional spheres. Antisemitic students at the University of Algiers invited all of their professors to join their student association as honorary members, except Professor Levy. The rector of the university urged the faculty not to accept the students' invitation. Following the rector's intervention, approximately 150 students protested in the city, yelling "resignation," even following Levy home.[40] On the morning of February 1, students of the law school protested.[41] They entered Levy's classroom, disrupting his lecture. The students voted to have Levy dismissed from his post, and publicized their decision in Drumont's *La Libre Parole* and *La France Libre* in Lyon. The student protestors also reached out to metropolitan students, from whom they received telegrams of support.[42]

Doors to the university remained guarded by police, who admitted only students registered for the current courses, while other students continued to protest in front of the university. Governor-General Cambon refused to see a delegation of students, stating that until they called off

[37] *L'Oeuvre des Antijuifs d'Alger* (Imprimerie Commerciale, 1899), 43–44.
[38] Henri Lazeau, "Max Régis: Mensonges et Vérités" (Issy-les-Moulineaux: Imprimerie Nouvelle), AIU 8JBr2162.
[39] E. Masson, *Max Régis et son Oeuvre* (1901), AN F/7/12459.
[40] Telegram 3665/13574 to *Echo* (Paris), Algiers, January 31, 1897, [C]entre des [A]rchives d'[O]utre [M]er FM F/80/1685. See also Gov-Gen Cambon to the Minister of the Interior, "No. 667, Re: Manifestations des Étudiants d'Alger," Algiers, February 5, 1897, CAOM FM F/80/1685.
[41] M. Fille to Presse Paris, "Telegram 13777," Algiers, February 1, 1897, CAOM FM F/80/1685
[42] Étudiants Algériens to Senator Treille (Paris), "Telegram 14632," Algiers, February 2, 1897, CAOM FM F/80/1685; see also Gov-Gen Cambon to the Minister of the Interior, "No. 667," Algiers, February 5, 1897, CAOM FM F/80/1685.

the strike he would not meet with them.[43] After several days of protests, the faculty met on February 6 to consider steps necessary to end the strike. They found Max and Louis Régis guilty of organizing and instigating the actions against Professor Levy and suspended them. Upon hearing of the suspensions, approximately 150 students protested and the police were called.[44] The "Algerian" students argued that the rector unfairly punished the Régis brothers.[45] Max Régis' leadership of the protests became the source of his instant popularity.[46]

Cambon feared the implications of the students' riots in Algiers and neighboring towns. He noted that "leaders of the antisemite party may try to take advantage of this emotion, it is important to use a lot of tact in all of this so as to be able to stop any unrest of such character." Cambon also indicated frustration with the mayor of Mustapha, who failed to adequately control the rioting students.[47] Telegrams from journalists to their newspapers indicate a high degree of complicity on the part of the mayors of Algiers and Mustapha with the students.[48] Students brought their protests from the local to national level when they demanded the "energetic intervention" of La Libre Parole.[49] Drumont took an active interest in these antisemitic demonstrations in the colony and in Max Régis' activities in particular.[50]

Upon being suspended for two years, Max Régis left the law school to devote his time to the antisemitic cause.[51] He gained notoriety through his editorship of the L'Antijuif Algérien, a newspaper popular among the néos and the colons alike. Régis managed to close the gap, at least partially, between colons and néos in the colony. French settlers elected Régis president of the Algiers Ligue antijuive, an organization similar to the metropolitan Ligue antisémitique française. Under Régis' leadership, the Ligue antijuive grew rapidly into a significant settler movement in Algeria.

---

[43] Gov-Gen Cambon to the Minister of the Interior, "No. 667," Algiers, February 5, 1897, CAOM FM F/80/1685.

[44] The Rector to Public Instruction (Paris), "Telegram 16704," Algiers, February 7, 1897, CAOM FM F/80/1685.

[45] Étudiants Algériens to Senator Treille (Paris), "Telegram 16638," Algiers, February 7, 1897, CAOM FM F/80/1685. See also Boue to Petit Parisien (Paris), "Telegram 17643," Algiers, February 9, 1897, CAOM FM F/80/1685.

[46] Hebey, Alger 1898, 97.

[47] Gov-Gen Cambon to Minister of the Interior, "Telegram 16763," Mustapha, February 7, 1897, CAOM FM F/80/1685.

[48] Boue to Petit Parisien (Paris), "Telegram 17643," Algiers, February 9, 1897; Muston to Agencia (Paris), "Telegram 16902," Algiers, February 7, 1897, CAOM FM F/80/1685.

[49] Étudiants Algériens to La Libre Parole, L'Intransigeant (Paris), "Telegram 16935," Algiers, February 7, 1897, CAOM FM F/80/1685.

[50] Busi, The Pope of Antisemitism, 146.

[51] Rector of Public Instruction of Algiers, "Telegram 16704," Algiers, February 7, 1897, CAOM FM F/80/1685.

Concurrently, antisemitism elsewhere in the colony intensified. In a June 1, 1897, article in *La Libre Parole*, Jean Drault detailed the activities of antisemites in Constantine. Drault likened Dreyfus to Judas, describing the long list of Jews who had betrayed their patrons, including France.[52] Just over a week later, 1,500 people met in Constantine to commemorate the anniversary of the death of the notorious Marquis de Morès, also the namesake of several antisemitic organizations that emerged following the onset of the Dreyfus Affair.[53] In attendance were the president of Constantine's *Ligue antijuive*, and Émile Morinaud, then a general council member who would later serve as an antisemitic deputy in 1898 and as mayor of Constantine during the 1934 pogrom. Speakers depicted the threat posed to France, and more particularly to Algeria, by the "preponderance of the Jewish race." They presented only one solution to such a threat: the abrogation of the Crémieux Decree.[54] This resulted in a petition to Governor-General Cambon signed by many antisemitic leaders throughout the colony. Although unsuccessful, the petition reveals the centrality of the Crémieux Decree – and what it represented (Jewish electoral rights and competition) – in the antisemites' program.[55] The collection of participants at these events indicates the convergence of diverse groups under the umbrella of antisemitism: *français d'origine*, administrators, military officers, municipal government members, and *néos*.

Antisemitism was already a powerful political force in 1897, as evidenced by the number of antisemites in municipal governments. Whether knowingly or unwittingly, Régis utilized the social geography of Algiers to gain supporters and followers, particularly during the theoretically spontaneous demonstrations that regularly followed his speeches or appearances. Although Algiers did not have an enclosed Jewish quarter, most Jews lived in the area between Rue de la Lyre and Rue Bab-Azzoun, which bordered the Lower Casbah and Marine Quarters, areas with a high European population. On the southern side of the Place du Gouvernment, which bisected the Rue Bab-Azzoun and Rue de Marine, was an area with many Italian immigrants, known as Petit Napoli. Spanish settlers formed a neighborhood of their own, known as

---

[52] Jean Drault, "À Constantine," *La Libre Parole*, June 1, 1897, AN F/7/12842.
[53] Wilson, *Ideology and Experience*, 172–173.
[54] Sec–Gen, Algiers, to the Minister of the Interior, "No. 3303, RE: Meeting organisé à l'occasion de l'anniversaire de la mort du Marquis de Morès," Algiers, June 18, 1897, CAOM FM F/80/1685. See also Bouveresse, *Un parlement colonial*, Vol. 1: 484–488.
[55] Gov–Gen Cambon to the Minister of the Interior, "No. 3706, RE: Police Gènèrale, Mouvement antisémitique," Algiers, July 8, 1897, CAOM FM F/80/1685. Gov-Gen Cambon to Minister of the Interior, "No. 3590, RE: Anniversaire de la mort du marquis de Morès, Manifestations Mustapha," Algiers, July 2, 1897, CAOM FM F/80/1685.

Petit Espagne, in the Bab-el-Oued quarter, to the east of the lower Casbah and Marine Quarter.[56] Over the course of 1897, Max Régis continued to establish himself as an antisemitic leader, emphasizing the economic competition of Jews. Régis led a meeting on the topic of the economic threat posed by Jews in the colony. One speaker proposed the creation of cooperative societies designed to undercut "Jewish commerce," and the publication of lists of Jewish merchants in Algiers, whom the antisemites would boycott. The president of the *Ligue antijuive* of Constantine, Monsieur Rejou, urged the candidates in the upcoming municipal elections to emphasize the Jewish question in their campaigns. Régis encouraged the union of all "Frenchmen" against the Jews.[57]

Régis' newspaper, *L'Antijuif Algérien*, made its debut on July 14, 1897.[58] Following the publication of the names and addresses of Jewish stores in Régis' paper, a Jewish butcher, Mantout, accused him of libel. Departing the courthouse, a crowd of approximately 300 cheered Régis, hoisting him onto the shoulders of a supporter. The crowd escorted Régis to a local café and then continued on toward the Rue de la Lyre, the central street in the Jewish area of Algiers, while shouting "À bas les Juifs!" (Down with the Jews!)[59] Régis led the crowd in cheers of "à bas les juifs! mort aux juifs! à bas Mantout! À mort le voleur Mantout!" (Down with the Jews! death to the Jews! down with Mantout! death to the thief Mantout!). Approximately 1,200 people had joined Régis' spontaneous demonstration, illustrating the widespread support of removing Jewish economic competition from the colony.[60]

Approximately 700 people attended the commemoration in September 1897 of Fernand Grégoire, a leading Algerian antisemite. In his eulogy, Régis depicted the Jews as lower than savage beasts and criticized other politicians, particularly the Algerian deputies, for their

[56] Zeynep Çelik, Julia Clancy-Smith, and Frances Terpak, eds., *Walls of Algiers: Narratives of the City through Text and Image* (Seattle: University of Washington Press, 2009), 50, 66. See also Zeynep Çelik, *Urban Forms and Colonial Confrontations: Algiers under French Rule* (Berkeley: University of California Press, 1997), 35, 38, 41–42, 64, 70. See also Berque, *French North Africa*, 208–210.
[57] Onesime Mohamed, a former municipal police agent (and Muslim), declared that his fellows Muslims "would always side with the French." Gov-Gen Cambon to the Minister of the Interior, "RE: Ligue anti-juive, réunion du 11 Juillet," Algiers, July 17, 1897, CAOM FM F/80/1685. Antisemites regularly sought the support of Algerian Muslims for their cause. See Ageron, *Les Algériens Musulmans*, 601.
[58] Ayoun, "Max Régis," 147; Wilson, *Ideology and Experience*, 232.
[59] Central Commissioner Paysant, "Report No. 645," Commissariat Central, Ville d'Alger, Algiers July 30, 1897, CAOM FM F/80/1685. See also Gov-Gen Cambon to Minister of Interior (Paris), "RE: Manifestation antisémitique à Alger," Algiers, August 6, 1897, CAOM FM F/80/1685. See also Çelik, *Walls of Algiers*, 66.
[60] Prefect of Algiers to the Gov-Gen, Algiers, July 30, 1897, AN F/7/12460.

lack of commitment to the antisemitic cause. Régis urged those in attendance to vote only for antisemitic politicians in the next municipal elections. He concluded by yelling, "à bas les Juifs, vive l'antijuif!" The
meeting ended with cries of "à bas les Juifs, à mort les Juifs, l'Algérie
aux Français, les Juifs en Palestine!" (Down with the Jews, death to the
Jews, Algeria for the French, the Jews to Palestine). Following the meeting, a crowd of 300 surrounded Max Régis cheering him and shouting "à
bas les Juifs!" Fearing potential violence, the police intervened, and
arrested two demonstrators.[61]

As Régis and other antisemitic politicians' power increased, the condition of Jews in Algeria sharply deteriorated.[62] At the end of September,
the Jewish consistory of Algiers requested aid for Jewish workers and
laborers who had been fired by their European employers.[63] Anti-
Jewish demonstrations occurred on September 26 and October 3, 1897,
in the town of Mustapha, just outside of the center of Algiers. The Prefect
of Algiers explained that the antisemitic demonstrations resulted from the
instigation of Régis' newspaper and its increasingly violent antisemitic
rhetoric. "Incitement to hatred of a category of citizens, for whom they
demand expulsion from French territory and the dispossession of their
property, replace the controversy and the study of legal solutions in the
new antisemitic press of Algiers."[64]

On September 26, Régis led a demonstration to the tomb of Fernand
Grégoire in Mustapha. A riot broke out as a result of the police's manage-
ment of the crowds. The Prefect blamed Régis for inciting the mob.
Afterward, Régis attacked functionaries and officials in *l'Antijuif*: "Foul
Prefect, Sinful Jewish Prefect, Despicable Brute, Prefect Assassin."[65]

---

[61] Approximately forty Arabs and several women were also in attendance. Central
Commissioner Paysant, Prefecture of Algiers, "Rapport au sujet du meeting antijuif,
réunion publique du Samedi 18 septembre," Algiers, September 19, 1897, CAOM FM
F/80/1685.

[62] Gov-Gen Cambon to Minister of Interior (Paris), "RE: Mouvement antisémitique,
Alger," Algiers, September 4, 1897; Sec-Gen to the Minister of the Interior (Paris),
"Telegram 122056," Algiers, September 19, 1897; Gov-Gen Cambon to the Minister of
Interior (Paris), "RE: Réunion antisémitique, Alger," Algiers, September 14, 1897,
CAOM FM F/80/1685.

[63] Gov-Gen Cambon to Minister of Interior (Paris), "Re: Antisémitisme; Réunion d'ouvr-
iers et employés israélites," Algiers, September 25, 1897.

[64] Prefect of the department of Algiers to the Minister of the Interior (Bureau de l'Algérie),
"Manifestation antisémite du dimanche 3 Octobre; Attitude de la Municipalité de
Mustapha; État des esprits à Alger au point de vue de l'agitation antisemite–Les
étrangers et les indigènes; Organisation défectueuse des services de police; Mesures
parait comporter à cette situation; Intervention du Conseil General," Algiers,
October 17, 1897, CAOM FM F/80/1685.

[65] Prefect of the department of Algiers to the Minister of the Interior, Algiers, October 17,
1897, CAOM FM F/80/1897.

Musette, the pseudonym for the author of the Cagayous series, Auguste Robinet, featured this demonstration in *Cagayous Antijuif*. Cagayous described how police beat the demonstrators "who don't want the Jews to control us and to steal our money. Why don't they want the people to speak when they are discontented?"[66] Cagayous continued, "we have the right to walk together and say that Dreyfus is a bastard and Zola is a sell-out."[67] In this scene, Musette links the growing antisemitic movement in Algeria to the events of the Dreyfus Affair in the metropole.

The Prefect of Algiers warned that given the widespread popularity of antisemitism in Algeria, it would be nearly impossible to prosecute it and control its violence. In the towns of Algiers, Mustapha, and St. Eugène, there were 25,982 non-French Europeans, including 15,028 Spaniards, who made up the bulk of the *néos*, as well as 26,372 Muslims, and 11,226 Jews, a relatively large concentration. The 1889 legislation increased the number of "French" in the area to 63,353, including the recently naturalized. As evidence of the pervasive nature of antisemitism in municipal governments, the Prefect identified the antisemitic leanings of the mayor of Mustapha, Monsieur Pradelle. The Prefect predicted the dangerous future of antisemitism in the colony, especially as an electoral force:

Tomorrow, it will probably be disorders in the street, in six months an anti-Jewish candidate elected by ... the most diverse elements, the dissatisfied of any origin, the least worthy ambitions and the most unscrupulous processes. I know in advance the boundaries of his electoral army.[68]

In this passage, the Prefect identifies Max Régis and his growing ranks of supporters as the threat they posed to the stability of the French administration in the colony.

À Bas Les Juifs! En Bas les Juifs! Antisemitic Violence in France and Algeria in 1898

The antisemitism of late 1897 reached a crescendo in the wave of riots throughout the metropole and in the colony in January and February of 1898. These events are generally associated with developments in the Dreyfus Affair, coinciding with the publication of Zola's *J'Accuse* on January 13, 1898.[69] The most significant anti-Jewish riots in the

---

[66] Musette, *Cagayous Antijuif*, 23.   [67] Ibid., 24.

[68] Prefect of the department of Algiers to the Minister of the Interior, Algiers, October 17, 1897, CAOM FM F/80/1897.

[69] Winock, *Nationalism, Anti-Semitism, and Fascism in France*, 141–142. See also Wilson, *Ideology and Experience*, 12–13.

metropole and in Algeria took place in the first wave.[70] Although anti-semitic conflicts had previously occurred in the metropole, for example, in Alsace and Provence, the scale of the 1898 riots was unprecedented.[71] While the famous antisemitic war cry was pronounced "*À bas les Juifs*" in the metropole, in the colony it was often pronounced "*En* bas les Juifs" by *néos*. The shared language of antisemitism had its particularities as well.

Steven Uran describes the 1898 antisemitic violence as having two faces; one was shaped by the influence and participation of the *néos* coupled with the separatist sentiment described by Ageron. The other face was a "hypernational" desire to prove their Frenchness.[72] As demonstrated in the previous chapter, participation in antisemitic events offered *néos* an opportunity to demonstrate their French iden-tities by eliminating the Jews, who competed with them for status and political power. The 1898 violence briefly connected the metropoli-tan and Algerian antisemitic movements. In Algeria, the 1898 riots further cemented the link between antisemitism and municipal governments.

In 1898, riots took place in fifty-five locations in metropolitan France, including Paris.[73] In Algeria, the riots shook the entire colony but were the most savage in Algiers under the leadership of Max Régis. In France and Algeria, shouts of *à bas les juifs* were followed by *vive l'armée*, emphasizing the rioters' patriotism.[74] This connection between antise-mitism and pro-army patriotism is reflective of the mutation of early *boulangisme* into the political antisemitism characteristic of Régis and his following.[75] In France, most demonstrations were on the smaller side, involving fewer than fifty participants; however, some demonstrations involved several thousand, including 4,000 in Marseille and 3,000 in Nantes.[76]

Although these riots and demonstrations are often considered sponta-neous reactions to the Dreyfus Affair and its proceedings, the growing coordination of antisemitic leagues in the period prior to 1898 questions that argument. The *Ligue antisémitique française* was active in Paris and Marseille. Régis was often in touch with the *Ligue antisémitique*'s leader-ship in Paris and received their support following the student protests of 1897. National antisemitic papers such as *La Libre Parole* also had pro-vincial subsections (including Régis' *L'Antijuif Algérien*) and incited

---

[70] Wilson, *Ideology and Experience*, 107–108.
[71] Arendt, *Origins of Totalitarianism*, 107–108; Wilson, *Ideology and Experience*, 107.
[72] Uran, "La réception de l'Affaire en Algérie," 527.
[73] Wilson, "The Antisemitic Riots," 790.   [74] Ibid., 792.
[75] Birnbaum, *The Antisemitic Moment*, 14–15.   [76] Wilson, "The Antisemitic Riots," 792.

support of these "patriotic" demonstrations.[77] More than half of the demonstrators in France were students and young people. The riots and demonstrations usually took place in the cities and towns of metropolitan France in which there was a sizeable Jewish population. Jews in Algeria also tended to concentrate in particular areas, often the sites of these demonstrations. The Algiers Jewish community was one of the largest and most significant in Algeria, and therefore was at the apex of the violence in the colony.[78]

In thirty towns in metropolitan France, the rioters attacked Jewish shops and businesses, breaking windows of shop fronts and occasionally looting their contents. These attacks on Jewish shops were thus a continuation of a long-sustained campaign against Jewish commerce led in many cities by the *Ligue antisémitique* and other antisemitic organizations.[79] Algerian antisemites paralleled the metropolitan antisemitic campaign against Jewish business and commerce. Flyers urged Frenchwomen to avoid shopping *chez les juifs*, and to financially support only French business owners.[80] Régis continued this boycott of shops after the January riot in Algiers and after his election as mayor. He used the power of the municipal government to encourage women to patronize only French shops.

The riots in Algiers were an extreme version of those in the metropole. From January 19 to 26, with the most intense days of rioting between January 22 and 24, Algiers was ravaged by disorder under the direction of Régis, who was later tried for his role as the main agitator. On January 16, Régis wrote in *L'Antijuif* that the coming year would be *une année terrible* (a terrible year) for the Jews.[81] Local authorities supported the riots, which caused 400,000 francs worth of damage to Jewish shops and homes, as well as several injuries and one Jewish death.[82] Riots occurred elsewhere in Algeria, but Algiers witnessed the most extreme violence.

Scholars have argued that the antisemitism in Algeria was more political than in the metropole. Some suggest that the antisemitic movement in Algeria was left-wing, linked to socialism, and anti-capitalist.[83] In reality, the situation in Algeria was much more complex.

---

[77] Ibid., 794. Bertrand Joly argued that the Ligue had absolutely no role in the 1898 violence. Joly, "La Ligue antisémitique de Jules Guérin," 411.

[78] Wilson, "The Antisemitic Riots," 796–797. See also Winock, *Nationalism, Anti-Semitism, and Fascism in France*, 91.

[79] Wilson, "The Antisemitic Riots," 798.

[80] "Chambre des Députés, 28e séance, 2e séance du vendredi 23 décembre," *Journel Officiel*, December 24, 1898, CAOM FM F/80/1687.

[81] Ayoun, "Max Régis," 150.   [82] Wilson, "The Antisemitic Riots," 803.

[83] Nadine Fresco, *Fabrication d'un antisémite* (Paris: Éditions du Seuil, 1999), 150–151.

The antisemitic movement in Algeria was primarily opposed to small-scale economic competition from Jews and to defeating Jews as political competitors. As a result, municipal governments played a central role in developing antisemitic power and facilitating antisemitic activities.[84] Elections were highly contested, and antisemites resented what they felt to be the undeserved rights of Algerian Jews.[85] Algerian antisemites therefore focused on reducing Jewish electoral and financial power in the colony, and improving colonist competition with Jewish commerce.

The 1898 demonstrations in Algeria began on January 19 in Mustapha, when students burned an effigy of Zola. Police intervened and arrested several students who were yelling *Vive l'Armée! À bas Zola! À bas les Juifs!*[86] In Algiers, demonstrators broke through police barriers, streaming onto the predominately Jewish Rue de la Lyre.[87] The next day, new riots occurred in Algiers and fights broke out between Jews and non-Jews, injuring many of those involved.[88] In Oran, students from the university and high school protested, yelling, *À bas Dreyfus, à bas le syndicat*, and Jewish shops closed early in the evening for fear of future violence.[89]

On January 21, the mayor of Algiers commended the "French fury" displayed by citizens during the riots. Three thousand people attended a meeting of antisemites in Mustapha, led by the mayor and Émile Morinaud, then a general council member of Constantine, who spoke against the "scheming of the Syndicat Dreyfus," "police provocations," and "demanding that the government recall the Governor General and the Prefect of Algiers." Following the meeting, mobs invaded Algiers and took over Bab-Azzoun and Bab-el-Oued streets, destroying shop fronts and continuing onto the quarter of the prefecture. Rue Bab-el-Oued served as an entryway into the Jewish area of Algiers from the predominately Spanish Bab-el-Oued quarter. Rue Bab-Azzoun was the southern street of the Jewish area of Algiers.[90] Jewish residents threw flower pots

---

[84] Ibid., 803–804; Wilson, *Ideology and Experience*, 231

[85] Consistoire Israélite de la Province d'Oran, "Résultat au point de vue israélite, des dernières élections du Conseil général et des Conseils municipaux de la Province," ACC Icc 40. Many of the early rioters were students.

[86] Havas to Havas (Paris), "Telegram 8988," Algiers, January 19, 1898, CAOM FM F/80/1686. According to a different telegram, the mannequin was actually supposed to be Dreyfus, Havas to Havas (Paris), "Telegram 8583," Algiers, January 19, 1898, CAOM FM F/80/1686. See also Minister of the Interior, "Les Faits," CAOM F/80/1685. Havas to Havas (Paris), "Telegram 8838," Algiers, January 19, 1898, CAOM FM F/80/1686.

[87] Minister of the Interior, "Les Faits," CAOM F/80/1685. See also Telegram 9216, Boue to *Petit Parisien* (Paris), Algiers, January 20, 1898, CAOM FM F/80/1686.

[88] Havas to Havas (Paris), "Telegram 9511," Algiers, January 20, 1898, CAOM FM F/80/1686.

[89] Pirignet to *La Libre Parole* (Paris), "Telegram 9556," Oran, January 20, 1898, CAOM FM F/80/1686.

[90] Çelik, *Urban Forms and Colonial Confrontations*, 64, 70.

and other household items from windows at the rioters below.[91] In spite of the considerable presence of armed police and troops, on January 22, the rioters ransacked and pillaged several Jewish shops. Some non-Jewish merchants closed their shops and placed signs in the window reading "This shop is not Jewish."[92]

The height of the rioting occurred on January 23–24. In Algiers, on January 23 a Jew allegedly shot and killed a mason named Cayrol.[93] Shops on Rue Bab-Azoun were pillaged. The military attempted to occupy the principal streets of the city. In Blida, 1,200 demonstrators broke windows of Jewish stores and markets. In Boufarik, rioters ransacked seven Jewish shops. In Oran, antisemites organized a meeting led by Monsieurs Bidaine, Subercaze, and Peffau. Following the meeting, 300 participants took to the streets of the city shouting *à bas les Juifs!*[94] M. Ladmiral, a general council member in Algiers, described the situation as "complete anarchy."[95] In the midst of the chaos, the British Consul requested the governor-general's assistance in guaranteeing the protection of British nationals (including Jews).[96] Municipal leaders were often complicit in the violence. On January 24, the Jewish socialist leader Henri Tubiana relayed the horrible conditions in Algiers as "full of looting, arson. Jews murdered, imprisoned. Mayor's inertia, only culprit."[97]

The unrest resumed in Algiers following Cayrol's funeral on January 25. The governor-general attended the funeral, along with 6,000–7,000 people at the cemetery in Saint Eugène, a city with a significant Jewish population. Although a separate municipality, it was right next to Algiers, just below the Basilica of Notre-Dame d'Afrique. As a result, many from Algiers were likely in attendance. Following the ceremony, two groups of mourners harassed and attacked Jews. Several Jews were seriously injured and one, Israel Chebat, died as a result of his injuries. Violence and destruction of property continued elsewhere as well.[98] The rioters were from a variety of backgrounds: some were *néos*,

---

[91] "Les Faits," CAOM F/80/1685.

[92] A rioter beat Police Commissioner Pelletier on the head with a cane and another police officer was injured. Isnardi to *Echo de Paris* (Paris), "Telegram 10288," Algiers, January 22, 1898, CAOM FM F/80/1686.

[93] Musette incorporated this accusation in *Cagayous Antijuif*, 54, 60.

[94] "Les Faits," CAOM F/80/1685.

[95] Conseiller gènèral Ladmiral to Deputy Thompson (Paris), "Telegram 10873," Algiers, January 23, 1898, CAOM FM F/80/1686.

[96] Gov-Gen to Foreign Affairs (Paris), "Telegram 10968," Algiers, January 23, 1898, CAOM FM F/80/1686.

[97] Tubiana to Jaurès, Clemenceau, *Aurore, Droits de l'homme* (Paris), "Telegram 11243," Algiers, January 24, 1898, CAOM FM F/80/1686. Jaurès' views regarding Jews and antisemitism had changed since his earlier publications on Jews in Algeria.

[98] "Les Faits," CAOM F/80/1685.

and there were rumors that many were foreigners or Muslims.[99] A reporter described the rioters as members of all *nations latines*, as well as Muslims.[100] To avoid being attacked in the chaos, non-Jewish shop owners again displayed signs in their windows identifying their businesses as "Maison française" or "Maison catholique."[101]

On January 25, the Chief Rabbi of the consistory of Algiers, Isaac Bloch, informed the Central Jewish Consistory in Paris that despite the presence of troops and police for three days and three nights Jewish stores had been looted. There had also been several arson attempts, including that of the synagogue of the quarter of Bab-el-Oued, which was ransacked. Bloch requested aid to deal with the "hideous misery" stemming from the absolute shutdown of Jewish commerce in the city.[102] Elie Drai, a Jew in Blida, wrote to Chief Rabbi of France Zadoc Kahn, expressing his frustration with the lack of official support and protection against the attacks upon Algerian Jews.[103] Jews in Algeria felt abandoned not only by their fellow Jews in France but also by the French colonial administration, which either supported the riots or remained passive in the face of the antisemitic violence. In another letter, Drai wrote that Régis was principally responsible for the disturbance.[104]

During the riots, Régis published editorials in the *L'Antijuif*, which added fuel to the fire of antisemitism already blazing in the colony.[105] Throughout the January riots, Régis was constantly involved in and encouraged the violence. Régis' popularity and his actions during the riots led to his election as mayor of Algiers in November 1898.[106] Cagayous proclaimed Régis the "King of the *Antijuifs*."[107] Régis' actions were emblematic of the wider linkages between municipal government and antisemitism during this period, as well as the misuse of municipal power by antisemites elected to municipal government. Other antisemitic mayors were already in office at the time of the January riots. Mayors like

---

[99] On January 24, the Havas news bureau reported that all foreigners arrested during the riots would be immediately expelled. Havas, Paris, "Telegram 921," Algiers, January 24, 1898, CAOM FM F/80/1686.

[100] Havas to Havas (Paris), "Telegram 9561," Algiers, January 24, 1898, CAOM FM F/80/1686.

[101] Muston to *Agencia* (Paris), "Telegram 4291," Algiers, January 24, 1898; Boue to *Petit Parisien* (Paris), "Telegram 11605," Algiers, January 24, 1898, CAOM FM F/80/1686.

[102] Bloch to Consistoire central Israelite, "Telegram 12138, Paris," CAOM FM F/80/1686.

[103] Drai wrote, "let me tell you, in my deep anguish, that you are unworthy of your duty." Elie Drai to Zadok Kahn, "Telegram 12136," CAOM FM F/80/1686.

[104] Elie Drai to Arthur Meyer, *Gaulois* Paris, "Telegram 13838," CAOM FM F/80/1686. See Winock, *Nationalism, Anti-Semitism, and Fascism in France*, 87.

[105] For example, Régis vilified the new Gov-Gen Lépine, dubbing him Isaac Lépine and accusing him of being bought by the Jews. Max Régis, "Isaac Lépine, Jacob Granet," *L'Antijuif Algérien*, Algiers, January 23, 1898, CAOM FM F/80/1686.

[106] Ayoun, "Max Régis," 153.   [107] Musette, *Cagayous Antijuif*, 67.

Pradelle used their positions of authority to encourage further violence and to ensure that rioters were not stopped by municipal police, who were under their control. In Régis' case, his antisemitic leadership secured his future mayoral post and he would use that role to intensify his antisemitic activity. The 1898 riots thus illustrate the deep relationship between antisemitism and municipal government.

Cagayous and Daniel Ulm: The 1898 Algiers Riots in Literature

Literary representations of the 1898 Algiers riots provide interesting insight into the causes, realities, and responses to the violence. Two books in particular represent different perspectives of the 1898 violence: *Cagayous Antijuif* (1898) and *Daniel Ulm: Officier Juif et Patriote* (1911). By reading these books contrapuntally, one can examine vastly dissimilar experiences during the riots.[108] Although fictional, these books offer two vastly different interpretations of the events. Fiction offers historians glimpses into the psyche of the time and the imagined realities as interpreted by an author. As fiction, they cannot be taken literally but can be mined for how events were understood, internalized, digested, remembered, and forgotten.

Cagayous Antijuif by Auguste Robinet, published in 1898, is among the most famous texts from the period. Robinet was a lawyer and public official in Algiers and through his work he regularly interacted with the lower classes of Europeans in Algiers, many of them *néos*.[109] From these interactions, Robinet developed the character of Cagayous, the son of a Frenchman and Spanish woman, who resided in the Bab-el-Oued neighborhood of Algiers. Cagayous became the symbol of the masses of *Algériens* in late nineteenth-century Algeria.[110]

Although fictional, *Cagayous Antijuif* constitutes an important "historical document" on the rise of Régis and Drumont as well as the riots in Algiers.[111] Cagayous represents a group in transition, expressing their new identity.[112] The *néos* used antisemitism to prove their Frenchness to the *français d'origine*.[113]

---

[108] Edward Said, *Culture and Imperialism* (New York: Alfred A. Knopf, Inc., 1993), 18, 66–67, 279.

[109] Emanuel Sivan, "Colonialism and Popular Culture in Algeria," *Journal of Contemporary History*, Vol. 14, No. 1 (January 1979): 21–22.

[110] Popular songs included lyrics such as "We Are All Cagayous." Sivan, "Colonialism and Popular Culture," 22.

[111] Prochaska, "History as Literature," 699.

[112] Dunwoodie, *Writing French Algeria*, 89, 143.   [113] Smith, *Colonial Memory*, 110.

Explaining his antisemitism, Cagayous exclaims, "all the time the Jews dabble in the affairs of Government. The French, who are a lot like ants, remain content to work and the Jews at every instant are pulling something, which brings misery, or war, or disputes."[114] Cagayous asserts that the *néos* were more antisemitic than the French. He describes the antisemites in Algeria as having "hotter blood than in France!"[115] Following Régis' lead, Cagayous encourages the boycott of Jewish-owned shops in the hopes that in a year there would be no Jews in Algiers.[116] By participating in antisemitic activities, the *néos* and other poor Europeans could remove the Jews as their competitors while simultaneously proving themselves as Frenchmen. Cagayous represented the zeitgeist of the *néos* who sought inclusion into French settler society.

Jean Steene's *Daniel Ulm: Officier Juif et Patriote* (1911) also deals with many of the themes of the period, including antisemitism in 1898. The main character, Daniel Ulm, is a Jew of Alsatian origin, born in Algiers. He thus represents an unusual category in the colonial population: a non-native Algerian Jew or Jewish *français d'origine*.[117] Coming from an entirely assimilated Jewish-French family, "Daniel had never considered being a Jew as a striking characteristic, the distinctive sign of a religious sect, not a race. One could be Jewish and French, as one could be French and Catholic or Protestant."[118] Completely assimilated, Ulm had rarely even practiced his religion. When he travels to France to become a military officer he encounters a great deal of antisemitism and regularly feels obligated to express his patriotism.[119] Steene uses Ulm as a loose representation of Dreyfus.

Faced with antisemitism in the metropole and colony during the 1898 riots, Ulm reexamines his ambivalent relationship with native Algerian Jews. Ulm's ardent patriotism and devotion to the army dissipate slightly as he reads his father's account of how the army was "visibly sympathetic with the rioters."[120] Ulm's father writes that "bands of Spanish and Maltese immigrants spread terror in Algiers and make no distinction

---

[114] Musette, *Cagayous Antijuif*, 24.

[115] Ibid., 25. During the riots, Cagayous depicts the booty that he and his friends collected from looting Jewish shops, including clothes, jewelry, and linens. Cagayous' friend Gasparette is injured by items thrown by Jews from windows at the rioters below. Musette, *Cagayous Antijuif*, 48–49, 52. Cagayous also attends the funeral of Cayrol, noting the eulogy given by Max Régis. He describes the crowd as "hotter than a sirocco." Musette, *Cagayous Antijuif*, 58.

[116] Musette, *Cagayous Antijuif*, 60–61.

[117] Ulm is the name of a city in Germany, thus "foreignness" is inscribed into the character's name. Ulm's parents both moved to Algiers from Alsace, married, and set up a successful small business selling linens and other "confections." Jean Steene, *Daniel Ulm: Officier Juif et Patriote* (Paris: Henri Fabre et Cie, 1911), 25–26.

[118] Ibid., 46.   [119] Ibid., 45–46.   [120] Ibid., 47, 94.

between us and the native Jews."[121] By describing the rioters as immigrants, he seeks to distinguish them from the *français d'origine*. Ulm's father requests that his son seek a month's furlough to visit his parents, stating that Ulm's uniform and therefore affiliation with the military would be "effective protection for your family, if rioting begins again."[122]

As his boat approaches Algiers, Ulm reads *Mort aux Juifs!* (Death to the Jews!) written in large red letters on the stone of the pier, clearly visible to all entering ships and throughout the port.[123] Reunited with his father, Ulm asks him his thoughts on the antisemitic violence in Algiers. Ulm's father grapples with the various sources of violence, including the Dreyfus Affair, and the role of *néos*.

Is it the Dreyfus affair? ... It seems. But it seems it was only a pretext ... Is it a lack of patriotism? But all Algerian Jews have been strong patriots. They have proved it in assimilating with astonishing speed the language, the customs and French ideas ... And what is this patriotism in whose name all Spaniards and Maltese naturalized yesterday act? ... Because almost all the rioters were composed of these guys ... The Arabs remained mostly indifferent. As for the French population, I believe that ultimately it regrets and disapproves of everything that happens, but it dares not say anything ... It seems that they are afraid.[124]

In his analysis, Ulm's father touches on several critical factors regarding the 1898 riots in Algiers. He weighs the issue of responsibility, blaming Spanish and Maltese immigrants for the violence, and identifying the French as complicit bystanders. As a Frenchman, however, Ulm's father is hesitant to place blame on the French, whom he describes as being afraid of the *péril étranger* and the growing strength of the *néos*. Furthermore, Ulm's father defends the Algerian Jews, who assimilated and embraced their French identity, unlike the *néos*, whose citizenship he emphasizes as recently received.

Ulm's father connects the 1898 violence in Algiers to the Dreyfus Affair, citing it as a "pretext." Algerian antisemites used the opportunity presented by the Dreyfus Affair to promote their own antisemitic program, one connected to that of the metropole but also different in character and purpose. This is a significant point because the Dreyfus Affair created an environment in which the Algerian antisemites could develop their particular brand of antisemitism and eventually elect more antisemitic municipal government officials. Ulm's father appears most distraught at the army's complicity. He depicts soldiers and officers laughing as rioters looted a Jewish home and applauding ten fishermen

---

[121] Ibid., 95.   [122] Ibid., 96.   [123] Ibid., 115.   [124] Ibid., 122–123.

who raped a young Jewish girl.[125] Although fictional, Ulm's story generally reflects the events of 1898.[126] Ulm's father expresses the outrage and concerns of the Jews in Algeria when he says, "today the world is upside-down. It is we who are cursed foreigners, and it is those ... from Italy and Spain who, once landed, become good French patriots ... They defend the morality, with batons in the streets, and save the French homeland by destroying the houses of peaceful people."[127] Administrators and the army in Algiers stood by or even promoted violence, illustrating the intersection of popular antisemitism and the actions (or inaction) of colonial administration.

Ulm is an amalgam of contemporary Jewish stereotypes, including Alfred Dreyfus, the Jewish assimilated ideal, but also the inassimilable Jew. Steene emphasized the perfectibility of Ulm's character and, by extension, Jewish character in general. Following the violence, Jews considered defenses against future violence, including regeneration, as well as defending themselves as an assimilated community.[128] Jewish leaders in Oran depicted the "regenerated" Jew as robust and strong, citing the example of Jewish self-defense during the 1897 violence. They countered the antisemitic cliché that Jews were incapable of physical work, insisting that Jews could excel even at the "harshest work." Jews also proved themselves to be intellectually adept; Jewish youth excelled in French primary schools.[129] The Jewish leaders were thus most concerned with improving the morality of Algerian Jews, specifically their participation in usury, gambling, alcoholism, and other vices, purportedly products of the local environment. Consequently, they recommended the creation of programs focused on Jewish youth in Algeria, such as apprenticeships and training in other foreign languages, and to provide scholarships that would bridge the gap between the proletarian and the wealthy Jew.[130]

A report written in 1899–1900 promoted moral, physical, and educational improvements on the part of Algerian Jews as a method of battling

---

[125] Ibid., 123. Ageron wrote that the antisemitism of the army stemmed from the Dreyfus Affair. Ageron, *Les Algériens Musulmans*, 596.

[126] In fact, Steene writes in a footnote, "All the facts reported in this book on the antisemitic disorders of Algiers, *are strictly authentic*." Steene, *Daniel Ulm*, 115.

[127] Ibid., 123.

[128] "Regeneration" was part of a rhetoric regarding the improvement of Jews in Europe in the nineteenth century. See, for example, Alyssa Goldstein Sepinwall, *The Abbé Grégoire and the French Revolution: The Making of Modern Universalism* (Berkeley: University of California Press, 2005). See also Schreier, *Arabs of the Jewish Faith*, 23.

[129] "Étude sur l'antisémitisme Algérien: Remèdes à y apporter," 1898, AIU Moscou C01.7. Joshua Schreier analyzed the role of the consistory in "regenerating" Jews in Algeria. See Schreier, *Arabs of the Jewish Faith*, 23.

[130] "Étude sur l'antisémitisme Algérien: Remèdes à y apporter," 1898, AIU Moscou C01.7. Languages would improve their futures if they chose to emigrate to France or Britain.

antisemitic attacks on Jews. The author cited the extreme antisemitism in the colony, the power of the antisemitic press, and the contested nature of elections as the main threats to Algerian Jews. The author recommended a two-tiered defense. He focused on developing the manual skills of Jews, both men and women, and the proper political comportment of Algerian Jews, specifically discouraging their involvement in petty brawls or reactions to antisemitic comments. The references to politics underline the significant role of electoral competition in municipal politics. The author suggested that the Jewish community should strategically align itself with the French to defend against the *néos*.[131] The report, along with the 1898 report from Oran, recommended Jewish self-improvement, or assimilation, as the best defense against future antisemitic violence.

Assimilation required absorbing and disproving antisemitic critiques. For example, the stereotype that Jews could not properly defend their country due to lack of patriotism could be debunked by participating in combat and receiving commendations for such actions. Following World War I, the Algerian Jewish leadership published a *Livre d'Or*, which included the name, rank, and commendation received for each Algerian Jew who participated in military action, highlighting those who died for their country.[132] Here was a powerful token of Jewish patriotism and combativeness. Daniel Ulm, a Jewish officer and patriot, emblematized a defense of Jewish patriotism and assimilability. *Cagayous Antijuif* shows quite the opposite. Moving forward following the 1898 violence, Jews chose to emulate the Ulm model, emphasizing assimilation and patriotism, in order to depreciate the value of antisemitism in the colony.

The Decline of Antisemitism in Algeria and France

Following the January riots, Algerian antisemites were at the peak of their success. In February 1898, metropolitan antisemites fêted Régis' role in the January riots in Algiers. Régis traveled to Paris, where he addressed a meeting of the *Ligue antisémitique française*. Régis outlined the political beliefs of Algerian antisemites, beginning by expressing the fraternal sentiments of the Algerian antisemites toward their metropolitan counterparts. He then attributed the 1871 Arab revolt to the Crémieux Decree, claiming that Sidi Mokrani revolted against France, which had made the Jew juridically superior to the Arab. Régis announced to his audience that hatred of Jews in Algeria was a unifying force: "there are no dissensions of parties – everyone is actually an antisemite

---

[131] Aron, "Affaires Algériennes," Oran, 1899/1900, AIU Moscou C01.8.
[132] Comité Algérien des Études Sociales, *Le livre d'Or du Judaïsme Algérien* (Algiers, 1919).

above all."[133] The recent riots reflected the fact that antisemitism managed to unite disparate elements of the Algerian populations under a common political, social, and economic ideology. To emphasize, his last point and the crucial role of electoral competition, Régis described Jewish behavior in municipal elections. He accused Jews of participating in the "commerce" of votes, which they sold to the highest bidder. Depicting the Jews as corrupt electors, Régis painted the *néo* and the Frenchman as the victims of fraudulent electoral practices. Régis did not tell his audience that the electoral economy thrived among all groups in the colony.

According to Régis, the riots were a reasonable response to the Jews' abuse of the good residents of the colony.

The Jews violate our women, murder our children! How can one not revolt? We first showed our discontent by taking over the streets of Algiers and shouting "death to the Jews" . . . the police intervened, and as a young man was arrested and driven to the station, he was cowardly attacked from behind by a Jew, stabbed. The indignation increased and finally the revolt exploded: in an instant we found ourselves in the street, revolvers, rifles or batons in hand.[134]

Continuing his diatribe, Régis turned to Governor-General Lépine, portraying him as the "protector of the Jews, who ordered his central brigades to serve against the people." Régis blamed Lépine for ending the riots in Algiers too early. However, the riots lasted as long as they did precisely because there was no significant military or administrative intervention.[135] Régis' speech justified and legitimated the antisemitic violence of the January riots, playing upon popular antisemitic stereotypes, while also reaching out to metropolitan antisemites.

For Régis, the abrogation of the Crémieux Decree was insufficient. He believed that "what is necessary is the expulsion of the Jews, or their extermination ... if there exists a Jew, there will be those who are duped, and if necessary, we will water the tree of our liberties with Jewish blood."[136] Régis may have adapted this line from Thomas Jefferson's 1787 quote in order to cloak his own political program in the language and symbol of patriotism and the struggle against tyranny. He certainly considered himself to be a great Algerian patriot, and for a brief period Algerian and metropolitan antisemites agreed with him.

Max Régis continued to enjoy his celebrity and the support of metropolitan antisemites even after his arrest and imprisonment in March 1898. On March 17, he was condemned to four months in prison and 1,000 francs in damages for brutality and defamation.[137] Régis

[133] "Rapport Salle Chaynes," February 23, 1898, AN F/7/16001/1.   [134] Ibid.
[135] Ibid.   [136] Ibid.   [137] Ayoun, "Max Régis," 155.

was released early, in mid-May, after the government abandoned certain charges in response to the continued demonstrations by supporters demanding his release and for fear of making him a martyr in the eyes of his followers.[138] A March 24, 1898, surveillance report detailed the candidacy of Drumont for the deputy seat in Algiers and the support he found among Algerian antisemites. The report suggested that Régis' arrest and imprisonment would instigate a violent campaign in Algeria against France, indicating the potential fragility of France's hold on the colony.[139] French authorities were increasingly worried about Régis' power and influence, as well as that of other antisemitic politicians in Algeria. Often associated with the separatist movement, the antisemitic moment of 1898 represented a potent threat to the security of the French administration.

Governor-General Cambon reported to the Interior Ministry that Régis' arrest and trial were part of an effort to remove him from the political scene. Cambon hoped that without Régis' support and backing, Drumont would be defeated in the coming elections.[140] At a meeting in Paris, the president of the *Ligue antisémitique française*, Jules Guérin, defended Régis' participation in the Algiers riots. Guérin sharply criticized the government for taking action against Régis and argued that he was innocent of inciting the Algerois to theft and pillage.[141] Guérin's defense of Régis reflected the growing connections between metropolitan and Algerian antisemites at their height in 1898.

Scholars have argued that Algerian antisemitism was inherently different from metropolitan antisemitism, which could occasionally instigate brief episodes of violence, but not a sustained violent populist antisemitic movement such as that of Algeria.[142] Indeed, they were different movements. Based on communication between Algerian and metropolitan antisemites, it is clear that there were connections across the Mediterranean between antisemites in the metropole and in the colony.

---

[138] Procurer General of Algiers to the Minister of Justice, "Telegram 38548," Algiers, March 23, 1898, CAOM FM F/80/1686; Procurer General of Algiers to the Minister of Justice, "Telegram 44439," Algiers, April 4, 1898, CAOM FM F/80/1686; Gov-Gen to the Interior Ministry, "Telegram 67011," Algiers, May 14, 1898, CAOM FM F/80/1686.

[139] "Report 500," March 24, 1898, AN F/7/16001/1. See also Central Police Commissioner of Grenoble to the Director of General Security, "Rapport," December 11, 1898; Central Police Commissioner of Grenoble to the Director of General Security, "Rapport," January 14, 1899, AN F/7/12460.

[140] Gov-Gen Cambon to the Interior Ministry, "Telegram 37791," Algiers, March 22, 1898, CAOM FM F/80/1686. See also "Intimidations Éléctorales," *Autorité*, March 24, 1898, CAOM FM F/80/1686.

[141] "Report 519," March 26, 1898, AN F/7/16001/1.

[142] Wilson, "The Antisemitic Riots," 804.

In the 1897–1898 police surveillance ledger of the Paris-based *Ligue antisémitique française*, Régis is mentioned in fourteen entries, Algeria ten times, and the Crémieux Decree just once.[143] The 1899 surveillance ledger contains sixteen entries on Régis, seven on Algeria or Algiers, and one entry on the Crémieux Decree.[144] In the 1900 surveillance ledger, Max Régis is mentioned in nineteen entries and Algeria in nine. Most of the entries regarding Régis also discuss his political ambitions in the metropole.[145] These statistics reflect the importance of Algerian antisemitism for French metropolitan antisemites during this period, yet also the differences in their political programs. While metropolitan antisemites welcomed Régis into their midst and celebrated the activities of Algerian antisemites, they were uninterested in the particularities of their efforts, such as abrogating the Crémieux Decree.

The zenith of antisemitic success and links between metropolitan and Algerian antisemites occurred in 1898. In May 1898, when Algeria won four deputy seats for which any French citizen could run, they were quickly filled by antisemitic leaders from Algeria and the metropole. Some metropolitan antisemites found more opportunities and political success in Algeria than in France. Among the newly elected antisemitic deputies was Drumont, who sought to further the Algerian antisemitic cause. Drumont modified his campaign and his approaches to appeal to his future constituents. Drumont and the deputy from Oran, Firmin Fauré, appealed to *néos* in their campaigns by "Italianizing" their names and signing posters and notices as "Edouardo Drumont" and "Firmino Fauré."[146] In a letter to the Minister of the Interior, Governor-General Lépine described Drumont's goal for Algeria as ensuring the success and continuation of the antisemitic movement in the colony.[147] The election of four antisemitic deputies and Régis' election as mayor of Algiers represented the apogee of Algerian antisemites' political prestige.

After his election as mayor in November 1898, Max Régis instituted a strong antisemitic program in Algiers, while also putting Algeria on the path to autonomy.[148] The Algerian antisemites' interest in Algerian independence threatened the connections made between them and the metropolitan antisemites.[149] The success and popularity of antisemitic leaders and the resulting fear on the part of the metropolitan government led to the dismissal of Algerian antisemitic leaders, such as Régis, from political

---

[143] "Ledger Ligue Antisémitique, 1897–1898," AN F/7/12882.   [144] Ibid.   [145] Ibid.
[146] Dermenjian, *La Crise antijuive Oranaise*, 91.
[147] Gov-Gen Lépine to the Minister of the Interior (Paris), Algiers, May 31, 1898, AN F/7/12460.
[148] Hebey, *Alger 1898*, 202.
[149] "Ledger Ligue Antisémitique, 1899," December 8, 1899, AN F/7/12882.

positions.[150] Following a series of trials and losing his seat as mayor, Régis fell out of favor with the metropolitan antisemites, who had supported him in earlier years. In 1899 Régis was exiled to Spain for a year following several guilty verdicts in Algeria and his failed appeal in Grenoble. In Grenoble, Régis was found guilty for "press offenses and glorifying murder and pillage at meetings in Algiers and Paris."[151] Protests occurred during the trial, evidence of Régis' continued popularity in the metropole.[152]

However, surveillance reports from France in December 1899 noted that Régis, Drumont, and other antisemites had begun amassing weapons in Paris in order to have a "new St. Barthelemy of Jews." The report acknowledged that that accusation was an exaggeration, but that antisemites in Paris had collected information on all the Jews in the city and in the province. The same report commented on the separatist efforts of Algerian antisemites. "In Algeria antisemites accused the French government of not having done anything to protect French nationals and Algerian natives against the Jews. It already looks like they still seek to make an independent Algeria."[153] Antisemites in the metropole welcomed Régis during his exile from Algeria, and his antisemitic collaborators in Algeria continued to agitate, even in his absence.

Régis returned to Algiers and was reelected mayor on May 10, 1900. Colonial bureaucrats were particularly concerned by Régis' excesses as mayor. As mayor, Régis used the power of municipal government to implement strongly antisemitic policies. He established an official boycott of Jewish shops and businesses, refused to allow Jewish cafés to use the sidewalk for their terraces, and even prohibited Jewish religious butchers from slaughtering animals. Régis went as far as to offer free passage to Marseille to Algiers' Jews, in hopes of encouraging a Jewish exodus. The colonial administration feared that the Algerian antisemites' efforts to encourage Algerian Muslim violence toward Jews could lead to another revolt like that of 1871, and the autonomist activities of some antisemites would put the colony at risk. As a result, the metropolitan government invoked special powers and subsequently dismissed several antisemitic mayors in Algeria, including Régis.[154] Although they were removed from their posts, many, including Régis, continued to be active in antisemitic

---

[150] Wilson, "The Antisemitic Riots," 804.
[151] "Max Régis Sentenced to Three Years," *The New York Times*, February 21, 1899.
[152] Central Police Commissariat of Grenoble to the Director of Sûreté Gènèrale, Grenoble, January 14, 1899, AN F/7/12460.
[153] Surveillance Report, December 8, 1899, Ledger Ligue Antisèmitique 1899, AN F/7/12882.
[154] Wilson, "The Antisemitic Riots," 804.

politics and sought election again. Certainly, the separatist element of the antisemites in Algeria would have been cause for concern for the French government seeking to tighten, not loosen, their colonial hold in Algeria. Colonial administrators sought to mollify tempers, not allow them to be excited by politicians such as Régis.

Régis' tenure as mayor illustrates the unprecedented power antisemites found in municipal government, although his dismissal by the governor-general shows the limits on municipal autonomy. Régis' use of his mayoral post to promote antisemitism was a model successfully followed by later antisemites such as Dr. Molle in Oran and Émile Morinaud in Constantine in the late 1920s and 1930s. In 1901, Régis set his sights on the metropole, announcing his candidacy for a legislative seat for the eleventh arrondissement of Paris. His loss set off his fall from grace.[155] In 1901, Régis spent much of his time in the metropole, embroiled in many disputes with fellow antisemites. As his prestige began to dwindle, so did relationships between metropolitan and Algerian antisemites.[156] Régis often appeared in newspaper articles that detailed his scandalous behavior. Régis challenged those he perceived as offenders to duels and was often injured.[157] After being attacked on the street, Régis used his injury to attempt to rally supporters, inviting the press into his bedroom so that his picture made it into the newspapers.

Régis was a notorious gambler, frequenting casinos in Algeria and the metropole, spending not only his family's modest fortune but also the funds of the *Ligue antijuive* and sums he borrowed from colleagues, friends, and even the *Ligue antisémitique française*. He was well known as a womanizer, and Paris police surveillance records show him in the presence of many different women, some single, many married. He lavished his mistresses with gifts, hotel rooms, and dinners.[158] Among Régis' mistresses (and benefactors) was supposedly a wealthy Jewish woman, Madame Darribat, although there is no clear evidence that a relationship occurred.[159] A rift developed between Drumont and

---

[155] Ayoun, "Max Régis," 156.
[156] In the police surveillance ledgers of 1901, Régis appears in sixty-four entries, whereas Algeria appears only nine times. "Ledgers Ligue Antisémitique, 1901," AN F/7/12882.
[157] "Réunion Régis à la salle des agriculteurs Rue d'Athènes," Paris, June 21, 1901, AN F/7/12461.
[158] "Ledger Ligue Antisémitique, 1904–1906," AN F/7/12883; "D'où vient l'argent?," *Le Petit Fanal*, Oran, February 22, 1899, CAOM F/80/1686.
[159] "Au Sujet de Max Régis," Algiers, December 31, 1904, AN F/7/12460. See also "Situation du parti antijuif à Alger," Paris, December 5, 1904, AN F/7/12460. Régis was also thought to be living in morally dubious conditions with a married couple in Paris, whose neighbors called the police several times because of worrisome noises coming from the home. "Ledger Ligue Antisémitique, 1904–1906," AN F/7/12883.

Régis in 1901.[160] Eventually Régis, who was the golden boy of the anti-semitic movement in the 1890s, became persona non grata at *Ligue antisémitique française* meetings and events. By 1905, he disappeared from the public record, permanently moving to France. In 1910, he founded the newspaper *La Grande France* in Nice, and managed a chain of hotels in the interwar period.[161]

Régis' career and the antisemitic violence it fostered can be used as a measure of different periods of Algerian antisemitism.[162] The antisemitic "moments" in Algeria in the 1920s and 1930s were largely temporary and localized, and, although intense, they were also short-lived. In August 1934 the Constantine "pogrom," the subject of Chapter 4, sent ripples of antisemitic violence into surrounding areas, but not to the same degree as 1898.[163] In 1934, the metropolitan antisemites did not seem to be as engaged with or as supportive of the Algerian antisemites as they were in 1898. No future political leader in Algeria experienced as much popularity as Régis, nor as much direct correspondence and coop-eration with the metropole. Even after Régis' disappearance in 1905 from the public eye, references were routinely made to him and to his activities well into the mid-twentieth century. By 1902, the political popularity of antisemitism waned. The antisemitic Algerian deputies such as Firmin Fauré and Drumont failed to be reelected in 1902. Future antisemitic politicians in Algeria were mainly based locally in Algerian municipal governments.

Historians have argued that 1898 represented the apogee of the anti-semitic movement in Algeria.[164] Indeed, antisemitism reached a zenith in 1898 because of the level of violence and popular support in the January riots on both sides of the Mediterranean. The context of the Dreyfus Affair created the optimal environment for the flourishing of antisemitism in the metropole and colony. Antisemites also learned an important lesson in the late 1890s: great power could be found in the control of

[160] "Au sujet des antisémites," Paris, October 30, 1901, AN F/7/12460.

[161] Hebey, *Alger 1898*, 287.

[162] There may be a significant urban foundation to late nineteenth-century antisemitism and to the links between metropolitan and Algerian antisemites in the 1890s. The late 1890s was a period of widespread power and influence for the antisemites throughout Europe who used municipal governments to promote their antisemitic campaigns. From 1897 to 1910 Karl Lueger, an Austrian antisemite and admirer of Edouard Drumont's, served as mayor of Vienna. Lueger's and Max Régis' terms as antisemitic mayors of significant cities overlapped in 1898. See Carl E. Schorske, *Fin-de-Siècle Vienna: Politics and Culture* (Cambridge: Cambridge University Press, 1981), 133–134.

[163] As in 1898, during the 1934 Constantine pogrom, the police were scandalously absent until a day into the violence. A. Sultan, "Lettre à M. le Président de l'AIU," August 15, 1934, AIU Algérie ICI.

[164] Uran, "La réception de l'Affaire en Algérie," 525.

municipal governments. Antisemitism continued to exist in the colony, nourished by competition for the scarce resources associated with control of municipal governments and with wider colonial economic conditions. Consequently, it is important to see beyond the antisemitism and the violence in 1898 and understand the layers beneath, those that center on identity, citizenship, and competition for control, status, and political power. Throughout the early 1900s *néos*, Jews, and Muslims demonstrated their developing identities through the development of new forms of self-defense and self-promotion. Periodic waves of antisemitic violence accelerated these developments.

3 Navigating Multiple Identities and Evolving French Patriotism

The period of the 1910s to early 1930s was a time of opportunity for Algerian Jews to prove themselves as Frenchmen. Following the violence of 1897 and 1898 and the increasing tensions between Jews and Europeans in the colony, some Algerian Jews moved assertively toward assimilation and formed associations to defend themselves against antisemitic attacks. Assimilation became increasingly necessary for survival and success in the colonial framework, and the lack of assimilation among certain elements of the Jewish community frustrated the elites. In order to educate Algerian Jews to be good French Jews, the Alliance Israélite Universelle (hereafter the Alliance) sponsored "religious" after-school programs to promote further modernization and assimilation. The next two decades offered other opportunities for Algerian Jews to prove themselves as Frenchmen and to disprove the antisemitic attacks that continued to plague them in the colony.

World War I was one such moment and opportunity. It allowed Jews to distinguish themselves as soldiers and patriots, offering their lives as a sacrifice to the glorious future of *la mère patrie*. Jews also secured leadership roles in municipal governments, by appointment and election. For example, a deputy mayor of Constantine in 1934 was a Jew. Such gains proved both transformative and costly. Although the period following the antisemitic "moment" of 1898 until World War I was one of relative calm between various groups in the colony, the postwar period witnessed increased political and electoral antisemitism among the French settlers and *néos*. At the same time, the growing pan-Islamic movement and the global economic crisis of the 1920s and 1930s fueled antisemitism in the colony.

While municipal government remained the crucible of antisemitic activity in the early 1900s, antisemitism infected other institutions, including universities and the military in Algeria. During this period, antisemitism was transformed from its violent late nineteenth-century incarnation into an insidious institutional twentieth-century form. As Jews' rights eroded as a result of antisemitic machinations, they established associations and programs to defend themselves. Their response was twofold: they sought election to municipal governments, and they formed self-defense groups, like the Comité Algérien des Études Sociales. Over the course of the early twentieth century, Jews became more skilled at articulating and defending their rights. With the support and leadership of the Alliance, Jewish defense groups, and left-wing metropolitan organizations, like the *Ligue des Droits de l'Homme*, Algerian Jews were better equipped to combat antisemitism on the local and colony-wide level.

The Alliance Israélite Universelle in Algeria

In the nineteenth century, the elite French Jewish leadership of the Alliance Israélite Universelle viewed their work as a crusade for human and Jewish rights. The Alliance's program of establishing schools for Jews outside of France internalized French Jews' devotion to state secularism and their belief that their own rights were intrinsically connected to the success of the French civilizing mission and the "regeneration" of their coreligionists in those regions. Established in 1860, and presided over in its early years by Adolphe Crémieux, the Alliance emphasized solidarity among Jews while simultaneously demonstrating their leaders' own acculturation to Republican ideals.[1]

Inspired by the emancipation of French Jewry, the Alliance philosophy emphasized that to be worthy of emancipation, Jews had to be "regenerated." Western Jews feared that they would be associated with their "backward" coreligionists – the "Jewish Eastern Question" – and that their own rights could then be at risk.[2] In its early years, the Alliance worked independently of the French government. The Alliance invested its early energy in the Levant and other countries of North Africa, particularly Morocco.[3] The Alliance leadership originally considered Algeria to be outside the scope of its mission because it was a French colony and therefore already had French schools. When the Alliance entered Algeria in 1900, its teachers collaborated with French officials, because their projects and goals overlapped.[4]

---

[1] Leff, *Sacred Bonds of Solidarity*, 153, 157–158.

[2] Aron Rodrigue, *Jews and Muslims: Images of Sephardi and Eastern Jewries in Modern Times* (Seattle: University of Washington Press, 2003), 9–10. See also Schreier, *Arabs of the Jewish Faith*, 4, 54.

[3] Michael M. Laskier, *The Alliance Israélite Universelle and the Jewish Communities of Morocco, 1862–1962* (Albany: State University of New York Press, 1983), 24.

[4] Rodrigue, *Jews and Muslims*, 12.

In Algeria, the Alliance had to deviate from its usual program of establishing primary schools to introduce western subject matter because after 1882 Algerian Jews attended French secular schools. Moïse Nahon, the director of the Alliance school in Algiers, feared that if the Alliance were to set up alternative educational facilities, they would merely arm their adversaries with further proof of Jewish "exclusivity." The Alliance leadership therefore focused their activity in Algeria on two essential aspects: religious instruction and occupational education.[5] During the early 1900s, the Alliance facilitated assimilation and social improvement among Algerian Jews in order to combat antisemitism. According to the Alliance's annual report of 1900–1901, its work in Algeria was a result of the sense of solidarity among Jews following the "antisemitic excesses of 1898." Nahon asserted, "Isn't Algeria a French land? Were not our coreligionists there called to the dignity of citizenship of the Republic? What more solid guarantee of security, what more fertile stimulation for regeneration could one hope for?"[6] Nahon's incredulity reflected the surprise of many Algerian Jews in response to the intensity of violence and the complicity of the administration during the 1898 riots.

Alliance schools in Algeria operated outside of regular school hours: in the afternoon on most days, all day on Sundays, and full-time during school vacations. The Alliance taught students Hebrew, translation of prayers and the Bible, religious history and practices, and the "moral responsibilities" of Jews. The goal of the Alliance in Algeria was "to instruct [students] on the attacks directed against our race and to prepare them to respond, to habituate them to proudly reclaim the name of Jew and Frenchman, and to demonstrate to them the need for human and Jewish solidarity." In this way, the Alliance schools prepared young Jews for self-defense in an antisemitic environment. The impact of the 1898 violence is clearly evident in these goals. Jewish students were also taught to be polite and respectful in order to differentiate themselves from the young Kabyles or Spaniards in the streets of Algiers.[7]

The Alliance reorganized the religious schools, the Talmud-Torahs, already in place. Seen as typical of the colony's religious instruction, the Talmud-Torah in Algiers was in terrible condition, housed in an old, dark building and in need of "radical reorganization." In July 1900 the Alliance took formal possession of the building and its teachers. The students of the original Talmud-Torah became the students of the Alliance school and Nahon encouraged children from wealthy families to enroll in order

---

[5] Moïse Nahon, "Rapport Annuel, 1900–1901 de M. Nahon, directeur de l'École de l'Alliance à Alger," Algiers, September 1901, AIU Moscou EN 01.2.
[6] Ibid.   [7] Ibid.

to help finance the school. Nearly all the applications for admission to the school came from poor and middle-class families as the upper class was "indifferent to issues of religion." When the school opened on July 22, 1900, it had a student body of 600.[8]

The establishment of Alliance schools created a rift between Alliance administrators and local religious leaders. Nahon bemoaned the fact that he was obligated to keep on the original teachers of the Talmud-Torah. The local consistory opposed his attempt to fire one of these teachers, Pariente, for his "disheartening stupidity." Local rabbis who made their livings tutoring students saw the Alliance as competition.[9] Although Alliance schools were entirely independent from the control of the local communities, resistance from local Jewish leaders and organizations could threaten the success of the Alliance schools.[10] In place since the 1840s, the consistory system both cooperated and competed with the Alliance. Because the consistory was also an extension of the French system, it worked together with the Alliance to encourage Algerian Jews to adopt European lifestyles. Consistories in Algeria, however, were often run by local Jewish leaders, who remained embedded in their immediate communities and promoted the interests of their rabbis, who were often resistant to Alliance schools. The consistory occasionally used its local influence to keep students from enrolling in Alliance schools.[11]

Contrary to the tendencies of the local rabbis, under Nahon's leadership, the Alliance school organized religious instruction for girls. The Alliance emphasized the important role of women as conduits of modernity.[12] Without exposure to modern religious instruction, women remained traditional and their practices and superstitions often collided with western modernity. Nahon described women in Algiers as confusing local superstition with Jewish tradition and dogma. Nahon therefore not only improved women's education but also created apprenticeship opportunities for them, as well as men. In cooperation with the Jewish society, "Le Travail," apprenticeship and training were part of the economic regeneration of Algerian Jews.[13] Nahon organized night courses on

---

[8] Ibid.   [9] Ibid.   [10] Rodrigue, *Jews and Muslims*, 13.

[11] Michael M. Laskier, *North African Jewry in the Twentieth Century: The Jews of Morocco, Tunisia, and Algeria* (New York: New York University Press, 1994), 13.

[12] Rodrigue, *Jews and Muslims*, 80.

[13] Nahon, "Rapport Annuel 1900–1901," AIU Moscou EN 01.2. See Albert Memmi, *Pillar of Salt* (Boston: Beacon Press, 1992), 159–162. In his book, Albert Memmi, a Tunisian Jew, educated in Alliance schools, described seeing his mother participating in a traditional dance as a traumatic, alien experience. Rebecca Rogers examines the role of women in the civilizing mission, particularly their involvement in the civilizing mission. She comments that colonial administrators considered Algerian Jews more open to European education than Muslim students, but this too was gendered. Rogers, *A Frenchwoman's Imperial Story*, 80.

French, arithmetic, and design for the apprentices. For girls, Nahon promoted apprenticeship opportunities in sewing/couture, embroidery, and laundry/pressing. In 1900, sixty girls enrolled in apprenticeship programs.[14]

Despite efforts to modernize Algerian Jews, antisemitism remained a potent and ever-present threat. In 1902, the president of the Algerian Alliance, Sylvain Benedict, described its significant role in combating Algerian antisemitism. Benedict highlighted the danger that their status competitors, the *néos*, posed to Algerian Jews.

The watchword was to starve, to exasperate the Jews in order to induce them to emigrate and leave the field open to those who pompously called themselves the French of France and were a bunch of Italians, Maltese, and Spanish, naturalized yesterday. Our fellow Jews, unprepared for this fight, were at a loss with little or no defenses ready to fight this smear.[15]

The Alliance thus viewed its role in Algiers as preparing Jews to fight antisemitism, particularly that of *néos*. Benedict concluded that the Alliance should expand its scope. "Our work of regeneration should not be confined to the capital of Algeria. Constantine waits impatiently for the Alliance to take charge of its moral and religious interests. Do not waste precious time."[16]

In 1902, the Alliance set about creating a similar school in Constantine; however, the task was more challenging than in Algiers. A.H. Navon of the Alliance reported that students in Constantine continued to speak a Judeo-Arabic dialect and were poorly behaved. In contrast to Jews at other Alliance schools who could discuss Hugo, Proudhon, and the like, Jews in Constantine could speak only of "insanities, filth that would make a monkey blush."[17] Navon blamed Algerian rabbis, who could not or would not encourage the assimilation of Algerian Jewish children. Despite the Ferry Law of 1882 that made secular education obligatory for all citizens in the colony, Navon depicted Algerian Jews racially as "half-European, half-African," caught between progress and the vices of

---

[14] Nahon, "Rapport Annuel 1900–1901," AIU Moscou EN 01.2.

[15] Sylvain Benedict, "L'œuvre d'éducation morale, religieuse et professionnelle," Algiers, April 1902, AIU Moscou EN 01.1.

[16] Benedict, "L'œuvre d'éducation morale, religieuse, et professionnelle," AIU Moscou EN 01.1. By 1930, the Alliance school in Algiers had 537 students with 172 paying tuition, out of the total Jewish community in Algiers of 25,000. A. Confino, "Rapport Financier de l'année 1930," Algiers, January 9, 1931, AIU Moscou EN 18.079. See also "Projet de Règlement des Écoles de l'Alliance Israélite à Tlemcen," Tlemcen, March 30, 1908, AIU Algérie IV B 27.

[17] A.H. Navon, "Talmud-Thora de Constantine," Constantine, August 15, 1902, AIU Moscou EN 01.1.

their native past.[18] The Alliance argued that the French schools were not sufficiently effective to turn Algerian Jews into Frenchmen; the Alliance was best suited for that task.

Navon attributed the lack of assimilation to antisemitism in Constantine. Jews were stunted by the "profound evil that this epidemic has caused and continues to cause in the economic, civil, and religious life of Jews in Constantine." Navon argued that education was one path to assimilation that even the Algerian antisemites could not suppress.[19] The Constantine school could serve as a "moral prophylactic" for Algerian Jewish children. The Alliance would impart to students the importance of the rights and obligations of the Jew for "his country of adoption, inculcate our young Algerians with the love of France, illustrate their responsibilities and rights as citizens."[20] The Alliance perceived its role as civilizing Algerian Jews to help them overcome the stunting effects of antisemitic fervor and make them worthy of their citizenship, a training that young Jews did not necessarily receive in French schools. The Algerian Jewish child "has so often heard the hideous slogan 'Down with the Jews! Death to Jews!' ringing in his ears. He is so used to the insult that he believes himself to be inferior."[21] Navon cited anti-semitic violence in Algiers, Oran, and Constantine as the source of Algerian Jews' isolationism and lack of assimilation.[22]

The Alliance in Constantine followed the model of Algiers and established apprentice schools and workshops to teach Algerian Jews marketable manual skills. The emphasis on teaching trades was part of a broader trend in colonial education in Algeria, particularly as it related to the education of girls. These workshops included bonnet-making, ironwork, carpentry, lingerie and dress-making, as well as night courses to teach the students basic reading, writing, and math. In 1924, David Nabon, the director of the Alliance schools in Constantine, wrote that the successful apprentice programs helped Jews in Algeria overcome their repugnance for manual labor, a common antisemitic accusation.[23]

---

[18] A.H. Navon, "Talmud-Tora de Constantine (suite)," Constantine, August 15, 1902, AIU Moscou EN 01.1. See also Deborah Reed-Danahy, *Education and Identity in Rural France: The Politics of Schooling* (Cambridge: Cambridge University Press, 1996), 110–111.

[19] Municipal council member Émile Morinaud led the antisemitic movement in Constantine at the time. Navon, "Talmud-Tora de Constantine (suite)," AIU Moscou EN 01.1.

[20] A.H. Navon, "Talmud-Tora de Constantine," undated, probably 1902, AIU Moscou EN 01.1.

[21] Ibid.   [22] Ibid.

[23] D. Nabon, "Rapport Annuel, Le Travail," Constantine, January 1924, AIU Algérie II B 10. See also Rogers, *A Frenchwoman's Imperial Story*, 128, 134, 136–137.

By introducing Algerian Jews to manual trades, furthering their education, and inculcating them with French ideals, Alliance leaders in Algeria worked toward their "regeneration." In addition to this project of regeneration, the Alliance also collaborated with Algerian Jewish leaders to defend and support Jewish rights in the colony and to encourage Jews to fulfill their rights and responsibilities as citizens, particularly during World War I.

Proving Patriotism: World War I, The Comité Algérien d'Études Sociales, and the *Livre d'Or*

In contrast to the economic crises and antisemitic successes of the 1890s, the period of economic growth in the early twentieth century offered opportunities to assimilating Jews in Algeria. Aided by improvements in agriculture, production reached its peak from 1909 to 1913; antisemitic activity in the colony concurrently decreased.[24] Following the Margueritte massacre on April 26, 1901, during which approximately one hundred Algerian Muslims attacked the settler village, the "native peril" took precedence over the "Jewish question" for many colonists.[25] At the same time, some Algerian Jews assimilated as Frenchmen, facilitated and supported by the Alliance.

World War I brought the metropole and colony closer together as colonial soldiers fought for France. It also underlined and emphasized the differences between the colonized and the colonizers. More than 500,000 men from the colonies served in France during the war.[26] The colonial soldiers occupied a complex place within French society: they were, for the most part, not citizens, but colonial subjects, but were engaged in the colonial process of assimilation by participating in the military. Through military service (whether obligatory or voluntary) they were exposed to French language, culture, traditions, and France's republican ideals, even if true participation remained beyond their reach. In the colonial troops' service lay the great paradox of France's exclusive inclusion practices: racial prejudice curtailed the progress of republicanism and universalism. Although serving France offered the camaraderie of the trenches, racial hierarchies controlled relationships and interactions within the military and maintained the colonial soldiers at the lowest ranks.[27] Throughout World War I, politicians debated

---

[24] Ageron, *Modern Algeria*, 84.   [25] Ageron, *Modern Algeria*, 64.

[26] Tyler Stovall, *Transnational France: The Modern History of a Universal Nation* (Boulder: Westview Press, 2015), 269–270.

[27] Richard S. Fogarty, *Race and War in France: Colonial Subjects in the French Army, 1914–1918* (Baltimore: The Johns Hopkins University Press, 2008), 2–3, 97. Blaise

offering greater access to nationality and citizenship to colonial troops. Although this debate was part of a larger discussion regarding compensation for colonial soldiers, the possibility of an easier path to citizenship caused great concern, especially among the French (and Europeans) living in the colonies who feared being outnumbered by naturalized colonial subjects. Algerians were at the heart of this debate regarding nationality for soldiers. The Europeans of Algeria fiercely opposed the idea of naturalizing Algerian Muslim soldiers. Moreover, the sénatus-consulte further complicated the paths to naturalization. Once again, personal status led to obstacles in Algerian Muslims' access to citizenship: if they maintained their personal status, they could not become citizens.[28]

While World War I provided limited improvement in the status of Algerian Muslims, it afforded assimilated Algerian Jews an opportunity to prove their civic and patriotic devotion to France. As citizens, Algerian Jews' role in the war has often been ignored as they were counted together with the French. In the major studies on the history of Algeria, there is virtually no mention of Jews in World War I.[29] Previously considered unworthy of their citizenship by antisemites, Algerian Jews proved themselves enthusiastic patriots by joining the war effort. The camaraderie of the trenches gave Jews hope that the antisemitic attacks of the 1890s were but memories and that their future in Algeria and France would now be assured. It also brought them into closer contact with Algerian Muslims, and thus put them in a tricky situation – feeling the connection with their former Muslim neighbors, while hoping for equality with their French counterparts.[30] Algerian Jews later used their sacrifices in World War I as evidence of their devotion to France to combat resurgent antisemitic attacks on Jews. Even after 1962, Algerian Jews proudly recalled the service of fathers, brothers, and husbands in the Great War.[31]

For Algerian Jews who answered the call of la mère Patrie, fighting for France symbolized the highest expression of their patriotism and value as French citizens. The Comité Algérien d'Études Sociales (CAES)

Diagne fought for access to the rights promised to Senegalese soldiers in exchange for military service. Joe Lunn, *Memories of the Maelstrom: A Senegalese Oral History of the First World War* (Portsmouth: Heinemann, 1999), 65–67.

[28] Fogarty, *Race and War in France*, 237–238, 242–245.

[29] Charles-Robert Ageron, *Histoire de l'Algérie contemporaine, Tome II: De l'insurrection de 1871 au déclenchement de la guerre de libération* (Paris: Presses Universitaires de France, 1979), 261. Ageron gives only statistics on the numbers of Algerian Muslims who served during the war and does not mention Algerian Jews.

[30] Ansky, *Les Juifs d'Algérie*, 65–66. See also Katz, *Jews and Muslims in the Shadow of Marianne*, 48, 58.

[31] Joëlle Allouche-Benayoun and Doris Bensimon, *Les Juifs d'Algérie: Mémoires et identités plurielles* (Paris: Éditions Stavit, 1998), 272–273. See Chapter 6 on Vichy for more detail on such appeals.

emerged out of this assimilationist and patriotic mentality as the proponent of universal equality under the French flag, and more particularly, as the defender of Algerian Jewish rights. In the perfect expression of universalism, all citizens would have equal access to rights as well as the resources of the state, such as voting, participation in associations, and equality in legislation. Antisemitism undermined such universalism by excluding particular groups from access to such resources of the state. The CAES worked to expose and destroy that particularism by employing the language of universalism and equal rights.

Founded in 1915, the CAES became the watchdog organization to protect Jewish rights in Algeria. Among the founders of the CAES were Lieutenant Léon Mayer, who was later killed on the front lines in World War I; Albert Confino, the director the Alliance in Algiers; and Dr. Henri Aboulker, a surgeon and member of a prestigious, assimilated, and influential Algiers-based Jewish family. All three men had strong ties to the metropole and were well respected by the Algerian Jewish community. In the context of the war, the CAES viewed its task as protecting the rights of Algerian Jews serving France and demanding recognition for this service. During wartime, Jews in Algeria and elsewhere were often the victims of scapegoating. In Algeria, one could find "men blinded by the hatred of the Jew, officers who forget their responsibilities, who, in the barracks, introduce passions, prejudices, and hostile sentiments."[32] Antisemitism in wartime was especially dangerous for Jewish assimilation.

At its start in 1915, the CAES's goals were threefold: to collect statistics on mobilized Jewish Frenchmen for all of Algeria; to provide moral support and assistance to the families of mobilized soldiers; and to attend to the social implications relating to antisemitism. Thus, in association with the Alliance, the CAES emphasized the importance of Jewish solidarity. "The spirit of solidarity is innate in the Jew," stated a report on the creation of the organization.[33] Identifying 1898 as a time of inaction on the part of the consistory and Jewish leadership, the CAES used the demands of war to encourage activism among Algerian Jews. "We must deploy a great deal of activity, patience, and tenacity to accomplish our task. We hope that our group will not fail."[34]

---

[32] "Rapport sur la fondation du Comité Algérien d'Études Sociales," Algiers, April 8, 1915, AIU Algérie IC2.

[33] David Cohen, "Les Circonstances de la Fondation du Comité Algérien d'Études Sociales ou la Prise de Conscience d'une Élite Intellectuelle Juive Face Au Phénomène antisémite en Algérie (1915–1921)" Revue des Études Juives, Vol. 161, No. 1–2 (January–June 2002), 184.

[34] "Rapport sur la fondation du Comité Algérien d'Études Sociales," Algiers, April 8, 1915, AIU Algérie IC2.

Despite their early ambitions, the CAES soon backtracked. Given the context of war, the Alliance's Central Committee in Paris urged Confino and the rest of the CAES leadership to be extremely prudent. The Central Committee advised the CAES to focus on accumulating and organizing the documentation necessary to "effectively combat the crisis of antisemitism, which is emerging in Algeria. But this said, the Committee encourages your organization to be extremely careful in its actions, lest it serve, by stirring inappropriate agitation, to cause what it purports to defend against."[35] The Alliance feared that the CAES would incite antisemitism by undermining the rhetoric of the sacred union of war.

Among their first actions, the CAES hoped to defend the rights of Jewish soldiers in Algeria against antisemitism within the military. In February 1915 they received a letter from a Jewish interpreter, A. Chemoul, who applied to be an Arabic interpreter in Battalion E in Bizerte.[36] The colonel called him for an interview, which Chemoul transcribed in his letter:

> The Colonel: "You know Arabic well?"
> Chemoul: "Yes, my Colonel, I write and read it well. I speak it and understand it easily; I have a certificate in Arabic and a certificate in Muslim law."
> The Colonel: "What do you call yourself?"
> Chemoul: "Chemoul, My Colonel."
> The Colonel: "You are Jewish, aren't you?"
> Chemoul: "Yes, my Colonel."
> The Colonel: "In that case, you are not my business."
> Chemoul: "Could you be obliged to indicate for me for what reason?"
> The Colonel: "Oh well! It is simple – I decided it is time to eliminate from my companies the entire Jewish element, at the present time, it is a done deal. I won't dwell on my decision and this is why I cannot do you any favors."

Chemoul expressed his hope that that the Jews, who generously spilled their blood for the benefit of others in France, would not always be the victims of antisemitism.[37]

When alerted to Chemoul's case, the Alliance Central Committee responded that the colonel was justified due to animosity between Arabs and Jews and strongly urged the CAES not to act on Chemoul's

---

[35] Central Committee, Alliance Israélite Universelle to M. Confino, Paris, March 10, 1915, AIU Algérie IC2. Confino responded that the CAES would use caution and act only with the greatest circumspection. A. Confino to the President of the Alliance Israélite Universelle, Algiers, April 2, 1915, AIU Algérie IC2.

[36] Bizerte was actually located in Tunisia; however, it is likely that Chemoul was an Algerian Jew and thus went to the CAES for support.

[37] A. Chemoul to M. Réné Scebat, Bizerte, February 5, 1915, AIU Algérie IC2.

behalf. In fact, they demanded that the CAES not intervene in similar situations "without first consulting us."[38] This demonstrates the Central Committee's concern that any political action against antisemitism in Algeria might have negative reverberations. After Henri Aboulker, who had been one of the main proponents of the CAES' activities, left the CAES to serve at the front, the organization became nearly dormant until 1919.[39]

For Jews, the "sacred union" established by fighting alongside other Frenchmen nonetheless gave them hope that antisemitism would disappear in Algeria. In 1915, members of the CAES wrote that "our fellow Jews, also do their share and their efforts are no less significant, they join with other Frenchmen in this outburst of generosity, of heroism and sacrifice, which prompts all Frenchmen to act as one man."[40] Jewish leaders hoped that this camaraderie during the war would translate into greater acceptance of Jews in general in colonial Algerian society. Algerian Jews departed in large numbers to fight on the various fronts of World War I. In some families, all the men went to war, leaving the women behind to support and run the household. In such cases, some women found themselves in desperate conditions and called upon Jewish organizations, including the Alliance and the CAES, for assistance.

In 1916, Madame A. Toubiana, a widow, wrote to the Alliance for aid following the mobilization of all of her brothers.[41] All five of Toubiana's brothers had either died for France or were serving in her armies. "I am proud that my brothers have fought and are fighting for our beautiful homeland, protector of the humble against the strong, the weak against the powerful, for freedom and civilization."[42] Madame Toubiana's letter illustrates the commitment of Algerian Jews in the face of war as well as that patriotism's impact at home. In some cases, when they were unable to serve, Algerian Jews donated to the cause. In a 1917 letter, the Jewish delegates of the Algiers Chamber of Commerce protested the lack of

---

[38] Central Committee, AIU, to A. Confino, Paris, March 10, 1915, AIU Algérie IC2.
[39] Cohen, "Les Circonstances de la Fondation du Comité Algérien d'Études Sociales," 186. Moïse D. Stora replaced Aboulker as president.
[40] Leaders of the Comité Algérien d'Études Sociales, "Letter to Coreligionists," Algiers, March 1, 1915, AIU Algérie IC2.
[41] Mme. Toubiana's brother, Abraham Edmond Oualid, had attended the Alliance's agricultural school established in Djedjeida, as had their four other brothers. Following the start of the war, all these brothers joined up to fight for France. In December 1914, as he led his company toward a German-occupied trench in Roulaincourt, he was killed. Another brother, Prosper, fought nobly at the Dardanelles, and received a promotion as a result. Madame A. Toubiana to the President of the AIU, Sétif, March 30, 1916, AIU Algérie II.I.
[42] Ibid.

recognition of Jewish donations of precious metals to the war. The Jewish delegates wrote,

We are all French in our heart, related to France by an unshaken and natural attachment, and indeed have always been ready to shed our blood for Her. The criticisms you have made against us have deeply affected us, because it suggests that the French of other faiths have a higher concept of their patriotic duty than we do, and it is not the case.[43]

Their protest indicates that they feared their support of the war was being ignored due to their religion. While serving their country, Algerian Jews also fought to have that commitment recognized by other Frenchmen in Algeria.

Among the most important tasks of the CAES was the organization and publication of the *Livre d'Or*. At the start of the war, the CAES began collecting statistics related to Algerian Jewish service during the war.[44] The members of the CAES framed the *Livre d'Or* project in terms of Jewish heroism and patriotism, describing Algerian Jewish participation in World War I as part of a "sacred union" between the colony and the metropole. They depicted World War I as the first opportunity for Algerian Jews to prove their worth as Frenchmen and their commitment to France. "For the first time since the Crémieux Decree we were called to fight in the ranks of the French army, side by side with the soldiers of the metropole, for the defense of the national soil . . . The French of the Jewish religion generously spilled their blood for their country." Citing the heroic efforts of Algerian Jews, the CAES leadership wrote that Algerian Jews "have demonstrated that the race has not degenerated at all and that they are worthy descendants of the Maccabees."[45] Alluding to the biblical Jewish warriors, the CAES used Jewish history to promote a French future: Algerian Jews were warriors for France. By highlighting the statistics of Jewish patriotism in World War I, the CAES developed its arsenal with which to fight antisemitism in the colony.

In 1919, the CAES published a *Livre d'Or* honoring the patriotism of Algerian Jews. Aboulker cited the statistics of the *Livre d'Or*: nearly 2,000 Algerian Jews were killed in battle; thirty-one Légions d'Honneur were

---

[43] The 1916 bulletin of the Chamber of Commerce recognized donations by *français d'origine*, not Algerian Jews. Jewish delegates to the Algiers Chamber of Commerce, Algiers, February 1917, AIU Algérie IC2.

[44] In 1915, the CAES sent out questionnaires to all Jewish families requesting information regarding their participation in the war. CAES, "Bulletin de Statistique," Algiers, April 8, 1915, AIU Algérie IC2.

[45] CAES to Algerian Jews, Algiers, March 1, 1915, AIU Algérie IC2. Signed by A. Confino, Henry Athon, Moise D. Stora, Maklouf Scebat, S. Lebar, Ch. Ziza, D. Solal, J. Kanoui, and Mathieu Levy.

awarded as well as 112 military medals, and a thousand various commendations. "We have contracted vis-à-vis our dead and our combatants ... a sacred debt. We must ensure that their sufferings and their sacrifices are used to establish a little more peace, a little more justice among men."[46] The preface lauded the commitment of Algerian Jewry. "To the calls to France, Algerian Jews eligible for mobilization replied with the greatest patriotic zeal. In all actions on all fields of battle, by land, sea, air, our coreligionists of all ranks shared the fate of the war with all the children of France."[47] The 300-page book listed medals and commendations awarded to Algerian Jews, as well as those who were wounded, dead, and missing. For each name in these lists, the CAES authors included a short homage including the date of their injury or death and, whenever possible, the story of their heroism.

For example, Youda Ben Barak, part of the 3e Zouaves, received a medal in a ceremony presided over by General Leguay, which took place in a military hospital filled with wounded Algerian, Moroccan, and Tunisian soldiers. Leguay commended Ben Barak's bravery, stating that he "gave the best example of patriotism and sacrifice." He then addressed the wounded soldiers in attendance, most of whom were Muslims: "Look, you other Arabs, it was a Jew who did this; you must be brave like him and imitate him." Ben Barak's citation in the Livre d'Or concluded with the note that despite being injured, he killed the two German soldiers who had attacked him. Approximately 1,500, or 12 percent, of Algerian Jewish soldiers fought alongside Muslim soldiers.[48]

The CAES leadership hoped that the Livre d'Or would provide concrete proof that "the Algerian Jews were just doing their duty, so that people will stop denying their courage and their patriotism, and recognize in all sincerity, that they are worthy of France and its traditions!"[49] Following the war, Algerian Jews sought election to municipal councils at an unprecedented rate and Algerian antisemites saw that engagement as a threat to their control of municipal government. By the 1930s, Jews represented a significant number of elected municipal and general council

[46] "Announcement of the Comité Algérien d'Études Sociales," Algiers, July 15, 1919, AIU Algérie IC2. See, for example, the concept of a "blood debt" in Gregory Mann, Native Sons: West African Veterans and France in the Twentieth Century (Durham: Duke University Press, 2006).

[47] Comité Algérien d'Études Sociales, Le Livre D'or de Judaïsme Algérien (Algiers: Publications of the Comité Algérien d'Études Sociales, September 1919), Preface. In a November 13, 1927, speech, the General of the Army increased the number of Algerian Jews who died in battle in World War I to 2,850, out of a total population of approximately 70,000 in 1914. "Le 'Livre d'Or' des Israélites Algériens de la Guerre 1914–1918" in Ministry of the Colonies files on the Crémieux Decree from 1942 to 1943, CAOM FM 1affpol/877.

[48] Katz, Jews and Muslims in the Shadow of Marianne, 64.

[49] CAES, Livre d'Or, Preface.

members in the colony.[50] Much to Jewish leaders' chagrin, the "sacred union" of war was fleeting.

The CAES and the Fight against Antisemitism in the Interwar Period

With Aboulker's return from the front in 1919, the CAES recommitted itself to advocacy on behalf of Algerian Jews. In addition to the publication of the *Livre d'Or*, Aboulker and the CAES sent announcements to Algerian Jews regarding the activities of the CAES. Explaining their goal, Aboulker wrote that "the peace and prosperity of Algeria cannot result except from the free and complete development of the activity of all French citizens, *including the Jews*. Above all, our mission is to react without weakness against antisemitism." He described antisemitism in the colony as the most "odious of civil wars." Vowing to respond to all acts of antisemitism, Aboulker and the CAES called upon the government in Algeria to join them in the fight.[51]

The CAES also dealt with discriminatory laws against Jews in the colony, particularly those preventing access to land designated for colonization (*terres domaniales*), elections of Financial Delegates, and Jewish voting privileges in merchant tribunal elections. Ultimately, the CAES worked to ensure that the equality inscribed in French laws be realized in Algerian lands. In 1919, for example, the CAES fought for the rights of Jewish students at the University of Algiers who had been excluded from the general student union. Aboulker wrote that "the Central Government and our fellow citizens in the metropole imagine that equality exists for all the French of Algeria ... The theoretical equality inscribed in law must become a reality in social as well as political life, from which we are generally excluded." Concluding his announcement with a plea for both moral and financial support, Aboulker once again emphasized the devotion of Algerian Jews to France: "The generous France, which we love, will see one more time that we are children worthy of her."[52] Aboulker's promotion of the activities of the CAES emphasized Jewish sacrifices as citizens for France – that sacred debt established in World War I – and thus France's reciprocal obligations to Algerian Jews.

---

[50] While there are constant references to Jewish elected officials in the colony in the 1930s, especially around the period of the Constantine pogrom, there are few references to Jewish municipal and general council members in the early 1920s. More research is needed to ascertain when exactly Jews pursued their own candidacies and were successful.

[51] "Announcement of the Comité Algérien d'Études Sociales," Algiers, July 15, 1919, AIU Algérie IC2.

[52] Ibid.

In May 1919, the CAES conducted its first major effort in combating institutional antisemitism in the colony promoted by the governor-general or local governments. The CAES began its defense efforts by lobbying on behalf of the Jewish students at the University of Algiers. As a faculty member at the university, Aboulker was personally involved in this case. On March 18, 1919, the General Association of the Students of Algiers refused to admit thirty out of thirty-two Jewish students. Muslim students joined only as "adherent" members, with no voting rights.[53] All professors and instructors at the university could theoretically also join the association as honorary members. There were four Jews eligible for such a position: one professor in the faculty and three departmental heads at the hospital (including Aboulker). The association excluded all four as honorary members, because they were Jewish.[54]

Aboulker criticized Governor-General Jonnart's support of the student association, stating that the title of General Association of Students was a misnomer. "It is not general and dissimulates behind this lying title an unspeakable spirit of xenophobia and antisemitism." In protest, fifty non-Jewish students joined the excluded Jewish ones in founding a General Union of Students and elected a Jew and a Muslim to its board. Aboulker concluded his note to Jonnart by emphasizing the patriotism of Algerian Jews.[55] In June 1919, Aboulker announced that the CAES had achieved its first major victory defending the rights of the Jewish students, who had finally been accepted to the General Association. He cautioned that the work of the CAES was still incomplete.

This is one poisoned fruit of the tree of antisemitism, which is now torn off . . . But the tree with poisonous fruit is nonetheless still standing . . . The antisemitism of this country has its roots in all the classes of society. But the trunk that supports the fruit is the Algerian administration . . . It seems to us necessary to put to task the administration. It is complicit with antisemitism by its action and by its desired and premeditated inaction.[56]

---

[53] Of the two Jews accepted, one was already a member of the General Association of Paris, and the other was admitted because he was not of Algerian origin. Dr. Henri Aboulker to M. Jonnart, Gov-Gen of Algeria, Algiers, May 3, 1919, AIU Algérie IC2.

[54] Of these instructors, two were commanders in the army, two were captains, and three of them had been decorated with the Légion d'Honneur, and all four received the Croix de Guerre. Among the students refused admission into the association, many were wounded veterans of World War I, and most had received commendations for bravery demonstrated on the battlefield. Four of the students were officers. Dr. Henri Aboulker to M. Jonnart, Gov-Gen of Algeria, Algiers, May 3, 1919, AIU Algérie IC2. See also A. Confino to the President of the Alliance Israélite Universelle, Algiers, May 7, 1919 (No. 336), AIU Algérie IC2.

[55] Dr. Henri Aboulker to M. Jonnart, Gov-Gen of Algeria, Algiers, May 3, 1919, AIU Algérie IC2.

[56] Ibid. In his description of the poisoned tree, Aboulker may have been referring to Max Régis' tree of liberties that he alluded to in his February 20, 1898 speech at the Salle

This was a bold statement for Aboulker and the CAES because it identified the colonial administration as the supporter and occasional proponent of antisemitism.

Following the success of their first concerted effort, the CAES defended the rights of Algerian Jews in the militarily annexed region of Aflou. The French conquered the M'Zab region of southern Algeria after the Crémieux Decree, and as a result, the decree did not extend to the Jews of that region, who remained French subjects. Due to the conditions of the annexation, the area was under military control.[57] In 1920, the Jews of Aflou complained of the antisemitism of the military officer in charge of the region, Captain Cottenceau, and his Algerian Muslim subordinates.[58] The Jewish elite of Aflou, all property owners and merchants, wrote to the governor-general to ask for assistance in dealing with Cottenceau. They accused his Muslim subordinates of using their power to harass the Jews. The Jewish elite concluded, "in the name of France, in the name of Justice, we energetically protest against Monsieur Captain Cottenceau and his style of administrative action."[59] In the Aflou region, the military administrator had significant and virtually unchecked power. Without the governor-general's intervention, Cottenceau's behavior would continue.

In 1921, the Jews of Aflou again appealed to Aboulker and the CAES regarding Cottenceau and his followers. They claimed that Cottenceau promoted virulent antisemitism in the region, and as a result, Jewish commerce in the region had become "paralyzed."[60] CAES petitioned the governor-general, and the military conducted an inquiry into Cottenceau's behavior.[61] Despite the efforts of the CAES, Cottenceau maintained his position. Their lack of success in this case indicates the limited impact of the CAES in Algerian colonial civil society, particularly in military affairs.

Chaynes in Paris. See Commissaire of Police M. Martin, "Au sujet d'une Réunion de la 'Ligue antisémite' à la Salle Chaynes," Paris, February 23, 1898, AN F/7/16001/1. A. Confino to the President of the Alliance Israélite Universelle (No. 337), Algiers, June 2, 1919, AIU Algérie IC2. In fighting for absolute equality, Aboulker and the CAES celebrated the fact that CAES managed to obtain rights for Serbian, World War I allies, and Muslim students of the university.

[57] Stein analyzes the difficult conditions of M'Zabi Jews relative to the Jews of northern Algeria. Stein, *Saharan Jews and the Fate of French Algeria*, 15, 60.

[58] According to the correspondence, the Muslim subordinates called the Jews "dirty Jews and dirty race," and physically attacked them. Jewish elite of Aflou to the Gov-Gen, Aflou, December 26, 1920, AIU Algérie IC2.

[59] Jewish elite of Aflou to the Gov-Gen, Aflou, December 26, 1920, AIU Algérie IC2.

[60] Jewish elite of Aflou to Henri Aboulker, President of the CAES, Aflou, March 20, 1921, AIU Algérie IC2. Stein notes the complicated situation of some M'Zabi Jews living in Aflou, Stein, *Saharan Jews and the Fate of French Algeria*, 15.

[61] A. Confino to the President of the AIU, Algiers, May 26, 1921, AIU Algérie IC2.

In 1919, the CAES identified three major factors that contributed to the state of Algerian antisemitism: first, the hostility of the European population; second, the indifference or antagonism of government representatives; and finally, the passivity of Jews. Aboulker described the population in Algeria as "irreducibly antisemitic."[62] Citing government complicity in antisemitism, Aboulker emphasized the inconsistent treatment of citizens in the colony. "The naturalized Italian or Spaniard, as a result of the law of 1889, who doesn't speak French and often left their family in their home country where they maintain an interest, have rights that are refused to Jewish workers, merchants, and intellectuals, born French ... and raised in the schools of the Republic." Aboulker contrasted the opportunism of the fortune-seeking *néos* with the ardent patriotism of Algerian Jews. The privileged status of the *néos* over the Jews was, to Aboulker, a product of antisemitism in the colonial administration. Although Aboulker spoke of the government in general terms, he directed much of the CAES efforts to the governor-general's office.[63]

On the eve of the arrival of the new governor-general, Jean-Baptiste Abel, in 1919, Aboulker hoped for a significant change in the nature of discrimination against Jews in the colony. The CAES believed that the cause of Algerian antisemitism was the "indifference or hostility of the representatives of the government of the Republic."[64] In 1920, Aboulker expressed frustration over the fact that the discriminatory measures of the 1890s remained active. Aboulker called upon metropolitan French Jews to come to their aid in fighting antisemitism and discrimination.[65]

In the 1920s, the first measure that the CAES contested was the exclusion of Jews from purchasing *terres domaniales*, tracts of land offered to French settlers to promote colonial agriculture. After seizing the land from Algerian Muslims, the colonial administration considered these lands part of the public domain and thus eligible for purchase by

---

[62] Henri Aboulker, "Note sur l'antisémitisme Algérien," 1919, AIU Algérie IC2.

[63] This strategy was likely due to the fact that combating the highly institutionalized nature of antisemitism in the municipal government would prove too great a challenge for the CAES. Henri Aboulker, "Note sur l'antisémitisme Algérien," 1919, AIU Algérie IC2. See also Musette, *Cagayous Antijuif.*

[64] Aboulker argued that Jews often had little choice in elections, merely due to the antisemitic tendencies of certain candidates. Dr. Henri Aboulker to the Sec-Gen of the AIU, Algiers, July 30, 1919, AIU Algérie IC2.

[65] Dr. Henri Aboulker to the President of the AIU, Algiers, August 9, 1920, AIU Algérie IC2. The final issue of inequality on which the CAES concentrated its efforts was the discrimination against Jewish participation in consular tribunals and elections, during which the CAES sought to promulgate the legislation of 1883 and extend universal suffrage to Algerians with regard to merchant tribunals.

Frenchmen.[66] The fight for Jewish access to *terres domaniales* began in 1919 with the efforts of E. Moatti, a Jewish agricultural engineer. Moatti failed to acquire such a tract based on the grounds that the law of 1904 permitted only Frenchmen of European origin or naturalized Europeans to obtain *terres domaniales*. As a result, Algerian Jews, despite their French citizenship, and naturalized Algerian Muslims were excluded.[67] CAES worked with Moatti to challenge these restrictions.

The CAES report highlighted the fact that the *néos* once again had access to more rights than Algerian Jews. The CAES recommended that the 1904 law be repealed and a new one instated that "removes the villainy from which we suffer."[68] In their fight for Jewish access to colonial lands, Aboulker and the leadership of the CAES sought the assistance of the *Ligue des Droits de l'Homme* (LDH), a human rights organization based in Paris.[69] The LDH acted as an intermediary between the CAES and the French government. The cooperation between the LDH and the CAES indicates the presence of wide networks of loosely linked civil society associations interested in ameliorating abusive conditions in the colonies. It also points to the way in which the CAES saw itself as operating within the larger metropolitan framework. The president of the LDH wrote to the Minister of the Interior in 1919 and 1920 protesting the exclusion of Algerian Jews and Muslims from acquiring *terres domaniales*, portraying Algerian Jews as great colonists and agriculturalists.[70] In 1924, Governor-General Steeg upheld the 1904 legislation in order to assure, "by way of metropolitan French settlement, the authority of France and her agricultural prosperity in Algeria."[71]

Despite the lack of progress on the issue of *terres domaniales*, the CAES focused on the discriminatory legislation regarding Jewish voting privileges in elections of Financial Delegates. The *Délégation Financière*, established by decrees of 1898 and 1900, was a source of significant settler

---

[66] John Ruedy, *Land Policy in Colonial Algeria: The Origins of the Rural Public Domain* (Berkeley: The University of California Press, 1967), 1, 87.

[67] E. Moatti to the Gov-Gen of Algeria, Algiers, September 16, 1919, AIU Algérie IC2.

[68] CAES, "RAPPORT I: Acquisition des Terres Domaniales," September 24, 1919, AIU Algérie IC2.

[69] Dr. Henri Aboulker to the President of the Ligue Française des Droits de l'Homme et du Citoyen (undated), AIU Algérie IC2.

[70] President of the Ligue des Droits de l'Homme to the Gov-Gen, Paris, 1920, BDIC-LDH F Delta Res 798/97; Dr. Henri Aboulker to the President of the AIU, Algiers, September 13, 1921, AIU Algérie IC2. See also CAES, "Colonisation," September 18, 1919, AIU Algérie IC2.

[71] Gov-Gen Steeg to the President of the Ligue des Droits de l'Homme, Algiers 1924, BDIC-LDH F Delta Res 798/97. The administration eventually revised the 1904 legislation, enabling Jewish and Muslim French citizens to acquire *terres domaniales*. See Cohen, "Les Circonstances de la Fondation du Comité Algérien d'Études Sociales," 204

control in the colonial administration, especially after a December 1900 law gave Algerian financial autonomy. The Financial Delegation gave advice regarding taxes and other fiscal issues and was composed of three bodies: two were European delegates and the third was Algerian Muslims. The Financial Delegation was 70 percent European. It was not until 1922 that Algerian Muslims were allowed to elect their own delegates, who were previously appointed or elected by a small Muslim electorate.[72] The budget was created by the governor-general, and voted on by the Financial Delegates before being settled in Parliament.[73] In 1900, when it was established, the Financial Delegation theoretically represented all sectors of the colony; however, Europeans were overrepresented and remained so.[74] The Financial Delegation discriminated against Muslim representatives in significant ways.[75] In addition, Algerian Jews were largely lost in the demarcations between the three bodies of representatives. Even in 1919, Frenchmen of metropolitan origin became electors for Financial Delegates at age 25, whereas Jews could not become electors until 33. Furthermore, the legislation lumped together Algerian Jews, who were born French, with naturalized Europeans within the second body of representatives.[76] Although this situation was discriminatory, it was not as extreme as the eradication of Jews from electoral lists.

As seen earlier, concerted efforts to exclude Jewish voters began in 1897. That year, antisemites revised electoral lists in order to maintain their control of municipal government. At the time, few excluded Jewish voters protested. Following World War I, however, Jews became better at articulating and defending their rights, especially with the support of the CAES. As the CAES fought against discrimination within the Financial Delegation, antisemites systematically removed Jews from municipal electoral lists in cities such as Constantine, Sétif, Berrouaghia, Médéa, Oran, and Algiers. Aboulker wrote that "the Algerian Jews do not demand to be accepted because they are Jews; they seek to be received by their fellow citizens in the municipal councils with the same status as the French of foreign origins ... They demand that they not be eliminated

---

[72] Ruedy, *Modern Algeria*, 86–87. See also Kaddache, *La vie politique à Alger*, 23.
[73] Collot, *Les Institutions de l'Algérie*, 203–205.   [74] Ibid., 218–219.
[75] Mohamed Adda-Djelloul outlines the discriminatory practices of the Financial Delegations directed toward Algerian Muslims. See Mohamed Adda-Djelloul, "Société colonisée et droit colonial: Les élus des délégations arabe et kabyle face au projet Albin Rozet," *Insaniyat*, Vol. 5, No. 187 (1998).
[76] Aboulker wrote that "the Algerian Jews do not have any other desire but to see these prejudices eliminated from Algerian politics." Dr. Henri Aboulker, "L'Exclusion des Israélites des Fonctions Electives," undated, AIU Algérie IC2. This is probably from 1919.

because they are Jews."[77] The CAES had limited success in the reinstatement of the eliminated voters. The issue of the elimination of Jewish voters came to the fore again in 1937 in Sidi Bel Abbès. Increasingly, the CAES identified the colonial administration as a central part of the persistence of antisemitic legislation.[78]

The CAES actively and boldly opposed the erosion of Jewish rights by lobbying the government directly and by coordinating with other groups, such as the LDH. Aboulker wrote that "we are at the most critical hour of the history of Algerian Judaism. Our generation has the weighty task of preparing for the future."[79] In 1919, the immediate postwar period, there was antisemitic resurgence in the colony, similar to that of 1898.[80] This increase in antisemitism stemmed from a variety of sources but echoed the status anxieties that fomented the antisemitic moment of 1898.

In campaigning and lobbying for the abrogation of discriminatory measures, actions, and legislation against Jews, the CAES also sought equal rights for other oppressed and victimized groups in the colony. Certain CAES leaders manifestly viewed its role as not only the defender of Algerian Jews but also as the champion of equality in the colony. Due to disagreement among the Committee members regarding the goals of the organization and its limited successes, the Committee dissolved in 1923.[81] Antisemitism, especially within municipal governments, continued to grow in the late 1920s and early 1930s. In the face of electoral antisemitism in the 1920s and 1930s and the revitalizing influence of the economic depression on antisemitism, Algerian Jews sought out more active forms of defense at a grassroots level.

---

[77] Ibid.

[78] The CAES next sought to redress economic discrimination in merchant tribunals. The merchant tribunal in Algiers was established in August 1834, and the governor-general named its members. The ordinance of October 24, 1847, gave the right to elect their own judges of the tribunal to the merchants. See Amalia D. Kessler, *A Revolution in Commerce: The Parisian Merchant Court and the Rise of Commercial Society in Eighteenth-Century France* (New Haven: Yale University Press, 2007). In Algeria, Jewish merchants were not allowed to vote for the judges. Alfred Ghighi, the associate director of CAES, proposed to extend universal suffrage to Algeria with regard to merchant tribunals to all citizens, including Jews. Alfred Ghighi, "Rapport III: Question des Tribunaux Consulaires," September 24, 1919, AIU Algérie IC2.

[79] "Announcement of the Comité Algérien d'Études Sociales," Algiers, July 15, 1919, AIU Algérie IC2.

[80] Cohen, "Les Circonstances de la Fondation du Comité Algérien d'Études Sociales," 212.

[81] Reeva Spector Simon, Michael Menachem Laskier, and Sarah Reguer, eds., *The Jews of the Middle East and North Africa in Modern Times* (New York: Columbia University Press, 2003), 464. See also Nahon, "Rapport Annuel 1900–1901," AIU Moscou EN 01.2.

The Depression and Antisemitism in the Interwar Period

During the 1920s, declining production led to an economic crisis in the Algerian colony. Annual grain production, European and native, had reached a peak in 1901–1910 at 19.6 million quintals. From 1921 to 1930, this amount decreased to 16 million.[82] In the postwar period, France struggled with inflation resulting from wartime advances and expenditures. The franc depreciated sharply after the war, with the greatest depreciation occurring in 1919–1920. The French currency reform in 1928 undervalued the franc, and France's subsequent embrace of deflation prolonged the depression. The problems caused by France's insistence on maintaining the gold standard worsened the conditions of the depression in France and her colonies.[83] In Algeria, population increase in the midst of reduced production deepened the impact of the depression. Strikes occurred in 1928, further weakening the sense of security in the colony.[84]

As often occurs in times of economic crisis, antisemitism increased alongside the depression and the uncertainty of the postwar period, including the arrival of Jewish refugees escaping Germany. The antisemitic revival of the 1930s gained its strength from middle-class groups seeking to close their ranks to the competition and economic threat posed by the refugees. By the end of 1933, 85 percent of the 25,000 German émigrés in France were Jews.[85] In 1933, Prime Minister Camille Chautemps sent a notice to Prefects of all French departments discussing the economic crisis and encouraging them to take measures to avoid any resultant conflicts.[86] In Algeria, rumors that Muslim employees would be replaced with German Jewish refugees fueled fears of economic stability in the wake of the depression.[87] This climate of competition and fear resulted in Parliament's promulgation of the July 19, 1934, law that established a two-tiered system of citizenship. This system granted fewer rights to recently naturalized citizens, while still requiring them to

---

[82] Ageron, *Modern Algeria*, 86.

[83] Kenneth Mouré, "The Gold Standard Illusion: France and the Gold Standard in an Era of Currency Instability, 1914–1939," in Mouré and Martin S. Alexander, *Crisis and Renewal in France, 1918–1962* (New York: Berghahn Books, 2002), 67, 69.

[84] Daniel Lefeuvre, *Chère Algérie: La France et sa colonie, 1930–1962* (Paris: Flammarion, 2005), 12–15. See also Samuel Kalman, *French Colonial Fascism: The Extreme Right in Algeria, 1919–1939* (New York: Palgrave Macmillan, 2013), 52–53.

[85] Vicki Caron, "The Antisemitic Revival in France in the 1930s: The Socioeconomic Dimension Reconsidered," *The Journal of Modern History*, Vol. 70 (March 1998): 27–29, 33.

[86] Camille Chautemps, letter to Prefects, Paris, February 10, 1933, CAOM Alg Oran 96.

[87] These rumors are examined in the following chapter as precursors of the violence in Constantine.

fulfill all responsibilities the status conferred. At the same time, antisemites called for the institution of quotas for non-French Jews.[88]

The already fraught conditions of the depression and the growing presence of Jews in commerce and on municipal councils stimulated the antisemitic revival in the colony. By the 1930s, Jews represented 12–13 percent of the population of Constantine; however, their relative success in commerce and politics in the city incorrectly suggested that Jews were more powerful than they actually were.[89] In 1926, the Constantine Jewish community consisted of more than 15,000 Jews, but Jews held many political posts, including one deputy mayor, seven municipal council members, one general council member, two judges, and two members of the Chamber of Commerce (vice president and treasurer).[90] These mostly elected posts afforded Jews previously untapped power within municipal governments, and concretized antisemitic fears of Jewish competition in municipal politics.

Called "Little Jerusalem" by the Europeans in the area, neighboring Ain-Beida became a major site of antisemitic rancor. David Nabon of the Alliance reported that all the Jewish candidates were elected to the municipal council, representing six out of sixteen councilors, and one mayor's deputy. Nabon suggested that Jews could have been even more numerous on the municipal council, but refrained from offering more candidates for fear of inciting jealousy and incurring antisemitic incidents.[91] Within this climate of economic turmoil and increased Jewish representation on municipal councils, politicians and antisemites responded with revitalized antisemitism.

Electoral Politics, Status Competition, and a Return to Municipal Antisemitism

As in the 1890s, the antisemitism of the 1920s developed out of competition for the scarce resources of municipal government, under the leadership of antisemitic politicians such as Dr. Jules Molle in Oran in the late 1920s. Molle was born in a small town in France, entered

[88] Caron, "The Antisemitic Revival in France in the 1930s," 41, 57.
[89] Charles-Robert Ageron, "Une émeute anti-juive à Constantine (août 1934)," *Revue de l'Occident Musulman et de la Méditerranée*, Vol. 13, No. 1 (1973): 23–24.
[90] There were three large synagogues and six smaller ones in Constantine. The Alliance-run Talmud Torah included 13 professors, 800 male students, and 100 female students, as well as a nursery. Seventeen social societies also provided various services to the community. Barkatz, President of the Jewish Consistory of Constantine, "Exposé sur la Communauté Juive à Constantine," Constantine, April 29, 1926, AIU Algérie II B 4.
[91] D. Nabon to the President of the AIU, "Communauté d'Ain Beida," Constantine, May 8, 1934, AIU Algérie II B 10.

politics as a republican, became a municipal councilor in 1908, and then moved to Algeria. His antisemitism emerged when he realized its popular electoral power.[92] In 1926, the total population of Algeria was 6,064,865, of which 872,439 were Europeans (this figure likely included *néos*). The Jewish population at the time was approximately 100,000; 30,000 in Oran, 20,000 in Algiers, 15,000 in Constantine, and 35,000 elsewhere in the colony.[93] Although still relatively small compared to the European population, Jews represented an important demographic of the voting population. Their ability to vote, and more significantly, their active voting record, posed a threat to the Europeans, particularly the *néos*, who viewed the Jews as status competitors.

As a result of the electoral power of the *néo* population in the city, Molle became mayor of Oran in 1921.[94] Molle had a long history as an antisemitic agitator and politician. On May 16, 1914, Molle founded the *Union Latine*, made up of *français d'origine* and *néos*, most of Spanish origin. The main goal of the *Union Latine* was to fight against the "electoral action of the Jewish bloc." Molle organized cocktail parties (known as *apéritifs*), banquets, balls, and parties for the members of the *Union*, who celebrated their shared "Latin" heritage and hatred of the Jew. Molle created an antisemitic anthem, the "Marseillaise Latine," which consisted of such lines as "The children of the Latin People / defend their destiny / and drive away the abhorred race ..." Molle addressed his *néo* followers in Spanish, which "flattered their national pride and further excited them against the Jews."[95] Molle's activities with the *Union* assured him a strong political base that led to his election and continued antisemitic activities while in office. In 1925, Molle's deliberately inflammatory tactics, such as excluding the names of Oran Jews who had died during World War I from a commemoration of a memorial, prompted a resurgence of antisemitic violence.[96] The LDH took

---

[92] Kalman, *French Colonial Fascism*, 32–33.

[93] A. Confino to the President of AIU, "Re: Demographics," Algiers, February 24, 1927, AIU Algérie IB4. Confino estimated that Jews of European origins made up approximately 3 percent of the total Jewish population.

[94] André Chouraqui, *Letter to an Arab Friend* (Boston: University of Massachusetts Press, 1972), 12.

[95] According to the LDH, during his electoral campaigns, Molle aimed his rhetoric at "enflaming Spanish fanatics and the reactionary and clerical party of Oran." Cited in Chouraqui, *Letter to an Arab Friend*, 12. See also "Marseillaise Latine," CAOM Alg Oran E227. Kalman states that the *Union* permitted Molle to dominate local politics, *French Colonial Fascism*, 32–33.

[96] A. Confino to the President of the AIU, Algiers, May 26, 1922, AIU Algérie IB4.

interest in the antisemitism of Molle and his followers because of its extreme nature.[97]

The municipal electoral campaign of 1925 witnessed a significant upsurge in antisemitic propaganda, sponsored by Molle and his supporters. The police files are filled with examples of tracts circulated in Oran supporting Molle and his fellow antisemitic candidates and urging Europeans, especially *néos*, to vote against Jews. A tract dated April 28, 1925, from a "group of merchants" was directed at other merchants, defaming Jews as economic exploiters. The tract emphasized not only the economic power of Jews but also their electoral power, due to the accusation that they voted as a bloc.

Sir, you are a merchant. You know from experience, what kind of SPECIAL competition . . . you have with the Jews. They are rich, powerful, clever, disloyal. Will you give them power and a new arrogance, by giving them the Mayor of Oran? Dr. Molle, the most favored candidate in Oran during the legislative elections, received 5,200 votes. Admittedly, Mr. Beranger could be elected with the same number, but it is indisputable that that number would include 3,600 Jewish votes. Want to tell me what he would refuse to the Jews? Nothing! Since he would only be the mayor because of the formidable appointment of the Jewish vote. Whatever your political ideas, your duty, your interest is not to deliver our city to JEWISH INFLUENCE. It is a matter of life or death for our country. We hope that you will do your duty on May 3 by VOTING for the anti-Jewish Doctor Molle candidate list.[98]

This tract echoes many similar piece of propaganda that demanded political and economic competition with Jews and clearly demonstrates the status anxieties that flourished at times of elections.

During his electoral campaign in April 1925, Molle spread rumors that the Alliance gave 80,000 francs to the Synagogue of Oran to bribe Jews to vote as a bloc. Molle accused Rabbi Weill of urging his congregants to vote for Molle's opponent, Beranger. On April 25, Molle published a call to his "Latin" electors, stating that "the *néo* is anti-Jewish and this is because all the settlers of foreign origin who contribute such a large part to the development of Algeria are horribly exploited by the Jews." Such calls echoed those of the late 1890s. Prior to the municipal elections, Molle and his supporters plastered posters directed at Latin voters throughout the city, which stated, "Municipal elections May 3, 1925: Latin Brothers: Attention! Be prepared for the Jewish Saint Barthelemy the day after our triumph!" Molle conjured up the wars of religion to

---

[97] Like Régis, Molle edited his own newspaper, *Le Petit Oranais*. "Rapport sur les Troubles Antisémites Déchaînés à l'Occasion de la Campagne Électorale du 3 Mai 1925," Oran, May 9, 1925, BDIC-LDH F Delta Res 798/71.

[98] Political tract, Oran, April 28, 1925, CAOM Alg Oran E227.

advocate for violence. On the days following the elections, May 4–6, Molle's followers attacked Jews throughout the city of Oran.[99] Molle won over 8,000 votes, beating his competitor by more than 2,000 votes.[100]

In August 1925, the Procurer General accused Molle and his newspaper, *Le Petit Oranais*, of inciting "murder and pillage" during the May violence. The Minister of Justice declared that the evidence against Molle was insufficient and dropped the case.[101] Like Régis before him, Molle realized that the status anxieties of the *néos* could be harnessed for his benefit in municipal elections and while in office. By unifying *néos* and *français d'origine* against the Jews, Molle capitalized on that competition.

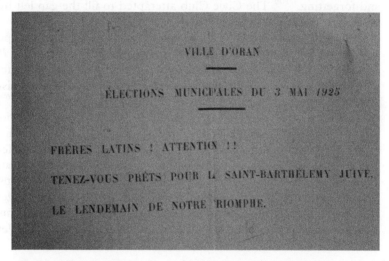

Political Tract, found in Oran, April 3, 1925. CAOM Alg Oran E 227.[102]

In the face of violent political antisemitism espoused by Molle, Jews in Oran established Jewish defense organizations. In 1928, a group of Jews founded the Club Civique d'Oran (Civic Club) to combat Molle's

---

[99] This statement alluded to the St. Bartholomew's day massacre in 1572 directed against the Huguenots in the midst of the French Wars of Religion. "Rapport sur les troubles antisémites," Oran, May 9, 1925, BDIC-LDH F Delta Res 798/71.

[100] Kalman, *French Colonial Fascism*, 33.

[101] Procurer General to the Garde des Sceaux, Algiers, August 24, 1925; Garde de Sceaux, Minister of Justice to the Minister of the Interior, "No. 57–201," March 4, 1926; CAOM FM 81F/864. See also L.Taourel to the President of the AIU, "No. 156," Oran, April 26, 1925, and the article "Coups d'Épingle," *Le Petit Oranais*, August 25, 1925, AIU Algérie IIC9.

[102] Report from the head of Departmental Security of Oran to the Prefect of Oran, "Report No. 799," Oran, April 30, 1925, CAOM Alg Oran E227.

antisemitic campaign and the rhetoric of *Le Petit Oranais*. The Prefect of Oran described the founders as "justifiably irritated by the excess and the persistence of this [antisemitic] campaign." They recruited young Jews in Oran to their organization.[103] The Civic Club cited the LDH as a source of inspiration and support. The Civic Club's central goal was to use peaceful and legal actions to combat antisemitism and contribute to the "moral and intellectual improvement of the citizen." The club planned to defend the rights of citizens through organizing conferences, interventions, and propaganda in the form of brochures, publications, and newspapers.[104] It emphasized the importance of actively combating antisemitism in contrast to those who passively approached it with "silence and forgetting."[105] The Civic Club attempted to fill the gap left by the CAES in the defense of Jewish rights.

Over the summer of 1929, the question of Jewish electoral power dominated the opinion section of the antisemitic newspaper *La Presse Libre*. Confino expressed concern over the first article on the subject, entitled "The Jewish Question: Should the Jews be considered a distinct ethnic or religious group in the midst of the French collectivity?"[106] This "Jewish Question" had originated in the era of Jewish emancipation in Europe and the concerns of lawmakers regarding the integration of a formerly autonomous group or the creation of a special status under the law.[107] On June 7, Dr. Molle's opinion on the "The Jewish Question" appeared in *La Presse Libre*. Molle wrote that one candidate, Monsieur Brunel, was elected because of the Jewish bloc. He cited 5,667 votes for Brunel, out of 6,000 Jewish voters. Such figures, although utterly unreliable, served to prove Molle's point of the dangerous power of the Jewish vote.[108]

---

[103] The Prefect added that in the face of past attacks during electoral periods, the Jews of Oran did not resort to violence, but sought to combat antisemitism through administrative channels. Prefect of the Department of Oran, Lambry, to the Gov-Gen "No. 2926," Oran, May 15, 1928, CAOM FM 81F/864.

[104] The Civic Club defined antisemitism as the "prejudices of races and all such dissolving theories or others, that is to say all things contrary to the spirit of our immortal revolution of 1789." Statutes, Club Civique Oranais, CAOM FM 81F/864.

[105] Chief of Departmental Security to the Prefect of Oran, "No. 967: Re: Réunion du 'Club Civique,'" Oran, May 14, 1928, CAOM FM 81F/864.

[106] A. Confino to the President of the AIU "No. 9469," Algiers, May 29, 1929, AIU Algérie IC2.

[107] Voltaire and his contemporaries debated the worthiness of Jews as citizens and feared that unless properly incorporated, they would create a "state within the State." Jacob Katz, *Out of the Ghetto: The Social Background of Jewish Emancipation, 1770–1870* (Syracuse: Syracuse University Press, 1998), 33, 98–99.

[108] Molle wrote, "The Jews always vote for men who commit to refusing to non-Jews that which they find excellent for themselves." There were 7,000 registered Jewish voters in Oran. Dr. Molle, "Après les Élections Municipales: La Question Juive: Les Israélites

Antonin Duboso, Molle's colleague, echoed such statements and questioned the Jews' right to citizenship. Duboso emphasized the religious connection between Jews, which cemented the voting power of the "Jewish Alliance." He warned future municipal candidates to "be sure of Jewish support, otherwise you are lost." Duboso attacked the Crémieux Decree as unjustifiable and contended that Jews should be considered juridically "*indigènes*," and therefore French subjects. He argued that Algerian Jews did not deserve French citizenship, but benefitted from the lobbying efforts of Jews in France.[109]

Duboso and Molle's analysis of "The Jewish Question" emphasized competition for control of municipal government as the core of Algerian antisemitism. The fact that in 1929, fifty-nine years after the Crémieux Decree, Algerian Jewish citizenship was still under debate indicates the potency of the Algerian antisemitic platform and the exploitation of status anxieties in order to gain votes. It also reflects the importance of voting rights and the power and benefits that votes could bring. By denigrating Algerian Jews' citizenship, political antisemites depreciated their electoral competitors' power and used antisemitism as a political platform. In this way, the political antisemitism of the 1920s and 1930s was an outgrowth of that of the 1890s.

The governor-general expressed concern over Molle's influence, which he termed a "veritable appeal for the reawakening of antisemitism" that would have "adverse consequences."[110] As evidence, the governor-general cited another article by Molle, which appeared in *Le Presse Libre d'Alger* in late June 1929. In the article, Molle again attacked Jewish confessional solidarity, which made a "shameful farce" of the electoral system. He depicted the Jew as the fat-cat banker, the enemy of the simple, patriotic Frenchman, particularly those of Latin blood. Antisemitism could unite the Frenchmen of Algiers with those of Oran

---

doivent-ils être considérés comme formant un groupe ethnique et religieux distinct aux milieux de la collectivité française? L'opinion de M. le Dr. Molle, maire-député d'Oran," *La Presse Libre*, June 7, 1929, AIU Algérie IC2. Molle echoed Count Clermont-Tonnere, who, in 1789, feared that Jews would constitute a "nation within the nation." Lynn Hunt, *The French Revolution and Human Rights: A Brief Documentary History* (Boston: Bedford Books/St. Martin's Press, 1996), 88. See also Schreier, *Arabs of the Jewish Faith*, 84.

[109] Duboso wrote that "the Jews of Algeria were not more prepared for naturalization as a bloc; they just benefit from a powerful political association," with the Alliance. He also suggested that "it is this latent, endemic antisemitism that penetrates all the classes of the nation." Antonin Duboso, "Après les Élections Municipales: La Question Juive: Les Israélites doivent-ils être considérés comme formant un groupe ethnique et religieux distinct au milieu de la collectivité française?," *La Presse Libre*, June 13, 1929, AIU Algérie IC2.

[110] Gov-Gen to the Minister of the Interior, Algiers, July 2, 1929, CAOM FM 81F/864.

because "the same Latin blood abundantly flows in the veins of one and the other." He prophesized that in the coming municipal elections, the "good people of Algiers will act against the Jews."[111] Under Molle, electoral competition reemerged as the foundation of antisemitism, facilitated by contemporary events around the colony and the world.

In the 1930s, as Hitler took power in Germany and antisemitism spread throughout Europe and Algeria, Henri Lautier, a virulent antisemite strongly influenced by Nazism, launched *L'Éclair Algérien*, an antisemitic newspaper.[112] Although a contemporary of Molle, Lautier was primarily an antisemitic agitator, and even though he had political aspirations, he did not have access to the same power and influence as Molle. In 1933, Lautier founded the *Ligue d'action latine* (LAC) and established its head-quarters in Constantine, which he nicknamed *Youpinville*.[113] The LAC allowed membership to both *français d'origine* and naturalized Frenchmen. Jews were obviously excluded.[114]

On November 25, 1933, Lautier published the statutes of the LAC, which codified the group's antisemitism.[115] The goal of the league was to "defend the Latin traditions, beliefs, and mores," and to combat Jewish competition by all necessary means, except violence, but primarily politically and commercially. All league members were required to participate in certain activities, or risk being removed. These requirements included "demonstrating his spirit of solidarity vis-à-vis Latin merchants and to abstain from making purchases from Jewish merchants. In the electoral period, he will cast his votes for candidates from the League."[116] Such requirements intertwined politics and economics in the antisemitic platform.

As a political agitator, Lautier followed the models of Régis and Molle. Lautier promoted popular political antisemitism in the colony, uniting *français d'origine* and *néos* by emphasizing shared *latinité* and unity against the common Jewish enemy. Like his forebears, Lautier incited popular

---

[111] Dr. Molle, "Une Lettre de M. le Dr. Molle, Député-maire d'Oran," *Presse Libre d'Alger*, June 30, 1929, CAOM FM 81F/864.

[112] Robert Attal, *Les Émeutes de Constantine: 5 août 1934* (Paris: Éditions Romillat, 2002), 69.

[113] *Youpinville* translates as a derogative term equating "Jew-ville." Prefect of Constantine to the Sec-Gen, "No. 81: Sociétés: Ligue d'Action Latine," Constantine, January 5, 1933, CAOM Alg Const B/3/250. See also Ageron, "Une émeute anti-juive," 36.

[114] Departmental Security, Constantine, "No. 3025: Au sujet de la création de la 'Ligue d'Action Latine," Constantine, November 16, 1933, CAOM Alg Const B/3/250.

[115] Henri Lautier, "La Ligue d'Action Latine," *L'Éclair Algérien*, November 25, 1933, CAOM Alg Const B/3/250.

[116] Lautier demanded that the members of LAC fight "against the intrusion of Jewish elements, considered to be the instigators of troubles and discords, and guilty of hatred and sectarianism, inassimilable in their great majority ..." Ibid.

opinion with salacious and libelous articles on the many misdeeds and nefarious activities of Jews in the colony, particularly in the realm of politics and commerce. Lautier encouraged his follow Latins to avoid shopping *chez le Juif*.

Lautier exploited current events to enflame feelings in the colony but relied on standards such as electoral and economic competition. In December 1933 Lautier published an article entitled "La Juiverie et les Elections Consulaires," in which he wrote that "the number of French merchants decreases every day, and after having infested France, the ghettos from Germany will poison the rest of our local commerce." For the upcoming election, Lautier encouraged his fellow French voters to vote against candidate lists that included Jews. In his rhetoric, Lautier synthesized economic fears with political competition.[117] Under the leadership of Lautier and Molle, *néos* once again became the foot soldiers of antisemitism in the 1920s and 1930s.

While antisemitism flourished again in the colony, Jewish defense activities also increased. In Constantine in April 1933, Jewish leaders organized a conference sponsored by the Universal Union of Jewish Youth (*Union Universelle de la Jeunesse Juive*) on the "Lessons of German Antisemitism." Approximately 250 people attended the meeting led by Monsieur Rabinovitch, a lawyer of the Court of Appeals in Paris. Rabinovitch set out three actions for Jews to take against Hitler: first, to aid German Jewish refugees in Paris; second, to boycott all German merchandise; and finally, to open the gates of Palestine to immigration and to colonization.[118] Jews in Constantine collaborated with the International League against Antisemitism (*Ligue Internationale contre l'Antisémitisme* – LICA) to prepare methods to combat Nazi antisemitism.[119] Jews cooperated with non-Jewish local leaders, including the pastor of the Episcopal Methodist Church, the local LDH, and the

---

[117] In the article, Lautier criticized Senator Henri Beranger for supporting the integration of 4,000 German Jewish refugees in France and the colony. Henri Lautier, "La Juiverie et les Elections Consulaires," *L'Éclair Algérien*, found in Departmental Security of Constantine, "Report No. 3307, Antisémitisme," Constantine, December 13, 1933, CAOM Alg Const B/3/250.

[118] Leymarie, Departmental Security of Constantine, "No. 955: Conférence organisée par l'Union Universelle de la Jeunesse Juive," Constantine, April 21, 1933, CAOM Alg Const B/3/249.

[119] Departmental Security of Constantine to the Prefect of Constantine, "No. 2415: Ligue Internationale contre l'antisémitisme," Constantine, September 9, 1933, CAOM Alg Const B/3/249. In 1935, LICA began its campaign against Hitler, antisemitism, and racism in earnest. See, for example, Fonds LICA, CDJC CMXCVI 12-14. From 1936 until 1940, Jews and Muslims collaborated against antisemitism in the work of the LICA. See Aomar Boum, "Partners against Anti-Semitism: Muslims and Jews Respond to Nazism in French North African Colonies, 1936–1940," *The Journal of North African Studies*, Vol. 19, No. 4 (2014): 554–570.

Section Française de l'Internationale Ouvrière (S.F.I.O., the French Section of the Workers' International), to organize a meeting to protest the persecution of German Jews.[120] The leaders organized an assembly on April 6, 1933, attended by over 1,200 people.[121] Cognizant of the growing antisemitism of many politicians, Jews in Algeria were careful to couch their critiques of Germany in words of praise for France.

Jewish leaders encouraged calm among the younger generation for fear of antisemitic reprisals.[122] On April 1, 1933, in the midst of a demonstration by approximately fifty young Jews, the police arrested seven Jews for yelling "Long live the war, Down with Hitler, Down with Germany, Long live France!"[123] It is likely that the Jewish elite, already concerned by the threat of boycott of their shops, feared that such overt political displays would put the Jewish community at risk.[124] The precautions taken by the Jews in Algeria were well founded – the colony had long developed a culture of episodic antisemitic violence. In the face of growing antisemitism, as well as increased competition in elections, Algerian Jews fought to develop their identities as loyal French citizens in order to combat the antisemitism of their status competitors, the *néos*.

In the face of the extreme antisemitism of Molle and Lautier, Jews also turned to violence. In Souk-Ahras in June 1934, after visiting the local president of *Action Française*, Lautier sought out a police officer to complain that a Jew had ripped up a package of his newspaper. While Lautier spoke to the police officer, a Jew, Albert Levy, walked up to the two men and asked Lautier, "Is it you, Monsieur Lautier? I am a Jew, and a veteran," and proceeded to punch Lautier in the face.[125] Levy's assault was a departure from the civilized defense of the CAES and other Jewish defense organizations that promoted peaceful resistance. That Levy

---

[120] Chief of Departmental Security of Constantine, "No. 818: Organisation d'une réunion contre l'action antisémite," Constantine, April 6, 1933, CAOM Alg Const B/3/249.

[121] Commissioner Hug, Departmental Security of Constantine, "No. 841: Réunion de protestation contre l'action antisémite Hitlerienne," Constantine, April 7, 1933, CAOM Alg Const B/3/249.

[122] Chief of Departmental Security in Constantine, "No. 821: Affiches au sujet de la protestation contre l'action antisémite Hitlerienne," Constantine, April 6, 1933, CAOM Alg Const B/3/249.

[123] Chief of Departmental Security in Constantine, "No. 773: Manifestation contre le movement antisémite allemande," Constantine, April 1, 1933, CAOM Alg Const B/3/249.

[124] Dr. Guedj to Israel Levy, Chief Rabbi of France, "Telegram," Constantine, April 3, 1933, CAOM Alg Const B/3/249.

[125] In the end, it was Lautier who was taken to the local prison – for his own protection. Police Commissioner of Souk-Ahras to the Director of General Security, Algiers, the Prefect of Constantine, the Sub-Prefect of Guelma, and the Mayor of Souk-Ahras, "No. 4331," Souk-Ahras, June 24, 1934, CAOM Alg Const B/3/250.

defined himself as a Jew and a veteran shows the duality of his identity and the importance of his service in World War I: he was a Jew *and* a Frenchman. Levy was not unique. In this period of heightened antisemitism, Jews used violence to demonstrate their identities and combat antisemitism in encounters with Algerian Muslims and the *néos*. Violence between Jews and Muslims escalated in the 1930s as unequal rights served as the catalyst of these conflicts, culminating in the 1934 Constantine pogrom.

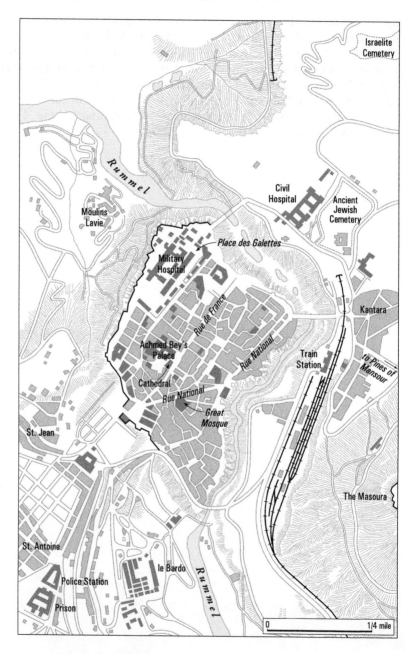

Constantine, ca. 1934

4   The Politics of Status Anxieties and Unequal Rights in Interwar Colonial Algeria

Jewish–Muslim Conflicts and the 1934 Constantine "Pogrom"

Jewish–Muslim relations deteriorated sharply during the interwar period as Muslim frustrations with the French colonial administration shifted onto Algerian Jews, whose citizenship and rights that had been denied to Algerian Muslim. Differences in status were the source of conflict in the interwar Algeria.[1] Small-scale episodes of violence, often over perceived personal slights or questionable economic exchanges, occurred regularly in Algeria in the 1920s and 1930s. Algerian Jews sometimes claimed that Muslims were not treating them with the respect their citizenship demanded. Algerian Muslims' campaign for rights, still inchoate in the 1920s and 1930s, shifted to a clearer political agenda in terms of the lack of Muslim rights in relationship to Jewish citizenship under the leadership of a new generation of educated and activist Algerian Muslims. Deteriorating economic conditions during the interwar period exacerbated status anxieties and sharpened competition for increasingly scarce resources.

The interwar period saw greater political mobilization among all groups in the colony, as well as an increase among the radical right wing, including the *Croix de Feu*. In this atmosphere, extreme violence between groups in the colony reflected the tensions between communities and politics – Jews competed with Muslims, the right competed with the left, Europeans competed with one another, *néos* competed with *français d'origine*, and so on. The violence of August 1934 must therefore be seen as the product of unequal access to political rights and the political power, increased political activities among competing groups, and the associated status anxieties that became heightened in the interwar period.

David Nirenberg's examination of violence between Jews and Muslims in Christian Spain in the Middle Ages offers a way to conceptualize the

[1] Jacques Berque emphasizes the centrality of issues of identity and status in colonial Algeria. He also identifies the role of "intimidation, maneuvers and secret discussions" in electoral affairs. Jacques Berque, *French North Africa: The Maghrib Between Two World Wars*, trans. Jean Stewart (New York: Frederick A. Praeger, Inc., 1967), 26–27.

role of violence in articulating identities in colonial Algeria.[2] In his argument, Nirenberg emphasizes that violence was a way of enforcing hierarchies and distinguishing difference. In colonial Algeria, Jews and Muslims used violence – rhetorical and physical – to enforce a perceived hierarchy vis-à-vis their victims. Benjamin Brower's analysis of the "multiple logic" of violence in colonial Algeria understands violence as representative of the social, political, and economic anxieties of colonial groups. He argues that the violence in Algeria was far more complex than the colonizers and the colonized binary. Brower focuses on the relationship between violence and power and the development of social and political inequalities.[3]

The subject of colonial violence – particularly that of Algeria – is a fertile topic for scholars, and much has been written on it in recent years. Samuel Kalman, in his work on the far right in Algeria, examines the way in which violence became an expression of extreme right politics in the colony.[4] Joshua Cole has extensively studied the causes behind the 1934 violence in Constantine. Cole argues that the 1934 riots must be understood within the context of the larger scope of access to and exclusion from rights within the colony. Although Cole and I use different sources in our analysis, our conclusions are similar.[5] We both argue that the local perspective in analyzing the 1934 violence in Constantine is crucial. We also believe that the violence must be examined in the larger framework of dialogues and debates regarding rights in the colony and the competition for access to rights and power among the various groups, particularly the settlers' efforts to undermine the political activities of certain communities. Violence in the colony in the interwar period must be studied in the context of shifting political and social hierarchies as well as perceived threats to the status quo.

This chapter examines interpretations and representations of violence between Jews and Muslims in the department of Constantine during the interwar period, reaching a crescendo in the violent pogrom in 1934.[6] I locate the 1934 Constantine pogrom within the trajectory of Algerian

---

[2] David Nirenberg, *Communities of Violence: Persecution of Minorities in the Middle Ages* (Princeton: Princeton University Press, 1996), 168–169.

[3] Benjamin Claude Brower, *A Desert Named Peace: The Violence of France's Empire in the Algerian Sahara, 1844–1902* (New York: Columbia University Press, 2009), 6–7.

[4] Kalman, *French Colonial Fascism*. See also Samuel Kalman, "Fascism and Algérianité: The Croix de Feu and the Indigenous Question in 1930s Algeria," in Martin Thomas. ed., *The French Colonial Mind, Volume 2: Violence, Military Encounters, and Colonialism* (Lincoln: University of Nebraska Press, 2012), 112–139.

[5] Cole, "Constantine before the Riots of August 1934: Civil Status, Anti-Semitism, and the Politics of Assimilation in Interwar French Algeria,": 839–841.

[6] The police files in the CAOM, especially those for Constantine, are particularly rich, more so than files for the departments of Oran and Algiers.

Muslim demands for citizenship, the growth of Jewish political activity, the continued power of municipal political antisemitism, and developing global antisemitism of the politically charged 1930s. This chapter also examines the Constantine pogrom's impact on the relationship between Algerian Jews and France. The inaction of the French administration during the violence forced Jews to recognize the limits on their position in the colony. For Constantine's Jews, August 5 created the first tear in the fabric of their French identities as they realized how deeply ingrained antisemitism was within the French administration.

The colonial city of Constantine serves as a microcosm through which to study similar trajectories of increasing status anxieties and violence throughout the colony. With 99,595 inhabitants in 1931, the city remained strongly traditional in certain areas, with little evident modernization and industrialization. Of the inhabitants, 36,092 were Europeans, 12,058 were Jews, and 51,445 were "natives."[7] Jews, Muslims, and Europeans lived within the city but separated into distinct quarters based on ethnic or religious identity.[8]

Despite these distinct quarters, there was significant interaction between the groups, particularly between Jews and Muslims. Sometimes the interactions turned violent. There is evidence of violent encounters between Jews and Muslims in the early 1910s. Violence increased dramatically during the interwar period in conjunction with political developments in Palestine and Europe as well as the development of the campaign to improve Muslims' access to rights in the colony increased tensions.

Governor-General Carde described Constantine's Jews in his October 1934 report on the events of Constantine.

The Jews, from the Crémieux decree of October 24, 1870 on, are French citizens. They form a disciplined community and occupy many public functions. They also play a large role in business, including the role they play as bankers and lenders, especially for the natives, whose lack of foresight and ignorance in matters of money we know, and who accuse the Jews of lending with usurious rates.[9]

The three most defining aspects of Constantine's Jews, according to Carde, include their status as citizens, their position and power within the administration, and their role as moneylenders. All three of these

---

[7] Gov-Gen Carde to the Minister of the Interior, "Report No. 4264," Algiers, October 19, 1934, CAOM Alg GGA 2CAB/3.
[8] Ageron, "Une émeute anti-juive à Constantine (août 1934)," 23–24.
[9] Gov-Gen Carde to the Minister of the Interior, "Report No. 4264," Algiers, October 19, 1934, CAOM Alg GGA 2CAB/3.

traits frustrated Muslims seeking access to rights and power within the colony.

The archives contain many examples of seemingly isolated cases of Jewish–Muslim violence and reflect its increasing pervasiveness in the interwar period. Why did such cases of violence become relatively common, and what does that increase indicate? As Joshua Cole asks, was colonial violence in the French colonial order systemic or circumstantial?[10] For example, in 1913 a Muslim, Ahmed ben Belkacem Slimini, bargained for a pair of shoes at a Jewish-owned shop. When Slimini decided not to purchase the shoes, the Jewish merchant hit him.[11] Following the incident, a group of Muslim municipal council members, merchants, and other elites protested the treatment of their fellow Muslims by Jews. Referencing the Slimini case, they wrote that Jews "lynched" him. They also emphasized that this incident was but one in a series of Jewish aggressions against Muslims.[12] The Slimini case reveals a climate of accepted violence between Jews and Muslims; it reflects tensions in the political and social hierarchies in colonial Algeria due in part to campaigns to promote Algerian Muslims' rights and their efforts to use the political and institutional channels available to them within the French colonial structure. This case also illustrates that Jews and Muslims lived in close proximity to and interacted with each other.

The key sources analyzed here include police reports that detailed the names, ages, and professions of the parties involved, provided the officer's analysis of the causes of the incident, and outlined any punitive measures taken. There were certainly more violent encounters than those reported by the police, and some files have undoubtedly been lost along the way. The reporting police officers were also subject to outside influences, including antisemitism and bribery. These factors may have led them to report certain cases, to overlook others, or to report in ways not

---

[10] Joshua Cole, "Massacres and Their Historians: Recent Histories of State Violence in France and Algeria in the Twentieth Century," *French Politics, Culture, and Society*, Vol. 28, No. 1 (Spring, 2010): 110.

[11] In 1913, in all five reported incidents between Jews and Muslims in Constantine, Jews attacked Muslims. Central Police Commissioner of Constantine, "Rapport journalier," Constantine, March 27–28, 1913, CAOM Alg Const B/3/248.

[12] Muslim notables to Prefect of Department of Constantine, Constantine, March 28, 1913, CAOM Alg Const B/3/248. With the start of war, more cases involved young Jews attacking Muslim soldiers. Commission of Police, "Rapport spécial à M. le Commissaire Central, No. 593," Constantine, February 7, 1914, CAOM Alg Const B/3/248. See also Central Commissioner Report, "No. 2045," Constantine, February 7, 1914; Departmental Security of Constantine, "Rapport No. 319: Au sujet d'une rixe entre tirailleurs et Israélites," Constantine, February 8, 1914; Commissioner of Police, "Rapport Journalier du 7–8 Fevrier: Bagarre de tirailleurs dans le quartier israélite," Constantine, February 7–8, 1914, CAOM Alg Const B/3/248.

necessarily reflective of the actual situation. As a result, the cases examined in this chapter are but a small sample of a wider phenomenon. Although violence can be examined through many different lenses, I use it to explore the ways in which the parties involved viewed their political and social status in the colony. Often the Jewish aggressors felt insulted by Algerian Muslims, whom they viewed as inferiors. These incidents are reminiscent of the violence that the *néos* perpetrated against Jews in the 1890s. Status anxieties were once again at the root of the violence of the interwar period.

Although technically citizens, most Europeans in the colony still considered Jews not entirely French. Many Europeans continued to lump Jews with Muslims in the category of *indigènes*. To borrow the words of Homi Bhabha, Jews were "almost the same, *but not quite.*"[13] Jews endeavored to distance themselves from Muslims in the eyes of Europeans. As a result, quotidian interactions between Jews and Muslim became violent when one or the other did not respect the Jews' new status, or when Muslims challenged the arbitrary nature of that change in status.

Néos remained similarly insecure in their status. Violence was one avenue to reassert one's position in that hierarchy, especially in the aftermath and rapidly changing world following World War I. Frenchness was constantly being redefined in the colony, whether the inclusion of Jews as citizens in 1870, or the naturalization of non-French Europeans in 1889. The colony needed a strong European presence to survive, and thus political inclusion and subsequent assimilation of non-French groups were necessary to maintain power. But that process of assimilation was slow, flawed, and inconsistent. Ambiguities over changing statuses in the colony were compounded by perceived increases in competition in politics and economics during the depression.

World War I, Blood Debt, and Algerian Muslim Demands for Rights

Algerian Muslims answered France's call in the First World War. Approximately 173,000 Arab and Berber soldiers served France during the war, often serving longer than French soldiers and receiving far less compensation. Following World War I, Algerian Muslims intensified their campaign for compensation for their service to France during the war and for rights in Algeria. The "blood debt" incurred between colonial soldiers and France forced French administrators and politicians to consider offering greater rights to those soldiers. The status of Algerian

---

[13] Bhabha, "Of Mimicry and Man: The Ambivalence of Colonial Discourse," 153.

Muslims had not significantly changed since the 1865 sénatus-consulte, which offered them French nationality but not the political rights of citizenship unless they gave up their personal status.[14] From the 1865 law until the end of the colonial period, only 6,000 Algerian Muslims successfully applied for naturalization.[15] The first major concession to these colonial soldiers in Algeria was the 1919 Jonnart Law, which provided Muslims with wider access to French citizenship, further shrinking the gap between Jews and Muslims in the colonial hierarchy.[16]

The February 4, 1919, law established an intermediate citizen status between the full French citizen and the French subject. These "half-naturalized" citizens had rights as "electors." According to the law, all indigenous Muslims could become electors if they were over the age of 25, maintained a residence for more than two consecutive years, and met one of several conditions that established their acculturated or educated status. The new law established a Muslim electoral body in Algeria of 421,000 new voters over the age of 25.[17] The law also altered access to naturalization and allowed Muslims to maintain their personal status, modifying the sénatus-consulte of 1865.[18] The procedure of applying for naturalization, however, remained complicated, and as a result, few Muslims applied.[19] Muslims who requested naturalization but sought to maintain their personal status could become "half-naturalized." The half-naturalized status provided exemption from the French code of administrative punishments, known as the *indigénat*, offered access to

---

[14] Laure Blévis, "Les avatars de la citoyenneté en Algérie coloniale ou les paradoxes d'une catégorisation," *Droit et Société*, No. 48 (2001): 561, 570. See also Blévis, "De la cause du droit à la cause anticoloniale. Les interventions de la Ligue des droits de l'homme en haveur des 'indigènes' algériens pendant l'entre-deux-guerres," *Politix*, Vol. 16, No. 62 (2003): 45.

[15] Laure Blévis, "La citoyenneté française au miroir de la colonization: étude des demandes de naturalization des 'sujets français' en Algérie colonial," *genéses* Vol. 4, No. 53 (2003): 26.

[16] Gosnell, *The Politics of Frenchness in Colonial Algeria, 1930–1954*, 26. Gilbert Meynier addressed the necessity of engaging Algerian Muslim soldiers due to the limited number of Europeans who enlisted for duty in World War I. Gilbert Meynier, *L'Algérie révélée: la guerre de 1914–1918 et le premier quart du XXe siècle* (Geneva: Librairie Droz, 1981), 260–261. See also Ageron, *Modern Algeria*, 80. On the subject of blood debts and colonial subjects' military service, see Myron J. Echenberg, *Colonial Conscripts: The Tirailleurs Sénégalais in French West Africa, 1857–1960* (Portsmouth: Heinemann, 1991), and Mann, *Native Sons*. See also Fogarty, *Race and War in France*, 237–238, 242–245.

[17] These conditions included (1) served in the military and received a decoration for service; (2) owned land, were a farmer or a sedentary merchant; (3) were employed by the state, the department, the commune, or were retired from such service; (4) were a member of the chamber of agriculture or of commerce; and (5) had a certificate of primary education or a university diploma. Charles-Robert Ageron, *Les Algériens Musulmans et la France (1871–1919)*, *Tôme Second* (Paris: Presses Universitaires de France, 1968), 1218.

[18] Ageron, *Les Algériens Musulmans*, 1221.   [19] Weil, *How to Be French*, 221.

public service employment opportunities, but did not include voting rights.[20] The law allowed Muslims to access certain rights, while limiting the number of Muslim representatives to ensure that they could never have a majority of votes.[21] Joshua Cole suggests that the Jonnart Law was at the root of the 1934 violence. Each improvement to Algerian Muslim status in the colony met severe opposition from those groups who felt threatened by such developments.

As a result of the improving status of Muslims in the colony, Jews endeavored to establish distance between themselves and Muslims by asserting their still-superior position as full French citizens in the colony. The economic crisis of the 1920s and 1930s exacerbated the already tense political and social conditions in the colony. President Morard of the Financial Delegation noted in December 1931 that Algeria's crisis went beyond economic dimensions, spilling into the political, social, and financial spheres.[22] A 1931 report from the Governor-General's Department of Indigenous Affairs stated that the generation of Algerian Muslims who served in World War I in the military or worked in factories in the metropole at the time were distancing themselves from the more religious tendencies of the older generation. The 1914 generation, as they were called, were more preoccupied with the economic situation.[23]

From the late 1920s into the early 1930s, the price of grain dropped significantly and small farmers in the Constantine area suffered. Creditors, among them Jews, benefited from the economic crisis as purchasers of buildings and other foreclosures. The economic crisis produced a mass of unemployed workers, a "floating population," whose misfortune could be politicized.[24] The economic crisis also led to an increase in interest among Muslims in the "neo-Marxist" rhetoric of communist organizations. The governor-general's cabinet reported a proliferation of pamphlets and tracts geared toward Muslim laborers that emphasized their exploitation by

[20] Ageron, Les Algériens Musulmans, 1223–1224.
[21] Joshua Cole, "Anti-Semitism and the Colonial Situation in Interwar Algeria: The Anti-Jewish Riots in Constantine, August 1934," in Martin Thomas, ed., The French Colonial Mind, Volume 2: Violence, Military Encounters, and Colonialism (Lincoln: University of Nebraska Press, 2012), 83. See also Cole, "Constantine before the Riots of August 1934," 840.
[22] Berque, French North Africa, 242. Berque notes that there was virtually no discussion of the economic crisis in the reports of the Arab delegation of the Financial Delegates at the time.
[23] Cabinet of the Gov-Gen, Department of Indigenous Affairs, "Rapport sur la situation politique et administrative des indigènes de l'Algérie au January 31, 1931," 39–40, CAOM Alg GGA 2CAB/3.
[24] M. Angel to the President of the AIU, "Oeuvres de Constantine," Constantine, September 30, 1934, AIU Algérie ICI. See also Ageron, "Une émeute anti-Juive," 34–35.

the French imperial program and Muslim elites.[25] The centennial celebrations of the French colony in 1930 proved a particularly fertile time for the frustrations of the Algerian Muslim population. In June 1930, the economic situation had reached a level of crisis. There was a serious shortage of wheat, as well as significant decline in the mining industry, which impacted employment and the colony's exports. The inequalities of wages led to strikes among dockers in Oran and Algiers from 1927 to 1929. The poverty of the Muslim masses paved the way for the emergence of Algerian Muslim political activists, such as Mohammed Salah Bendjelloul, who sought to work within the system to gain rights.[26]

In the face of important, yet limited, advances in the situation of Muslim rights in the colony, certain Algerian Muslim leaders began articulating the demands of the nascent Algerian independence movement. In the midst of shifting political, economic, and social alliances, Algerian Muslims organized into political groups with divergent demands regarding their rights. In the early twentieth century, the évolués, a group of secularized elite Muslims who had adopted French customs and values as a result of a French education, coalesced into the Young Algerians. They opposed the official Muslim establishment, the Old Turbans, and the Algerian administration. The Young Algerians' goal focused on political equality for assimilated Algerian Muslims. As one of their first political activities, the Young Algerians supported the February 1912 establishment of conscription for Algerian Muslims.[27]

In 1927 the Young Algerians formed the Fédération des élus indigènes. The Fédération emerged in response to the perceived lack of support for the Jonnart Law in 1919 by the Association of Algerian Mayors. The 1919 law was a turning point in the politicization of Algerian Muslim opinion.[28] In 1931, the governor-general described the Fédération as initially combative, but by 1930, it was "nothing more than a weakened and artificial organization," under the direction of Dr. Bentami, a general council member.[29] The Fédération emphasized its main goals, including

---

[25] Cabinet of the Gov-Gen, Department of Indigenous Affairs, "Rapport sur la situation politique et administrative des indigènes de l'Algérie au January 31, 1931," 58–59, CAOM Alg GGA 2CAB/3. The report focused on articles appearing in the newspaper L'Humanité that appeared in 1930.

[26] Younsi, Caught in a Colonial Triangle, 142. See also Berque, French North Africa, 223, 241–242, 269.

[27] Ageron, Modern Algeria, 77. See also Claude Collot and Jean-Robert Henry, Le Mouvement national algérien, Textes 1912–1954 (Paris: L'Harmattan, 1978), 18, 23.

[28] Ali Merad, Le Réformisme musulman en Algérie de 1925 à 1940 (Paris: Mouton & Co., 1967), 44–45.

[29] Cabinet of the Gov-Gen, Department of Indigenous Affairs, "Rapport sur la situation politique et administrative des indigènes de l'Algérie au January 31, 1931," 75, CAOM Alg GGA 2CAB/3.

demanding Algerian representation on elected bodies, particularly the Financial Delegations. Despite its weakness, the *Fédération* incubated the next generation of leaders. Mohammad Salah Bendjelloul and Ferhat Abbas studied at the University of Algiers; Bendjelloul became a doctor, and Abbas, a pharmacist. Both succeeded in local politics, winning elections to municipal and general council positions. Both gained notoriety by 1935 and were involved in the riots in Constantine and Sétif, respectively.[30]

Bendjelloul served on municipal and departmental councils and became the president of the *Fédération des élus musulmans de Constantine* in 1932. One of his goals was to unify Muslim elected officials and to campaign for full citizenship rights Muslims, especially for *évolués*, while allowing them to maintain their legal religious status.[31] Although Bendjelloul pursued an assimilationist agenda, the administration distrusted him and linked him to wider pan-Islamic agitation. In the 1935 report, written in the aftermath of the Constantine riots, the author cited a telegram to Bendjelloul from the Damascus ultra-nationalist deputy, Fakhri bik El Baroudi, that appeared in the Egyptian newspaper *El-Djihad* on March 9, 1935. The telegram praises the "glorious attitude that you have shown against the colonists" and praised Bendjelloul for showing "the world that the Arab does not sleep under oppression, even if for a time, he was reduced to slavery. May God favor your struggle." The report also indicated a growing union between the reformists, such as Bendjelloul, and the Ulamas.[32]

A movement for Islamic renewal had emerged in Constantine in the early 1930s led by Abd al-Hamid Ben Badis. His movement, the Association of Algerian Muslim Scholars, emphasized a return to the original form of Islamic tradition, which put them at odds with the French administration, as well as the *Fédération* under the leadership of Bendjelloul. Ben Badis preached that Algerian culture had deteriorated and risked collapsing, like Algeria's economy. The remedy was a return to

---

[30] Mohammad Salah Bendjelloul had a complicated role in the 1934 Constantine pogrom. Ferhat Abbas was living in Sétif during February 1935 riots there. Ruedy, *Modern Algeria*, 133. See also James McDougall, *History and the Culture of Nationalism in Algeria* (Cambridge: Cambridge University Press, 2006), 78. Julien Fromage argues that if Bendjelloul and Abbas did not exactly line up with Algerian nationalism, they contributed to that ultimate goal. See Julien Fromage, "Innovation politique et mobilisation de masse en 'situation coloniale': un 'printemps algérien' des années 1930? L'expérience de la Fédération des Élus Musulmans du Département de Constantine," *Insaniyat* / إنسانيات, Vol. 57–58 (2012): 167–174.

[31] Cole, "Anti-Semitism and the Colonial Situation in Interwar Algeria," 87–88.

[32] President of the Ministers' Council, care of the Minister of the Interior, "Situation politique en Algérie," 2, May 10, 1935, CAOM GGA 2CAB/3. See also Report #August 3, 2614, 1934, same file.

Islam. Ben Badis published a newspaper, *Ech-Chihab* (the Meteor), which featured articles in line with his organization's goals. The 1931 Governor-General reported that *Ech-Chihab* published articles "impregnated with a latent wahabism," reflecting the conservative nature of Ben Badis' politics.[33] Although Ben Badis' traditionalist stance did not mesh with that of Bendjelloul, the two spoke at a meeting in Constantine on May 16, 1934, just months before the Constantine riots.[34] A 1935 report identifies Ben Badis as one of the "most ardent propagandists in favor of Bendjelloul." *Ech-Chihab*'s press also published a tract that honored Bendjelloul's efforts: "Bendjelloul is a great leader, if God wishes, he will deliver us. He will bring the end of the terror in which Algeria lives." The report saw cooperation between Ben Badis and Bendjelloul indicating a shift from the progressive reformist movement toward an "ulterior and latent nationalism, his claims are a clever disguise for his anti-French agitation plan." Ben Badis had declared that naturalization was apostasy.[35]

In contrast to the *Fédération*, the *Étoile Nord-Africaine*, led by Messali Hadj, was influenced and supported by the Communist Party. Unlike the *Fédération*, the *Étoile* garnered many of its supporters from outside of the colony, predominately Algerian workers in metropolitan France, like Messali Hadj himself. Hadj was born in 1898 in Tlemcen and served in the French army in World War I. Returning to Algeria after the war, he became frustrated with the status of Algerian Muslims and in 1924 moved to Paris. In 1926, he became the secretary-general of the *Étoile*, which he founded that year.[36] In February 1927, Hadj delivered the *Étoile*'s first list of demands, which included independence for Algerian Muslims, the building of a national army, abolition of the *indigénat*, and an Algerian parliament elected through universal suffrage. While the *Fédération*'s main concern was the integration of the Algerian elite, the *Étoile* focused on the situation of rural Algerians and the goal of independence.[37]

---

[33] Cabinet of the Gov-Gen, Department of Indigenous Affairs, "Rapport sur la situation politique et administrative des indigènes de l'Algérie au January 31, 1931," 16–17, CAOM Alg GGA 2CAB/3. See also Berque, *French North Africa*, 228. See also Merad, *Le Réformisme Musulman*, 80–90.

[34] Cole, "Anti-Semitism and the Colonial Situation in Interwar Algeria," 89.

[35] President of the Ministers' Council care of the Minister of the Interior, "Situation politique en Algérie," 3–4, May 10, 1935, CAOM GGA 2CAB/3.

[36] Jacques Simon, *Messali Hadj (1898–1974): Chronologie commentée* (Paris: L'Harmattan, 2002), 25–33. See also Benjamin Stora, *Messali Hadj: pionnier du nationalism algérien (1898–1974)* (Paris: Le Sycomore, 1982).

[37] Ruedy, *Modern Algeria*, 137.

Hadj and the *Étoile* did not develop a strong following in Algeria until the mid-1930s.[38] The Communist Party in Algeria had a complicated relationship with the nationalist movements. Some of the *Étoile*'s co-founders, including Hadj Ali Abdel-Kader and Hassan Issad, had been members of the Parti Communiste Français (PCF). In fact, the PCF's success among Algerian workers in the metropole between 1926 and 1929 developed a base of support for the Étoile; 4,000 former PCF members joined the *Étoile*.[39] The *Étoile* did not have a branch in Algiers until 1932, when members of the Communist Party of Algeria began reading *Étoile*'s newspaper, *El Ouma*. They formed the National Revolutionary Party (*Parti nationale révolutionnaire*) in May 1933, which joined the *Étoile* in January 1934.[40] During the interwar period, there were far more members of fascist groups than members of communist organizations. In the spring of 1936, the Communist Party in Algeria had only 1,300 members, whereas the fascist groups had more than 30,000 members. These numbers were partly responsible for the lack of support for the Popular Front in Algeria. Despite the International Communists' commitment to the anticolonial fight, there was little support for communism among Algerians.[41]

The various movements of Algerian Muslims demanding rights led Léon Blum and his Minister of State and former Governor-General of Algeria, Maurice Viollette, to pen the hotly contested Blum-Viollette Plan in 1936. The plan would offer citizenship to some 25,000 Algerian Muslim *évolués*. The PCF and the Muslim Congress initially threw their support behind the Plan. However, communists and the leadership of the *Étoile* eventually withdrew their support in favor of universal suffrage.[42] Europeans in the colony rallied against the new legislation, which threatened the existent political and social hierarchy in the colony. Algerian Muslims' campaigns for rights coincided with significant political changes around the world, including conflicts in Palestine and Hitler's rise to power in Europe. This wider context helps explain the events in Constantine.

---

[38] Ibid., 138.
[39] Emmanuel Sivan, *Communisme et nationalism en Algérie, 1920–1962* (Paris: Presses de la Fondation Nationale des Sciences Politiques, 1976), 66, 71.
[40] Jean-Louis Planche, "Les lieux de l'algérianité," in Jean-Jacques Jordi and Jean-Louis Planche, eds., *Alger 1860–1939: Le modèle ambigu du triomphe colonial* (Paris: Éditions Autrement, 1999), 187–189.
[41] Jean-Louis Planche, "Le Parti communiste d'Algérie et la question nationale au temps du Congrès musulman et du Front populaire," in *Cahiers d'histoire de l'Institut de recherches Marxistes*, Vol. 36 (1989): 16–17.
[42] Ruedy, *Modern Algeria*, 141. See also Planche, "Le Parti communiste d'Algérie," 25–26.

Reverberations from Palestine and Europe

The police files of Constantine are relatively quiet on Jewish–Muslim violence between 1914 and 1928. In this period, there appeared to be coexistence, perhaps influenced by the "sacred union" between Jews, Muslims, and *colons* developed in the trenches of World War I. Violence increased sharply after 1928, around the same time that the Algerian organizations demanding rights for Muslims gained influence. The majority of cases of violence during the interwar period occurred between 1929 and 1930. The boycott of Jewish shops in Algeria in the late 1920s is an example of the ripple-effect of the situation in Palestine. In 1929 riots broke out in Mandate Palestine over access to the Western Wall in Jerusalem. The area immediately adjacent to the section of the Wall where Jews prayed was known as the Maghrebi quarter, named for the Maghrebi pilgrims and scholars living there.[43] The proximity of the North African Muslim quarter to the 1929 events resulted in reverberations in Algeria and brought the conflict home for Algerian Jews and Muslims. Throughout the conflicts in Palestine, Algerian colonial officials and police reported on how local newspapers covered these events.

The riots, known as the Western Wall or Buraq Uprising, began over the Jewish insertion of a *mechitza*, or customary screen that separated men and women during prayer, at the Western Wall on September 24, 1928, for their Yom Kippur service.[44] Muslim religious leaders saw this as an infraction of an old Ottoman rule that forbade Jews from constructing religious structures at the Western Wall. Muslim leaders reportedly told British administrators that unless the *mechitza* was removed, they could not be responsible for the actions of their coreligionists. Hajj Amin al-Husseini, the mufti of Jerusalem, took advantage of this incident and established the Committee for the Defense of the Noble Buraq Wall.[45] The strong Muslim reaction emerged from growing fears and rumors that Jews planned to claim the entire Temple Mount as a Jewish holy site.[46] The Prefect of Constantine reported on an article in the Arabic newspaper *An Nadjah* that called for Muslim support for the defense of Buraq.[47]

---

[43] Gudrun Krämer, *A History of Palestine: From the Ottoman Conquest to the Founding of the State of Israel* (Princeton: Princeton University Press, 2008), 225.

[44] Muslims called the section of the Wall which is the site of the dispute *al-buraq al-sharif* named for Mohammed's horse, which he tethered to that part of the Wall during his night journey. See Krämer, *A History of Palestine*, 225. The French documents often refer to the riots as *l'Affaire Bourag*, using the Arabic title.

[45] Krämer, *A History of Palestine*, 228–229. See also Howard M. Sachar, *A History of Israel From the Rise of Zionism to Our Time* (New York: Alfred A. Knopf, 2007), 173.

[46] Krämer, *A History of Palestine*, 227, 230.

[47] Mami Smain, "Mon voyage au Maroc et en Andalousie," *An Nadjah*, No. 662, November 9, 1928. See also Prefect of Constantine to the Gov-Gen, "Affaires

On August 15, 1929, during the Jewish fast of Tisha B'av, groups of approximately 300 Jews, including some members of the right-wing Betar movement, met in front of the Western Wall chanting "the Wall is ours" and singing the Zionist anthem "Hatikvah." Rumors circulated that Jewish youth beat up Muslims and cursed the Prophet in the Maghrebi quarter. The next day 2,000 Muslims, organized by their leaders, marched to the Wall, attacked Jewish worshippers, and destroyed Jewish religious texts, including a Torah scroll.[48] Rumors spread that Jews planned to attack the al-Aqsa Mosque. On August 23, thousands of Muslims, encouraged by religious leaders, attended Friday prayer on the Temple Mount armed with sticks, clubs, knives, rifles, and other weapons. One rumor circulated that the mufti himself called for Arabs to defend the mosque.[49] The next day, upon hearing rumors that Jews killed their fellow Arabs in Jerusalem, Arabs attacked Jews in Hebron, murdering 64. Over the course of the riots, approximately 116 Arabs and 133 Jews were killed.[50]

These events in Palestine had a significant impact in Algeria, where relations between Jews and Muslims were already strained. On August 29, 1929, the governor-general wrote the Prefect of the Department of Constantine regarding the press' coverage of the situation in Palestine and ordered the Prefect to notify him immediately if there were any "repercussions" in his department.[51] Different administrators and elected officials in the colony reported that Muslims and Jews in their regions read about and discussed the events in Palestine with great interest. They noted, however, that relations remained peaceful, for the most part.[52]

Indigènes, No. 18386: Presse Arabe: An Nadjah No. 662," Constantine, November 21, 1928, CAOM Alg Const B/3/248.

[48] Krämer, A History of Palestine, 230; Sachar, A History of Israel, 173; Philip Mattar, "The Role of the Mufti of Jerusalem in the Political Struggle over the Western Wall, 1928–29," Middle Eastern Studies, Vol. 19, No. 1 (January 1983): 113. At the same time, another incident further incensed already flared tempers. An Arab beat a Jewish boy who accidentally kicked a ball into an Arab woman's garden. The Jewish boy died of his injuries and Jews took revenge by stabbing an Arab child. Krämer, A History of Palestine, 230–231.

[49] Krämer, A History of Palestine, 231–232; Mattar, "The Role of the Mufti," 114; Sachar, A History of Israel, 173–174.

[50] Mattar, "The Role of the Mufti," 115; Krämer, A History of Palestine, 232. Again, there is much disagreement on the numbers of casualties. Mattar and Krämer agree with the stated figures. Sachar cited 133 Jews killed, 399 wounded, and 87 Arab fatalities, Sachar, A History of Israel, 174. Ilan Pappé gave the figures 300 Jewish dead and a similar number of Arabs, Ilan Pappé, A History of Modern Palestine: One Land, Two Peoples (Cambridge: Cambridge University Press, 2004), 91.

[51] Gov-Gen to the Prefect of the Department of Constantine, "No. 21829a: Au sujet des troubles qui ont éclaté en Palestine," Algiers, August 29, 1929, CAOM Alg Const B/3/248.

[52] Mayor of Sétif to the Prefect of Constantine, "No.31," Sétif, September 1, 1929, CAOM Alg Const B/3/248; Commissioner of Police of Ain-Beïda to the Prefect of Constantine,

Although it is challenging to track what Jews and Muslims in Algeria were reading at the time, Algerian newspapers published articles on the situation in Palestine. In one popular paper, *L'Echo d'Alger*, the word "Palestine" was mentioned in 89 articles in 1929. *L'Echo d'Alger* was created in 1912, had a politically left-leaning readership, and was one of the few to include photographs in its early years.[53] The newspaper also covered the events related to the Balfour Declaration in 1917. Events in Palestine continued to be reported on in *L'Echo d'Alger*, 78 articles in 1933 and 60 additional articles in 1934, the year of the Constantine pogrom. Some articles described Jews in Jerusalem and Hebron as victims of Muslims, while others mentioned that "repercussions are possible in Muslim countries."[54] The newspaper reported on protests occurring in sympathy, and cited Grand Rabbi Israel Lévy of France as suggesting that the violence in Palestine reflected a long-planned attack.[55]

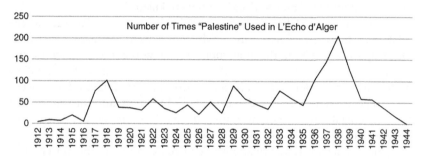

"No. 866: Objet: Troubles de Palestine," Ain-Beïda, September 5, 1929, CAOM Alg Const B/3/248; Commissioner of Police of Tebessa to the Prefect of Constantine, "Au sujet des évènements de Palestine," Tebessa, September 7, 1929, CAOM Alg Const B/3/248; Sub-Prefect of Philippeville to the Prefect of Constantine, "No. 4220: A.S. des troubles qui ont éclaté en Palestine," Philippeville, September 10, 1929, CAOM Alg Const B/3/248; Sub-Prefect of the Arrondissement of Batna to the Prefect of Constantine, "No. 6384: A.S. des troubles qui ont éclaté en Palestine," Batna, October 4, 1929, CAOM Alg Const B/3/248. On August 29, 1929, Elissa Rhaïs published an article in *Annales Coloniales*, entitled "Les musulmans nord africains blament les tueries de Palestine." The Sec-Gen noted that the fact that Rhaïs was Jewish reduced its impact on a Muslim audience. Sec-Gen on behalf of the Prefect of Constantine to the Gov-Gen, "Presse: au sujet d'un article des Annales Coloniales sur les évènements de Palestine," Constantine, September 9, 1929, CAOM Alg Const B/3/248.

[53] On the topic of *L'Echo d'Alger*, see Idir Bouaboud, *L'Écho d'Alger, cinquante ans de vie politique française en Algérie 1912–1961* (Lille: Presses universitaires du Septentrion, 1999).

[54] "Juifs et Musulmans sont aux prises en Palestine: Les sanglantes bagarres d'Hebron et de Jerusalem forcent le gouvernement britannique à prendre des mesures de rigueur," *L'Echo d'Alger*, August 28, 1929, 1.

[55] "Les Troubles de Palestine: Juifs et Musulmans aux prises," *L'Echo d'Alger*, August 29, 1929, 1.

The situation in Palestine received extra attention due to the development of pan-Islamism in North Africa. The colonial administration was concerned that the neo-Wahabist movement among Algerians grew in appeal alongside the older pan-Islamic program following the 1931 Congress of Jerusalem and that the independence movement in Algeria evolved alongside that of the Levant. It points to evidence of coordination between a leader of the Ulamas of Algeria, possibly Ben Badis or one of his associates, who was welcomed by the Pan-Arab Committee of Mecca, and meetings with leaders of Tunisia, Egypt, and Syria.[56] While it is difficult to assess how the wider Muslim population received the ideas of independence or pan-Islamism at this time, the actions of their leaders indicate certain trends.

Zionism was not among the major causes for discord between Jews and Muslims in the Algeria. Although most Jews in Algeria generally saw their future in France rather than Palestine, a small number were Zionists. Algerian Jews first expressed an interest in Zionism in 1897, when antisemitism threatened Jewish security in the colony. That year a Constantine Jew, Edouard Attali, attended the first Zionist Congress. In Algiers in 1920, Zionists established the *L'Union Sioniste Algérienne*.[57] As citizens, Algerian Jews were focused on defending their citizenship and civil rights against antisemitic attacks rather than engaging in Zionist ideologies.[58] Zionists competed with the Alliance, which supported the assimilation of Algerian Jewry and was more established in the colony than Zionist organizations.[59] Zionists from France, however, traveled to Algeria to promote the cause. In 1923, Dr. Sussman of the Palestine Foundation Fund/Keren Hayessod spoke in Algiers and requested the CAES' support. Confino wrote that the CAES decided not to publicly support Keren Hayessod and the Zionist program "because of its political character and the negative impact it could have on relations between Muslims and Jews in this country."[60] Confino and the CAES feared that Zionism would worsen the already troubled relationships between Jews and Muslims.

---

[56] President of the Ministers' Council care of the Minister of the Interior, "Situation politique en Algérie," 4, 6, May 10, 1935, CAOM GGA 2CAB/3.
[57] The activities of the organization were limited to supporting the Jewish National Fund, whose representatives visited Algeria. David Cohen, "Algeria," in Simon, Laskier, and Reguer, eds., *The Jews of the Middle East*, 469; Moshe Davis, ed., *Zionism in Transition* (New York: Arno Press, 1980), 197–198, 202.
[58] Cohen, "Algeria," 469.
[59] In the face of growing antisemitism in the mid-1920s, Zionist activity decreased in Algeria and throughout North Africa. Davis, ed., *Zionism in Transition*, 203.
[60] A. Confino to the President of the Alliance Israélite Universelle, Algiers, February 13, 1923, AIU Algérie IB4.

Despite the misgivings of the CAES leadership, the number of Zionist meetings in Constantine increased concurrently with events in Palestine in 1929 and 1930. A surveillance report lists four Zionist presentations between 1930 and 1934.[61] It was not until the late 1930s, in the aftermath of the Constantine pogrom, that Zionism gained popularity in the colony. Most of the Zionist presentations in Algeria reported during this time period featured women from the metropole. It is possible that Zionism in Algeria found support primarily among women, who did not share the same benefits as citizens, such as voting.

Following the 1928 Buraq uprising in Palestine, the Prefect of Constantine feared its impact on his department, where Jewish–Muslim relations were already fraught.[62] In late August 1929, immediately following the bloodshed in Jerusalem, Hebron, and Safed, he wrote that repercussions would develop "where Jews and Muslims find themselves in contact. The government cannot remain indifferent to these events, notably in Algeria where one finds latent antagonism, ready to manifest itself at the first occasion."[63] Given the history of antisemitism in his town, the mayor of Sétif and his fellow administrators feared problems would arise as a result of the events in Palestine. He recommended that the Prefect censor the French and Muslim presses' presentation of events in Palestine.[64] The police commissioner of Ain Beida feared that "the contagion might come from Oran, where the population is known for its antisemitic sentiments."[65]

---

[61] Departmental Security of Constantine, "Manifestations d'activité et de propagande parmi l'élément israélite de Constantine au cours des années 1930–1933–1934," CAOM Alg Const B/3/250. See also Departmental Security, Commissioner of Bône, "No. 108: Surveillance politique des indigènes," Bône, March 8, 1934, CAOM Alg Const B/3/250.

[62] Prefect of Constantine to the Gov-Gen, "No. 18386: Presse Arabe: An Nadjah No. 662," Constantine, November 21, 1928, CAOM Alg Const B/3/248. See also Smain Mami, "Mon Voyage au Maroc et en Andalousie," An Nadja No. 662, November 9, 1928, CAOM Alg Const B/3/248.

[63] Prefect of the Department of Constantine, "Affaires Indigènes, No. 17871, Très Confidentiel," Constantine, August 27, 1929, CAOM Alg Const B/3/248. See also Gov-Gen, "Memo No. 21829a, Au sujet des troubles qui ont éclaté en Palestine," Algiers, August 29, 1929, CAOM Alg Const B/3/248.

[64] Mayor of Sétif to the Prefect of Constantine, "No. 31," Sétif, September 1, 1929, CAOM Alg Const B/3/248.

[65] The police commissioner of Ain Beida wrote that the conflicts in Palestine increased emotions among the Jewish population and that literate Muslims carefully followed news published on the topic. Commissioner of Police of Ain Beida to the Prefect of Constantine, "No. 866: Object: Troubles de Palestine," Ain Beida, September 5, 1929, CAOM Alg Const B/3/248. See also Commissioner of Police of Tebessa to the Prefect of Constantine, "Au sujet des événements de Palestine," Tebessa, September 7, 1929, CAOM Alg Const B/3/248. The police commissioner's comment about Oran is an allusion to Dr. Jules Molle's antisemitic activities in Oran in the late 1920s.

In this climate of developing nationalistic ideologies, albeit ones with little traction on the ground, violence between Jews and Muslim reemerged. In 1928, the Constantine police files include four such cases, all of which involved Jewish aggressors. These cases mostly concerned Jews attacking Muslims who entered the Jewish quarter.[66] In 1929, the number of cases of violence between Jews and Muslims rose to twentyone. Fifteen of the cases involved Jewish aggressors. Upon leaving a party sponsored by the workers' union on New Year's Day, a group of Jews stumbled upon two Muslims, both of whom were editors of the newspaper *Ech-Chihab*. After exchanging insults, the two groups began to fight.[67] Afterward, the Prefect called a meeting in which he urged the assembled Jewish and Muslim leaders to encourage calm among their coreligionists. Henri Lellouche, a Jewish general council member, assured the Prefect that he and his fellow leaders would not support any Jew involved in aggressions against Muslims and that they would independently punish such individuals. In a sermon, the mufti similarly preached calm to his followers.[68] The Prefect's effort to unite Jewish and Muslim leaders in condemning the violence indicated that its prevalence already warranted proactive measures.

Some Jewish aggressors needed no motive for violence other than the fact that their victim was Muslim. On April 14, 1929, a group of Jews stopped a Muslim former general council member, Allaoua Lounissi. One of the Jews, Eliaou Zaffran, age 30, demanded whether Lounissi was a Jew or a Muslim and when Lounissi responded that he was Muslim, Zaffran punched him in the face.[69] The Prefect demanded that the Jewish deputy mayor of Constantine, Monsieur Barkatz, stop his coreligionists from attacking Muslims.[70] The Prefect's letter emphasized that

---

[66] On December 23, 1928, a band of inebriated Jews attacked three Muslims. Prefect of Constantine to the Central Commissioner of Constantine, "No. 20813: Object: au sujet d'incidents entre Indigènes Musulmans et Israélites," Constantine, December 29, 1928, CAOM Alg Const B/3/248. See also Amar ben Belcacem Hamel, Alile Zouati, Mostefa ben Daoud to the Prefect of Constantine, Constantine, December 24, 1928, CAOM Alg Const B/3/248.

[67] Central Commissioner of Constantine Cayol to the Prefect of the Department of Constantine, "No. 4C," Constantine, January 4, 1929, CAOM Alg Const B/3/248.

[68] Prefect of Constantine to the Gov-Gen, "No. 258: Au sujet aggressions commises par des Israélites contre des indigènes musulmans," Constantine, January 5, 1929, CAOM Alg Const B/3/248.

[69] Central Police Commissioner E. Aschbacher to the Prefect of Department of Constantine, "No. 46: Incident entre indigène et Israélite," Constantine, April 15, 1929, CAOM Alg Const B/3/248. See also Central Commissioner Aschbacher to Prefect of Constantine, "Report No. 47," Constantine, April 16, 1929, CAOM Alg Const B/3/248.

[70] Prefect of Constantine to Deputy Mayor Barkatz, "No. 16328," Constantine, August 9, 1929, CAOM Alg Const B/3/248.

a sense of Jewish superiority over Muslims was the real cause of such violence.[71] Most of the cases involving Muslim aggressors centered on trivial issues, such as an altercation over the ripeness of a melon.[72] Regardless of the purported causes, inequality of rights and status in the colony were at the root of such encounters. *La Voix Indigène*, an Algerian Muslim newspaper popular among elites and a proponent of Franco-Muslim union, published an article on the escalating violence between Jews and Muslims titled "Let's be reasonable."[73] The author wrote of a problematic trend: "Jewish youth, when they are in a group, too often quarrel with the Arabs who venture alone in their neighborhoods."[74]

These Jewish youth, like the members of the self-defense-oriented Civic Club of Oran, may have seen their actions more as self-defense than aggression. This is an important issue: how did young Jews see themselves in the climate of increasing violence between Jews and Muslims? Were they impacted by Zionist ideals of "muscular Judaism" espoused by Max Nordau and seen within the Jewish scouting movements?[75] Young Jews felt themselves called upon to defend themselves and their community against increasing provocations from the antisemitic press, such as *La Tribune* and *Le Silhouette*. Colonial officials called upon Jewish leaders, both religious and civic, to demand that their coreligionists avoid violence. On December 5, 1929, the Prefect of Constantine requested that Rabbi Eisenbeth, the Head Rabbi of

---

[71] While Jews were often the aggressors in the cases in 1929, Muslims were also guilty of assaults against Jews. In one example, on August 28, two or three Muslim youth broke windows at the Alliance school in Constantine. Central Commissioner of Constantine Aschbacher to the Prefect of Constantine, "No. 126," Constantine, August 29, 1929, CAOM Alg Const B/3/248.

[72] Central Commissioner of Constantine E. Aschbacher to Prefect of Constantine, "No. 134," Constantine, September 10, 1929, CAOM Alg Const B/3/248. Commissioner of Police of the Second Arrondissement of Constantine to the Central Police Commissioner of Constantine, "No. 6149: A.S. de deux jeunes filles israélites parties avec 2 indigènes," Constantine, December 13, 1929, CAOM Alg Const B/3/248; Prefect of Constantine to Henri Lellouche, General Council Member of Constantine, Constantine, December 18, 1929, CAOM Alg Const B/3/248.

[73] Gosnell, *The Politics of Frenchness*, 110.

[74] "Soyons raisonnables," *La Voix Indigène*, December 12, 1929, CAOM Alg Const B/3/248.

[75] On the Jewish scouting movements in France in World War II, see Daniel Lee, *Pétain's Jewish Children: French Jewish Youth and the Vichy Regime, 1940–1942* (Oxford: Oxford University Press, 2014), 74. See also Michel Alain, "Qu'est-ce qu'un scout juif? L'éducation juive chez les Éclaireurs israélites de France, de 1923 au début des années 1950," in *Archives Juives*, Vol. 35, No. 2 (2002): 77–101. A branch of the Revisionist Zionist group Betar was established in Algeria in 1936 by Josué Cohen-Aloro. See Haim Saadoun, "Le sionisme en Algérie (1898–1962): une option marginale," *Archives Juives*, Vol. 45, No. 2 (2102): 72.

Constantine, intervene again to calm his community.[76] As Cole shows, banal incidents could become far more significant when interpreted as politically motivated.[77]

In 1930, significantly more cases of Jewish violence against Muslims occurred: twenty-seven cases in contrast to one case of Muslim assault on Jews.[78] Reports of bands of Jews committing violence continued into 1930 often without any provocation, the lines between self-defense and ruffianism became increasingly blurred for the Jewish community.[79] The governor-general feared that the growing number of incidents between Jews and Muslims in Constantine could lead to a revival of antisemitism.[80] His fears proved warranted with the Constantine Pogrom in 1934.

In response to the 1930 violence, *La Voix Indigène* published an article by Mohammed el Mourtada, who criticized the actions of Algerian Jews, writing that "calm is reestablished in Palestine, but doesn't seem to have appeased certain spirits. The secular union of Muslims and Jews seems to have dissolved to the great detriment of the public peace ... These cowardly aggressions, in which Muslims are victims of the Jews, are truly regrettable." In particular, Mourtada pointed to the "bands of rascals," groups of young Jews responsible for much of the violence. Mourtada discouraged vengeance; rather, he recommended that "it would be better if we remain good friends."[81] Although there is no evidence that the violence was due to reverberations of events in Palestine, Mourtada implied that all clashes between Jews and Muslim could be interpreted as politically motivated. In August 1930, the governor-general concluded that "we should take energetic measures to stop" the violence

---

[76] The Prefect noted that he made the same request of Muslim religious leaders. Prefect of Constantine to Rabbi Eisenbeth, "No. 25313," Constantine, December 5, 1929, CAOM Alg Const B/3/248. The Prefect sent a similar letter to the Mufti of Constantine that same day. Prefect of Constantine to the Mufti of Constantine, "No. 25314," Constantine, December 5, 1929, CAOM Alg Const B/3/248.

[77] Cole, "Constantine before the riots of August 1934," 847.

[78] Central Police Commissioner, Constantine, to the Prefect of Constantine, "No. 199: Re: Incident entre Musulmans et Israélites," Constantine, January 30, 1930, CAOM Alg Const B/3/248.

[79] The twelve young Jews between ages 16 and 22 punched and kicked the Muslims, tore off their caps, which they threw in the ravine. Central Police Commissioner, Constantine to the Prefect of the Department of Constantine, "No. 328: Objet: Incident entre indigènes et israélites," Constantine, September 2, 1930, CAOM Alg Const B/3/248.

[80] Gov-Gen to the Prefect of Constantine, "No. 27833a," Algiers, September 15, 1930, CAOM Alg Const B/3/248. This letter was actually written by Marcel Peyrouton, who was then serving as the Sec-Gen.

[81] Md. el Mourtada, "Lâche Agression," *La Voix Indigène*, September 18, 1930, CAOM Alg Const B/3/248. See also Chief of Departmental Security to the Prefect of Constantine, "No. 2099," Constantine, October 19, 1930, CAOM Alg Const B/3/248.

between Jews and Muslims. He found a certain number of Algerian Jews were routinely involved in the violence and referred to "bands" of Jews. Unrest continued into 1931, with seven cases in the Constantine police files, six of which involved Jewish aggressors.[82]

These cases of violence reflect several important features of Jewish–Muslim relations in the colony. The situation in Palestine may have exacerbated tensions in Algeria, which had a culture of violence. Such altercations served as a terrain upon which groups acted out their status anxieties and frustrations. As Algerian Muslims worked to improve their access to rights and to make a case for their inclusion, some Jews feared that their position of power would weaken. Some Jews used violence as a way to exert their superior colonial status and to maintain distance from Muslims in the colony. Antisemites in the colony also provoked violence between Jews and Muslims. Joshua Cole has convincingly argued that the violence in Constantine in 1934 has to be understood in context with the evolving relationships and competitions between settlers, Jews, and Muslims in the colony, particularly in the aftermath of shifting rights due to the Jonnart Law.[83]

Emile Morinaud, the longtime mayor of Constantine, is a prime example of such shifts. At times a strong antisemite, Morinaud was elected as deputy for Algeria in 1898 alongside the other antisemitic candidates, including Drumont. However, as mayor of Constantine, Morinaud formed an alliance with the president of the Jewish consistory, M. Narboni, after Narboni encouraged Jewish voters not to vote as a bloc in the 1904 municipal elections – a sign of his willingness to work with Morinaud.[84] Morinaud needed Jewish voters to support him in order to remain in office – even though his memoirs detail his career-long efforts to abrogate the Crémieux Decree. In his memoirs, Morinaud repeatedly asserts that his antisemitism was political in orientation – that his efforts to abrogate the Crémieux Decree and his actions in Constantine were not part of a "racial war, nor a religious war," but a war against the Jewish bloc.[85] In the 1930s

---

[82] Gov-Gen to the Prefect of the Department of Constantine, "No. 25038a," Algiers, August 9, 1930, CAOM Alg Const B/3/248. Most of the cases were low-level altercations that often resulted in violence. Central Commissioner of Constantine to the Prefect of the department of Constantine, "No. 1114M: Incident entre indigène et israélite," Constantine, February 11, 1931, CAOM Alg Const B/3/248.

[83] Cole, "Anti-Semitism and the Colonial Situation in Interwar Algeria," 78; Cole, "Constantine before the riots of August 1934," 839.

[84] Emile Morinaud, *Mes Mémoires: Première Campagne contre le Décret Crémieux* (Algiers: Éditions Baconnier Fréres, 1941), 331–336.

[85] Morinaud, *Mes Mémoires*, 286.

and 1934 in particular, Morinaud nonetheless bent to pressure from right-wing organizations, such as the *Croix de Feu*, to reassert his anti-semitic roots.[86]

It is therefore important to see the Jewish–Muslim violence in Constantine of the late 1920s as the enactment of status anxieties and the inequality of rights. The context is crucial: violence increased between the two groups as Algerian Muslims developed a more active campaign for rights and acceptance within the existing political structure in the colony, and as the alliances between Jews and settlers disintegrated. The Constantine pogrom of 1934 can only be understood as part of a longer history of Jewish–Muslim relations, colonial violence, shifting political allegiances, and status anxieties.

Hitler's Growing Popularity in Colonial Algeria

In 1930, the French administration in Algeria celebrated the centennial of the capture of Algiers. Throughout the spring and summer of 1930, colonial administrators organized celebrations, including parades, unveilings of commemorative monuments, and a visit by the French president Gaston Doumergue in May. The centennial celebration fêted the "Frenchness" of the colony, which only increased Algerian Muslims' frustration with their status in the colony.[87] Brawls broke out between Jews and Algerian Muslim soldiers (*tirailleurs indigènes*) in August and December 1930.[88] At the same time, Hitler's propagandists capitalized on Algerian Muslim dissatisfaction with the French colony and renewed antisemitism.

In April 1933, the police found antisemitic pamphlets in a café in the city of Khenchela.[89] A few months later, the mayor reported growing unrest among Algerian Muslims. Flyers in Arabic urged Algerian Muslims to boycott Jewish shops, suggesting that money spent there bought bullets to kill Muslims in Palestine. Such accusations promoted violence among younger Algerian Muslims.[90] By late July 1933, the

---

[86] Cole, "Constantine before the Riots of August 1934," 846.

[87] Gosnell, *The Politics of Frenchness*, 19–21; and Attal, *Les Émeutes de Constantine*, 55.

[88] Commissioner of Police, Constantine, "No. 433: Incident entre Tirailleurs Indigènes et Israélites," Constantine, December 20, 1930; Commissioner of Police, Constantine, to the Prefect of Constantine, "No. 320: Incident entre indigène et israélite," Constantine, August 17, 1930, CAOM Alg Const B/3/248.

[89] Khenchela was in the department of Constantine. Prefect of Constantine to the Gov-Gen, Constantine, April 28, 1933, CAOM Alg Const B/3/249.

[90] One of the first reactions was throwing stones at windows of Jewish-owned apartments. Dr. Maurin, Mayor of Khenchela, to the Prefect of the Department of Constantine,

boycott in Khenchela was under way and Muslims attacked those frequenting Jewish shops. A local inspector, Defendini, described the incendiary influence of the flyers, which stated:

O Arabs, for every five franc piece that you spend at the Jews, five pennies will go to Palestine and serve the purchase of arms to kill the Arabs. O Arabs, the Jew is your enemy and the enemy of Islam, if you buy something from them, you will no longer be under the protection of the Prophet. Whoever buys anything from the Jews, it is like he is buying the death of his brothers. God said: You will certainly not find stronger animosity towards believers than among the Jews and the polytheists; by consequence, he who purchases from the Jews buys a bullet that kills an Arab in Palestine.[91]

The author of the flyers was a French mechanic and well-known antisemite in Khenchela.[92] The fact that the man responsible for the flyers was French indicates the particular role of European antisemites in intensifying, and taking advantage of, tensions between Jews and Muslims in the colony.

Rumors also circulated in 1933 that the JOB cigarette factory planned to fire all Muslim employees to replace them with Jewish refugees from Germany.[93] Another rumor spread that the JOB factory advertised that Algerian Muslims "love JOB cigarettes as much as their prophet" and that the factory's proprietor, Monsieur Job, was a Jew. Algerian shop owners refused to sell these cigarettes to their fellow Muslims, instigating the widespread boycott of the brand.[94]

In these boycotts, French antisemites capitalized on Muslim status anxieties and world events to promote antisemitism. Although the

"No. 1046," Khenchela, July 16, 1933, CAOM Alg Const B/3/249. See also Prefect of Constantine to the Gov-Gen, Constantine, July 19, 1933, CAOM Alg Const B/3/249.

[91] Report of Principal Inspector Defendini, Khenchela, July 21, 1933, CAOM Alg Const B/3/249. The flyer cited the Qur'anic sura 5:82.

[92] Defendini, Khenchela, July 21, 1933, CAOM Alg Const B/3/249. See also report of Commissariat of the Police, "Mouvement antisemite, Secret Rapport Special, No. 1918," Khenchela, July 11, 1933, CAOM Alg Const B/3/249; Prefect of Constantine to the Procurer of the Republic, "No. 6012," Constantine, August 5, 1933, CAOM Alg Const B/3/249. On the appearance of the flyer elsewhere in the colony see letter Gov-Gen to the Prefect of Algiers, "Au sujet du boycottage de commerces israélites," Algiers, July 20, 1933, CAOM Alg Alger 2i/38.

[93] Gov-Gen to the Prefect of Constantine, "No. 13031b: Au sujet de la Croix Gammée," Algiers, June 2, 1933, CAOM Alg Const B/3/249.

[94] Departmental Security to the Prefect of Constantine, "No. 1370/1374: Au sujet du boycottage des produits d'une manufacture de tabacs," Constantine, June 9, 1933, CAOM Alg Const B/3/249. Commissioner of Police to the Prefect of the Department of Constantine, "No 2–2256: Au sujet du boycottage des produits de la Maison JOB," Bougie, June 18, 1933, CAOM Alg Const B/3/249. The police commissioner in Ain-Beida attributed the boycott to the deteriorating relationship between Jews and Muslims in the colony. Commissioner of Police of Ain-Beida, to the Prefect of Constantine, "No. 462," Ain-Beida, June 19, 1933, CAOM Alg Const B/3/249.

colonial administration long feared the possibility of an Algerian Muslim uprising, they did little to quell the rising antisemitism. The administration likely welcomed the redirection of Algerian Muslims' frustrations onto Jews.

At the same time as the JOB boycott, swastikas appeared and cheers of "Vive Hitler" reverberated throughout the colony. In 1932, Hitler's *Mein Kampf* was translated into Arabic and distributed in large numbers under the title *El Hitler*.[95] Already in September 1932, Jacques Taïeb and Alfred Levy, editors and directors of the newspaper *Souk-Ahras Republicain*, received an antisemitic letter along with a swastika. The author of the letter blamed the "perpetual excitations" of Jews for the recrudescence of antisemitism among other "races," motivating them to act against the Jews. The letter was signed by the initials M.A.J., which could represent "Death to the Jews" (*Mort aux Juifs*), a common rallying cry of earlier antisemitic demonstrations.[96] Starting in 1933, National Socialists began a campaign to win over former German colonies in southwest Africa and to gain support elsewhere in Africa.[97] This increase in antisemitism among Muslims was less about the actions of Jews and more about the machinations and provocations of European antisemites.

Throughout the summer of 1933, swastikas appeared throughout the department of Constantine. In June 1933, two trucks bearing swastikas traveled through Batna. In Constantine, young Algerian Muslims openly wore armbands adorned with swastikas, greeting each other with *Tu as le bonjour de Hitler*.[98] The governor-general connected the appearance of swastikas, references to Hitler, the boycott of the JOB cigarette factory, and the rumors circulating regarding German Jewish refugees as a worrisome trend.[99] In July, the police commissioner of Batna reported that some young Algerian Muslims supported Hitler's rise to power in Germany and attributed the boycott of the JOB products to the latent discord between Jews and Muslims in the colony.[100]

In late August and September 1933 the BASTOS cigarette factory started selling packages of cigarette paper printed with a swastika.

[95] Attal, *Les Émeutes de Constantine*, 69.
[96] Alfred Levy to M. Landel, Sec-Gen of the Prefecture, Constantine, Souk-Ahras, September 13, 1932; Prefect of Constantine to Alfred Levy, Director of *Souk Ahras Républicain*, "No. 6848," Constantine, September 16, 1932, CAOM Alg Const B/3/249.
[97] L. Smythe Barron, ed., *The Nazis in Africa: Lost Documents on the Third Reich Volume III* (Salisbury: Documentary Publications, 1978), i. See also Charles-Robert Ageron, *L'Algérie algérienne de Napoléon III à de Gaulle* (Paris: Éditions Sindbad, 1980), 168–190.
[98] Can be translated as "Best regards from Hitler."
[99] Gov-Gen of Algeria to the Prefect of Constantine, "No, 13031b: Au sujet de la croix gammée," Algiers, June 2, 1933, CAOM Alg Const B/3/249.
[100] Commissariat de Police de Batna to the Sous-Prefect, "No. 3950: Camions portent la croix gammée," Batna, June 21, 1933, CAOM Alg Const B/3/249.

The governor-general ordered the halt to sales of such packages due to its implicit support of Hitler.[101] The Sub-Prefect of Bougie argued that the BASTOS factory wanted to take advantage of the rumors regarding the JOB factory in order to widen their clientele and to advertise the "anti-Jewish" nature of the BASTOS factory. He feared that the anti-Jewish sentiments of the Algerian Muslims in the colony would further Hitler's growing success and popularity and create "political agitation."[102]

Bastos Cigarette Papers, c. 1930s

Jacob Saffar, a Jewish merchant in Bougie, reported that the BASTOS factory, whose primary owners were of Spanish origin, "sought to encourage and assist the antisemitic movement and as well as the anti-French movement."[103] Saffar's concerns indicate the continued role of *néos* as the leaders of the antisemitic movement in the colony.

In July 1934, just weeks prior to the August 5 pogrom, the director of German foreign propaganda and "racial philosopher," Dr. Alfred Rosenberg, visited North Africa, Yemen, and Syria.[104] Although the

---

[101] Gov-Gen to the Prefect of the department of Constantine, "No. 18436B: Au sujet des cahiers de papier à cigarettes portant l'insigne de la croix gammée," Algiers, September 1933, CAOM Alg Const B/3/249.

[102] Sub-Prefect of Bougie, Richardot, to the Prefect of Constantine, "No. 6174: Mouvement antisémite," Bougie, August 25, 1933, CAOM Alg Const B/3/249.

[103] Jacob Saffar to the Sub-Prefect of the Arrondissement of Bougie, Bougie, August 24, 1933, CAOM Alg Const B/3/249.

[104] Jonathan Trigg, *Hitler's Jihadis: Muslim Volunteers of the Waffen-SS* (Gloucestershire: The History Press, 2008), 24.

impact of his visit to Algeria is not clear, his intention – to promote tensions – was evident. The governor-general remarked on Hitler's popularity among Muslims in those areas, "Mr. Hitler is known by all the leaders and they speak with great admiration of modern Germany. Racism is now adopted by the Arabs." The Prefect of Algiers considered Hitler's success in North Africa a reaction to the growing Jewish presence in Palestine.[105] At the end of July 1934, the Commissioner of Police in Kolea reported that Algerian Muslims demonstrated great "affection" for the image of the swastika as an emblem of anti-Judaism. He added that the Algerian Muslims in Oran supported Hitler's anti-Jewish measures taken in Germany. However, the commissioner concluded that Algerian Muslims' alleged antisemitism and support of Hitler did not preclude their loyalty to France.[106] Not all administrators in Algeria agreed with him.

Hitler propagandists drew upon the "latent" antisemitism of Algerian Muslims who blamed their poor status and conditions on the nefarious political and economic activities of Jews in the colony. An administrator in Cherchell believed that Algerian Muslims supported Hitler because they considered Nazi Germany as the only credible threat to French control in Algeria.[107] This assessment hints at the French colonial administrators' growing fears regarding independence efforts among Algerian Muslims in the colony. For the most part, however, administrators did not seem concerned with Algerian Muslim antisemitism – in fact, some likely welcomed the idea.

The presence of Nazi propaganda in the colony increased after the August 5 pogrom. In October 1934, the governor-general noted the increase in swastikas appearing throughout the colony.[108] While the source of the swastikas was unclear, they likely came from right-wing Europeans.[109] In November 1935, surveillance records indicated that Dr. Bendjelloul, who figured in the events of August 5, had received

---

[105] Prefect of Algiers, "No. 14823," Algiers, July 19, 1934, CAOM Alg Alger 2i/38.

[106] Commissioner of Police of Kolea to the Prefect of Algiers, "No. 1781," Kolea, July 25, 1934, CAOM Alg Alger 2i/38. Although inconsistent, some administrators used "anti-Judaism" in place of "antisemitism" when discussing Jewish-Muslim conflicts.

[107] Administrator of the Mixed Commune of Cherchell to the Prefect of Algiers, "No. 2662: Au sujet de l'existence d'un mouvement raciste chez les indigènes, Titus Panaitescu," Cherchell, July 25, 1934, CAOM Alg Alger 2i/38.

[108] The Gov-Gen suggested that Goebbels was the mastermind of such activities in the colony. Gov-Gen to the Prefect of Algiers, "No. 16267b: Au sujet de la propaganda hitlerienne en Algérie," Algiers, October 17, 1934, CAOM Alg Alger 2i/38.

[109] Administrator of the Mixed Commune of Cherchell to the Prefect of Algiers, "No. 4706: Au sujet de la propaganda hitlerienne," Cherchell, October 29, 1934, CAOM Alg Alger 2i/38. The administrator in Cherchell suggested an anti-French sentiment rather than an antisemitic or pro-Nazi opinion.

a package of antisemitic newspapers, *L'Éclaireur Aryen*, from Germany.[110] The 1935 report on the political situation of Algeria also noted "ardent sympathy" for Hitler among Muslims.[111] In 1935, the police commissioner of Algiers reported the appearance of flyers displaying various phrases such as "Mort aux Français et aux Juifs," "Vive Hitler et Mussolini sauvers des indigènes," and "Vive Mussolini, Vive l'Algérie indépendante."[112] Such phrases appeared throughout the colony, scrawled on walls, shouted during protests, and whispered on the streets.[113]

Relations between Jews and Muslims deteriorated in the years and months prior to the August 5 violence, evolving into a crescendo of frustrations and hatreds. In April 1934, the governor-general reported the appearance of flyers in Arab markets in the department of Constantine that read "Muslims, France loves you and the Jews hate you." The governor-general noted that the flyers were likely produced by members of the antisemitic movement and worried that it could incite Algerian Muslim fear and anger toward Jews.[114] The administration also believed that the Algerian Muslim leadership was at least in part to blame. A report by Governor-General Carde to the Minister of the Interior on August 9, 1934, immediately following the violence, detailed the results of his personal inquiry. In the report, Carde argued that there was a certain "preparation" in advance of the violence, conducted by some elected Muslim leaders, and by the leaders of the Ulamas, including their president, Ben Badis. Carde asserted that Ben Badis and other leaders preached the return to the purity of Islam but were in fact "agents of a xenophobic nationalism." Ben Badis' actions, Carde continued, created in the department of Constantine, a kind of "politico-religious psychosis among the believers."[115] In a 1935 report on the political situation in Algeria, the author stated that even if the reformist and neo-

---

[110] Departmental Security of Algiers, "Report No. 7639: Propagande Allemande," Algiers, November 30, 1934, CAOM Alg Alger 2i/38.

[111] President of the Ministers' Council care of the Minister of the Interior, "Situation politique en Algérie," 11, May 10, 1935, CAOM GGA 2CAB/3.

[112] Police Commissioner of Algiers, Bethcessahar, to the Sec-Gen of Affaires Indigènes, Algiers, April 6, 1935, CAOM Alg Alger 2i/38. It is unclear why that Frenchman was targeted.

[113] Samuel Kalman identifies a surge in membership of the Croix de Feu after 1934. Kalman, *French Colonial Fascism*, 60–61. Aomar Boum noted that Algerian antisemites endeavored to cause tension and discord between Jews and Muslims in the colony. Boum, "Partners against Anti-Semitism," 557.

[114] Gov-Gen to the Prefect of Constantine, "No. 6170B: Au sujet des papillons antisémites," Algiers, April 25, 1934, CAOM Alg Const B/3/250.

[115] Gov-Gen of Algeria Carde to the Minister of the Interior, "Telegram," Algiers, August 9, 1934, CAOM Alg GGA 2CAB/3.

Wahabist leaders were not responsible for organizing the Constantine riots, their propaganda had at the very least weakened the "sense of discipline, excited the instincts and allowed the populace to believe that the freedom of social criticism allowed to their leaders also meant freedom for the crowd to murder and pillage."[116]

Another report from Governor-General Carde argued that political developments and competing parties created an intensely charged environment in which many of the incidents between Jews and Muslims were provoked by "barely conciliatory, even insolent, attitude shown by some Jews who do not deny themselves the pleasure of insulting, in the street, the natives, often unknown to them, or humiliate them by taunts and threats." He added that because the Jews spoke the same language as Muslims, they knew what would insult them most. These minor incidents increasingly turned violent. In addition, Carde argued that the Algerian Muslims were far more impacted by the economic crisis than the Europeans and that Muslim antisemitism was intensified by the actions of the *Croix de Feu*.[117] It is within this environment that the August 5th violence can best be understood. Small-scale altercations in Constantine occurred with great regularity in the months leading to the pogrom.[118] The machinations of the antisemitic movement intensified this fraught environment.

The 1934 Constantine Pogrom

Constantine Jews and left-wing groups referred to the August 5 violence as a pogrom, a Russian word meaning to wreak havoc.[119] The term is generally applied to Eastern European episodes of violence perpetrated by non-Jews against Jews. The anthropologist Paul R. Brass' definition of a pogrom involves interethnic violence supported or sponsored by the police or administration. The 1934 Constantine bloodshed meets such criteria.[120] Over the course of August 5, Algerian Muslims attacked Jews in Constantine while the police surveyed the violence without

---

[116] President of the Ministers' Council care of the Minister of the Interior, "Situation politique en Algérie," 9, May 10, 1935, CAOM GGA 2CAB/3.

[117] Gov-Gen Carde to the Minister of the Interior, "Report No. 3359: Situation morale de l'Algérie," Algiers, August 11, 1935, CAOM Alg GGA 2CAB/3.

[118] Small-scale violent encounters continued in the months before the August 5 pogrom. Central Police Commissioner to the Prefect of Constantine, No. 3425, "Incident entre Indigène et Israélites," Constantine, June 7, 1934, CAOM Alg Const B/3/240.

[119] Ellen Land-Weber, *To Save a Life: Stories of Holocaust Rescue* (Champaign: University of Illinois Press, 2007), 297.

[120] Paul R. Brass, *Theft of an Idol: Text and Context in the Representation of Collective Violence* (Princeton: Princeton University Press, 1997), 4–5, 11.

intervening. The local police were employees of the municipal administration, including a few remaining Jewish policemen. The inaction of Constantine's police demonstrated the inherent antisemitism in the municipal government and the French colonial administration more broadly. More significantly, the term "pogrom" reflects the way in which Algerian Jews understood the violence and interpreted it through the lens of global Jewish history, thus writing their story into that of their European coreligionists.

The political constructions and interpretations of the 1934 violence provide an unparalleled illustration of the competition between colonial groups and the ways in which political antisemitism manifested itself. The goal of this section is not to present a detailed recounting of the history of the pogrom. Rather, this analysis uses previously unexamined sources in conjunction with well-known accounts to examine the Constantine pogrom through the prism of political antisemitism and the intense competition for rights in the colonial context. This section is therefore less about the violence itself and more about violence as the enactment of political frustrations, competition, and antisemitism, and its interpretations.

Many of the administrative reports concluded that the violence occurred as a result of locally based clashes and explained away as the inevitable consequence of long-standing Jewish–Muslim conflicts. Historians, including Joshua Cole, Charles-Robert Ageron, and Rochdi Ali Younsi, use these administrative analyses, concluding that the violence, although tragic, was of localized origin, but also reflective of the larger issues of Jewish–Muslim relations.[121] Joshua Cole rightly identifies that the key issue at play behind the Constantine violence was that of access to rights and Muslims' frustrations with the partial citizenship offered by the Jonnart Law in 1919.[122] These historians rely heavily on administrative reports, published narratives, and contemporary Algerian Muslim analyses.

However, there are other sources that have been ignored by historians: for example, the responses to a questionnaire on the causes and events of August 5 by mayors and administrators in the department of Constantine provide insight into the local conditions and administrative interpretations of Jewish–Muslim relations. Jewish reports illustrate the ways in which they understood the causes of the pogrom, and the actions – or inaction – of the French administration. These accounts

---

[121] Ageron, "Une émeute anti-juive à Constantine," 40; Rochdi Ali Younsi, *Caught in a Colonial Triangle: Competing Loyalties within the Jewish Community of Algeria, 1842–1943* (Dissertation, University of Chicago, 2003).

[122] Cole, "Anti-Semitism and the Colonial Situation in Interwar Algeria," 78, 83.

demonstrate the broader implications of the pogrom, specifically bringing the question of rights to the fore of political debates at the time.[123]
August 5 represents a climax of the growing tensions between Jews and
Muslims in the colony following the evolution of administrative and
municipal antisemitism in the 1920s and 1930s. In particular, it reflects
the ways in which antisemites exploited those tensions to further their
own agenda.[124]

Central to the increasing tensions between Jews and Muslims was the
issue of citizenship. At the time of the pogrom petitions circulated for the
abrogation of the Crémieux Decree.[125] Many contemporary reports
described the violence of August 5, 1934, as caused by the frustrations
felt by Algerian Muslims toward Algerian Jews' political status in the
colony. The ways in which the different groups in the colony experienced,
deconstructed, and interpreted the pogrom illuminate the meanings and
limits of citizenship in the colony.

The Power of Rumors: The Immediate Causes
of the August 5 Pogrom

The Constantine pogrom originated out of a web of rumors, which fed
upon local tensions. Rumors are particularly effective in inciting public
opinion because they play upon fears, concerns, and frustrations.[126]
The rumors that circulated around the Constantine pogrom reflect
a climate of status anxiety. The immediate causes of the August 5 pogrom
can be traced to the dissemination of versions of an altercation between
a Jewish soldier and Muslims at a mosque. Algerian Muslims considered
the incident a serious affront to their religion and status in the colony.
Jews feared that it would be used as a pretext for attacks on their community. Europeans, and particularly the administration, reacted to the
episode and the resulting violence without significant interest or
intervention.

---

[123] Younsi, *Caught in a Colonial Triangle*, 142.
[124] It is also closely linked to the economic crisis in the late 1920s and 1930s.
The depression and economic crisis in the 1920s are dealt with in the previous chapter.
[125] Ageron, "Une émeute anti-juive à Constantine," 32. The fact that the pogrom occurred
on the anniversary of Bendjelloul's 1933 delegation to Paris to demand rights for
Algerian Muslims must be taken into account in understanding its causes. This delegation will be explained later in the chapter.
[126] Foucault, "Governmentality," 92. See also Luise White, *Speaking with Vampires: Rumor
and History in Colonial Africa* (Berkeley: University of California Press, 2000), 43, 86;
Brass, *Theft of an Idol*, 19; and George Rudé, *The French Revolution: Its Causes, Its
History, and Its Legacy after 200 Years* (New York: Grove Pres, 1998), 47.

Each colonial group understood the pogrom itself in different ways and placed blame on a range of actors. Jews blamed Algerian Muslim leaders for vilifying them. Algerian Muslims blamed the Jewish soldier for instigating the violence. Europeans blamed ethnic hatred. Some Jews and administrative officials blamed European antisemites' provocations, especially Henri Lautier's *L'Éclair* and its propagation of antisemitic rhetoric such as "Everything bad comes from the Jews . . . It is the Jews who should be slaughtered."[127] Due to the divergent interpretations of the pogrom, it is difficult to find a single, unbiased account of the events.[128]

Administrative reports often took sides, despite being fact-finding missions supposedly uninfluenced by politics. The Vigouroux report is one such example. Jean Vigouroux was a government advisor, appointed by Governor-General Carde to lead a commission in investigating the pogrom.[129] In his analysis, Vigouroux resuscitated old antisemitic arguments, such as the accusation that Jews voted in blocs according to the direction of their religious leaders.[130] Vigouroux's report has been criticized for being too dependent on the Algerian Muslim version of the pogrom, concluding that the Jews were to blame. Historian Robert Attal suggests that Vigouroux's conclusions covered up the failures of the French administration.[131] The Vigouroux commission was made up almost entirely of local administrators, whose proximity to the violence, and their potential involvement, certainly made their impartiality questionable. Marcel Régnier, the Minister of the Interior in 1934, criticized the report, citing Vigouroux's own antisemitic sentiments. Régnier demanded that another inquiry be made by a public or parliamentary figure named by the French government, who would examine the role of the administrators in particular.[132]

Despite his historical training, Attal's analysis is profoundly shaped by his personal experiences as a "son of 'August 5'," and ultimately its orphan. He describes the attacking mob of Muslims; his family's escape,

---

[127] Fédération de France du Front de Libération Nationale, "FLN Documents: Les Juifs d'Algérie dans le Combat pour l'Independence nationale," CDHA 296 FRO.

[128] Brass, *Theft of an Idol*, 5, 8. I have endeavored, however, to leave my opinions out of this analysis and to let the documents speak for themselves.

[129] Attal, *Les Émeutes de Constantine*, 169. There is very little available information on Vigouroux. It is possible that he was previously the director of the interior of the Gov-Gen's cabinet in 1931. "M. Le Gouverneur Jules Carde a inauguré, hier, les nouveaux groups d'immeubles édifiés par l'Office public d'habitations à bon marché de la ville d'Alger," in *L'Echo d'Alger*, December 15, 1931, 3.

[130] Attal, *Les Émeutes de Constantine*, 172.   [131] Ibid., 178, 181.

[132] Marcel Régnier, "Voyage en Algérie de M. Régnier, Ministre de l'Intérieur, Note sur les massacres de Constantine," February 28, 1935, CAOM FM 81F/864. Régnier's report seems to draw heavily from Jewish reports, including Sultan's and Confino's.

divided into groups to increase chances of survival; the image of his mother pounding on the door of their neighbor's home, the curtain being pulled aside and quickly returned; his father's body bleeding out on the floor of the truck once their family had been rescued; his little sister crying out for their father.[133] Like many of the documents that emerged out of the wreckage of the August 5 pogrom, Attal's account is tinged with personal loss and horror. Attal emphasizes that the main causes were the political climate and the economic depression, which made the Jew the ideal victim.[134]

Unlike Attal, Rochdi Ali Younsi centers his analysis of the "disputed" pogrom on the Vigouroux report. Younsi rightly identifies the pogrom's main causes as growing Algerian Muslim nationalism, increasing demands for political rights, and the embedded nature of anti-Jewish attitudes within the Muslim population.[135] However, Younsi points to the Algerian Jews' harassment of Algerian Muslims as another cause. In the aftermath of the disturbances each side attempted to paint themselves as the victims.[136] Historians have the challenging task of wading through the personal to access the details of the events. As my analysis is primarily about Algerian Jewish experience, Jewish reports of August 5th will receive special attention. Régnier's report offers some of the least biased contemporary reports and as such is a good starting point for this analysis.

Régnier began his analysis of the pogrom with his version of the immediate cause: the altercation involving the Jewish *zouave*, Eliaou Kalifa, and the worshippers of the Sidi Lakhdar Mosque.[137] On the evening of August 3, Kalifa returned to his home in an inebriated state. His home faced the mosque. In order to enter his apartment, Kalifa had to pass through a corridor with two windows looking onto the courtyard where Muslims made their ablutions. Normally, the windows were closed, yet that evening the windows were open. Kalifa requested that the windows be closed. The manner in which he made the request differed based on the source. Régnier cited the muezzin of the mosque who stated that Kalifa declared "Cursed be your religion." Régnier denounced the claims made in many newspapers that Kalifa then urinated on the wall of the mosque; however, this rumor appears to have circulated widely throughout the department of Constantine.[138] Albert Confino, the director of the Alliance Israélite

---

[133] Attal, *Les Émeutes de Constantine*, 73–76.   [134] Ibid., 185–186.
[135] Younsi, *Caught in a Colonial Triangle*, 142–143.   [136] Ibid., 160–161189.
[137] Depending upon the report, the Jewish *zouave*'s name is spelled differently, ranging from Eliaou Kalifa, to Elie Khalifa, to Elie Khalifat.
[138] Régnier, "Note sur les massacres de Constantine," CAOM FM 81F/864.

Universelle schools in Algiers, also commented on the rumor, stating that the muezzin formally declared that Kalifa had indeed offered insults, but had not entered the mosque, nor had he urinated on the mosque.[139]

Régnier rightly argued that the Kalifa incident was relatively minor and should not have served as the spark for the August 5 attacks. Nonetheless, the "standard" version of events, subsequently published in newspapers, was that Kalifa drunkenly entered the mosque, insulted Islam, urinated, and, after being chased out, called upon fellow Jews to attack Muslims.[140] Governor-General Carde believed that the Kalifa incident was minor enough that had communal leaders worked to calm the subsequent fervor, the incident could have passed with little consequence.[141] The spread of the urination rumors incensed public opinion, leading to a massive and violent gathering at the Place des Galettes, which was in the Jewish quarter, bordering the Muslim quarter.[142] If they circulated for the goal of inciting violence or intensifying already tense moments, rumors in Algeria constituted political tools.

During the evening of August 3, after 8:30 pm, a fight broke out at the Place des Galettes, where the police department of the second arrondisse-ment was located.[143] Many of the injured Jews were police officers who intervened in the fighting, at the orders of M. Landel, the Secretary-General of the Prefecture.[144] This is a significant point: although the municipal government of Constantine was increasingly antisemitic, there were still some Jews on the police force, a holdover from the period of more cooperation between Jewish officials and Morinaud.[145] Henri Lellouche, General Council member and president of the Jewish consistory of Constantine, arrived at the scene along with the mufti, French authorities, and Bendjelloul, the Algerian Muslim–elected General Council member. Lellouche and the mufti called for unity and calm.[146] Bendjelloul found

---

[139] Albert Confino to the President of the Alliance Israélite Universelle, Algiers, August 15, 1934, AIU Algérie ICI.

[140] Rumors spread that Kalifa was actually the illegitimate son of a Jewish mother and Muslim father. Régnier, "Note sur les massacres de Constantine," CAOM FM 81F/864.

[141] Gov-Gen Carde to the Minister of the Interior, "Report No. 4264," Algiers, October 19, 1934, CAOM Alg GGA 2CAB/3.

[142] Younsi, *Caught in a Colonial Triangle*, 145.

[143] According to Régnier, twenty-three participants were injured, including fourteen Jews, eight Arabs, and one Italian. Ageron includes vastly different numbers than Régnier: 15 injured, which included three police agents. Ageron, "Une Emeute anti-Juive," 25.

[144] Gov-Gen Carde to the Minister of the Interior, "Report No. 4264," Algiers, October 19, 1934, CAOM Alg GGA 2CAB/3.

[145] Morinaud, *Mes Mémoires*, 331–336.

[146] Régnier, "Note sur les massacres de Constantine," CAOM FM 81F/864.

an Algerian Muslim being arrested for attacking a Jew and harangued the arresting police officer for harassing one of his electors. Disappointed with the officer's response, Bendjelloul slapped him.[147] Algerian Muslims saw Bendjelloul's intervention as an act of defiance against the colonial regime. Most, however, chose to ignore the fact that the slapped officer was a Muslim named Gassab.[148] Bendjelloul's demands for Muslim rights as French citizens made him extremely popular among Algerian Muslims. To some of his followers, his action both betrayed the weakness of the French authorities and revealed his "contempt" for the French.[149]

The day following the Kalifa incident, Muslim and Jewish leaders worked to calm their respective communities while preaching unity and coexistence. The morning of August 4, the most widely read newspaper of the city, *La Dépêche de Constantine*, published the alleged urination account of the Kalifa incident. Read by a large number of Algerian Muslims, the article further incensed the Muslim population and served as a catalyst in inciting the subsequent violence.[150] Lellouche later arrived at the mayor's offices, along with fellow Jewish leaders, where they found approximately thirty Muslim leaders and notables already assembled.[151] At the meeting, Monsieur Sultan, a Jewish delegate, decorated veteran, and president of the Constantine section of the LDH, spoke of unity and coexistence between Jews and Muslims in Algeria. Sultan offered encouragement, pointing to "this harmony and understanding between Jews and Muslims ... I hope to work in unity and harmony under the

---

[147] Ibid. See also Ageron, "Une émeute anti-juive," 25; Attal, *Les Émeutes de Constantine*, 82–83.

[148] Younsi, *Caught in a Colonial Triangle*, 146.

[149] Although Bendjelloul was western-educated, he emphasized his rootedness in Algeria as the descendent of the Bey of Constantine. Régnier, "Note sur les massacres de Constantine," CAOM FM 81F/864. Albert Confino of the Alliance felt that the events of August 3 were a pretext for looting. Six Jewish-owned jewelry stores had been broken into and ransacked, a sign of premeditation in Confino's opinion. He suggested that the stores had been marked in advance. Albert Confino to the President of the AIU, Algiers, August 14, 1934, AIU Algérie ICI.

[150] Régnier pondered if this was the intent of the editors of the *Dépêche de Constantine*. Régnier, "Note sur les massacres de Constantine," CAOM FM 81F/864. That morning Monsieur Lellouche visited all the synagogues in Constantine, urging his coreligionists to avoid demonstrations, gestures, and "imprudent words." A. Confino to President AIU, Algiers, August 15, 1934, AIU Algérie ICI.

[151] Muslim religious leader and president of the association of the Ulamas of North Africa, Ben Badis, began the session by complaining about violent incidents instigated by Jews during the previous five years. Central Commissioner of Police, Constantine, "No. 113, Incidents entre indigènes et israélites," Constantine, August 6, 1929, CAOM Alg Const B/3/248. Régnier, "Note sur les massacres de Constantine," CAOM FM 81F/864. It is possible that much of Régnier's theories and arguments in his report are too tinged by a teleological outlook on the events of August 1934.

aegis and protective guardianship of France."[152] Even though Jewish and Muslims leaders urged calm, it was not enough to slow the rush of events.

In the afternoon on August 4, French administrators met to discuss the protocol for maintaining calm in the city of Constantine. At the meeting, the Jewish delegates demanded that General Kieffer request reinforcements. Kieffer agreed and requested that 200 tirailleurs Sénégalais from Philippeville be directed toward Constantine.[153] M. Landel, the Secretary-General of the Prefecture, telephoned M. Souchier, the Secretary-General of the Government, to inform him of the decisions made at the meeting. Souchier approved them, but urged them to do all they could to avoid employing their weapons. According to Governor-General Carde, the situation at the time, while serious, "wasn't alarming."[154] Confino emphasized that the Jewish delegation explicitly requested that only Senegalese soldiers be sent, rather than Algerians.[155] This was a calculated request; in the past there had been violent encounters between Algerian Jews and Algerian Muslim tirailleurs.[156]

Police Commissioner Fusero announced that the situation was growing more serious and that reinforcements were needed immediately. Algerian Muslim tirailleurs threatened to scale the walls of their barracks in Constantine in order to invade the Jewish quarter. In the end, Kieffer was able to produce only 150 tirailleurs to serve as reinforcements.[157] Jewish leaders accused French administrators of failing to confront the growing threat of violence. French administrative failure, they argued, was due to criminal neglect and complicity in the violence. At the time, Constantine's mayor, Émile Morinaud, was away. His subordinates

---

[152] A. Confino to President AIU, Algiers, August 15, 1934, AIU Algérie ICI.

[153] Régnier, "Note sur les massacres de Constantine," CAOM FM 81F/864.

[154] Gov-Gen Carde to the Minister of the Interior, "Report No. 4264," Algiers, October 19, 1934, CAOM Alg GGA 2CAB/3.

[155] A. Confino to President AIU, Algiers, August 15, 1934, AIU Algérie ICI.

[156] See, for example, cases of violence between Jews and Algerian Muslim soldiers (Tirailleurs indigènes): Constantine, Consistoire Israélite Constantine to the Consistoire Central of Paris, May 24, 1875, CC Icc 39; Constantine, Consistoire Israélite Constantine to the Consistoire Central, Paris, Constantine, June 18, 1878, CC 2E-boite 2; Tlemcen, April 1903, AN F/7/12460; Tlemcen, R. Ardette to the Chief Rabbi of the Consistoire Israélite, Paris, August 29, 1912, CC 2E-Boite 1; Constantine, Daily report of Commissaire of the Police of Constantine, February 7–8, 1914, CAOM Alg Const B/3/248; Constantine, Commissariat Central de Police, "Rapport No. 433," December 20, 1930, CAOM Alg Const B/3/248; Sétif, February 1935, See Simon Bakhouche to the Chief Rabbi of the Consistoire Central, Constantine, February 7, 1935, AIU Algérie ICI.

[157] A. Confino to President AIU, Algiers, August 15, 1934, AIU Algérie ICI; Régnier, "Note sur les massacres de Constantine," CAOM FM 81F/864.

alerted him to the situation so that he could return to Constantine in time to deal with any potential problems. On August 4, thousands of Algerian Muslims participated in a meeting at the central Mosque, where Bendjelloul spoke.[158] As Régnier described, "an atmosphere of riot and of pogrom weighed upon the city."[159]

August 5

During the early morning hours of August 5, 1934, Algerian Muslims congregated in the forest outside of Constantine known as the Pines of Mansours. According to Régnier, the meeting was to assemble forces for the impending pogrom; the participants were armed with clubs and after the meeting they descended upon the city. Régnier noted that the police could easily have prevented the rioters from entering the city, but failed to do so.[160] Coincidentally, the funeral for Monsieur Narboni, the former president of the Constantine consistory and municipal council member, was scheduled for the morning of August 5. It is important to note that Narboni and Morinaud had earlier developed a truce, despite Morinaud's antisemitic leanings.[161]

As Jews made their way to the funeral home, many observed large groups of Algerian Muslims heading toward the Pines of Mansours. Fearing for their coreligionists' safety, Jewish leaders called upon the police. The majority of the Constantine Jewish population attended the funeral, as well as four to five Muslim municipal council members. As the cortege made its way to the cemetery, Algerian Muslims descended upon the central street of the city, Rue Nationale, and began their assault on Jewish shops.[162]

Rumors quickly spread regarding the meeting at the Pines. One rumor stated that Jews strangled two Algerian Muslims.[163] Another rumor centered on Bendjelloul, who had been expected at the meeting, suggesting that Jews had killed him, and served as an opportunity to seek revenge on the Jews.[164] The events of August 3–5 illustrate the power of rumors in

---

[158] A. Confino to President AIU, Algiers, August 15, 1934, AIU Algérie ICI.

[159] Régnier, "Note sur les massacres de Constantine," CAOM FM 81F/864.

[160] Ibid. See also Younsi, *Caught in a Colonial Triangle*, 150.

[161] Morinaud put a different spin on the violence in his *Mes Mémoires*, 336.

[162] A. Confino to President AIU, Algiers, August 15, 1934, AIU Algérie ICI. Confino wrote that the rioters looted a salon and barber shop, destroying the interior, and taking all of the razors in the shop, which he claimed they later used to stab Jewish victims.

[163] A. Confino to President AIU, Algiers, August 15, 1934, AIU Algérie ICI.

[164] Régnier, "Note sur les massacres de Constantine," CAOM FM 81F/864. Attal also notes a similar rumor of Bendjelloul's assassination. Attal, *Les Émeutes de Constantine*, 141. See also Younsi, *Caught in a Colonial Triangle*, 151. Rumors such as these proved a powerful tool in the colonial climate. White, *Speaking with Vampires*, 17, 43.

inciting public opinion and fanning fears. In their contemporary analyses, Régnier, Confino, and Sultan emphasized the importance of the meeting at the Pines and the suspicious nature of what occurred there. In contrast, Younsi and Ageron considered an altercation that took place between Jewish women and Muslim merchants the morning of August 5 to be the catalyzing force.[165] According to this version, a quarrel broke out at the market at the Place des Galettes in the Jewish quarter. Jews fired gunshots and injured several Muslim market attendees. Jews then attacked Arab boutiques situated in the Jewish quarter, shouting "Death to Bendjelloul," which was misunderstood as announcements of Bendjelloul's death. The rumors of Bendjelloul's death reached the meeting participants at the Pines and beyond. From there, cries of "Let us avenge Bendjelloul, who the Jews are going to kill." Some even accused Bendjelloul of spreading the rumors himself.[166] A report from the Police Commissioner of Khroub noted that two Muslims arrived in a truck at 10 am and announced that the "Jews" had killed Bendjelloul and they had to immediately avenge his death.[167]

An altercation did occur between Jews and Muslims on the morning of August 5, but the connection to the meeting of the Pines and the escalation of violence is tenuous at best. Police interviews with some of the Jewish women involved and witnesses suggest that the Jews did not start the violence but were its victims. Reine Atlan, a 26-year-old Jewish housewife, explained that she and two other Jewish women were at the Place des Galettes where they bargained for melons. Suddenly, she was hit on the back with a club. She could not identify her assailant but noted that there were numerous Algerian Muslims present. She abandoned her bags and took flight, seeking refuge at the police station, chased by Algerian Muslims yelling "Kill her! Kill her!" The two other women followed her to the station. There they found a Jewish police agent, Joseph Sebbah. Atlan heard the rioters saying "Go to the Place des Chameaux! That is where we're going to kill everyone."[168]

---

[165] Younsi, *Caught in a Colonial Triangle*, 151.

[166] Ageron, "Une émeute anti-juive," 26. Ageron excuses Bendjelloul's possible involvement, stating that as he learned of the meeting, he sent emissaries ordering its dispersal. A 1935 report on the political situation of Algeria held Bendjelloul largely responsible for the increasing tensions in Algeria at the time of the Constantine violence and beyond. President of the Ministers' Council, Minister of the Interior, "Situation politique en Algérie," 17, May 10, 1935, CAOM GGA 2CAB/3.

[167] The Police Commissioner of Khroub to the Gov-Gen, "Rapport Spécial No. 2291," Khroub, August 7, 1934, CAOM Alg GGA 2CAB/3.

[168] Henri Coquelin, Chief of the Departmental Security, Constantine, "Procès Verbal d'Audition, Préfecture de Constantine, Atlan, Reine," Constantine, September 11, 1934, CAOM Alg Const B/3/250.

After taking another report, Sebbah left the station only to find Algerian Muslims armed with clubs running toward Rue Vieux. At that time he heard more gunshots and hurried back into the station to call the central police station for reinforcements. A half hour later, the reinforcements arrived, but Algerian Muslims had already "disemboweled" Jewish shops.[169] Police agent Chaou El Beze reported that he received orders to push back the crowds of Algerian Muslims.[170] El Beze was eventually joined by another Jewish police officer, Maurice Barkatz. Upon hearing cries coming from the street, Barkatz looked out the window to see a group of Algerian Muslims throwing stones at the Jews in the street.[171] Governor-General Carde reported that at the Place des Galettes, after a few altercations, gunshots were fired from the second story of a building. Because the Place des Galettes was in the Jewish quarter, the implication of such an accusation is that the gunfire came from a Jew. Afterward, groups of Jews attacked about ten Muslim-owned shops in the quarter, which the Muslim proprietors either fled or barricaded themselves within. Two Muslims were shot and injured by Jews. Further exacerbating the situation, rumors spread that Bendjelloul had been killed. From there, the situation snowballed, as Muslims from the neighboring quarter flooded the Place des Galettes.[172]

These reports do not provide conclusive evidence that Jews attacked Muslims near the Place des Galettes. Although the morning's altercation may have exacerbated the later violence, it is unlikely that it was the instigating factor, as Ageron and Younsi contend. These reports do demonstrate, however, that Jews played a role in the Constantine police force and within municipal services in general. The presence of Jewish police was, however, a crucial issue that no doubt frustrated some Algerian Muslims and reinforces the centrality of competition and inequalities in political rights and access to power.

The descriptions of the violence are startling. Régnier described the ensuing violence succinctly, stating that "the morning, from nine am, the natives invaded the city, rushing toward Jewish boutiques and

---

[169] Henri Coquelin, Chief of the Departmental Security, Constantine, "Procès Verbal d'Audition, Sebbah, Atlan," Constantine, September 12, 1934, CAOM Alg Const B/3/250.

[170] Henri Coquelin, Chief of the Departmental Security, Constantine, "Procès Verbal d'Audition, El Beze, Chaou," Constantine, September 15, 1934, CAOM Alg Const B/3/250.

[171] Ibid.

[172] Gov-Gen Carde to the Minister of the Interior, "Report No. 4264," Algiers, October 19, 1934, CAOM Alg GGA 2CAB/3.

stores, and until three pm – in the suburbs, until five pm – pillaged, massacred, slaughtered, disemboweled, attacked, burned, under the watch of the troops of the police." Upon calling the police, the mayor, and the fire station for help, Jews received the same response: "the necessary will be done, be assured." According to Régnier, "by two pm there are 13 bodies, horribly mutilated, murdered children, young girls slashed, the men with smashed skulls. Outside, the troops and police are waiting for orders. Through the closed shutters of windows, one can see the corpses in the street."[173] Confino described the Rue Nationale at noon as "a battlefield," upon which "heaps of goods are scattered on the ground, ripped open safes, records destroyed, promissory notes burned. Nothing can withstand the fury of the assailants. Woe to those who dare to defend themselves."[174] Looting and burning promissory notes suggest economic motivations in the violence of August 5.

Monsieur Sultan provided the most chilling report of the events. A veteran and politician with great faith in France, Sultan was shocked by the lack of administrative response. After attending Narboni's funeral, Sultan and other Jewish leaders were alerted to the developing horrors at the Place des Galettes. Accompanied by Lellouche, Sultan arrived at the scene where they were warned that they would be in grave danger. Sultan's home was situated on a street that had already been taken over by rioters. Thinking that these warnings were exaggerations, Sultan returned home. Along the Rue de France, Sultan witnessed police and soldiers carrying injured Jews on stretchers. A "fellow citizen," a *français d'origine*, protected Sultan. Earlier that morning Sultan's wife repeatedly telephoned the authorities for help. Through the closed shutters, she witnessed an old Jewish man beaten to the ground, where his crushed body formed "one large wound. His body was exposed to all the dirt and not removed until 5pm." Sultan wrote,

Every minute the same scenes were repeated, the "you-you" shouted by native women, amassed on terraces, mingling with the shouts of pillagers and incendiaries ... Those discovered in their apartments were ruthlessly slaughtered ... Nothing has been spared in the Jewish quarter itself, we knew that the Jews would defend themselves to the death.[175]

---

[173] Régnier, "Note sur les massacres de Constantine," CAOM FM 81F/864.
[174] A. Confino to President AIU, Algiers, August 15, 1934, AIU Algérie ICI.
[175] A. Sultan, "Les Événements de Constantine," Constantine, August 9, 1934, AIU Algérie ICI.

Sultan criticized the inaction of the police and the troops who surveyed the violence but did not intervene to stop it. It was not until 3 pm that Mayor Morinaud and General Kieffer ordered police and soldiers to stop the violence.[176]

Sultan's report, written just a few days after the pogrom, captures his and other Jews' exasperation and sense of betrayal. "An entire population has been delivered without defense, with the horrible illusion of being protected by a force that remained *immobile* ... A veritable pogrom has been organized and realized." Sultan doubted that the administrative inquiry would correctly identify the causes of the violence or attend to the central issue of the "deficiency" of the authorities and their response.[177] Sultan continued,

it is inconceivable that from 9am until 5pm the bandits were the masters of the street, that they could ransack, destroy, pillage more than 100 stores ... beat or slaughter twenty-four people, including five women and four children, that they had the *time to do this without anyone intervening or making arrests* ... Here is the other crime![178]

Sultan criticized the administration's inaction, attributing it to "incompetence, cowardice, or complicity." He concluded, "*France was absent from Constantine from 9am to 5pm.*"[179] General Kieffer, who commanded the immobile troops, dismissed Sultan and Lellouche's critiques as unpatriotic and provocative. Kieffer's report represents the antisemitism of the French administration. He suggested that the Jews "demonstrated a certain sense of triumph." Kieffer's report is a classic example of blaming the victim.[180] Even Governor-General Carde admitted that it was unfortunate that military response was not more immediate and that administrators had not anticipated that such violence could occur.[181]

Confino's report began with the statistics: twenty-five dead, a large number of wounded, four burned buildings, more than 150 million pieces of merchandise pillaged or destroyed, and families reduced to poverty. He surmised that had the authorities "acted responsibly, if they had heard the call of Jewish leaders who begged them to bring the Sénégalais, if the troops had acted, if the cavalry had charged,

---

[176] The violence stopped in the city but continued in the suburbs until 5 pm. Sultan, "Les Événements de Constantine," AIU Algérie ICI.

[177] Sultan was likely describing the Vigouroux report, which held the Jews largely responsible for the violence.

[178] Sultan, "Les Événements," AIU Algérie ICI. Emphasis his own.   [179] Ibid.

[180] General Kieffer, Commander of the Constantine Division, "Lettre à M. Le Député–Maire de la Ville de Constantine, No TS/398," Constantine, August 10, 1934, CAOM Alg Const B/3/250.

[181] Gov-Gen Carde to the Minister of the Interior, "Dépêche Télégraphique," Algiers, August 9, 1934, CAOM Alg GGA 2CAB/3.

even without firing one shot, the assailants would have taken flight and we would not have to note the loss of human life and the accumulating ruin."[182] Sultan and Confino's accusation of the administration's complicity in the pogrom led to administrative review of the events.

L'appartement de M. J. Sebbah, avenue Forcioli, après le passage des pilleurs.

Le Populaire, September 13, 1939, AIU Algérie I C 6a[183]

---

[182] A. Confino to President AIU, Algiers, August 15, 1934, AIU Algérie ICI. Régnier adds further statistics noting that three Algerian Muslims died, that 150 Jews and two Arabs were wounded, and 150 shops were pillaged. Régnier, "Note sur les massacres de Constantine," CAOM FM 81F/864.

[183] It is impossible to verify, but it is possible that this was the same J. Sebbah who had complained of the Bastos factory's activities. This could potentially indicate an effort at retribution.

Jewish victims of August 5 pogrom, *Dépêche de Constantine*, August 11, 1934, AIU Algérie I C 6-c

The Post-Mortem on the Pogrom: Causes, Responsibilities, and Unequal Rights

Governor-General Carde enumerated the results of the riots in his report: twenty-five Jews had been killed and fifty-eight wounded. Three Muslims were killed and eighty-two were injured. Sixty-three soldiers or policemen were wounded, most of them slightly. One European, who had been mistaken for a Jew, had been killed. Two hundred shops had been pillaged. Two hundred and forty-two arrests were made, of which 187 were detained.[184]

Following the pogrom, the Prefect of Constantine sent mayors and administrators in the department a questionnaire asking them to assess

---

[184] Gov-Gen Carde to the Minister of the Interior, "Report No. 4264," Algiers, October 19, 1934, CAOM Alg GGA 2CAB/3.

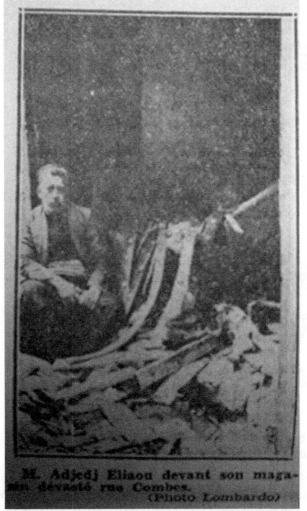

Dépêche de Constantine, August 14, 1934, AIU Algérie I C 6-c

the reasons for the riot based on the opinions of the Muslim population.[185] Of the forty-seven responses reviewed in the archives,

[185] The questionnaire asked, "according to the information collected from native milieu in your commune, was the incident that began the movement (the profanation of a holy Muslim space by a Jew) actually the veritable cause of the riot?" Prefect of Constantine to the Mayors and Administrators of the Department, "No. 5265," Constantine, August 8, 1934, CAOM Alg Const B/3/250.

thirty-five cited the Kalifa incident as the cause of the pogrom. Thirteen of those suggested that the Kalifa incident was merely a pretext, part of a premeditated and well-organized program of violence.[186] Many administrators pointed to usury and Jewish "arrogance" as the sources of Algerian Muslim anger toward the Jews.[187] The administrator of Chateaudun noted that Algerian Muslims in his commune felt that Jews had become too arrogant, treating them "like dogs," and that the Kalifa rumor served as a pretext for violence.[188]

The police commissioner of Khroub had a more nuanced analysis of the causes based on his discussions with Muslims. The long-term cause was the latent hatred of the "Jews" among Muslims. The first cause was the malaise in Algeria caused by the economic crisis, the second cause was the partiality shown by some functionaries in their dispersion of patronage. Although he does not indicate the source of such favoritism, it can be assumed that he implies that Jews were the recipients of such benefits. The report suggests that a further cause was Bendjelloul's political campaign in Constantine. However, the determining factor was the "arrogant attitude of the Jews of Constantine in particular," while the pretext was the "history" of the Jewish soldier, Kalifa.[189] However, the commissioner maintained the party line among administrators that Jews were to blame due to their arrogant or superior attitude demonstrated toward Muslims.

Other administrators pointed to European antisemites' activities in the colony as another cause of the violence. The administrator of Khenchela suggested that European antisemites in the colony exploited Algerian Muslims' frustrations with Jews. After the pogrom, Europeans refused to contribute to funds for the Jewish victims and organized a boycott of

---

[186] Administrative reports in response to the Prefect's questionnaire (August 8, 1934), CAOM Alg Const B/3/250.

[187] The accusation of usury is reflective of the economic crisis' impact on the colony. Usury was a long-standing antisemitic accusation. Administrator of the mixed commune of Ain-Touta to the Prefect of Constantine, "No. 3550: Au sujet des incidents antijuifs des 5 et 7 août," MacMahon, August 21, 1934. Mayor of Bône to the Prefect of Constantine, "No. 11635," Bône, August 18, 1934, CAOM Alg Const B/3/250. See also Administrator of the mixed Commune of Sefia to the Prefect of Constantine, "No. 4193," Laverdure, August 10, 1934, CAOM Alg Const B/3/250.

[188] The administrator of Chateaudun noted a variety of rumors which excited the Algerian Muslims of his commune, including "the Jews burned a mosque," "Algerian Muslim schools were burned, and the children murdered," "Upon arriving in Constantine the Gov-Gen reprimanded M. Morinaud and embraced Dr. Bendjelloul," and "The Algerian Muslims had received the order to ransack but not to steal." Administrator of the Mixed commune of Chateaudun to the Prefect of Constantine, "No. 2645: Au sujet des événements de Constantine," Chateaudun, August 20, 1934, CAOM Alg Const B/3/250.

[189] The Police Commissioner of Khroub to the Gov-Gen, "Rapport Spécial No. 2291," Khroub, August 7, 1934, CAOM Alg GGA 2CAB/3.

Jewish merchants.[190] The administrator argued that Europeans may have incited violence by preying upon the "latent antisemitism of every Muslim." In order to benefit from the attacks.[191] Régnier attributed some responsibility to antisemitic groups, such as the *Action Française*, which produced propaganda on the abrogation of the Crémieux Decree and were likely involved in the organization of the riot.[192] The *Croix de Feu* also participated; its members in Constantine incited the rioters to violence.[193] Many colonial administrators attempted to explain away the riots by citing preexisting Muslim antisemitism. The administrator of the mixed commune of Ain-M'lila wrote that "the Jewish community of Constantine is detested as much by natives as by the great majority of the European element and that the points of friction are numerous."[194] The administrator of the mixed commune of Akbou responded that "the hatred of the Jew is at the heart of every Muslim." He pointed to the unequal rights for Jews and Muslims in the colony as being the central issue.[195]

Colonial administrators agreed that antisemitism and the troubled economic climate were the primary causes of the pogrom. They did not directly attribute the violence to the issue of rights in the colony in part because this implied that the violence could have been avoided if the

[190] Administrator of the mixed commune of Khenchela to the Prefect of Constantine, "No. 5824: Au sujet des incidents antisémites," Khenchela, August 11, 1934, CAOM Alg Const B/3/250.

[191] "Rapport sur les événements qui se sont produits à Khenchela à l'occasion des troubles antisémites de Constantine," Khenchela, August 17, 1934, CAOM Alg Const B/3/250. The administrator of Maadid agreed that Europeans sought to excite the antisemitic sentiment of Muslims, who used the Kalifa incident as a pretext for the August violence. Administrator of the mixed Commune of Maadid to the Prefect of Constantine, "No. 3734: Objet: Surveillance politique des indigènes, au sujet des événements de Constantine," Bourdj-bou-Arreridj, August 14, 1934, CAOM Alg Const B/3/250.

[192] Ibid.

[193] Samuel Kalman, *The Extreme Right in Interwar France: The Faisceau and the Croix de Feu* (Hampshire: Ashgate Publishing Limited, 2008), 216. See also Kalman, *French Colonial Fascism*, 66, 70–71. Kalman cites the case of the Croix de Feu leader named Bagnères, who hoped to "recreate" the August 1934 riot by urging Muslims to attack Jews.

[194] Administrator of the mixed commune of Ain-M'lila to the Prefect of Constantine, "No. 6054: Surveillance des indigènes, émeutes de Constantine du 3 au 5 août," Ain-M'lila, August 14, 1934, CAOM Alg Const B/3/250.

[195] The administrator of Akbou indicated that the comparison of Algerian Muslims and Jews' access to citizenship was a popular subject in newspapers and in conversations. Administrator of the mixed commune of Akbou to the Prefect of Constantine, "No. 37: Au sujet des troubles Constantinois," Akbou, August 15, 1934, CAOM Alg Const B/3/250. The mayor of Akbou suggested that the Jews bullied their Muslim neighbors, and that some Muslims believed that during the violence, "the Jews only got the lesson they deserved." Mayor of Akbou to the Prefect of Constantine, "No. 1265: Rapport sur la repercussion dans la commune, des événements de Constantine," Akbou, August 14, 1934, CAOM Alg Const B/3/250.

inequalities of access to citizenship had been addressed. For the administrator of Sidi-Aich, the pogrom was merely "a revolt of the hubris of the Arab population of Constantine and its surroundings."[196] In the poor economy that plagued the colony, many Algerian Muslims suffered from unemployment and poverty, which only increased their resentment of Jews, whom they saw as prospering.[197]

From these initial reports, it is evident that there were essentially four general causes for the August 5 pogrom: first, the Kalifa incident, seen by some as a pretext for premeditated violence; second, the economic crisis and frustration with perceived Jewish economic success, usury, grain speculation, or a general sense of Jewish superiority; third, antisemitism, built upon secular and religious beliefs, but primarily stemming from social issues, such as the presence of Jews in civil service, in the administration, or in elected positions; and fourth, the sense of unfairness among Muslims regarding their inferior rights.[198] The frustrations resulting from unequal rights melded with antisemitism and were fueled by the influence of Nazism in North Africa and the economic crisis.[199] Although the August 5 pogrom and its precursors are often depicted as the result of interethnic and religious hatred, the issue of access to rights is actually at the heart.

The *Ligue des Droits de l'Homme* (LDH) emphasized the role of unequal rights in its analysis of the August 5 pogrom. According to LDH member Monsieur Deroulède, who served as defense counsel for a Muslim involved in the riots, the lack of Muslim citizenship rights was the central cause of their "discontentment and exasperation." Deroulède hoped that the trials would result in a measure ending the "terrible state of affairs from which the natives of the three Algerian departments suffered."[200] The LDH leaders in Algiers considered the *indigénat* to be a motivating factor for Muslim participation in the violence. The *indigénat* represented the ongoing inequality of Jews and Muslim in the colony.[201]

---

[196] Administrator of the mixed commune of Sidi-Aich, to the Prefect of the Constantine, "No. 7661: Evénements de Constantine," Sidi-Aich, September 11, 1934, CAOM Alg Const B/3/250.

[197] Administrator of the mixed commune of Souk-Ahras to the Prefect of Constantine, "No. 2508: Au sujet des événements de Constantine," Souk-Ahras, August 21, 1934, CAOM Alg Const B/3/250. See also Mayor of the commune of El-Kseur to the Prefect of Constantine, El-Kseur, August 10, 1934, CAOM Alg Const B/3/250.

[198] Bostom, ed., *The Legacy of Islamic Antisemitism*, 51, 150.

[199] Younsi, *Caught in a Colonial Triangle*, 143.

[200] The post-pogrom trials served as the occasion to highlight the administration's "abuses of power committed each day." M. Deroulède, Defense of Boufedjil, "Événements de Constantine," Paris, October 2, 1934, BDIC-LDH F Delta Res 798/169.

[201] Note LDH Algiers to LDH Paris, "Constantine–Pogrome," V/1, November 3, 1934, BDIC-LDH F Delta Res 798/169. On the *indigénat*, see A. I. Asiwaju, "Control

An August 11, 1934, article titled "The Explanation of the Riots of Constantine" in *L'Éclaireur de Nice* connected the recent violence to the allegedly preponderant electoral role of Jews and the Muslims' quest for rights. According to the article, Jews made up 40 percent of the electoral body in Constantine, Ain-Beida, and Sétif, which resulted in the election of French mayors and Jewish deputies and the appointment of many Jews in the police force and in other municipal posts. "A Frenchman is always the leader, but he is encircled by Jewish collaborators who lead him to their bidding . . . In Constantine, they [the Jews] have been the masters for some ten years." The article contrasted the conniving Jews with the patriotic Algerian Muslims and accused Governor-General Carde of supporting Jews at the expense of Arabs.[202] According to the article, assimilated Muslims wanted to be French, but felt it was unfair to require them to give up their personal status.[203] The article, written by an "Algerian" of metropolitan origins and published in the metropole, reflects the degree of interest in the issue of Algerian Muslim rights in France.

Seizing upon the hotly contested issue of rights, Henri Lautier used his newspaper to rally antisemitic sentiments, especially regarding the Crémieux Decree and the alleged large numbers of the Jews in municipal positions. At the end of August 1934, a petition circulated throughout the city of Constantine demanding the abrogation of the Crémieux Decree. It received 1,200 signatures.[204] At the same time, Lautier

---

Through Coercion: A Study of the Indigénat Regime in French West African Administration, 1887–1946," *Bulletin de l'I.F.A.N. T.*, Vol. 41, *ser.* B (1979): 35–71. See also Mann, "What Was the *Indigénat?*," 331–353.

[202] The article stated that "in each incident the Jew is innocent and the Arab imprisoned, thanks to the reports established by the judges, agents of Judaism." "L'explication des émeutes de Constantine," *L'Éclaireur de Nice*, August 11, 1934, CAOM Alg Const B/ 3/687.

[203] The reluctance of Muslim colonial subjects to give up their personal status was not limited to Algeria. Muslim notables in colonial Senegal sought to maintain their personal status and Muslim tribunals. See Dominque Sarr and Richard Roberts, "The Jurisdiction of Muslim Tribunals in Colonial Senegal, 1857–1937" in Kristin Mann and Richard Roberts, eds., *Law in Colonial Africa* (Portsmouth: Heinemann Educational Books, 1991), 131–145. In two years, the author of the article contended, Jews would become the majority in Constantine and in five years, the majority in Algiers and Oran. 'L'explication des émeutes de Constantine,' August 11, 1934, CAOM Alg Const B/3/687.

[204] At the same time a rumor circulated that traces of blood and a chechia, a hat commonly worn by Arabs in North Africa, were discovered along the Boulevard de l'Abime. The rumor accused local Jews of having taken the corpse and cutting it into tiny pieces so as to make it easier to carry. The episode was reminiscent of blood libels. Departmental Security of Constantine, Report No. 2727, "Antisémitisme," Constantine, August 29, 1934, CAOM Alg Const B/3/687.

prepared an article titled "The Battle of Constantine," which reflects the spin that antisemites wished to put on the events: by using the term "battle," the Jewish victims could be conflated with aggressors and the violence could then be explained as self-defense. Lautier also prepared his electoral campaign for the upcoming General Council elections, which he based on the hatred of the Crémieux Decree and made allusions to the pogrom.[205] Sixty-four years following its promulgation, the Crémieux Decree still played a significant role in the politics of the colony.

Regarding the issue of rights, Régnier cited Bendjelloul's failed mission to Paris to lobby for Muslim rights exactly one year before the pogrom as one of its central causes. Minister of the Interior Chautemps refused to grant Bendjelloul and his entourage an audience, which they perceived as an affront. The delegation consisted of "young Turks," who, according to Régnier, endeavored to differentiate themselves from the more conservative "Ulama." The Ulama leadership sought access to citizenship rights without losing personal status, while the Young Turks believed that their personal status should not play such an integral role. Their goal was independence. Régnier linked the meeting at the Pines to the one-year anniversary of the delegation's visit to Paris.[206] However, as other reports indicated, there may have been more cooperation between the reformists and the Ulama leadership than Régnier indicated.

Confino ascribed responsibility to the pan-Islamic movement and to the anti-French sentiment and antisemitism among Algerian Muslim leadership, including Bendjelloul.

Hatred against the French, hatred against the Jews, who became French citizens and enjoy all the privileges that this entails, does one need more to excite the masses against a minority that is envied and hated by the weak of the country? For their leaders, antisemitism has been, if not a determining factor, at least one of the factors that they have been careful not to neglect in their calculations.[207]

Confino accused the colonial administration of blatant antisemitism: "If this had not been a case involving Jews, do you think they would have tolerated such a slaughter?" He noted that although the "stooges" of the pogrom had been arrested and sentenced to several years in prison,

---

[205] Departmental Security of Constantine, Report No. 2727, "Antisémitisme," Constantine, August 29, 1934, CAOM Alg Const B/3/687.
[206] Régnier, "Note sur les massacres de Constantine," CAOM FM 81F/864.
[207] A. Confino to President AIU, Algiers, August 15, 1934, AIU Algérie ICI.

the main architects of the violence, including Bendjelloul, remained free.[208]

Other Algerian Muslim leaders sought to distance their efforts to gain citizenship rights from the violence.[209] Ferhat Abbas argued that tensions emerged because French legislators made Jews citizens, while Muslims remained colonial subjects. The French should have upheld the sénatus-consulte of 1865, he argued, which had equal requirements for Jewish and Muslim naturalization. Some Muslim leaders believed that certain Jews in the administration created obstacles to restrict Muslims from attaining French citizenship and therefore retain their privileged position in the colony.[210] Although Jews were the object of these attacks, their ultimate target was France's unequal standards for colonial citizenship.

As victims of the violence of August 3–5, Jews felt a profound sense of abandonment by the French administration. Monsieur Angel, the director of the Alliance's Constantine school, described how in the climate of escalating antisemitism in the region during and after the pogrom, some Jews chose to leave rather than confront these conditions. "It is a heavy atmosphere in which we live, charged with much sadness."[211]

Premeditation or Spontaneity: The Origins of the Pogrom and the Inaction of the French Administration

The lack of response from the French administration weighed heavily upon the Jewish community in Constantine. Régnier cited the social, psychological, and political toll of the violence and the Jews' sense of abandonment. He quoted a Jewish notable and veteran, who said,

We were targeted for being French, but we see now that we are only poor Jewish refugees. At the most grave moment of our lives, when we were attacked because we are French, we were abandoned by France ... Ah, if the object of this attack had been French "Europeans"! What a violent reaction the authorities would have had. But, the moment it involves the Jews, they find a thousand pretexts to remain passive and to sacrifice the eternal scapegoat. We are the French for the Arabs, and the poor Jews for the French. That is our tragedy.[212]

---

[208] Confino wrote that no one "put a hand on the collar of the truly guilty, on Bendjelloul, who seems to be the soul of the movement." Confino to President AIU, Algiers, August 15, 1934, AIU Algérie ICI.

[209] Younsi, *Caught in a Colonial Triangle*, 159–160.   [210] Ibid, 164–165, 167.

[211] M. Angel, Letter to the President of the AIU, "Oeuvres de Constantine," Constantine, September 30, 1934, AIU Algérie ICI.

[212] Régnier, "Note sur les massacres de Constantine," CAOM FM 81F/864.

Like the veteran cited by Régnier, for Sultan, the pogrom was not just a product of antisemitism; rather it was a premeditated attack on the French authority in Algeria.[213] Even after the pogrom, the French administration continued to ignore the Jewish victims. When Governor-General Carde arrived in Constantine following the pogrom, he did not make an official visit to the victims' families or attend the funerals. This insensitivity on the part of the government, Sultan feared, would send a message of tacit approval to the rioters of August 5.[214] According to the leaders of the LDH, some perpetrators had been arrested and judged; however, many others still remained free, including those who, due to their "inertia or their incapacity, allowed a pogrom, like those known only in Russia, Poland, or the Balkans, to unfold on French land."[215] LDH members and other organizations empathized with Constantine's Jews.[216]

The publication of the Vigouroux report, which blamed Jews for inciting the August 5 violence, sharpened the Jews' sense of betrayal. Sultan accused the report over covering up the failures of the local authorities.[217] Governor-General Carde echoed the findings of the Vigouroux report in his October 1934 assessment. He too blamed the Kalifa incident as the starting point of the violence, and pointed to certain groups of Jews who had been the first to shoot into the crowd of Muslims or pillaged Muslim shops. The rioters' response was unsurprising, Carde continued, as

[213] A. Sultan, Letter to the President of the LDH, Constantine, August 11, 1934, BDIC-LDH F Delta Res 798/169.

[214] Ibid.

[215] The president of the LDH emphasized the premeditated nature of the pogrom and the lack of administration response. To the LDH, the division of labor involved in the pogrom was evidence of its premeditation. The first group consisted of blacksmiths and boilermakers, who broke metal doors, shutters, and safes. The second set included butchers who slit throats, even those of "four year old children." The third category was responsible for finding and destroying account books, documents in portfolios, and deeds. The fourth and final group lacerated fabrics. President LDH to the Minister of the Interior, Paris, August 29, 1934, BDIC-LDH F Delta Res 798/169.

[216] J. Weil, a member of the LDH in Nancy, expressed his concern over the situation and questioned whether French citizens in Algeria, Jews in particular, could count on the protection of the authorities. J. Weil, Nancy, to M. V. Basch, President of the LDH, Paris, Nancy, August 16, 1934, BDIC-LDH F Delta Res 798/169. The LDH president also received a letter from the Red Cross International, written by J. Chauvet, who wrote that perhaps they should send a commission of inquiry of their own to seek out the actual causes of the violence, rather than the official French version which centered on the Kalifa incident. Secours Rouge Internationale, J. Chauvet, Paris, August 28, 1934, BDIC-LDH F Delta Res 798/169.

[217] Vigouroux's report emphasized the "spontaneous," antisemitic nature of the violence. It found Jews guilty of firing gunshots into the crowd at the Place des Galettes and "provoking the pogrom." Police reports, as shown previously, did not reach the same conclusions. A. Sultan, Letter to the President of the LDH, Paris, "Affaire événements de Constantine 5 août 1934," Constantine, February 16, 1935, BDIC-LDH F Delta Res 798/169.

Constantine was "fertile ground with a frustrated population, suffering from the economic crisis, the demands of usurers and hurt by Jewish bullying." Carde explained away the violence and "murderous frenzy" shown by the rioters as characteristics of their "race" and a result of "religious excitation." Carde belittled the accusations made by Jewish leaders of administrative failure. "France was not absent for six hours, during which the riot was the sovereign mistress of the city," he wrote.[218]

Carde defended the actions of the Secretary-General of the Prefecture, but criticized his failure in not anticipating the violence of August 5. Carde believed that troops should have already been in place – and removed M. Landel as a result of this oversight. He emphasized that the local administrators should have been more cognizant of the deterioration of relations between Jews and Muslims.[219] However, Carde commended the actions of the troops and asserted that the Jewish quarter had been well defended, and if it had not, the number of Jewish deaths would have been much higher.[220]

In contrast, the LDH and Jews were convinced that the pogrom was premeditated. A group of Jews wrote to a Constantine judge, "the Constantine Jewish population is convinced that the massacre, of which they were the victims, is a crime that was premeditated well before the incident at the Sidi-Lakhdar Mosque. The murders, pillage, and robbery of which the Jews were the object seem to be the result of an anti-French campaign." The authors pointed to evidence of premeditation. For example, on August 1, a Muslim tradesman emptied his store of the majority of his merchandise, under the pretext of cleaning.[221] Régnier agreed that "the Constantine pogrom was premeditated, organized, and executed with a method and a system to which the Arabs are generally not

---

[218] Gov-Gen Carde to the Minister of the Interior, "Report No. 4264," Algiers, October 19, 1934, CAOM Alg GGA 2CAB/3.

[219] Carde did maintain Vigouroux's conclusions that Jews were in large part responsible for setting off the riots by their actions in the Place des Galettes. Ibid.

[220] Ibid.

[221] They gave other examples, such as Madame Soliveres, who declared in a police statement that the Arab butchers on Rue Combes told her eight days before the troubles began that Jews would be the victims of a massacre. "Un Group de JUIFS à M. le Juge d'Instruction, Constantine," Constantine, August 11, 1934, included in a letter from the Prefect of Constantine to the Commander of the Gendarmerie, No. 5466, Constantine, August 16, 1934, CAOM Alg Const B/3/250. The police in Constantine followed up on the information included in the letter of August 11, and interviewed relevant witnesses. See Brigade de Constantine, No. 3880, "Témoin KRIEF Simon," Constantine, August 29, 1934, CAOM Alg Const B/3/250. See also R. Adt-chef Touret, 19e Légion, 3e Compagnie, Section de Constantine, Brigades de Constantine, No. 3880, "Procès Verbal: de renseignements sur la prétendue préméditation de l'élément musulman dans les troubles antisémites (Enquête administrative)," Constantine, August 30, 1934, CAOM Alg Const B/3/250.

accustomed," leading him to believe that the violence was the result of cooperation or direction by another group, likely the Europeans. The rioters, he argued, seemed well informed regarding Jewish owned houses and shops.[222]

The blame game flourished as the different parties involved held the others liable for the slow and inadequate response to the violence on August 5. The Chief of the Departmental Security of Constantine emphatically denied Mayor Morinaud's accusation that he and the Prefectural Authorities did not respond to the signs of preparation and "lacked energy" in their response once the violence began. Morinaud and others suggested that there was evidence, such as the closure of certain Muslim-owned shops in advance of the violence, or the fact that the riots occurred on the anniversary of Bendjelloul's delegation's failed visit to the Minister of the Interior in 1933. The Chief denied that he knew that Bendjelloul had declared that "the next August 5, we will show them what we are worth!" The report stated that while the French population of Constantine celebrated the pillage of Jewish shops by the rioters, they deplored the death of children and women. They would not, however, offer reparations to the victims of the violence, arguing that it was the responsibility of the Jewish community to support its own.[223]

In his report, the Chief of Departmental Security asserted that the violence was a direct response to the fact that a Muslim had been shot by a Jew – something he witnessed himself. He stressed that other Muslims claimed that a Jewish police officer had shot at the crowd of Muslims and that other Jews had followed suit.[224] This report indicates that there was a wide range of interpretations on the cause of the violence and on the responsibility of the administration.

Although nongovernmental reports are nearly unanimous that the Constantine pogrom was premeditated, they were less certain of who was behind it. Some blamed Bendjelloul; others looked to Émile Morinaud, the suspiciously absent mayor of Constantine, who had a strong antisemitic background.[225] Maurice Eisenbeth, the Chief Rabbi of Constantine, believed that Morinaud was behind the pogrom: "for those who know the politics practiced by this man, this could not be surprising." Eisenbeth concluded that "the power of Morinaud constitutes a real

---

[222] Régnier, "Note sur les massacres de Constantine," CAOM FM 81F/864. Confino's report included testimonies similar to those included in Régnier's report, which describe certain indications of premeditation. See A. Confino to President AIU, Algiers, August 15, 1934, AIU Algérie ICI.

[223] Chief of the Departmental Security of Constantine, "Report No. 2453: Antisémitisme," Constantine, August 8, 1934, CAOM Alg GGA 2CAB/3.

[224] Ibid.   [225] For more on his activities, see Chapters 1 and 2.

danger, not only for our coreligionists, but also for French sovereignty in North Africa." He added that should Morinaud be removed from power, Jewish–Muslim relations would automatically improve.[226] The deputy of Constantine, Paul Cuttoli, who owed his elected position in part to Jewish voters, added his voice to the criticisms of the police's failure to intervene. Cuttoli noted that in the months prior to the pogrom, he and others had been warned of the mounting frustrations of Algerian Muslims. Like many Jewish leaders, Cuttoli pondered "if this aggression had been directed against the *français d'origine*, would we have left them to be slaughtered under the indifferent watch of the armed forces?" He concluded that Algerian Jews deserved the same treatment as *français d'origine* in the colony because they too "are French and need to be protected in the same way as all citizens."[227] Cuttoli argued that antisemitism was the motivating force behind the lack of administrative response during the violence.

Following the violence, a noted Jewish leader in Constantine, André Bakhouche, reported on antisemitism among the *tirailleurs indigènes* (Algerian Muslim soldiers), whose actions also indicated premeditation. On Saturday, August 4, the *tirailleurs indigènes* in the garrison in Constantine hid their weapons in order to retrieve them later that night and escape over the walls of the barracks to join the rioters. According to Bakhouche, although some 400 *tirailleurs* arrived to halt the riots, many actually participated in the violence: some collected fallen clubs and handed them to rioters. A police officer arrested two *tirailleurs indigènes* ransacking a Jewish apartment.[228] Bakhouche blamed the French administration, particularly the military leadership, for the casualties and damages of the riot. In the aftermath of August 1934, a small number of Algerian Jews moved to the metropole; others turned to Zionism and Palestine.

Many Jews and Muslims reiterated the rote belief that their two communities had lived in perfect harmony before the arrival of the French colonists.[229] Immediately following the violence, Muslim leaders, among them Bendjelloul, published a proclamation decrying the pogrom in *La*

---

[226] Maurice Eisenbeth, "Rapport de M. Eisenbeth sur le rôle de M. Morinaud dans les événements de Constantine," Constantine, November 21, 1934, AIU Algérie ICI. This same letter was sent on to the Sec-Gen of the LDH by the National Committee for Aid for German Refugees Victims of Antisemitism on December 17, 1934, BDIC-LDH F Delta Res 798/63.

[227] Cuttoli wrote that "Algeria wants to know what the Government will do to protect all those who seek the shelter of the French flag." Cuttoli, Deputy of Constantine, to the Gov-Gen of Algeria, October 8, 1934, AIU Algérie ICI.

[228] André Bakhouche to the Sec-Gen of the AIU, "No. 8220/3," Constantine, August 27, 1934, AIU Algérie ICI.

[229] See, for example, Bahloul, *The Architecture of Memory*.

Voix Indigène. They stated that "the sane population of Constantine deplores the riots and their monstrous excesses." The authors emphasized their willing collaboration with Jewish leaders and French administrators and spoke out against the ensuing boycotts of Jewish shops. "It is criminal to allow the regrettable events of August to degenerate into a war of races with an economic point of view." The proclamation concluded with the hope that "the past be forgotten, the future envisioned ... for the greatest prestige of France." Muslim leaders tried to appease not only Jewish concerns but also the French administration's fears of an insurrection led by Algerian Muslim nationalists.[230]

Soon after the violence, Bendjelloul and other Muslim elected officials met with Governor-General Carde. Bendjelloul declared his and his fellow Muslim leaders' deep sadness at the events and reassured French officials of their "profound attachment to our Mother country and to the Republic." The governor-general reported that he accepted their efforts but urged them to refrain from promoting further dangerous propaganda among their ranks. He also warned that should similar events occur and if Muslim leaders did not intervene to calm their coreligionists, the repression would be far more intense.[231]

Carde then met with Jewish representatives. The meeting was less conciliatory. Jewish leaders demanded that Carde bring justice to the victims of violence and destruction of property. Earlier in his report, while Carde identified the role of propaganda among Muslim leaders as a key cause in the violence, he also blamed Jews, who also "committed many blunders." Carde also urged the Jewish leaders to demand calm among their coreligionists and cautioned them that even though in Constantine "they found themselves in safety under the shield of bayonets" if the provocations and violence continued throughout the colony, "I would be helpless, due to a lack of resources, to curb unrest before there were many victims." Jewish leaders assured him that they would demand calm and peace.[232]

For his part, Régnier suggested that the machinations of European antisemites destroyed the natural harmony between Jews and Muslims in colony. "The antisemitic movement in Algeria did not come from the Arabs; it is the work of reactionary French." As evidence, Régnier quoted a relative of the murdered Halimi family on the issue of Jewish–Muslim coexistence: "Our home has been here for forty years

[230] Elected Muslim Officials, "Proclamation," in *La Voix Indigène*, August 16, 1934, AIU Algérie IC6-c.
[231] Gov-Gen Carde to the Minister of the Interior, "Dépêche Télégraphique," Algiers, August 9, 1934, CAOM Alg GGA 2CAB/3.
[232] Ibid.

and we have never had even the smallest misunderstanding with the natives."[233] That harmony, however tenuous, ended with the violence of the pogrom.

Jews in Algiers expected the violence to spill over from Constantine, even though administrators were hopeful that it would not.[234] The leaders of the Jewish consistory of Constantine sent a telegram to their colleagues in Algiers alerting them to the plans for the funeral for the Jewish victims of the Constantine violence. The Algiers consistory informed its adherents that they should not close their shops as a sign of mourning, but that prayers for the victims would be said in all synagogues in Algiers on August 11. They also called upon their followers to avoid all provocations. The President of *Fédération des Élus Musulmans* of Algiers, Mehieddine Zerrouk, along with Cheik Tayeb el Okby, similarly warned their coreligionists to avoid all possible conflicts with Jews – even though some Muslims in Algiers wanted to protest the military presence, especially that of the *tirailleurs sénégalais*, in Constantine. Jews and Muslims in Algiers continued to discuss the events of Constantine. Indeed, the Chief of Departmental Security in Algiers reported an altercation between a Jew and a Muslim who were arguing over the situation of Constantine.[235] Members of the Jewish consistory in Algiers met with the Secretary-General of the Prefecture to demand his assurance that measures would be taken in order to avoid similar violence in their city.[236] Jewish youth in Algiers bought weapons, nearly emptying the stores of gunsmiths.[237]

Despite the presence of the military, looting and violence continued in the Constantine department. On August 6, the day of the weekly market of Jemmapes, a group of Muslims looted the fabric store of Abraham Guedj, a Jewish merchant. Guedj, and other Jewish merchants, managed to close their shops before more damage was done. When two police officers attempted to apprehend one of the pillagers and bring him to the police headquarters, a group of Muslims began to throw items at them and attacked one of the officers. Looting continued in Jemmapes and

---

[233] Régnier, "Note sur les massacres de Constantine," CAOM FM 81F/864.
[234] Chief of Department Security, Algiers, "Report No. 4529," Algiers, August 6, 1934, CAOM Alg GGA 2CAB/3.
[235] Chief of Department Security, Algiers, "Report No. 4559," Algiers, August 8, 1934, CAOM Alg GGA 2CAB/3.
[236] Confino to the President of the AIU, No. 8189, Algiers, August 8, 1934, AIU Algérie ICI. The president of the Jewish Consistory in Bône, Benabu, sent a telegram to the Gov-Gen, expressing the Jewish community's fear for the safety in the aftermath of the August 5 violence. Benabu to the Gov-Gen, in Gov-Gen to the Prefect of Constantine, "No. 3365," Algiers, August 23, 1934, CAOM Alg Const B/3/250.
[237] Régnier, "Note sur les massacres de Constantine," CAOM FM 81F/864.

throughout the department, despite the efforts of the local police and administration to stop it.[238]

Looting also spread to the countryside. Two Jewish farms, belonging to Daniel and Elie Dokhan, were looted. Albert Dokhan recounted, "Forty natives came to attack me. They ransacked the farm. As you realize, everything has been looted. The furniture in my private apartment was destroyed or taken. Myself, they wanted to grind me in the harvester. I was saved by one of my servants." The looters took flour from Dokhan and the police report details those found in possession of the stolen grain. One of them declared that "when we saw that Elie Dokhan's grain was being taken, we wanted to take our part."[239] This attack reflects an economic element at play. In September 1934, Jews in Constantine distributed weapons among the Jewish community.[240] These grassroots-organized efforts to prepare Jewish self-defense indicate that Jews felt they could not count on the administration to defend them in cases of future violence.

As Jewish communities prepared self-defense, antisemitism escalated throughout the colony. In October, Bakhouche reported that the anti-semitic newspapers *L'Éclair* and *Le Tam-Tam*, as well as the reactionary *L'Opinion Libre*, threw "oil on the fire." Boycotts of Jewish shops increased under the leadership of Mozabite merchants, who saw Jews as their main economic competitors. Young Algerian Muslims received payment to prevent any non-Jews from patronizing Jewish-owned shops. Bakhouche wrote that local authorities did nothing to stop the boycotts as they also had vested interest in reducing Jewish economic power.[241] The slogan of the boycott read, "To have the Jew, not a penny to the Jew."[242] Sergeant Chief Perrier reported on the growing tension between Jews and Muslims in his district of Algiers. His forces overheard Algerian Muslims threatening that "in some time, there won't be a Jew left in Aumale," and "the Jews should not be among the

---

[238] Chief of Mobile Brigade of Philippeville, "Rapport Spécial No. 1051: Jemmapes: Troubles antisémitiques," Philippeville, August 8, 1934, CAOM Alg GGA 2CAB/3.

[239] Chief of Mobile Brigade of Ain-Beida, "Rapport Spécial No. 523: Troubles antisémites: Pillage des fermes Dokhan Daniel et Dokhan Elie," Ain-Beida, August 11, 1934, CAOM Alg GGA 2CAB/3.

[240] Central Commissioner Constantine to the Prefect, No, 5791, Constantine, September 13, 1934, CAOM Alg Const B/3/250. See Central Commissioner of Constantine to the Prefect, No. 5991, "Armes vendues à Israélites," Constantine, September 18, 1934, CAOM Alg Const B/3/250. Jews elsewhere in the colony also bought large quantities of weapons. Administrator of Azazga to the Sub Prefect of Tizi-Ouzou, "No. 3988: Surveillance politique des indigènes," Azazga, August 22, 1934, CAOM Alg Alger 2i/38.

[241] André Bakhouche, "Lettre adressée par M. André Bakhouche à M. Confino, Representant de l'Alliance Israélite à Alger," Constantine, October 3, 1934, AIU Algérie ICI.

[242] Confino to the President of the AIU, Algiers, October 17, 1934, AIU Algérie ICI. See also Confino to the President of the AIU, Algiers, October 5, 1934, AIU Algérie ICI.

functionaries."[243] These comments reflect the centrality of unequal rights in the deteriorating Jewish–Muslim relations in the colony.

The electoral period of October 1934 was marked by increasing anti-semitism among candidates, some of whom were members of the *Croix de Feu*. Monsieur Angel, of the Alliance, feared that Jews would not vote in the election.[244] In the end, Constantine Jews voted for several Republican candidates. Angel's report reflects the continued importance of the Jewish vote and the general significance of the right to vote in the colony – a right still out of reach for Algerian Muslims.

Encore: Sétif, 1935

The intensification in antisemitic activity following the Constantine pogrom led to a recrudescence of anti-Jewish violence in Sétif in February 1935. The atmosphere at the times of the General Council elections in October 1934 and the Financial Delegation in January/February 1935 showed the continued frustrations of the Algerian Muslims. Even though the candidates of the Muslim reform party were elected to the General Council as well as two seats on the Financial Delegation, tensions regarding eligibility to vote and Muslims rights mounted. The 1935 report on the political situation in Algeria commented that the "political results of these elections are less harmful than their psychological and social consequences. The election campaign, in fact, was conducted with bitterness and a particular violence, and has deeply shaken the public peace in the douars." Propaganda urged Muslim voters to vote for the reformists, which would be a vote for Islam. Such statements appeared alongside others that suggested a vote for candidates loyal to France would be like voting for Jews. The report sums up the nature of propaganda aimed at Muslim voters as follows: "to vote for the outbound lists, is to vote for the Administration, which is sharply dependent on the Jews."[245]

On February 1, *tirailleurs indigènes* and some civilians attacked Jewish shops and threw stones at the windows of Jewish homes in Sétif. Although Jews were the primary victims of the soldiers, the rioters also attacked

---

[243] Sergeant Chief Perrier, "No 4/4: Objet: État d'esprit des Indigènes," CAOM Alg Alger 2i/38.
[244] Angel to the President of the AIU, Paris, "No. 8318/3: Oeuvres de Constantine," Constantine, October 19, 1934, AIU Algérie, ICI. Angel noted that although not elected, Lautier received 129 votes in the suburbs. In the same district, M. Valle was elected, due to the votes of Jews, with 1,152 votes, while his antisemitic competitor, M. Rival, received 910 votes. Although the antisemitic candidate was not elected, these figures indicate that many voters still voted for antisemitic leaders.
[245] President of the Ministers' Council care of the Minister of the Interior, "Situation politique en Algérie," 14–15, May 10, 1935, CAOM GGA 2CAB/3.

Europeans. After killing a police officer, the *tirailleurs indigènes* yelled that they had to kill "all the French," not specifically the Jews. Patrols of European soldiers halted the violence. The Sétif riot occurred after Ferhat Abbas' election to the General Council. Abbas later played a critical role in Algeria's war of independence, serving as the nation's first president. The Sub-Prefect of Sétif linked Muslim nationalism led by Abbas to the antisemitic movement in the region led by Monsieur Masselot. "Through the method of troubling the peace, the so-called super-French meet in a perfect union with the efforts of the anti-French."[246] Unlike Constantine, where the links between European antisemites and Algerian Muslims were tenuous, Sétif demonstrated cooperation between the two groups.

In his capacity as General Council member, Abbas submitted his own report on the events of Sétif. Abbas explained the violence as originating from an argument between a drunken *tirailleur indigène* named Massaoud Saoula and a police officer, which resulted in Saoula's death. A false rumor spread that a Jewish police officer killed Saoula. Soon, a group of *tirailleurs*, assisted by civilians, attacked Jewish-owned cafés. Abbas wrote that Algerian soldiers did not ransack any Jewish shops with the exception of two Jewish-owned cafés, where the *tirailleurs* often went to drink. Abbas emphasized the harmony between Jews and Muslims, but added that money was the one source of conflict between the two groups – an obvious allusion to complaints of usury and economic competition on the part of Jews.[247] However, these were only minor issues. The deeper cause of the violence of Sétif was the inequalities of access to rights in the colony.

Abbas described a malaise among Algerian Muslims that could be improved only by the "emancipation" of Algeria.[248] In June 1935, Abbas responded to the LDH's accusations that he was an antisemite and involved in the activities of the *Croix de Feu*. In his defense, Abbas emphasized the inequality of Jewish–Muslim rights in the colony and the fact that Algerian Muslims did not have any rights as citizens. "I am careful not to profess this doctrine for the simple reason that, having

---

[246] Sub-Prefect of the Arrondissement of Sétif to the Prefect of Constantine, "No. 66C, Confidential," Sétif, February 7, 1935, CAOM Alg Const B/3/656. See also "Rapport d'autopsie de l'agent Colas, tué le 1er février 1935 à Sétif," CAOM Alg Const B/3/656.

[247] The rioters yelled at the police attempting to stop them, shouting, "Are we dogs? Are we not children of the flag? Why do you shoot at us?" Abbas suggested that the actual problem lay in the fluctuating population of Sétif as well as the powerful influence of unregulated prostitution. Ferhat Abbas, "Rapport de Monsieur Ferhat Abbas, Conseiller General de Sétif, sur les événements du premier février 1935," Sétif, February 8, 1935, CAOM Alg Const B/3/656. Kalman identifies the antisemitism of the Front Paysan as key influence here, as the Front Paysan emphasized the economic culpability of Jews in the depression. Kalman, *French Colonial Fascism*, 86–87.

[248] Ferhat Abbas, "Rapport de M. Ferhat Abbas, Conseiller Général de Sétif sur la politique général de la France en Algérie," Sétif, March 7, 1935, CAOM Alg Const B/3/656.

myself suffered racial prejudice, I cannot do the same to the Jewish minority."[249] Abbas pointed to the fact that with their electoral power, Jews could bring sympathetic politicians to power, whereas Muslims would always be the victims of whims of elected officials because of their lack of electoral rights. Once again, unequal rights were at the root of Jewish–Muslim conflict.

Developments in Palestine exacerbated the already tenuous relationship, as did evolving political ideologies among Algerian Muslim leaders. The machinations of European antisemites provided additional tensions. The distance between Jews and Muslims in the colony widened in the 1920s and 1930s, as Jews became more involved in municipal governments while Muslims became acutely aware of their own lack of rights. Although Jews were not themselves responsible for the lack of Algerian Muslim rights, they became the victims of that frustration. As a result of the antisemitism of the French administration, Jews became the victims of Algerian Muslim colonial subjects' anti-colonial frustrations. The issue of rights remains central to the history of the Constantine pogrom in 1934, the riots in Sétif in 1935, and the development of the Muslim independence movement in Algeria, which accelerated during that time.

Efforts by the Popular Front to improve the rights of Algerian Muslims met with resistance from antisemites who challenged Léon Blum's government in the second half of the 1930s. After 1936, antisemites across the Mediterranean once again united against the political threat posed by Jews. Algerian Jews faced increased antisemitism in the colony as they discovered that their rights were intertwined with those of Algerian Muslims. As antisemites and *colons* combated Blum's attempts to give Algerian Muslims greater rights, they once again looked to their perpetual foe: Algerian Jewish citizenship.

---

[249] Ferhat Abbas, General Council Member, to the Prefect of Constantine, Sétif, June 25, 1935, CAOM Alg Const B/3/656.

5 The Popular Front, Algerian Nationalism, and Evolving Institutional Antisemitism, 1935–1940

In the years preceding the Constantine Pogrom of 1934, Jews in Algeria began to see the rewards of their assimilationist efforts. The most assimilated found employment in liberal professions, civil service, universities, and elected positions in municipal governments. After the pogrom, however, increasing institutional antisemitism in the colonial and municipal government eroded Algerian Jews' improved status. Not only had their Algerian Muslim neighbors attacked them, the French administration had forsaken them by failing to act in a timely and effective manner to protect them. In the years between the pogrom and the era of Vichy, the tone and tenor of antisemitism in the colony intensified, as antisemitic European leaders once again called upon the *néos* to serve as foot soldiers.

In the late 1930s, electoral antisemitism reached new heights. Municipal governments systematically removed Algerian Jews from electoral lists. Violence erupted between Jews and European antisemitic league members. The 1930s in Algeria witnessed a revival of many of the antisemitic tactics used by municipal governments in the 1890s. The election of the Popular Front in 1936 became a lightning rod for mounting antisemitism in the metropole and the colony. Antisemitism and hatred of the Popular Front united various right-wing groups in the colony and metropole.[1] Hitler's consolidation of power in Germany and beyond encouraged antisemitic activities in the colony.

In the climate of the depression and Hitler's rise to power, the population was primed for the appeal of antisemitism. Antisemitism and political competition coalesced in a night of violence in Paris on February 6, 1934, led by right-wing, antisemitic organizations in response to the newly formed government of Edouard Daladier. Members of the militant *Action Française* (AF) and *Croix de Feu* (CF) were active in the February violence.[2] These groups, together with Jacques Doriot's *Parti Populaire Français* (PPF), founded in 1934, shared a hatred of the Jewish Léon

---

[1] Kalman, *The Extreme Right in Interwar France*, 199.
[2] Julian Jackson, *The Popular Front in France: Defending Democracy, 1934–1938* (Cambridge: Cambridge University Press, 1988), 1, 22.

Blum and his Popular Front government.[3] These groups found fertile ground in Algeria, where antisemitism was already deeply embedded in daily and political life. As the Constantine Pogrom raged, French organizations such as the AF and PPF garnered new members in Algeria. The late 1930s witnessed both intensified electoral antisemitism and revitalized Jewish defense in Algeria. In the aftermath of the Constantine Pogrom, the Comité Algérien d'Études Sociales (CAES) collaborated with metropolitan organizations such as the *Ligue des Droits de l'Homme* (LDH) and the *Ligue Internationale Contre l'Antisémitisme* (LICA) to confront political antisemitism in the colony. Throughout the 1910s and 1920s the consistory warned against taking bold, public actions against antisemitism. By the 1930s the consistory leadership finally took steps to protect Jews. The Alliance Israélite Universelle continued its activist role in Algeria, and its Algiers representative, Albert Confino, helped to reorganize the CAES in 1937. In order to confront the new extremes of institutional antisemitism, Algerian Jews developed their arsenal of defense methods and began to reach outside their immediate circle for assistance. This chapter reinserts the history of municipal antisemitism into existing histories of Algeria during this period.

The late 1930s represented a formative period in the development of competing political philosophies in the colony. The rise and fall of the Popular Front and its efforts to improve Algerian Muslim rights in the colony met with significant challenges by Algeria's increasingly antisemitic and fascist leagues. Opposition to the Popular Front was expressed in various ways, including antisemitism and rejection of Muslim rights. In Algeria, these trends played out within municipal governments.

The Communist Party spawned two very different and often competing organizations. On the one hand, Jacques Doriot, formerly a leader of the colonial section of the French Communist Party (PCF), founded the fascist *Parti populaire Français* (PPF). On the other hand, Messali Hadj and other Muslim Communists formed the independence-oriented *Étoile Nord Africaine* (ENA). Both groups protested the work of the Popular Front in Algeria.

Jacques Doriot began his political career in the Communist Youth, becoming one of the most popular leaders of the organization. In 1936, a journalist described him as "the living incarnation in France of the man with a dagger clenched between his teeth."[4] Doriot's efforts in the Communist Party in the 1920s focused on the battle against war and

[3] Jackson, *The Popular Front in France*, 251.
[4] Gilbert D. Allardyce, "The Political Transition of Jacques Doriot," *Journal of Contemporary History*, Vol. 1, No. 1 (1966): 56.

imperialism. The year 1929 marked a turning point for Doriot as he clashed with the party's leadership and became increasingly cynical about the party's goals and methods. When he was elected mayor of Saint Denis in 1931, his popularity grew. From 1929 to 1934, Doriot became increasingly distant from the party's leadership.[5] Leaders in Moscow of the Communist International pushed members of the party away from his leadership. Doriot believed that French Communists needed to follow a French path. When the Popular Front formed in July 1935, it was associated with the Soviet pact and therefore was in opposition to Doriot's previous campaign for peace. Doriot endeavored to distance the Popular Front from the Soviet Union, or to decrease popular support for the Popular Front. In the process, Doriot became increasingly nationalistic. Upon its formation on June 28, 1936, the PPF developed a form of France-centered "peace fascism" – a mix of the battle of the classes, the power of the crowd, and a willingness to fight for their goals. After Doriot took leadership of the PPF in 1936, he shifted further to the right.[6]

Even as it distanced itself from Doriot, the PCF also found itself in a complex position as it related to the question of Algerian independence. At first the Section Française de l'Internationale Ouvrière (SFIO) and the PCF were largely indifferent to the colonial question. The PCF initially found support in Algeria among the Europeans of the colony, especially those of non-French origin who were the working poor. These supporters of the PCF were opposed to the anticolonial stance of some Algerian Muslim adherents. The Sidi-Bel-Abbès manifesto of 1922, which called for the end of colonialism, created tension within the PCF. Historian Emmanuel Sivan argues that the PCF's "sacrosanct myth" of the proletarian revolution was entirely in opposition to the desires of the majority of its members, the Europeans of the colony.[7]

Some communists who called for an independent Algeria formed the *Étoile Nord Africaine* (ENA) in 1926 and recruited members from among Algerian workers in the metropole. In 1927, a schism formed between those who followed the anticolonial orientation that demanded an independent Algeria and its more right-leaning members. The split increased when the French government cracked down on communism in the late

---

[5] Allardyce, "The Political Transition," 57–59. See also Gilbert Allardyce and Andrée R. Picard, "Jacques Doriot et l'esprit fasciste en France," *Revue d'histoire de la Deuxième Guerre mondiale, 25e Année*, No. 97 (Visages de fascistes français) (1975): 34–36.

[6] Allardyce, "The Political Transition," 68–74. See also Allardyce and Picard, "Jacques Doriot," 32.

[7] Emmanuel Sivan, *Communisme et nationalisme en Algérie, 1920–1962* (Paris: Presses de la foundation nationale des sciences politiques, 1976), 21–23, 27, 40.

1920s.[8] In 1929, the colonial question was no longer part of the agenda at the PCF's congress. The ENA eventually distanced itself from the PCF in 1933 and joined the socialist and revolutionary Left. In February 1934, it joined the Popular Front. However, the Popular Front's efforts at improving Muslim rights in the colony did not meet the demands of the developing nationalism of the ENA.[9] Algerian nationalism strengthened in response to the realization that the French colonial government would not bring equal rights for Algerian Muslims.

The shifts in the PCF and the organization of the ENA were further complicated by the Constantine pogrom. Jews were active members of the Communist Party in Algeria. Many, such as Constantine Jewish Communist leader Lucien Sportisse, had joined because of a sense of solidarity with Algerian Muslims' condition in the colony. They were shocked by the events of August 1934 and the fact that their perceived comrades had attacked them. Sportisse seemed baffled by the violence against him and his coreligionists, as well as the lack of intervention by the PCF. Some leaders of the PCF, such as Albert Ferrat, even suggested that the pogrom was a good sign that Algerian Muslims were rising up against their oppressors. Sportisse suggested that the PCF leadership was unprepared by the rise of antisemitism and feared cutting themselves off from their supporters.[10] As antisemitism continued to develop in the colony in the late 1930s, Jewish communists became unsure of their place between the PCF and the ENA.

In the Aftermath of the Pogrom: Jewish Electors, *Croix de Feu*, and Elections in 1935

Following the pogrom, Algerian Jews, Muslims, *néos*, right-wing groups, and Popular Front supporters jockeyed for power and influence. Soon after the Sétif riots, Simon Bakhouche complained that the colonial administration refused to acknowledge the anti-French and anticolonial aspects of these cases, attributing the violence to antisemitism.[11] In March 1935, Jewish representatives in Constantine echoed Bakhouche in their letter to the Minister of the Interior. They argued that Algerian Muslims had been influenced by external forces, such as

---

[8] Jacques Simon, *Le PPA (Le Partie du people algérien), 1937–1947* (Paris: L'Harmattan, 2005), 13. Sivan, *Communisme et nationalisme*, 47–48, 50, 54–55.

[9] Sivan, *Communisme et nationalisme*, 65–68, 72–73.

[10] Sivan, *Communisme et nationalisme*, 79–80. Ferrat depicted Jews in Algeria as the "quartermasters of imperialism." Planche, "Le Parti communiste d'Algérie et la question nationale au temps du Congrès musulman et du Front populaire," 20, 22.

[11] Simon Bakhouche to the Chief Rabbi of France, Constantine, February 7, 1935, AIU Algérie ICI.

Hitler's propaganda, the situation in Palestine, the action of antisemitic groups, and the anti-Jewish press in Algeria. Extensive poverty made Muslims particularly susceptible to such rhetoric. "On this Algerian land, continuation of France, no one can be permitted to create discord, hatred, or to set one group against another, the inhabitants of one country, the servants of one flag, all sons of one *Patrie*."[12] The Jewish leaders urged the government to take action.

The Jewish representatives described the impact of the boycott of Jewish shops. They believed it was organized by Hitler's agents in the colony.[13] Most Jews in Constantine were very poor, still living in dilapidated ghettos. Those who could afford the modest rent of the municipally controlled housing projects, the *Habitations à Bon Marché*, moved out of the ghetto.[14] Given the poverty among Constantine's Jews, the boycott motivated some Jews to move to France or to less antisemitic regions of Algeria. Local Jewish politician Henri Lellouche reported that contrary to antisemitic rhetoric, Jews were not overrepresented in public employment. In fact, in Constantine, the municipal government employed no Jews as electricians, city-cleaners, in gas works, and with electric trams.[15] At the municipal casino, there was only one Jewish employee out of fifty. Jews, who constituted 12 percent of Constantine's population, held only 12 percent of the administrative positions in the municipality.[16]

Jewish leaders in Sétif also presented their concerns to the minister. They depicted a long history of Jewish–Muslim cooperation and unity based on shared traditions and morals and blamed the recent tensions on the influence of "criminal agitators," who used the press and politics to their advantage. As a result, the Jews in Sétif "live in the uncertainty of the hour … Profoundly French, in this land of Africa, extension of the metropole, we want to live in the shadow of the tricolor flag in security of property and persons that should be conferred to all Algerians."[17] The minister responded that the Jews of Algeria could count upon the government to prevent renewals of violence. He assured the representatives that he would personally ensure the security of each French citizen.[18]

---

[12] Alliance Jewish delegation to the Minister of the Interior, March 10, 1935, AIU Algérie ICI.
[13] Ageron, *L'Algérie Algérienne*, 168.
[14] Maurice Eisenbeth, *Les Juifs de l'Afrique du Nord: Démographie & Onomastique* (Alger: Imprimerie de Lycée, 1936), 39.
[15] Angel to President of the AIU, "Déclaration des Élus de Constantine," Constantine, March 15, 1935, AIU Algérie ICI.
[16] Alliance Jewish delegation to the Minister of the Interior, March 10, 1935, AIU Algérie ICI.
[17] Angel to President of the AIU, Constantine, March 15, 1935, AIU Algérie ICI.
[18] "Déclaration des Élus de Constantine," Constantine, March 15, 1935, AIU Algérie ICI.

In response to demands for legislation regulating antisemitic propaganda, Marcel Régnier, former Minister of the Interior and author of the eponymous report from 1934, submitted a decree that would punish demonstrations against French sovereignty or attempts at creating racial discord. It included a stipulation that if the offender was a functionary, the punishment would be doubled, and that the offender would be banned from public service for five to ten years.[19] The fact that the Régnier Decree was enacted only in Algeria and carried a harsh penalty for functionaries reflects Régnier's assessment of French administrators' guilt in the Constantine pogrom.[20]

Despite the government's calming rhetoric and decrees, the Alliance, headed by Albert Confino in Algiers, prompted Jewish self-defense.[21] Confino feared that the growing popularity of Zionism in the colony might undermine France's willingness to protect Algerian Jews and could depreciate their status as Frenchmen. Another Alliance member, Sylvain Levi, urged Confino to "warn our brethren against the spirit of nationalism that would likely have us alienate the sympathies of the metropole."[22] Zionism, however, remained peripheral among Algerian Jews. Of greater concern was the continued assimilation and education of Algerian Jews. Confino expressed his frustration that the Jews of Constantine were not as "evolved" as Jewish communities in Algiers and Oran and continued to resist French as their new language.[23] In September 1935, Jews in Constantine established the "Society for the Reeducation of the Jewish Population of Constantine."[24] The Society attacked traditions that made Jews appear backward or uncivilized.[25] The Society was strongly influenced by the Alliance's work in cultivating Algerian Jews as Frenchmen and women and saw assimilation as

[19] Decree of March 30, 1935 (Decret Régnier), CAOM FM 81F/864.

[20] Decree of Daladier Government, May 24, 1938, CAOM FM 81F/864. In 1938, attempts would be made to extend it to the rest of the country, through the project of Daladier.

[21] A. Confino to M. Halff, Alliance, Algiers, March 6, 1935, AIU Algérie ICI.

[22] Jews who had left Constantine following the violence threatened a mass emigration to Palestine. A. Confino to M. Halff, Alliance, Algiers, March 6, 1935, AIU Algérie ICI.

[23] A. Confino to M. Halff, Alliance, Algiers, March 6, 1935, AIU Algérie ICI. Confino ordered his colleagues in Constantine to instate a penalty of a penny for each student who spoke Arabic during recess, based on actions he had instituted during his time working for the Alliance in Persia.

[24] The founding members were doctors, pharmacists, professors, and teachers, who hoped that "old Jewish customs would be abandoned in terms of dress and the use of Arabic." Central Commissioner of Constantine to the Prefect of Constantine, "No. 6651: Objet: Réunion au sujet de la Constitution d'une Société de Rééducation de la Population Israélite de Constantine," Constantine, September 10, 1935, CAOM Alg Const B/3/390.

[25] For example, the Society began their activities by dealing with Jewish women who sat on the sidewalks of Rue de France on Saturday afternoon and evenings. Pedestrians harassed these women. Commissioner of Department Security of Constantine, "Rapport No. 3369: Intellectual Israélites rééducation de la masse," Constantine, September 16, 1935, CAOM Alg Const B/3/390.

the best defense against antisemitism. However, as municipal governments once again became the stronghold of antisemitism, assimilation could not defend against the extreme measures taken by municipal politicians.

Sidi Bel Abbès in the department of Oran was such a municipality. Until 1929, Sidi Bel Abbès had a Jewish mayor, M. Lisbonne, considered to be radical. Lisbonne's "republican action" list in the 1929 municipal elections received 1,752 votes, while the antisemitic Lucien Bellat and his list received 1,928 votes. By 1935, when Bellat ran for reelection as part of the "Economic and Social Union" party, his list received 3,159 votes against 1,540 votes for his competitor, the communist list. Bellat's fellow antisemitic politicians were similarly successful. In the October 1934 General Council Elections, the antisemitic candidate was elected over the candidates from the Radical Socialist party and the communist SFIO. In the May 1936 Legislative elections, Bellat's favored antisemitic candidate beat the former radical mayor of Tlemcen. In the Financial Delegation elections of February 1938, Paul Bellat, Mayor Bellat's son, won over G. Lisbonne (son of former Mayor Lisbonne) with 1,896 votes to 1,449 votes.[26]

These elections reflected significant electoral competition. Algerian Jewish voters, who favored the Popular Front candidates, could potentially sway the outcome. In his 1938 report to the governor-general, Perier de Feral, the Inspector General of the Administration of Algeria, assessed the activities of antisemites in Sidi Bel Abbès and identified an ongoing conflict between antisemites and Jews in the municipality, especially after Bellat *père* won the 1929 election over Lisbonne *père*. This further pitted the Jewish population against the European population. The Union Latines, composed largely of those of Spanish origin and under the leadership of Mayor Bellat's son Paul, further intensified this conflict. De Feral described this as a "period of open battle." Raoul Follereau, the General President of the League of the Union Latine of France and the Colonies, attended several meetings of the Sidi Bel Abbès Union Latine to lend his support and to encourage its propaganda. Electoral competition continued to be the bedrock of the Union Latine' actions. De Feral noted that elections created moments of intense "antagonism," even violence, between Jews and antisemites.[27]

In 1935, Jewish leaders of Sidi Bel Abbès confronted renewed threats to Jews' ability to perform their rights as citizens, particularly in terms of voting. Mayor Bellat was the honorary president of the Union Latine and many municipal councilors were members. At a meeting of the Union

---

[26] Perier de Feral, Inspector General of the Administration of Algeria, "Report No. 222, to the Gov-Gen of Algeria," Algiers, April 20, 1938, CAOM Alg GGA 3CAB/52.
[27] Ibid.

Latine, a speaker announced that the municipal government wanted to build an "arc de triomphe" in the central square. It was to be carved with the slogan "Foreigners, come to Bel Abbès – there are no more Jews here!"[28] Article one of the 1932 Statutes of the Union Latine of Sidi Bel Abbès stated their primary goal as protecting all "citizens of the latin race," against the "aims of the Jewish electoral bloc."[29] The municipal government's overt patronage of antisemitic leagues indicated an intensification of political antisemitism.

Despite growing antisemitism, elections in Oran in May 1935 were the calmest in many years. Abbé Lambert, who would later realize the power of antisemitic politics, based his candidacy on a program of "the fusion of races."[30] In contrast, the elections in Constantine in May 1935 brought antisemites to power. Although four Jewish candidates were elected, Alliance director Angel argued that this was at the cost of "too many humiliations for the dignity of our people and will be costly to the future of calm and peace ..." Angel contended that the political ambitions of certain Jews put the entire community at risk by drawing undue attention to them and encouraging antisemitism through political competition.[31]

In Constantine's municipal elections, several groups competed for power: the "Republican Union," sponsored by Émile Morinaud, faced opposition from the leftist republican "antifascists." The *Croix de Feu* nominated candidates, and Henri Lautier, the antisemitic editor of *L'Éclair*, ran in the election. The Republican Union candidates, among them four Jews, expected the electoral support of Constantine's Jews. Only twenty-two of the thirty-four Republican Union candidates were elected, and following the elections Morinaud's paper, *Le Republicain*, published a "declaration of war against all the Jewish element of Constantine."[32] The election of the new government heralded a new era of municipal antisemitism.

---

[28] Sidi Bel Abbès LDH President Martaing to the Sec-Gen, "Objet: Excitations antisémites de Sidi Bel Abbès," Sidi Bel Abbès, February 23, 1935, BDIC-LDH F Delta Res 798/96. See also Laure Blévis, "Une citoyenneté française contestée–reflexion à partir d'un incident antisémite en 1938," in Association Française pour l'histoire de la Justice, ed., *La Justice en Algérie, 1830–1962* (Paris: La Documentation française, 2005), 116. See also untitled report on the situation in Sidi Bel Abbès in the Gov-Gen's files, likely dated 1938, CAOM Alg GGA 3CAB/52.

[29] "Statuts des Unions Latines de Sidi Bel Abbès," CAOM Alg GGA 3CAB/52.

[30] Toledano to A. Confino, Director of the École de l'Alliance Israélite, Algiers, Oran, May 8, 1935, AIU Algérie ICI.

[31] Angel to the President of the Alliance, Constantine, May 17, 1935, AIU Algérie ICI.

[32] Ibid. This election shows that Algerian Jews did not vote as a bloc. They ran with and voted for different parties. Although Morinaud was antisemitic, Algerian Jews still voted for his party.

M. Angel wrote that "we lived in very hard times during this election period." When the outgoing municipal government threw a banquet in honor of Morinaud, Jewish council members were excluded. Consistory leaders begged those Jewish politicians, Lellouche and Sultan, to resign from the government and Angel pondered, "What role will the Jewish elected officials play in a municipal assembly that is nearly entirely hostile towards them?"[33] The press campaign intensified against the Jews of Constantine, especially in Lautier's "infected" antisemitic weekly *Tam-Tam*.[34] In previous elections, Jews experienced power as elected members of municipal governments. In 1935, this trend changed as antisemites put up obstacles to Jews' election and limited their power in government.

Conditions for Jews deteriorated elsewhere in the departments of Constantine and Oran. In August 1935, groups of the Front Paysan, the Union Latine, and the *Croix de Feu* launched a new propaganda campaign that stressed the suffering of those impacted by the depression. The Union Latine revived antisemitic accusations of Jewish–Freemason collaboration against the honest French colonist. Making matters worse, Monsieur Haze, the new Sub-Prefect of Sidi Bel Abbès, was known for his "antisemitic tendencies."[35] The director of the Alliance school in Sidi Bel Abbès, Monsieur Cohen, reported that posters appeared demanding "death to the Jews, they are the cause of the crisis, they steal from the workers." Following an attack on a Jewish café "there were Jewish arrests, not arrests of others," likely the work of the antisemitic Sub-Prefect.[36] The Sub-Prefect was not alone – the majority of the municipal government of Sidi Bel Abbès was antisemitic, led by Mayor Lucien Bellat, who was reelected in 1935.[37]

Monsieur Bluamou, the president of the Consistory of Sidi Bel Abbès, commented on the extent of the antisemitism of the municipal government and its involvement in recent skirmishes between Jews and antisemites. He identified the main culprits as the mayor and his associates, all of whom were antisemitic, and the mayor's son, who founded the Union Latine section in the city. In addition, the mayor's private secretary, many municipal employees, and police officers were members of an antisemitic society. The mayor's offices served as the headquarters for all antisemitic groups in the city. Bluamou criticized "the unjust

---

[33] Ibid.
[34] Ibid. See also Letter M. Angel to the President of the Alliance Israélite Universelle, Constantine, May 19, 1935, AIU Algérie ICI.
[35] On August 7, 150 people armed with clubs broke into a café, owned and frequented exclusively by Jews. A. Confino to the President of the Alliance Israélite Universelle, Algiers, August 14, 1935, AIU Algérie ICI.
[36] M. Cohen to A. Confino, Sidi Bel Abbès, August 13, 1935, AIU Algérie IC2.
[37] Blévis, "Une citoyenneté française contestée," 116.

attitude of the municipal police, which has shown a flagrant bias against the Jews, supported the provocateurs by all means, even making false testimonies that undermine our own."[38] The entrenched nature of antisemitism in the municipal government motivated Jewish leaders to utilize other avenues to combat such acts. The Jewish community of Sidi Bel Abbès filed a legal claim against an antisemite for incitement to murder.

Taking an antisemite to court marked an important transition. In the late nineteenth century the Jews in Algeria rarely defended themselves against antisemitic attacks. In the late 1910s, Jews developed defense groups, such as the CAES, but their impact was limited. The lawsuit by the Sidi Bel Abbès Jewish community indicates an important development in their defense strategy: the use of non-Jewish intermediaries (legal counsel) and the French courts. This strategy demonstrates the Algerian Jews' understanding and use of state institutions to protect themselves. The local LDH president, however, commented that he had no confidence in the impartiality of government inquiries into antisemitism as their primary informants, the police and the municipal government, were biased and often culpable themselves.[39]

Confino identified the *néos'* successors, the "Latins," as the driving force of antisemitism throughout the colony. "Antisemitism has made alarming progress in Algeria, not among Muslims, as some may imagine, but in the French population of Latin origin and especially among intellectuals and civil servants." The shift from the everyman *néo* to the municipal official illustrates the transition from popular to political/municipal antisemitism. Antisemitic leaders used the context of the depression in their appeals, calling upon the economic frustrations of the Latins. In Algiers posters appeared attacking the Jews, who "monopolize any situation: trade, industry, politics, administrator, professional." Antisemites also attempted to establish quotas in Algeria's professional schools, which would have further eliminated Jews as their economic and status competitors.[40]

Although primarily concerned with the activities of European antisemites, Algerian Jews remained apprehensive in their dealings with local

---

[38] M. Bluamou, on behalf of the Association Cultuelle Israélite, Consistory Israélite of Sidi Bel Abbès to the Chief Rabbi Liber, of the Consistory Central of Vieux-Moulin (Oise), August 17, 1935, AIU Algérie ICI.

[39] Sidi Bel Abbès LDH President Martaing to the President of the LDH, Paris, "Object: Oran–Éxcitation antisémite," Sidi Bel Abbès, August 17, 1935, BDIC-LDH F Delta Res 798/96.

[40] A. Confino to the President of the Alliance Israélite Universelle, Algiers, October 31, 1935, AIU Algérie ICI. The posters appeared on the eve of Rosh Hashanah, the Jewish New Year, and accused Jews of being traitors, citing Dreyfus and Blum. The imposition of quotas became part of Vichy's antisemitic legislation.

Muslims. In an article on Jewish–Muslim relations, Ferhat Abbas wrote that Muslims did not blame Jews for their unequal status in the colony. "The injustice that is at the base of the Crémieux Decree was committed by the French Parliament, that is to say the French nation. The Jews did not demand anything." Despite absolving Jews of any responsibility in terms of their higher political status in the colony, Abbas contended that the Crémieux Decree set in motion the development of a powerful Jewish bourgeoisie, which "today is everywhere. In the judiciary, in the administration, in the army, in commerce, in the banks, in agriculture, in the postal service, in the railways, in welfare, wherever the citizen-elector may enter, the Jew has found a place."[41] As the competition for the scarce resources of municipal government intensified, status anxieties deepened among all the groups of the colony. Like the Latins who begrudged Jewish representatives in government, Algerian Muslims resented their relative lack of power in such institutions.

In late November 1935, Chief Rabbi Maurice Eisenbeth met with the head of the governor-general's cabinet to present the concerns of Algerian Jews. He conveyed the Jews' lack of security in the colony, especially as a result of the growing extremism of right-wing groups such as the *Croix de Feu* and the *Volontaires Nationaux*. Eisenbeth suggested that the Constantine pogrom was actually the "work of French antisemites" and was a harbinger of future disorders. "If civil war breaks out in the Metropole," Eisenbeth argued, "Jewish blood will freely flow in Algeria." Algerian Jews remembered the lessons learned in 1898 when disturbances in the metropole caused violent reverberations in the colony.[42] In 1936, the *Croix de Feu*, the *Volontaires Nationaux*, and other right-wing groups used developments in the metropole, such as the election of Blum and the Popular Front, to revive political antisemitism in the colony. Increasingly antisemitic municipal governments supported such efforts. Elections in 1936 represented opportunities for violence, boycotts, and the establishment of thoroughly anti-Jewish municipal governments.

The Rise of Right-Wing Organizations, Electoral Antisemitism, and the Popular Front

Over the course of 1935 and 1936, the *Croix de Feu* and other antisemitic organizations gained considerable traction in Algeria. Elections provided

---

[41] Abbas also accused Jews of not supporting Muslims' campaign for rights in the colony. Ferhat Abbas, "Juifs et Musulmans d'Algérie," *La Dépêche Algérienne*, November 10, 1935, AIU Algérie ICI. See also Ruedy, *Modern Algeria*, 133.
[42] Rabbi Maurice Eisenbeth, "Résumé, No. 9236/4," Algiers, December 3, 1935, AIU Algérie ICI.

opportunities for the intensification of their rhetoric, and they gained followers during those fraught political occasions. Although predominately European, the *Croix de Feu* incorporated propaganda aimed at Muslims to increase their ranks but lacked a coherent policy on Muslims' roles in the organization.[43] Under Lieutenant Colonel François La Rocque after 1930, *Croix de Feu* leadership in France emphasized the acceptance of all races and creeds into its ranks, the antisemitism of its members in Algeria informed the group's politics. The *Croix de Feu* in Algeria cooperated with other antisemitic organizations such as the *Action Française* (AF), the *Parti Populaire Français* (PPF), and the *Rassemblement Nationale d'Action Sociale* (RN), led by the increasingly antisemitic Abbé Lambert. The rhetoric, terminology, and propaganda used by the *Croix de Feu* in the 1930s closely mirrored that of Algerian antisemites of the 1890s.[44]

In May 1936, the Popular Front in France come to power. In the two years that it governed, under the leadership of Léon Blum, its foreign policy focused on avoiding war at all costs, and preparing for war in the eventuality that it was necessary.[45] When the Spanish Civil War broke out in July 1936, Blum's cabinet was deeply divided. Blum himself wanted to send aid to the Spanish Republic. However, he soon acquiesced to his cabinet and diplomatic forces and accepted a policy of nonintervention, even though it received a serious backlash from communists. Tears in the fabric of the Popular Front's coalition in France quickly appeared.[46]

The Spanish Civil War also had reverberations in North Africa. General Franco had colonial experience in Spanish Morocco and brought his brutal tactics with him to Spain. When Mussolini and Hitler lent their support and weapons to Franco, they further encouraged antisemites' support in Algeria. As Franco's troops brutalized the Republicans, carrying out many atrocities, French *colons* appreciated Franco's military style. The centrality of the Church and Catholicism in the Nationalist zone, with its hostility to freemasonry, liberalism, socialism, and communism, further appealed to Algerian antisemites, who wished to follow such

---

[43] Muslims made up only 10 percent of the Croix de Feu's membership in Algeria. Kennedy, *Reconciling France against Democracy*, 62. See also Kalman, *The Extreme Right in Interwar France*, 216. In late 1935 in Algiers, the Central Police Commissioner reported on the appearance of tracts distributed throughout the town inciting Muslims against Jews. The tracts read, "Muslims: the Frenchman is not your oppressor. Your enemy is the Jew, who robs and ruins you." Central Commissioner to the Sec-Gen of Affaires Indigènes et Police Générale, Algiers, December 24, 1935, CAOM Alg Alger 2i/38.

[44] Kalman, *The Extreme Right in Interwar France*, 210–212.

[45] Mary Dewhurst Lewis, *The Boundaries of the Republic: Migrant Rights and the Limits of Universalism in France, 1918–1940* (Stanford: Stanford University Press, 2007), 216.

[46] Jackson, *The Popular Front in France*, 10.

policies in the colony. This support was especially rampant in Oran and Sidi Bel Abbès, where there was a large population of néos of Spanish origin as well as Spanish citizens.[47]

Antisemites in the metropole and in Algeria attacked Blum's Jewish background. Although Blum's parents were of Alsatian Jewish descent, he later abandoned Judaism. In the face of antisemitic attacks, Blum did not shy away from declaring his Jewishness, stating that he was born in France to a long line of French ancestors and spoke only French.[48] Despite his lack of religious observance, Blum's mere Jewishness provided antisemites with ammunition against the Popular Front. Despite the Popular Front's identity as the union of the French people, it afforded the right-wing groups an opportunity to contrast their Frenchness with the perceived "foreign-ness" of the Popular Front, which allowed into France refugees from Germany, Spain, and Central Europe. With Blum at its head, the Right depicted the Popular Front as intrinsically "other": socialist, Jew, foreigner, immoral, anti-class, and communist.[49]

In the climate of the lingering depression, the activities of the Popular Front, and increasing antisemitism in the metropole and the colony, membership of the *Croix de Feu* in Algeria grew considerably. In the department of Algiers, in December 1933 there were 2,500 *Croix de Feu* members, increasing to 8,440 in July 1935, and 15,000 in June 1936. In the department of Constantine, in December 1933 there were 2,000 members; 3,000 in July 1935; and in June 1936, 7,000. The department of Oran had 1,500 members in December 1933, 2,520 in July 1935, and 6,000 in June 1936.[50] The exponential growth of *Croix de Feu* members over the course of three years indicates the power of antisemitism and the appeal of fascism in the colony. By 1935, *Croix de Feu* militants terrorized Jewish neighborhoods, yelling "Long live La Rocque," and "Long Live Hitler," and making fascist salutes. Although La Rocque attempted to discourage antisemitism, his efforts had little or no impact in Algeria. The *Ligue Internationale Contre l'Antisémitisme* (LICA),

---

[47] Paul Preston, *The Spanish Civil War: Reaction, Revolution, and Revenge* (London: Harper Perennial, 2006), 79, 119, 137–144, 207, 219. Although many Spanish resistance supporters fled to France in 1939, it is not clear whether they also went to Algeria. If they had, they would likely support the left-wing groups, rather than the antisemites. Shirley Mangini, *Memories of Resistance: Women's Voices from the Spanish Civil War* (New Haven: Yale University Press, 1995), 151. See also Chief of the Active Brigade of Administrative Research, Social and Economic, "Report No. 340," Algiers, February 26, 1937, CAOM Alg GGA 3CAB/52.

[48] Jackson, *The Popular Front in France*, 54–55.   [49] Ibid., 249–251.

[50] Kennedy, *Reconciling France against Democracy*, 87.

a left-wing metropolitan organization, became concerned with the *Croix de Feu*'s activities in Algeria.[51]

In 1929, the LICA shifted its orientation to be more broadly concerned with antisemitism and racism.[52] In July 1935, it organized a meeting in Oran to introduce Jews to the role that LICA could play on their behalf. One of the LICA's first endeavor in the colony was to encourage the boycott of German "Hitlerian" products, based on a successful boycott in Paris.[53] The LICA increased its actions in 1936. During a meeting in Oran in February 1936, Bernard Lecache, the head of the LICA, commented that "Jews were regarded by some as 'second class' Frenchmen and their examples of bravery during the 1914–1918 war and their decorations have been criticized."[54] Like other Jewish organizations, the LICA was primarily concerned with defending Algerian Jews' rights as citizens. Lecache was committed to fighting injustice more generally.

In March 1936, Algerian *Croix de Feu* delegate, A. Debay, declared "that among our ranks there are Algerian antisemites, it would be futile to deny," but emphasized that the organization was open to all French patriots "without distinction of party, race, or religion."[55] A few weeks later, Debay blamed Jews' political activities, particularly in municipal governments, for the problems in the colony. Debay accused Algerian Jews, specifically those in Constantine, of provoking peaceful *Croix de Feu* members. Most importantly, he portrayed the Jews of Constantine as fomenting discord through municipal elections and the use of their "professional politicians, who use electoral weapons."[56] Debay linked Jews

---

[51] Ibid., 62. Although the LICA also sought to encourage Muslim involvement by evolving into the Ligue Internationale Contre le Racisme et l'Antisémitisme (LICRA), it remained a predominately Jewish organization.

[52] Emmanuel Debono, "Bernard Abraham Lecache, président fondateur de la Ligue internationale contre l'antisémitisme. (Paris (3e), 16 août 1895–Cannes, 16 août 1968)," *Archives Juives*, Vol. 40, No. 1 (2007): 141.

[53] Central Commissioner of Oran to the Prefect of Oran, "No. 947C: Object Réunion de la Ligue Internationale contre l'Antisémitisme," Oran, July 22, 1935, CAOM Alg Oran 424.

[54] Central Commissioner of Oran to the Prefect of Oran, "No. 94C: Objet: Conférence par M. Bernard Lecache," Oran, February 12, 1936, CAOM Alg Oran 424. The report on the meeting estimated that the majority of the 1,500 attendees were Jews; there were also approximately 300 women, and the mayor of Oran, Abbé Lambert (whose own antisemitism was building), and the General Council members Dubois, as well as several European and Muslim municipal council members, were in attendance.

[55] A. Debay, "Mouvement Croix de Feu," *La Dépêche Algérienne*, March 25, 1936, AIU Algérie ICI. See also A. Confino to M. Halff, Alliance Israélite Universelle, Algiers, March 26, 1936, AIU Algérie ICI.

[56] A. Debay "Le Mouvement Croix de Feu et l'antisémitisme: Une lettre du commandant Debay, délégué pour l'Algérie du Comité directeur au Gouverneur General," April 8, 1936, AIU Algérie ICI. Although not specified, it appears that this article was published in *La Dépêche Algérienne*.

and the Popular Front, further tying Algerian Jews to conflicts in the metropole.[57] More significant, however, was his emphasis on the pivotal role of municipal politics and the role of Jewish politicians.

The electoral period of 1936, with legislative elections on April 26 in Algiers, was marked by antisemitism and violence. In late March, Lecache recommended to Charles Aboulker, the president of the LICA in Algeria, that the LICA submit a "symbolic candidate" in the upcoming elections. This candidate would enter the election in order to respond to the attacks of antisemites in the election.[58] In Algiers, the conflict centered on the anti-Jewish candidate Henry Coston. The LICA and Jewish organizations worked together to undermine Coston's propaganda campaign.[59] Some efforts bordered on the illegal, including a group of young Jews who broke into his headquarters. The community treated them as heroes.[60] Aboulker stated "that the Jewish youth [in Algeria] have shown that they do not want to repeat the troubles of 1898."[61] In these electoral contests, Jewish youth took on a decidedly active role, including a tilt toward violence.

The elections also paved the way for boycotts in Constantine. Morinaud's *Le Republicain de Constantine* published articles demanding the boycott of Jewish shops. One article accused Jewish council member Lellouche of forcing his coreligionists to vote against Morinaud, concluding with a call for boycotts: "in the face of this declaration of war, don't bring your money to anyone other than the French!" Although the article was directed mostly at Europeans in Constantine, it also reached Muslims. The author used the Crémieux Decree to negate the Frenchness of the Algerian Jews. "Defend ourselves, since we are facing enemies who, 65 years after the Crémieux Decree ... want to control the French majority!"[62] The allusion to the Crémieux Decree characterized

---

[57] Jackson, *The Popular Front in France*, 7, 9.

[58] Bernard Lecache to Charles Aboulker, March 27, 1936, CDJC CMXCVI-105.2 (Fonds LICA).

[59] LICA Secretary E. Yaffi to Bernard Lecache, Algiers, April 18, 1936, CDJC CMXCVI-105.2 (Fonds LICA).

[60] On April 21, 300–400 people, mostly young Jews aged 16 to 25, protested outside of Coston's campaign headquarters on Rue d'Isly. The next day, protests turned violent. Six to ten "Europeans, mostly Jews," broke into Coston's headquarters. Central Commissioner of Police to the Sec-Gen (Affaires Indigènes et Police Générale), "Rapport No. 429," Algiers, April 21, 1936, CAOM Alg Alger F410. See also Central Commissioner of Police to the Sec-Gen (Affaires Indigènes et Police Générale), "Rapport No. 434," Algiers, April 22, 1936, CAOM Alg Alger F410.

[61] Department Security of Algiers, "Rapport No. 2427: Réunion Électorale Fiori," Algiers, April 22, 1936, CAOM Alg Alger F410.

[62] "Entre Français d'une part Hai Lellouche et sa Troupe de l'Autre: L'Abime! Le demi fou Lellouche a délibérément creusé cet abime," *Le Républicain*, April 28, 1936, CAOM Alg Const B/3/656. The next day, *Le Républicain* published a report on the boycott,

the Jews as the other in the colony, the unworthy beneficiaries of arbitrary French citizenship law, rather than deserving Frenchmen.

Morinaud used the boycott and the elections to intensify anti-Jewish rhetoric in the press. *Le Républicain* constantly made reference to the Crémieux Decree, which remained the bête noire of European antisemites in the colony because it provided Jews with competitive electoral power. In order to "counterbalance the bloc vote of the Jewish electors," French electors had to vote in great numbers.[63] Calling upon Frenchmen to follow the insular example of Jews in Algeria, one author encouraged Frenchmen to patronize only French-owned shops. "Look at the Lellouches and imitate their example ... The Jew helps no one but the Jew ... Frenchmen first, French solidarity, to assure the French predominance."[64] The French organizers of the boycott also encouraged Muslim participation by connecting the boycott to the situation in Palestine.[65] In an article entitled "Bloc against Bloc," the authors called upon Frenchmen to act against the Jewish bloc: "Since they [the Jews] had the audacity to declare war, you have proudly accepted the challenge – on all fronts, political, economic, and social!"[66] With this call to battle, *Le Républicain* articulated a political and economic war against the Jews in Constantine.

In the face of increased antisemitic agitation, Jews reorganized their defense. They protested against the boycott and Jewish veterans sent telegrams to the governor-General, bringing his attention to Morinaud's and *Le Républicain*'s provocations and demanding that the government act to prevent a reenactment of the August 5 violence.[67] In the department of Constantine, skirmishes broke out between Jews and members of right-wing groups during the April 26

connecting it to strikes in Palestine, which related to the impact of the Arab Rebellion. See "Le boycottage," *Le Républicain*, April 29, 1936, CAOM Alg Const B/3/656.

[63] In "The dream of a half-fool," *Le Républicain* emphasized the dangers of the Jewish vote, providing the statistics for Constantine: 50,000 Frenchmen, 50,000 Muslims, and 10,000 Jews, who were Frenchmen because of the Crémieux Decree. As a result, the French electoral lists contained 8,333 electors, among whom there were 2,747 Jews. Of these 2,747 Jewish voters, 2,381 voted in the past election, "all who could vote voted." Out of 5,586 French voters, 4,424 actually voted. "Le rêve du demi-fou," *Le Républicain*, April 30, 1936, CAOM Alg Const B/3/656.

[64] "Solidarité Nécessaire," *Le Républicain*, May 1, 1936, CAOM Alg Const B/3/656.

[65] In an article entitled "The Jews in Palestine" the author quoted Dr. Hussein al-Khalidi, the mayor of Jerusalem and president of the Arab Reform Party, who stated "the Jews cannot consume all the products of their industry. Their economic plan includes the opening of shops in the Near East, which will be indispensable for them to live. We will close the doors of the Levant to them." "Les Juifs en Palestine," *Le Républicain*, May 1, 1936, CAOM Alg Const B/3/656.

[66] "Bloc contre Bloc," *Le Républicain*, May 2, 1936, CAOM Alg Const B/3/656.

[67] Anciens Combattants Français Israélites, Constantine, to Le Beau, Gov-Gen of Algeria, CAOM Alg Const B/3/656. They sent similar telegrams to ministers in Paris, the president of the LDH, and to Bernard Lecache, LICA.

elections.[68] On election day, *Croix de Feu* members intimidated Jewish voters in an effort to prevent them from voting.[69] Numerous new recruits, especially *néos*, joined the *Croix de Feu*.[70] Violence increased in the days following the election. On April 29 four separate altercations broke out between *Volontaires Nationaux* and Jews in Constantine.[71] On May 27, Jewish LICA members and their *Action Française* adversaries got into a gunfight.[72]

Antisemitism intensified throughout the colony. By July 1936 the boycott of Jewish shops in Constantine spread to Algiers. One flyer posted on a storefront read, "Do not enter, it is a Jew – He is ashamed of his name." Another stated, "French, do not buy anything from the Jews. You will control them through boycott," and others warned "Attention!!! This is a Jewish shop. Danger!!!"[73] The boycott received support from antisemitic mayors and municipal governments, such as the notoriously antisemitic government of Sidi Bel Abbès.[74] After Blum and the Popular Front took office on June 14, a parade traveled through Sidi Bel Abbès. Union Latine members attacked the participants, using toxic gas and injuring fifty people.[75] The municipal government tacitly, and occasionally actively, encouraged such acts.

The Popular Front's actions upon taking office in May 1936 exacerbated tensions in Algeria. The Popular Front banned right-wing organizations such as the *Croix de Feu*, which later reorganized as the *Parti Social*

---

[68] On April 26, Croix de Feu and Volontaires Nationaux members, including some 200 Muslims, staged a demonstration in Khenchela yelling, "Down with the Jews, the sellouts, the traitors ... We are now the masters, the fortress of Khenchela is demolished!" The Khenchela police commissioner reported that the demonstration was "symptomatic of a state of spirit which could have grave consequences." Commissioner of Police of Khenchela to the Prefect of Constantine, "Rapport No. 929," Khenchela, April 27, 1936, CAOM Alg Const B/3/656. See also LICA Secretary, E. Yaffi, to Bernard Lecache, Algiers, April 18, 1936, CDJC CMXCVI-105.2 (Fonds LICA).

[69] Central Commissioner of Constantine to the Prefect of Constantine, "Rapport No. 3489, Objet: Élections Législatives 1936," Constantine, May 4, 1936, CAOM Alg Const B/3/656.

[70] Departmental Security in Constantine, "Rapport No. 1680: Antisémitisme (confidential)," Constantine, May 1, 1936, CAOM Alg Const B/3/656.

[71] Departmental Security of Constantine, "Rapport No. 1661: Antisémitisme," Constantine, April 30, 1936, CAOM Alg Const B/3/656.

[72] Commissioner of Police Spiteri to Sec-Gen (Affaires Indigènes et Police Générale), "Rapport No. 588RS," Algiers, May 27, 1936, CAOM Alg Alger F410. See also Mobile Police of Algiers, Third Brigade to the Chief of the Mobile Police of Algiers, Algiers, May 27, 1936, CAOM Alg Alger F410.

[73] Police Commissioner of the Third Arrondissement Le Boul to the Central Police Commissioner, "Rapport No. 777R.S.," Algiers, July 10, 1936, CAOM Alg Alger F410.

[74] President of the LDH in Paris to the Minister of the Interior, Paris, June 13, 1936, BDIC-LDH F Delta Res 798/96.

[75] Ibid.

Français.[76] In spite of – or perhaps because of – the Popular Front's actions, violence erupted between Jews and *Croix de Feu* members. On June 27, members of right-wing organizations excluded Jews from a public celebration, informing them that "this party is only for Frenchmen and not for *Youpins* [Jews]." Other incidents, including the looting of several stores, occurred over the next few days, without intervention by the municipal government. According to Lellouche, antisemitic groups were responsible, and "naturally no one says anything and no arrests were made."[77]

Many in the colony, including numerous municipal employees, opposed the Popular Front. In Souk-Ahras, a French officer, Marrès, interrupted a presentation of a film on the Popular Front yelling "Death to the Jews" and "Down with the Popular Front!"[78] In another case, the municipal police in Perregaux openly expressed their hostility to the Popular Front, yelling "Long Live Hitler," and making the fascist salute. One police officer stated, "We wait for Hitler to come to Algeria and rid us of those dirty Jews and Reds."[79] Anti-Popular Front sentiment melded easily with antisemitism, especially as municipal governments became even more antisemitic. In the face of that increasing antisemitism, Jews felt the dire quality of their situation in the colony and the need for self-defense. As Algerian Jews defended their status in the colony, Algerian Muslims continued to articulate their own demands for rights in the hopes that the Popular Front would be more receptive than previous governments.

The Blum-Viollette Bill and the Quest for Muslim Rights

The development of Muslim-oriented nationalist movements in Palestine and Morocco in 1936 resonated in Algeria. Algerian Jews worried about how the Arab revolt beginning in 1936 would impact the colony. The first

---

[76] Jessica Wardhaugh, *In Pursuit of the People: Political Culture in France, 1934–39* (New York: Palgrave MacMillan, 2009), 122–123.

[77] Henri Lellouche to M. Vanikoff in Paris, Constantine, July 2, 1936, CDJC DCCXXI-1 (Fonds Vanikoff). See also Henri Lellouche to the Prefect of Constantine, Constantine, July 2, 1936, CDJC DCCXXI-1 (Fonds Vanikoff); Vanikoff to M. Lellouche, July 3, 1936, CDJC DCCXXI-1. Lellouche noted that the night of July 1, swastikas were drawn on Jewish shops in indelible black ink. See also President Consistory of Constantine to the Prefect of Constantine, Constantine, June 30, 1936, CDJC DCCXXI-1 (Fonds Vanikoff).

[78] LDH President Victor Basch to the Minister of the Interior, Paris, September 17, 1936, BDIC-LDH F Delta Res 798/171.

[79] Georges Munch, Committee of the Popular Front in Perregaux to M. Victor Basch, President of the LDH in Paris, Perregaux, October 10, 1936, BDIC-LDH F Delta Res 798/171.

phase of the Arab revolt in Palestine lasted from mid-April to November 1936, and included a boycott of Jewish shops and "goods," as well as attacks on Jews and British forces.[80] At the same time, the boycott of Jewish shops in Constantine and Algiers continued, supported by Europeans and Muslims. Jewish leaders expressed concern that the nationalist "agitation" in Morocco could also pose serious problems in Algeria.[81] In this context, Algerian Muslims rearticulated their demands for rights in the colony. The year 1936 was a significant year for the ENA: in June it organized strikes of factories in the metropole, and in July it participated in a republican parade in Paris and published its program in its newspaper, *El Ouma*, which demanded the abrogation of the *indigénat*. Throughout the summer of 1936, the ENA recruited new members in Algeria.[82]

In June 1936, the first Algerian Muslim Congress met in Algiers. In July, the Congress adopted its official program, named the "Charter of Demands of the Muslim Algerian People." The Charter demanded universal suffrage, a single electoral college, Muslim representatives in Parliament, and amnesty for political prisoners. Bendjelloul led a delegation from the Congress to Paris to present the Charter, where they were welcomed by Blum and former Algerian Governor-General Maurice Viollette.[83] While the Charter demanded improved rights for Muslims, it did not require independence. As a result of his work with the SFIO in the 1920s, Blum developed his philosophy that colonization was justified only if it prepared subjects for eventual self-rule. As the governor-general of Algeria, Viollette was nicknamed *l'Arbi* (the Arab) due to his pro-native politics. Both politicians ultimately sought the improvement of Algerian Muslims' rights – a relatively unpopular attitude at the time.[84]

The Blum-Viollette Bill built upon Viollette's original 1931 bill, offering French citizenship to a small cadre of well-educated and "evolved"

---

[80] Charles D. Smith, *Palestine and the Arab-Israeli Conflict* (Boston: Bedford Press, 2001), 138.

[81] The co-director of the antisemitic *Libre Parole* published posters demanding "For the Jews out of Palestine, an economic boycott is required." A. Sultan to M. Vanikoff, Paris, Constantine, November 18, 1936, CDJC DCCXXI-1 (Fonds Vanikoff).

[82] Simon, *Le PPA*, 14. See also Sivan, *Communisme et nationalisme*, 95–96.

[83] Ruedy, *Modern Algeria*, 141. Communists rejected this act as an "imperialist ruse." Sivan, *Communisme et nationalisme*, 94–95. See also Planche, "Le Parti communiste d'Algérie," 26–27.

[84] As Bendjelloul worked to develop support for the Blum-Viollette bill, the Parti Populaire Français, led by Jacques Doriot, and his Algerian representative, Victor Arrighi, developed a strong base of support in Oran. F. Tostain, "Algeria: The Popular Front and the Blum-Viollette Plan, 1936–7," in *French Colonial Empire and the Popular Front: Hope and Disillusion*, Tony Chafer and Amanda Sackur, eds. (New York: St. Martin's Press, Inc., 1999), 220–225.

Algerians without forcing them to give up their personal status. As a result, the Bill had a limited, and largely symbolic, impact: out of the five million Algerian Muslims in the colony, approximately 25,000 received citizenship.[85] The Muslim Congress organized a huge rally in the Algiers Municipal Stadium on August 2, 1936, to support the Bill. Messali Hadj, the leader of the ENA, spoke at the Stadium of Algiers, where he argued against the idea of attachment to France, the goal of the more assimilationist Muslim organizations, such as the Muslim Congress and the *Fédération*, who were in closer alignment with the PCF.[86] Europeans in the colony opposed the idea of allowing Algerian Muslims into their electoral ranks. In response to the Muslim Congress' rally on August 9, 1936, right-wing groups organized a massive political rally to protest the Bill, attended by 25,000 people.[87] *Croix de Feu* groups, reorganized since the June ban as the *Parti Social Français* (PSF), rejected the Bill's attempt to create equality between Europeans and Muslims in the colony. PSF members accused Blum of colluding with Algerian Jews to lure Muslims to communism.[88]

Most municipal politicians opposed the Bill. In December 1936, all but two members of the Congress of Mayors of Algeria, organized by Abbé Lambert, rejected the Blum-Viollette Bill.[89] Despite its general unpopularity in the municipalities, some politicians including Cianfarini, suggested that since the Blum-Viollette Bill only admitted certain elites as citizens, it therefore represented "the will of France to take a step closer to the fusion of races" and could appease frustrated Algerian Muslims seeking independence.[90] Furthermore, he added, as a Jew, Blum's efforts proved that Jews were not enemies of Muslims.[91] The ENA opposed the project, calling it an attempt to divide and conquer the Algerian Muslims. The Blum-Viollette Bill ultimately became a defining moment for Muslim communists and their relationship to the state.[92]

---

[85] Ibid., 220–222.

[86] Ruedy, *Modern Algeria*, 142. See also Sivan, *Communisme et nationalisme*, 95–96. See also Planche, "Le Parti communiste d'Algérie," 31–32.

[87] Tostain, "Algeria: The Popular Front," 223, 226.

[88] Kalman, *The Extreme Right in Interwar France*, 213–214. See also Kennedy, *Reconciling France against Democracy*, 153.

[89] Ruedy, *Modern Algeria*, 141. See also Chafer, *French Colonial Empire and the Popular Front*, 226.

[90] Commissioner of Police of the First Arrondissement of Philippe to the Central Police Commissioner, "No. 1871: Au sujet d'une conférence 'Le Droit de Citoyenneté des Indigènes,' par M. Cianfarini," Philippeville, February 30, 1937, CAOM Alg Const B/3/656.

[91] Police Commissioner of the Second Arrondissement of Philippeville to the Central Police Commissioner, Philippeville, February 24, 1937, CAOM Alg Const B/3/656.

[92] Sivan, *Communisme et nationalisme*, 96, 103.

Politically left-wing organizations, such as the LICA, expressed their support for the Blum-Viollette Bill. Bernard Lecache contended that the Bill was a way for the Popular Front to demonstrate its commitment to Algerian Muslims and its colonial subjects in general. Lecache criticized the fascist groups, who claimed to have Algerian Muslim interests at heart, and pilloried Abbé Lambert, who organized the Congress of Mayors of Algeria against the Bill. He disparaged the self-proclaimed "super-French" of Oran, whose French identities did not prevent them from sporting the swastika. As an example, Lecache told of a French officer in Constantine, who proclaimed that he would prefer to become Hitler's subject than to live under the "occupation of the Popular Front."[93] The LICA remained one of the central supporters of the Blum-Viollette Bill and of Jewish–Muslim coexistence in the colony.[94] The LICA continued to champion the Bill, even after its initial defeat.[95]

The LDH similarly supported the Bill and campaigned for improved access to rights for Algerian Muslims throughout the 1920s and 1930s. Sociologist Laure Blévis concludes that although the LDH and similar political left-leaning organizations had no intention of cooperating with the developing anticolonial or independence movements in Algeria, their actions on behalf of Algerian Muslims ultimately did just that. The LDH, in combating discrimination, pointed to the inherent inequalities of the legal system in Algeria that gave Algerian Muslims French nationality, but restricted their access to the rights of French citizens. Similarly, in 1937, the LDH intervened on behalf of Messali Hadj, whose election to the General Council of Algiers was rejected by the French government.[96]

---

[93] At a LICA meeting, a Muslim speaker encouraged his Muslim brothers to "march with the Popular Front, because it will give us rights and to not return to the fascists who wish to suppress us and our religion." Police Commissioner of the Second Arrondissement to the Central Police Commissioner, Philippeville, March 10, 1937, CAOM Alg Const B/3/656.

[94] Central Police Commissioner to the Sec-Gen (Affaires Indigènes et Police Générale), "No. 277R.S.," Algiers, March 20, 1937, CAOM Alg Alger F410. See also Central Police Commissioner of Algiers to the Sec-Gen (Affaires Indigènes et Police Générale), Algiers, March 21, 1937, CAOM Alg Alger F410. See also Departmental Security, "Rapport No. 3141, Assemblé Général des Membres de la LICA," Oran, April 1, 1937, CAOM Alg Oran 2541. See also Police Commissioner of Orléansville, "Rapport Spécial: No. 2475: Re: Antisémitisme: Réunion publique organisée par la LICA," Orléansville, May 16, 1937, CAOM Alg Alger F410.

[95] Special Police of Oran, "Report No. 275: Ligue Internationale contre l'Antisémitisme (LICA) Assemblée Générale de la section d'Oran," Oran, January 16, 1939, CAOM Alg Oran 2541.

[96] Laure Blévis, "De la cause du droit à la cause anticoloniale. Les interventions de la Ligue des droits de l'homme en haveur des 'indigènes' algériens pendant l'entre-deux-guerres," Politix, Vol. 16, No. 62 (2003): 40, 55–56. See also Blévis "Sociologie d'un droit colonial. Citoyenneté et nationalité en Algérie" (PhD Dissertation: Institut d'Études Politiques, 2004).

Algerian Muslim leaders continued to lobby for the Bill to succeed in some form. After the government dissolved the Étoile Nord-Africaine in January 1937, Messali Hadj founded the Parti du Peuple Algérien (PPA). Initially, the PPA demanded liberation of Algeria from France and derided those who supported the Blum-Viollette Bill. On April 10, 1937, it published its "Declaration of the Political Office of the PPA," in which it articulated its three goals: the refusal of assimilation, sovereignty for the Algerian people, and total emancipation. The PPA sought to engage those Muslims who were frustrated by the limited accomplishments of the Popular Front government on their behalf. The PPA had few allies in Algeria – pro-assimilation Muslim groups were put off by the aggressive nature of the PPA's goals. The PCF continued to see the PPA as competition and even accused them of allying with Doriot's PPF. The PPA followed what historian Jacques Simon calls the "messalism" ideology, which he describes as a mixture of populism, spontaneism, arabo-islamism, and the sacralization of the people. The government banned the PPA in September 1939, but it continued to operate clandestinely.[97]

In July 1938, Ferhat Abbas founded the Union Populaire Algérienne, which demanded emancipation and to have Algeria reconstituted as a French province. In 1938, the Federation of Mayors again protested the Blum-Viollette Bill. Even after Blum's return to power, he could not push the legislation forward, given the weakness of his government. After so many obstacles, the Blum government abandoned the legislation.[98] The failure of the Blum-Violette Bill further fractured the various Algerian Muslim organizations. In 1939, Bendjelloul and other Muslim elites again raised their voices to demand citizenship rights for Muslims, even at the expense of their personal status.[99] It was not until Charles de Gaulle came to power that legislation like the Blum-Viollette Bill went into effect on March 7, 1944.[100]

The Intensification of Extreme Electoral Antisemitism and the Bellat Affair, 1937–1938

Over the course of 1936 and 1937 as debates raged over the Blum-Viollette Bill, the Popular Front became increasingly unpopular in

---

[97] Simon, *Le PPA*, 16–19, 27, 65, 70–71. See also Planche, "Le Parti communiste d'Algérie," 34–35.

[98] Ruedy, *Modern Algeria*, 143–144.

[99] Prefect of Oran, "Rapport No. 51: Renseignements au sujet de la réaction des Indigènes en face du décret du 17 janvier et représentation des Indigènes au Parlement," Oran, January 27, 1939, CAOM Alg Oran 5i/50.

[100] Tostain, "Algeria: The Popular Front," 226–227.

Algeria. Antisemites in Algeria used Blum's unpopularity to intensify their efforts in the colony. Antisemitic politicians took control of several municipalities. Right-wing organizations, such as the PSF (formerly the *Croix de Feu*) and Jacques Doriot's PPF, supported antisemitic electoral campaigns. When Doriot established the PPF in 1936, he was interested in the situation of the empire.[101] Algeria therefore served as a crucial terrain in the PPF's war on the Popular Front. Mobilized armies of *Latins* elected antisemites to high municipal offices. These developments heralded a period of extreme municipal antisemitism, including the removal of many Jewish voters from electoral lists in late 1937 and early 1938.

One of the most efficient ways to reduce the electoral power of Jewish voters was to employ the 1871 restrictions on the Crémieux Decree to remove Jewish voters from electoral lists, a project Lucien Bellat undertook as mayor of Sétif. The 1871 Lambrecht Decree was the second modification of the Crémieux Decree, which followed the Charles du Bouzet modification of October 7, 1871. The Lambrecht Decree sought to further regulate the Jews in Algeria who were eligible for citizenship by demanding proof of birth or parental (or ancestor) birth in Algeria before 1830. This decree combined *jus soli* and *jus sanguinis* as the legal basis for access to citizenship within the Algerian colonial legal system. The Lambrecht Decree required "proof" in the form of witnesses to attest to the "indigenous" status of the Jew in question. This legal issue continued to be a significant tool for antisemites and was resurrected in the heyday of antisemitism in the 1890s in Algeria. In 1895, two Algerian deputies, Samary and Forcioli, wished to revive such a method to eliminate Jewish voters. Governor-General Cambon responded to their demands in a series of circulars in 1895 that prescribed the revision of electoral lists under the supervision of municipal commissions. As a result of this revision, that year 900 Jewish electors out of 1,100 in Constantine were removed from electoral lists.[102]

Under pressure from the deputies, Cambon published the "Circular relating to the revision of electoral lists regarding Jews." The December 12, 1895, circular modified previous ones on June 1 and 6, 1895, given the "irregularities" regarding Jews that had occurred since 1870 regarding the establishment of electoral lists. The December 1895 circular firmly established control of electoral lists in the hands of

---

[101] Wardhaugh, *In Pursuit of the People*, 134, 143. See also Allardyce and Picard, "Jacques Doriot," 32.

[102] Blévis, "Une citoyenneté française contestée," 115–116; Blévis, "De la cause du droit à la cause anticoloniale," 561; Todd Shephard, *The Invention of Decolonization: The Algerian War and the Remaking of France* (Ithaca: Cornell University Press, 2006), 28–29.

municipalities.[103] The governor-general justified the new legislation as an effort to remove from electoral lists Jews from Morocco, Tunisia, and other countries, who came to Algeria hoping to benefit from the Crémieux Decree of 1870. In the circular, Cambon clarified that the 1870 law was a naturalization decree while the October 7, 1871, law was a "measure of exception" regarding the special rules for the inclusion of Jews as recent citizens on electoral lists. The 1895 legislation clarified the provisions of the 1871 decree and prohibited its retroactive application. However, Cambon did not find fault with the removal of non-Algerian indigenous Jews or those of regions, such as the M'Zab, which had been annexed after the 1870 law. The M'Zab Jews could still benefit from the 1865 sénatus-consulte in order to become naturalized.[104]

The timeline described in the 1871 law, as well as the 1895 circular, called for a yearly revision of electoral lists. According to Article 5 of the October 7, 1871, law, Algerian Jews who were removed from electoral lists for having failed to satisfy the requirements of proof of indigeneity laid out in the law could prove their indigenous status and be reconsidered for inscription on the electoral list. However, this would be available to them only at the "next revision," which could be annually but was also at the discretion of the municipal commission charged with regulating the electoral lists. Proof still required an "act of notoriety" by a judge, a birth certificate, or proof from the civil state proving their birth in Algeria before the French occupation. Proof from family members or military service would not suffice for reinscription on electoral lists.[105]

The next governor-general, Louis Lépine, reevaluated the situation of Jews and their status or removal from electoral lists in a circular published on December 7, 1897. Lépine's circular was a reassessment of the debate in Parliament on February 21, 1895, by Samary and Forcioli, as well as Cambon's circulars. He confirmed Cambon's stance that Jews from M'Zab would not benefit from the Crémieux Decree, but could become naturalized via the 1865 sénatus-consulte. Jews from European countries would benefit from the 1889 legislation regulating naturalizations of foreigners. By contrast, Jews coming to Algeria from Muslim countries could not be naturalized if they wished to maintain their

---

[103] Gov-Gen Cambon, "Circulaire du Gouverneur Général: Relative à la revision des listes électorales en ce qui concerne les israélites," December 12, 1895, CAOM Alg GGA 3CAB/52. See also Blévis, "Une citoyenneté française contestée," 115–116.

[104] Gov-Gen Cambon, "Circulaire du Gouverneur Général: Relative à la revision des listes électorales en ce qui concerne les israélites," December 12, 1895, CAOM Alg GGA 3CAB/52. See also Stein, *Saharan Jews and the Fate of French Algeria*, 46, 51.

[105] Gov-Gen Cambon, "Circulaire du Gouverneur Général: Relative à la revision des listes électorales en ce qui concerne les israélites," December 12, 1895, CAOM Alg GGA 3CAB/52.

personal status. As such, they had the same requirements as Muslims for access to naturalization.[106]

As for "native" Algerian Jews, Lépine concluded that the October 7, 1871, law was "abusive" and that those Jews who had been impacted by the law's limits could benefit again from the common law and could be reinscribed on electoral lists. However, he maintained that Jews who had not fulfilled the requirements imposed by the 1871 law could be removed from electoral lists. After removal, impacted Jews who could prove their indigenous status would be reinscribed at the next revision of the electoral lists. In a footnote, Lépine noted that the Algerian Jew who failed to prove his indigenous status within the time period outlined in the 1871 law could no longer acquire citizenship based on the Crémieux Decree, but only through the 1865 sénatus-consulte or by the 1889 legislation. However, the son of such a Jew would be considered, based on the 1889 law, a French citizen, as long as he had completed his military service.[107] These circulars served as an opportunity for municipal antisemites to eliminate Jewish voters from electoral lists, and, as a result, from competition for access to municipal services and power. Bellat took this route, calling upon the precedent of the 1895 and 1897 circulars that gave him, as mayor, the power to revise electoral lists.

Under Bellat, Sidi Bel Abbès was an epicenter of the renaissance of antisemitic municipal activity. Since his election in 1929, Lucien Bellat conducted antisemitic activities under the auspices of his electoral office, including firing Jewish municipal employees.[108] In 1936, the town's population was 49,306 inhabitants, of whom there were 23,495 French citizens: 1,462 from the metropole, 21,801 from Algeria, and 232 from other colonies. Counted among the total number of Frenchman were approximately 3,500 Jews. The vast majority of the non-Jewish Frenchmen were of Spanish origin, going back one or two generations. In addition, there were 803 recently naturalized Frenchmen, of whom 632 were Spanish, 31 were Italians, and 84 were of other origins. Among the naturalized were 38 Muslims and 8 Kabyles, bringing the total number of French citizens (by origin or naturalization) to 24,298. The population also included 18,647 Muslims, who were French subjects. There was also a population of 6,361 foreigners, who were neither French citizens nor subjects. Among the foreigners were 940 Muslims

---

[106] Gov-Gen Lépine, "Circulaire du Gouverneur Général relative à l'inscription des israélites sur les listes électorales ou à leur radiation des dites listes," December 7, 1897, CAOM Alg GGA 3CAB/52.

[107] Ibid.

[108] "Report on the Election of the Municipality of Bellat," undated (probably 1938), CAOM Alg GGA 3CAB/52.

and 5,421 non-Muslim foreigners, of whom 5,119 were Spaniards. The numbers of the Frenchmen of Spanish origin and Spanish citizens living in Sidi Bel Abbès made them a powerful group. Jews, by contrast, made up only 7 percent of the general population. Only men of voting age who met the requirements of citizenship could actually vote. As a result, the electoral lists of Sidi Bel Abbès in 1937 included 5,718 electors, of whom 605 were Jews. As such Jews were in fact but 10.6 percent of the voting population. While this is a relatively small percentage, it still exerted power at the polls, and as such, posed a threat to antisemitic politicians, such as Bellat.[109]

With the support and encouragement of the antisemitic mayor of Sidi Bel Abbès, violence occurred in the town on August 6–7, 1935. The cause of the violence was the publication of an antisemitic poster and its dissemination through the town. The poster was directed at "latin" workers and employees. It stated, "Communists who seem to take your interests in hand, in fact take you to the bankruptcy of all your good feelings. Communism is only instituted to defend Jewish international capitalism." The poster identified the worst Jewish offenders: Blum, Grumbach, Rothschild, and Dreyfus. The poster also provided statistics for Sidi Bel Abbès: "Out of four solicitors, two are Jewish. Out of eight lawyers, five are Jewish. And almost all clerks are Jewish. Merchants in lingerie, hosiery, are all Jews ... The Jews do not build, they place their fortune abroad." While the poster began with appeals to reduce the economic role of Jews within Sidi Bel Abbès, toward the end, it called for violence against Jews. "It is best that we slaughter the Jews who are Bolsheviks and preach the revolution. Latins who are concerned about the future of your children and the whole country, let us unite to drive the Jews and their Freemason accomplices out of France." The poster ended with "Down with the Bolsheviks, Death to the Jews and Freemasons, Long Live the tricolor flag, Long Live France."[110]

Throughout the morning and afternoon of August 7, fights broke out between Unions Latines members and members of the Francist movement. The Francist movement, organized by Marcel Bucard

---

[109] Laure Blévis' numbers are problematic. She gives the following statistics: In 1929, the town of Sidi Bel Abbès had 45,000 inhabitants, 30,000 of whom were Europeans, 15,000 were Jews, and 14,000 Muslims. These numbers do not add up correctly, and are countered by the 1938 report of Perier de Feral, the Inspector General of the Administration of Algeria. See Blévis, "Une citoyenneté française contestée," 116. Perier de Feral, Inspector Général of the Administration of Algeria, "Report No. 222, to the Gov-Gen of Algeria," Algiers, April 20, 1938, CAOM Alg GGA 3CAB/52.

[110] The Commissioner of General Security, Chief of the Mobile Brigade of Sidi Bel Abbès Palous, "Rapport Special, Sidi Bel Abbès, Provocation au meurtre," Sidi Bel Abbès, August 17, 1935, CAOM Alg GGA 3CAB/52.

in September 1933, was a French fascist movement supported and inspired by Benito Mussolini and the Italian fascists, and were also known as the *chemises bleues* (blue shirts) and gave the Roman salute. The Francists were involved in the violence in Paris in February 1934 following the Stavisky Affair. While not initially antisemitic, they became increasingly anti-Jewish and collaborated with the German occupiers in World War II. Fights also developed when Jews attempted to tear or take down the posters. A delegate of the Financial Delegation of Algeria wrote to the governor-general urging him to take immediate action, fearing that if left unchecked, there could be a repeat of the events of Constantine and Sétif. After the municipal police intervened, the violence stopped.[111] However, Jews continued to feel insecure.

Following the violence, the General Security and Mobile Brigade services of Sidi Bel Abbès were charged with identifying who the author of the poster was, which press produced the poster, and who distributed it. The Commissioner of General Security identified that the posters came from the Roidot press and that only Alfred Vidal could have produced them. Vidal was 35 years old and most likely of Spanish origin.[112] Although Vidal was responsible for the publication of the posters, accusations were made against almost all groups in Sidi Bel Abbès. Marcel Bremond, a Financial Delegation member of Sidi Bel Abbès, defended Vidal and identified Jews as the instigators of the violence. He also stated that the posters, while inflammatory, were not incorrect in identifying Jewish power in certain fields, especially legal and judicial positions in the city. Bremond also wrote of his support for Mayor Bellat, whose task of maintaining order in Sidi Bel Abbès was extremely challenging. Bremond's letter reflects the widespread antisemitism in Sidi Bel Abbès as well as the popular beliefs that Jews had inordinate control over certain aspects of governance.[113]

The Prefect of Oran described the rising tensions at play in the violence of August 1935, organized in part by the communists. He noted that there had been several protests of unemployed men in the preceding days. Furthermore, on August 8, 1,500 people attended a meeting for the members of the Popular Front in Oran. As the people left the meeting,

---

[111] Ibid. See also Financial Delegation of Algeria Delegate (name illegible), "Letter to the Gov-Gen of Algeria," Sidi Bel Abbès, August 7, 1935, CAOM Alg GGA 3CAB/52. Stanley Payne, *A History of Fascism* (London: University College London Press, 1995), 400–401.

[112] The Commissioner of General Security, Chief of the Mobile Brigade of Sidi Bel Abbès Palous, "Raport Special, Sidi Bel Abbès, Provocation au meurtre," Sidi Bel Abbès, August 17, 1935, CAOM Alg GGA 3CAB/52.

[113] Marcel Bremond, "Letter of Monsieur Carde, Gov-Gen of Algeria," Sidi Bel Abbès, August 21, 1935, CAOM Alg GGA 3CAB/52.

violence occurred between members and the police sent there to keep the peace. The Prefect of Oran noted that a large number of the communist militants were Jews. "Their double quality of Communists and Jews has increased the antagonism towards them from the right wing parties, the *Croix de Feu*, the Volontaires Nationaux, and the members of the Action Française, who are mostly antisemites."[114] Ultimately, politics and antisemitism were behind the increase in violence in 1935.

Conflicts continued in Sidi Bel Abbès in 1936 and 1937 with Mayor Bellat looming in the background. On May 27, 1936, M. Smadja, the president of the Jewish Consistory of Oran, received word from Jewish and Muslim leaders in Sidi Bel Abbès that the "lies" of articles and police reports in *L'Echo d'Oran* could provoke violence between Muslims and Jews. A meeting occurred between Jewish members of the Consistory of Sidi Bel Abbès and Muslim leaders sought to defuse tensions. Djillali Talem, the cousin of a Muslim Financial Delegation member in Tlemcen, and Mohamed Lalout, a municipal council member of Sidi Bel Abbès, commented that the situation was deteriorating. They added that "the Muslims of Sidi Bel Abbès are apparently calm, but the Bellat municipality wants to create violent incidents, with flowing blood."[115] The meeting between Jewish and Muslim leaders points to collaboration and cooperation between the two groups.

On February 25, 1937, violence sponsored by Bellat resurfaced in Sidi Bel Abbès. Over two days, groups of antisemites, many of whom were employees of the municipality, harassed Jews and shouted, "Down with the Reds! Down with the Jews! Long Live Doriot!" A crowd of possibly 1,500 people, including some 500 to 600 Muslims, gathered to protest these aggressions. At the same time, a group of Rassemblement National members formed nearby. As police officers attempted to calm the protestors, a gunshot rang out. Some municipal police officers then opened fire on them with their personal revolvers, not their regulation arms. The LDH accused Mayor Bellat of encouraging the violence.[116]

---

[114] The Prefect of the Department of Oran, "Report No. 4528 to the Gov-Gen of Algeria," Oran, August 9, 1935, CAOM Alg GGA 3CAB/52.

[115] Chief of the Departmental Security of Oran, "Report No. 3329 to the Prefect of Oran: Incidents de Sidi Bel Abbès," Oran, May 28, 1936, CAOM Alg GGA 3CAB/52. In a truly bizarre letter to Léon Blum in September 1936, Mayor Bellat defended his actions with regard to Jews, stating that he and his municipal government held the Jews in high esteem. See Mayor Lucien Bellat, "Letter No. 8391 to Léon Blum," Sidi Bel Abbès, September 2, 1936, CAOM Alg GGA 3CAB/52.

[116] President LDH, "Rapport sur les événements sanglants du 25 février 1937 à Sidi Bel Abbès," Sidi Bel Abbès, March 6, 1937, BDIC-LDH F Delta Res 798/171; Director of the Algerian Railways Ardoin, "Report to the Gov-Gen of Algeria," Algiers, March 2, 1937, CAOM Alg GGA 3CAB/52. See also Inspector General of the Administration of

The Inspector General of the Administration of Algeria reported on the violence in February 1937. All members of the city were split between two political parties: on the one hand was the Popular Front, and on the other was the Rassemblement National, the composite of the Parti Populaire Français, the Parti Social Français (formerly the *Croix de Feu*), and the Union Latine, led by Paul Bellat, the son of Mayor Bellat, and a member of the Financial Delegation. Most of the leaders of these groups were also employees of the municipality under Bellat. The inspector general described the Popular Front supporters as "disciplined," whereas the actions of the Rassemblement National were shaped by "nervousness and acrimony" toward communists.[117]

The Spanish Civil War contributed to the charged environment in part because of the large Spanish population in Oran and Sidi Bel Abbès. The inspector general noted that "these events certainly have a great influence on the Rassemblement National, who supports General Franco and ardently hopes for his success," and were as responsible for the graffiti, destruction of Jewish shop windows, and the general harassment of Jews. The Popular Front supporters believed that the Rassemblement National controlled the mayor and profited from the relationship. Furthermore, members of the Popular Front believed that the "municipal police, devoid of impartiality, is fully under the orders of the Mayor, and bullies, on all occasion, those who do not think like the Municipality."[118] As punishment, the governor-general removed the administration of the police from the municipality's purview. Angered by this action, the municipal government blamed Jews for the reduction in their control of the municipal services and focused on "reducing the role of Jews in public life."

At a meeting in Algiers in March, Lecache of the LICA chided Jews for their lack of support of the Blum-Viollette Bill.[119] At an April 1937 LICA meeting, Cheikh el Hadi of Tlemcen spoke in Arabic on the importance of unity between Jews and Muslims in the face of intensified antisemitism. He pointed a finger at mayors in Algeria who fomented antisemitism in

Algeria, Department of Oran, "Report No. 90, to the Gov-Gen of Algeria: Incidents du 25 février à Sidi Bel Abbès," Algiers, March 3, 1937, CAOM Alg GGA 3CAB/52.

[117] Inspector General of the Administration of Algeria, Department of Oran, "Report No. 90, to the Gov-Gen of Algeria: Incidents du 25 février à Sidi Bel Abbès," Algiers, March 3, 1937, CAOM Alg GGA 3CAB/52.

[118] Ibid.

[119] Departmental Security Report, "Rapport No. 1623: Au sujet de l'Assemblée Générale de la LICA," Algiers March 16, 1937, CAOM Alg Alger F410. See Central Police Commissioner "Rapport No. 277R.S.," Algiers, March 20, 1937; Police Commissioner of Blida, "Rapport No. 1621: Objet: Réunion publique organisée par la LICA," Blida, March 20, 1937; Central Police Commissioner to the Sec-Gen, Algiers, March 21, 1937, CAOM Alg Alger F410.

their cities.[120] Benhoura, another Muslim Conference member, also warned his coreligionists that "everything that is anti-Jewish is anti-Muslim." In May 1937, the LICA shifted its attention to Abbé Lambert and his mobilization of antisemitism, which Lecache described as "a dangerous contagion that will one day attack France, but first Oran."[121] The LICA clearly identified municipal governments as crucibles of antisemitism.

"A Group of *Latins*" wrote a letter to Lecache in which they renamed him "Belzebuth Nakach." Depicting Lecache as the representative of "Jewish finance" and "Jewish commerce," they accused Jews of seeking only to enrich themselves at the expense of Frenchmen. The *Latins* accused Jews of controlling the Popular Front. "The Jews are two percent of the population of France, but in the ministerial officers of Blum, they hold fifty-two percent of the positions." Seeking the support of Arabs, the *Latins* claimed that "under the pretext of defending the Arabs and the workers, Belzebuth Nakach wants to assure in Oran and elsewhere the supremacy of the Jew."[122] In Affreville, antisemitic flyers appeared on Jewish shops that called for yet another Jewish boycott. One read, "Parents! Guard your daughters if they work for Jews." Another stated that "if you have a Jewish friend, he will cheat on you with your wife . . . or with his word of honor." Another warned "A non-Jew is ruined by bankruptcy! A Jew is enriched by bankruptcy!"[123] The boycott continued throughout the colony, and by connecting the boycott to the situation in Palestine, antisemites gained support among Muslims.[124] The rhetoric of antisemites enflamed tensions between Jews and

---

[120] Police Commissioner of Nemours to the Prefect of Oran, "Rapport No. 986," Nemours, April 13, 1937, CAOM Alg Oran 5i/50. The LICA also called upon Communists and Algerian Muslims to join the fight against antisemitism. Departmental Security of Algiers, "Rapport No. 3675: Ligue Internationale contre l'Antisémitisme," Algiers, May 24, 1937, CAOM Alg Oran 5i/50.

[121] Departmental Security of Oran, "Rapport No. 4182: Ligue Internationale Contre l'Antisémitisme, Conférence de M. Bernard Lecache dans la Salle du Cinéma Familia," Oran, May 12, 1937, CAOM Alg Oran 2541. See also Police Commissioner of Perregaux, "Rapport No. 1426: Conférence publique par M. Bernard Lecache," Perregaux, May 13, 1937, CAOM Alg Oran 2541.

[122] A Group of Latins, "Le Juif Belzebuth Nakach (dit Bernard Lecache), Président de la Ligue pour l'Antisémitisme, vient provoquer en Oranie, la guerre de religion," Ain Temouchent, April 11, 1937, CAOM Alg Oran 424. It is unclear why the authors of this letter called Lecache Nakach. It is possible that they sought to make his name sound more Algerian than French. Or, possibly they were alluding to the Algerian Jewish swimmer, Alfred Nakache, who, after 1936, became one of France's top swimmers. See Joseph Seigman, *Jewish Sports Legends* (Dulles: Brassey's Press, 2000), 151–152.

[123] Police Commissioner of Affreville to the Sub-Prefect of Miliana, "Rapport No. 1366," Affreville, May 12, 1937, CAOM Alg Alger F410.

[124] Prefecture of Oran, "Rapport No. 151: Renseignements au sujet d'antisémitisme," Oran, July 28, 1937, CAOM Alg Oran 5i/50.

Muslims, despite the unity efforts of the LICA. As of April, the majority of incidents involving Jews transitioned from being between Jews and Europeans to Jews and Muslims.[125]

Over the course of 1937 in Constantine, violent encounters continued between Jews and Muslims, and between Jews and Europeans. An interesting encounter between Jews and French officers illustrates the ways in which Jews considered themselves Frenchmen above all else: upon hearing a French officer say the word "Jewry" (*Juiverie*) in a derogatory manner, a Jewish man responded, "at your service, my Commandant." He continued, "I heard the word 'Jewry' and I saw you turn towards me; we're French. I also wear a civil uniform, I am a judge."[126] Although not violent, this exchange exemplifies several important elements: the antisemitism of French officers as well as the fact that Jews held significant civil service positions in the colony. It also demonstrates the way in which Jews valued their French identities and defended their Frenchness in the face of antisemitic attacks and slights.[127]

Amid increasing violence and successes of antisemitic campaigns, Jews reassessed their approach to self-defense in the colony with the assistance of organizations such as the Alliance, the LICA, and, eventually, the CAES. In the late 1930s, Zionism still was not a popular movement in North Africa, especially in Algeria.[128] Most Jews saw self-defense as the best strategy of dealing with antisemitism and ensuring a French future for Jews in Algeria. The vice president of the Alliance, Georges Leven, described the evolution of the Alliance from its educative origins to a defense organization. Since 1933, the Alliance recognized the need to respond to the "worldwide recrudescence of antisemitism," influenced by

---

[125] Central Police Commissioner of Constantine to the Prefect of Constantine, "Rapport No. 2005: Objet: Incident à signaler," Constantine, April 21, 1937, CAOM Alg Const B/3/656. In Algiers in August 1937, a small incident quickly turned into a dangerous mob provoked by Brahim ben Yahia Moknine, who encouraged the crowd to "get the Jew who hit one of ours," and to do "as in Constantine." "Incident entre Arabes et Juifs à Alger," Algiers, August 27, 1937, CAOM Alg Oran 5i/50.

[126] Central Commissioner to the Prefect of Constantine, "No. 445: Objet: Incident entre Officiers et Israélites," Constantine, January 21, 1937, CAOM Alg Const B/3/656.

[127] For a strange case of a young Jewish man who sought to join the Spanish military, see Commissioner of Police of Batna to the Sub-Prefect of Batna, "Rapport No. 745," Constantine, February 1, 1937, CAOM Alg Const B/3/656.

[128] As antisemitism developed, so did hopes for a future Jewish homeland in Palestine. Departmental Security Oran, "Rapport No. 12: Oeuvre Israélite," Oran, January 3, 1937. See also Departmental Security, Oran, "Rapport No. 3901: Passage à Oran de M. STERN Maurice, délégué du Comité Central de Paris du Keren Kayemeth Leisrael," Oran, March 30, 1937, CAOM Alg Oran 2539. See also Departmental Security Oran, "Rapport No. 3230: Keren Kayemeth Leisrael, Causerie faite par M. Stern au Cinéma Rio," Oran, April 5, 1937, CAOM Alg Oran 2539.

Nazi propaganda.[129] In 1937, the editors of *La Juste Parole* argued that antisemites would never accept Jews' assimilation. "Even if you spilled your blood for your country on the battlefield ... even if you abandoned Judaism and received a Christian baptism ... in the eyes of antisemites you are part of a cursed race, a hated race, eternally chased, and you will not escape the hatred of antisemites."[130] Even Jewish assimilation, the previous method of combating antisemitism, could no longer compete with the rhetoric of antisemites, especially as they gained control of municipal governments.[131]

In the absence of other major Jewish defense organizations in the colony, the CAES reemerged in 1937. In the early 1920s the CAES disbanded due to internal conflicts.[132] The CAES reemerged with a tripartite program of combating antisemitism in Algeria: providing information, coordinating Jews in defense efforts, and "fighting for the respect of human dignity and the rights of French Algerian Jews." The CAES also planned to work with Algerian Muslims on a "project of rapprochement and mutual comprehension."[133]

At the end of 1937, Section President Richard Hell and Secretary-General Lucien Sebbah of the Constantine Section of the LICA submitted a report on the intensification of antisemitism in Algeria. The report depicted the impact of Nazi antisemitic propaganda in Constantine, and provided a picture taken of families of workers, posing and smiling in front of a large swastika and the inscription "Down with the Jews." Hell and Sebbah's report also described the municipal governments' efforts to remove Jews from electoral lists in order to eliminate them as competitors in elections. In conclusion, Hell and Sebbah recommended that pro-fascist elements in the Algerian administration be removed from their posts.[134] The opposite would occur.

---

[129] "M. Georges Leven, Vice Président de l'Alliance Israélite Universelle, à Alger," *Bulletin de la Fédération des Sociétés Juives d'Algérie*, No. 33 (May 1937): 6–7.

[130] "S.O.S. Dites-Vous Bien Ceci," *Bulletin de la Fédération des Sociétés Juives d'Algérie*, No. 33 (May 1937): 15.

[131] Division Chief of Departmental Security of Oran to the Prefect of Oran, "Rapport No. 9411: Re: Foyer Intellectuel Israélite conférence de Mlle BABIS Rachel," Oran, November 18, 1937, CAOM Alg Oran 2539.

[132] In the aftermath of the 1934 pogrom, Confino described the group's necessity, but the organization would not be active for another three years. Cohen, "Algeria," 464.

[133] "Assemblée Générale du Comité Juif Algérien d'Études Sociales," *Bulletin de la Fédération des Sociétés Juives d'Algérie*, No. 33 (May 1937): 23. Although the CAES had left out the "Juif" from its title, in 1937 they reinserted the Jewish aspect of the committee. This is likely due to the new leadership of Levy-Valensi, whereas Henri Aboulker was more concerned with assimilation of Jews, rather than emphasizing their Jewishness.

[134] Hell and Sebbah also demanded that the Blum-Viollette Bill be promulgated in the interest of the future of the nation and racial harmony. Richard Hell and Lucien Sebbah,

Among the most extreme cases of such municipal antisemitism was the removal of Jews from electoral lists in Sidi Bel Abbès at the end of 1937 and into 1938, which LICA representatives named the "Bellat Affair." The "Bellat Affair" demonstrated the politicization of the municipal commission responsible for the revision of the electoral lists. According to Perier de Feral, the Inspector General of the Administration of Algeria, Bellat accused the Sub-Prefect, whose responsibilities included choosing a delegate for the commission, of being influenced by a Jew, M. Choukroun, who was a court employee. In the end, Bellat claimed that no delegate had been assigned. His municipal government took matters into their own hands and revised the electoral lists even before the first meeting of the official Commission.[135]

Over the course of 1937, Jewish electors in Sidi Bel Abbès were called to the mayor's office and told to bring proof of identity with them. Upon arriving at the City Hall, officials asked for information on their origins, their parents, grandparents, and great-grandparents, theoretically to regulate their military eligibility. Many Jews found the situation suspicious and refused to respond to the call. A second call went out to more Jews, many of whom were known for their pro–Popular Front politics. By early 1938, approximately 372 Jewish electors were removed from electoral lists, supposedly due to the fact that the Jewish voters did not meet the requirements set forth in the October 7, 1871, law modifying the Crémieux Decree.[136]

The Sub-Prefect and the administration were aware of the problematic and unethical efforts of Bellat and his commission to remove Jewish electors. The Sub-Prefect of Sidi Bel Abbès placed a delegate, M. Pfister, on the commission as his representative. When Pfister arrived at the

"Brèves Observations de la Section Constantinoise de la LICA (600 membres) sur la situation en Algérie, suivies des remèdes proposes," Constantine, December 29, 1937, CDJC CMXCVI-123.3.

[135] Perier de Feral, Inspector General of the Administration of Algeria, "Report No. 222, to the Gov-Gen of Algeria," Algiers, April 20, 1938, CAOM Alg GGA 3CAB/52. See also Mayor Bellat of Sidi Bel Abbès, "Letter to Minister of the Interior re: Revision of the Electoral Lists of Sidi Bel Abbès for 1938," Sidi Bel Abbès, February 24, 1938, CAOM Alg GGA 3CAB/52.

[136] The mayor called the commission to meet initially on January 7. Mayor of Sidi Bel Abbès (by his assistant Contraire) to the Sub-Prefect of Sidi Bel Abbès, "No. 111," Sidi Bel Abbès, January 6, 1938, CAOM Alg GGA 3CAB/52. See also The LICA, "Affaire Bellat de Sidi Bel Abbès, Rapport sur Radiations," Sidi Bel Abbès, 1937, CDJC CMXCVI-135.2. The numbers prove challenging to confirm. Laure Blévis identifies only 323 Jewish voters removed from the electoral lists; however, the LICA's report seems more accurate. It is also confirmed by Perier de Feral's report. See Blévis, "Une citoyenneté française contestée," 117. See also Perier de Feral, Inspector General of the Administration of Algeria, "Report No. 222, to the Gov-Gen of Algeria," Algiers, April 20, 1938, CAOM Alg GGA 3CAB/52.

commission's meeting on January 8, 1938, he learned from Mayor Bellat that "a number of voters would be removed on the initiative of the Commission itself. He was told that these particular removals involved voters of Jewish origin, on the grounds that these voters had not proven their French citizenship." Bellat stated that to his knowledge, throughout the entire colony, only forty Algerian Jews had met the requirements of the 1871 law. Pfister argued that Bellat was using a far too strict interpretation of the 1871 law and that there were other means by which those Jews could have proven the requirements of citizenship. Pfister added that the commission could not remove those voters unless it could prove that they were indeed *not* citizens, and the fact that they were already on the electoral lists indicated that they indeed were citizens. The mayor and council members ignored Pfister's points. In advance of the commission's first meeting, the names of the Jewish voters had already been marked in red, whereas all other names under consideration for removal were marked in purple.[137] Pfister made a formal objection to the plan of the commission, arguing that the removal of the Jewish voters was unjust and that the eliminated voters were not offered due process.[138] His formal protest was in vain, however, as the mayor and the municipal council members serving on the commission formed the majority.[139]

When on February 4, 1938, the Sub-Prefect demanded the reinstatement of the Jewish voters, the electoral commission responded by returning only a small number to the list.[140] At the same time, Abbé Lambert, then the mayor of Oran, began publishing articles under a pseudonym in the newspaper *Oran Matin*, regarding the elimination of Jewish voters. The articles concluded that the Jews had been given universal suffrage too early and that to avoid allowing this group to "impose their wishes" on the rest of the population, the revision of the electoral lists was necessary.[141] Abbé Lambert clearly hoped to follow Bellat's model, which was exactly what the Sub-Prefect had feared.

---

[137] M. Pfister, "Declaration produced for Perier de Feral," Sidi Bel Abbès, April 5, 1938, CAOM Alg GGA 3CAB/52. See also Perier de Feral, Inspector General of the Administration of Algeria, "Report No. 222, to the Gov-Gen of Algeria," Algiers, April 20, 1938, CAOM Alg GGA 3CAB/52.

[138] M. Pfister, "Exposé de M. Pfister, délégué de l'Administration, Commission administrative de revision des listes électorales de la commune de de Sidi Bel Abbès pour l'année 1938," Sidi Bel Abbès, January 11, 1937, CAOM Alg GGA 3CAB/52.

[139] Perier de Feral, Inspector General of the Administration of Algeria, "Report No. 222, to the Gov-Gen of Algeria," Algiers, April 20, 1938, CAOM Alg GGA 3CAB/52.

[140] Sub-Prefect of the Arrondissement of Sidi Bel Abbès, "Letter to the Mayor of Sidi Bel Abbès, No. 1579," Sidi Bel Abbès, February 4, 1938, CAOM Alg GGA 3CAB/52.

[141] Perier de Feral, Inspector General of the Administration of Algeria, "Report No. 222, to the Gov-Gen of Algeria," Algiers, April 20, 1938, CAOM Alg GGA 3CAB/52. See also Kalman, *French Colonial Fascism*.

Mayor Bellat expressed his frustration regarding the challenges he faced in a letter to the Minister of the Interior, detailing the interference of the Sub-Prefect and his demand that the municipal commission reinstate 300 electors to the electoral lists. These electors, Bellat continued, were ones that the majority of the administrative commission had decided did not meet the requirements of the "quality of French citizenship," because they did not prove their "indigenous" status according to the regulations of the October 7, 1871, law. Bellat further complained that the Sub-Prefect's request that he submit to him the names of the voters who had been removed from the lists so that the Sub-Prefect conduct an independent inquiry was an unnecessary burden on the municipality.[142]

In a letter to the Prefect of Oran, the Sub-Prefect of Sidi Bel Abbès responded to Mayor Bellat's accusations, suggesting that his complaints were merely a tactic to subvert the Sub-Prefect's authority over the activities of the municipal electoral commission. The Sub-Prefect argued that he had followed protocol

because the attitude and circumstances of the Municipality of Sidi Bel Abbès much exceeds the concern for legality and the framework of the city. In doing so, the Mayor of Sidi Bel Abbès wanted, at least this is my feeling, to exercise through political bullying a grudge against the Jew; he hoped, and probably still hopes, to be followed by many of the Algerian municipalities. This gesture, along with other vexing examples, has caused an emotion that extends far beyond Sidi Bel Abbès and may cause undesirable reactions for maintaining order.[143]

The Sub-Prefect clearly sought to prevent the antisemitic machinations of Bellat and his municipal government.

The LICA joined the Sub-Prefect and argued, "It is undeniable that the actions taken by the administrative commission and confirmed by the municipal commission constitutes a case of bullying with regards to Jews." They pointed out that many of the Jewish victims were veterans of World War I. The Sidi Bel Abbès electoral commission and the municipality as a whole sought not only to remove Jews from the electoral lists but also to strip them of their citizenship, refusing to allow Jews to serve as witnesses in courts under the pretext that they were not Frenchmen. The authors of the report called for an immediate inquiry into the situation and demanded that the administration make examples

---

[142] Bellat complained that the committee examined the files several times. Mayor Bellat of Sidi Bel Abbès, "Letter to Minister of the Interior re: Revision of the Electoral Lists of Sidi Bel Abbès for 1938," Sidi Bel Abbès, February 24, 1938, CAOM Alg GGA 3CAB/52. See also Sub-Prefect of the Arrondissement of Sidi Bel Abbès to the Prefect of Oran, "Report No. 2468," Sidi Bel Abbès, February 28, 1938, CAOM Alg GGA 3CAB/52.

[143] The Sub-Prefect of the Arrondissement of Sidi Bel Abbès to the Prefect of Oran, Sidi Bel Abbès, April 5, 1938, CAOM Alg GGA 3CAB/52.

of the offenders involved.[144] The Sidi Bel Abbès commission's actions were indicative of the new radical nature of municipal antisemitism. Several other groups defended the Jewish voters of Sidi Bel Abbès. In 1938, the LDH examined the case to assess how they might protect the rights of Jews involved.[145] Among the cases they examined was that of Levi Henri Pinto, one of the impacted Jewish voters.[146] After being removed from the electoral list, Pinto submitted a request to be reinstated, which the commission rejected. Pinto provided proof of his right to French citizenship: born in Oran on March 3, 1899, he satisfied his military service, and had been on the electoral lists in Oran for many years. Following Pinto's complaint, the electoral commission responded that they did not contest the fact that Pinto was French, but the law required him to show proof of his French citizenship. Despite providing the necessary documentation, the commission still removed Pinto from the electoral lists.[147] For many Jews, supplying documentation regarding their citizenship was impossible because they either did not have the documents that the commission required or that such documentation never existed.

At the request of the Sub-Prefect, the case of the eliminated Jewish voters came to the court on March 19, 1938. Alfred Ghighi, the lawyer and Jewish General Council member of Oran, argued that the Jewish voters should be protected by the assumed permanence of electoral lists. Furthermore, the commission for the revision of the electoral lists had falsely applied judgments coming from cases at the appeals court of April 27, 1896. Ghighi emphasized that the removal of the Jewish voters was an abuse of power by the commission. The Jewish voters were descendants of citizens who had completed the requirements of the October 7, 1871, law or were citizens based on the June 26, 1889, legislation on naturalizations. They were therefore French – "there are no more indigenous Jews in Algeria – in the territories of the three Algerian

---

[144] Ibid.
[145] Sec-Gen LDH to M. Bertrand, President of the LDH, "Re: Sidi Bel Abbès protestation contre radiation d'israélites sur listes électorales," Paris, February 1, 1938; Secretary LDH Sidi Bel Abbès to the Sec-Gen LDH, Paris, Sidi Bel Abbès, January 24, 1938, BDIC-LDH F Delta Res 798/169.
[146] President Martaing, LDH Sidi Bel Abbès, to the Sec-Gen of the LDH, Paris, "Objet: Radiation de 372 électeurs israélites à Sidi Bel Abbès," Sidi Bel Abbès, March 5, 1938, BDIC-LDH F Delta Res 798/169.
[147] In addition, Pinto's father, Aaron Pinto, born on March 3, 1862, in Oran, was naturalized. D. Philippe Martinez, "Copie de la sommation de M. Pinto à M. le Président de la Commission de révision des listes électorales," Sidi Bel Abbès, February 28, 1938, BDIC-LDH F Delta Res 798/169. This proof of citizenship had to be based on the law of October 7, 1871, or his naturalization or that of his predecessors by virtue of the sénatus-consulte of July 14, 1865.

departments – since October 24, 1870," he contended. Furthermore, Mayor Bellat had not followed the governor-general's directions set forth in the June and December 1895 circulars. M. Lisbonne, acting as the lawyer of the eliminated Jewish voters, argued that the electoral lists were presumed permanent, and the revision of such lists was an abuse of power.[148]

On March 30, 1938, the judge refused to reinstate all the Jewish voters as the law was technically on the side of Bellat and his antisemitic coterie. He ruled that there was a distinction based on Article 7 of the civil code between civil rights and political rights. He also concluded that the burden of proof of citizenship rested with the Jewish voters eliminated by the commission. The judge ruled that some Jews be reinscribed on the electoral lists if they had become French by way of naturalization, or if they were the sons of foreigners who became naturalized via the 1889 law. Seventeen of the affected Jews could be returned to the electoral lists because they had succeeded in proving their "indigeneity." The vast majority of the victims, however, had not succeeded in proving their quality of French citizen based on the requirements of the October 7, 1871, law.[149]

Inspector General De Feral noted the larger possible impact of the judgment. "The decision of Sidi Bel Abbès magistrate is likely to have a large scope since it admits that 68 years after the decree law of October 24, 1870 and the Decree of October 7, 1871, the quality of the French citizenship of the indigenous Jews of Algeria can be questioned." Furthermore, the judgment presented a dangerous precedent by forcing Jews to prove their rights to citizenship based on the requirements of the 1871 decree. De Feral contended that the continued emphasis on the 1871 decree was illogical. "Algerian Jews are French citizens and they can be nothing else: the category of indigenous Jewish French subjects has *legally disappeared*." Furthermore, he continued, the decisions by Mayor Bellat and the justice of the peace of Sidi Bel Abbès were "without juridical foundation." De Feral anticipated that there would be significant political repercussions, and that many other Algerian municipalities would follow suit.[150] Even the Minister of Justice admitted in 1939 that the requirement to provide witnesses to attest to a Jew's indigenous status

---

[148] Perier de Feral, Inspector General of the Administration of Algeria, "Report No. 222, to the Gov-Gen of Algeria," Algiers, April 20, 1938, CAOM Alg GGA 3CAB/52. See also the Sub-Prefect of Sidi Bel Abbès, "Letter to the Justice of the Peace of Sidi Bel Abbès, No. 2733," Sidi Bel Abbès, March 10, 1938, CAOM Alg GGA 3CAB/52.
[149] Perier de Feral, Inspector General of the Administration of Algeria, "Report No. 222, to the Gov-Gen of Algeria," Algiers, April 20, 1938, CAOM Alg GGA 3CAB/52.
[150] Ibid. Emphasis in the original.

verged on the ridiculous. However, the law had to be upheld, especially in the context of the efforts regarding the Blum-Viollette Bill. Any alterations or openings offered to Jews would likely have to be offered to Muslims, something the government was reluctant to consider at the time.[151] In the legal sphere, the situation of Jews and Muslims remained inextricably linked.

Leaders of antifascist organizations in Sidi Bel Abbès submitted a letter of protest on behalf of the Jews, detailing the long history of Jewish patriotism and military service in the colony. They considered Bellat responsible, given his role as mayor, president of the electoral commission, and leader of the antisemitic movement in the region of Oran. "The decision he has made has caused legitimate concern in both the Jewish and Republican circles. Since 1870 (the Crémieux Decree), never and under no government has the quality of French citizen been contested for a group of electors/citizens." Despite being entirely illegal and unethical, the authors feared that the case of Sidi Bel Abbès would serve as a model to be replicated in other municipalities in the colony. "If Mr. Bellat's approach only gives rise to a legal controversy without administrative sanctions, we are confident that many reactionary municipalities in Algeria will follow his example."[152]

Bernard Lecache, the president of the LICA, wrote directly to Governor-General Le Beau regarding the actions of the Sidi Bel Abbès antisemites. "You can see, like me, the gravity of what such a precedent could do, and I am confident that you would not tolerate as such its existence much longer."[153] Le Beau responded that he was well aware of the situation and had already met with a delegation of Jewish leaders regarding the situation. He added that he remained very attentive to all developments on the incident, "which, in addition, happily has only occurred in a single commune of Algeria."[154] The CAES used the Sidi Bel Abbès affair to highlight their concern over the escalation of municipal antisemitism in the colony. In particular, they pointed to Henri Lautier's antisemitic activities, including his campaigns for the abrogation of the Crémieux Decree.[155]

---

[151] Blévis, "Une citoyenneté française contestée," 117–118, 121–122.

[152] Leaders of antifascist organizations in Sidi Bel Abbès to the President of the Rassemblement Populaire, Paris, Sidi Bel Abbès, March 4, 1938, BDIC-LDH F Delta Res 798/169.

[153] Bernard Lecache to the Gov-Gen of Algeria Le Beau, Paris, March 18, 1938, CAOM Alg GGA 3CAB/52.

[154] Gov-Gen Le Beau to Bernard Lecache, "No. 103," Paris, March 19, 1938, CAOM Alg GGA 3CAB/52.

[155] Elie Gozlan, Sec-Gen, CAES, to the President of the Centre de Documentation et Vigilance, Paris, Algiers, February 4, 1938, CDJC DCCVVI-2.

Imposing sanctions on Mayor Bellat was legally challenging. The administration could not invoke religious persecution, as Bellat could claim that he was not discriminating against the Jews based on their faith, but on their "indigenous" status. Inspector General De Feral stated that he had no doubt that Mayor Bellat was personally behind the abuses, but legally, he had never taken action on his own, but as a member of an administrative commission. Therefore, responsibility rested with the commission and not with Bellat.[156] In February 1939, the Prefect of Oran assured the governor-general that the situation in Sidi Bel Abbès was "purely local" and that there was no sign there would be other cases.[157] This was not, however, true. Although the Sidi Bel Abbès case was the most extreme, there were other cases of antisemitic municipalities removing Jewish electors.

But removing Jewish electors was only part of Bellat's objective. Bellat also directed a campaign to restrict Jews from completing their military service. The Sub-Prefect of Sidi Bel Abbès reported on March 12, 1938, that several young Jews had not been included on the census lists of the draft class of those born in 1918. Mayor Bellat was responsible for this, as it was the mayor's responsibility to organize the lists. The Sub-Prefect presented two cases: that of Charles Chlous, born May 10, 1918, and Jacob André Charbit, born March 9, 1918. Both young men were born in Sidi Bel Abbès. Bellat and his revision commission explained that the two men were considered indigenous Jews and therefore could not be considered part of the census lists of 1938. Instead, they would only be added to the class of 1939, under the category of "native." Inspector General De Feral demanded that Bellat produce the birth certificates of the individuals in question and noted that none of the certificates listed the individual as "indigenous Jew." Thirty-two young men born in 1918 found themselves in this situation.[158]

Bellat's tactics prevented young Jewish men from completing their military service and therefore were unable to prove their value as French citizens. The requirement for active service for citizens was two years; if categorized as "indigenous Jews," the young men would not be able to complete their service. Inspector General De Feral concluded that based on his actions and his abuse of power Mayor Bellat "continues to

---

[156] Perier de Feral, Inspector General of the Administration of Algeria, "Report No. 222, to the Gov-Gen of Algeria," Algiers, April 20, 1938, CAOM Alg GGA 3CAB/52.

[157] Prefect of the Department of Oran, "Letter No. 2023, to the Gov-Gen of Algeria," Oran, February 23, 1939, CAOM Alg GGA 3CAB/52.

[158] Perier de Feral, Inspector General of the Administration of Algeria, "Report No. 222, to the Gov-Gen of Algeria," Algiers, April 20, 1938, CAOM Alg GGA 3CAB/52. See also Mayor Bellat of Sidi Bel Abbès, "Report to the Sub-Prefect No. 2887," Sidi Bel Abbès, March 30, 1938, CAOM Alg GGA 3CAB/52.

administer a systematic policy against his Jewish constituents that tends to deprive them of exercising the rights granted to them by law." Given all of Bellat's abuses, De Feral believed that the mayor deserved to be sanctioned. If not sanctioned, De Feral feared that the situation would only worsen and likely be emulated by other municipal governments.[159]

With the Sidi Bel Abbès Affair, antisemites had discovered a new tool to undermine the Crémieux Decree and the citizenship it provided. Alfred Ghighi lobbied Inspector General De Feral and asked that a decree be published criticizing the actions of the municipality of Sidi Bel Abbès. De Feral stated that he was opposed to such an idea as it might in fact *"reopen* the *Jewish question* in Algeria."[160] In February, Alliance, CAES, and consistory leaders met with the governor-general to formulate an intervention on behalf of the Sidi Bel Abbès Jewish voters. The governor-general "deeply moved by the flawless plea ... assured us of his benevolent feelings towards our coreligionists." He assured the Jewish delegates that the administration would not allow similar actions to take place in the future.[161]

Even the Minister of War and National Defense reviewed the situation of Jewish voters in Sidi Bel Abbès and found Bellat and the municipal council completely irresponsible.

This situation is wrong, in breach of Article 26 of the Act of March 31, 1928, and a manifest excess of power that the revision commission made in relation to young people mentioned, the conditional nature of these decisions, and I cannot, for these reasons, but persist based on the findings of my efforts, to request a cancellation, in the interest of the law, of the decisions so reached.

Many of the Jewish voters removed by Bellat's electoral commission were eventually returned to their status as citizens.[162] However, many others remained off of the electoral lists[163] The debates regarding their position on the electoral lists continued into 1939. *La Dépêche Algérienne* reported on January 13, 1939, that the Court of Appeals maintained the elimination of 128 Jewish voters from Sidi Bel Abbès.[164] On January 17, 1939,

---

[159] Perier de Feral, Inspector General of the Administration of Algeria, "Report No. 222, to the Gov-Gen of Algeria," Algiers, April 20, 1938, CAOM Alg GGA 3CAB/52.

[160] Ibid. Emphasis in the original.

[161] M. Eskenazi to the Sec-Gen of the Alliance Israélite Universelle (No. 871/3), Oran, March 24, 1938, AIU Algérie IIC9.

[162] The Minister of War and National Defense to the President of the Litigation Section of the State Council, "No. 6059/10," July 15, 1938, CAOM Alg GGA 3CAB/52. See also

[163] Members of the Electoral Commission, "Decision: Qui rejette une demande en reinscription sur les listes électorales des citoyens français," Sidi Bel Abbès, February 24, 1938, CAOM Alg GGA 3CAB/52.

[164] "La Cour de cassation maintient la radiation des listes électorales de 128 israélites algériens de Sidi-bel-Abbès," in *La Dépêche Algérienne*, January 13, 1939, CAOM Alg GGA 3CAB/52.

President Albert Sarraut decreed that Algerian Jews no longer needed to furnish proof of their indigeneity as required by the 1871 legislation, thus ending Bellat's action.[165] At the same time, the antisemitic press praised Bellat's actions. *Le Petit Oranais* published an article entitled "L'Invasion Juive," (The Jewish Invasion) on January 20, 1939, in which they suggested that Bellat was taking the necessary steps to protect the French of the colony: "We believe that the French government, instructed by the Jewish peril that menaces us, would profit from such judicial decisions to assure the French predominance in our colony."[166]

Others added their voices in defense of the Sarraut Decree, including Ferhat Abbas, who published an article expressing his support in *L'Entente* on February 2, 1939. Abbas emphasized the hypocrisy of Bellat questioning the Frenchness of Algerian Jews when his own origins were Spanish. Bellat, "Gallic via Spain – wanted to contest the rights of Algerian Israelites, living in Algeria for five or six centuries. These Algerians of French nationality since 1830, the period in which M. Bellat was still Spanish, had become French citizens by the application of the Crémieux Decree." Abbas cited the assimilation of Algerian Jews over time, stating that "the descendants were more evolved, more educated, and submit themselves to the French civil law. And since, all Algerian Jews have been considered French." Bellat's requirement that Algerian Jews prove their status by providing evidence, Abbas continued, was impossible. As a result, they were in a difficult position "outside of the law. Because if these natives could not benefit anymore from the civil law, neither could they benefit from the special law of 1919 because this only applied to Muslim natives. This was therefore purely a return to the past and towards social anarchy." Abbas praised the Sarraut decree, which defined Algerian Jews as Frenchmen, much to the chagrin of those mayors who hoped to follow the actions of Bellat. Abbas concluded by arguing that the "néo-Français" should be allowed to remain among the Algerians, and to prosper and succeed, but "to be racist in Algeria against the Algerians, stop there! Otherwise, the Republic could very well become angry and send them back to Spain."[167]

Abbas' assessment and support for the impacted Algerian Jews indicated a sense of camaraderie among certain Jews and Muslims in the colony, as well as his position that assimilation in the colony should be

---

[165] Quoted in "Après les radiations de Sidi-bel-Abbès: Un decret du 17 janvier 1939 fait echec aux manœuvres des racistes algériens," in *Oran Républicain*, January 18, 1939, CAOM Alg GGA 3CAB/52.

[166] "L'Invasion Juive," in *Le Petit Oranais*, January 20, 1939, CAOM Alg GGA 3CAB/52.

[167] Ferhat Abbas, "Du Décret Crémieux au décret Sarraut," in *L'Entente*, February 2, 1939, CAOM Alg GGA 3CAB/52.

rewarded with rights and citizenship. Although in 1938 the governor-general assured Lecache that no other similar situations were taking place in the colony, in a letter to the Prefect of Oran on February 25, 1939, Alfred Ghighi noted that because Bellat had not been punished dozens of other mayors were prepared to strip Jews from electoral lists.[168] Municipal antisemitism continued to intensify, with municipally sponsored antisemitic organizations as the motors of that acceleration.

The Power of Antisemitic Organizations

The Sidi Bel Abbès electoral commission's elimination of over 300 Jewish voters indicated the great strides of electoral antisemitism in the colony. Since Dr. Jules Molle in the 1920s, antisemitism had become entrenched in Oran's municipal government. When Abbé Lambert first entered politics, he campaigned against antisemitism and preached the union of races. Lambert created the Amitiés Lambert and encouraged Jews, Muslims, and Catholics to join its ranks. Following the elections of 1936, many members of Lambert's entourage pushed him to join the battle against the Jews. He refused and lost to the candidate sponsored by the *Croix de Feu* and Union Latine. Lambert soon recognized that political success depended upon harnessing the popular strength of electoral antisemitism. In November 1937, he established a new group oriented toward electoral politics, named the Amitiés Latines.[169] Lambert's propaganda centered on organizing a French electoral bloc to guarantee the election of antisemites and the exclusion of Jews.[170] The best way to ensure antisemitic electoral success was to remove Jews as political competitors, as the Sidi Bel Abbès government had done. In February 1938, the governor-general recognized the danger posed by antisemitic propaganda in Oran because of the involvement of right-wing groups.[171]

Despite this recognition, antisemitic right-wing groups continued to proliferate in the colony. The RN cooperated with various right-wing parties that opposed the Blum-Viollette Bill. In Oran, the RN joined the PPF, the PSF, and other similar groups under the leadership of Abbé

---

[168] Alfred Ghighi to Prefect of Oran, February 25, 1939, CAOM Alg GGA 3CAB/52.

[169] Prefect of Oran, "Rapport sur le Mouvement antisémitique dans le Département d'Oran," Oran, March 1, 1938, CAOM Alg Oran 5i/50.

[170] Prefect of Oran, "Rapport relatif à la Propagande antisémitique dans le département d'Oran, au cours du mois de Juin 1938," Oran, July 13, 1938, CAOM Alg Oran 5i/50.

[171] Gov-Gen to the Prefect of Oran, "No. 3663s, au sujet: mouvement antisémitique," Algiers, February 21, 1938, CAOM Alg Oran 424. In order to monitor the escalation of antisemitic activity, the Gov-Gen requested that the Prefect send him a detailed report on the 15th of each month.

Lambert. The RN became increasingly antisemitic in orientation; its meetings concluded with cries of "Long Live Hitler."[172] During the April 1938 General Assembly of the RN, Monsieur Viniger, president of the RN and a General Council member, called for greater unity between the groups that made up the RN, arguing that their disunity risked "giving power to the Jacobs and the Isaacs." Viniger urged his compatriots to ride the wave of antisemitism developing in the metropole in response to Blum and other Jewish politicians. Viniger demanded of his audience, "What will be your attitude? Ours will be to remain a union against the Jews; we must be a bloc against the Jewish bloc in all branches of their activity: politics, economy, society, and particularly in commerce. With the boycott, Jews will not live long."[173] The RN's goal was the complete elimination of Jews as competitors from all spheres in the colony.

Other antisemitic groups also emerged during this period. The Paris-based Front de la Jeunesse incorporated youth into the right-wing groups and organized meetings in Oran, Sidi Bel Abbès, and Mostaganem. The Prefect of Oran reported that the Front de la Jeunesse's President Jean Charles Legrand's visit to the colony coincided with the municipal elections in Tiaret on June 26, 1938. At those elections, the Union Latine candidate list won.[174] Such examples indicate cooperation between metropolitan and colonial branches of antisemitic organizations. These organizations also reached out to Algerian Muslims to garner wider support, even if they could not vote themselves. In 1938, the Amitiés Latines organized its Muslim Section, most of whom were employees of the municipality, further indicating the overlap between antisemitic organizations and municipal governments in the colony.[175]

---

[172] William B. Cohen, "The Colonial Policy of the Popular Front," *French Historical Studies*, Vol. 7, No. 3 (Spring 1972): 381.

[173] Police Commissioner of Tiaret to the Prefect of Oran, "Rapport No. 2824," Tiaret, April 24, 1938, CAOM Alg Oran 424. At the meeting, Viniger cited an article about Minister Marx Dormoy's comments in Parliament in which Dormoy stated, "A Jew is worth a Breton." Viniger concluded the meeting by stating, "Next to a Breton, the Jew is shit."

[174] Gov-Gen to the Prefect of Oran, "No. 2572SP: Antisémitisme, Conférénce de M. Jean Charles Legrand," Algiers, June 5, 1938. See also Letter Prefect of Oran to the Gov-Gen, "No. 12097: Objet: Le Front de la Jeunesse, Mostaganem," Oran, June 28, 1938, CAOM Alg Oran 424.

[175] Prefect of Oran, "Rapport relatif à la Propagande antisémitique dans le département d'Oran, au cours du mois de Juin 1938," Oran, July 13, 1938, CAOM Alg Oran 5i/50. In courting Muslim members to their antisemitic organizations, leaders frequently alluded to the situation in Palestine. Affaires Indigènes, "Rapport 17204: CIE: Évènements de Palestine à le GGA, d'Alger," Oran, August 30, 1938, CAOM Alg Oran 5i/50. In November 1938, the Gov-Gen noted that relations between Jews and Muslims began to deteriorate as a result of events in Palestine and increasing Zionism in

In November 1938, however, Lautier intensified his antisemitic propaganda campaign with the publication of a poster entitled "Jewish Failure," which incorporated antisemitic tropes of Jewish cosmopolitanism and economic power. Lautier depicted the Jew as "the master of the beautiful buildings of Algiers and master of the commerce of Algiers, and even master of medicine and law." Lautier encouraged his followers to "denounce the Jew, boycott the Jew, hunt the Jew, expel him, and spit in his face, at any time, in the street, the café, in trams – this is now our attitude." The posters promised that antisemites would restitute Muslim property taken through Jewish usury. Utilizing the language of racial cleansing, the posters outlined Lautier and his compatriots' goal to return Jews to their "ghettos" and remove them from society. Concluding that "the torches are ready," Lautier not only called antisemites to boycott the Jew but also encouraged outright violence.[176]

In December 1938, the governor-general reported on the condition of electoral antisemitism in Algeria, indicating that the departments in Constantine and Oran were particularly influenced by antisemitic propaganda. The police kept surveillance records of political events and noted antisemitism in their reports. Based on these reports, the governor-general concluded that the ultimate goal of antisemites was "to free France and Algeria of Jews." Antisemitic groups in the colony focused on taking over municipal and administrative governments. Despite the courtship of antisemitic parties, Algerian Muslims rarely joined. The governor-general noted that Muslims appeared to be following the directions of their leaders to avoid antisemitic activities.[177]

certain communities. Gov-Gen, "Rapport No. 1899: Renseignements au sujet d'état d'esprit chez les Israélites," Algiers, November 25, 1938, CAOM Alg Oran 5i/50. Zionism made greater inroads in Algeria in 1938 than in previous years. Division chief of the Departmental Security of Oran to the Prefect of Oran, "Rapport No. 71: Re: Conférence: Keren Hayessod LeIsrael," Oran, January 5, 1938, CAOM Alg Oran 2539. See also Division Chief, Departmental Special Police to the Prefect of Oran, "No. 3468: Keren Hayessod: Conférence à Oran de Mlle Erlich Sassia, avocet à Paris," Oran, April 29, 1938; Division Chief, Departmental Special Police to the Prefect of Oran, "No. 3628: Keren Hayessod, Conférence de Melle Sassia Erlich, avocat à la Cour de Paris," Oran, May 4, 1938, CAOM Alg Oran 2539.

[176] The posters proclaimed, "It is necessary, by all means, to hunt this Hebraic rot that comes from the four corners of the universe to our land." Special Police of Algiers, "Rapport No. 8499, au sujet des affiches de Henri Lautier," Algiers, November 22, 1938, CAOM Alg Oran 5i/50. Although Lautier's antisemitic rhetoric was extreme, it was not unique. Also in the metropole, antisemitic propaganda proliferated in 1938. See "Qui Veut la Guerre? Le Juif!," 1938, AN F/7/15134. See also "Note sur la Question de la Propagande antisémite," 1938, CDJC DCCXXI-3 (Fonds Vanikoff).

[177] Gov-Gen to the Minister of the Interior, "Rapport No. 21253S: Rapport sur l'Antisémitisme en Algérie," Algiers, December 10, 1938, CAOM FM 81F/864.

In summer and fall 1938, antisemites focused their efforts on abrogating the Crémieux Decree. Morinaud published an antisemitic campaign in *Le Républicain*, in which he urged his fellow Europeans to "denounce the Jewish pretension of governing us." At the October PSF congress in Constantine, one speaker emphasized the necessity of fighting Jews on the "electoral terrain." In order to remedy the alleged Jewish bloc voting, the speaker recommended the revision of the Crémieux Decree. This recommendation was vigorously supported by the 5,000 people in attendance. In November, the PPF held their congress in Algiers, where the speakers also dealt with the Jewish question. One passionately demanded the abrogation of the Crémieux Decree, while another emphasized nativism in response to the "invasion of our chairs, legal bars, and faculties by strangers and Jews." The Moroccan delegate, Monsieur Queyrat, condemned the "invasion of administrative posts in the protectorate by Jews." Doriot encouraged his followers to "remake France." To do so required the abrogation of the Crémieux Decree. Such platforms were popular, because, as the governor-general observed, "antisemitism is anchored in the minds of some of the European and indigenous populations."[178] This was especially true in the late 1930s.

The left-wing organizations, such as CAES, the LICA, and the LDH, reacted to the machinations of antisemitic organizations. In May 1938, the CAES sent a delegation to Paris to report on the dangers posed by the antisemitic campaign raging in the colony.[179] In response, Daladier's government developed a decree in May 1938 to punish activities that threatened the security of the metropole and the colony, as well as any efforts to encourage "racial hatred."[180] Although aimed primarily at antisemitic organizations, this law was vague and did not have a significant impact on the growth of antisemitic activity in the colony. As antisemitism and fascism gained traction in the colony, leaders of left-

---

[178] Ibid.

[179] Gov-Gen, "Rapport No. 686: Renseignements: Antisémitisme: Inquiétude manifestée par le Comité Juif d'Études Sociales d'Alger, Projet d'Envoi d'une délégation à Paris," Algiers, May 19, 1938, CAOM Alg Oran 5i/50. The CAES also sent 20,000 francs to the Bernard Lecache and the LICA.

[180] "Décret ayant pour but de réprimer les atteintes à l'intégrité du Territoire Nationale ou à l'Autorité de la France sur les Territoires ou cette Autorité s'exerce," Paris, May 24, 1938. See also "Congrès de l'Union Socialiste et Républicaine de Bordeaux." Minister of the Interior, "Note sur une proposition tendant a compléter le décret du 30 mars 1935 réprimant les manifestations contre la souveraineté française," Paris, June 22, 1938, CAOM FM 81F/864. On June 24, an article appeared in the *Oran Républicain*, entitled "Anti-Jewish propaganda in Arab lands," which was unleashed by the activities of Germans and Italians in the Middle East and North Africa. M.S. Zahiri, "La Propagande anti-juive dans les pays arabes," *Oran Républicain*, June 24, 1938, CAOM Alg Oran 5i/50.

wing organizations became increasingly concerned with Jews' safety in the colony. Remaking on the spread of fascism in Europe, an LDH member in Mostaganem feared that "one day North Africa will go on its own into the arms of Hitler, as Austria did."[181] At the end of the 1930s, antisemites remained in control of several municipal governments, and their influence continued to grow as Hitler and Mussolini gained control of Europe and North Africa.

Prelude to Vichy, 1939–1940

As France dealt with the specter of a possible war, Algerian Jews realized that the war provided another opportunity to prove themselves as patriots and, in so doing, to combat antisemitism. Jewish communities throughout the colony prepared their sons, fathers, and husbands for battle. As a response to the Sidi Bel Abbès affair and to the need for more soldiers, on January 17, 1939, the French government passed a decree certifying Algerian Jews' French citizenship by altering the requirements of proof of indigenous status set forth in the Lambrecht Decree. In the 1939 revision, the inscription of a Jew's father or other ancestor on the electoral lists would serve as sufficient proof. In anticipation of war, the Consistory of Oran published a statement of the commitment of Jews to France: "When our beloved country needs more than ever the union of its children, we are ready to spill the last drop of our blood to defend the influence of our country's liberal ideas and the integrity of its territory."[182] In spite of the antisemitic attacks on their citizenship, Algerian Jews remained patriotic and optimistic that their service could finally put antisemitic accusations to rest in the colony.

While the 1939 decree appeased Jewish spirits, it enhanced the disappointment of Algerian Muslims, whose status remained unchanged. Bendjelloul and other Muslim leaders expressed their frustration that the administration passed this decree certifying Jewish citizenship quickly, while the Blum-Viollette Bill continued to face opposition.[183]

---

[181] Gustave Marie to President Victor Basch, Mostaganem, June 13, 1938, BDIC-LDH F Delta Res 798/167.

[182] Fédération des Cultuelles Israélites du Département d'Oran to the President of the Republic, the President of the Council, the Vice President of the Council, the Minister of the Interior, the Minister of Justice, the Gov-Gen of Algeria, Oran, January 22, 1939, CAOM Alg Oran 2539. See also Fédération des Cultuelles Israélites du Département d'Oran to M. Boujard, Prefect of Oran, Oran, January 22, 1939, CAOM Alg Oran 2539 and Blévis, "Une citoyenneté française contestée," 122.

[183] Prefecture of Oran, "Rapport 51: Renseignements au sujet de la réaction des Indigènes en face du décret du 17 janvier et représentation des Indigènes au Parlement," Oran, January 27, 1939, CAOM Alg Oran 5i/50.

In spite of such inequality, Jewish and Muslim religious leaders met French Cardinal Jean Verdier to emphasize the importance of solidarity in the colony. On the occasion of Verdier's visit to Algiers, Rabbi Eisenbeth expressed the great respect of Algerian Jews toward the Pontiff and the cardinal.[184] This was a significant tactical move in the context of the approaching war: Verdier was overtly antifascist, despite the official connections between the papacy and both Fascist Italy and Nazi Germany, through the concordats of 1929 and 1933 respectively.[185] Verdier's visit also prompted antisemitic commentary. E. Bermin, a Frenchman in Algiers, wrote a letter to Eisenbeth, calling the patriotism and Frenchness of Algerian Jews into question:

We, Algerians, know what you are doing better than the naive French who are misled so easily by fine words; we know that any nation into which the Jew enters is doomed to gangrene by your solvent action; … we know that you are not and cannot be patriots … we have the right and duty to hold suspect all your fine words, honeyed as they are. We know that hypocrisy is your best virtue.

Bermin stated that he was 200 percent antisemitic because he was 100 percent French.[186] For many antisemites in Algeria, being French was synonymous with being antisemitic.

In spite of such attacks on their patriotism, Algerian Jews prepared for the coming war. In April 1939, rabbis in Algeria contacted the central consistory in Paris to request military chaplaincies in their towns so that they could continue to serve their communities as well as their fellow Jews in the military.[187] When France declared war on Germany on September 3, 1939, Jews in the metropole and the colony answered the call to military service. On September 4, the rabbi of Oran, D. Askenazi, and president of the consistory, Albert Smadja, published a letter urging Jews to mobilize, stating that "our country is in a time of extreme gravity … It is our desire to

---

[184] "Les Chefs Religieux Musulmans, L'Association Cultuelle et les représentants des Associations Cultuelles Israélites d'Alger sont reçu par S.E. le Cardinal Verdier," *Bulletin de la Fédération des Sociétés Juives d'Algérie*, No. 39 (May 1939): 2–3. See also "Hommage des Israélites d'Alger à son Éminence le Cardinal Verdier," Algiers, April 2, 1939, CDJC CMXCVI-109.1.

[185] Frank J. Coppa, *The Papacy, the Jews, and the Holocaust* (Washington: Catholic University Press, 2006), 154. When Germany invaded France in 1940, Verdier commented that "the war is a crusade." "Foreign News: Crusade," *Time* magazine, February 19, 1940.

[186] E. Birmin, to Rabbi Eisenbeth, Algiers, May 7, 1939, CDJC LIII-27a.

[187] Rabbi Eisenbeth to the Central Consistory in Paris, Algiers, April 18, 1939, ACC ACP-4. See also Sec-Gen Oualid of the Union of Jewish Religious Associations of France and Algeria to the President of Jewish Associations (form letter), Paris, April 20, 1939, ACC ACP-4.

peacefully rise to the occasion." Calling upon the French identity of Algerian Jews, Smadja and Askenazi exhorted Jews to "give the highest testimony of their love and their devotion to the country that so generously welcomed them . . . each must, according to his abilities and his physical age, be determined to serve in the military or civilian formations."[188] Expressions of patriotism had long been the key component in the Jews' arsenal for combating antisemitism.

Despite such calls to service by Jewish leaders, the Prefect of Oran commented that Jewish strategies in the face of the war could further provoke antisemitism. He wrote that "one must acknowledge the public rumor that attributes to them a tendency of seeking posts that are out of the shadow of danger." He gave the example of a rumor circulating among Muslims and Europeans that Jews ate soap so as to be excluded from military service.[189] In October, rumors spread that Jews in the garrison in Oran continued to trick doctors into removing them from service. This was contrasted with a gathering of Algerian Muslims on September 26 that ended with shouts of "Long Live France!"[190] The period of mobilization coincided with an increase in antisemitic statements such as "The Jews have succeeded in having their war," "We are going to have to fight for the Jews," "Jewish finance has succeeded in forcing us into a war against Hitler."[191] Conscripted Jews experienced antisemitism from their officers. In battalions of Zouaves in Algiers, Constantine, and Oran, Jewish soldiers were separated from European and Muslim soldiers. Jewish leaders provided soldiers with guidelines for proper conduct and contended that antisemitism in the military will be proven unfounded as Jews felt the need to "personally" seek vengeance against Hitler.[192]

---

[188] Rabbi D. Askenazi, President of the Consistory of Oran, Albert Smadja, "Appel aux Israélites Protégés Français," Oran, September 4, 1939, CAOM Alg Oran 5i/50.

[189] Prefecture of Oran, "Rapport No. 342: Renseignements au sujet: question Israélite," Oran, September 14, 1939, CAOM Alg Oran 5i/50.

[190] Prefecture of Oran, "Rapport No. 1751: Bulletin de Renseignements Produits le 28 septembre 1939, par M. l'Administrateur de la Commune Mixte de Frenda," Oran, October 2, 1939, CAOM Alg Oran 5i/50. See also Préfecture of Oran, "Rapport No. 423, Renseignements au sujet de l'antisémitisme," Oran, October 16, 1939, CAOM Alg Oran 5i/50.

[191] European antisemites also used Nazi propaganda to encourage antisemitism among Muslims, stating that "You will see, that the Jews are the masters of the governments of France and England, and will succeed in expediting Muslims to the front to sacrifice them while they don't even go to the front." Prefect of Oran to the Gov-Gen, "No. 27256: Objet: Antisémitisme septembre 1939," Oran, October 18, 1939, CAOM Alg Oran 5i/50.

[192] "Lettre d'Algérie," Bulletin de la Fédération des Sociétés Juives d'Algérie, Algiers, November 20, 1939, CDJC LIII-27b.

Antisemites continued to make the Jew the scapegoat for the war.[193] The author of an article in the *Bulletin de la Fédération des Sociétés Juives d'Algérie* lauded the fact that most Algerian Jews, "with the exception of a few black sheep, have, since the first days of war, shown their sentiments of ardent patriotism ... to complete the most pious of responsibilities: the defense of *la Patrie*." Despite the devotion of Jews, antisemitism continued to spread and Nazi propaganda influenced many in the colony, including Muslims. The article concluded with a call for the government to intervene in the situation to deter the growth of antisemitism.[194] Concerns regarding institutionalized antisemitism in the military proved warranted in the months before the German invasion of France in June 1940. Antisemitic officers found a new outlet for their hatred. In March 1940, the Prefect of Oran reported that a rumor spread regarding a French officer who demanded to be placed in charge of a unit of Muslim *tirailleurs*, rather than be forced to work with Jewish soldiers.[195]

Abbé Lambert summed up this mentality on the eve of war when he stated, "I love Arabs and I regret not having had more love for them, but I do now. In contrast, I hate the Jews and I feel regret for not having had more contempt for them, but I will in the future."[196] Antisemitism was no longer just entrenched in municipal governments; it had long ago spread to the military as well. Jews feared the new levels of antisemitism that the war could bring. These concerns would be realized after the establishment of Vichy and the subsequent abrogation of the Crémieux Decree. Upon being reduced from French citizens to French subjects after seventy years of citizenship, Algerian Jews would have to prove their patriotism and assert their French identity in new ways.

---

[193] "The famous lie, heard since the first days of the war, is that the war was wanted by the Jews and caused by them, continues to reach the mean spirits who are always ready to exhale their resentment, their rancor, their hatred of the eternal scapegoat: the Jew." "Le Malaise Continue," *Bulletin de la Fédération des Sociétés Juives d'Algérie*, CDJC LIII-27g.

[194] Comments circulated, such as "If the French would carry out an expulsion of Jews, peace would return." Ibid. It is very likely that these two reports ("Lettre d'Algérie" and "Le Malaise Continue") were written by Elie Gozlan.

[195] Prefecture of Oran, "Rapport No. 197, Note: Au sujet de l'antisémitisme," Oran, March 18, 1940, CAOM Alg Oran 5i/50.

[196] Prefecture of Oran, "Rapport No. 220: Renseignements au sujet de l'antisémitisme à Oran," Oran, March 26, 1940, CAOM Alg Oran 5i/50.

6   Rupture
Vichy, State Antisemitism, and the Crémieux Decree

In spite of the numerous calls of antisemites to abrogate the Crémieux Decree in the seven decades that followed its promulgation, Algerian Jews never imagined that could actually happen. However, in October 1940, the Vichy government removed Algerian Jews' civil rights by abrogating the Crémieux Decree.[1] From 1870 to 1940, many Algerian Jews assimilated to the expectations of the French Republic and its modernizing agenda; they learned French, attended French schools, integrated into the colonial administration, municipal governments, and high economic echelons, and served in two major wars. For Algerian Jews, Vichy's leaders and the antisemitic legislation promulgated by the regime did not represent their *patrie*. Although the 1940 abrogation of the Crémieux Decree marked a decisive rupture for Algerian Jews, they maintained faith that the "true France" would reemerge and they would be once again recognized as French sons and daughters. In the years preceding Vichy, Algerian Jews confronted increased electoral antisemitism and efforts of antisemitic municipalities to restrict or eliminate their rights as citizens. As traumatic as those years were, they could not compare with the scale of institutional antisemitism under Vichy.

Vichy marked the transition from municipally oriented antisemitism to a government formally established upon an antisemitic foundation. Antisemitism was no longer a tool used by politicians to draw votes; under Vichy, antisemitism became an official state project. Xavier Vallat, the leader of the Commissariat Général des Questions Juives (CGQJ), captured this orientation when he stated, "I am a state antisemite, not a passionate antisemite."[2] In Vallat's mind, there was a difference between the antisemite of the state, who was rational and educated, and the passionate antisemite, which evoked images of religiously charged violent irrationality. While there was certainly a degree of opportunism among certain state and local officials engaged in enforcing antisemitic legislation, Algeria was home to a long-standing and powerful antisemitic movement engaged in municipal governments. For these

---

[1] Ansky, *Les Juifs d'Algérie*, 87–88.   [2] Ibid., 118.

officials, it was an easy transition to Vichy, and the local police, who were likely hired by antisemitic politicians, were happy to implement Vichy's laws. State antisemitism informed the promulgation of the legislation that removed Jewish rights. It was an act of governmentality. In practical terms, the transition from municipally based to institutional antisemitism meant that antisemites were no longer members of the far right or fervent antisemites such as Molle or Régis, but statesmen leading the Republic. They wielded power far greater than previous antisemitic politicians ever hoped to access. Antisemitism was no longer only locally based – it was to be the political program of the French empire.

However, it is important to emphasize that there was a kind of synergy of institutional/state-sponsored antisemitism and that of municipal governments. Municipal antisemitism did not disappear or become subsumed by Vichy. Municipal governments sometimes worked alongside national governments (or occupying authority) to carry out antisemitic legislation in World War II. Historians Michael Marrus and Robert O. Paxton identify the important role of mayors and municipalities in the enforcement of anti-Jewish laws under Vichy. They also note the professionalization of mayors under Vichy, due to the enormous responsibility to regulate and surveil Jews, as well as to enforce the Aryanization process.[3] The role of the municipal in assisting the national has often been overlooked in studies of the Holocaust. In recent years, however, historians have begun to examine the local dimensions of the Holocaust and the role of municipalities. Historian Wolf Gruner demonstrates that municipalities, particularly mayors and local officials, in Germany implemented antisemitic legislation and measures even before being told to do so by the national government. Until 1938, the German Council of Municipalities played an important role in promoting and pushing for discriminatory legislation and actions. Similarly, municipalities were expected to organize local Aryanization efforts and sequestration of Jewish property, as well as organize the isolation of Jewish residents in Jewish houses and provide names for compulsory labor. Municipal governments worked alongside and for national governments and particular ministries.[4]

---

[3] Their assessment of the role of the municipal under Vichy gets only limited attention – one page – in their seminal work. Michael R. Marrus and Robert O. Paxton, *Vichy France and the Jews* (New York: Basic Books, 1981), 148.

[4] Wolf Gruner, "Local Initiatives, Central Coordination: German Municipal Administration and the Holocaust," in *Networks of Nazi Persecution: Bureaucracy, Business and the Organization of the Holocaust*, Gerald D. Feldman and Wolfgang Seibel, eds. (New York: Berghahn Books, 2005), 269–271, 275–277. See also Yuri Radchenko, "Accomplices to Extermination: Municipal Government and the Holocaust in Kharkiv, 1941–1942," *Holocaust and Genocide Studies*, Vol. 27, No. 3 (2013): 443–463.

Like Gruner's work on German municipalities, historian Donna E. Ryan emphasizes the importance of examining the local as well as the national, as "the Vichy experience was varied and complex." Ryan examines the city of Marseille, which was in the unoccupied zone, and the interaction between municipal officials and Vichy leaders in the implementation of antisemitic legislation and actions. She emphasizes the fact that because laws had to be enforced at the prefectural level, it is necessary to study the local – as well as the senior administration of Vichy, such as that of Paxton and Marrus.[5] The interactions of the different levels of authority show the necessity of cooperation and clear communication in the successful execution of Vichy legislation.

Implementing the census mandated by the *statut des juifs* is a perfect example of such collaboration, as well as the quotas put into place on various professions. Ryan shows the layers of responsibility in fulfilling the requirements and enforcing the quotas. The same was essential for the economic Aryanization projects, which were conducted by local officers in tandem with Vichy. The local police also served as intermediaries between the prefecture and the CGQJ, the central branch responsible for executing anti-Jewish legislation. Vichy attempted to ensure success by placing known leaders in positions of local power, especially the role of police intendant. Without successful communication and cooperation between these levels of government, anti-Jewish laws could not be enforced.[6] In the case of colonial Algeria, there were often gaps in the flow of communication between the various branches and levels, and the prefects were occasionally confused as to how to properly execute orders from the CGQJ.

How new was Vichy's institutional antisemitism?[7] As demonstrated in this book, political and electoral antisemitism had a long history in Algeria, dating back at least to the 1890s in its most virulent form. Political antisemitism, in its various incarnations such as municipally based, electoral, and ultimately the institutional form under Vichy, had

---

[5] Donna E. Ryan, *The Holocaust and the Jews of Marseille: The Enforcement of Anti-Semitic Policies in Vichy France* (Urbana: University of Illinois Press, 1996), viii–xii; Paxton and Marrus, *Vichy and the Jews.*

[6] Ryan, *The Holocaust and the Jews of Marseille*, 43–45, 60, 65, 75.

[7] Marrus and Paxton, *Vichy France and the Jews*, emphasize the deep roots of French antisemitism as a precursor to the Vichy regime, tracing this legacy back to the Revolution, the Dreyfus Affair, and the virulence of antisemitism in the 1930s, xvii, 26–27. Julian Jackson similarly argued that there was a long history of antisemitism in France before Vichy, emphasizing the role of the Dreyfus Affair. Julian Jackson, *France: The Dark Years: 1940–1944* (Oxford: Oxford University Press, 2001), 25. Michel Ansky and Henri Msellati, among other historians, assert that Vichy represented a new era in Algeria with its institutional antisemitism. Msellati, *Les Juifs d'Algérie sous le régime de Vichy*, 47.

deep roots in the colony. The election of antisemitic officials, from Drumont as a deputy for Algeria in 1898 to Dr. Molle and Abbé Lambert in the 1920s and 1930s, demonstrates the deeply engrained nature of antisemitism in the governmental apparatus of Algeria. These politicians implemented antisemitic policies during their terms, such as Sidi Bel Abbès Mayor Bellat's removal of hundreds of Jews from voter lists in 1937. The administration's lack of response to the Constantine violence of August 1934 reveals the state's toleration, if not the support, of antisemitism. Antisemitism during these periods was not on the same scale as under Vichy, as it was largely locally sourced and supported. However, to suggest that Vichy inaugurated institutional antisemitism is to ignore the long history of state-sponsored antisemitism from the fin-de-siècle into twentieth-century France and Algeria. Vichy's success was due in large part to the overwhelming support it found in certain areas – Algeria in particular. The long-standing antisemitic movement in the colony had created a fertile environment for Vichy's efforts.

This chapter examines Algeria during the Vichy era. The immediate post-Vichy period under Generals Giraud and de Gaulle will be discussed in Chapter 7. This chapter charts the ways in which antisemitic legislation, specifically the abrogation of the Crémieux Decree, impacted Jews in the colony and their relationships with France and their Muslim and European neighbors. Following the abrogation of the Crémieux Decree, Algerian Jews were initially surprisingly acquiescent in comparison to their earlier defense efforts. Perhaps Jews felt more equipped to challenge antisemitism in municipal government but were unprepared to challenge antisemitism from the French government itself. Indeed, the intensity of the state-organized antisemitism was something most Algerian Jews could not have imagined. They had developed the tools to fight municipal antisemites, but fighting state antisemites was beyond their capabilities. Rather than combat the legislation, the Jewish community turned inward to deal with issues such as supporting fired administrative employees, teachers and other professions, and students expelled from their schools as a result of Vichy-imposed quotas.[8]

At the same time, Jews also took individual measures, invoking their commitment to France and loyalty to Pétain to plead for the reinstatement of their citizenship. These personal requests, as well as the correspondence between Jews on the subject of the antisemitic measures, provide a unique insight into the mentality of Algerian Jews, the meanings they attributed to citizenship, and the results of their assimilation. One particularly fascinating subsection of these appeals consists of Jews in

---

[8] Ansky, Les Juifs d'Algérie, 109.

interfaith marriages who had converted to Christianity. These letters demonstrate the profound transformation of the Algerian Jewish community from that of an insular, Judeo-Arabic speaking, non-westernized collective to a diverse group including some Jews who had assimilated so fully to their French identity that they left Judaism entirely. This group was not large, but it indicates the impact of assimilation on some Algerian Jews. Although the degree of assimilation among Algerian Jews was quite diverse, most felt strongly about the importance of their French citizenship. Other letters, from veterans of the French army, indicate the embeddedness of the concept of military service and the performance of citizenship responsibilities in the Algerian Jewish identity in the early 1940s.

Philosopher Jacques Derrida remarks that "citizenship does not define a cultural, linguistic, or, in general, historical participation ... But it is not some superficial or superstructural predicate floating on the surface of experience. Especially not when this citizenship is, through and through, *precarious, recent, threatened*, and more artificial than ever."[9] Losing their citizenship meant the loss of a key aspect of their identities. An Algerian Jew who experienced the rupture of losing his citizenship under Vichy (at age 10), Derrida illustrates the complicated sense of self of Algerian Jews. Some Algerian Jews maintained certain cultural and religious aspects of their pre-Crémieux Decree existence, while antisemites simultaneously sought to keep Algerian Jews outside of the French citizenry by emphasizing their "otherness."

The abrogation of the Crémieux Decree created a profound, internal rupture for Algerian Jews, separating formerly cohesive elements of their identity: Jews, Frenchmen, and Algerians. Algerian Jews confronted an unfamiliar form of antisemitism, one far more extreme than that of municipalities. Previously, Jews encountered the passionate and popular antisemitism of the street, extending to politicians and administrative officials. But they were not prepared to lose their citizenship status.[10] In spite of the rupture created by this drastic change in their status, for the next three years Algerian Jews fought for the government to reinstate the Crémieux Decree. Even following the return of their citizenship in 1943, the memory of the rupture remained.

[9] Jacques Derrida, *Monolingualism of the Other, or, the Prosthesis of Origin* (Stanford: Stanford University Press, 1998), 14–15, emphasis in original.
[10] Michael Abitbol, *The Jews of North Africa during the Second World War* (Detroit: Wayne State University Press, 1989), 62.

The Fall of France and the Men of Vichy

Fleeing the imminent arrival of German troops, the French government evacuated Paris on June 10, 1940. German troops entered the city four days later, and on June 22 the French government signed an armistice with Germany. Following the armistice, France was divided into two parts: the northern three-fifths of the country occupied by German troops, and the Vichy government in control of the unoccupied zone, under the leadership of Marshal Philippe Pétain. Pétain blamed France's surrender to Germany on "moral laxness."[11] France's quick defeat was due in large part to the fact that France was ill-prepared for war.[12] France was also determined to reduce potential loss of life, especially after the enormous losses it suffered in World War I. Historian Ernest R. May argues that this lack of preparation was due to a sense of confidence among the French that Germany would not attack and that if it should, France would win. This belief was shared by Marc Bloch, executed by the Germans in 1944, who wrote of his experiences in 1940 in an essay entitled "Strange Defeat."[13]

On July 10, the Parliament voted to give Pétain full powers, transforming French republican politics into a nondemocratic regime.[14] In contrast, Charles de Gaulle declared his opposition to the Vichy government, and, as of June 18, he could be heard promoting his cause to his fellow Frenchmen over the airwaves.[15] Vichy's relationship with Hitler's Germany was that of "collaboration," both in form and in the articles of the armistice agreement. From the start, Pétain portrayed himself as the "protector" of the country, developing the National Revolution for the revival of France in the aftermath of defeat. Pétain was in many ways the figurehead of the Vichy regime, but never protested the antisemitic legislation implemented by his staff, his government, and its ministers.[16] Recent evidence unearthed by historian and lawyer Serge

---

[11] Julian Jackson, *The Fall of France: The Nazi Invasion of 1940* (Oxford: Oxford University Press, 2003), 2. See also Ernest R. May, *Strange Victory: Hitler's Conquest of France* (New York: Hill and Wang, 2000), 3.

[12] Jackson, *The Fall of France*, 219, 221.

[13] May, *Strange Victory*, 8–10, 255–256. Marc Bloch wrote of his shock at seeing so many cities given over to the occupiers and at the "peaceful cohabitation" of German officers and Frenchmen. Marc Bloch, *L'Histoire, la guerre, a la résistance*, eds., Annette Becker and Étienne Bloch (Paris: Éditions Gallimard, 2006), 540.

[14] Jackson, *France: The Dark Years*, 139.

[15] Philippe Burrin, *France under the Germans: Collaboration and Compromise* (New York: The New Press, 1996), 9–10, 16. See also Robert O. Paxton, *Vichy France: Old Guard and New Order, 1940–1944* (New York: Alfred A. Knopf, 1972), 8.

[16] Paxton, *Vichy France*, 19. Burrin, *France under the Germans*, 69, 73. Pétain himself was not necessarily a virulent antisemite. See also May, *Strange Victory*, 446.

Klarsfeld in October 2010 indicates that Pétain himself intensified the severity of antisemitic legislation.[17]

Vichy was more than a collaborationist regime; it was an organic reaction to previous French governments.[18] Vichy's first one hundred days occurred without the direct orders of the occupiers. Even beyond that, Vichy pursued its own particular goals, which often coincided with those of Hitler. The men of Vichy had four objectives: protection, sovereignty, status, and regime.[19] They used antisemitic policies to achieve these objectives. However, despite France's long history of antisemitism, there was also a degree of opportunism among Vichy officials who jumped on the bandwagon of institutional antisemitism in order to develop their own careers. As was the case for municipal politicians in Algeria, under Vichy, antisemitism promised political success and power. Vichy leaders implemented measures to remove groups they considered outside the nation, including Jews and some foreigners. On July 22, Vichy officials organized a commission to revise naturalizations after 1927. Between 1940 and 1944 the commission eradicated the citizenship of 15,000 people, including 6,000 Jews.[20] The Vichy regime did so without the direct orders of Germany, which indicates the "indigenous" quality of Vichy's antisemitism.[21]

The British attack on the French fleet at Mers-el-Kebir, near Oran, on June 25 shifted the tides of war. Vichy could cite the need to protect the country in order to justify its actions against perceived enemies.[22] The Mers-el-Kebir attack brought the reality of the war into the lives of those in Algeria.[23] In the months following the British attack, some politicians and their followers accused Jews in Algeria of Anglophilia and British support. In September 1940, the governor-general reported that the Jews in Algiers and surrounding areas were "ferociously hostile to

---

[17] Maïa de la Baume, "Vichy Leader Said to Widen Anti-Jewish Law," *New York Times*, October 6, 2010, A6. See also Laurent Joly, Benn E. Williams, "The Genesis of Vichy's Jewish Statute of October 1940," *Holocaust and Genocide Studies*, Vol. 27, No. 2 (Fall 2013): 287.

[18] Paxton, *Vichy France*, 20.

[19] Ibid., 48–49, 51–53. Burrin, *France under the Germans*, 80.

[20] Jackson, *France: The Dark Years*, 150. In his correspondence with the UGIF in 1941, historian Marc Bloch noted his confusion regarding the "Jewish problem." He wrote to Jean Ullmo on April 2, 1941 that "The French Jews are French as others, and for the vast majority of them, are good Frenchmen." March Bloch, *L'étrange defaite: Témoignage écrit en 1940* (Paris: Éditions Gallimard, 1990), 307–308.

[21] Paxton, *Vichy France: Old Guard*, 48–49.

[22] Burrin, *France under the Germans*, 25; Paxton, *Vichy France*, 41–44.

[23] Cantier, *L'Algérie sous le Régime de Vichy*, 7. Vichy extended its National Revolution to its colonies. See Eric T. Jennings, *Vichy in the Tropics: Pétain's National Revolution in Madagascar, Guadeloupe, and Indochina, 1940–44* (Stanford: Stanford University Press, 2001).

Marshal Pétain and demonstrate, with regards to Britain, sentiments that seem to exceed that of platonic admiration." According to the report, Jews in Algeria hoped that Britain would defeat the Germans and that de Gaulle would take power in France.[24] A few Algerian Jews looked to de Gaulle and elsewhere for help, especially following the abrogation of the Crémieux Decree in October 1940.[25] Jews' presumed lack of faith in Vichy France and their lack of patriotism served as fodder for antisemitism.

Like the attack on Mers-el-Kebir, the massive turnover of colonial administrators under Vichy also brought the realities of the regime change to the colony. Of the ninety-four French Prefects in 1940, Vichy leaders pushed twenty-six into retirement, revoked twenty-nine, and moved thirty-seven to other posts. Algeria was no exception to this rule: only one Prefect remained, Louis Boujard in Oran.[26] Weathering the political transitions as a Prefect under both the Third Republic and the Popular Front, Boujard made a smooth transition into Vichy and obediently executed the legislation directed against Jews. Boujard emblematizes the political opportunism of some administrators. Under the Popular Front, Boujard emphatically criticized the antisemitic mayor of Oran, Abbé Lambert. However, as a man of Vichy, Boujard oversaw the stripping of Algerian Jews' citizenship – one of Lambert's demands during his tenure.[27] Max Bonnafous became Constantine's new Prefect. A socialist with a degree in philosophy, Bonnafous nonetheless proved himself to be such an asset to Vichy that Minister of State Pierre Laval promoted him as Minister of Food and Agriculture in April 1942. General Valin, a notorious Doriot supporter, replaced Bonnafous as Prefect, cementing the continued strength of antisemitic leagues in Algeria.[28]

The selection of new governors-general of Algeria reflected Vichy's effort to populate its administrative ranks with antisemites who would oversee the regime's institutional antisemitism implemented in legislation. Forced out of his position on August 1, 1940, Governor-General Le Beau was known as a generous administrator with a particular interest in the Jewish and Muslim populations of the colony. On the eve of his departure, Le Beau addressed the Jews of Algeria, encouraging them to maintain hope and faith in their future in France. Admiral Jean Abrial

---

[24] Gov-Gen, "CIE: No. 970: Renseignements: A/S Courant d'Anglophilie parmi les Juifs," Algiers, September 4, 1940, CAOM Alg Oran 5i/50.

[25] Paxton, *Vichy France*, 44–45.

[26] Cantier, *L'Algérie sous le Régime de Vichy*, 52. See also Marc-Olivier Baruch, *Servir l'État français. L'administration en France de 1940 à 1944* (Paris: Librairie Arthème Fayard, 1997).

[27] Msellati, *Les Juifs d'Algérie*, 52   [28] Ibid., 53.

succeeded Le Beau and served from August 2, 1940 to July 15, 1941. Famous for his time as a prisoner of the Germans at Cherbourg and his liberation at the request of Vichy officials, Abrial used the regime's anti-Jewish legislation to oppress the Jews under his jurisdiction. On the day of the publication of the abrogation of the Crémieux Decree, Abrial ordered troops to shoot Jews if they demonstrated against the new legislation.[29]

Following Abrial, General Maxime Weygand assumed leadership of the colony, serving only from July 17 to November 18, 1941. Weygand's politics, like that of Vichy, reflects the pervasive nature of French anti-semitism among some politicians. For example, in 1899 Weygand supported the anti-Dreyfusards.[30] As early as June 1940, Weygand demanded the development of anti-Jewish legislation in Algeria. During his term as governor-general, Weygand acted upon his early demands and pursued his antisemitic agenda. Algeria adopted a quota for Jewish students in higher education that was more severe than that of the metropole and other colonies. He also extended the quota to primary and secondary schools. On August 14, 1941, Weygand established an Algerian Service for Jewish Questions to enforce and process antisemitic legislation in the colony.[31] As a state antisemite, Weygand implemented antisemitic legislation in Algeria with an intensity that exceeded that of the metropole.[32] The results of his actions brought the harsh reality of Vichy's antisemitism into sharp relief for Algeria's Jews.

Yves Châtel served as governor-general from November 18, 1941, to January 17, 1943. As former Resident General in Tonkin, Châtel was a veteran colonial administrator. He was also strongly antisemitic and did not hesitate to apply harsh measures against the Algerian Jews. One of his closest advisors during his tenure was a leader of the PPF.[33] Châtel's support for the PPF cemented the significant role that Algeria played in the party's revised program under Vichy, especially after Doriot convened a congress of the PPF in Vichy on August 8, 1940. Algeria served a crucial front for its redevelopment – the North African delegate of the PPF, Jean Fossati, was integral in the party's reorganization.[34] Under the leadership

---

[29] Ibid., 53–54. See also Ansky, *Les Juifs d'Algérie*, 90.
[30] Cantier, *L'Algérie sous le Régime de Vichy*, 94–95.
[31] Msellati, *Les Juifs d'Algérie*, 55. See also Gov-Gen Weygand, "Arrêté No. 5934," August 14, 1941, CAOM FM 81F/846.
[32] Cantier, *L'Algérie sous le Régime de Vichy*, 131.
[33] The advisor was known as Monsieur Canavaggio. Msellati, *Les Juifs d'Algérie*, 56. See also Cantier, *L'Algérie sous le Régime de Vichy*, 150.
[34] Cantier, *L'Algérie sous le Régime de Vichy*, 219. Following Admiral Darlan's assassination in December 1942, General Giraud named Marcel Peyrouton as the new Gov-Gen, with the support of Dwight D. Eisenhower. Msellati, *Les Juifs d'Algérie*, 56.

of these governors-general, Algerian Jews saw their citizenship stripped away and their livelihoods threatened.

Vichy Legislation, 1940–1941: The Abrogation of the Crémieux Decree and the *Statut des Juifs*

After the war of 1939–1940, Vichy officials described the legislation they enacted as a form of self-defense, a "pre-emptive" strategy to maintain French control and avoid further German encroachment.[35] In reality, Vichy's anti-Jewish measures were of their own making and Vichy's representatives in Algeria took this legislation to the extreme. The collaboration between Vichy and Hitler allowed what historian Robert O. Paxton calls "an indigenous French antisemitism" to use its "own venom." Paxton emphasizes that Vichy's antisemitism evolved *sui generis*.[36] As Algeria was an extension of the metropole, Jews were subject to legislation impacting their coreligionists in France proper, but also suffered from laws in Algeria specifically aimed at reducing their status in the colony, the most significant example of which was the abrogation of the Crémieux Decree. The goals of the past several decades of municipal antisemites in the colony were finally realized under Vichy.

As early as summer 1940, rumors circulated in the colony regarding Algerian Jews' future under Vichy. Such rumors also represented an effort to encourage different groups in the colony to choose political sides. In particular, Algerian Muslims were split in their opinions.[37] A Muslim newspaper, *El Balagh el Djezairi*, published an article criticizing Great Britain and the Jews.[38] For some Muslims, the anti-Jewish stance of Vichy represented an opportunity to express antisemitic sentiment in order to gain favor with the new regime. Some Muslims, however, accused Jews of working with Europeans to organize a pro-English movement. Others responded to calls for unity put forth by Algerian Jews. At the end of August 1940, Governor-General Abrial noted that some Jews and Muslims encouraged cooperation, especially under the sponsorship of the *Cercle du Progrès*, led by Dr. Loufrani and Elie Gozlan.[39]

---

[35] Henry Rousso, *The Vichy Syndrome: History and Memory in France since 1944* (Cambridge: Harvard University Press, 1991), 7. See also Marrus and Paxton, *Vichy France*, xvii, 9.

[36] Paxton, *Vichy France*, 174.

[37] In July 1940, urban Algerian Muslims discussed the possibility of the abrogation of the Crémieux Decree. Departmental Center for Information, "No. 2548," Oran, July 11, 1940, CAOM Alg Oran 5i/50.

[38] *El Balagh el Djezairi*, No. 487, July 12, 1940, CAOM Alg Oran 5i/50.

[39] Gov-Gen, "CIE No. 955: Renseignements les Juifs, les *Colons*, et l'Angleterre," Algiers, August 29, 1940, CAOM Alg Oran 5i/50.

In Algiers, Muslim leaders associated with the *Cercle du Progrès* encouraged their coreligionists to avoid any actions against Jews. Dr. Bendjelloul urged support for the government. A surveillance report emphasized that although "deep within every Muslim is an anti-Jew who wants the most extreme measures, if not violence, taken against the Jews," Algerian Muslims remained calm.[40] Such a report was likely conjecture as such broad statements could not be quantified. Furthermore, the author of the report likely hoped to create a firm demarcation between Jews and Muslims in the colony. The Prefect of Oran, Louis Boujard, reported that the Muslims of Oran demonstrated their support for France and the abrogation of the Crémieux Decree, which had positioned them "in a state of inferiority with regards to their former vassals for seventy years." Boujard accused the Jews of critiquing Pétain, Vichy, and supporting Britain. In contrast, he commented that "the Algerian Muslim is very impressionable, he is a big child who always needs good advice," and should be used to gain support for the administration.[41] Boujard's racist commentary on Muslims served two purposes: the first was to continue to emphasize disunity, if not animosity, between Jews and Muslims to ensure that they did not cooperate in seeking rights. The second purpose was to reiterate the official discourse that Muslims were not capable of the free thought necessary for political inclusion.

Antisemitism escalated in the weeks before the announcement and publication of the October 1940 legislation. One of the causes of this intensification was that Vichy repealed the Marchandeau law, which penalized acts of inciting racial hatred. This facilitated the PPF's reinvigoration of its antisemitic activity in the metropole and the colony, as well as the concurrent renewal of Muslim antisemitism. On the evening of September 11, mobs broke the windows of twenty Jewish-owned shops in Algiers.[42] In late September, police reported that walls in

---

[40] The report quoted Muslim leaders stating, "We do not wish to be the instruments to others' grievances, because we would only have to bear the consequences; Satan continues to excite the French against the Jews, we'll just be spectators." Gov-Gen, Center of Information, "No. 1004: Renseignements (source Indigène, bonne), Les Indigènes se tiennent à l'écart du Mouvement d'antisémitisme à Alger," Algiers, September 14, 1940, CAOM Alg Oran 5i/50. The use of the term "anti-Jew" is significant in that it was important for Muslims to differentiate between Jew and Semite.

[41] Prefect of Oran, Centre for Information, "CIE, No. 823: Note A/S État d'esprit entre Indigènes et Israélites," Oran, October 5, 1940, CAOM Alg Oran 5i/50.

[42] Cantier, *L'Algérie sous le Régime de Vichy*, 73. The Administrator of Ain-M'lila reported that "the indigenous psychology is profoundly moved by serious or fallacious news reported by demobilized soldiers and is moving very much towards antisemitism." Administrator of the Mixed Commune of Ain-M'lila to the Gov-Gen, "No. 11041/R-10/B; Rapport Hebdomadaire," Ain-M'lila, September 11, 1940, CAOM Alg Const B/3/688.

Batna had been painted with "Down with the Jews! Death to the Jews! Thieves! Are you leaving or not?"[43] Those responsible for the graffiti were not identified, but the slogan was reminiscent of chants heard in the late nineteenth century and throughout the 1930s. Jews became increasingly concerned for their future in the colony.

Among Vichy's first antisemitic laws was the October 3, 1940, *Statut des Juifs* (Jewish Statute). The law defined Jews racially: to be considered part of the "Jewish race," one had to have three Jewish grandparents, or have two Jewish grandparents and be married to another Jew. Those who met such criteria could no longer hold administrative positions, be a teacher, or serve in the army as officers. The law outlined the exceptions to this rule, which included veterans of World War I or the 1939–1940 war, as well as recipients of the Legion of Honor or the Military Medal. Jews could continue to practice liberal professions as long as they did not exceed the quotas to be determined later. Jews could no longer be editors of print journals or work in the entertainment industry. Article Nine extended the law's reach to Algeria and other colonies, protectorates, and mandate territories.[44] In contrast to the German occupiers' ordinance, which defined Jewishness in religious terms, Vichy defined it racially to make it more inclusive and severe.[45] By doing so, the assimilated and sometimes nonobservant Algerian Jews were still victims of the legislation.

Promulgated on October 7 and published the next day, the abrogation of the Crémieux Decree in Algeria was actually the first of the antisemitic laws to become official. In contrast, the Jewish Statute took ten days to go into effect. By abrogating the Crémieux Decree, the law of October 7 undermined many significant principles of French law, particularly that of the imprescriptible nature of French citizenship in the absence of an individual reason.[46] According to Article Two of the law, Jews' new "native status" would be regulated by the laws governing the political rights of native Algerian Muslims. However, Article Three contradicted that regulation by stating that Jews' civil rights, their real and personal status, would remain governed by French law. This meant that Algerian Jews did not have the same rights as Algerian Muslims in that they continued to be governed by French law but did not receive the

---

[43] Sub-Prefect of Batna to the Prefect of Constantine, "No. 757 P.G.R.8/F: Objet: Antisémitisme," Batna, September 26, 1940, CAOM Alg Const B/3/688.
[44] Philippe Pétain, "Loi Portant le Statut des Juifs," Vichy, October 3, 1940, CAOM Alg Const 93/3G3.
[45] Marrus and Paxton, *Vichy France*, 12.
[46] Cantier, *L'Algérie sous le Régime de Vichy*, 72–73. See also Joly and Williams, "The Genesis of Vichy's Jewish Statute," 284, 290.

concomitant benefits of citizenship. Nor did they benefit from personal status, like their Muslim counterparts, which allowed them to be governed by religious law. The exceptions to the abrogation were the same as the October 3 Jewish Statute. According to Article Six, the new law applied to all the beneficiaries of the 1870 Crémieux Decree and their descendants but not those naturalized by the sénatus-consulte of 1865 or via individual naturalization.[47]

The October 7 law represented the importance of Algeria in the eyes of Vichy but also served as a way of garnering greater support from the European population of the colony and Muslim populations in the three North African territories. By retracting their French citizenship, Jews were no longer superior to their Muslim counterparts.[48] Algerian Muslims' status in the colony was actually better than Jews' as they retained their personal status and their communal institutions. Anticipating potential loopholes in the October 7 legislation, Vichy legislators promulgated a second law on October 11, which excluded Jews from accessing political rights via the Jonnart law of February 4, 1919.[49] Had Jews been eligible to benefit from the 1919 law, a significant percentage could have maintained their citizenship.[50] The October 7, 1940, law applied to the Jews of the three departments of Algeria, and not to the Jews of the M'Zab, who were not beneficiaries of the Crémieux Decree.[51]

It is important to emphasize that with the abrogation of the Crémieux Decree, Vichy ensured that the treatment of Algerian Jews would be far harsher than that of Jews in the metropole. Robert Paxton and Michael Marrus emphasize that Vichy actually felt pressured by Algeria in terms of promulgating antisemitic legislation, in an effort to appease the antisemitism in the colony.[52] Echoing Paxton's analysis of the organic quality of Vichy's antisemitism, Jacques Derrida, an Algerian Jew who was 10 at the time of the abrogation of the Crémieux Decree, noted that "citizenship in essence does not emerge like that. This is not natural. . . . The withdrawal of the French citizenship from the Jews of Algeria, with all that ensued, it was the fact only because of the French. They decided this on their own,

---

[47] Philippe Pétain, "Loi portent abrogation du Décret du Gouvernement de la Défense Nationale du 24 Octobre 1870 et fixant le statut des juifs indigènes des départements de l'Algérie," Vichy, October 7, 1940, CAOM Alg Const 93/3G6.

[48] Abitbol, *The Jews of North Africa*, 59–60.

[49] Philippe Pétain, "Loi du 11 octobre 1940 portant suspension de la procédure instituée par les articles 3 à 11 de la loi du 4 février 1919 en ce qui concerne les israélites indigènes de l'Algérie," Vichy, October 11, 1940, CDJC LXXXVII-153.

[50] Msellati, *Les Juifs d'Algérie*, 67.

[51] Gov-Gen Abrial to the Prefect of the Department of Constantine, "No. 1676P: Loi du 7 octobre 1940: Statut des juifs du M'Zab," CAOM Alg GGA 6CAB/1.

[52] Marrus and Paxton, *Vichy France and the Jews*, 194.

in their heads, they had dreamed of it forever, they implemented it on their own."[53] The abrogation of the Crémieux Decree was a Vichy project, not a German one.

Responses to the Abrogation

The various groups in the colony responded to the abrogation in divergent ways. Europeans and Muslims expressed satisfaction, sometimes even joy, at the decline in the Jews' status in the colony. Émile Morinaud, a veteran of antisemitism in the colony since the 1890s, wrote of the joy among some Frenchmen in the colony upon learning of the abrogation.[54] Jews, predictably, were disheartened by the new reality that they faced under Vichy.[55] The administrator of the mixed commune of Souk-Ahras reported that he increased surveillance to ensure that Jews were not harassed after the news of the abrogation.[56]

The city of Bône was a microcosm in which the various reactions to the abrogation emerged. Some Jewish shops were closed on October 8 and 9 as a sign of mourning. Some Jews in the area blamed German influence for the new legislation, and others voiced support for the British. While some Europeans in the region were pleased with the abrogation, members of the Left, specifically socialists, argued that the new legislation went against principles of humanity. Frustrated by their own failed attempts to receive citizenship and fueled by long-standing resentment of Jews' former privileged status in the colony, certain Muslims were content with the abrogation. However, others feared that upon being reduced to "native" status, Jews would be included in the Muslims' electoral college, further depreciating the already limited influence of Muslim electors.[57] These

---

[53] Paxton, *Vichy France*, 174. Derrida, *Le monolinguisme de l'autre*, 34–35.

[54] Marrus and Paxton, *Vichy France and the Jews*, 193–194.

[55] An administrator in the department of Constantine reported that when the news of the abrogation appeared in the press, few were surprised. Jews immediately reached out to Muslims in hopes of finding support, stating that "they have lowered us, and now we are equal!" The Administrator of the Mixed Commune of Sedrata to the Gov-Gen and the Prefect of Constantine, "No. 132: Objet: Rapport hebdomadaire," Sedrata, October 9, 1940, CAOM Alg Const B/3/688.

[56] Administrator of the Mixed Commune of Souk-Ahras to the Prefect of Constantine, "No. 6371: Rapport sur la situation politique et économique," Souk-Ahras, October 9, 1940, CAOM Alg Const B/3/688.

[57] The Commissioner of the Departmental Police of Bône, "Rapport Journalier, dès 8 et 9 Octobre 1940, No. 2280: Répercussion du Décret Abrogeant le Décret Crémieux," Bône, October 9, 1940, CAOM Alg Const B/3/688. See also Central Police Commissioner of Bône to the Director of General Security of Algeria, "No. 19360: Objet, Repercussion du décret abrogeant le décret Crémieux," Bône, October 10, 1940, CAOM Alg Const B/3/688. See also Central Police Commission of Bône to the

responses demonstrate the long-standing importance of the issue of access citizenship in the colony as well as competition for political resources.

Many Jews in Algeria did not publicly respond to the abrogation, in part because they knew that there was little they could do to fight it. Jews were hesitant to protest the abrogation as they feared that they might be forced to leave Algeria and France, like Jewish refugees from Germany and Eastern Europe. In spite of the abrogation, Jews still envisioned their future in France. The limited Jewish protest against the abrogation came in the form of support for Britain. Some expressed hope for a British victory and the fall of the Vichy government. The Prefect of Constantine reported that Jews clandestinely sent their gold to support the British forces. In response to the Jewish Statute and the abrogation of the Crémieux Decree, Jews in Constantine also began selling their shops and buying gold.[58] Perhaps they feared the eventual Aryanization of businesses and sought to gain as much as they could before having their businesses usurped.

Jewish intellectuals articulated their frustration with the abrogation, arguing that Jews had always served France faithfully. Jewish veterans were especially disappointed by the news, given their patriotic service of the country.[59] The question of the exemption of certain Jewish veterans from the abrogation resurrected arguments regarding blood debts and military service that had been brought to the forefront after World War I, particularly with regard to Muslim service. Certain Muslims were displeased that some Jews, among them decorated veterans, remained Frenchmen as a result of the exceptions to the October 7 legislation. They were critical of these decorations, stating that Jews often benefited from the efforts of others, including Muslim soldiers, who rarely received parallel commendations. Although the disparity between their statuses in the colony shrank as a result of the decree, the relationship between Jews and Muslims did not improve. As a way of relating their respective

Prefect of Constantine, "No. 46Z/A.I.R./10/B: Objet: État d'Ésprit de la population," Bône, October 10, 1940, CAOM Alg Const B/3/688.

[58] Prefect of Constantine, Departmental Center for Information, "No. 3002/S: Compte Rendu Journalier du 23 Octobre 1940," Constantine, October 23, 1940, CAOM Alg Const B/3/688; Police Commissioner of Guelma to the Mayor of Guelma, "No. 838 A.I./ R.10/B: situation politique et économique des indigènes (Secret)," Guelma, October 25, 1940, CAOM Alg Const B/3/688.

[59] Commissioner of the Departmental Police of Constantine, "No. 6291: Surveillance des Milieux israélites," Constantine, October 20, 1940, CAOM Alg Const B/3/688. Some European officials feared for their positions if they had been brought to office by a Jewish majority vote, one of the features of the antisemitic rhetoric of the previous century. The Prefect of Constantine, Center for Information, "No. 1105: Renseignements sur le Statut des Juifs," Constantine, October 21, 1940, CAOM Alg Const B/3/688.

struggles, some Jews warned Muslims that they would be Vichy's next victims.[60] Bendjelloul encouraged Muslims to avoid the "Jewish question."[61] Muslim leaders hoped to keep the Muslim community on the sidelines of what had become an explosive matter in the colony.

In contrast, antisemites used the opportunity presented by the abrogation to increase their ranks. PPF members lured Muslim support by publishing flyers that celebrated Pétain for making the Muslims equal, if not superior, to Jews.[62] These efforts to increase Muslim participation in the PPF were not very successful. For the most part, Algerian Muslims were wary of the PPF's activities in the colony. The PPF's campaign to garner Muslim support competed with Jewish efforts at encouraging Muslim-Jewish unity in the colony. In Algiers, police reported on a non-Algerian Jew, who spoke impeccable Arabic, who urged Muslim solidarity with Algerian Jews by depicting both groups as the present and potential victims of Vichy. Using the language of rights, this man encouraged Muslim cooperation in the campaign to get access to citizenship for both groups. "We Jews, we are the brothers of the Muslims, now that France has rejected us, we have become natives ... We need to take one another's hands and act to obtain all of our rights ...."[63] He continued that if the Germans or Italians gained control of Algeria, Muslims would be their next victims. His efforts highlight the fact that, as had been the case in recent decades, Muslim and Jewish rights were intertwined.

In their efforts to encourage Muslim-Jewish cooperation, Jews emphasized that they were now equal to Muslims. Jews' status was actually worse than that of Muslims in the colony, in that they did not have access to rights associated with personal status, which allowed them to be ruled by religious law rather than the French civil code. As a result, Algerian Jews were still ruled by French civil law and brought their disputes before French courts headed by Vichy magistrates. In their unity campaign, Jews

[60] Prefect of Constantine, Department Center for Information, "Compte Rendu Journalier du 22 Octobre 1940, No, 2995S, Statut des Juifs, I. Impressions générales et réactions de la population musulmane," Constantine, October 22, 1940, CAOM Alg Const B/3/688.
[61] Administrator of the Mixed Commune of Guelma, "Rapport sur la Situation Politique et économique de la commune mixte, au 23 Octobre 1940," Saint-Arnaud, October 23, 1940, CAOM Alg Const B/3/688.
[62] Special Departmental Police Commissioner of Bône, "Rapport No, 2399A/S d'un tract du PPF," Bône, October 26, 1940, CAOM Alg Const B/3/688; Police Commissioner of Guelma, "No. 882: Rapport Journalier du 9 au 10 Novembre 1940," Guelma, November 10, 1940, CAOM Alg Const B/3/688. In November, police found young men putting up signs stating, "This is a Jewish shop," on storefronts in Sétif. Police Commissioner of Sétif to the Gov-Gen and the Prefect of Constantine, "No. 14.114: Objet: Affiches Antijuives," Sétif, November 10, 1940, CAOM Alg Const B/3/688.
[63] Central Police Commissioner of Algiers to the Prefect of Algiers, "No. 2/091R.S.," Algiers, November 4, 1940, CAOM Alg Const B/3/688.

suggested that France, "in order to distract the French masses, gave the Jews in a holocaust" and that Muslims would be the next scapegoats.[64] The use of the term "holocaust" is notable as it indicates a certain awareness of the increasingly precarious situation of Jews in 1940. While the use of the term "holocaust" is almost terrifyingly prescient, it was likely used to reference its more religious connotations but still emphasized the wholesale sacrificing of a group in hopes of accomplishing a goal. In Relizane, Jews illustrated the fragility of rights in the colony as they reached out to Muslims, entwining the fate of their statuses. "France took our rights away in order to not give you yours. The decision that she made against us is also directed against you."[65]

Despite these attempts at unity between Jews and Muslims, Muslim antisemitism flourished. Muslim antisemitism may have been part of an effort to distinguish themselves from Jews under Vichy's new order. Or perhaps it was an attempt to seek favor in the eyes of Vichy officials.[66] In Oran, Muslims threatened to remove Jewish names from a World War I memorial, challenging Jewish assertions of patriotism.[67] In the month following the announcement of the abrogation of the Crémieux Decree, cases of Muslim violence against Jews increased. In Constantine, a 55-year-old Jewish fabric merchant, Julien Bacri Cohen, complained that he had been shoved and called a "dirty Jew" by a Muslim.[68] A Jewish woman, Zernouda Nakache, age 59, complained that she had been slapped by a Muslim who told her that "You Jews, you don't count anymore and you just got what you deserved."[69] In these two cases, Muslims treated Jews as inferiors in the colonial hierarchy. While some Muslims may have been pleased to see Jews lose their citizenship, it did

[64] Captain Ben Daoud to the General Commandant of the Division of Oran, "État d'esprit des indigènes et propagande anti-Française dans les milieux israélites," Oran, October 9, 1940, CAOM Alg Oran 5i/50.

[65] Prefect of Oran, Center of Information, "No. 861: Renseignement A/S de l'Abrogation de décret Crémieux," Oran, October 18, 1940, CAOM Alg Oran 5i/50.

[66] Antisemitism was also present among Algerian Muslims living in the metropole. One Algerian Muslim in Marseille stated, "We distinguish their [the Jews] secret work to divide you [the French]. Today, they spread their money among us to have us join with them. They sow money as we sow wheat for the harvest. They also say you will expand their rights for French citizenship, but us, our rights, when will you think of that?" Prefecture of Bouches-du-Rhône, "No. 328: Renseignements: L'antisémitisme parmi les Musulmans de Marseille," Marseille, March 26, 1942, CAOM Alg Oran 5i/50.

[67] Chief of the Squad, Roubaud, Company of Oran, "No. 858/2," Oran, October 18, 1940, CAOM Alg Oran 5i/50.

[68] Police Commissioner of the Second Arrondissement of Constantine to the Central Police Commissioner, "No. 6098," Constantine, October 15, 1940, CAOM Alg Const B/3/688.

[69] Police Commissioner of the Second Arrondissement of Constantine to the Central Police Commissioner, "No. 6198," Constantine, October 15, 1940, CAOM Alg Const B/3/688.

not improve their political situation. Vichy's actions with regard to Jews was an indication that the government would further limit access to rights to those not considered properly – and purely – French.

After the abrogation of the Crémieux Decree, Europeans also reminded Jews of their new inferior status. These altercations ranged from small scale, such as the French student who called his Jewish classmate a "dirty Jew," to broader efforts at encouraging antisemitism.[70] In Oran, a group of "Frenchmen" wrote a letter to Pétain, celebrating his leadership, his "specifically French work," and demanding even more stringent treatment of Jews in the colony. They entreated the modification of the racial definition of Jews in Article One of the Jewish Statute, because Algerian Jews "will not hesitate, in order to arrive at their goals, to profit from the qualifications of this article by creating mixed homes ... We want a French Algeria." They described their antisemitism as a natural reaction to and defense against the insolence of Jews in the colony.[71]

The authors of the letter argued that due to the different demographics of the metropole and the colony, the Statute needed to be adapted to fit the unique situation of the colony. They called upon the earlier tropes of antisemites that included the accusation of Jewish bloc voting.

200,000 Jews currently constitute a formidable "ethnic minority" for the 800,000 Europeans. A homogenous bloc, which rigorously obeys the orders coming from different consistories ... the Algerian Jews don't have any patriotic sentiment, in these conditions how can they love and serve France, which welcomed them? In the French crucible, they have not, nor have they ever wanted to assimilate.[72]

In this passage, the authors capitalized on accusations of Jews' unwillingness to assimilate and their lack of patriotism and service to France. The electoral challenges posed by Jews to European hegemonies are also evident here. However, the statistics were inflated in this letter – in reality the numbers were closer to half those stated. These false statistics served to prove a point of the danger of Jewish political power felt by Europeans. Furthermore, using the racial calculations of the Jewish Statute, antisemites emphasized an irreducible Jewish nature. They

[70] Police Commissioner of the Second Arrondissement of Constantine to the Central Police Commissioner "Re: Incident entre deux lycéens israélites et un lycéen Français," Constantine, October 23, 1940, CAOM Alg Const B/3/688; Police Commissioner of the Second Arrondissement of Constantine to the Central Police Commissioner, Constantine, March 29, 1941, CAOM Alg Const B/3/688.

[71] They wrote, "Our ANTISEMITISM is a natural reflexive defense because there is an aggressive and insolent SEMITISM, particularly violent in Algeria." "A Group of Frenchmen of Oran," to Marshal Pétain, "Consideration sur le statut des Juifs en Algérie," CAOM FM 81F/847. Emphasis in the original. Although the letter is undated, it was likely written soon after the implementation of the legislation in 1940.

[72] Ibid.

posited that children born of a marriage between a Jewish man and a European woman would inherit not only the "physical characteristics of the Jewish race, but also all the moral and intellectual dispositions." They observed that if a child was "only one quarter Jewish, he still showed a clear tendency consistent with the Jewish spirit, especially if he had a Jewish name." They proposed that the revised first article of the Jewish Statute consider anyone with two Jewish grandparents a Jew and urged banning intermarriage. "Without hatred, only because we want France to remain sovereign in Algeria, we demand other measures that do not allow Jews to continue to cause the immense evil that they create in our country."[73] Even after the abrogation of their citizenship, Jews still presented a threat to Europeans in the colony. Antisemites sought to capitalize on an antisemitic national government to remove Jews from all positions of power and influence.

An anonymous "Frenchman" wrote to the Prefect of Constantine in March 1941 to complain that Jews remained in the administration, when there were non-Jewish Frenchmen available to replace them. "There are true Frenchmen, are they not worthy of replacing the Jews in our truly French administration? We beg you, Monsieur the Prefect, to reserve for them these positions ... Vive la France! Vive l'Algérie Française!"[74] This complaint echoes the expressions of status anxiety among the néos in the decades prior. Antisemitism abounded in all spheres in the colony. A Muslim man reproached a Muslim woman for working for Jews. "Could you not find work elsewhere? Don't you know that it is a dishonor to work for the Jews? It would be better if you returned to us; we would pay for your trip."[75] In the era of Vichy, Algerian Jews became increasingly maligned in colonial society, suffering a form of "social death."[76]

In the face of such antisemitic efforts, Jewish leaders focused their efforts on support, defense, and solidarity for those impacted by the Jewish Statute.[77] Following the abrogation of the Crémieux Decree,

---

[73] Ibid.

[74] Anonymous letter to the Prefect of Constantine, "Re: Justice," Guelma, March 7, 1941, CAOM Alg Const 93/3G19. Many denunciations under Vichy were submitted anonymously.

[75] El Hocine ben Abdelmalek to Colomb Bechar, Kaddour ben Belkacem, "Intercepted telegram No. 193: Re: Activités Indigènes, Reproche addresses á une musulmane qui travaille chez un juif," Oran, November 23, 1941, CAOM Alg Oran 5i/50.

[76] Patterson, *Slavery and Social Death*. Marion Kaplan also used the concept of "social death" to describe the Jews' excommunication from non-Jewish society in Germany. Kaplan, *Between Dignity and Despair*, 5.

[77] Police Commissioner of Constantine to the Prefect of Constantine, "No. 6832: Surveillance des milieux israélites," Constantine, November 25, 1940, CAOM Alg Const B/3/688.

Chief Rabbi of France Moïse Schwartz submitted a letter of protest to the leaders of Vichy that incorporated familiar tropes of Jewish patriotism and service. "We cannot adhere to the principle of a racial legislation ... We affirm that we are not a racial minority, nor a political minority, but a religious community." To defend this statement, Schwartz enumerated the similarities between Judaism and the ideals of the new Vichy government. Despite these shared characteristics, Jewish "men of science, judges, officials ... who chose to enter government service ... will now find themselves excluded and unemployed, often without resources." Schwartz emphasized the long history of Jewish service and their significant efforts in the last two wars. In spite of the legislation imposed by Vichy, Schwartz promised an "unfailing devotion to the homeland."[78]

Around the same time, the CAES leaders submitted a letter to Marshal Pétain in response to the abrogation of the Crémieux Decree. They outlined the history of Jewish commitment to France since the very early days of French presence in Algeria. "The promoters and the authors of the Crémieux Decree were not wrong in according the status of citizen to Algerian Jews. In a general manner, the new citizens have helped to cement French authority in Algeria." In analyzing the new legislation, the CAES members pointed out the problems that the exceptions to the abrogation posed, primarily the fact that such exceptions could divide families. By pointing to their former status competitors, the Jewish representatives indicated the prejudice of the legislation. "In Algeria, a French citizen for 70 years, who experienced the same joys and the same agony as his countrymen, who fought in two wars, is now rejected for French citizenship while the son of foreigner retains his rights; even worse, a naturalized citizen who has not participated in the two wars is still a French citizen." By contrasting their long history of patriotic service to the lack thereof among the descendants of non-French Europeans, the CAES accused the men of Vichy of antisemitism. Nonetheless, they concluded their letter with an expression of their unerring loyalty to France. "If the October 7, 1940 decree of abrogation withdraws our rights, we will maintain our responsibilities. We will accomplish them all, as in the past, in all unselfishness, motivated only by the greatness of France."[79] To continue to distinguish themselves from the "undeserving" naturalized Europeans, Jews remained loyal

---

[78] Chief Rabbi of France, Moïse Schwartz, to Marshal Pétain, the Head of State, and to the members of Government, "Le Grand Rabbin de France, Chevalier de la Légion d'Honneur à le devoir d'adresser au Chef de l'État et aux Membres du Gouvernement la déclaration suivante au nom des Français israélites," Vichy, October 22, 1940, CAOM FM 81F/846.

[79] Rabbis and Consistory Presidents of Algeria, under auspices of the CAES, "Mémoire à Monsieur le Marechal Pétain, Chef de l'État Français," Algiers, undated, CDJC LXXXIV-1.

patriots, even if they did not have the benefits of French citizenship. For them, their assimilation was not just to prove their worth as citizens; it was because over the seventy years of their citizenship, they had truly become Frenchmen.

Intensification of Institutional Antisemitism in Algeria

On November 20, 1940, Vichy promulgated a subsequent Jewish Statute for the Jews of Algeria. The new law created deadlines for Jews who sought exemptions from the abrogation of the Crémieux Decree. Algerian Jews had one month following the promulgation of the new law to demonstrate that they met the requirements for exemption and to provide all the necessary documentation to support their request to a Justice of the Peace. If the judge did not accept their request, the individual then had three days to submit another request to the president of the Tribunal of their arrondissement. Article Four retracted Jews' previous voting privileges, for which they had fought to maintain in recent years. The law established a commission to be led by a Member of the State, charged with examining requests for exemption.[80] Algerian Jews' experiences mirrored that of German Jews following the Nuremberg laws, in that both lost their rights as citizens.[81] French metropolitan Jews' status was less explicit than the Jews in Algeria: even though they could not practice their citizenship rights, they remained citizens in name. As Derrida recounted, because Algerian Jews' citizenship was so new and fragile, its loss was traumatic.[82]

The implementation of the abrogation of the Crémieux Decree and the Jewish Statute had severe implications for Jews in Algeria and for the colonial administration as well. The mayor of Constantine reported in December 1940 that in accordance with the October 7 law, his service marked all certificates of Jews with the word *Juif*.[83] The definitions of nationality and of citizenship would later cause much confusion for administrators and Vichy officials, especially during the period of the 1941 census. The statistics of the Jewish community in Algeria a decade before Vichy reflects Jews' place within the colony following a generation of assimilation and integration. In 1931, there were 110,127 Jews in Algeria, 850,279

---

[80] Philippe Pétain, "Statut des Juifs d'Algérie," Vichy, November 20, 1940 (published in the Journel Officiel of Algeria on November 26, 1940), CAOM Alg Const 93/3G7. The retraction of voting privileges had little real impact on the situation of Algerian Jews, as under Vichy there were no elections.

[81] Marrus and Paxton, *Vichy France and the Jews*, 193.

[82] Derrida, *Monolingualism of the Other*, 14–15.

[83] Mayor of Constantine to the Prefect of Constantine, "No. 361: Objet: Certificates de Nationalité," Constantine, December 6, 1940, CAOM Alg Const 93/3G7.

Europeans, and 5,593,045 Muslims.[84] Jews in all three departments were concentrated in certain occupations such as jewelers, merchants, and other similar professions; Jews also represented a significant portion of administrative and municipal employees. By 1940 and the Vichy antisemitic legislation, these numbers had grown significantly.

Statistics of Jewish Administrative Employment in Algiers, Constantine, and Oran in 1936

Field of Employment	Jews employed in the Department of Algiers	Jews employed in the Department of Constantine	Jews employed in the Department of Oran
Police	16	40	40
Railroad	34	95	45
P.T.T. (Postes, télégraphes, téléphones)	204	147	200
Administrative positions	162	120	157

Source: Maurice Eisenbeth, Grand Rabbin d'Alger, *Les Juifs de l'Afrique du Nord: Démographie et Onomastique* (Alger: Imprimerie du Lycée, 1936), 16.

Governor-General Abrial reported on January 22, 1941, that the October 3 Jewish Statute removed 423 Jews from official positions. Of those Jews removed, 108 were based in Algiers, 176 in Oran, and 139 in Constantine.[85] Based on the 1936 statistics of Jewish professions, nearly all Jews in the administration would have lost their jobs. The men of Vichy were not ignorant of the problems posed by such a purge of administrative personnel. At the end of December 1940, then Secretary of State Peyrouton warned of the implications of the upcoming termination of Jewish administrative employees in Algeria. "A large proportion of clerks, attorneys, notaries, and bailiffs currently serving the Algerian departments are indeed of the Jewish race. So far, this situation raises a series of problems that must be addressed quickly."[86] Peyrouton's office followed up in a subsequent letter that tried to work out the complexities of the legislation. "In certain Algerian administrations, the simultaneous eviction of all the Jews also risks creating important gaps and will disrupt the effective functioning of the service."[87]

---

[84] Eisenbeth, Grand Rabbin d'Alger, *Les Juifs de l'Afrique du Nord*, 16.

[85] Gov-Gen of Algeria, "Services Communaux (statistiques sur le nombre et la répartition des juifs dans les services publics, loi 3 octobre 1940)," Algiers, January 22, 1941, CAOM FM 81F/846.

[86] Secretary of State Peyrouton to the Minister of Justice, "Re: Officiers ministeriels israélites en Algérie," Vichy, December 24, 1940, CAOM FM 81F/847.

[87] Bergen, Director of Peyrouton's cabinet to the Sec-Gen, "Re: Statut des Juifs application de la loi du 3 octobre 1940 en Algérie," Vichy, January 2, 1941, CAOM FM 81F/847.

These concerns demonstrate the extent to which Algerian Jews had integrated into French society in the colony. They represented such an integral part of the administration that the implementation of the Vichy legislation and the Jewish officials' subsequent termination posed significant problems for effective governing of the colony. However, in the eyes of the legislators, the ultimate goal of removing Jews from the administration was more urgent than the possible repercussion.

By October 1941, the numbers of terminated Jewish administrative employees had increased dramatically. According to the governor-general, of the 2,671 Jews who had been employees of the administration, by October 13, only 469 remained.[88]

Statistics of Jews Removed from All Positions within Algerian Administration (October 1941)

	Titled	Auxiliary	Total
Number of Jews in the administration	1890	781	2671
Jewish agents terminated December 19, 1940	1400	491	1891
Jewish agents terminated December 10, 1941	11	142	153
Jewish agents affected by the law of June 2, 1941	78	47	125
Total Jewish agents eliminated in application of the Jewish Statute	1489	680	2169
Jews terminated following normal procedure (retirement, discipline)	9	24	33
Jews remaining in the administration	392	77	469

Source: CAOM FM 81F/847

Beyond the administrative challenges caused by the termination of Jewish employees, the actual implementation of the legislation caused confusion. Officials were perplexed as to what they should do with Jews who were citizens not by the Crémieux Decree. The Minister of Justice clarified this issue: all beneficiaries of the Crémieux Decree and their descendants would be impacted by the abrogation. Those who became naturalized individually before the promulgation of the Crémieux Decree, Jews born outside of Algeria who relocated to the colony and benefited from individual naturalization, and the descendants of both groups were not impacted by the law. The Minister of Justice added that according to the meeting of the State Council on January 29, 1941, underage children of Jews exempted from the October 7 law could also maintain their citizenship.[89] However, in processing individual files, Vichy officials rarely applied these exemptions.

---

[88] Gov-Gen to the Secretary of State, "No. 465QJ: Objet: Statut des Juifs A/S de l'application aux fonctionnaires de la loi du 3 juin," Algiers, October 13, 1941, CAOM FM 81F/847.
[89] Minister of Justice to the Secretary of State, Vichy, February 8, 1941, CAOM Alg Const 93/3G7.

Confusion over definitions of citizenship and nationality came to the fore during the 1941 census ordered by the law of June 2, 1941, which also expanded the list of prohibited professions. For the census, all those considered Jewish had one month to present themselves to the Prefect of their department or the Sub-Prefect of their arrondissement. There they had to provide a written declaration indicating that they were Jews, detailing their civil status, their marital and family status, their profession, and their property holdings. Nonparticipants in the census faced imprisonment for up to a year, and a fine between 100 and 10,000 francs.[90] Pétain extended this law to Algeria on July 18.[91]

Even before the July 18 promulgation of the law, Prefect of Constantine Max Bonnafous submitted a set of guidelines to the administrators in his department regarding how to process the census. These guidelines were more rigorous than those in the first set of Jewish Statute. To prove nonpractice of Judaism, individuals had to provide proof of participation in another religion, which included baptism certificates and letters of certification from priests.[92] At the end of August 1941, Bonnafous circulated a new set of guidelines for the census to be implemented between September 1 and 10, 1941. All Jews were required to participate. Men would make declarations for their wives and underage children.[93] During the census 117,656 Jews participated, of which 33,095 were children under age 15.[94] The large number of youth in the Jewish community impacted the quota placed on Jewish students in primary and secondary schools in Algeria, further exacerbating the Jewish sense of rupture.

Mayoral reports to Bonnafous reflected administrative confusion regarding the processing of the census. Mayor Huguon of Batna reported reluctance among the 1,062 Jews making declarations in his city due to confusion regarding the attribution of nationality and citizenship.[95]

---

[90] Philippe Pétain, Admiral Darlan, "Loi du 2 Juin 1941 Prescrivant le Recensement des Juifs (No. 2333)," Vichy, June 2, 1941, CAOM Alg Const 93/3G4.

[91] Philippe Pétain, Admiral Darlan, "Décret du 18 Juillet 1941 étendant à l'Algérie la loi du 2 Juin 1941 Prescrivant le recensement des Juifs (no. 3032)," Vichy, July 18, 1941, CAOM Alg Const 93/3G4.

[92] Regardless of the religion currently observed by the individual, if he or she had three Jewish grandparents, or two Jewish grandparents but was married to a Jew, he or she would be considered Jewish. Prefect of Constantine to administrators in the Department of Constantine, "No. 4780," Constantine, July 11, 1941, CAOM Alg Const 93/3G3.

[93] Prefect of Constantine to administrators in the Department of Constantine, "No. 13.501A.C.2: Objet: Recensement des Juifs," Constantine, August 29, 1941, CAOM Alg Const 93/3G4.

[94] Cantier, L'Algérie Sous le Régime de Vichy, 316.

[95] Mayor of Batna to the Prefect of Constantine, "No. 6: Re: Recensement des Juifs," Batna, September 19, 1941, CAOM Alg Const 93/3G4. Huguon reported that the Muslim and European populations in his city were pleased with the steps taken in "putting the Jews in their place." The Prefect of Oran did not report similar issues; he

The misunderstanding stemmed from the categories applied to Jews on nationality certificates following the Vichy legislation, which included "non-naturalized native Algerian Jew," "naturalized native Algerian Jew," and "naturalized or non-naturalized Moroccan or Tunisian Jew."[96] In November, Bonnafous alerted his departmental administrators that all certificates and identity cards provided for Jews should be marked by one of three categories "Jew-French citizen," "Jew-Algerian native," and "Jew-foreign." He also reminded them that a person's status might change in accordance with the Jewish Statute. For example, someone with only two Jewish grandparents would not be considered a Jew, unless he or she married a Jew, in which case that status would change.[97]

The issue of what rights could be inherited further confused colonial administrators. There was little uniformity among different officials' interpretations, and confusion passed down the line of command. In April 1941, the mayor of Bône asked the Prefect for clarification as to the status of the children of Algerian Jews who maintained their citizenship. The mayor needed additional information to process the large number of requests from Jews to join the *Chantiers de la Jeunesse*, a paramilitary youth group in France and Algeria that was open only to French citizens.[98] The Prefect responded that the children of Algerian Jews who retained their citizenship could not inherit their parents' citizenship. In contrast, Pétain's deputy, Admiral Darlan, ruled that the under-age Jewish children could inherit French citizenship if their parents benefited from the exceptions to the abrogation. As a result of the conflicting verdicts, the mayor was at a loss for how to deal with the requests inundating his office.[99] There were other examples of confusion among officials regarding the implementation of the legislation.

To deal with the complicated nature of Algerian Jews' status, Governor-General Weygand established a Service for Jewish Questions, modeled on the General Commissariat of Jewish Questions in the metropole. The Service was responsible for studying the political, administrative,

reported 51,316 Jews in his department. See Prefect of Oran, "No. 729 d/2: Note pour Monsieur le Directeur du Cabinet, Objet: Recensement des Juifs," Oran, March 4, 1942, CAOM Alg Oran 3363.

[96] Prefect of Constantine to the Gov-Gen of Algeria, "No. 6033: Statut des Juifs, Certificat de nationalité," Constantine, March 22, 1941, CAOM Alg Const 93/3G7.

[97] The Prefect of Constantine to the Mayor and Administrators, "No. 23002," Constantine, November 7, 1941, CAOM Alg Const 93/3G7.

[98] Mayor of Bône to the Prefect of Constantine, "No. 6502," Bône, April 10, 1941, CAOM Alg Const 93/3G6. The *Chantiers de la Jeunesse* were also intended to replace military service. On the *Chantiers de la Jeunesse*, and the position of Jews within it under Vichy, see Lee, *Pétain's Jewish Children*.

[99] Mayor of Bône to the Prefect of Constantine, "No. 15963," Bône, August 9, 1941, CAOM Alg Const 93/3G6.

economic, and social implications of the Vichy legislation regulating Jewish status and interpreting issues specific to Algeria. The Service reviewed Jews' applications to retain their citizenship and ensured that there were no infractions of the Jewish Statute, especially with regard to professions barred to Jews. The Service for Jewish Questions also controlled the process of Aryanization in Algeria and oversaw the liquidation of Jewish property and belongings.[100] The regulation of Algerian Jews' status was complicated for colonial administrators, but it was even more difficult for the Jews themselves, who suffered from the ambiguity of their status and future in the colony.

The persistent confusion surrounding the Algerian Jews' status led to the promulgation of another law on February 18, 1942. The law clarified the issue by confirming the abrogation of the Crémieux Decree; however, impacted Jews could request naturalization via the sénatus-consulte of 1865, a complicated and lengthy process, but not the 1919 Jonnart Law. The February 18 law exempted from the abrogation Jewish widows or orphans of soldiers who died for France. It also clarified the question of citizenship inheritance: children of those Jews who retained their citizenship inherited that status, unless opposed by the governor-general. Nonbeneficiaries of the Crémieux Decree who retained their citizenship were not exempted from the Jewish Statute in Algeria.[101] Vichy officials clearly had trouble understanding how to implement and manage the range of Jewish statuses and identities in the colony. Nonetheless, the multiple laws from Vichy regarding their status and citizenship had a significant impact on the Jews of Algeria. The sense of rupture that these Jews felt can best be understood in their own words in their appeals to Vichy and colonial officials and in their correspondence with one another.

Appealing to Vichy: Jewish Letters and Petitions

A particularly rich source for interpreting the range of Algerian Jewish identities, statuses, and experiences under Vichy is the body of letters and petitions sent by Jews to Vichy officials claiming exemptions from the abrogation of the Crémieux Decree and the Jewish Statute. This

---

[100] Gov-Gen Maxime Weygand, "Arrête No. 5934," Algiers, August 14, 1941, CAOM FM 81F/846.

[101] The law reaffirmed the particular exemptions available to Jews from the earlier legislation, under the condition that the applicants had never been found guilty of a crime. In addition, non-Algerian Jewish women who acquired French nationality by marrying native Algerian Jewish men would have the same political and civil status as their husbands. Philippe Pétain, "Loi No. 254 du 18 février 1942 fixant le statut des Juifs indigènes d'Algérie," Vichy, February 18, 1942, CAOM Alg Const 93/3G6.

correspondence illustrates the rupture that they experienced and the supplicant tones they used in their appeals. The rupture was immediate and traumatic, yet Jews maintained a sense of hope for a continued future in France's empire, calling upon the France of their past and hopefully their future to grant them clemency.[102]

The June 2, 1941, Jewish Statute excluded Jews from various liberal professions, such as medicine and law, serving as officers and NCOs in the military, and reduced the number of Jews allowed to attend schools and serve in the administration. Sergeant Réné Boukobza, a soldier stationed in Bedeau (Oran), wrote to Suzanne Amoyel soon after the June 1941 legislation. "You have read, my dear, that we [Jews] no longer have the right to be an officer or even a NCO ... Since I can no longer perform my duties, a single solution presents itself, to demobilize ..."[103] Elie Gozlan denounced the treatment of Jewish soldiers, particularly those who were held as prisoners after the war of 1939–1940. Jewish career soldiers and veterans were particularly incapacitated by the legislation.[104]

Another decree promulgated on November 5, 1941, applied quotas for Jews in primary and secondary schools in Algeria.[105] These new realities overwhelmed Jewish communal leadership who not only had to support Jews terminated from their occupations but also had to care for children who could no longer attend state schools. The June 1941 law instituted a 3 percent quota for Jews in each faculty of universities. Governor-General Weygand set the quota for Jewish students in primary and secondary schools in Algeria at 14 percent in 1941 but reduced it to 7 percent in 1942.[106] The harsher quota in the colony reflects the impact of Algerian antisemitism on the implementation of Vichy-inspired legislation.[107] In the light of such restrictions, the responsibility for educating Jewish children fell to the Jewish community. Elie Gozlan wrote in the Jewish monthly *Bulletin de la Fédération des Sociétés Juives* that "our

---

[102] There are parallels in metropolitan France. For example, Rabbi H. Palan of Cusset wrote to Xavier Vallat on July 31, 1941. In his letter, he outlined the ways in which philosophers approved of Judaism and the issues of the antisemitic Vichy legislation. Rabbi H. Kaplan to M. Xavier Vallat, Commissaire Général aux Questions Juives, Cusset, July 31, 1941, [Y]ad [V]ashem [A]rchives, O.26 (Collection on North Africa).

[103] Sergeant Réné Boukobza to Suzanne Amoyel, Bedeau, June 16, 1941, CAOM Alg Oran 5i/50.

[104] "Our children fought to defend their country, they have endured thousands of sufferings while in captivity, they dream of their release and their return to the motherland. Much grief and sadness awaits them." Elie Gozlan, "Quand nos Prisonniers reviendront," *Bulletin de la Fédération des Sociétés Juives d'Algérie*, No. 69 (May 1941): 1, CDJC BIB 9001.

[105] Cantier, *L'Algérie Sous le Régime de Vichy*, 132–133.   [106] Ibid., 317.

[107] Msellati, *Les Juifs d'Algérie*, 55.

children must not remain ignorant and we have the responsibility to provide them with instruction for all degrees. ... It is within instruction that the Jewish spirit has its safeguard, it is through education that it regains its unity."[108] As Jews in Algeria clustered in certain areas, they often represented a large portion of students in urban schools. The imposition of the quota greatly reduced their proportion of the student body.[109] Establishing Jewish schools in the aftermath of the quotas was an enormous task.

André Bakouche, the president of the Jewish Consistory of Constantine, submitted a report to Governor-General Châtel in September 1941, in which he emphasized the crisis caused by the Jewish quotas in education, particularly primary and secondary schools. "How do we support them ... morally and materially? ... It is a generation in total disarray." Bakouche outlined the efforts of Jews to develop schools of their own. Among them were professional training programs, in the manner of the Alliance, including apprenticeships, an artisan society, and a farm school in the department of Constantine. He emphasized Algerian Jews' devotion to Pétain and the men of Vichy, as well as the administrators of Algeria, and Constantine in particular.[110] On December 31, 1941, Pétain promulgated a law that placed private Jewish schools under the jurisdiction of the French government. The governor-general thus had the power to temporarily or permanently shut down any Jewish private school.[111] The governor-general's commission that supervised the Jewish schools could reject Jewish teachers based on various aspects of their past, particularly their political activities and affiliations.[112]

[108] Elie Gozlan, "Pour nos Enfants," *Bulletin de la Fédération des Sociétés Juives d'Algérie*, No. 75 (December 1941): 1, CDJC BIB 9001.

[109] President Attali, Association Culturelle Israélite de Constantine, to M. Szarka, Cannes, "RE: Entr'aide juive pour l'organisation des écoles libres israélites," Constantine, January 31, 1942, CAOM Alg Const 93/3G29.

[110] Bakouche wrote of Jews' faith in Vichy leaders: "It is to them that we look, along with all the French of this country, for our unity of purpose, inspiration, and guidance." André Bakouche, "Mémoire par M. André Bakouche, President du Consistoire Israélite de Constantine, à M. le Gouverneur Châtel, Gouverneur Général Adjoint de l'Algérie," Constantine, September 12, 1941, CAOM Alg Const 93/3G3. Once education fell to the Jewish community, Jewish aid groups, such as the *Association d'Assistance et d'Entr'aide* in Oran, organized fund-raisers to establish Jewish schools. Albert Smadja, President Jewish Consistory to the Prefect of Oran, Oran, December 18, 1941, CAOM Alg Oran 1S/41.

[111] Teachers had to be French and approved by the Gov-Gen or the Prefect on the recommendation of the rector of the Academy of Algiers. Philippe Pétain, "Loi No. 5535 du 31 Décembre 1941 relative à l'enseignement privé Juif en Algérie," Vichy, December 31, 1941, CAOM Alg Const 93/3G29.

[112] For example, Réné Kahn, father of two children, a literature professor, was rejected because of his past as a member of the SFIO. "Candidats Enseignement Privé: René Kahn," Bône, November 21, 1942, CAOM Alg Const 93/3G29.

Students and their parents wrote of their frustrations following the school quotas. Madame Aboab-Azerad expressed her sadness over the situation of Jewish children, her daughter among them, but continued to emphasize her faith in France and the strength of her French identity. "The time is fertile with sadness. However, we are no less confident in the France of Montaigne, of Pascal, of Descartes, of Renan, of Pasteur."[113] The student-run Zionist organization *Qol Aviv* protested the exclusion of Jewish students from the University of Algiers on the basis of the racial legislation. They questioned the definition of identity based on race rather than nationality, pointing to the fact that in the colony most Europeans were naturalized citizens. The students questioned whether those natur-alized Europeans were more French than they were. "We are accused of not having a French mentality. Did our fathers and our ancestors not fight for France in 1914–1918? Many of us have fought for France more recently."[114] The Zionist students highlighted the Vichy government's use of antisemitic definitions of nationality in order to remove Jews from society. *Qol Aviv* was more critical of Vichy and more defensive of Algerian Jewish patriotism than most contemporary Algerian Jewish organizations.

The June 1941 Jewish Statute limited the number of Jews who could serve in certain liberal professions. Dr. J. Salama described the anguish that he felt upon learning of his exclusion from the College of Physicians. "Despite my courage, yesterday was a day of mourning at home . . . Our hopes are dashed."[115] While Salama was overwhelmed by uncertainty, Gaston Aboucaya, a senior lawyer, faced the quotas with confidence that Vichy would end and true France would return. "Today was my last day; I have removed my plaque and hung up my robe at home. It was not without emotion, but my morale is good because I have confidence in the repossession of France and her recovery."[116] For Jews formerly employed within the administration, the realities of their termination were profound and discouraging. In particular, those impacted by the Jewish Statute lost access to their pensions. A group of Jewish men who worked for the

---

[113] Madame Aboab-Azerad to M. Joseph Lévy (Nice), "Intercepted Telegram No. 5281: RE: Application du 'Numerus-Clausus' et opinion," Oran, November 3, 1941, CAOM Alg Oran 5i/50.

[114] Representatives of *Qol Aviv*, "Aux Étudiants de l'Université d'Alger," *Bulletin de la Fédération des Sociétés Juives d'Algérie*, no. 70 (June–July 1941): 7, CDJC BIB 9001.

[115] Dr. J. Salama to M. J. Skalli (Oran), "Intercepted Telegram No. 229: RE: Doléances d'un médécin juif sur l'application du numerus-clausus," Tiaret, February 6, 1941, CAOM Alg Oran 5i/50.

[116] Gaston Aboucaya, ancient bâtonnier, to Alphonse Aboucaya (Algiers), "Intercepted Telegram No. 412: Re: consideration sur l'application du 'numerus-clausus' aux avo-cats," Oran, February 15, 1942, CAOM Alg Oran 5i/50.

Postes, Télégraphes, Téléphones (PTT) protested the loss of their pensions. "We are old servants of the state. We had conscientiously done our duty as officials and we will always remain disciplined, faithful and devoted."[117] Some Jews remained hopeful, especially in public, but many were lost as to how to sustain their families in the face of such hardship.

After the abrogation of the Crémieux Decree and the Jewish Statute stripped them of their citizenship and terminated their employment, some Jews appealed directly to Pétain to maintain their citizenship, based either on their own contributions or that of their parents or spouses. Many of the appeals came from women. These appeals are inflected with suppliant tones, Vichy rhetoric, and plaintive requests. Rénée Zerbib, the widow of a World War I veteran and PTT employee and mother of four children, appealed to Pétain directly. "Monsieur the Marshal of France and dear father, I dare to count on your kindness to get a favorable opinion to my query, and during this wait, I assure you of my deep respect and my complete dedication as a passionate Frenchwoman."[118] Zerbib's appeal was one of thousands that engaged in the style of "suppliant appeals." They can be used to examine the ways in which their authors crafted the narrative of their dilemmas, and, to use historian Natalie Zemon Davis' work, the "fiction" of their situation – expressing love and devotion of Pétain and Vichy.[119] Similarly, they must be read *against* and, as historian Ann Stoler argues, *along* the grain of the archives and these letters in order to understand the goals of these suppliants and the very conscientious way in which they described their plight. While they are appeals that seek a particular outcome – exemption from the Jewish Statute or other antisemitic legislation – these letters also reveal a highly assimilated Algerian Jewish identity.[120]

One particularly interesting subsection of these appeals was a wave of letters and appeals to Vichy on behalf of interfaith couples confused by their status in light of the Jewish Statute, the abrogation of the Crémieux

---

[117] All of the ten men listed on the letter had at least four children; some had as many as eight. Simon Allouche, Sakhar Aouizerate, David Zaouche, Simon Zaouche, Maklouf Halimi, Ephraim Elbeze, David Derai, Benoun Chemba, Maklouf Guedj, Askil Abrahami to the Prefect of Constantine, Constantine, March 25, 1941, CAOM Alg Const 93/3G19.

[118] Zerbib's brother-in-law, a retired police inspector, maintained his citizenship rights because he received a Croix de Guerre and a Medal of Honor for courage and devotion, as well as a Medal of Honor from the police. As Zerbib lived with her brother, who helped her raise her four children, she used his status as the basis for her appeal. Rénée Zerbib to Philippe Pétain, Constantine, May 5, 1941, CAOM Alg Const 93/3G30.

[119] Natalie Zemon Davis, *Fiction in the Archives: Pardon Tales and Their Tellers in Sixteenth-Century France* (Stanford: Stanford University Press, 1987), 2–3.

[120] Ann Laura Stoler, *Along the Archival Grain: Epistemic Anxieties and Colonial Common Sense* (Princeton: Princeton University Press, 2008).

Decree, and the 1941 census. These interfaith couples reflect the depth of assimilation of some Algerian Jews over the seventy years of their French citizenship as well as the complicated realities of Vichy's antisemitic legislation and their impact on families. Marcel Tubiana, a lawyer in Bône, married the Catholic daughter of a French officer in 1939, with whom he had two children. He did not declare his children during the 1941 census; however, the governor-general ruled that his children were considered Jewish.[121] While he was serving in the army in 1940, his wife gave birth to a daughter. Since he was away, his wife chose to wait to baptize their daughter until his return. His wife gave birth to a son in February 1941, and both children were baptized on June 14, 1941. According to the Jewish Statute, for baptisms to be considered valid, they had to be conducted before June 1940. Tubiana wrote that his children "have been and will be raised in the Catholic religion."[122]

He added that he, as well as his brothers, received a Catholic education, even though he was technically Jewish. "From a young age, the Catholic religion was more familiar to us than that of the Jewish religion." Concluding that regardless of the outcome of his appeal, he would raise his children with a love of France. "No one has the power, I think, to stop me from making my children into good Frenchmen and women, whatever happens. My essential desire is that they can also be, without restriction, good servants of the country."[123] The governor-general eventually ruled that while Tubiana's son qualified as a non-Jew because of his timely baptism, his daughter would be considered a Jew.[124] The Tubiana case shows the subjectivity of the implementation of Vichy legislation, to the point where siblings, separated in age by one year, could be divided between two religions and statuses in the eyes of the law.

Other cases of intermarriage reveal the complexities of interpretation and execution of the Vichy antisemitic laws.[125] The confusion regarding

---

[121] Gov-Gen to the Prefect of Constantine, "Objet: Recensement des Juifs–A/S de M. Marcel Tubiana, Avocat à Bône," Algiers, November 25, 1941, CAOM Alg Const 93/3G6.

[122] Marcel Tubiana to the Mayor of Bône, Bône, February 5, 1942, CAOM Alg Const 93/3G6.

[123] Ibid.

[124] Gov-Gen to the Prefect of Constantine, "No. 2857QJ: Objet: Recensement de M. Tubiana Marcel," Algiers, April 20, 1942, CAOM Alg Const 93/3G6.

[125] For cases similar to the Tubiana case, see Jeanne Abecassis to the General Commissioner of the Jewish Questions, Constantine, October 21, 1941; Mayor of Constantine to the General Commissioner of Jewish Questions (Vichy), "No. 3491/C Objet: Application de la loi du 2 Juin 1941 dans 3 cas particuliers," Constantine, November 10, 1941, CAOM Alg Const 93/3G8; M. Albert Perrot to the General Commissioner of the Jewish Questions (Vichy), Constantine, November 4, 1941; Mayor of Constantine to the General Commissioner of the Jewish Questions (Vichy),

definitions of nationality and citizenship became apparent again in the case of Raymond Bernard. Bernard, a non-Jewish Frenchman, married a Jewish woman who had three Jewish grandparents. His wife converted to Catholicism before June 1940, and their four children were raised as Catholics. He wrote to the governor-general demanding French nationality for his wife by virtue of their marriage. Bernard alluded to the Constantine municipal government's antisemitism, suggesting that it may have influenced its decision in regard to his wife. "Perhaps the interpretation of the law is not understood in Constantine? That would not be surprising."[126] The Prefect of Constantine wrote that Bernard had confused the issue of nationality with that of citizenship. Given that his wife had three Jewish grandparents, by the Jewish Statute, she was considered Jewish. "If her grandparents are of Algerian origin and benefited from the Crémieux Decree, she is a native Algerian Jew. This quality is independent of nationality."[127] The nuances of the nationality and citizenship proved complicated for both residents and the administrators of the colony. The fact that Jews remained French nationals but lost their French citizenship created a confusing status for these Jews and they were often unsure as to what rights they retained as French nationals.

The Jewish Statute had a clearly powerful impact on Algerian Jews, but it also deeply affected their spouses, especially when their spouses were not Jewish.[128] For example, in 1941 Madame Chicheportiche wrote to the governor-general to request clarification of her status. She was a French Catholic woman from Paris who married an Algerian Jew. At the time of their marriage, her husband was a French citizen. Her letter expressed the anxiety of those non-Jews married to Algerian Jews regarding their own status and their own sense of rupture.

The Crémieux law was still in place, and I married a man of French nationality . . . Today, what remains of all this? I apologize, Mr. Governor General, for abusing your kindness, but I'm sure you understand my painful situation, and that you will answer me with what I can do. My husband loves France; he married a Frenchwoman; is it possible that the final decree concerning the Jews will impact

---

"No. 3491/C Objet: Application de la loi du 2 Juin 1941 dans 3 cas particuliers," Constantine, November 10, 1941, CAOM Alg Const 93/3G8.

[126] M. Raymond Bernard to the Gov-Gen, Constantine, September 10, 1941, CAOM Alg Const 93/3G8.

[127] Prefect of Constantine to Raymond Bernard, "No. 7854," Constantine, October 10, 1941, CAOM Alg Const 93/3G8.

[128] The issue of marriages between "colonizers" and "colonized" has a literature all its own. See, for example, Ann Laura Stoler, *Carnal Knowledge and Imperial Power: Race and the Intimate in Colonial Rule* (Berkeley: University of California Press, 2002), 42–44 and Rachel Jean-Baptiste, *Conjugal Rights: Marriage, Sexuality, and Urban Life in Colonial Libreville, Gabon* (Athens: Ohio University Press, 2014).

him too? ... I left my whole family in Paris, I have been separated from my real race and although this life gave me a companion, I don't yet understand the full meaning of this abolition.[129]

Many non-Jewish spouses never anticipated being faced with this difficult reality. Madame Chicheportiche's letter depicts the ambivalence of the position of non-Jewish spouses of Algerian Jews following the abrogation of the Crémieux Decree, as well as the impact of racial propaganda from Vichy on individuals in the colony.

Some non-Jewish spouses of Algerian Jews not only felt concern for their own status but also fought for their spouses to maintain their citizenship. Léonie Delphine Zekri, a non-Jewish woman born in Paris, wrote to Marshal Pétain to request that her husband, Abraham Zekri, remain a French citizen. Her husband served in the French army from 1930 to 1934, during the general mobilization in 1939, and was currently a German prisoner. "I come to you, Monsieur the Marshal, in the hope that you might comfort me by telling me that the rights of French citizenship will not be taken from my husband and upon his liberation, you will allow him to have a position in the administration, or to have a profession without him being refused because of his origins."[130] Particularly illustrative, this letter indicates the highly assimilated nature of some Algerian Jews, who not only married non-Jews but also served in the French military and sought to remain part of the administration, even in the face of antisemitic legislation.

Some Jews married to non-Jews appealed to maintain their citizenship on the basis of their marriage, conversion, and their service to France. Salomon Marcel Kharoubi, a bailiff of the civil courts of Bône for twelve years, who served in the military from 1939 to 1940, based his appeal to the Prefect of Constantine on his service, as well as his conversion to Catholicism and marriage to a French, Catholic woman. "French by birth and heart ... I left the Jewish society and community very young, I ardently desire not to be returned to it ... Not being Jewish but by Jewish law, I am, however, a Frenchman in my heart, Catholic by religion."[131] Particularly interesting in Kharoubi's letter is his frustration that the Jewish Statute would return him to the Jewish identity from which he sought to escape. In his assessment of Kharoubi's request, the mayor of Bône noted that he had not provided the country with any

---

[129] Madame Chicheportiche to the Gov-Gen, in letter Prefect of Oran to the Prefect of Constantine, "No. 2897," February 8, 1941, CAOM Alg Const 93/3G8.

[130] Madame Zekri to Marshal Pétain, Philippeville, June 24, 1941, CAOM Alg Const 93/3G8.

[131] Salomon Marcel Kharoubi to the Prefect of Constantine, Bône, September 1942, CAOM Alg Const 93/3G23.

exceptional service.[132] The Jewish Statute created an ambiguous reality for Jews who married non-Jews or had converted themselves. The long delays of appeals prolonged their uncertain status.

These cases are profoundly illustrative of the sense of rupture experienced by Algerian Jews, their spouses, and children as a result of the Jewish Statute and the abrogation of the Crémieux Decree. The annihilation of their previous identities, which were the result of a long process of assimilation and integration, ripped Jews from their connection to France and their history in the colony. The cases discussed here demonstrate that some Jews had assimilated to such a degree that intermarriage was relatively common and both Algerian Jewish men and women entered into mixed marriages with French Catholics. In their appeals and demands to Vichy and colonial administrators, Algerian Jews made the case for their continued participation in the French nation as citizens based on the intensity and extent of their French identities. Despite the rupture and the feeling of alienation, they maintained their hope for France to once again recognize them as sons and daughters of the *mère Patrie* and reintegrate them into her ranks.

Jewish Loss and the Role of Local Leadership in Enforcing Vichy Law

The laws regulating Jewish status and citizenship in Algeria created a deep sense of rupture for Algerian Jews. The sense of confusion regarding the applications of these laws plagued Jews and administrators alike. These laws restricted Jews' ability to own property, work in certain professions, and even their freedom in certain cases. Some Jews were sent to thirty-six labor camps in Algeria, including Bedeau, which was an internment camp for Algerian Jewish soldiers.[133] On November 5, 1941, a new law restricted the number of Jewish lawyers in Algeria to 2 percent of the 800 total lawyers in the colony. Similarly, Jewish midwives were restricted to 2 percent.[134]

---

[132] Mayor of Bône, "Rapport confidential: Kharoubi," Bône, January 1943, CAOM Alg Const 93/3G23.

[133] Susan Slyomovics, "French restitution, German compensation: Algerian Jews and Vichy's financial legacy," *The Journal of North African Studies*, Vol. 17, No. 5 (2012): 893–896. The subject of labor camps in Algeria is currently understudied. But scholars are starting to study the subject in recent years. There is not space here for me to deal with the subject with enough detail. For more on the subject, see Norbert Bel Ange, *Quand Vichy internait ses soldats juifs d'Algérie: Bedeau, sud Oranais, 1941–1943* (Paris: L'Harmattan, 2006).

[134] Secretary of State of the Colonies to the Commissariat Général aux Questions Juives, "No. 5861/D.P. Objet: Admission des avocats juifs aux colonies," Vichy, October 8, 1941, Ministry of the Colonies, Direction of Political Affairs, USHMMA RG-43.062M. See also Michael M. Laskier, "Between Vichy Antisemitism and German Harassment:

The process of economic Aryanization further demonstrated to Algerian Jews that their situation and position within the colony was no longer guaranteed and their property no longer theirs. The Vichy Law of July 22, 1941, legislated the process of economic Aryanization in order to "eliminate all Jewish influence in the national economy." The law allowed the Commissariat General of Jewish Questions (CGQJ) to assign provisionary administrators to control Jewish property, who were advised to find "French" buyers of such properties.[135] Marshal Pétain and Xavier Vallat of the CGQJ continued to adapt the July 22 law in order to clarify the process of assigning administrators of Jewish property and the process by which they could be taken. Vallat communicated these changes to the Minister of the Colonies over 1941 and 1942.[136] Even though Vallat visited Algeria in August 1941, where he met with Jewish leaders, including Head Rabbi Maurice Eisenbeth and war veterans, he had no intentions of creating more lenient legislation in Algeria. Ultimately, the purpose of his visit was to prepare for the regulation of Article 4 of the *statut des juifs*, which gave his service the "power, in conjunction with the competent departments taking into account the needs of the Algerian economy, the administration and the liquidation of Jewish property in cases where these operations are prescribed by law." This law extended to Algeria on November 21, 1941.[137]

The law identified three categories of property that could be taken: all industrial, commercial, real estate, or artisanal businesses; buildings, titles, and leases; and properties, securities, and investment rights. According to Article 1 of the law, the governor-general of Algeria could name a provisional administrator to control Jewish property. Jews could maintain control of bonds and government security as well as their private homes and the contents within them. However, they could no longer control their businesses, a measure taken by Vichy to "eliminate all Jewish influence in the Algerian economy."[138] A decree of December 15, 1941, created the Economic Aryanization Service, which was responsible for the

The Jews of North Africa during the Early 1940s," *Modern Judaism*, Vol. 11, No. 3 (1991): 360–361.

[135] "No. 3086: Loi du 22 juillet 1941 rélative aux entreprises, biens et valeurs appartenant aux juifs," *Journel Officiel de l'État Français*, No. 237, August 26, 1941, Ministry of the Colonies, Direction of Political Affairs, USHMM RG-43.062M.

[136] Xavier Vallat, CGQJ, "Modification de l'article 5 de la loi du Juin 1941 et de la loi du 22 juillet 1941," Vichy, November 14, 1941, Ministry of the Colonies, Direction of Political Affairs, USHMM RG-43.062M.

[137] Jean Laloum, " 'En vue d'éliminer toute influence juive dans l'économie algérienne . . .'," *Les cahiers du judaïsme: Spoliations: Nouvelles Recherches*, No. 27 (2009): 105.

[138] "Mesures concernant les biens, décret du 31 novembre 1941 étendant à l'Algérie la loi du 22 juillet 1941 relative aux entreprises, biens et valeurs appartenant aux juifs,"

Aryanization measures of Jewish business, goods, and capital. There were three departmental directors located in Algiers, Oran, and Constantine. Roger Franceschi was the regional director, named by Governor-General Châtel on December 17, 1941. Franceschi and his departmental directors had a great deal of latitude to intensify the enforcement of the Aryanization measures.[139]

Approximately 384 temporary administrators were named custodians of 2,537 Jewish businesses in Algeria: 1,457 (57.4 percent) in the department of Algiers; 593 (23.4 percent) in Constantine; and 482 (19 percent) in Oran. Most of the administrators were Europeans, of French, Italian, Spanish, and Maltese ancestry – meaning many of them were those who had considered Jews status competitors in previous decades.[140] The role of the temporary administrator of Jewish property was a nebulous one. The administrators had to fill out a questionnaire for the local director of the Economic Aryanization Service, which detailed their personal finances and politics, as well as those of their ancestors. The administrators were allowed to "pay" themselves with the profits of the businesses they had taken over, until they could find a suitable European buyer.[141]

In December 1942, Governor-General Châtel and Regional Director of Economic Aryanization Franceschi grappled with the question of what should be done in the case of an administrator, M. Laussel, who could not fulfill his obligations due to health issues. The Jewish owner of the business, Raphaël Douieb, was unsure of what would happen to his property should Laussel no longer be its administrator. While the Regional Director did not feel that Laussel should lose control of the property, the governor-general believed that in the case in which an administrator could not carry out his obligations, the property in question would be returned to the original Jewish owner, in this case Douieb. This complex decision reflected the difficulty of enforcing the Aryanization of property in the colony.[142] Those Jews who had their businesses or belongings taken by the economic Aryanization measures or were impacted by the quotas placed on professions, as well as those who were interned in the Algerian

November 25, 1941, *Journal Officiel d'Algérie*. See also Laskier, "Between Vichy Antisemitism and German Harassment," 361. See also Laloum, "En vue d'éliminer," 106.
[139] Laloum, "En vue d'éliminer," 106–107.
[140] Ibid., 107–108, 111. Laloum examines the numbers of various industries taken over from Jews in great detail.
[141] Ibid., 112–113.
[142] Algiers Regional Director of Economic Aryanization, "No. 10189: Note pour Monsieur le Directeur des Affaires Réservées," Algiers, December 18, 1942, CAOM Alg GGA 6CAB/1. See also Gov-Gen Yves C. Châtel, "No. 4501," December 20, 1942, CAOM Alg GGA 6CAB/1. See also Laloum, "En vue d'éliminer," 112–113.

camps, were eligible to receive reparations, although that in itself was a very complicated process.[143]

The municipal governments and local police played an integral role in executing the Aryanization processes, as well as enforcing rationing efforts. For example, a report by the Prefect of Algiers on July 1942 to the Director of Departmental Economic Services noted that Jews were consuming nearly as much milk as Europeans and Muslims. He requested that the mayor follow up on the issue.[144] Ultimately, the CGQJ was dependent on the cooperation of local officials to execute the anti-Jewish laws and especially the Aryanization of Jewish property.

In 1941, prefects in the colony conducted a study of the "political tendencies" of the mayor and municipal councils of communes in their department, as well as the statistics of the European population. The reports on the political orientation of the mayors reflect an effort to replace mayors who may not have supported Vichy and the National Revolution with more cooperative leaders. For example, in the commune of Ain-El-Turck, which had a European population of 1,766, the comments on the political situation of the municipality read, "Former mayor a radical independent. Had rallied to the politics of the Marshal, but was not maintained for the reason of his ineptitude at dealing with multiple problems relating to the administration of the resort of Ain-El-Turck-Plage. Was replaced by his brother, former mayor." In Renan, a commune with 321 Europeans, the report read, "Mayor of a tendency Popular Front. Was replaced by a National notable. Old municipal council without clearly determined tendency. Was partially reworked." In Mascara, which had a European population of 9,758, "the former mayor was radical socialist (Popular Front). Municipality an entente of radical socialist-socialist SFIO – Municipality suspended. Replaced by a special delegation, then by a new municipality entirely national."[145]

---

[143] On June 2, 1944, Jewish leaders published an article in *Alger Républicain* in which they discussed the necessity of restoring property to Jewish owners. They thanked their Muslim colleagues for supporting this project. Zevaco, Belaiche, and Baretaud, "Restoration of Property to the Victims of Vichy," in letter from Marcel Belaiche to A. Leon Kubowitzki, Algiers, June 6, 1944, CZA C2\1904 (Rescue and refugees Correspondence with the ICRC and other organizations and individuals regarding the situation of the Jews in Argentina and North Africa, agreement). Nehemiah Robinson, *Indemnification and Reparations: Jewish Aspects* (New York: Institute of Jewish Affairs of the American Jewish Congress and World Jewish Congress, 1944), 198–209. See also Susan Slyomovics, *How to Accept German Reparations* (Philadelphia: University of Pennsylvania Press, 2014).

[144] Prefect of Algiers to the Director of Economic Services of the Department, "No.781/D/ D.S.E.," Algiers, July 21, 1942, CDJC LXXXI-43, USHMM RG-43.024M Reel 36.

[145] Prefect Louis Boujard of Oran, "Renouvellement des corps municipaux en Algérie: Situation Politique," Oran, September 18, 1941, CAOM Alg GGA 5CAB/56.

Although Vichy enforced state-level antisemitism, it needed the support and cooperation of municipal governments, which remained vital for the successful application of Vichy legislation. If the mayor or municipal council were deemed inappropriate, they were replaced by those who would support the National Revolution and Vichy. The same situation occurred in the Department of Algiers, Oran, and Constantine.[146] This reorganization of the local-level governments indicates their crucial importance in the operation of Vichy.

Operation Torch and the Jewish Insurgents' Role

Even after the abrogation of the Crémieux Decree, most Algerian Jews maintained their allegiance to France. Many believed that Vichy was an aberration and did not represent true France. In the ensuing years, Charles de Gaulle became a symbol of hope for the future, and the Free French encapsulated all that was positive about France before the arrival of the Germans and the imposition of antisemitic Vichy legislation. That faith was cemented by de Gaulle's statement on October 4, 1941, in honor of the 150th anniversary of the emancipation of the Jews of France. de Gaulle confirmed the politics of the Free French regarding Jewish rights, stating "the celebrated decree of the emancipation of the Jews of France, similarly, the proclamation of the Right of Man and of the Citizen remain always in place and cannot be abrogated by the men of Vichy." Such laws, he continued, were unconstitutional and illegal. The Free French were "resolved to reestablish, after the Victory, equality in dignity ... of all the citizens in all French territories."[147] Although de Gaulle did not explicitly promise to restore the Crémieux Decree, this statement gave Algerian Jews hope that one day they would again be French citizens. As a result, they sought avenues to support de Gaulle and the Free French. One such method of support came in the form of paving the way for the Allied landings in Algeria in November 1942 as part of Operation Torch.

On January 4, 1941, Governor-General Abrial decreed that Jews could not buy and collect weapons.[148] Abrial's decree limited the scope of

---

[146] Prefect of Algiers to the Gov-Gen of Algeria, "No. 88500, A.S. des communes," August 29, 1941, CAOM Alg GGA 5CAB/56.

[147] Charles de Gaulle, October 4, 1941, CDJC-XC-15.

[148] Gov-Gen Abrial to the Secretary of State, "Re: Juifs Algériens, armes," Algiers, January 4, 1941, CAOM FM 81F/846. See also President of the Departmental Union of the Légion Française de Combattants et des Volontaires de la Révolution Nationale, Oran, to General Martin, Provincial President of the Légion Française de Combattants, Algiers, "No. 1146/D3, Objet: A/S questions juives," Oran, August 25, 1942, CAOM FM 81F/846.

Jewish self-defense, which in the face of rising antisemitism was becoming ever more a concern. Throughout 1941 and 1942 relations deteriorated between Jews, Muslims, and Europeans in the colony and low-level violence erupted between the groups with growing regularity. For example, a French captain, Léon Guibert, complained that he had been insulted by a Jewish cobbler, André Ifrah. After an altercation, Guibert shoved Ifrah and told him, "There is a big difference between me, a Frenchman, and you, a Jew."[149] Algerian Jews tried to hold fast to their former dignity, defending themselves against perceived attacks on their identities. Antisemitic slurs also troubled Jewish youth.[150] Other altercations emerged as a result of wartime austerity and accusations of the lack of Jewish patriotism. The Jews' reduced status penetrated daily conversations and encounters between Jews and Muslims. Waiting outside a dispensary, a Muslim man and a Jewish woman got into an argument over whose turn it was in line. When the woman tried to assert her priority, the Muslim man told her, "Don't yell so loud, the luck of the Jews is now over."[151]

Accusations of Jewish treason prompted a propaganda campaign among antisemitic groups. Antisemites organized a demonstration in Khenchela, in the department of Constantine, on July 13, 1941. At a rally, cheers of "Vive la France, Vive Marshal Pétain" soon devolved into cries of "Vive la France, Down with the Jews!" Rally attendees descended upon the Jewish quarter, throwing stones at Jewish homes and shops. Some of those involved were actually the sons of naturalized Italian fathers, evidence of the ongoing divides between former status competitors.[152] Members of the local Muslim scouting group also participated in the demonstration.[153] Some organizers of the event argued that the violence was in response to Jewish demonstrations of support for the British.[154] Jewish support for Britain provided fodder for antisemites,

---

[149] Commissioner of Police of the Second Arrondissement to the Central Police Commissioner, "No. 8150," Constantine, January 2, 1941, CAOM Alg Const B/3/688.

[150] Commissioner of Police of Souk-Ahras, to the Sub-Prefect of Guelma, "No. 321: Propos injurieux à l'égard du Chef de l'état et des Français," Souk-Ahras, January 16, 1941, CAOM Alg Const B/3/688.

[151] Police Commissioner of the First Arrondissement to the Central Police Commissioner, "No. 1594: Incident entre Bertali Ahmed et Madame Alimi," Constantine, February 22, 1941, CAOM Alg Const B/3/688.

[152] Police Commissioner of Khenchela to the Prefect of Constantine, "No. 72: Objet: Manifestations antijuive," Khenchela, July 16, 1941, CAOM Alg Const B/3/688.

[153] Sergeant Tabaud, Commandant of the Khenchela Brigade, "Rapport No. 34/4 sur un incident survenu entre arabes et juifs," Khenchela, July 15, 1941, CAOM Alg Const B/3/688.

[154] Sub-Prefect of Batna to the Prefect of Constantine, "No. 558Z.PG.R.8/F: Objet: Manifestations antijuives de Khenchela P.E.," Batna, July 18, 1941, CAOM Alg

especially after the attack on Mers-el-Kebir. In March 1942, police reported graffiti in tar on walls of Constantine that included "Vive Pétain, down with the Jews, down with Britain," "The Jews to Borneo," and "Churchill is a bastard."[155] In May, the local head of the PPF declared antisemitism part of the organization's official doctrine.[156]

By late 1941, Jews believed that they had a few options available to them. Antisemitism was embedded in government and in their quotidian lives, and most Jews in Algeria focused on supporting one another through the implementation of each antisemitic law and prayed for a better future. A number of Jews considered a future elsewhere, or at least entertained the possibility of leaving the colony, but few actually did.[157] While many Algerian Jews tried to adjust to their diminished civil status, a small group of Jews actively demonstrated their faith in de Gaulle by working alongside the Allies to fight against Germany and, by extension, Vichy. In June 1942, Allied propaganda appeared to be making inroads in Oran. The police commissioner reported Croix de Lorraine and "V" graffiti in the city.[158] Bolstered by increased Allied activity, Algerian Jews formed self-defense organizations to protect themselves against antisemitic groups. In Constantine, Jews established an "association of fighting," and Jewish scouting groups oriented themselves increasingly toward physical education and defense.[159] Such activities created the foundation for Algerian Jews' efforts to pave the way for Allied landings in North Africa.

On July 24, 1942, the Combined Chiefs of Staff, approved by President Roosevelt and Prime Minister Churchill, decided to launch Operation Torch in North Africa under the leadership of General Dwight D. Eisenhower. The main purpose was to relieve beleaguered British

Const B/3/688. See Commissioner of Police to the Mayor of Khenchela, Khenchela, July 15, 1941, CAOM Alg Const B/3/688.

[155] Commissioner of the Special Departmental Police of Constantine, to the Prefect of Constantine, "No. 1175: Journée du 8 mars," Constantine, March 10, 1942; Central Police Commissioner to the Prefect of Constantine, "No. 3353: Objet: Inscriptions faites sur les murs de la Ville au cours de la nuit du 7 au 8 mars 1942," Constantine, March 10, 1942, CAOM Alg Const B/3/688.

[156] Prefect of Constantine to the Gov-Gen, "No. 1282 AR.2 Secret: Objet: Antisémitisme à Constantine," Constantine, May 11, 1942, CAOM Alg Const B/3/688.

[157] "I would leave for South America without hesitation. At my age, 70 years, what else awaits me!!!" Joseph Kanoui to Madame J. Serfaty, "Intercepted Telegram No. 4351: Re: Recriminations des Juifs indigènes," Tanger-Marbe, September 14, 1941, CAOM Alg Oran 5i/50.

[158] Central Police Commissioner to the Prefect of Oran, "No. 275/S Objet: A/S de la propaganda Gaulliste," Oran, June 11, 1942, CAOM Alg Oran 424.

[159] Gov-Gen to the Prefect of Constantine, "No. 11300: Objet: Surveillance des milieux israélites," Algiers, April 28, 1942; Prefect of Constantine, "Rapport No. 3191: Action Juive, Institution Bergson," Constantine, June 6, 1942, CAOM Alg Const B/3/688.

forces there.[160] The specific goals of the operation were to occupy French Morocco and Algeria, and later Tunisia, and to gain complete control of North Africa, from the Atlantic to the Red Sea.[161] North Africa represented a strategic location for Allied operation.[162] An Allied North Africa would serve as a staging ground for the campaign against southern Italy, Europe's soft underbelly. Roosevelt hoped that North Africa would become the locus of French anti-German activity.[163] He imagined secretly recruiting French army units stationed in North Africa. Plans for Operation Torch included a complex matrix of intelligence contacts and resistance organizations centered around American diplomat Robert Murphy and a group of American vice-consuls, known as the twelve apostles, who served as intelligence agents in North Africa.[164]

In late 1941, a clandestine insurgent movement in North Africa made connections with the apostles. This movement was diverse; its members were businessmen, professionals, civil servants, workers, intellectuals, and military officers of various ranks. One of the most important, and most overlooked, subgroups consisted of young Jewish men from Algiers.[165] Throughout 1941, Murphy reached out to Frenchmen frustrated with Vichy, such as Colonel Germain Jousse, who joined the growing French Resistance in 1941. With the aid of André Achiary, the head of the secret police, Murphy widened his circle of contacts in Oran.[166] The small Oran group consisted of army officers, such as Henri d'Astier de la Vigerie, a non-Jew, and Lt. Bernard Karsenty, as well as young local Jews, like Roger and Pierre Carcassonne.[167] Murphy

---

[160] Arthur Layton Funk, *The Politics of Torch: The Allied Landings and the Algiers Putsch, 1942* (Lawrence: The University Press of Kansas, 1974), 3.

[161] Rick Atkinson, *An Army at Dawn: The War in North Africa 1942–1943, Volume One of the Liberation Trilogy* (New York: Henry Holt and Company, 2002), 22. See also Keith Sainsbury, *The North Africa Landings, 1942: A Strategic Decision* (Newark: University of Delaware Press, 1976), 43; Funk, *The Politics of Torch*, 5.

[162] General Marshall, "Reference Cable 3412," HIA RMF, Box 47, File 8, General Cables. In a series of cables organizing speeches by Roosevelt and Eisenhower to be broadcast in North Africa, the common themes are of friendship and the desire to fight the Germans, not to change the French government. HIA RMF, Box 47, File 8, General Cables.

[163] Franklin D. Roosevelt, "Directive for Mr. Robert D. Murphy," September 22, 1942, HIA RMF, File 10, General Directives.

[164] Funk, *The Politics of Torch*, 3. See also Norman Gelb, *Desperate Venture: The Story of Operation Torch, the Allied Invasion of North Africa* (New York: William Morrow and Company, Inc., 1992), 43. See also Sophie Roberts, "Jews, Vichy, and the Algiers Insurrection," *Holocaust Studies: A Journal of Culture and History*, Vol. 12, No. 3 (Winter 2006).

[165] Gelb, *Desperate Venture*, 55–56. See also Roberts, "Jews, Vichy, and the Algiers Insurrection."

[166] Achiary became a Prefect after the fall of Vichy. He was responsible for the massacre of hundreds of Muslims in May and June 1945 in Guelma. See Chapter 7 for more details.

[167] Funk, *The Politics of Torch*, 19–20.

also made an effort to reach out to Admiral Jean-François Darlan. Darlan was one of the chief architects of Pétain's policy and the supreme military commander in North Africa. Although outwardly pro-collaboration, Darlan was opportunistic and Murphy believed he could serve the Allied cause.[168]

Following the U.S. decision to enter the war in December 1941, the Resistance groups in North Africa grew more active.[169] At this same time, another figure entered the already complicated web of connections. Henri Honoré Giraud, a distinguished general, had escaped imprisonment in Germany and clandestinely approached both Allied agents and members of the French underground.[170] By early June, Giraud's interest galvanized the Resistance and sparked the Allies' interest.[171] Murphy and the Resistance leaders organized a meeting with the Allied military leadership. Set for October 21, the meeting took place in the Algerian beachfront town of Cherchell.[172] On the French side, the delegation included General Charles Mast, Giraud's delegate, and Colonel Jousse, his chief of staff. U.S. General Mark Clark and Murphy led the Allied side, and Henri d'Astier and José Aboulker ran security.[173] General Clark promised the earliest possible delivery of 2,000 small arms with ammunition to the vicinity of Cherchell in order to arm the insurgents.[174] In the end, only a few supplies arrived, mostly through Murphy's diplomatic connections. The Americans did not inform their French allies of the time or exact locations of the landings until four days before, seriously impairing the Resistance's preparations.[175] Nonetheless, plans for the Allied invasion were in motion.

One of the resistance organizations integral in the Allied plans in North Africa was the almost exclusively Jewish Géo Gras Group (GGG), which produced the major leaders and the bulk of the insurgents. Three young Jewish men – André Temime, Émile Atlan, and Charles Bouchara – founded the sports club in 1940 as a front for political purposes. Under Vichy restrictions, sports clubs were among the few organizations tolerated.[176] Temime, Atlan, and Bouchara bought the gym in the center

---

[168] Ibid., 23–24. See also "Telegram from American Embassy, Paris," March 4, 1941, HIA RMF, Box 47, File 5, Envoy-office files: U.S.-French Negotiations.

[169] Funk, *The Politics of Torch*, 42. See also Colonel Jousse, "La libération de l'Afrique du Nord et la résistance nord-Africaine," *Esprit* (January 1945): 194–201.

[170] Funk, *The Politics of Torch*, 45.   [171] Ibid., 55–56; Gelb, *Desperate Venture*, 81–82.

[172] Gelb, *Desperate Venture*, 146.   [173] Jousse, "La Libération," 202–204.

[174] General Mark Clark, "Report on Cherchell," HIA RMF, Box 47, File 3.

[175] Sainsbury, *The North African Landings*, 146–148.

[176] See, for example, Naval Admiral, Secretary of State to the Minister of the Interior, "Administration et Direction d'un Syndicat Professionnel par des Juifs algérienne," May 24, 1941, USHMMA, Microfilm 1998.A.0087, Reel 1, Afrique du Nord.

of Algiers and employed Géo Gras as its director.[177] Gras was a non-Jewish Frenchman on excellent terms with the Vichy leadership and most right-wing groups in Algiers. A middle-weight boxing champion of France, Gras gave the gym credibility and served as a front for its covert activities.[178] Members were recruited clandestinely. According to founding member Aharon Mesguich, a potential member went through an interview, had to receive recommendations from at least two people, and appear before a committee of twelve members. He then took an oath vowing to fight to the death in defense of Algerian Jewry, the liberation of France, and the defeat of the Third Reich.[179]

Originally the GGG focused on responding to local attacks on Jews.[180] The group dreamed of fighting against Vichy and the Nazis and attempted to contact de Gaulle in London to no avail. The group trained themselves to fight, collected weapons, and committed various acts of sabotage. For example, they spoiled goods that were on their way to the German occupation army in France. They distributed leaflets in Algiers stating "the Resistance is watching," and posted anti-Vichy, anti-German placards.[181] By 1942, the Géo Gras Group had grown to around 250 members organized into five-man cells. To maintain secrecy, the members of the group only knew the others in their group. Captain Alfred Pilafort, who was not Jewish, served as the GGG's central commander.[182]

Familial networks played an important role in the GGG and the insurgents' network. Pilafort knew Raphaël and Stéphane Aboulker, José Aboulker's cousins, prior to the war. Pilafort informed them of a possible Allied landing in North Africa and the necessity of supporting this operation from inside Algeria. The leadership of the GGG agreed to help but wanted to maintain their group's independence.[183] Approximately 100 young men from the GGG served as insurgents.

---

[177] "Rapport sur le rôle joue dans la préparation et l'exécution des opérations du 8 Novembre par un groupe du combat d'Alger, dit 'Groupe de la Salle Géo Gras'," USHMMA, Microfilm 1998.A.0087, Reel 1, Afrique du Nord, 1. This anonymous report was most likely written by one of the leadership of the Géo Gras Group, perhaps Temime, Bouchara, or even Raphael Aboulker.

[178] Gitta Amipaz-Silber, La Résistance Juive en Algérie, 1940–1942 (Jerusalem: Presses Daf-Chen, 1986), 65–66. See also Funk, The Politics of Torch, 174. "Rapport sur le rôle joue dans la préparation," USHMMA, Microfilm 1998.A.0087, Reel 1, Afrique du Nord.

[179] "Rapport sur le rôle joue dans la préparation," USHMMA, Microfilm 1998.A.0087, Reel 1, Afrique du Nord. See also Amipaz-Silber, The Role of the Jewish Underground, 65–66.

[180] Ibid.   [181] Amipaz-Silber, The Role of the Jewish Underground, 67.

[182] Funk, The Politics of Torch, 174. "Rapport sur le rôle joue dans la préparation," USHMMA, Microfilm 1998.A.0087, Reel 1, Afrique du Nord. Pilafort received the Legion of Honor for bravery in single-handed combat in 1932.

[183] "Rapport sur le rôle joue dans la préparation," USHMMA, Microfilm 1998.A.0087, Reel 1, Afrique du Nord. Pilafort received the Legion of Honor for bravery in single-handed combat in 1932.

They were organized into four sections led by young Jewish reserve officers and a deputy. In addition to organizing and recruiting new members, the Jewish leaders provided the Allies with military information on the defense and surveillance of the coast, places suitable for the landings, and the locations of the Vichy army barracks.[184]

Other Jewish insurgent groups organized during the same period. In Oran, a group of Jewish professionals headed by Roger and Pierre Carcassonne prepared for the landings. Roger Carcassonne recruited Henri d'Astier, a non-Jew involved in the resistance. In 1940, D'Astier worked with small resistance groups in France; after being captured by the Germans, he escaped to Algeria and found a position on the security staff of Oran. In a conversation with his cousin José Aboulker in Algiers, Roger Carcassonne realized that the two were involved in similar activities. José was a medical student and the son of the Algiers Jewish community leader and respected doctor, Henri Aboulker. After his father lost his job at the University of Algiers Medical School as a result of antisemitic legislation, José connected with other outraged young Jews. He organized a resistance group consisting of fellow students of the University of Algiers.[185]

Jacques Soustelle, Commissioner of Information for de Gaulle in London, later wrote of Carcassonne and Aboulker that "never before were more vast and dangerous undertakings discussed with more composure by more amateur conspirators, who, nevertheless, as demonstrated by their success, surpassed the most experienced specialists in this field."[186] Soon the Algiers and Oran groups merged and recruited new members, both Jews and non-Jews. Henri d'Astier met José Aboulker after he transferred to Algiers in the spring of 1942 to work under Colonel Van Hecke of the *Chantiers de la Jeunesse*.[187] The participants of the Algiers Insurrection were a diverse group, including several officers from the regular French army such as General Mast, General de Monsabert, Colonel Jousse, and Colonel Baril, as well as officers on inactive duty. In addition, the organizers of the Insurrection counted on the aid of a few hundred young Frenchmen in the *Chantiers de la Jeunesse*. The bulk of the forces included students, refugees from France, and Algerian Jews.[188]

In the week preceding the Allied landings, Raphaël and Stéphane Aboulker went several times to the beaches of Algiers to receive the

---

[184] Office of Strategic Services, Washington D.C., "Allied Landing in North Africa," January 28, 1943, USNARA, RG 226, Entry 97, Box 5, File 77.

[185] Amipaz-Silber, *The Role of the Jewish Underground*, 69–70.

[186] Jacques Soustelle, *Envers et contre tout: Souvenirs et Documents sur la France libre*, Tome 2 (Paris: Presses R. Laffont, 1950), 426.

[187] Funk, *The Politics of Torch*, 174–175.   [188] Ibid., 172.

weapons promised by General Clark, which never arrived.[189] On the night of the Allied landings, of the 800 resistance members originally involved in the movement, only about 350 appeared, in addition to the GGG members. The insurgents were led by José Aboulker, Henri d'Astier, and Colonel Jousse. According to Aboulker, the insurgents' mission was to rupture communications, arrest Vichy officers capable of organizing defense, and occupy important government and army buildings and arrest their staff. The insurgents wore armbands with "V.P." inscribed on them, indicating the *Volontaires de Place*, a civil defense group.[190] They had 900 very old Lebel rifles and 25,000 cartridges stolen by order of Colonel Jousse.[191]

On the evening of November 7, the insurgents listened intently to the radio for word of the Allies' arrival.[192] The insurgency was to begin at 1:30 am on November 8 and the insurgents were to be replaced by Allied troops two hours later. In the absence of the designated leaders, Aboulker assumed the leadership of the operation. He led his team to the Central Police Commissariat where they arrested police agents and cut the telephone lines, keeping only the official line intact. From the Police Commissariat, Aboulker contacted the other teams.[193] Police stations throughout Algiers called in to the Central Station asking for information. Posing as an official switchboard operator, Aboulker gave them the following orders: all the police chiefs must come to the Central Commissariat, where the insurgents detained them.[194] The insurgents believed that they had achieved their goals.[195] During the day, fifty insurgents were arrested and two insurgents – Alfred Pilafort and Jean Dreyfus – were killed in action.[196] American troops finally arrived and by 7:45 pm they defeated the regrouping Vichy forces.[197] The Jewish-led insurrection in Algiers played a crucial role in the Allied victory because it disrupted the Vichy command's ability to marshal its defense. Yet the

---

[189] "Rapport sur le rôle joue dans la préparation," USHMMA, Microfilm 1998.A.0087, Reel 1, Afrique du Nord.

[190] Funk, *The Politics of Torch*, 172; "Allied Landing in North Africa," USNARA, RG 226, Entry 97, Box 5, File 77.

[191] José Aboulker, "La part de la résistance française dans les événements de l'Afrique du Nord," *Les Cahiers Français* (1943): 18.

[192] Ibid., 23–24. See also William B. Breuer, *Operation Torch: The Allied Gamble to Invade North Africa* (New York: St. Martins Press, 1985), 107. See also "Memo on alert," HIA RMF, Box 47, File 3.

[193] Aboulker, "La Résistance," 25. See also "Les événements de la nuit du 7 au 8 Novembre 1942 à la Grande Poste," USHMMA, Microfilm 1998.A.0087, Reel 1, Afrique du Nord.

[194] Aboulker, "La Résistance," 18, 27.   [195] Ibid., 27.

[196] "Allied Landing in North Africa," USNARA, RG 226, Entry 97, Box 5, File 77.

[197] Aboulker, "La Résistance," 29.

Allies failed to recognize or reward them. Some insurgents were even punished for their involvement.

After the landings at Algiers, the Allied command wanted little responsibility in organizing a new political regime in North Africa. In correspondence known as the Giraud-Murphy agreement, the Allies agreed to name General Giraud commander in chief of the French forces.[198] However, on November 10, Darlan and Clark began negotiations. By the afternoon of November 11, German forces crossed the Line of Demarcation in France and proceeded to occupy the southern zone. As soon as Darlan learned of the German action, he accepted Clark's "mild armistice" terms and the leadership of North Africa.[199] Frustrated with the continued power of Vichy leaders, former insurgents sought to topple the new Darlan government. They planned to assassinate Darlan under the leadership of Fernand Bonnier de la Chappelle, a veteran of the Algiers Insurrection. Bonnier succeeded in firing two fatal shots at Darlan on December 24, 1942. He was arrested, tried, and executed the next day.[200] Giraud took power after Darlan's assassination.

The insurgents feared reprisals and felt abandoned by their former allies. Henri Aboulker commented that Murphy "shuns us like a case of an extremely contagious disease."[201] A.J. Liebling, a journalist for *The New Yorker*, interviewed the insurgents. One of them explained that since the government remained in the same hands as before, they feared retribution:

The army brass hats and the people of the Prefecture whom we arrested hate us. They hate us because we know what cowards they are. You should have seen how miserably they acted when they saw the tommy guns, the brave Jew-baiters. The chief of the secret police, who, of course, has been restored to his position, knelt on the floor and wept, begging one of my friends to spare his life. Imagine his feeling toward the man who spared him! Another friend, a doctor, is to be mobilized – in a labor camp of course – under military jurisdiction of the general whom *he* arrested.[202]

The day after Liebling's interview, at least fifteen of his interlocutors were arrested, including Dr. Henri and José Aboulker, Raphaël Aboulker, the

[198] Arthur Funk, "Negotiating the 'Deal with Darlan'," *Journal of Contemporary History* Vol. 8, No. 2 (April 1973): 104–105, 107.
[199] Ibid., 111–113. See also "Note sur les évènements qui se sont déroulés à partir du 8 Novembre 1942," HIA RMF, Box 47, File 2.
[200] D'Astier, *Qui a tué Darlan?*, 35–37, 41–42. See also "Notes sur les évènements d'Alger dans la nuit du 29 au 30 décembre 1942," YVA O.26 (Collection on North Africa).
[201] A.J. Liebling, *The Road Back to Paris* (Garden City: Doubleday, Doran and Co., Inc, 1944), 228.
[202] Ibid., 228–229.

founders of the GGG, and Henri d'Astier.[203] Murphy finally intervened and the men were released in February 1943, three months later. José Aboulker left for England after he was released and gave De Gaulle a written report of the insurrection. De Gaulle sent Aboulker on a mission to occupied France, where he played a role in the liberation of France.[204] The Jewish insurgents believed that their actions would bring back the true France and that they would once again become citizens. This was not yet to be the case.

From 1940 to 1943, Algerian Jews had their identities torn apart. One moment, they were French citizens, highly assimilated, and integrated into French society. The next moment, with the stroke of a pen, they were reduced to their pre-1870 status as French subjects. Most Algerian Jews had lived only as French citizens and knew no other existence. Even after combating antisemitic attempts to remove or reduce their citizenship over the seventy years between the Crémieux Decree and the organization of the Vichy government, Algerian Jews never believed their citizenship to be truly threatened.

During that period of rupture, Algerian Jews reached out to Jews outside of the colony and the metropole to form international bonds. In spite of their alienation by Vichy, Algerian Jews paved the way for Allied troops to land on Algerian shores, taking risks that few non-Jewish Europeans in the colony even considered. Algerian Jews' activities in the Allied landings as well as their efforts to be reinstated as French citizens illustrate the profound assimilation of Algerian Jews following the Crémieux Decree. They achieved what Adolphe Crémieux promised they would: they became Frenchmen, even as Vichy and Giraud continued to belittle their Frenchness.

---

[203] Ibid., 229. See also "Rapport sur le rôle joué dans la préparation," USHMMA, Microfilm 1998.A.0087, Reel 1, Afrique du Nord.
[204] Amipaz-Silber, *The Role of the Jewish Underground*, 167. Georges-Marc Benamou, *C'était un temps déraisonnable: Les premiers résistants racontent* (Paris: Imprimerie Robert Laffont, 1999), 224.

7 Broken Identities
Post–World War II and the Algerian War

The aftermath of World War II left the Algerian Jewish community in a precarious position. Even after regaining their French citizenship under de Gaulle in 1943, being stripped of their citizenship profoundly altered Algerian Jews' identity. Despite the rupture caused by the abrogation of the Crémieux Decree, Algerian Jews remained loyal to France. In the context of the Algerian War, many, but not all, chose France over their *terre natale*. A few sided with the Algerian nationalists, and some chose Israel over France.

In the immediate period after the war, Algerian Jews focused on rebuilding and healing from the wounds of that period. They remained patriotic, but not in the same manner as before World War II. Many held a shimmer of doubt as to whether France would return and protect them as Frenchmen. The rupture of Vichy could never be completely healed. At the same time, Zionism became a more enticing philosophy and possibility. Ultimately, Jews faced an impossible choice: they could remain with France, which had abandoned them during Vichy, and move to the metropole, a homeland they had never known; they could accept and support a nascent independent Algeria and whatever their status might be under Muslim rule; or they could move to a brand new Jewish state currently besieged by its neighbors. At the start of the Algerian War in 1954, Algerian Jews remained apprehensive, but faithful to France.

Although pleased with their renewed status as French citizens in 1943, the memory of rupture and alienation shaped Algerian Jews' post-Vichy identity and activities. In order to expunge the remnants of Vichy's antisemitic acts, the governor-general ordered the Prefect of Oran to destroy Vichy files in the presence of Jewish leaders.[1] All files ranging from requests to maintain citizenship following the Vichy 1940 abrogation of the Crémieux Decree to declarations for the 1941 census were subsequently destroyed starting on July 11, 1944.[2] However, even the

---

[1] Gov-Gen to the Prefect of Oran, "No. 1104 IJ/3: Objet: Destruction des documents se rapportant aux déclarations des Israélites," Algiers, May 22, 1944, CAOM Alg Oran 2539.

[2] Councilor of the Prefecture to the Prefect of Oran, "Rapport á M. le Prefect/ Procès-Verbale," Oran, July 12, 1944, CAOM Alg Oran 2539. These actions explain the lack of such documents in the archives. It is likely that the Prefect of Algiers executed

destruction of Vichy documents could not eradicate its memory. Jews feared that resurrecting antisemitic accusations of Jewish separatism would again endanger their citizenship. Jews asserted their patriotism and commitment to France through celebrations of their fallen brethren. In December 1944, Jews in Oran organized a memorial for fallen Jewish Scouts. Chief Rabbi David Askenazi gave a sermon emphasizing Jewish commitment and patriotism even under the racial laws of Vichy, and celebrated the Jewish patriots who died in the effort "to save the country, in communion with the ideas of all the members of the true French family."[3] By celebrating the memory of the fallen, Algerian Jews continued to assert their patriotism and worth as French citizens.

The Giraud Era: The Renewed Abrogation of the Crémieux Decree and Lobbying Efforts for the Reinstatement of the Crémieux Decree

After the Allied landings, Jewish leaders rearticulated their demands for the reinstatement of their citizenship. On November 14, 1942, Maurice Eisenbeth, the Chief Rabbi of Algeria, wrote to the governor-general regarding the psychological impact of the abrogation of the Crémieux Decree on Jews. "Innocent victims of discriminatory legislation from which they have truly suffered, my coreligionists in Algeria wait for you to remove, with the shortest possible delay, all the laws and regulations that impact them as 'Jews'."[4] André Bakouche, president of the Consistory of Constantine, also demanded the restoration of Algerian Jews' citizenship. He outlined the severe economic and social implications of the antisemitic legislation. "The Jews in Algeria have demonstrated, throughout their misfortunes, dignity and composure drawn from their patriotic faith, and feel that their just cause is mingled with the liberation of the Motherland and the Empire."[5] Jewish leaders were disappointed with the lack of change after the Allied success in Algeria.

Prior to his arrest after the Insurrection, Dr. Henri Aboulker resumed his activities on behalf of the CAES. On December 7, 1942, he wrote to Darlan to request the abrogation of antisemitic Vichy legislation.

---

a similar measure, while the Prefect of Constantine did not. The largest number of remaining Jewish declarations in the archives can be found in the Constantine files at the COAM.

[3] General Information Police, Oran, "No. 7945: Rapport: Objet: Cérémonie au temple israélite d'Oran," Oran, December 7, 1944, CAOM Alg Oran 2539.

[4] Chief Rabbi of Algeria Maurice Eisenbeth to the Gov-Gen, Algiers, November 17, 1942, CDJC LXXXIV-9.

[5] André Bakouche, President of the Constantine Consistory, to Gov-Gen Châtel and Admiral Darlan, Constantine, November 25, 1942, CAOM Alg GGA 6CAB/1.

Aboulker used the example of his own military service to depict the deep distress of Jews who lost their citizenship under Vichy.[6] Following Darlan's assassination, Rabbi Eisenbeth expressed Algerian Jews' hope that Giraud would bring with him the restitution of their citizenship. They were disappointed. "The era of the liberation seems to open up to us. However, since November 8, no effort has been made to abrogate the laws of Hitlerian spirit." Eisenbeth also protested the arrest of the Jewish insurgents whose patriotism, he argued, was undeniable.[7]

Algerian Jews' disappointment continued into the New Year. On January 7, 1943, the CAES reported that antisemitic legislation in the colony persisted and that Jews were permitted to participate in the military only as workers in separate groups. The CAES leaders added that after the Allied landings, antisemitism continued to rise, arguing that "if the Germans had occupied Algeria, they would have taken the same measures that are about to be applied."[8]

The continued implementation of the Vichy antisemitic legislation remained the central focus of Algerian Jews. To that end, Algerian Jewish leaders organized a meeting with Governor-General Peyrouton to detail their grievances. Peyrouton dismissed the discussion, stating that fighting the war was the highest priority and the situation of Algerian Jews would be dealt with after the war.[9] Peyrouton emphasized that the anti-Jewish measures were a necessary requirement of the Armistice and argued that abrogating the laws would cause discontent among Muslims. Furthermore, he argued, Algeria was still an integral part of France and no separate legislation could be introduced. However, Peyrouton proposed several improvements to Algerian Jews' status, including improving the quotas, returning Jewish property, and permitting some Jews to return to their professions. He informed the Jewish delegation that he could not "guarantee that he could obtain all that he had proposed, because he no longer had the powers of a Governor before 1939." Dr. André Levy-Valensi, one of the Jewish leaders in attendance, informed Peyrouton that he had been misinformed regarding Muslim resentment of the Crémieux Decree, should it be reinstated. He stated, "Perhaps we would see some discontent at the subject of the

---

[6] Dr. Henri Aboulker to Admiral Darlan, Algiers, December 7, 1942, CDJC LXXXIV-14.
[7] Chief Rabbi Eisenbeth to the High Commissioner General Giraud, Algiers, December 31, 1942, CDJC LXXXIV-21.
[8] Comité Algérien des Études Sociales, "Rapport sur la Situation Générale Actuelle des Juifs en Algérie," Algiers, January 7, 1943, CDJC LXXXIV-26.
[9] "Entretien avec Monsieur Marcel Peyrouton, Gouverneur Général de l'Algérie, étaient présentes pour y avoir été convoqués: M. le Grand Rabbin M. Eisenbeth, E. Balensi, Marcel Belaiche, Dr. Benhamou, Dr. André Levi-Valensi, Charles Levy, Intendant Général Levy," January 28, 1943, CDJC LXXXIV-36.

re-establishment of the Crémieux Decree, but for the rest, one can't believe that, and this you can be assured if you consider the letters written by Muslim notables." He continued, "The laws were presented by the French administration as imposed by the Germans; no Jew could comprehend today why they are still maintained."[10] On January 14, Giraud ordered that identity cards and certificates no longer use the term *juif*, but note only three distinctions: "French, citizen," "French, non-citizen," and "Foreigner."[11] The possibility of improving the Jews' status caused concern among some Algerian Muslims. They feared that Jews would become citizens once again and that Muslims would remain subjects.[12] Algerian Muslims renewed their own demands for rights. These measures barely scratched the surface of repairing the damage done by Vichy.

Over the course of February 1943, lawyers, doctors, university students and professors, former administrators, and administration employees submitted   petitions   to   the   governor-general   requesting   their reintegration.[13] The status of Jews' eligibility to serve in the military remained unclear. Alfred Ghighi of the CAES submitted two petitions to the governor-general. The first, on January 8, cited the long history of Jewish military contributions and demanded that Jews be reintegrated into the military so that they could fight for France in the war against Germany.[14] In his second petition, Ghighi expressed his hope that if allowed to fight together, the camaraderie of soldiers on the battlefield would cement "French cohesion, more necessary than ever."[15] These early efforts failed to bring about change.

After the "liberation" of Algeria, many Jews were even more frustrated with their circumstances than they had been under Vichy. A surveillance

---

[10] Meeting between Marcel Peyrounton, Grand Rabbin Eisenbeth, E. Balensi, Marcel Belaïche, Dr. E. Benhamou, Dr. André Lévy-Valensi, Charles Levy, Intendant Général L. Levy, "Entretien avec Mr. Marcel Peyrtoun (Gr. Gal. de l'Algérie)," January 28, 1943, YVA, O.26 (Collection on North Africa).

[11] Gov-Gen to the Prefect of Constantine, "No. 1003 pol.RG.I," Algiers, January 14, 1943, CAOM Alg Const 93/3G6.

[12] Gov-Gen, Center for Information, "No. 181 CIE: Renseignements: Abrogation de certaines mesures anti-juivés," Algiers, February 1, 1943, CAOM Alg Oran 5i/50.

[13] "Motion, Les Avocats Israelites du Barreau d'Oran," CDJC LXXXIV-44; "Motion (CJAES)," Algiers, February 11, 1943, CDJC LXXXIV-43; "Motion-Médecins," Algiers, February 15, 1943, CDJC LXXXIV-48; "Réunion des médecins juifs non-éliminés," Algiers, February 18, 1943, CDJC LXXXIV-49; Jewish students of Algiers to the Gov-Gen, Algiers, February 20, 1943, CDJC LXXXIV-50; "Motion-Membres de l'enseignement Public," Algiers, February 20, 1943, CDJC LXXXIV-51; "Motion-Membres de l'Université Français," Oran, February 25, 1943, CDJC LXXXIV-55; "Motion-Fonctionnaires de toutes catégories," February 28, 1943, CDJC LXXXIV-56.

[14] Alfred Ghighi to the Gov-Gen, Oran, January 8, 1943, CAOM Alg GGA 8CAB/71.

[15] Alfred Ghighi to Gov-Gen Peyrouton, Oran, February 14, 1943, CAOM Alg GGA 8CAB71.

report identified four political groups among Algerian Jews at the end of February 1943. The first group included leaders such as Henri Aboulker who hoped for a return of the pre-Armistice government. The second group directed its efforts at a common Jewish–Muslim front under French or Anglo-American dominion. The third group, supported by Elie Gozlan, preferred American control over the colony, followed by the British, or, as a last resort, French rule. The fourth and final group looked toward Palestine and exhibited "Zionist and Anglophilic tendencies."[16] These groups began to develop different political programs to attain their goals, further fracturing the Jewish community.

On March 14, 1943, Giraud took one step toward remedying the wrongs of Vichy and one step backward with regard to the Jews of Algeria's citizenship status. To illustrate the goals of his new government, Giraud repealed Vichy's antisemitic legislation, describing it as a "consequence" of the German occupation. As a result, all distinctions made on the quality of being Jewish in terms of access to and exercise of certain professions, attendance at schools, and involvement in the administration were abolished. Fired employees of the administration were to be reintegrated. Jewish property and goods confiscated as part of the Aryanization program would be returned to their owners. This act signaled a major transition from the era of Vichy to that of Giraud and the Allies.[17]

Many applauded this important gesture to remedy Vichy injustices. However, Algerian Jews discovered that Giraud also promulgated two contradictory ordinances regarding their status that same day. Giraud's first declaration of March 14 canceled Vichy's abrogation of the Crémieux Decree, which should have returned Algerian Jews to their French citizenship status. However, Giraud's second decree re-abrogated the Crémieux Decree. As with Vichy's original abrogation, Jews had three months in which to submit exemption requests.[18] Under Giraud, official state antisemitism continued even as his government shed layers of Vichy legislation.[19] Jewish lawyer Alfred Ghighi reported that Giraud's re-abrogation was nearly identical to Vichy's abrogation.[20]

---

[16] Gov-Gen, "CIE No. 388: Renseignements Tendances actuelles des Juifs Algérois," Algiers, February 24, 1943, CAOM Alg Oran 5i/50.

[17] Henri Giraud, "Déclaration et ordonnance du 14 mars 1943 relative aux mesures prises à l'encontre des juifs," *Journal Officiel du Commandement en Chef Français*, March 18, 1943, CAOM Alg Const 93/3G7.

[18] Henri Giraud, "Ordonnance du 14 Mars 1943 portant abrogation du décret du 24 Octobre 1870 relatif au statut des israélites indigènes de l'Algérie," in *Journal Officiel du Commandement en Chef Français*, March 18, 1943, CAOM Alg Const 93/3G7.

[19] Msellati, *Les Juifs d'Algérie*, 223, 230.

[20] Alfred Ghighi, "Renseignements, A/S du Statut des Juifs," Oran, March 29, 1943, CAOM Alg Oran 5i/50.

Giraud's staff explained that the rationale of the re-abrogation was to avoid inciting Muslim anger in wartime. As had been the case for decades prior, antisemites continued to use Muslim frustration as justification for reducing or eliminating Algerian Jews' status. Algerian Jews again turned to Jewish–Muslim unity efforts, as they had done after the initial Vichy abrogation. Jews sought to garner Muslim support by emphasizing their shared status as victims of racism but without much success.[21]

The re-abrogation of the Crémieux Decree enlarged the rupture between Algerian Jews and France. It was inconceivable that Giraud would put an end to Vichy but maintain its most offensive act for Algerian Jews. The CAES leadership emphasized its illegality by asserting that the quality of citizen was imprescriptible. "The French Republic made Algerian Jews French citizens, its will remains sovereign. The Algerian Jews solemnly declare that they are and remain integrally French."[22] Their protests against the Giraud abrogation were reiterations of those used against the Vichy abrogation.

Giraud's renewed abrogation of the Crémieux Decree thrust the issue onto the world stage. In April 1943, the *New York Times* published a letter by philosopher Jacques Maritain, then president of the Executive committee of the École des Hautes Études of New York. Among his conclusions, Maritain wrote that the abrogation was unwarranted and went against traditional French law. He suggested that long-standing antisemitism in the colony was responsible for the re-abrogation. "Antisemitism is the carrier of all the Nazi poisons, and there cannot be, under any circumstances, any concessions to it." Maritain recommended that the new government in Algeria not only declare the abrogation null but also work toward "a just and equitable solution for the Muslim population."[23] Maritain rightly pointed out that the issue of Jewish rights was inextricably linked to that of Muslim rights and that any reevaluation of Jewish citizenship should be accompanied by a reconsideration of Muslim access to rights. Although Muslim rights long served as an excuse for degrading Algerian Jewish rights, the re-abrogation of the Crémieux Decree was motivated in part by the desire to appease the right-wing elements of French Algeria.

---

[21] Gov-Gen, "No. 817CIE: Renseignements Activité de Docteur Loufrani," Algiers, April 7, 1943, CAOM Alg Oran 5i/50; Prefect of Algiers, "No. 2426: Relations Judeo-Musulmans, A/S Dr. Loufrani," Algiers, May 18, 1943, CAOM Alg Oran 5i/50.

[22] CAES, "L'Action du Comité Juif d'Études Sociales," *Bulletin de la Fédération des Sociétés Juives d'Algérie*, No. 89 (August–September 1943), CDJC BIB 9001.

[23] Jacques Maritain, "Le *New York Times* publié la lettre suivante du philosophe Français Jacques Maritain, President du Comité exécutive de l'École des Hautes Études de New York," New York, April 25, 1943, CAOM FM 1affpol/877.

The Free French (now the "Fighting French" – *France Combattante*) and de Gaulle also criticized Giraud's abrogation of the Crémieux Decree. The Fighting French, under the leadership of Captain Pierre Bloch, denounced the argument that the re-abrogation had Muslims' rights at heart. "The position of Algerian Jews has become worse. General Giraud goes further than the Vichy government."[24] During roll call of the General Council of Algiers, council member Belaiche stood and announced, "I realize that, in view of the abrogation of the Crémieux Decree, I shall no longer be qualified to exercise my functions because I am a Jew."[25]

Giraud's re-abrogation reverberated throughout the wider Jewish world and received the attention of activists and intellectuals. George Hexter, of the Community Service Unit of the American Jewish Committee (AJC), distributed a memo on the re-abrogation, accompanied by an article by Hannah Arendt. In the memo, Hexter analyzed the long history of colonial antisemitism and its clear influence on the new legislation.

These French colonials, traditionally reactionary, have long been imbued with racial theories. Not only has it been their policy to keep the Arabs in subjection, but they also have a persistent record of antisemitism. Both before and after the Dreyfus Affair, as well as during it, antisemitism on the part of the French in Algeria was far more virulent than in France itself ... The claim that the revocation of the Crémieux Decree was necessary in order to prevent discord among Algerian Arabs is regarded by those who are familiar with conditions in North Africa as a smokescreen thrown up by the French reactionaries there.[26]

Hexter very rightly identified antisemitism among French and naturalized European colonists as being at the root of the impetus behind Giraud's re-abrogation. Arendt shared this analysis.

In "Why the Crémieux Decree Was Abrogated," Arendt analyzed Giraud's abrogation of the Crémieux Decree as a continuation of anti-semitism in the colony. Arendt argued that French colonists first resisted the Crémieux Decree because they feared it would reduce their own power in the colony. "They were anti-native in general but became anti-Jewish when equality was given to native Jews."[27] Arendt outlined the history of antisemitic politics and politicians in the colony, from Régis in

---

[24] Jewish Telegraph Agency, "Fighting French Voice Severe Criticism of Abrogation of Crémieux Decree," April 16, 1943, CDJC CCCLXXXV-1.

[25] Jewish Telegraph Agency, "Algiers Council-Général Embarrassed by Gen. Giraud's Abrogation of Crémieux Decree," April 23, 1943, CDJC CCCLXXXV-1.

[26] George J. Hexter, "Letter and Memo," April 1, 1943, CDJC CCCLXXXV-1.

[27] Hannah Arendt, "Why the Crémieux Decree Was Abrogated," *Contemporary Jewish Record* (April 1943): 118, CDJC CCCLXXXV-1.

1898 to Molle in the 1920s. She cited Viollette's 1935 statement that Europeans were behind antisemitism in Algeria.[28] In her analysis of the legal and political problems posed by the abrogation of the Crémieux Decree, Arendt emphasized that Algerian Jews no longer had recourse to representation in political bodies. In contrast, Algerian Muslims had elected representatives as a result of the 1919 Jonnart Law. Arendt firmly denounced the claim that Giraud abrogated the Crémieux Decree in order to create equality between Jews and Muslims in the colony. She accused Giraud of acting as an "agent of those French colonials," who sought to exert their own control of the colony.[29] She argued that the state antisemitism of Vichy continued under Giraud's supervision with the complicity of the American forces in Algeria.

Henry Torrès, a French-Jewish lawyer made famous for his defense of Simon Schwartzbard, also commented on Giraud's abrogation.[30] Originally published in the *Free World*, his article encouraged American readers to relate to the situation of Algerian Jews.

What would be the reaction of the American public opinion if it were to discover that American citizens of two or three generations' standing, with a record of having heroically carried their country's flag on the battlefields ... and contributed at least their share to the civilization of their motherland ... had been suddenly stripped of their American citizenship? Would it accept as valid the excuse offered by the perpetrator of this arbitrary decision that such a step, directed against a single category of citizens, had been taken to appease Indians or Negroes and to resolve political problems that concerned them?[31]

Like Arendt, Torrès contradicted Giraud's rationale for the abrogation and emphasized Algerian Jews' long history of service to France. Torrès denounced the abrogation as a regressionist approach to dealing with the issue of Arab rights. By retracting Algerian Jewish citizenship in order to appease Algerian Muslims, Giraud went against the history of assimilation in French colonialism and actually handicapped Algerian Muslims' path to emancipation. Like Arendt, Torrès also emphasized the long history of antisemitism in Algeria, from Drumont to Doriot's PPF, which he described as the "Vassals of the Nazis." Torrès described the

---

[28] Ibid., 121.

[29] "The French colonials, in other words, took advantage of France's defeat and their freedom from the control of the mother country in order to introduce in Algeria a measure that they would never have been able to obtain through legal channels." Ibid., 123.

[30] Laura Jockusch, *Collect and Record!: Jewish Holocaust Documentation in Early Postwar Europe* (Oxford: Oxford University Press, 2012), 29–30.

[31] Henry Torrès, "The Abrogation of the Crémieux Decree," *Free World*, CDJC CCCLXXXV-1. This article also appeared in *The Canadian Jewish Chronicle* on May 7, 1943.

re-abrogation as "a crime against history, a burden on the present, a portentous warning for the future . . . a vestige of Vichy, a concession to Nazism."[32] By depicting the Algerian Jews as the allies of Allied forces and fellow enemies of the Axis powers, Torrès encouraged public support of Algerian Jews.

In addition to its publicity campaign, the AJC lobbied American political leaders on behalf of Algerian Jews. Joseph M. Proskauer, the president of the AJC, wrote to Undersecretary of State Sumner Welles in March 1943 to protest Giraud's abrogation. Proskauer noted that he and the AJC were concerned with the implications of the abrogation, specifically that it sought to create equality between Jews and Muslims by denying citizenship to both groups. The situation of the Algerian Jews was "of so grave a nature, affecting not only the status of Jews in Algeria, but possibly of other lands."[33] The fact that the American government appeared to support Giraud's abrogation was unacceptable to the AJC. "That means it has approved the following: that a group of French citizens, over 100,000 in number, that has enjoyed over 70 years of such citizenship, is now deprived of citizenship solely on the ground that they are Jews." Proskauer emphasized the dangerous similarities between such legislation and that of Nazi Germany and the Nuremberg laws. The "present situation is wholly inconsistent with the principles announced by the Allied nations."[34] Proskauer enclosed a statement prepared by the AJC.

The AJC argued that among the most significant implications of the abrogation were that Jews could no longer vote for deputies to the French Parliament and could no longer properly serve in the military. The eradication of Algerian Jews from voter lists would reduce the number of eligible voters in Algeria by 11 or 12 percent. As Jews often voted for Republican candidates, their elimination from elections could transfer power to the anti-Republicans. The AJC statement concluded that the Giraud abrogation created a precedent for excluding groups of citizens on the basis of religion or race. "This is the first time that a non-totalitarian regime has deprived native born citizens of their citizenship."[35] Welles responded to that by stating the Americans did not have any involvement in the decision to abrogate the Crémieux Decree and did not express approval for such an act.[36]

---

[32] Ibid.

[33] Joseph Proskauer, President of the American Jewish Committee, to Undersecretary of State Sumner Welles, New York, March 17, 1943, CDJC CCCLXXXV-2.

[34] Joseph Proskauer to Sumner Welles, New York, May 17, 1943, CDJC CCCLXXXV-2.

[35] AJC, "Statement Regarding the Abrogation of the Crémieux Decree, submitted to Sumner Welles," May 17, 1943, CDJC CCCLXXXV-1.

[36] Undersecretary of State Sumner Welles to Joseph Proskauer, Washington, D.C., May 20, 1943, CDJC CCCLXXXV-2.

The abrogation of the Crémieux Decree also became a central issue for the World Jewish Congress (WJC). In June 1943, the Advisory Council on European Jewish Affairs and the French Jewish Representative Committee, represented by Henry Torrès and Paul Jacob, created a Memorandum on Giraud's abrogation, which they described as a "concession to Fascism and Nazism." In their report, the WJC representatives wrote that the re-abrogation constituted racial discrimination and that "the retraction of citizenship is the most extreme measure that one can take against a citizen such as a criminal, a spy, or a traitor of the country."[37] Antisemitism in the colony, they argued, was the product of French colonists, particularly the naturalized non-French Europeans. Torrès and Jacob highlighted the injustice that the Italian, Spanish, and Maltese naturalized French citizens, even those very recently naturalized, were allowed to keep their citizenship while Algerian Jews lost theirs.[38] Emphasizing the link between antisemitic activity and anti-French agitation, Torrès and Jacob demanded action.[39]

The CAES also used the platform provided by the WJC to present their own report in June 1943. The CAES leadership outlined the activities of the Jewish community in Algeria in dealing with the repercussions of antisemitic legislation under Vichy and under Giraud. Antisemitism increased after the Giraud abrogation, worsening conditions of Algerian Jewry. Jews feared reprisals from leaders and officials from the Vichy period in Algeria who remained in their positions. "The continuation of the discriminatory laws is incompatible with the liberation of African France and the presence of the Allies. It is impossible to fight simultaneously against the Axis on the outside and maintain the spirit of the Axis powers on the inside." The CAES believed that Giraud's administration did not provide the Allies with accurate information on the situation.[40]

World War II presented an unparalleled opportunity for Algerian Jews to bring their plight onto the world's stage. Algerian Jews directed previous efforts to speak out against antisemitic measures at the municipal or Algerian administration's levels, occasionally calling for assistance from

---

[37] Henry Torrés, Paul Jacob, World Jewish Congress, French Jewish Representative Committee, "Mémorandum: Une Concession au Fascisme et au Nazisme: L'Abrogation du Décret Crémieux," June 1943, CDJC XC-6.

[38] Torrés and Jacob, "Mémorandum: Une Concession au Fascisme et au Nazisme: L'Abrogation du Décret Crémieux," June 1943, CDJC XC-6.

[39] "It is the duty of all democrats and all democracies to fight and to reduce the contagion of fascist and Nazi propaganda, weapons of Axis war, which is the only reason for such an unjust, painful, and unnecessary condemnation." Ibid.

[40] CAES, "Report on the Present General Situation of Jews in Algeria, presented to the Advisory Council on European Jewish Affairs, World Jewish Congress," June 1, 1943, CDJC XC-7.

their fellow Jews in the metropole. Gaining the support of Jewish organizations such as the AJC and the WJC to their situation represented a major transition from insular defense to creating bonds with worldwide Jewry. Algerian Jews also fostered connections with Jewish American and British soldiers stationed in Algeria by celebrating holidays together. In April 1943, 800 American soldiers attended Passover services at the Grand Synagogue of Oran. Chief Rabbi of Oran Askenazi gave a speech in which he stated that "today, all of the Jewish population comes together to celebrate both the deliverance of the Jews from Egypt and slavery as well as from Nazi laws."[41] The work of these organizations on behalf of Algerian Jews also indicates the development of Jewish cooperation and collaboration in the face of the devastation of World War II.

The lobbying efforts of Jewish organizations within and outside of Algeria forced French leaders to reexamine the impact of antisemitic legislation. In May 1943, Algerian surgeon and French colonel Jules Abadie, who served in Giraud's government and later de Gaulle's Comité Français pour la Libération Nationale (CFLN), considered the tactical importance of Algerian Muslim and Jewish status. He acknowledged that it was critical to ensure Algerian Muslim support of France and their cooperation. Abadie suggested that rather than privilege Algerian Jews, the government should also make Algerian Muslims citizens.[42] Abadie's analysis responded to protests voiced by Algerian Jewish representatives, such as Alfred Ghighi, who submitted several reports outlining the dangers and legal ramifications of the abrogation.[43]

Abadie's opinions changed between his first report on May 28 and his second on June 6, 1943, as power shifted to de Gaulle during the period of Giraud–de Gaulle cooperation in leading the CFLN. In the second report, Abadie argued that the question of European antisemitism needed to be sidelined, although he acknowledged that it had played a role in the colony since the Dreyfus Affair and was often the

---

[41] He also honored the Allied soldiers, "who came from far away to save France and humanity." Special Police of Oran, "No. 1624; RAPPORT Objet: Cérémonies célébrées au Grand Temple à l'occasion des fêtes de Pâques," Oran, April 20, 1943, CAOM Alg Oran 2539.

[42] J. Abadie, Secretary of the Interior, "No. 213C.I.: Note au Sujet de l'abrogation du Décret Crémieux," Algiers, May 28, 1943, CAOM Alg GGA 8CAB/71.

[43] As a result of the re-abrogation, Jews could no longer serve in the army, but could serve as forced workers. Alfred Ghighi, "Note Remise à M. le Docteur Abadie, Secrétaire d'État à l'Intérieure, Situation militaire des Français de confession Juive," Oran, June 1, 1943, CAOM Alg GGA 8CAB/71. The issue of work camps for Algerian Jews under Vichy and Giraud became a contentious issue, but one that cannot be dealt with adequately in this chapter. For more information, see Norbert Bel Ange, *Quand Vichy Internait ses Soldats Juifs d'Algérie, Bedeau, sud oranais, 1941–1943* (Paris: L'Harmattan, 2005). See also declaration of Jews in Bedeau (undated), YVA O.26 (Collection on North Africa).

cause of local problems during electoral periods. Instead, the report focused on the role of Algerian Muslims. He suggested that the question of Muslim rights was more critical than ever in terms of military action: there were 120,000 Jews in the colony in contrast to the seven million Muslims. Abadie supported Giraud's argument that the abrogation would put Jews and Muslims on equal footing.[44]

Abadie's change in opinion from questioning the abrogation of the Crémieux Decree to supporting it may have been meant to consolidate support for Giraud in the face of Charles de Gaulle's arrival in Algiers on May 30, 1943. In the midst of the de Gaulle–Giraud rivalry after June 3, the abrogation of the Crémieux Decree presented an opportunity for de Gaulle to distance himself from Giraud.[45] Algerian Jews were optimistic that de Gaulle's arrival might usher in improvements to their status. Muslims similarly hoped that it would be an opportune time to demand their own rights. In July 1943, under the leadership of Ferhat Abbas and others, Muslims in Blida and Tlemcen called for greater rights.[46]

General Catroux replaced Vichy's Peyrouton as governor-general as de Gaulle arrived in Algiers. Ghighi immediately provided Catroux with documents regarding the politics of Algerian Muslims and the situation of Algerian Jews. In anticipation of the discussion of the Giraud's abrogation scheduled for the next meeting of the Senate of the CFLN, Ghighi rearticulated his analysis that the abrogation was illegal.[47] In July 1943, Abadie submitted another lengthy report on the impact of Giraud's abrogation in which he argued that "the most complex question remains that of the future rules for access to French citizenship." He proposed that the 1919 Jonnart law be extended to Algerian Jews, which would guarantee French citizenship to those who met certain conditions. The alternative to this proposal would be to suspend Giraud's abrogation.[48]

---

[44] J. Abadie, "Note Relative aux solutions a donné à l'ordonnance du 14 Mars 1943, portent abrogation du décret Crémieux," June 6, 1943, CAOM Alg GGA 8CAB/71.

[45] Msellati, *Les Juifs d'Algérie*, 248.

[46] General Catroux, "No. 2440CIE: Objet: Situation des militaires indigènes," Algiers, July 1, 1943, CAOM Alg GGA 8CAB/71.

[47] Alfred Ghighi to General Catroux, Oran, July 11, 1943, CAOM Alg GGA 8CAB/71. Of the fifteen members of the CFLN, twelve were in favor of restoring the Crémieux Decree, while General Catroux hoped for a "compromise." General Georges and General Firaud were opposed to restoring the Crémieux Decree. Albert Cohen, "To the Political Committee," London, July 18, 1943, CZA Z4\31461 (Politics. Correspondence on persecution of Jews in North Africa).

[48] J. Abadie, "Étude Concernant l'ordonnance du 14 Mars 1943 portant abrogation du Décret Crémieux," July 20, 1943, CAOM FM 1affpol/877. In his analysis, Abadie outlined the legal aspects of the applying a retroactive abrogation.

Giraud's abrogation of the Crémieux Decree thrust the issue of citizenship into the consciousness of colonial subjects and colonial administrators alike. The question of Algerian Jewish citizenship became inextricable from issues of increasing access to citizenship for Muslims. The Commissioner of the Colonies suggested that Algerian administrators take into consideration the system of offering citizenship to Africans in the *communes de plein exercice* in Senegal. He wrote that the case of Senegal indicated that they should "occasionally adapt our rather rigid legislation to the conditions of the people placed under our protection." To this end, he argued that the title of French citizen should not always require the renunciation of personal status, pointing to the fact that in those four communes in Senegal, courts managed to judge cases in accordance with Muslim custom. "The most essential goal is achieved when the citizen of a French country, whatever the nuances of his citizenship, participates completely in honor of the French name, and wherever he is, in the rights and burdens that it entails."[49] The American forces worried that the retraction of the abrogation would enflame Muslim reaction. Colonel Truchet of the CFLN feared that the reestablishment of the Crémieux Decree would lead to "agitation at an inopportune moment," because of the antisemitism of the European and Muslim populations in the colony. Muslim leaders, such as Ferhat Abbas, waited for the reinstatement of the Crémieux Decree in order to demand their own rights.[50]

Rumors circulated that the Americans planned to put greater pressure on the French administration to immediately reinstate the Crémieux Decree.[51] Robert Murphy sent a representative of the State Department, Lieutenant Colonel Harold Boies Huskins, to negotiate the return of rights to Algerian Jews. The French leaders explained to Huskins that there were insurmountable obstacles to reinstating the Crémieux Decree because wartime conditions made it impossible to risk Muslim agitation.[52] French administrators used the threat of

---

[49] Commissioner of the Colonies to the Commissioner of Justice, National Education and Public Heath, "No. 2/COLALG/Circ: Objet: Décret Crémieux," Algiers, August 9, 1943, CAOM FM 1affpol/877.

[50] Truchet recommended that they broaden access to citizenship for Algerian Muslims, but establish definite limits on their involvement in the administration. Colonel Truchet to Gov-Gen Catroux, "No. 41, CAM," Algiers, August 9, 1943, CAOM FM 1affpol/877.

[51] A. Leon Kubowitzki to Baron Easterman, British Section, World Jewish Congress, September 24, 1943, CZA C2/14 (American Jewish Congress Correspondence, 1943).

[52] "Note pour le Général Catroux," August 11, 1943, CAOM Alg GGA 8CAB/71. See also Director of Muslim Affairs and the Southern Territories to Head of Legislative Service and Administrative Legislation, "GGA CIE, No. 3342CIE: Objet: Application de l'ordonnance du 14 mars 1943, portent abrogation du décret Crémieux," Algiers, September 18, 1943, CAOM Alg GGA 8CAB/71.

Muslim agitation as an excuse for prolonging their decision regarding the status of Algerian Jews.[53]

The lobbying efforts of Algerian Jews, their American and French counterparts, as well as American officials finally brought results. In early October 1943, Giraud lost his co-presidency of the Comité de la Libération Nationale as de Gaulle consolidated power.[54] On October 20, 1943, the Comité de la Libération Nationale nullified Giraud's abrogation, returning Algerian Jews to their pre-Armistice status as French citizens.[55] The declaration also reserved the right of the French authorities to redefine the status of Algerian Jews, as well as other Algerian populations.[56] This maneuver not only reinstated Algerian Jews' French citizenship but also gave the illusion that Algerian Muslims' rights would be addressed in the future.

Jewish leaders throughout the world celebrated the news of the Crémieux Decree's restoration. Baron Alex Easterman of the British section of the WJC sent Rabbi Irving Miller, of the New York branch, a cable that read, "We are officially advised by French national authorities Algerian Jews Rights Restored."[57] Although Algerian Jews were pleased to be reinstated as citizens, they did not publicly express their happiness.[58] It was likely a calculated decision by Algerian Jewish leadership who feared that public celebrations might anger their Muslim neighbors. Despite the paucity of overt celebrations, Algerian Jews immediately expressed their gratitude for the return of their French citizenship. Ghighi sent letters of appreciation to Catroux and to de Gaulle, in which he thanked his fellow Oran General Council members for their support, singling out his Muslim colleagues, who provided him with "unanimous and spontaneous" support and aid.[59]

---

[53] Gov-Gen Catroux to the Commissioner of the Interior, "No. 2332-CC: Objet: Application de l'ordonnance du 14 mars 1943 portant abrogation du décret Crémieux," Algiers, September 29, 1943, CAOM Alg GGA 8CAB/71. Gov-Gen Catroux maintained his hard-line stance that the Giraud abrogation remain in effect in order to avoid grave repercussions.

[54] Bruce D. Graham, *Choice and Democratic Order: The French Socialist Party, 1937–1950* (Cambridge: Cambridge University Press, 1994), 256.

[55] According to the declaration, the laws of the Republic remained in effect; there was no need to reestablish the Crémieux Decree. Msellati, *Les Juifs d'Algérie*, 250. Baron A.L. Easterman spoke of his frustration at not being updated immediately regarding the reinstatement of the Crémieux Decree, which illustrates the profound interest world Jewry had in the situation of Algerian Jews. A.L. Easterman to Rabbi Irving Miller, World Jewish Congress, ALE/MB/1o-185, November 26, 1943, CZA C2/14 (American Jewish Congress Correspondence, 1943).

[56] Ansky, *Les Juifs d'Algérie*, 318–319.

[57] Cable from Alex Easterman to Irving Miller, October 22, 1943, CZA C2/14.

[58] Msellati, *Les Juifs d'Algérie*, 252.

[59] Alfred Ghighi to General de Gaulle, Oran, October 23, 1943, CAOM Alg GGA 8CAB/71. See also Alfred Ghighi to Gov-Gen Catroux, Oran, October 23, 1943, CAOM Alg GGA 8CAB/71. The Jewish Consistory of Tlemcen sent a telegram to de Gaulle expressing their "indefectible attachment to the project you are undertaking for the liberation of

At a ceremony for Simchat Torah attended by 3,000 Jews at the Main Synagogue of Oran, the Chief Rabbi gave a sermon in which he connected the holiday to the reinstitution of their status. "We are again French citizens. The Republic is now what it should be in reality, that is to say, fully free, great, and generous in justice." The Chief Rabbi then offered a prayer asking God to aid de Gaulle and the Comité de la Libération Nationale in their task of liberating France.[60]

The AJC also expressed their gratitude. On October 22, Proskauer congratulated de Gaulle and the CFLN "on their courageous rectification of an error and humane righting of a wrong."[61] The French Jewish Representative Committee of the WJC published a statement of their support as well.[62] The president of the American Jewish Congress, Stephen S. Wise, and the president of the WJC, Nahum Goldman, sent a telegram to the Comité de la Libération Nationale. "The American and the World Jewish Congress never doubted that the spirit of France, which framed the Crémieux Decree, would never permit its annulment."[63] Wise and Goldman also sent a similar telegram to Algerian Jewish leaders, including Henri Aboulker.[64]

Muslims were not pleased by the restitution of French citizenship for Algerian Jews. In Oran, Muslim elites and intellectuals expressed their frustration that Algerian Jews' status improved while theirs remained unsatisfactory.[65] In Bône, Muslims were disappointed and right-wing Europeans criticized the reinstatement of the Crémieux Decree and its discriminatory privileging of Jews over Muslims.[66] In Mascara, certain Muslim leaders believed that the decision of the Comité de la Libération

our motherland and the restoration of republican principles." Jewish Consistory of Tlemcen to General de Gaulle, "Telegram," Tlemcen, October 25, 1943, CAOM Alg GGA 8CAB/71.

[60] Principal Commissioner of Oran to the Prefect of Oran, "No. 4982: Objet: Remise en vigeur du Décret Crémieux, État d'esprit en milieux Israélite et musulman d'Oran," Oran, October 23, 1943, CAOM Alg Oran 2539.

[61] Joseph Proskauer, "AJC Press Statement," October 22, 1943, CDJC CCCLXXXV-2.

[62] Henry Torrés, Paul Jacob, Edouard de Rothschild, "Resolution of the French Jewish Representative Committee of the World Jewish Congress," October 23, 1943, CDJC XC-14.

[63] Stephen S. Wise and Nahum Goldman to the Comité de la Libération Nationale, October 22, 1943, CDJC XC-14.

[64] "We greatly rejoice over the long awaited abrogation of the act that annulled the Crémieux Decree. Glorious France could have done nothing else." Stephen S. Wise and Nahum Goldman to Henri Aboulker, Elie Gozlan, and Joseph Kanoui, October 22, 1943, CDJC XC-14.

[65] Principal Commissioner of Oran to the Prefect of Oran, "No. 4982," October 23, 1943, CAOM Alg Oran 2539.

[66] Special Departmental Police of Bône to the Commissioner of Constantine, "No. 1606: Objet: A/S du rétablissement du décret Crémieux," Bône, October 26, 1943, CAOM Alg GGA 8CAB/71.

Nationale indicated a positive future for Muslim rights.[67] According to a surveillance report, the supporters of Algerian nationalists Abbas and Messali Hadj "now constitute a powerful majority and see the return of the Crémieux Decree as a justification and argument for a tentative dissociation of the two elements, Jew and Arab, a justification of their anti-French sentiments ... Even the *évolués*, even the Muslims most loyal to the French ideal are discouraged."[68] In the end, Algerian Muslims yet again felt slighted by the French government. Muslim leaders recognized that their community would not receive equal rights under the French colonial system and intensified their demands for independence after World War II.

Rising Muslim Nationalism and May 8, 1945, in Sétif and Guelma

Although the reinstatement of the Crémieux Decree was a springboard for the revival of Algerian Muslim rights, many scholars agree that 1945 was a major turning point for Algerian Muslim nationalism. This transition pivots on the violent events of Sétif and Guelma in May 1945, during which Algerian Muslims were massacred by French forces. At this point, Algerian nationalists, and even the more conservative assimilationists, realized that Algerian political enfranchisement could not succeed under French imperialism.

Historian James McDougall described the relationship between colonizer and colonized as "constitutively marked by violence. But far from being a simple matter of the 'monologic' imposition of an unchanging European will on similarly unchanging, perennially passive or unyieldingly resisting others, colonialism was a relationship within which new, dialogical discursive practice of self-fashioning emerged."[69] This relationship became ever more complicated as decolonization occurred elsewhere. While Algerian nationalism had been steadily developing in the interwar period, it slowed during World War II. The violence that exploded on May 8, 1945, in Sétif and Guelma, on the day of celebration of the end of war in Europe, ushered in a new awakening of nationalist efforts. Some scholars suggest that decolonization did not begin in 1954 with the start of the Algerian War but rather on May 8, 1945. Historian

---

[67] State Police of Mascara to the Sub-Prefect of Mascara, "No. 8537: Objet: repercussion du rétablissement du Décret Crémieux," Mascara, October 29, 1943, CAOM Alg Oran2539.
[68] Gov-Gen CIE: "No. 3719 CIE: Renseignements: A/S du Maintien en Vigueur du Décret Crémieux," Algiers, October 25, 1943, CAOM Alg Oran 5i/50.
[69] McDougall, *History and the Culture of Nationalism*, 6.

Jean-Pierre Peyroulou concluded his study of Guelma in 1945 by arguing that "a political conscience was born after the events of May 8, 1945" and that Algerian nationalism entered a new period of intensity.[70] The interwar period was a time of developing articulations of Muslim demands for rights. This accelerated during the post-Vichy period when Jews and Muslims simultaneously made their case for regaining or receiving citizenship in the colony. While they made their respective cases on vastly different bases, as Jules Abadie's assessment of colonial rights illustrated, the question of Jewish rights was inextricable from that of Muslims.

With the Allied landings of 1942, the tides of the war changed dramatically. The arrival of the Allies, and particularly the anti-colonial politics of the American forces, gave hope to Algerian Muslim leaders. However, independence was not yet the goal.[71] In his memoirs, journalist and activist Henri Alleg describes the frustration felt with the "French style apartheid" present in the colony. At the top of the hierarchy were the "true" French, followed by those naturalized Europeans, and below them the Jews, and at the bottom, "the natives, uniformly called 'Arabs.' "[72] Alleg recalls that in 1943, "whenever we spoke of Independence, it seemed to be in the distant future."[73]

At that point, Ferhat Abbas shifted his politics from his more assimilationist efforts toward nationalism. Abbas had been a proponent of assimilationism in the 1920s and 1930s, even declaring in 1936 *la France, c'est moi*. During the highly politicized events of the early 1940s, his approach changed. On February 10, 1943, Abbas presented his document "L'Algérie face au conflit mondial," subtitled the *Manifeste du peuple Algérien* (Manifesto of the Algerian People), signed by thirty Algerian Muslim notables. On March 31, Governor-General Marcel Peyrouton accepted Abbas' document as the "basis for reforms to come" and encouraged Abbas and the other signers to make the document even more precise in terms of their demands. They completed this task on May 26 and gave the revised document to the new French authorities on June 10, 1943. The Manifesto demanded an Algerian nationality and citizenship, a constitution that would grant liberty and equality to all

---

[70] Jean-Pierre Peyroulou, *Guelma, 1945: Une subversion française dans l'Algérie coloniale* (Paris: Éditions la Découverte, 2009), 244.

[71] Malika Rahal, "Ferhat Abbas, de l'assimilationisme au nationalisme," in Abderahmane Bouchène, Jean-Pierre Peyroulou, Ouanassa Siar Tengour, Sylvie Thénault, eds., *Histoire de l'Algérie à la période coloniale (1830–1962)* (Paris: Éditions la Découverte, 2012), 444.

[72] Henri Alleg, *The Algerian Memories: Days of Hope and Combat* (London: Seagull Books, 2012), 147.

[73] Ibid., 90.

inhabitants of Algeria, and recognition of Arabic as an official language. The revisions submitted in May and June also recommended the creation of a democratic and liberated Algerian state at the end of the war, one that would be federated to France. The Manifesto of February 10, 1943, has been called the "birth of an Algerian nation."[74]

Abbas believed that the American forces in Algeria would support his efforts and considered Robert Murphy's expressions of American anti-colonialism a sign of encouragement. Abbas even hung a picture of Roosevelt in his pharmacy in Sétif.[75] According to Marcel Reggui, a French naturalized Muslim whose family later perished in the Guelma massacre, the Allied landings gave Algerian Muslims the courage to pursue their campaign for improved rights. "The Allied landings in North Africa created a favorable climate for the awareness of Muslims who wanted to overcome the inferiority complex that the Europeans of Africa, by their attitude, had inculcated until then."[76] Although the American and British forces perhaps intellectually supported the Algerian Muslims' cause, they endeavored to avoid French colonial politics.

While some Algerian Jews hailed Charles de Gaulle as their savior and the representative of "true" France, he was not necessarily seen as such by some Algerian Muslims. After his arrival in Algiers on May 30, 1943, de Gaulle imposed the CFLN on Giraud on June 3, and subsequently removed Peyrouton from his post. With Peyrouton's departure, Abbas' hopes for realizing the demands of his Manifesto were quashed. Governor-General Catroux succeeded Peyrouton, but his commitment to Algerian Muslims was more limited than that of his predecessor. The CFLN was very cautious in its treatment of Muslim rights for fear of antagonizing Europeans in the colony. Furthermore, the situation of Algerian Jews had not yet been resolved. In August 1943, twenty-seven Communist deputies asked de Gaulle to return Jews to their status as citizens. He responded that the "practical application is delicate," because the problem of Jewish rights was linked to the problem of Muslim rights.[77]

With de Gaulle's arrival, Algiers became the capital of Free France. The great irony of this is that as Abbas made his transition to nationalism, de Gaulle reaffirmed the centrality of Algeria to the French republic.

---

[74] Peyroulou, *Guelma 1945*, 25–26.
[75] Ibid., 25–27. See also Jean-Louis Planche, *Sétif 1945: Histoire d'un massacre annoncé* (Paris: Éditions Perrin, 2006), 61.
[76] Marcel Reggui, *Les Massacres de Guelma: Algérie, Mai 1945: Une enquête inédite sur la furie des milices colonials* (Paris: Éditions la Decouverte, 2006), 66.
[77] Planche, *Sétif 1945*, 73–74.

The year 1943 was marked by de Gaulle and his compatriots' complete preoccupation with ending the war and beating Hitler. Algerian Muslim rights were largely sidelined due to the intensity of this singular goal.[78]

As shown in Abbas' Manifesto, the central interest of Algerian Muslims was oriented around their commitment to receiving Algerian citizenship. Some Algerian Muslim leaders were no longer as wedded to the idea of a future in French Algeria, but a future in an Algeria federated to France. This is also a key difference between the Algerian Muslim and Jewish campaigns for rights in the Giraud/de Gaulle period, and one of the central reasons why Algerian Jews were successful in achieving their goals and not Algerian Muslims. Algerian Muslims were frustrated with the extremely limited access they had to French citizenship, which required them to give up their personal status, a consistently central issue in debates regarding Muslims' rights and status. In 1936, only 7,817 Muslims had gained French citizenship via naturalization. This was out of a population of approximately 7,200,000. In 1943, there were 6,000 Muslim *élus* in the Second College in mixed communes, and 18,000 members of *djemaas* (assemblies of douars of mixed communes), which totaled approximately 24,000 Muslims participating in the colonial political system in Algeria. These numbers reflect the extreme imbalance of Algeria's political system and represent one of the key reasons for the transition from the politics of assimilation among Algerian Muslims to nationalism in 1943.[79]

In 1943, there was no unified Algerian nationalist movement. There were essentially three branches of Algerian nationalism: the more conservative approach of Abbas and his community, the independence oriented nationalists led by Messali Hadj, and the Ulamas led by Bachir Brahimi, the successor of Cheikh 'Abd al-Hamid Ben Badis (1889–1940). The Association of the Algerian Muslim Ulama (*Association des Ulama Musulmans Algériens*, AUMA) was founded in Algiers in May 1931 by Ben Badis. The AUMA focused its efforts on gaining control of cultural authority in order to define and direct "the true religion" in Algeria. They would gain further power over that domain after independence, but in the 1930s and 1940s, they focused on "resurrecting" Algerian Muslim society by focusing on education. Although not overtly nationalistic, this reformist movement focused on the reduction of the colonial cultural hegemony imposed upon Algerian Muslims.[80] Assimilationism reigned as the logic among Muslim elites since

---

[78] Peyroulou, *Guelma 1945*, 27–28.   [79] Ibid., 30, 33.
[80] McDougall, *History and the Culture of Nationalism*, 12–14; Shepard, *The Invention of Decolonization*, 38.

Bendjelloul's efforts with the *Fédération des élus*, but the limited influence of Muslims in Algerian politics fueled the popularity of more nationalist movements, such as the *Étoile Nord Africaine*, formed by Messali Hadj in 1926 in Paris, and its successor, the *Parti du Peuple Algérien*.[81]

Although Algerian nationalism was divided in 1943, Abbas' Manifesto created hope for unity among Algerian Muslim leaders. Unity, however, posed a threat to the continuation of French Algeria, and de Gaulle sought to appease these leaders without losing control of the colony. For de Gaulle, the realities of colonial control were pressing: the ratio of Frenchmen to Algerian Muslims threatened French control, especially with Algerian Jews no longer recognized as French citizens. In particular, the department of Constantine was largely Muslim, with only scattered French *colon* presence. According to the 1936 census, the European population in the colony was 946,013, of which there were 188,354 in the Constantine region. In comparison, there were 2,494,653 Algerian Muslims in the department of Constantine. In the colonial mind, this ratio threatened the security and authority of Europeans in the region. The fact that most of the Algerian Muslim nationalists (in their varied degrees of nationalism) were based in the Constantine area further concerned French colonial officials. As a result, de Gaulle set about to "reconquer" those French territories that had become more Muslim in demographics, particularly Constantine.[82]

In the face of de Gaulle's priorities, cracks began to form in the limited unity experienced by Algerian Muslim nationalisms in the period following Abbas' Manifesto. The assimilationists, those French-educated Muslim professionals and intellectuals, who had found moments of unity, increasingly splintered as they redefined their goals. The first generation of the assimilationists, organized pre-1914 by the Young Algerians, which included Dr. Benthami Ould Hamida and Chérif Benhabylès, were overshadowed by the more prolific second-generation leaders, including Dr. Bendjelloul, Ferhat Abbas, Ahmed Boumendjel, and Ahmed Francis. These men sought to achieve equality for Muslims within the French framework and hoped to extend the same emancipation enjoyed by Jews before Vichy to Algerian Muslims. However, as Abbas and his colleagues shifted the direction of their goals in the Manifesto and in the face of the changing power structure with de Gaulle's arrival, Bendjelloul took his name off the Manifesto. Abbas announced the rupture of their leadership on September 16, 1943.

---

[81] Peyroulou, *Guelma 1945*, 35–37; Shepard, *The Invention of Decolonization*, 39.
[82] Peyroulou, *Guelma 1945*, 30, 40. See also Anthony Clayton, "The Sétif Uprising of May 1945," *Small Wars and Insurgencies*, Vol. 3, No. 1 (Spring, 1992): 2.

Perhaps Bendjelloul was aware of the coming repression; Abbas was arrested on September 23, just seven days after the split.[83]

As Algerian Muslim leaders faced increased challenges to their demands for improved rights and status, Algerian Jews succeeded in their lobbying efforts to be returned to their pre-Vichy status as French citizens on October 20, 1943. This frustrated Algerian Muslim leaders, both assimilationists and nationalists. de Gaulle quickly implemented legislation to ameliorate the Algerian Muslim legal situation, but these reforms did not meet the demands made by the Manifesto. In Constantine on December 12, 1943, de Gaulle announced the plan to widen citizenship ranks to Muslims. On December 14, Governor-General Catroux instituted a commission charged with proposing a series of reforms to the CFLN that would allow an elite group of Algerian Muslims to become citizens. The work of the commission concluded in the March 7, 1944, ordinance of the Provisional Government of the French Republic (GPRF) that extended citizenship, with its own peculiarities and limitations, to 65,000 Muslims, many of whom had served France in the past wars, who were allowed to maintain their local civil status. The 1944 ordinance established a new category, the "Muslim French from Algeria," and made all civil statuses theoretically equal in the eyes of French public law.[84]

The limited progress of the March ordinance frustrated Algerian Muslim leaders, even the more assimilationist among them. Henri Alleg described them as a "few very minor positive modifications."[85] Although the reforms including abolishing aspects of the hated *indigénat* and offered access to military and civil positions, they did not extend citizenship to the vast majority of Algerian Muslims. On March 14, 1944, Ferhat Abbas renewed his demands made in the Manifesto by founding a movement in Sétif, *Amis du Manifeste et de la liberté* (AML). The new organization quickly gained 500,000 adherents, most of whom came from the surrounding region, who also subscribed to the movement's journal, *Égalité*, whose first issue appeared in May 1944. Sétif became the headquarters of the AML, the most active nationalist/assimilationist Algerian Muslim movement in Algeria at the time, and it is this centrality that set the stage for the violence of May 8, 1945.[86]

---

[83] Peyroulou, *Guelma 1945*, 42; McDougall, *History and Culture of Nationalism*, 74. See also Ruedy, *Modern Algeria*, 145–146.

[84] Peyroulou, *Guelma 1945*, 42–43; "La Commission des réformes musulmanes a entendu des représentants des populations d'Algérie," *L'Echo d'Alger*, January 4, 1944, 1; "Les Français musulmans d'Algérie jouissent de tous les droits et sont soumis à tous les devoirs des français non musulmans," *L'Echo d'Alger*, March 8, 1944, 1; Shepard, *The Invention of Decolonization*, 38–39.

[85] Alleg, *The Algerian Memories*, 109.

[86] Clayton, "The Sétif Uprising," 4; Peyroulou, *Guelma 1945*, 45–46.

Albeit a limited shift toward including Algerian Muslims within the electoral ranks, the March 1944 ordinance was quickly met with resistance from Europeans in the colony, who feared the impact that the new voters would have on upcoming elections. The new governor-general, Yves Chataigneau, came to power on September 9, 1944, and immediately faced the concerns regarding the new bloc of 65,000 Muslim voters and how their votes might impact the coming elections. Mayors and municipal councils were especially concerned. They feared that the presence of Muslim voters at the polls would fundamentally shift the balance of power of the municipalities, especially in regions in which the new Muslim voters were concentrated, such as Constantine. These concerns regarding the voting tendencies of the new citizens echoed the status anxieties demonstrated by Frenchmen and *néos* in the 1890s and 1920s with regard to Jewish votes. The same accusations of voting as a bloc were leveled against Muslim voters. Once again, status anxieties intensified in municipal councils as European officials feared the potential impact of the new cadre of Muslim voters and their presumed communal power. In the face of the opposition of Europeans to their new, but limited, citizenship, Algerian Muslim leaders reemphasized the importance of unity. In January 1945, the PPA and the AML achieved rapprochement and began to collaborate. At the same time, the AML began to radicalize its program through its association with the PPA, shifting further and further away from assimilationism and more toward nationalism.[87]

From January 1945 on, four primary factors shaped the radicalization of the AML and the Algerian Muslim population more generally: the economic situation of the 1940s, particularly the extreme food shortages from 1942 onward; the development of Muslim nationalist organizations; the status anxieties of the various colonial constituencies in the colony alongside the shifting power structures; and, finally, the intensification of colonial repression. These factors merged, feeding one another in the general climate of tension in the final months of war. As Marcel Reggui wrote in his 1946 inquiry into the events of Guelma, "the repression in Guelma reached a scale never registered in Algeria, not even after the revolts of 1871 and 1917 ... The events of 8 May broke out not in an atmosphere of peace but in a climate of latent hostility."[88]

The economic climate at the end of the war was especially dire in colonial Algeria. Historian Martin Thomas identifies the roots of the violence in Sétif in the issue of political economy and the chronic food supply crisis that plagued Algeria in the winter and spring of 1944–1945. Those who participated in the riots and violence in Sétif were largely farm

[87] Peyroulou, *Guelma 1945*, 48–49, 55–57.   [88] Reggui, *Les Massacres de Guelma*, 49.

workers, sharecroppers, and other food producers, ultimately those Muslims who suffered as a result of the preferential treatment given to settler farmers. In the region of Constantine, more than 80 percent of the colonial land in the region as owned by just 25 percent of the population of European farmers. As a result, Europeans had a firm grip on the agricultural economy. As famine and food shortages challenged Algeria, Muslims were left with few resources. Furthermore, French colonial officials acted with the needs of the Europeans in mind. In this atmosphere, chronic food shortages and famine are often accompanied by intense politicization in response to state inaction.[89]

The French colonial leadership was fully aware of the growing danger of the food supply situation in the colony. Little was done to improve or alter the situation. From 1940 to 1942, there were a series of bad harvests and a typhus epidemic, all of which were exacerbated by the demands of wartime on agriculture. From 1943 onward, Sétif faced a major meat shortage, bread rations, and an almost nonexistent supply of fruit. As early as February 1945, surveillance reports commented on the worsening hardship and incipient famine experience among Muslims in the colony. As of April 1945, Algeria was entirely dependent on imported wheat to supply the country's bread requirements, further evidence of the failing agricultural system. Furthermore, Muslims were at the bottom of the rationing hierarchy, as the colonial leadership believed poor Muslims to be incapable of political protest. They were mistaken as the Muslim poor were the most impacted by the growing rhetoric and efforts of the Muslim political organizations in the area. In his analysis of the Sétif violence, historian Anthony Clayton argued that the hunger and general deprivation of Algerian Muslims, contrasted with the relative riches and abundance of the French *colons*, served as a catalyst for the violence in Sétif.[90]

In this climate, the three main branches of Algerian nationalism – the AUMA, the AML, and the PPA – began to cooperate more. Even though the PPA had been banned since 1939 and Messali Hadj was in prison, it still had an active popular base. Ferhat Abbas emerged as the central Algerian Muslim leader, particularly in Eastern Algeria. In the spring of 1945, despite the AML's continued commitment to nonviolent reform, the PPA organized demonstrations and encouraged AML support by

---

[89] Martin Thomas, "Colonial Minds and Colonial Violence: The Sétif Uprising and the Savage Economics of Colonialism," in Martin Thomas, ed., *The French Colonial Mind, Volume 2* (Lincoln: University of Nebraska Press, 2011), 141–143; Peyroulou, *Guelma 1945*, 31.

[90] Thomas, "Colonial Minds and Colonial Violence," 144–147, 157; Clayton, "The Sétif Uprising," 2.

arguing that divisions between their organizations would be unproductive in reaching their goals of change. In addition, the *Fédération des Scouts Musulmans Algériens* (FSMAC) brought together the large numbers of young Muslims in the region. The young people, mostly male, felt further alienated by the French colonial government in the face of limited access to rights and the food shortages that never seemed to improve. The FSMAC engaged in nationalist parades and paramilitary activities and thus provided unity and action for the disenfranchised Muslim youth in the colony. It also found support among the PPA and AML leadership. From March 1945 onward, the AML made significant inroads in Constantine, particularly in mixed communes where the food shortages and unequal rights were most sharply felt. On May 1, 1945, a crowd of nearly 500 protested the inadequacy of the distribution of emergency relief supplies and flour rations outside the Sub-Prefecture of Orléansville. Many of the protesters were peasant sharecroppers. The protests devolved into attempts to storm two *boulangeries*, signifying the centrality of food shortages and impossible economic conditions.[91]

The economic climate created an ideal environment for the mobilization of movements such as the AML in Guelma. The local AML section included virtually all of the Algerian Muslim population of the city. In the larger region, PPA members dominated the leadership of the AML. In fact, to not be an active and paying member, approximately 120 francs per family at that time resulted in ostracism for nonparticipation. Young people were especially involved in Guelma – they participated in the FSMAC as well as the AML – and revealed generational divisions in terms of the goals and strategies among AML members. On May 8, 1945, as the elder leaders of the AML remained in a café, the young people actively protested.[92]

In Marcel Reggui's analysis of the Guelma violence in 1945, he emphasizes economics and status anxieties as two of the key causes for the violent repression. Reggui wrote that the French of the region had a history of exploiting the colonial hierarchy and continually asserting their superiority over Muslims. He noted that the concept of "European" in the colony was a tricky one as it often encompassed what he called both the "true French" and the "néo-Français." In the Vichy period, the Europeans in the colony were particularly pleased with the ramifications of the racial politics that offered them "an unexpected opportunity to victimize the Jews, whose intelligence, skill, wealth, and unity they envied."[93] Under Vichy, some Europeans became increasingly

---

[91] Thomas, "The Colonial Mind and Colonial Violence," 149–151, 154, 158–159.
[92] Peyroulou, *Guelma 1945*, 85–87, 114.   [93] Reggui, *Les Massacres de Guelma*, 46.

antisemitic, but also "arabophiles." In the aftermath of the racial laws that removed Algerian Jews' citizenship, Reggui asserted that Muslims had more opportunities to improve their material situation, especially in the black market and in taking over some jobs and businesses that had been held by Jews. With the Allied landings in November 1942, Muslims' material situation changed yet again.[94]

While Reggui identified increased status anxieties and the actions of Europeans and Jews in the repression of Guelma in May 1945, he ultimately blamed what he called "the problem of civilization." Reggui, who was baptized as a Catholic, French-educated and naturalized, firmly believed in a French future for Algeria when he wrote his inquiry in 1946. However he recognized the fundamental failure in colonial Algeria was colonialism itself: "To colonize is to civilize, therefore the Guelma tragedy put into opposition those two concepts of colonization."[95] At the core of the "problem of civilization" was the inability of Muslims to truly improve their situation within the colonial hierarchy. "The Europeans, humiliated, deprived by the economic rise of Muslims, could not wait for a chance to take exploding revenge. The Jews, blocked more and more by the rise of Muslims, sought to regain their commercial primacy. The ones and the others were more and more worried by the young dynamism shown by the Muslims of Guelma."[96] Status anxieties amid the tense economic conditions of the end of war created the perfect environment for the intense repression of the protests of Guelma and the violence of Sétif.

In the face of the developing Algerian Muslim nationalist movements, as well as the urgent need to reaffirm French control over Algeria, the French colonial leadership was primed to promote strong repression of any perceived threat. The *indigénat* outlawed rallies as acts of rebellions and established required police approval. When the Arab League was founded on March 20, 1945, the news was welcomed by Algerians.[97] In the atmosphere of anticolonial activities circulating through the Middle East and North Africa, de Gaulle ordered General Henry Martin to repress all nationalist movements' activities in North Africa. Independence seemed at hand. The intent of the French government to repress all nationalist activity in Algeria was embodied by Sub-Prefect André Achiary of Guelma.

Achiary arrived in Guelma on March 22, 1945, in his new position of Sub-Prefect. Born in Tarbes on July 10, 1909, Achiary had a background

---

[94] Ibid., 53–54.   [95] Ibid., 69.   [96] Ibid., 71–72.
[97] Jean-Pierre Peyroulou, "Preface," in Reggui, *Les Massacres de Guelma*, 9–11; Peyroulou, *Guelma 1945*, 103.

in the police, having become commissioner in 1934, and subsequently the chief of the surveillance brigade of the territory (*brigade de surveillance du territoire*, BST) in Algiers from 1938 to December 1942. He was also one of the principal actors involved in the Algiers Insurrection in November 1942. He was therefore an odd hybrid: both a celebrated resistant and an establishment man. In Guelma, he faced a legacy of police abuse in the region. On April 14, Achiary reactivated the civilian militia, known as the *Volontaires de Place*, which consisted of approximately 300 people. The original goal of the militia was the "protection" of Europeans in the region. The group was mostly made up of men aged 35 to 50, of various social classes, unified against the "native" peril. This militia was among the principal groups responsible for the massacre of Muslims in the region in May 1945.[98] Reggui identified Achiary as one of the key orchestrators of the extremely violent repression in Guelma in 1945, writing that "if, in the place of Achiary, had been found another Sub-Prefect, never would the city of Guelma have known such a terrible tragedy. He alone set if off, and caused, by his requirements, the most ruthless repression Algeria has ever known."[99]

As four factors combined – economic hardship, status anxieties, Algerian nationalism, and a culture of French repression – the stage was set for the unprecedented violence in Sétif and Guelma in May 1945. Peyroulou argues that the cases of Sétif and Guelma were distinct and that Guelma was an entirely different situation. However, even the names of the town are rarely mentioned without the other, especially with regard to the events of May 1945. In this discussion, more emphasis will be placed on Guelma because of the activities of the militia, which acted upon the status anxieties that had shaped colonial society in Algeria from the 1890s to 1945, and beyond.

Concerns regarding nationalist activity primed colonial officials, especially prefects and Sub-Prefects, such as Achiary, to put down any rallies or protests in their regions. While some officials were worried about nationalist activities, the decision to transfer Messali Hadj to El-Goléa on April 21 was due to the idea that it would "decapitate" the nationalist movement. Despite official repression, in the week leading up to May 8, 1945, a series of rallies took place in the Constantine region. On May 1, protests for the liberation of Messali Hadj occurred, during which the PPA ordered the use of the Algerian flag (the green crescent that had been used by Abd'el-Khader). Similar protests took place throughout Algeria. Most of these protests were quickly put down by local forces. In Algiers

---

[98] Peyroulou, *Guelma 1945*, 89–98, 128; Alleg, *The Algerian Memories*, 65–66.
[99] Reggui, *Les Massacres de Guelma*, 127.

there were twelve deaths; at the Oran protest of nearly 10,000 people there was only one death, but many injuries. There were similar numbers elsewhere, including approximately 5,000 protestors in the department of Constantine, where the protests ended peacefully through negotiation. When calm reigned, protestors dispersed; when the police used force, violence ensued. AML leaders encouraged calm responses, while some leaders of the PPA demanded active responses to police force, rather than negotiation. This difference in opinion led to a split between moderates and PPA leadership on May 4.[100]

May 8 was meant to be a day of celebration of the end of world war; it was to be treated like France's July 14. The streets would be spaces of celebration. Rallies were planned in advance and submitted to the Sub-Prefect in order to meet the requirements of article 1 of the decree of October 23, 1935. Rallies that had not been authorized would be considered illegal and were to be put down immediately. In Sétif, the spontaneous nature of the rallies could not be approved in advance and thus were considered illegal. As the numbers of participants increased from 4,000 to more than 6,000, some carried Algerian flags and banners with slogans such as "Free Messali," "Long Live the United Nations," and "We want to be your equals." The twenty police officers present intervened and demanded that the more "seditious" banners be taken down. At that point, a police officer named Oliviéri grabbed the banner of a protestor and a fight ensued. It is not clear, however, who shot first. Peyroulou describes the violence that followed as that of "vengeance and despair."[101]

Clayton describes the next moments as attacks on Europeans in the streets of Sétif among cries of "kill the Europeans." By 11 am, twenty-one Europeans had been killed. Similar political rallies in Bône and Constantine were also put down by police or troops. Bands of Algerian Muslims then took to the countryside in the next few days, attacking European farmers in the department of Constantine. While Clayton depicts the aggressors as "insurgent groups," Martin Thomas identifies their actions as direct responses to the harsh economic conditions facing Algerian Muslims at the end of World War II. In the end, 102 Europeans were killed.[102] Henri Alleg described traveling through Sétif in the afternoon on May 8. "None of us could have imagined what had happened

---

[100] Clayton, "The Sétif Uprising," 2; Peyroulou, *Guelma 1945*, 105–107.
[101] Peyroulou, *Guelma 1945*, 109–112; Clayton, "The Sétif Uprising," 7.
[102] Clayton, "The Sétif Uprising," 1, 7–8; Thomas, "The Colonial Mind and Colonial Violence," 141. See also Planche, *Sétif 1945*, 139; See also Charles-Robert Ageron, "Les troubles du nord-constantinois en mai 1945: Une tentative insurrectionnelle," *Vingtième Siècle. Revue d'histoire*, No. 4 (1984): 25–26.

that very morning. During the victory celebration, the police had opened fire on the crowd in an authorized Muslim parade, killing demonstrators. After the shooting, various groups, mainly farmers on their way to the market, had spread out in the city and attacked Europeans."[103] Although Alleg's account does not entirely match those commonly used, it does reflect the unexpected nature of the violence. These events, alongside those of Guelma, led to the massive repression by the French military and the civilian militia in Guelma.

The situation in Sétif began before the protests in Guelma and primed Achiary and his team to respond strongly. The Prefect had alerted Achiary that morning and ordered him to disperse any nationalist demonstrations or rallies. By afternoon, Achiary was told to put down any disorder in Guelma by force, if necessary. The rally in Guelma began with the goal of honoring the war dead. However, by 6 pm, a procession moved into the city with Algerian flags, as well as Allied flags and signs demanding the liberation of Messali Hadj and that read "Vive Algérie." At 6:30 pm, Achiary met the rally at the center of the city with a group of police officers as well as city leaders, demanding that the participants disperse. Ali Abda, the 20-year-old younger brother of a local leader of the AML, shoved Achiary. The crowd then threatened the officers; Achiary took out his revolver and shot it into the air, and the policemen followed suit, then charged. In the end, an AML leader was killed and six Algerian Muslims were hurt. Elsewhere conflicts between PPA members and the police took place and many protestors were arrested. Achiary ordered that troops be placed in each neighborhood, closed all cafés, and instated a curfew of 9:30 pm.[104]

It is important to note that the majority of the police officers were in fact Algerians. The police forces were under the purview of the municipal authority, a bastion of local power. They were recruited by the municipality and it was one of the few opportunities for Algerian Muslims to hold a position within the municipal government at the time. There were also two Jews on the police force in May 1945. The demographics of the police force indicates that the police acted within their role and did not conduct extralegal activities. Rather, the local militia that Achiary had reassembled on April 14 took on that role. On May 9, Achiary called his militia into action. The militia consisted of seventy-eight well-armed members and 120–180 others. Of the seventy-eight armed militias, the majority were European, but included eleven Jews, including M. Attali, the leader of the local consistory, and one Muslim, named Taïeb. The militias took up positions around Guelma to stop Algerian Muslim

[103] Alleg, *The Algerian Memories*, 117.   [104] Peyroulou, *Guelma 1945*, 113–115.

movement and interaction.[105] The motivations of the militia will be discussed later.

At the same time, Algerian Muslims attacked Europeans outside the city of Guelma. General Raymond Duval called in the air force, which conducted "intimidation flights," meant to scare away groups of protestors. However, on May 9, the flights began bombing and shooting Algerian peasants. Also on May 9, Achiary and leaders of the militia, including Attali, set up a tribunal to charge and condemn Algerian Muslims who had been arrested. The tribunal, modeled upon the tribunals set up after the fall of Vichy to try collaborators, operated May 9–18. The tribunals worked swiftly and executions took place within a day of judgment. During its operation, 25,000 Muslims came before the tribunal, many of whom were found guilty and summarily executed.[106]

The murders of Europeans led to calls for revenge. On May 11, the "European revolt" began to "save French Algeria." This consisted of the wholesale murder of Algerian Muslims. Achiary excused the violent extremes as necessary actions. Alleg depicted the activities of the militia, which "hunted down Arabs, shameless and without qualms killing everyone on their way, including children. They also shot and killed whoever they thought a suspect, without burdening themselves with undue considerations ... André Achiary, who, before becoming a Gaullist resistant, had tortured Communist militants – encouraged these self-appointed avengers, saying, 'Messieurs les *colons*, take your revenge!' "[107]

The days of May 13–19 were the bloodiest – the heart of the massacre. At that stage, Achiary and the militia had the support of the prefect. Aerial bombings continued despite general calm. The executions determined by the militia tribunal also continued. The killings would have actively continued if it had not been for the Tubert Commission, charged with studying the massacre by the government. Although the commission did not complete its task, Achiary disbanded the militia on May 19. By May 18, the militia and civil forces of Guelma had already killed at least 540 Algerians. By June 8, the number of Muslim dead had grown to 642. That number, however, has been challenged by various sources. The police listed that number as 800 in Guelma and 15,000–20,000 in the region more generally. In general, the statistics of dead tell a very clear story: there were 102 Europeans killed, most of whom were in Sétif. The inability to produce a similarly accurate number of Algerian Muslims killed illustrates the ferocity of the massacre. Governor-General Yves Chataigneau used General Raymond Duval's 1945

---

[105] Ibid., 123, 128–133.   [106] Ibid., 135–136; Planche, *Sétif 1945*, 197, 203.
[107] Alleg, *The Algerian Memories*, 121–122.

estimate of 1,165 dead. The Allies estimated 6,000 dead and 14,000 hurt in the region in their report on May 24, 1945. The *New York Times* listed the number first at 7,000–8,000, later increasing it to 15,000–20,000. In 1948, Ferhat Abbas cited the latter number. In the end, eighty-nine militia were ultimately found guilty for the deaths of at least 636 Algerians, in what Peyroulou calls "politicide."[108]

Who constituted the militia and why did they engage in a massively violent repression of seemingly peaceful protests on a day of national celebration? Given the many proclamations of Muslim-Jewish coexistence, particularly in the Giraud period, how could Jews, especially prominent Jews such as Attali, participate in the militia's activities? This returns us to the issue of status anxieties. Peyroulou argues that following the Constantine pogrom in 1934, Jews in the region were perpetually fearful of Muslims and they chose Europeans over Muslims in 1945. In addition, he points to the shifting status of Jews in the colony and the relationship between Jewish and Muslim rights. The issue of rights was further conflated in 1943 and 1944, after Jews regained their rights as French citizens and Muslims demanded either inclusion or autonomy. Peyroulou writes that "a half century apart, the two issues go hand in hand." Peyroulou rightly points to the intractability of Muslim and Jewish rights in the colony. He even goes so far as to suggest that the violent use of the streets to suppress Muslims in 1945 was similar to that of 1898, when the antisemites attacked Jews in Algiers.[109]

Perhaps Jews participated in the militia in May 1945 in order to assert their Frenchness, so recently returned to them, and to seek out allies among the European population in putting down the threat posed to their status by Muslims. Reggui identified concerns over control of the municipality following Vichy as the unifying motivation between Europeans and Jews against the potential electoral power of the new Muslim citizens.[110] Once again, control over municipal government and status anxieties served to rationalize the violence and abuse of a perceived threat to local authority.

In the end, there was little repercussion or punishment for Achiary and his militia. Alleg asserts that "the powerful landowners wanted the riots and even helped to incite them, so that, after the bloodbath, they could regain control over a population that was becoming increasingly defiant."[111]

---

[108] Peyroulou, *Guelma 1945*, 164–173, 186, 198–199, 201; Peyroulou, "Preface," 8, 19. On the issue of statistics, see also Charles-Robert Ageron, "Mai 1945 en Algérie. Enjeu de mémoire et histoire," *Matériaux pour l'histoire de notre temps*, No. 39–40 (1995): 52–53.

[109] Peyroulou, *Guelma 1945*, 140.   [110] Reggui, *Les Massacres de Guelma*, 47.

[111] Alleg, *The Algerian Memories*, 122.

Achiary was arrested, tried, and released twice. Achiary left the Sub-Prefecture on March 23, 1946, and was not arrested until December 23, 1949. He was then tried for torture and for involvement in the death of Fernand Bonnier de la Chappelle, Darlan's assassin. At the time, few denounced his involvement or the work of the militia. In fact, one of the very few to denounce the Guelma massacres was Achiary's former fellow resistant, José Aboulker, who criticized Achiary and the violence in Guelma at the National Assembly on July 19, 1945. Even after Achiary's arrest in 1949, Aboulker continued to denounce his involvement in an article in *Alger Republicain*, entitled "À qui profite! Affaire Achiary," which appeared on February 16, 1950. Upon his release, Achiary remained involved with the Europeans of Algeria, organizing the protest against the new Governor-General Guy Mollet on the February 6, 1956 "day of tomatoes." Achiary promoted the *Organisation de la resistance de l'Algérie française* (ORAF), which placed the first bomb on the Rue de Thèbes in the Casbah of Algiers on August 10, 1956, and participated in the creation of the OAS in Madrid in February 1961.[112]

Reggui identified Achiary as the central culprit in the massacre that took the lives of his brothers and sister. Despite these deaths, Reggui believed in Algeria's future with France. In a section entitled "Will Algeria Live?," which paid homage to former governor-general Maurice Viollette's 1931 text, Reggui pondered the future of French Algeria. "It had never been a question for the Algerians whether to restrict the French presence in Algeria. They knew well why they needed France. But they believed legitimately, that they had the right, themselves, to direct the affairs of their country."[113]

Writing in 1946, Reggui looked to the future for colony, outlining a series of six recommendations to improve the "daily relations of French and Algerians." These suggestions included: the government needed to eliminate the concept of "disappeared" in the violence of Guelma and acknowledge its victims; Muslims needed to have their own inquiry; the government need to indemnify the victims of May 8 and their families; more schools had to be opened in Guelma; Muslims had to have "exactly the *same rights*" as Europeans, so that all could share in rights and responsibilities in the colony; and, finally, the government had to commit to combatting racism, and to treating the Muslims as equals.[114]

Reggui concluded that French colonial officials had to deal directly with the situation of Muslims in the colony or face the possibility of losing

---

[112] Peyroulou, *Guelma 1945*, 250, 301–303; Peyroulou, "Preface," 25.
[113] Reggui, *Les Massacres de Guelma*, 129.   [114] Ibid., 131–133.

control altogether. "If France wants to maintain her presence in Algeria, not by shots of the canon, but peacefully, she must audaciously address the people of Algeria and listen to their agents. It is in the name of hundreds of Algerians that we cry: FRANCE, BEWARE OF LOSING YOUR EMPIRE!"[115] That Achiary was not punished for the events in Guelma indicated the government's tacit approval of his actions. In fact, violent repression became the new policy in the colony. Maurice Papon, a man of Vichy, was appointed the deputy director of the Interior Ministry's Algeria Subdivision on October 1945. He embodied the colonial state's willingness to violently repress challenges to its authority in post–Sétif and Guelma Algeria.[116]

Although de Gaulle offered a small olive branch in the form of Muslim entry into the second Electoral College, which expanded their access to citizenship on October 5, 1946, it was not enough to slow the progress of Muslim nationalism in the colony. French officials worried about the fragility of the empire and the future of Algeria. For Algerian nationalists, the trauma of 1945 determined what would come in 1954.[117] From the "politicide," the unparalleled violent repression in the region, a new political consciousness was born. Many historians agree that the massacres of Sétif and Guelma started the next stage of modern Algerian history – that of armed revolution.[118]

Negotiating Identities: Zionism, Citizenship, and Nationalism

As Algerian nationalism developed, Algerian Jews endeavored not to bring too much attention to their community, especially after regaining their citizenship. They believed that they were still in a precarious position. In preparation for the 1944 meeting of the WJC, Algerian Jewish leaders debated whether it would be wise to send delegates. Some argued that participation in the Congress would feed the fires of antisemitism by giving the indication of the existence of a Jewish race working through international channels to promote the Jewish cause. Algerian Jews also remained divided on the issue of Zionism. Most Algerian Jews were against the creation of a Jewish state and did not want to participate in

[115] Ibid., 134.   [116] Thomas, "The Colonial Mind and Colonial Violence," 162, 165.
[117] Ageron, "Les troubles du nord-constantinois," 32, 38. See also Alain Ruscio, "Les communists et les massacres du Constantinois (Mai–Juin 1945)," *Vingtième Siècle. Revue d'histoire*, No. 94 (2007), 271, 220.
[118] Peyroulou, *Guelma 1945*, 228, 244, 329; McDougall, *History and the Culture of Nationalism*, 29; Jean-Pierre Peyroulou, "Les massacres du nord-Constantinois de 1945, un événement polymorphe," in Bouchène, Peyroulou, Tengour, Thénault, eds., *Histoire de l'Algérie*, 502.

the WJC, which would champion that cause.[119] Nonetheless, Algeria sent six delegates to the meeting of the WJC in Atlantic City in November 1944.[120]

For a few Algerian Jews, however, the experience of rupture under Vichy and Giraud proved too profound. They turned to Zionism as an alternative to continued devotion to a France that had betrayed them. One of the first postwar Zionist groups, the *Foyer Intellectuel Israélite*, developed in October 1943 in Oran. The *Foyer* organized conferences on Jewish issues, taught Hebrew, and celebrated the heroism of Jewish biblical figures.[121] In 1944, the *Foyer* leadership formally separated from consistory leaders, who opposed Zionism, and focused its efforts on a form of "militant" Judaism that emphasized Zionism.[122] The Algerian Zionist Federation, led by Benjamin Heler, urged Algerian Jews to support their cause in June 1944.[123] In September, Jews in Algiers organized the *Nouvelle Organisation Sioniste d'Algérie* (New Zionist Organization of Algeria, NOSA), which supported a Jewish state in Palestine and free immigration there.[124] Jews in Algiers also organized a *Fédération des Éclaireurs Juifs d'Algérie BETAR*, which focused on the physical and Zionist education of Jewish youth.[125]

Membership in Zionist organizations in Algeria remained limited. By 1945, government surveillance reports noted discussions regarding the possibility of the formation of a Jewish State in Palestine. Flyers in French and English appeared in the colony urging their support.[126] Most Zionist activity took place in Algiers, where the Algerian Zionist Federation had an office. There were also three Zionist youth organizations in Algiers: a Halutzim group that had 90 members between the ages

---

[119] Police of General Information, Oran, "No. 1740: Objet: A/S du congrès Mondial Juif de New York: Protestation formulé par l'Entr'aide Israélite d'Oran," Oran, March 4, 1944, CAOM Alg Oran2539.

[120] Resolutions, War Emergence Conference of the World Jewish Congress, Atlantic City, New Jersey, November 26–30, 1944, CDJC XC-3. The delegates included André Bakouche, Rabbi Maurice Eisenbeth, Benjamin Heler, Alfred Ghighi, Elie Gozlan, and Réné Roubache.

[121] Special Police of Oran to the Prefect of Oran, "No. 4898: Objet: Activité Sioniste–Foyer Intellectuel Israélite," Oran, October 20, 1943, CAOM Alg Oran 2539.

[122] "Exposé de la Situation crée par le F.I.J. Œuvre de Judaïsme militant à Oran," Oran, October 13, 1944, CAOM Alg Oran 424.

[123] Fédération Sioniste, Algérienne, "Appel de l'Organisation Sioniste au Peuple Juif," June 1944, CAOM Alg Oran 424.

[124] Nouvelle Organisation Sioniste d'Algérie, "No. 3409," Algiers, September 21, 1944, CAOM Alg Oran 424.

[125] "Statuts de la Fédération des Éclaireurs Juifs d'Algérie BETAR, LE BETAR," June 2, 1944, CAOM Alg Oran 5i/50.

[126] Gov-Gen of Algeria to the Minister of the Interior, "No. 5052/SG: Objet: Reprecussion en Algérie des événements d'Egypte et de Tripolitaine," Algiers, November 15, 1945, CAOM FM 81F/864.

of 15 and 18, a Betar group of 300 members, and 150 members belonging to the Éclaireurs de France, whose members engaged in the Jewish National Fund (JNF) work. A report by David Saltiel on Zionist activity in North Africa noted that "during the Vichy period there had been signs of a strong Zionist trend, especially among young people. Following the abolition of the anti-Jewish laws, and especially owing to the fact that all young men have been drafted into de Gaulle's army, the Zionist mood has practically evaporated."[127] Despite the surge in Zionist activity in the postwar period, most Algerian Jews did not support Zionism. Instead, most focused on the current situation on the ground in Algeria.

In the aftermath of the violence of May 1945, Jewish leaders feared that there would be more attacks on Europeans and, by extension, on Algerian Jews in the colony. To avoid tensions between their groups, Jewish and Muslim leaders urged cooperation and coexistence. In 1946, the *Comité Régional d'Union Sémite* in Algiers encouraged unity among Semites in Algeria through cultural, economic, and communal activities. They endeavored to work together to battle racism and gain rights as citizens for all Semites. The contentious issue of Palestine, which they considered central to friction between Semitic brothers, could be easily resolved by allowing all religious groups to rule themselves. They resolved that Jerusalem would remain a religious and free city, available to all, and independent. With Palestine as a democracy, divisions between Jews and Muslims in Algeria could be mended.[128]

This effort at cooperation was ultimately inadequate in the face of growing tensions between Jews and Muslims in Algeria. The PPA intensified its demands for independence. The March 7, 1946, ordinance established a new category of Algerian Muslims, known as "Muslim French from Algeria," who were given full political rights and were allowed to maintain their local civil status. The number of the new "Muslim French" consisted of 65,000 elite men. The law of May 7, 1946, and article 80 of the Constitution of the Fourth Republic made all other Algerians with local civil status French citizens. This was part of the broader project of transitioning "overseas France" into the "French Union." The October 1946 Constitution of the Fourth Republic established French Union citizenship.[129] These changes were universally rejected by nationalist and Islamic groups, as well as groups of Europeans in Algeria. The law

---

[127] David Saltiel, "Report on the Position of Jews in North Africa," London, November 24, 1944, CZA Z4/30703 (Politics. Correspondence on situation of Jews in North Africa and immigration to Palestine).

[128] A. Hedef, Principal Commissioner of the Police of Oran, General Surveillance, "Rapport No. 6332," Oran, September 19, 1946, CAOM Alg Oran 424.

[129] See especially Cooper, *Citizenship between Empire and Nation*.

of September 20, 1947, declared the departments of Algeria and the Southern Territories of the Sahara their own particular form of departments. However, M'Zabi Jews still did not have French citizenship. On March 26, 1948, 125 heads of Jewish families in Ghardaïa wrote to the governor-general of Algeria to demand French naturalization.[130]

Even as Jewish and Muslim rights in Algeria reached a level of equality, coexistence between the two groups, and with the European population, did not accompany these developments. In March 1947, a wave of arsons destroyed synagogues in Algeria. The North African Surveillance Department reported that the alleged guilty party, the PPA, might not actually be responsible. Rather, the report suggested that certain "French colonialists" were behind the arsons, but framed the PPA in order to foment clashes between Jews and Muslims and to discredit the developing independence movement.[131] It is not clear who was actually responsible for the violence; however, it is clear that the Europeans had the greatest status anxieties as a result of the developments regarding Jewish and Muslims rights in the colony.

Antisemitism intensified after the announcement of the United Nations' General Assembly Resolution 181, better known as the Partition Plan, on November 29, 1947. This plan recommended the partition of British-Mandate Palestine into a Jewish State and an Arab State. Just over a week after the Resolution passed, the governor-general of Algeria commented on the situation of Zionist activity and antisemitism in the colony. Antisemitic activity flourished at the time because Moroccan and Tunisian Jews were not allowed to depart for Palestine and traveled instead to Algeria in order to emigrate, thus increasing the numbers of Jews in Algeria. The governor-general also noted his concern that foreign agents might cause conflicts between Jews and Muslims. He was especially concerned that anti-Jewish agitation in the streets would lead to violence.[132]

---

[130] Shepard, *The Invention of Decolonization*, 39–41. See Frederick Cooper, *Decolonization and African Society: The labor question in French and British Africa* (Cambridge: Cambridge University Press, 1996). See also Cooper, *Citizenship between Empire and Nation*, 30–32. The 1947 decree created an even more complicated position for the M'Zabi Jews of the Southern Territories, who were still viewed as more "indigenous" or "Muslim" than Jewish, and still very different from their northern coreligionists. See Stein, *Saharan Jews and the Fate of French Algeria*, 103. Jews of M'Zab represented by Rabbi Jacob Ben Meyer Partouche, Vice President of the Consistory of Ghardaïa to the Gov-Gen of Algeria, "Objet: Demande de naturalization française," Ghardaïa, March 26, 1948, CZA C10/337 (The Algerian Division–Jacques Lazarus).

[131] General Surveillance Department, North Africa Section, "Objet: Commentaires nord africains au sujet des recents incendires de synagogues en Algérie," March 26, 1947, CAOM FM 81F/864.

[132] Gov-Gen of Algeria to the Ministry of the Interior, "No. 2013/ADC A/S des mouvements antisémites en Algérie," Algiers, December 8, 1947, CAOM FM 81F/864.

The Governor-General and the Minister of the Interior, as well as the other administrators who weighed in on the issue of Zionism, were aware of the growing significance of Palestine. The Minister of the Interior was similarly concerned with the developments of the two-state solution and its echoes in Algeria, especially as the PPA intensified its demands. The minister believed that the emigration of Jews from Algeria could not continue without repercussions. The minister hoped to avoid provoking antisemitism and proposed to require Zionist leaders to organize departures from other ports, including those in the metropole.[133]

When Israel became a state on May 14, 1948, the already fraught relations between Jews and Muslims in the colony increased. In April 1948, Benjamin Heler of the Zionist Union of Algiers wrote to Judge Levinthal, the president of the Zionist Federation of the United States, to request that representatives be sent to Algiers.[134] The *Comité Juif Algérien des Études Sociales* (CJAES)-sponsored Jewish monthly *Information Juive* covered the situation in Israel and Zionist activities in Algeria, as well as Morocco and Tunisia. The CJAES was not a Zionist organization; however, the attention paid to the issues in Israel on the pages of *Information Juive* reflects the fact that Algerian Jews continued to be interested in the situation there.[135]

Although few Algerian Jews were actually Zionists and even fewer had any intention of moving to the new country, many Algerian Jews were accused of Zionist proclivities. Algerian nationalists sided with Palestinians, especially after the violence of Deir Yassin on April 9, 1948. As a result, tensions between Jews and Muslims in the colony escalated.[136] These developments set the stage for the hardening of political positions that would be drawn during the Algerian War and further exacerbated by wider decolonization in the 1950s. The 1950s witnessed enormous changes for the French empire. Even before the collapse of the Fourth Republic in 1958 and the return of Charles de

---

[133] Minister of the Interior, "Objet: Mouvement antisémite en Algérie," Paris, December 22, 1947, CAOM FM 81F/864.

[134] Benjamin Heler, Zionist Union of Algiers, to Judge Levinthal, President of the Zionist Federation of the US, Algiers, April 9, 1948, CZA Z4\30703.

[135] Jacques Lazarus, "Theodore Herzl, nôtre guide," *Information Juive*, No. 57 (July 1954): 5 and "Les conditions d'immigration pour Israël," *Information Juive*, No. 58 (July 1955): 3, YIVO.

[136] The massacre at Deir Yassin played a pivotal role in later Israel–Palestine relations. It occurred before Israel became a state, and involved Israeli forces entering the Palestinian Arab village in order to circumvent an Arab blockade on Jerusalem. Upward of 200 villagers were killed in the violence and it became a lightning rod in the Arab world. Michael Brenner, *Zionism: A Brief History* (Princeton: Markus Weiner, 2003), 159–160. See also Benny Morris, *1948: The First Arab-Israeli War* (New Haven: Yale University Press, 2008), 125–128.

Gaulle to power as president of the Fifth Republic, colonial independence movements unsettled the empire. The French reeled following their defeat at the Battle of Dien Bien Phu that raged from March to May 1954, culminating in the Geneva Accords, which led to the French withdrawal from Indochina. This was a major defeat for the French, which emboldened the already thriving nationalist movements throughout the empire, particularly the PPA in Algeria. It was the beginning of the end for France's empire.

The Algerian War: Increasing Conflict and Jewish Attempts at Neutrality

At the start of the Algerian War in 1954, the Jewish community had healed, to some degree, from the rupture they experienced under Vichy. The beginning of the clashes between the French and Algerian Muslims would bring about new debates as to their identities, and whether they were more French than Algerian or vice versa. The debates would question the hybrid nature of their identities and ultimately force them to choose between them. By 1954, the Algerian Jewish leadership argued that Algerian Jews were no longer just the beneficiaries of the Crémieux Decree, but that they were French based on *jus sanguinis* or by paternity. In many ways, they were peripheral to the two central groups involved in the war: they were not Algerian enough for the Algerians or French enough for the French. They were among the French of Algeria, but not considered true Frenchmen. Both the Algerian Front de Libération Nationale (FLN) and the French Organisation de l'Armée Secrète (OAS) inherited and used earlier antisemitic tropes in order to emphasize Algerian Jews' otherness in the conflict. Upon leaving Algeria at the end of the war, Jews would discover the degree to which they were not considered French by the metropolitan French.[137]

In 1954, the Jewish population in Algeria consisted of approximately 126,000 people, or 12 percent of the population classified as "European" in the colony. At that time, the majority of Jews lived in urban areas and made up 10 percent of the population of Oran and Constantine and about 5 percent of the population in Algiers. Many Jews were middle class, employed as artisans, in various trades and professions, and some served in the administration or municipal governments.[138] Approximately 3,000 Algerian Jews worked within the public sector and 4,000 worked in

---

[137] Shepard, *The Invention of Decolonization*, 171, 181.
[138] Richard Ayoun, "Les Juifs d'Algérie pendant la guerre d'indépendance (1954–1962)," *Archives Juives*, Vol. 29, No. 1 (1996): 18.

medicine, law, dentistry, or held government office. These careers reflect the important transformations of the Jewish community of Algeria under the French. These Jews were French-educated, urban, assimilated, and belonged to a variety of political parties, putting an end to the antisemitic accusation that Jews followed blindly the orders of their religious leaders.[139]

These varying political affiliations led to conflicted responses by the Jewish community when the FLN launched their armed revolts against France and issued their proclamation demanding a sovereign Algerian state on October 31–November 1, 1954. That day, bomb blasts ripped through Algiers, killing eight people and wounding four more. Thus began the war.[140] The FLN and its military arm, the National Liberation Army (Armée de la Libération Nationale, ALN), claimed responsibility. The proclamation demanded complete independence and declared that it was ready to use all necessary means, including terrorism, to achieve its goals. The FLN announced that the "National Movement" had arrived at its final phase.[141] The FLN proclamation emphasized the mistreatment of Algerian Muslims by the French, the necessity of "restoring the Algerian state" through armed battle, and bringing the suffering of the Algerian to the attention of the world. Interior Minister François Mitterrand's response on November 5, 1954, stated that the only solution to the problems laid out by the Algerian leadership was war.[142]

Following the FLN's proclamation, the CJAES reorganized in order to represent the voice of Algerian Jews in the developing conflict. However, Algerian Jews did not have a unanimous opinion on the matter. In 1954, Information Juive covered the commemoration held in Algiers on May 9 for the sixth anniversary of the creation of the State of Israel. At the commemoration, attended by more than 1,000 people, Zionist leader Benjamin Heler connected the anniversary of Israeli independence to the revolt of the Warsaw ghetto as well as the end of the "heroic resistance of Dien Bien Phu."[143] That Heler described the anti-imperial resistance as brave illustrates the diversity of political opinions among Algerian Jews as the onset of the Algerian War. As in the early days of Vichy, the CJAES leadership recommended prudence and calm among its constituents.

---

[139] Sung Choi, "Complex Compatriots: Jews in post-Vichy French Algeria," The Journal of North African Studies, Vol. 17, No. 5 (2012): 865.

[140] Shepard, The Invention of Decolonization, 43.

[141] "La Première Proclamation du FLN," October 31, 1945, reproduced in Mohammed Harbi, Gilbert Meynier, Le FLN: Documents et Histoire, 1954–1962 (Paris: Librairie Arthème Fayard, 2004), 36–37.

[142] Ayoun, "Les juifs d'Algérie," 16.

[143] Information Juive, No. 44, May 1944, 3, YIVO.

A meeting of Jewish leaders, organized by André Narboni, reached the conclusion that Jews and Jewish organizations should take all measures possible to avoid taking sides, but remain faithful to their obligations as French citizens.[144] That orientation continued into 1955 as well.

As the conflict deepened, Algerian Jews were thrust into a challenging and emotionally difficult situation. In spite of the recent memory of Vichy, for many Algerian Jews, especially the younger, more assimilated generations, French citizenship was a source of pride and the foundation of their identities. Older generations, however, maintained stronger ties to their Muslim neighbors, remembering a time of sustained coexistence and commonality in a shared past, language, and way of life.[145] Choosing between France and Algeria would be choosing between two inextricable parts of their identity. It would, however, be a choice they eventually had to make.

The Prefect of Constantine noted in his report to the governor-general on February 14, 1955, that the general spirit of Muslims was highly excitable and could deteriorate into violence very quickly.[146] Although Algerian Jews hoped to remain outside of the conflict between France and the FLN, over the course of 1955 the violence hit close to home. In July 1955, FLN members attacked the rabbi of Batna. Alongside the violence that killed more than 120 Europeans in Philippeville in August 1955 and led to retaliation killings of over 1,200 Muslims, a Jewish family was among the victims.[147] This was a part of the wider trend of ALN fighters (*moudjahidine*) and those whom the French authorities termed bandits (*fellaghas*) and outlaws (*hors-la-loi*) who attacked inhabitants of "colonial centers."[148] In the October 1955 edition of *Information Juive*, the head rabbi of Algeria offered a message for Yom Kippur. "This year has been sad for all those who live in Algeria, the blood has flowed, and the calm has not yet returned."[149] It was among the very first mentions of the conflict in the Jewish monthly. Further fanning the

---

[144] Benjamin Stora, *La guerre d'Algérie expliquée à tous* (Paris: Éditions du Seuil, 2012), 33. See also Shepard, *The Invention of Decolonization*, 171. The Jewish community in Algeria was not unanimous in its opinions regarding the developing conflict.

[145] Ayoun, "Les juifs d'Algérie," 17. Joëlle Bahloul charted the experience of her Jewish family living alongside Muslims in Sétif. She states that in Sétif many houses were shared between Jews and Muslims. Bahloul, *The Architecture of Memory*, 14–15.

[146] Prefect of Constantine to the Gov-Gen, "Report," February 14, 1955, SHAT 1H1944, reproduced in Harbi, Meynier, *Le FLN*, 167.

[147] Ayoun, "Les Juifs d'Algérie," 24–25. See also Clement Henry Moore, "The Maghrib," in *The Cambridge History of Africa Volume 8: From c. 1940 to c. 1975*, ed. Michael Crowder (Cambridge: Cambridge University Press, 1984), 579–580.

[148] Shepard, *The Invention of Decolonization*, 43.

[149] "Message de kippour de Monsieur le grand rabbin d'Algérie," *Information Juive*, No. 71 (October 1955): 4, YIVO.

flames of the Algerian revolution was the independence of Morocco on March 2, 1956, and that of Tunisia on March 20, 1956. Algerian nationalist leaders were inspired by such successes and aligned their revolution with that of the broader revolution of North Africa.[150]

Internal divisions within the FLN and the various factions associated with it and the lack of a cohesive policy for the group led to a congress held in the Soummam Valley in August 1956. There, sixteen delegates reorganized the FLN, creating the *Comité de Coordination et d'Éxecution* (CCE), the core leadership committee, and the *Conseil Nationale de la Révolution Algérienne* (CNRA), a parliamentary group overseeing the direction of the revolution that included thirty-four elected delegates. The Soummam platform emphasized the centrality of Algerian independence and refused any cease-fire before that goal had been achieved. It also planned to expand strikes directed at European civilians. In addition, it called for an independent Algeria in its current borders, including the Sahara, and that the European population of the colony would not be offered the possibility of dual-citizenship. This congress also produced literature on the goals of the revolution and issued appeals to non-Muslim groups in the colony, including Algerian Jews.[151]

The Soummam declaration outlined the political position of Algerian Jews in the future independent Algeria. The delegates sent letters to Chief Rabbi Eisenbeth of Algiers, consistory members, as well as elected officials and leaders of the Jewish community. In these letters, the FLN leadership affirmed the Jewish community's place in the future Algerian nation. After detailing the mistreatment of Algerian Jews in World War II, it emphasized Muslim support and tolerance for Jews. While under Vichy Jews were treated as worse than "animals," their future in Algeria would be one of acceptance.[152] By emphasizing the rupture of the Vichy era, the leaders of the Algerian revolution sought to remind Algerian Jews that France had abandoned them and could certainly do so again in the future. The declaration argued that FLN leaders stopped tensions from developing in recent years between Jews and Muslims in the colony, claiming responsibility for the lack of violence in response to the Arab–Israeli conflict. The tolerance offered by the Algerian Muslim leadership was contrasted with the long history of racism and antisemitism of the Europeans in the colony: "the disappearance of the colonial regime, which availed itself of the Jewish minority as a buffer to mitigate the anti-

---

[150] Harbi, Meynier, *Le FLN*, 36.

[151] Alistair Horne, *A Savage War of Peace, 1954–1962* (New York: The New York Review of Books, 2006), 143–145. See also Harbi, Meynier, *Le FLN*, 18, 247; Shepard, *The Invention of Decolonization*, 43–44.

[152] Friedman, *Colonialism and After*, 93–94. See also Ayoun, "Les Juifs d'Algérie," 22.

imperialist shocks, does not necessarily mean it will be pauperized."[153] The Soummam Congress platform promised Algerian Jews a place and economic security within the new independent country.

The Jewish leadership in Algeria hesitated before responding to the appeal of the Soummam Congress. Although the appeal encouraged Jewish support for the FLN, Jews were skeptical of the FLN's claims. Despite periods of Jewish–Muslim coexistence in the colony, Jews still remembered violent encounters with Muslims, including the 1934 Constantine pogrom. The threat of future Muslim antisemitism, especially as the situation with Israel and her neighbors worsened, made Jews hesitant to join the FLN. The consistory leadership remained silent, because they were primarily responsible for Jews' spiritual and religious interests and abstained from remarking on political issues. In the August–September 1956 edition of *Information Juive*, the front page featured wishes for the Jewish new year. "At the moment at which drama distresses Algeria, we are affected, like the other communities, but perhaps even more profoundly in our own. This is why, even as grave as the situation is, no one here wants to despair ... it is with hope that we turn towards He who presides over the destinies of all."[154] This statement reflects the complex situation of the Jews of Algeria as they attempted to navigate the increasing tensions and violence between Algerian nationalists and European and French forces. In abstaining from politics, Algerian Jewish leaders called upon God to guide them.

After nearly three months, at the end of November 1956, the CJAES published its response in its monthly newsletter, *Information Juive*. Like the consistorial leadership, the CJAES emphasized the fact that the Jewish community was extremely diverse religiously, culturally, and politically, and therefore no one body or person could speak on its behalf. Due to the divergent political opinions within the Jewish community, the CJAES could only promote the basic hope of Algerian Jews as a whole for a peaceful resolution to the increasing violence and a respect for all human rights, which it described as a core value of Judaism. Furthermore, the CJAES argued that as a persecuted people, the Jews of Algeria could only encourage respect for all groups involved in the conflict and asserted their allegiance to both France and Algeria. "The Jews, having lived in this country for more than two thousand years, deeply grateful to France, to which they owe so much," only hope

---

[153] "The Question of the Jewish Minority in the FLN platform of the Soummam Congress, August 1956" reproduced Norman A. Stillman, *Jews of Arab Lands in Modern Times* (Philadelphia: Jewish Publication Society, 2003), 537–539. See also Katz, *Jews and Muslims in the Shadow of Marianne*, 257–260.

[154] "Algérie 5717," *Information Juive*, No. 80 (August–September 1956): 1, YIVO.

to continue to live peacefully beside the "two other religious communities, Muslims and Christians. Their firm hope is to continue to live in close friendship with both." The CJAES authors highlighted their support of Muslim rights in the colony and once again offered their commitment to maintain Jewish–Muslim harmony in Algeria.[155] The CJAES leaders understood that Algerian Jews were in a significantly precarious position and did not want to risk alienating any potential allies.

The Jewish leaders were particularly interested in remaining on the periphery of the conflict as violence intensified between French and Algerian forces in 1956 and 1957. In those years, the *Armée de la Libération Nationale* (ALN), the armed wing of the FLN, stepped up its campaign against French forces. In addition, FLN members targeted urban areas in their efforts to take control of major cities, such as Algiers.[156] As the FLN, and primarily the ALN, intensified their campaigns, the colonists also responded with their frustration at the lack of appropriate repercussions for the FLN. On February 1, 1955, Guy Mollet became prime minister and General Georges Catroux was appointed minister resident in Algeria. Former governor-general Jacques Soustelle's departure was met with protests by the Europeans of the colony, particularly the right-wing groups. Upon Mollet's visit to Algiers on February 6, right-wing Europeans, led by André Achiary, protested against his neutral approach to the situation in Algeria by throwing tomatoes and other items at the new prime minister. The protest became known as "the day of tomatoes," and in its aftermath Mollet transitioned from neutrality to seeking peace in Algeria.[157] Mollet realized that the situation in Algeria was direr than he had realized and hoped to avoid an all-out war, especially as he dealt with a series of other conflicts involving France.

The years 1956 and 1957 were among the most intense in the Algerian War, particularly in Algiers. At the same time, the conflicts between the French army and the FLN intensified in Algeria. The repression by the French army drove more Algerians into the guerrilla forces of the ALN. On November 15, 1956, Mollet appointed General Raoul Salan, a veteran of Indochina and an expert on subversive warfare, to improve the French response to the guerrilla warfare. His appointment signaled the new extreme phase of the war. Mollet unveiled a declaration in late December, later published on January 9, 1957, which outlined France's stance on the issue of Algeria. The declaration backed the

---

[155] Stora, *Les Trois Exils*, 213–215.
[156] Benjamin Stora, *Algeria, 1830–2000: A Short History* (Ithaca: Cornell University Press, 2005), 62–63.
[157] Stora, *Algeria, 1830–2000*, 45–46; Reggui, *Les massacres de Guelma*, 25.

French army's activities in Algeria, and specifically in Algiers, but also emphasized that Algeria's future would inevitably involve France and that his government's goal was to bring reconciliation. The beginning of 1957 witnessed the intensification of the "Battle of Algiers," which began on September 30, 1956, when three FLN female militants carried out a series of bomb attacks on European civilian targets in Algiers. On January 7, 1957, 8,000 paratroopers arrived in Algiers to police the area. On January 9 and 10, two explosions rocked the city. The violence reached a crescendo on January 26 when two additional explosions occurred in a bar and a café in the center of the city. A European mob lynched two Muslims in retaliation, and on January 28, the FLN leadership ordered an eight-day strike. Bombings and attacks continued into the summer, eventually slowing in late September 1957 as a result of the brutal tactics and torture used by the French.[158]

Mollet's government was plagued by several conflicts: the ongoing conflict in Algeria and the Suez-Sinai campaign in October and November 1956, which brought France and Israel into collaboration and resulted in a major United Nations controversy. The military and intelligence cooperation between France and Israel emerged in part because of Egypt's endorsement of the FLN. In exchange for tanks and fighter planes, the French demanded that Israel help to counteract FLN activity, especially its international campaigns.[159] Starting in 1955, the Mossad created a special force that operated in North Africa, known as *Misgeret*, or framework. *Misgeret* worked throughout Morocco, Algeria, and Tunisia, organizing emigration of Moroccan and Tunisian Jews, and developing Algerian Jewish self-defense groups. In the department of Constantine, there were approximately one hundred Algerian Jewish members, led by unit commanders who received training in France or Israel, many of whom were French reservists. The *Misgeret* established weapons caches in the colony and unit commanders had access to the Israeli leadership. As the FLN violence increased from 1956 until the end of 1961, the *Misgeret* worked with Algerian Jews in order to neutralize the threat posed by the FLN to the Jewish community.[160] In 1958, David Ben Gurion, Israel's first prime minister, stated that the French should not trust Algerian Arabs, regardless of how "assimilated" they had become.

---

[158] Martin Evans, *Algeria: France's Undeclared War* (Oxford: Oxford University Press, 2011), 192. See also Stora, *Algeria, 1830–2000*, 48–50. See also Horne, *Savage War of Peace*, 184.

[159] Michael M. Laskier, "Israel and Algeria amid French Colonialism and the Arab-Israeli Conflict, 1954–1978," *Israel Studies*, Vol. 6, No. 2 (2001): 1–2.

[160] Laskier, "Israel and Algeria," 2. See also Choi, "Complex Compatriots," 873–874. Katz writes of how the situation in Israel complicated relationships between Jews and Muslims in Algeria. Katz, *Jews and Muslims in the Shadow of Marianne*, 285–286.

This comment further tied Israel's struggles with her Arab neighbors to that of France and the Algerian nationalists.[161]

Self-defense became increasingly necessary for the Jewish community. In 1957, the FLN killed the head rabbi of Médéa, Jacob Chekroun. In April 1957, *Information Juive* reported that "over the course of the last months, many of our coreligionists, in effect, have been the victims of attacks on this community." The article continued that the deaths of Jews in Médéa were especially tragic, because Jewish–Muslim relations had been strong there, even "quasi-familial." The author noted several other Jewish victims: Daoud Elbaz, who had been killed while driving his bus, and Réné Obadia, who was killed while driving his car, among others.[162] The August–September edition of *Information Juive* included a short report entitled "Attacks." The article included details regarding the deaths of David Chiche in Algiers and Mardochée Dayan, who was the president of the Consistory of Palikao. It also listed several victims in Bône.[163] These reports, often buried in the middle of the monthly, reflected the continued attempts of the Jewish community to remain outside the conflict, but that the realities of the violence were hitting very close to home, especially as Jewish leaders became targets.

In 1957, a young man who fought in the 1948 Israeli war of independence helped Batna Jews establish a self-defense group alongside the *Misgeret*. In the case of the Batna group, its members were anti-Organisation de l'Armée Secrète (OAS) and its antecedents, but in favor of Algeria remaining French. The OAS was the French group of militants who fought to keep Algeria French. They mobilized in the streets and tried to take control of cities in order to thwart FLN/ALN activities, chanting *Algérie française*. The OAS was organized in Madrid in January 1961 by Raoul Salan and others, including André Achiary. Some members were described as fascists and many were antisemitic.[164]

Jews were generally opposed to the OAS in part because the organization echoed the early antisemitism of the *néos*. They also avoided the organization because they wanted to remain neutral in the French-Algerian conflict. Some of the self-defense groups eventually worked alongside the OAS after 1961.[165] Israel's association with France further influenced Algerian Jews' allegiance. Most were in favor of Algeria remaining under France's control. The efficacy and impact of the *Misgeret*'s development of networks of self-defense groups among

[161] Shepard, *The Invention of Decolonization*, 176.
[162] *Information Juive*, No. 87 (April 1957): 5, YIVO.
[163] "Attentats," *Information Juive*, No. 90 (August–September 1957): 4, YIVO.
[164] Shepard, *The Invention of Decolonization*, 86, 89; Reggui, *Les massacres de Guelma*, 25.
[165] Friedman, *Colonialism and After*, 95–96.

Algerian Jews remain unclear. In their appeal to Algerian Jews, the FLN suggested that they were responsible for protecting Jews, whereas the *Misgeret* took credit for defending Jews in Algeria. In some ways, the Israeli organization inserted a wedge between Algerian Jews and Muslims.

Although the *Misgeret* worked with some Algerian Jews to combat the FLN, a small number of Jews actually worked with the FLN. Some Jews who joined the FLN were members of the Algerian Communist party. Rumors circulated about Jewish involvement with the FLN, including that Jewish doctors treated wounded FLN guerillas and that Jews gave money or goods to the FLN. Few Algerian Jews admitted to such activity after the war. Those Jews who joined the FLN often cited their experiences in Algeria following the Allied landings and the re-abrogation of the Crémieux Decree by Giraud as a key motivation. For those Jews, the rupture of Vichy was irreparable and a Muslim Algeria was more appealing than a French future.[166]

That was the case for Daniel Timsit, a young Algerian Jew and FLN member. Timsit and his parents experienced both European and Muslim antisemitism. His father grew up in the era of Edouard Drumont and Max Régis and developed a distrust of the Europeans in the colony as a result. His mother survived the 1934 Constantine pogrom, and raised her children with a fear of Arabs. The deciding factor for Timsit was the Vichy era, during which he saw his father, a veteran of World War I, cry at the announcement of the armistice in 1940. Timsit and his brothers were excluded from their schools as a result of the quotas put into place by Vichy. At his new school, run by the Jewish community, the children of well-off Muslim families also attended. There Timsit befriended Taleb Ibrahimi, the son of Cheikh Ibrahimi, who became the future Algerian minister of foreign affairs. Through his friendship with Ibrahimi, Timsit became involved in the FLN.[167] In the history of the Algerian War of Independence, Timsit's case was fairly unique, but reflects the diversity among the Jews of Algeria. While many remained neutral, some Jews supported the OAS and others the FLN. Violence against Jews also continued in 1958. Two members of the Jewish Agency in Algeria, Jacob Hassan and Raphael Ben Guera, were killed, and a grenade was thrown into the synagogue of Boghari.[168] Jewish attempts to remain outside the violence were failing.

---

[166] Ibid., 96–97. See also Ayoun, "Les juifs d'Algérie," 23.
[167] Jean Laloum, "Portrait d'un Juif du FLN," *Archives Juives*, Vol 29, No. 1 (1996): 65–66.
[168] *Information Juive*, No. 100, August–September 1958, 3; *Information Juive*, No. 101 (October 1958): 3, YIVO.

The Changing Tide of War: De Gaulle and the Beginning of the End

On April 26, 1958, with the Fourth Republic on the verge of collapse, several thousand European demonstrators marched on Algiers to demand a new government. The day before, General Salan announced that the army sought the total destruction of the FLN's fighters. In May, Salan took control of the "Committee of Public Safety," which had as its primary goal the return of General de Gaulle to power. On May 15, 1958, de Gaulle announced that he was prepared to take control of the Republic again. From June 4 to 7, de Gaulle visited Algeria, where he declared that "I have understood you" and "Long live French Algeria." On December 21, 1958, de Gaulle was elected president of the Fifth Republic.[169] The 1958 Constitution of the Fifth Republic reaffirmed the laws of 1944, giving all Algerians who had "local civil status" full citizenship and extended enfranchisement to women. Articles 3 and 75 emphasized that the French Republic still included Algeria.[170]

On September 16, 1959, de Gaulle televised a speech in which he announced that after analyzing the situation in Algeria, he believed that self-determination was the only resolution to the conflict. Self-determination offered three choices: first, secession and partition; second, Algeria could remain in the French community; and, finally, a government of Algerians to lead a new country, but supported by French aid and a continued relationship between France and Algeria in terms of the economy, defense, and foreign relations. Historian Todd Shepard argues that de Gaulle's announcement reflected the "invention" of the meanings of decolonization as de Gaulle located the shift in historical determinism. Ultimately, for de Gaulle, Algerians and Algeria could never be truly French and therefore had to be let go. The speech signaled a major change in the tide of the war in that it made it appear that there would be open negotiations with the FLN and the opportunity for Muslim Algerians to determine their own future.[171]

Although a major step toward peace, Algerian self-determination caused great concern among Algerian Jews, whose current hybrid identities in Algeria would be untenable. They realized that very soon they would be faced with a choice between Algeria and France. In November 1959, the CJAES met to determine a collective Jewish position on the future of Algeria. They debated how to deal with the

---

[169] Stora, *Algeria, 1830–2000*, 70–73.
[170] Shepard, *The Invention of Decolonization*, 45–46.
[171] Choi, "Complex Compatriots," 871; Shepard, *The Invention of Decolonization*, 75–77. Stora, *Algeria, 1830–2000*, 74–76.

FLN, but focused their deliberations on whether Jews would be able to retain their French citizenship. Their primary concern was with retaining their French identities, even if that meant abandoning their ancestral home. France would ultimately determine their future on the basis of their French status.[172]

On December 1, 1959, the FLN published a brochure aimed at Jews in the colony entitled "Documents addressed to the French people, the Jews of Algeria in combat for national independence." Addressing the "Jewish Algerians," the FLN depicted their primary goal as establishing a democracy in Algeria that would grant equality to all its citizens, without discrimination. The FLN denigrated the French colonial enterprise and its discriminatory practices. "The colonialist policy, always racist, occasionally antisemitic, compelled to 'justify' in the eyes of the world the unjustifiable war it is waging against the Algerian people, dares to pretend that today in refusing us our most sacred rights, it is defending yours." It continued its appeal to Algerian Jews by identifying them as fellow Algerians. "You are an integral part of the Algerian people. It is not a question for you of choosing between France and Algeria, but of becoming effective citizens of your true country." The publication emphasized the inextricable nature of Jewish and Muslim rights, criticizing the French colonial administration's antisemitic and racist treatment of them. It appealed to the average Jew, not the leaders of the community who remained at least superficially neutral.[173] In the February 1960 edition of *Information Juive*, Jacques Lazarus published "Algerian Realities." In the article, he explained the journal's effort to avoid politics in its articles. "Since the beginning, in this journal we have made it a rule to avoid all polemics on politics ... The Jewish community of Algeria is not a political entity." This had been the mantra of the CJAES throughout the conflict. Sensing the emerging reality of change, Lazarus repeated the party line, but also emphasized Jews' French patriotism.[174]

After 1960, Algerian independence emerged as a real possibility and maintaining Jewish intermediaries became less important. As the FLN began negotiations with France in late June 1960, a new phase in the war began. Algerian Jews slowly accepted the fact that most of their coreligionists would choose France when the time came.[175] Beginning on the eve of Yom Kippur in 1959, violence against the Jewish community intensified

[172] Choi, "Complex Compatriots," 872–873.

[173] "An Appeal by the FLN for the Support of Algerian Jewry," November 25, 1959, reproduced in Stillman, *Jews of Arab Lands in Modern Times*, 540–541.

[174] Jacques Lazarus, "Réalités algériennes," *Information Juive*, No. 116 (February 1960): 1, YIVO.

[175] Ayoun, "Les juifs d'Algérie," 21–23; Stora, *Algeria, 1830–2000*, 78.

after 1960. That evening someone threw a grenade into the synagogue of Bou Saada, killing the 6-year-old granddaughter of the rabbi and injuring several others. In December 1960, de Gaulle's visit to Algeria resulted in riots by Europeans in the colony, as well as a major uprising of Algerian Muslims, who shouted "Muslim Algeria!" and "Long Live the FLN." On December 12, 1960, in the midst of the nationalist celebrations, rioters attacked and desecrated the Great Synagogue of the Algiers, destroying a Torah scroll that had been brought to Algeria by Jews leaving Spain in 1391. The rioters raised the Algerian nationalist flag in the synagogue and scrawled "death to the Jews" and a swastika on the walls.[176] In this increasingly dangerous climate, some Algerian Jews began leaving Algeria. In Constantine in 1960, police noted that Jews were leaving without the intention of returning. From January 1961 on, the Jewish Agency was active in encouraging and facilitating Algerian Jewish emigration to Israel. The Jewish Agency's activities led to a diplomatic kerfuffle when the Minister of State for Algerian Affairs refused visas for ten delegates of the Jewish Agency. Israeli prime minister Golda Meir demanded an explanation from the French ambassador in Tel Aviv.[177]

In the aftermath of growing violence against Jews, the war developed another dimension: an internal French conflict between those who supported Algeria's self-determination, de Gaulle among them, and those who rejected the idea of an independent Algeria. On January 8, 1961, de Gaulle's self-determination-based Algerian policy came to a referendum vote. It passed by a majority. Those Frenchmen who refused to accept the capitulation by the French government also began to make plans. Among them, General Salan made contacts with other Europeans in the colony to establish the OAS, which would operate outside the French army in order to combat the FLN. After de Gaulle formally announced decolonization as the resolution to the Algerian war, a group of generals who opposed this decision, including Generals Challe, Jouhaud, Zeller, and Salan, attempted a coup d'état on April 21, 1961. By April 26, the generals acknowledged the failure of their putsch, but their actions had paved the way for the OAS to intensify its activities in Algeria. Among the OAS's primary goals was organizing popular protests in September 1961, and to ultimately break up the Evian negotiations, which began on May 20, 1961.[178]

---

[176] Ayoun, "Les juifs d'Algérie, 25; Evans, *Algeria: France's Undeclared War*, 322–323; Phillip C. Naylor, *France and Algeria: A History of Decolonization and Transformation* (Gainesville: University Press of Florida, 1990), 44. See also Stora, *Algeria, 1830–2000*, 79.

[177] Shepard, *The Invention of Decolonization*, 174–175.

[178] Stora, *Algeria, 1830–2000*, 80–82. For more on the role of policing during the era of Algerian nationalism, see Roger le Doussal, *Commissaire de police en Algérie (1952–1962): Une grenouille dans son puits ne voit qu'un coin du ciel* (Millau: Riveneuve éditions, 2011).

In the spring of 1961, as preparations for negotiations began, debates regarding Jews' situation in Algeria and their future there resumed. In a conversation with former prime minister Guy Mollet, de Gaulle made a distinction between Jews and Frenchmen in Algeria. Once again, Jewish leaders were forced to argue their Frenchness. The Alliance leadership argued that Jews should be treated as French individuals and not a distinct ethnic community. Jewish leaders used both *jus soli* and *jus sanguinis* to prove Algerian Jews' Frenchness. Bernard Tricot, a diplomat on de Gaulle's staff and a negotiator at Evian, included Algerian Jews in the definition of Europeans in the Accords.[179]

As the final phase of war escalated, more Jews considered leaving. To avoid losing a potential constituency and source of financial support, the FLN reached out to Jews in spring and summer 1961. In a letter sent to Jews in Algiers in April–May 1961, the FLN emphasized that colonialism had come between Jews and Muslims, succeeding in pitting the two groups against one another as in the case of the 1934 Constantine pogrom. The FLN recalled Vichy's treatment of Jews. "It would be absurd for colonialism to take you down with it. Be clear. Before it is too late, orient yourself to the future, a common future, a future of liberty, of dignity, of prosperity for all." The letter concluded by urging Jews to follow the path of their coreligionists in Morocco and Tunisia and donate to support the FLN.[180] A similar demand for financial support was sent to two Jewish leaders in Bou Saada during the summer of 1961. The letter stated that should the leaders see a future in free and democratic Algeria, they had to immediately change their comportment. It demanded 1,200,000 francs and that they establish a Jewish municipal council.[181] A tract was sent to Jews in the Wilaya 4 region. It stated that Jews were "authentic children of Algeria," and called upon "Algerians of the Jewish Confession" to unite alongside their Muslim compatriots. Another letter sent to Jews in 1961 reminded Jews that they "have been Algerians for centuries."[182]

In October 1961, the OAS attempted to gain the support and participation of Algerian Jews, and even some Algerian Muslims, by including

[179] Shepard, *The Invention of Decolonization*, 170–172.
[180] "Personalized letter to Jews in Algiers," April/May 1961, reproduced in Harbi, Meynier, *Le FLN*, 594–596.
[181] "Demand for contribution of Two Notable Jews of Bou Saada," Summer 1961, SHAT 1H1650-2, reproduced in Harbi, Meynier, *Le FLN*, 600–601. The intended significance of the Jewish municipal council is unclear, other than the legacy of municipal councils as the locus of power in the colony.
[182] "Tract of Wilaya 4 for Jews," 1961, reproduced in Harbi, Meynier, *Le FLN*, 599–601; "Model letter to a Jew of the liberal profession, merchant, industrial, or artisan," 1961, reproduced in Harbi, Meynier, *Le FLN*, 601–602.

both groups into their definition of the French people of Algeria. Although few Jews actually joined the OAS, it was an appealing proposition to be united with other Frenchmen in the colony without religious distinction. The OAS even argued that the Algerian independence movement was part of a larger conspiracy to destroy Israel. The OAS's effort to reach out to Jews impacted the far right in the colony as well. In this last phase of the Algerian War, the Algerian far right depicted Algerian Jews as French and an integral part of the "French of Algeria." This was a far cry from their nineteenth-century treatment of Jews and their antisemitic municipal activities of previous decades. French bureaucrats took a similar path in their discussions of Algerian Jews and stopped describing them as a group distinct from the French of the colony. Some scholars have attributed this transition as a response to the Israeli government's efforts to emphasize Jewish difference in their attempts to encourage Algerian Jewish immigration to Israel. The French government initially attempted to prevent mass departures from Algeria, but when they eventually accepted that inevitability, Algerian Jews joined the other "French of Algeria" on the journey to metropolitan France.[183]

Despite competing appeals to Jews by both the OAS and the FLN, through 1961 and 1962, Jews were increasingly the victims of the activities of both groups. In October 1961, Alex Easterman of the WJC wrote to Isaiah Berlin on the situation in North Africa. In terms of Algeria, he wrote that "the solution of this problem is ultimately, of course, migration, and it is on these lines that we are all working. There are great difficulties, however, both political and financial. The wealthy and middle-class Jews are heading for France; the poorer class – the vast majority of Algerian Jews – will have to be emigrated to Israel."[184] Although Easterman expected the majority of Jews of Algeria to go to Israel, most would actually be "repatriated" to France.

Beginning in November 1961, the attacks on Jews became more numerous. That month, the FLN killed Adolph Lévy, the president of World War II Veterans group in Algiers. They also killed David Zermati, a lawyer and the president of the Jewish community of Sétif. Zermati was a friend of Ferhat Abbas' and had been used as a symbol of the cooperation and friendship that could be possible in an independent Algeria. His death was therefore a serious blow to the idea of a Jewish future in an independent Algeria. After Zermati's assassination, Jews began to leave Sétif. Of the 2,400 Jewish residents of Sétif in 1954, only 700 remained by

---

[183] Shepard, *The Invention of Decolonization*, 177–181.
[184] Alex Easterman to Isaiah Berlin, October 10, 1961, CZA C2/1730 (North Africa Correspondence with Isaiah Berlin on Jewish communities in North Africa).

the end of 1961. On June 22, 1961, an FLN commando shot 48-year-old Raymond Leyris as he shopped with his daughter in Constantine. Leyris was known as Cheikh Raymond, a gifted oud player with a powerful voice, whose music was popular among Jews and Muslims. Just a month before, pro-independence Algerian Jews used Leyris as an example of the common culture of Jews and Muslims, a sign of the possibility of a future home together.[185] Other Jews departed as well. The Secretary of State for Algerian Affairs kept track of Jews leaving Algeria indefinitely, especially those going to Israel. His records show that out of 1,913 Jewish departures in September 1961, 302 were going to Israel. In October 1961, 173 out of 2,086 Jews leaving were going to Israel. In December 1961, that number was 21 out of 2,530 Jewish departures.[186] Jews were increasingly leaving Algeria, but the numbers going to Israel were decreasing, perhaps due to the dwindling activities of the Jewish Agency or the realization that the metropole seemed a less disruptive choice.

Leaving also posed a danger, especially by the hand of the OAS. In December 1961, Moïse Choukroun, the vice president of the Jewish community of Maison Carrée, was murdered. The OAS was responsible for other deaths of Algerian Jews whose politics supported independence. In November 1961, the OAS killed William Lévy, the secretary-general of the Algiers chapter of the SFIO. Lévy's son was killed by the FLN. The OAS was also likely responsible for several other mysterious deaths of Algerian Jews. The OAS and the FLN continued their violence against Jews in the first few months of 1962 before the Evian talks were to begin again. In January 1962, two Jewish students were killed in the midst of FLN attacks on the Jewish quarters of Oran and Mostaganem. In February, a grenade was thrown into a market in the Jewish quarter of Constantine. The FLN, although mostly disinterested in Jewish participation by 1962, equated the OAS with the fascism of the Holocaust.[187] Jews remained caught in the crossfire between the FLN and the OAS.

The Evian negotiations began on March 7, 1962, as the OAS stepped up its violent campaign in Algeria. The negotiations ended on May 19 with a cease-fire proclaimed in Algeria. Despite concessions made on each side, including a period of dual nationality for certain Europeans as well as continued economic aid from France for Algeria, fighting between the FLN and the OAS continued until June. In late March, European supporters of French Algeria, led by the OAS, took over the

[185] Ayoun, "Les juifs d'Algérie," 26–27; Evans, *Algeria: France's Undeclared War*, 322–323.
[186] Shepard, *The Invention of Decolonization*, 176.
[187] Ayoun, "Les juifs d'Algérie," 26–27; Naylor, *France and Algeria*, 44; Evans, *Algeria: France's Undeclared War*, 324.

Algiers suburb of Bab-el-Oued, known as the "Battle of Bab-el-Oued," which resulted in 35 deaths and 150 injuries. Jews continued to be the victims of violence as well. In May, two Jewish siblings aged 2 and 6, were killed by their Muslim nanny. The OAS took on a "scorched-earth policy" as they moved through the country. The battle between the FLN and the OAS finally ended in an accord signed in Algiers on June 18. OAS members in Oran rejected the truce and robbed six banks. In the chaotic aftermath of the truce, OAS leaders prepared to leave Algeria.[188]

The future of independent Algeria was put to a vote for non-European Algerians on July 1, 1962. Approximately six million voters expressed their support for an independent Algeria on the basis of the conditions decided upon at Evian on March 19. Only 16,534 voted against it. The results were made public at a ceremony on July 3, 1962, during which a French representative passed a letter from de Gaulle to Abderrahmane Farès, the president of the provisional governing body formed after the Evian agreement. In his letter, de Gaulle expressed his good wishes for the future of the newly independent Algeria. Although the transfer of power marked a new period of peace, it did not last long. On July 5, 1962, a mob attacked the European section of Oran. However, by this time, many Europeans, including most Jews, had already left.[189]

Exile or Exodus: Jewish Departures

In the weeks before Algeria's independence in July, the majority of Jews in Algeria, approximately 130,000, departed for France leaving behind their homes, neighbors, and history. Benjamin Stora recounted his departure with his family in 1962: "My father locked the door, and he slipped the key into his pocket, we each carried our two bags and we left. It was like we were going on vacation. But we knew well that this was the end, that we would never return. This was the most important moment in our life, a jump into the unknown."[190] Over the course of late 1961 and 1962, most Jews took the same actions as Stora and his family. From September to December 1961, 6,529 Jews left Algeria, 496 of whom headed to Israel.[191] For most Algerian Jews, Israel was not really an option, despite the Israeli government's efforts to bring Algerian Jews to the new Jewish state. By 1969, Israel had received at most only 10 percent of Jews who had left Algeria.[192]

---

[188] Stora, *Algeria: 1830–2000*, 97–101; Ayoun, "Les juifs d'Algérie," 26.
[189] Stora, *Algeria: 1830–2000*, 104–106.   [190] Stora, *Les Trois Exils*, 131, 167.
[191] Shepard, *The Invention of Decolonization*, 176.
[192] Choi, "Complex Compatriots," 874.

Most Algerian Jews joined the nearly one million *pieds noirs*, European settlers, in the bizarre and ill-named process of "repatriation." These French of Algeria were repatriated to France, a country in which most had never lived. But in the rhetoric of decolonizing France, Algeria was no longer part of France, so the repatriates were coming home to France from foreign Algeria. Even M'Zabi Jews, who had been outside the purview of the Crémieux Decree, were welcomed as French repatriates. They had been made French citizens by the law 61–805 of July 28, 1961. They left France in May–June 1962.[193] Although they superficially seemed to blend in among the other repatriates, Jews continued to be singled out as such. They moved to France because of their Frenchness, but their arrival and early experiences in their new home were shaped by their Jewishness. Even within the Jewish community, they were different. The rapid and traumatic transition from their ancestral home to a new one, by which they felt simultaneously welcomed and alienated, further exacerbated the sense of their broken identities. In France, the arrival of Algerian Jews significantly increased Jewish communities. In Marseille, for example, the Jewish community grew from 10,000 to 70,000 and twenty new synagogues were built. However, the Algerian Jewish community remained largely a group apart, an internal other within the French Jewish community, as they had been among the Europeans in Algeria.

Nostalgia colors both the Jewish and *pied noir* experience. Jews continued to look back to their lost homeland. The Algerian War broke down the hybrid identities of Algerian Jews. As the war progressed and Jews were forced to choose sides, they were pushed further onto the Europeans side and farther away from their Algerian heritage. One thousand years of shared culture and ancestry gave way to 132 years of French rule. The Algerian part of their identity was ultimately in the past.[194]

In his *The Algerian War Explained to Everyone*, Benjamin Stora responded to the question regarding his reasons for leaving Algeria. "We left because we were the French of Algeria, and since Algeria was becoming independent, we had to 'follow France' ... but it was not easy ... I was a child and I knew that it was an exile without return, and that I was leaving behind me the country that had seen me be born."[195] It was not just that Algerian Jews had known no other country than

---

[193] Shepard, *The Invention of Decolonization*, 217, 243–246. However, Stein emphasizes, the French government lacked access to the proper records, registers of Jewish births, to identify who was a Southern-born Algerian Jew, and therefore who was eligible for repatriation. Stein, *Saharan Jews and the Fate of French Algeria*, 119.

[194] Sussman, "Jews from Algeria and French Jewish Identity," 218–219, 221–222. See also Katz, *Jews and Muslims in the Shadow of Marianne*, 268, 272; Friedman, *Colonialism and After*, 98; Naylor, *France and Algeria*, 44; Evans, *Algeria: France's Undeclared War*, 325.

[195] Stora, *La guerre d'Algérie*, 14.

Algeria; it was that their lives had been based upon proving their worth as Frenchmen, while still seeking coexistence with their Muslim neighbors, particularly in the form of shared traditions and cultures.[196] Denis Guénoun wrote of the distress of his father, who had supported the insurrection, at the possibility of a future without Algeria. "Papa never imagined not finishing his days in Algeria."[197] It is important to recall that this was the second in a series of ruptures in the last twenty years of Algerian Jewish experience. Vichy was an extreme rupture; upon having their rights returned to them in 1943, Algerian Jews slowly recovered from the trauma. However, in 1961 and 1962, there was no other option but to follow France and leave their ancestral home. The strength of their French identities proved stronger than their allegiance to their native land. The law of December 20, 1966, reaffirmed that all Algerian Jews were French.[198] The goal of Adolphe Crémieux and the decree named for him in 1870 had been achieved. From the indigenous Jews of Algeria had emerged a community of Frenchmen repatriated to metropolitan France.

---

[196] David Cohen, "Le Comité Juif Algérien d'études sociales dans le débat idéologique pendant la guerre d'Algérie (1954–1961)," *Archives Juives*, No. 29/1 (1996): 46.
[197] Denis Guénoun, *Un Sémite* (Clamency: Circé, 2002), 113.
[198] Shepard, *The Invention of Decolonization*, 247.

Conclusion

"My heart bled because I felt how much recent events have impacted me. I thought with despair 'but I'm the same, I did not change.' " These words, written by the young schoolteacher Edmond to his parents after the abrogation of the Crémieux Decree, emblematize the deep rupture and trauma felt by Algerian Jews upon losing their citizenship in 1940. His anguish reflects the impact of the abrogation as well as the seventy years of assimilation, political activity, and defense against the threat of political antisemitism upon Algerian Jews. Edmond was the product of French education, a patriotic Frenchman, so rooted in French culture and society that he devoted himself to the education of the next generation of Frenchmen and women. His despair at the idea of no longer being able to work with his students, and at the broader implications of no longer being a French citizen, reflected his embeddedness in French society in colonial Algeria. While Edmond and his ancestors had faced many antisemitic challenges to their inclusion in French civil society, they had persevered to become the Frenchmen that Adolphe Crémieux and others believed they could be.

From the 1890s until the reinstatement of the Crémieux Decree by Charles de Gaulle in 1943, Algerian Jews faced an endless series of challenges to their role as citizens, electors, and Frenchmen by a particular brand of political antisemitism, uniquely poisonous in the context of the colony and particularly potent in municipal governments. Even upon regaining their citizenship under de Gaulle, Algerian Jews did not have much reprieve before facing the ultimate decision at the end of the Algerian War: to stay in Algeria or to commit to their French identity and move to France.

In Algeria, French *colons, néos* and their *Latin* sons, Algerian Jews, and Algerian Muslims competed for economic advantage and political control in this extension of the metropole. Municipal governments in Algeria provided a singular political space in which *colons, néos,* and Jews struggled over power and patronage. French citizens in Algeria elected representatives to the National Assembly, but it was far away in Paris.

Colonial institutions dominated the political landscape in Algeria through the operation of the governor-general. Control over municipal government offered more immediate and tangible benefits to French citizens in Algeria. As such, municipal elections were consistently fraught as electors sought ways to reduce competition from other groups and parties. As citizens, Algerian Jews and their alleged cohesive voting practices threatened the supremacy of French *colons*, and after 1889, the *néos* as well in municipal politics.

Over the years, especially following World War I, Algerian Muslims made increasing demands for political rights so that they could be represented in government rather than continue to exist as a maligned and marginalized majority. Algerian antisemites insincerely promised Algerian Muslims improvements in their status in exchange for their cooperation in combating the aggressive integration of Jews into politics, civil service, the military, and the economy. Antisemites called upon the frustrations of Algerian Muslims to act out their resentment of the Jew as citizen. One result of this rhetoric was the Constantine pogrom in 1934.

In the crucible of municipal governments, Algerian Jews' rights as electors and the competition that those rights represented served as a catalyst in producing political antisemitism. In the 1890s, antisemites discovered that by gaining control of local governments, they could undermine Algerian Jewish citizenship. Antisemitism became deeply embedded in Algerian colonial society, especially in the political arena. Antisemitism manifested itself most dramatically surrounding elections for Algerian municipalities.

Antisemitism in Algeria combined several forms, melding race, religion, and status. In 1898 Max Régis dreamed of an Algeria free of Jews, by violent means if necessary. Municipal governments thrived on antisemitism as a political force: it elected mayors and municipal councilors, it fostered systems of patronage, it even allowed municipal leaders to remove Jews from the administration and from voter lists. When antisemitism became part of municipal or national policy, it became institutional in nature. As such, antisemitism under Régis in Algiers under his mayorship was institutionalized, as it was under other antisemitic politicians such as Molle, Bellat, and others. Institutional antisemitism blossomed under the auspices of anti-Jewish municipal governments that worked to remove the Jews as political and status competitors. Mayor Bellat led his antisemitic electoral commission in removing over 300 Algerian Jewish voters in Sidi Bel Abbès in 1937. Without the concerted efforts of Algerian Jewish defense organizations, the French colonial administration would have remained uninvolved in this egregious abuse of power. Bellat and his compatriots would have been free to establish further obstacles to the Algerian Jews' practice of their citizenship.

Antisemitic violence in 1898 and 1934 forced Jews to face the tenuousness of their status in the colony and the fragility of their citizenship. The colonial administration failed to come to their aid. Jews called out to administrators for help only to be reassured that the necessary would be done. The fatal neglect of the administration in the face of antisemitic violence further illustrated to Jews that they had to be responsible for their own defense. Elite Jews established organizations, such as the Comité Algérien des Études Sociales, to defend their rights against infringements by municipal politicians and the administration as a whole. Other Jews realized that defense meant more than battling for their rights; it meant defending themselves physically through the establishment of groups such as the Géo Gras Group. Algerian Jews also reached out to Algerian Muslims and sought common ground in the face of discrimination and persecution. Jewish-Muslim alliances were developed but rarely gained traction in the ever-changing dynamic of colonial Algeria during two world wars and the Great Depression.

Algerian Jews responded to the threats posed to their rights by antisemitism by accelerating their assimilation at the behest of their leaders. To combat the accusations of backwardness, corporatism, and inappropriate voting practices, Algerian Jews had to become Frenchmen above reproach. They aggressively responded to attacks on their patriotism by pointing to service to their country in the military and civil service. In particular, they found the greatest defense of their rights in military service, mobilizing in great numbers in both World War I and the war of 1939–1940 before the fall of France to Germany. In 1919, to document commitment to France, the CAES published a *Livre d'Or* detailing the commendations, medals, and heroic deeds of Algerian Jews in defense of France in World War I.

Under Vichy in Algeria institutional antisemitism reached its apogee when it enacted decrees in the colony far harsher than in the metropole. Its Jewish Statute set firm quotas for Jewish employment in professions and in the civil service and severely limited attendance of Jews in schools and universities. The governor-general at the time, Peyrouton, went beyond those restrictions imposed by Vichy in the metropole in order to further restrict the position of Jews within the colony. Actions such as this reflected the nature of Algeria's fertile terrain for antisemitism. It also reflects the significance of the local situation in the colony, even during the Vichy era. The men of Vichy in the colony had the latitude to implement harsher legislation than their colleagues in the metropole. The municipal governments and local prefects in turn carried out those laws, carrying over the antisemitism of previous municipal governments into the era of Vichy.

In 1940, Algerian Jews experienced the deepest rupture of their relationship with France caused by the Vichy government's abrogation of the Crémieux Decree and the elimination of their identities as French citizens. Their expressions of mourning in the days following indicated how intensely they experienced the circumcision of their connection to France. With the stroke of pen, seventy years of assimilation, integration, and patriotism were erased by the state-sponsored antisemitism of Vichy. The abrogation of the Crémieux Decree reduced Algerian Jews to the status of colonial subjects. In the process of assimilating over the past seventy years, Algerian Jews left behind their communal institutions and "traditional" leaders. As French citizens, Jewish communal institutions, built over centuries of Muslim and Ottoman rule, had withered. Algerian Jews could not legally or socially function again as colonial subjects.

Algerian Jews appealed to Vichy to reinstate them as citizens on the basis of patriotism and assimilation. They begged Pétain and other leaders, both national and local, to allow them to remain "in the shadow of the tricolor flag." In the process of assimilating, some Jews illustrated their deep commitment to France through marrying non-Jews and converting to Catholicism themselves. These cases of appeals of intermarried and converted Jews illustrate the rigidity of Vichy's institutional antisemitism and the limits of Algerian Jews' assimilation. Even those who did not directly seek exemption from the antisemitic legislation reflected the deep sense of rupture felt by Algerian Jews in their correspondence to one another. Edmond, the school teacher forced out of his position by the Jewish Statute, shared his sorrow with his parents, as he considered leaving his students behind. His shock and confusion at the possibility of no longer being considered French, despite his deep commitment to France and his own French identity, were overwhelming for him and so many others.

In response to Vichy's institutional antisemitism, in 1942 a group of Algerian Jews joined an underground movement to pave the way for the Allied landings in Algeria, believing that in doing so true France would return and reinstate them as French citizens. The Jewish underground members played a vital role in the Allied victory in Algeria. Even after the fall of Vichy, Algerian Jews remained the victims of lingering antisemitism. José Aboulker and his father, Henri, a leader of the Algerian Jewish community since the early 1910s, were imprisoned for their efforts, further victimized for their commitment to France. Algerian Jews mobilized political support from Jewish intellectuals, such as Hannah Arendt, and recently established Jewish political organizations, such as the World

Jewish Congress, to pressure the Allies and the Free French to reinstate their citizenship. It was nearly a year after their demonstrated bravery and patriotism that Algerian Jews finally regained their citizenship. Over the course of their integration as citizens, Algerian Jews discovered that antisemitism, especially virulent in its political form, posed the greatest threat to their status and the practice of their rights as citizens.

Even after regaining their citizenship in 1943, Algerian Jews were hesitant to trust France as fully as they had before Vichy. The process of lobbying internationally for the return of the Crémieux Decree illustrated for Algerian Jews the fragility of colonial citizenship. When they successfully returned to their status as French citizens, some Algerian Jews recognized the continued exclusion of Algerian Muslims as political actors, even as Algerian Muslim leaders made stronger demands for rights and access to citizenship. The past seventy-three years had shown Algerian Jews that their rights could never be discussed separately from those of Algerian Muslims. Their political fates were always intertwined and always threatened. Algerian Muslim leaders increasingly shifted ideologically from assimilationism to independence, especially after World War II. The extreme violence against Muslims by the French in Sétif and Guelma in May 1945 rang the death knell of a future for Algerian Muslims in French Algeria. Independence increasingly became the ultimate and only goal.

Although Algerian Jews' wounds began to heal from the rupture of the Vichy period, the Algerian War questioned their loyalty, solidarity, and identities. In the Algerian War, Jewish leaders attempted to keep the community on the periphery of the conflict. However, rabbis and other Jewish leaders became targets of both the FLN and the OAS. These two organizations questioned the ability of Algerian Jews to commit to either side. Although native to Algeria, Algerian Jews were Frenchmen – Frenchmen of Algeria. However, as the conflict reached an end and independence became the only solution, Algerian and French leaders questioned how Algerian Jews could choose between the two. In the end, nearly a century of French education, military service, and the development of their identity as citizens in the face of antisemitism in municipal and institutional forms led most Algerian Jews to choose to be repatriated to France, a country most only knew in theory. Even upon their arrival in France, Algerian Jews remained on the outside of not only the *pieds noirs* community but also the Jewish community.

This book has explored the complexities of citizenship in the colonial context, the pursuit of rights by various groups, and the competition between them for control of local governments. Citizenship did not exist in a vacuum. Political antisemitism developed alongside the articulation of the Algerian Jews' citizenship as electors and members of civil society. Stemming from a variety of sources and influences, antisemitism emerged as the dominant political ideology for Europeans in the colony who sought the rewards of the patronage system endemic in municipal politics. Algerian Muslims expressed their resentment of the Jews' superior status and their concomitant frustrations with their lack of rights in the colony through political antisemitism. Through its diverse sources of nourishment, the tree of antisemitism grew strong and fruitful, extending its roots throughout all realms of Algerian colonial society: politics, economics, the military and civil service, and daily life.

Algerian Jews experienced decades of integration and assimilation in the colony, aggressively entering the economy and politics, and rising in the military and civil service. They discovered, however, that their path of assimilation was not without obstacles. Political and institutional antisemitism in the colony placed the greatest limits on the practice of their citizenship. Concurrently antisemites learned that they could harness the unprecedented power of the *néos*, French *colons*, and Algerian Muslims to their advantage. Like Hélène Cixous' Jewish trapezists outfitted in the tricolor flag, Algerian Jews desperately reached out across the abyss and grasped for France. Algerian antisemites plucked the trapeze of citizenship from the Algerian Jews' hands, highlighting the realities of their fragile status and the limits of their citizenship. Despite their assimilation and embrace of France, Algerian Jews recognized that antisemitism created severe limits on their identities as Frenchmen and the practice of their French citizenship. As long as antisemitism existed in the colony, regardless of its source, they would never be allowed to be fully French citizens. Even after being "repatriated" to metropolitan France, Algerian Jews' Frenchness continued to be questioned. They were always on the periphery of Frenchness, close but not quite fully French in the eyes of other Frenchmen, regardless of their efforts.

References

Archives

Archives de l'Alliance Israélite Universelle, Paris, France

Algeria Files

AIU Algérie IB4 – Alger 1918–1939

AIU Algérie ICI – 1934–1936: situation politique

AIU Algérie IC2 – 1870s–1920s: antisémitisme

AIU Algérie IC6-c – Troubles de Constantine: Constantine 1934 Journaux d'Algérie

AIU Algérie IIB4 – Constantine Consistoire 1920, 1926–1929: Talmud Torah; Écoles

AIU Algérie IIB10 – Œuvre de l'Alliance, Nabon 1923–1925

AIU Algérie IIC8 – Antisémitisme: Mostaganem

AIU Algérie IIC9 – Antisémitisme: Oran, 1864–1937

AIU Algérie ILI – Demandes de Secours

AIU Algérie IVB27 – Tlemcen 1863–1934

Moscow Files

AIU Moscou EN 01.1 – Algérie, Alger/Constantine, Sylvain Benedict

AIU Moscou EN 01.2 – Algérie, Alger 1900–1901, Directeur Moise Nahon, Correspondence

AIU Moscou EN 18.079 – Informations centrales

AIU Moscou C01.7 – Algérie, Oran, 1898, Antisémitisme

AIU Moscou C01.8 – Oran, 1899–1900, Antisémitisme

Library

AIU 8JBr2162 – Lazeau, Henri. *Max Régis: Mensonges et Vérités.* Issy-les-Moulineaux: Imprimerie nouvelle, ND.

AIU 8UBr1271 – Taupiac, C. *Les Israelites Indigènes: Réponse a la Pétition de M. Du Bouzet, ancien Préfet d'Oran, Ancien Commissaire extraordinaire de laRépublique par C. Taupiac, Avocat.* Constantine: Chez L. Marle Libraire; Paris: Chez Challemel, Librairie, 1871.

AIU 8JBr878 – Consistoire Israélite du département d'Alger: *Installation de M. Moise Weil, Grand Rabbin, 16 avril 1891, 8 nissan 5651*. Alger: Imprimerie Franck et Solal, 1891

AIU 8JBr 1778 – Crémieux, Adolphe. *Réfutation de la pétition de M. Du Bouzet*. Paris: Imprimerie Schiller, 1871

Archives de la Consistoire Centrale, Paris, France

CC ACP-4 – Communauté Israelite avant 1939
CC 2E-Boîte 1 – Algérie
CC 2E-Boîte 2 – Algérie
CC Icc 38 – Consistoire d'Alger 1885–1905
CC Icc 39 – Consistoire de Constantine 1857–1905
CC Icc 40 – Consistoire d'Oran 1855–1895

Archives Nationales, Paris, France

Antisémitisme
AN F/7/12459 – Antisémitisme-1890–1907
AN F/7/12460 – Antisémitisme-1880–1900
AN F/7/12461 – Antisémitisme, antisémitic groups-France
AN F/7/12463 – Affichages and propagande antisémitisme 1898–1906
AN F/7/12842 – Newspapers late 1890s–1910s
AN F/7/12882 – Antisémitisme 1897–1901
AN F/7/12883 – Antisémitisme 1902–1906
AN F/7/15134 – Prospectus antisemites 1934–1940
AN F/7/16001/1 – Max Régis

Culte Israélite
AN F/19/11143 – Préparation et exécution de l'ordonnance du 9 novembre 1845, 1842–1845
AN F/19/11144 – Rapports situation et l'organisation du culte des israélites 1942–1872
AN F/19/11145 – Culte Israélite
AN F/19/11146 – Culte Israélite
AN F/19/11031 – Plaintes et réclamations contre faits de l'intolérance

Central Zionist Archives, Jerusalem, Israel

CZA C2/14 – American Jewish Congress correspondence 1943
CZA Z4\31461 – Politics: Correspondence on persecution of Jews in North Africa

CZA C2\1904 – Rescue and refugees correspondence with the ICRC and other organizations and individuals regarding the situation of the Jews in Argentina and North Africa, agreement

CZA C10\337 – The Algerian Division (Jacques Lazarus) (The Algerian Jewish Committee of Social Studies) correspondence, reports, and news bulletins concerning the WJC's activities in North Africa

CZA C2\1730 – North Africa correspondence with Isaiah Berlin on Jewish communities in North Africa, and reports on the first WJC North African Conference

CZA Z4/30703 – Politics: Correspondence on situation of Jews in North Africa and immigration to Palestine

Centre des Archives d'Outre Mer, Aix-en-Province, France

Administration des Indigènes

CAOM Alg Alger 2i/38 – Antisémitisme 1934–1940

Department of Algiers

CAOM Alg Alger F410 – Questions Israélites (1934–1939)

CAOM Alg Alger F512 – Services des Questions Juives (1940–1942)

Department of Constantine

CAOM Alg Const B/3/240–

CAOM Alg Const B/3/248 – Affaires Indigènes: Antisemitism 1896–1931

CAOM Alg Const B/3/249 – Affaires Indigènes: Antisemitism 1932–1933

CAOM Alg Const B/3/250 – Affaires Indigènes 1934

CAOM Alg Const B/3/390 – Société de Rééducation de la Populations Israelite 1935

CAOM Alg Const B/3/656 – Événements antisémite à Sétif 1934/ Antisémitisme 1936

CAOM Alg Const B/3/687 – Antisémitisme 1933–1934 – Lautier-L'Éclair Algérien

CAOM Alg Const B/3/688 – Antisémitisme 1941–1942

Prefecture of Constantine

CAOM Alg Const 93/3G3 – Instructions (1940–1942)

CAOM Alg Const 93/3G4 – Opération de recensement (1941–1942)

CAOM Alg Const 93/3G6 – Demandes de Maintien et décisions 1940–1942

CAOM Alg Const 93/3G7 – Instructions et pièces justificatives 1940–1943

CAOM Alg Const 93/3G19 – Recensement, enquêtes, licensements (1940–1942)

CAOM Alg Const 93/3G23 – Demandes de dérogation au titre de l'art.
8 de la loi 2 juin
1941 (dossiers individuels)
CAOM Alg Const 93/3G29 – Enseignement des Juifs 1942–1943
CAOM Alg Const 93/3G30 – Affaires particulières suivies par le Service
(1941–1943)

Department of Oran

CAOM Alg Oran 96 – Surveillance des Italiens
CAOM Alg Oran 424 – Antisemitism; Front populaire, Amitiés
Lambert, Rassemblement national, Union Latine, Amitiés Latines,
LICA, Front de la jeunesse, Gaullisme, Sionisme, Police des ques-
tions juives, destruction des documentations fonde sur la qualité juif
CAOM Alg Oran 2539 – Consistoire Israélite d'Oran 1934–1944
CAOM Alg Oran 2541 – Ligue internationale contre le racisme et
antisémitisme
CAOM Alg Oran 3363 – Police statistique sur population Israélite par
commune Mars 1942
CAOM Alg Oran 5i/50 – Questions Israélites-action antisémites
1936–1943
CAOM Alg Oran 1S/41 – Ecoles privées juives (1942)

Fonds Ministériels

CAOM FM F/80/1685 – Antisémitisme 1897
CAOM FM F/80/1686 – Antisémitisme 1898
CAOM FM F/80/1687 – Antisémitisme 1898
CAOM FM 81 F/864 – mouvement et manifestation d'antisémitisme,
lutte contrel'antisémitisme dans la population européen et musulman
d'Algérie, surveillance (1928–1949)
CAOM FM 81 F/846 – Statut des Juifs – Application a l'Algérie
(1940–1943)
CAOM FM 81 F/847 – Statut des Juifs – Application en matière d'accès
á la fonction publique et á certaines professions en Algérie, textes
réglementaires et correspondance (1940–1942)

Fonds Ministère des Colonies – Affaires Politiques

CAOM FM 1affpol/877 – 1942–1943

Fonds Gouverneur Gènèral d'Algérie

CAOM Alg GGA 6CAB/1 – Juifs 1940–1943
CAOM Alg GGA 8CAB/71 – Décret Crémieux 1943

Centre de la Documentation de l'Historique sur l'Algérie, Aix-en-Provence, France

CDHA 296 FRO – FLN Documents: Les Juifs d'Algérie dans le Combat pour l'Indèpendence Nationale. Éditè par la Fédération de France du Front de Libération Nationale

Centre de la Documentation Juive Contemporaine, Paris, France

CDJC CMXCVI 12-14 – Fonds LICA
CDJC CMXCVI-105.2 – Fonds LICA
CDJC CMXCVI-109.1 – Fonds LICA
CDJC CMXCVI-123.3 – Fonds LICA
CDJC CMXCVI-135.2 – Fonds LICA
CDJC DCCVVI-2 – Fonds Vanikoff
CDJC DCCXXI-1 – Fonds Vanikoff
CDJC DCCXXI-3 – Fonds Vanikoff
CDJC LIII-27b – Afrique du Nord – Algérie
CDJC LIII-27a – Afrique du Nord – Algérie
CDJC LXXXIV-1 – Juifs d'Algérie
CDJC LXXXIV-9 – Juifs d'Algérie
CDJC LXXXIV-14 – Juifs d'Algérie
CDJC LXXXIV-21 – Juifs d'Algérie
CDJC LXXXIV-26 – Juifs d'Algérie
CDJC LXXXIV-36 – Juifs d'Algérie
CDJC LXXXIV-43 – Juifs d'Algérie
CDJC LXXXIV-44 – Juifs d'Algérie
CDJC LXXXIV-48 – Juifs d'Algérie
CDJC LXXXIV-49 – Juifs d'Algérie
CDJC LXXXIV-50 – Juifs d'Algérie
CDJC LXXXIV-51 – Juifs d'Algérie
CDJC LXXXIV-55 – Juifs d'Algérie
CDJC LXXXIV-56 – Juifs d'Algérie
CDJC-LXXXIV-75 – Juifs d'Algérie
CDJC LXXXVII-153 – Commissariat Généraux aux Questions Juives: Lois, Décrets, Arrêtes de la Période de l'Occupation Allemande, 1940–1944
CDJC XC-3 – Fonds Congres Juif Mondial – Brochures et Bulletins
CDJC XC-6 – Fonds Congres Juif Mondial – Brochures et Bulletins
CDJC XC-7 – Fonds Congres Juif Mondial – Brochures et Bulletins
CDJC XC-14 – Fonds Congres Juif Mondial – Brochures et Bulletins
CDJC-XC-15 – Fonds Congres Juif Mondial – Brochures et Bulletins
CDJC CCCLXXXV-1 – Algérie

CDJC CCCLXXXV-2 – Algérie

CDJC BIB 9001 – *Bulletin de la Fédération des Sociétés Juives d'Algérie 1941–1947*

Hoover Institution Archives, Stanford University, Stanford, CA

RMF, Box 47, File 2 – Robert D. Murphy Papers
RMF, Box 47, File 3 – Robert D. Murphy Papers
RMF, Box 47, File 5 – Robert D. Murphy Papers
RMF, Box 47, File 8 – Robert D. Murphy Papers
RMF, Box 47, File 10 – Robert D. Murphy Papers

Ligue des Droits de l'Homme Archives-BDIC, Nanterre, France

BDIC-LDH F Delta Res 798/63 – Communautés Juives
BDIC-LDH F Delta Res 798/96 – Algérie
BDIC-LDH F Delta Res 798/97 – Algérie
BDIC-LDH F Delta Res 798/169 – Algérie – Fédérations
BDIC-LDH F Delta Res 798/171 – Algérie – Fédérations

United States National Archives and Records Administration, College Park, MD

RG 226, Entry 97, Box 5, File 77 – Operation Torch

United States Holocaust Memorial Museum and Archives, Washington, DC

Microfilm 1998.A.0087 – Afrique du Nord

YIVO Institute for Jewish Research Library and Archives, New York, NY

CJH ALEPH 015007116 – *Information Juive*

Yad Vashem Archives, Jerusalem, Israel

O.26 – Collection on North Africa

Newspapers and Periodicals

Information Juive
L'Antijuif Algérien

L'Autorité

Bulletin de la Fédération des Sociétés Juives d'Algérie

La Dépêche de Constantine

La Dépêche de Toulouse

La Libre Parole

L'Éclair Algérien

L'Éclaireur de Nice

Free World

La Gazette des Tribunaux

Le Petit Fanal Oranais

Le Peuple Français

Le Populaire

Time Magazine

La Verité

Published Sources

Abitbol, Michael. *The Jews of North Africa during the Second World War*. Detroit: Wayne State University Press, 1989.

Aboulker, José. "La part de la résistance française dans les événements de l'Afrique du Nord." *Les Cahiers Français* Vol. 47 (August 1943): 3–45.

Adda-Djelloul, Mohamed. "Société colonisée et droit colonial: Les élus des délégations arabe et kabyle face au projet Albin Rozet." *Insaniyat*, Vol. 5, No. 2 (1998): 171–186.

Adida-Goldberg, Josy. *Les Deux Pères*. Paris: Orizons, 2008.

Ageron, Charles-Robert. *De l'Algérie 'Française' à l'Algérie Algérienne*. Paris: Éditions Bouchève, 2005.

L'Algérie Algérienne de Napoléon III à de Gaulle. Paris: Éditions Sindbad, 1980.

Les Algériens musulmans et la France 1871–1919. 2 vols. Paris: Éditions Bouchène, 2005.

Histoire de l'Algérie Contemporaine, Tome II: De l'insurrection de 1871 au déclenchement de la guerre de libération. Paris: Presses Universitaires de France, 1979.

Histoire de l'Algérie Contemporaine. Paris: Presses Universitaires de France, 1999.

"Mai 1945 en Algérie. Enjeu de mémoire et histoire." *Matériaux pour l'histoire de notre temps*, Vol. 39–40 (1995): 52–56.

Modern Algeria: A History from 1830 to the Present. London: Hurst and Company, 1991.

Politiques Coloniales au Maghreb. Paris: Presses Universitaires de France, 1972.

"Les troubles du nord-constantinois en mai 1945: Une tentative insurrectionnelle." *Vingtième Siècle: Revue d'histoire*, Vol. 4 No. 1 (1984): 23–38.

"Une émeute anti-juive à Constantine (août 1934)." *Revue de l'Occident Musulman et de la Méditerranée*, Vol. 13, No. 1 (1973): 23–40.

Akoun, André. *Né à Oran: Autobiographie en troisième personne*. Paris: Éditions Bouchene, 2004.

Alain, Michel. "Qu'est-ce qu'un scout juif?. L'éducation juive chez les Éclaireurs israélites de France, de 1923 au début des années 1950." *Archives Juives*, Vol. 35, No. 2 (2002): 77–101.

Allardyce, Gilbert D. "The Political Transition of Jacques Doriot." *Journal of Contemporary History*, Vol. 1, No. 1 (1966): 56–74.

Allardyce, Gilbert and Andrée R. Picard, "Jacques Doriot et l'esprit fasciste en France." *Revue d'histoire de la Deuxième Guerre mondiale*, 25e Année, No. 97, Visages de fascistes français (1975): 31–44.

Alleg, Henri. *The Algerian Memories: Days of Hope and Combat*. London: Seagull Books, 2012.

Allouche-Benayoun, Joëlle and Doris Bensimon. *Les Juifs d'Algérie: Mémoires et Identités Plurielles*. Paris: Éditions Stavit, 1998.

Amipaz-Silber, Gitta. *La Résistance Juive en Algérie, 1940–1942*. Jerusalem: Presses Daf-Chen, 1986.

Amselle, Jean-Loup. *Affirmative Exclusion: Cultural Pluralism and the Rule of Custom in France*. Ithaca: Cornell University Press, 2003.

Anonymous. *L'Oeuvre des Antijuifs d'Alger*. Algiers: Imprimerie Commerciale, 1899.

Ansky, Michel. *Les Juifs d'Algérie du décret Crémieux a la Libération*. Paris: Éditions du Centre, 1950.

Arendt, Hannah. *The Origins of Totalitarianism*. New York: Meridian Books Inc., 1958.

Asiwaju, A. I. "Control through Coercion: A Study of the Indigénat Regime in French West African Administration, 1887–1946." *Bulletin de l'I.F.A.N.*, Vol. 41, ser. B (1979): 35–71.

Assan, Valérie. "Les synagogues dans l'Algérie coloniale du XIXe siècle." *Archives Juives, revue d'histoire des Juifs de France*, Vol. 37, No. 1 (2004): 70–85.

Atkinson, Rick. *An Army at Dawn: The War in North Africa 1942–1943, Volume One of the Liberation Trilogy*. New York: Henry Holt and Company, 2002.

Attal, Robert. *Les Émeutes de Constantine: 5 août 1934*. Paris: Éditions Romillat, 2002.

  Regards sur les Juifs d'Algérie. Paris: L'Harmattan, 1996.

Au, Sokhieng. *Mixed Medicines: Health and Culture in French Colonial Cambodia*. Chicago: Chicago University Press, 2011.

Ayoun, Richard. "Les Juifs d'Algérie pendant la guerre d'indépendance (1954–1962)." *Archives Juives*, Vol. 29, No. 1 (1996): 15–29.

Ayoun, Richard and Bernard Cohen. *Les Juifs d'Algérie: Deux mille ans d'Histoire*. Paris: Éditions Jean-Claude Lattès, 1982.

Bahloul, Joëlle. *The Architecture of Memory*. Cambridge: Cambridge University Press, 1996.

Barron, L. Smythe ed. *The Nazis in Africa: Lost Documents on the Third Reich Volume III*. Salisbury: Documentary Publications, 1978.

Barthelemy-Saint-Hilaire, Jules "Minister of Foreign Affairs to His Excellency M. le Duc de Fernan-Nunez, Spanish Ambassador to Paris, July 23, 1881." In *Affaires Étrangères: Documents Diplomatiques. Affaires de Saida (1881–1882)*, 8–10. Paris: Imprimerie Nationale, 1883.

Baruch, Marc-Olivier. *Servir l'État français. L'administration en France de 1940 à 1944*. Paris: Librairie Arthème Fayard, 1997.

Begley, Louis. *Why the Dreyfus Affair Matters*. New Haven: Yale University Press, 2009.

Beiner, Ronald ed. *Theorizing Citizenship*. Albany: State University of New York Press, 1995.

Bel Ange, Norbert. *Quand Vichy Internait ses Soldats Juifs d'Algérie, Bedeau, sud oranais, 1941–1943*. Paris: L'Harmattan, 2005.

Benamou, Georges-Marc. *C'était un temps déraisonnable: Les premiers résistants racontent*. Paris: Imprimerie Robert Laffont, 1999.

Béquet, M. *Organisation de Culte Israélite en Algérie, Rapport au Conseil de Gouvernement par M. Béquet, Conseiller-Rapporteur*. Algiers: Imprimerie de Gouvernement, 1888.

Berque, Jacques. *French North Africa: The Maghrib Between Two World Wars*. Translated by Jean Stewart. New York: Frederick A. Praeger, Inc., 1967.

Bhabha, Homi. "Of Mimicry and Man: The Ambivalence of Colonial Discourse." In *Tensions of Empire: Colonial Cultures in a Bourgeois World*, ed. Frederick Cooper and Ann Laura Stoler. Berkeley: University of California Press, 1997.

Birnbaum, Pierre. *Anti-Semitism in France: A Political History from Léon Blum to the Present*. Oxford: Blackwell Publishers, 1992.

The Antisemitic Moment: A Tour of France in 1898. New York: Hill and Wang, 2004.

"French Jews and the 'Regeneration' of Algerian Jewry." *Studies in Contemporary Jewry: Jews and the State: Dangerous Alliances and the Perils of Privilege*, Vol. 19 (2003): 88–103.

The Jews of the Republic: A Political History of State Jews in France from Gambetta to Vichy. Stanford: Stanford University Press, 1996.

Birnbaum, Pierre and Ira Katznelson. *Paths of Emancipation: Jews, States, and Citizenship*. Princeton: Princeton University Press, 1995.

Blévis, Laure. "Les avatars de la citoyenneté en Algérie coloniale ou les paradoxes d'une catégorisation." *Droit et Société*, No. 48 (2001): 557–581.

"La citoyenneté française au miroir de la colonization: étude des demandes de naturalisation des 'sujets français' en Algérie colonial." *Genèses*, Vol. 4, No. 53 (2003): 25–47.

"De la cause du droit à la cause anticoloniale. Les interventions de la Ligue des droits de l'homme en faveur des 'indigènes' algériens pendant l'entre-deux-guerres." *Politix*, Vol. 16, No. 62 (2003): 39–64.

"Sociologie d'un droit colonial. Citoyenneté et nationalité en Algeria (1865–1947): Une exception républicaine." PhD Dissertation, Institut d'Études Politiques, Aix-en-Provence, 2004.

Bloch, Marc. *L'étrange defaite: Témoignage écrit en 1940*. Paris: Éditions Gallimard, 1990.

L'Histoire, la guerre, a la résistance, ed. Annette Becker and Étienne Bloch. Paris: Éditions Gallimard, 2006.

Bostom, Andrew G. ed. *The Legacy of Islamic Antisemitism: From Sacred Texts to Solemn History*. Amherst: Prometheus Books, 2008.

Bouaboud, Idir. *L'Écho d'Alger, cinquante ans de vie politique française en Algérie 1912–1961*. Lille: Presses universitaires du Septentrion, 1999.

Boum, Aomar. "Partners against Anti-Semitism: Muslims and Jews Respond to Nazism in French North African Colonies, 1936–1940." *The Journal of North African Studies*, Vol. 19, No. 4 (2014): 554–570.

Bouveresse, Jacques. *Un parlement colonial? Les Délégations financières algériennes (1898–1945)*. Mont-Saint-Aignen: Publications des universités de Rouen et du Havre, 2008.

Brass, Paul R. *Theft of an Idol: Text and Context in the Representation of Collective Violence*. Princeton: Princeton University Press, 1997.

Bredin, Jean-Denis. *The Affair: The Case of Alfred Dreyfus*. Translated by Jeffrey Mehlman. New York: George Braziller, 1986.

Brenner, Michael. *Zionism: A Brief History*. Princeton: Markus Weiner, 2003.

Brett, Michael. "Legislating for Inequality in Algeria: The Senatus-Consulte of 14 July 1865." *Bulletin of the School of Oriental and African Studies, University of London*, Vol. 41, No. 3 (1988): 440–461.

Breuer, William B. *Operation Torch: The Allied Gamble to Invade North Africa*. New York: St. Martin's Press, 1985.

Brower, Benjamin Claude. *A Desert Named Peace: The Violence of France's Empire in the Algerian Sahara, 1844–1902*. New York: Columbia University Press, 2009.

Brubaker, Rogers. *Citizenship and Nationhood in France and Germany*. Cambridge: Harvard University Press, 1992.

Burns, Michael. *Dreyfus: A Family Affair, 1789–1945*. New York: HarperCollins Publishers, 1991.

Rural Society and French Politics: Boulangism and the Dreyfus Affair, 1886–1900. Princeton: Princeton University Press, 1984.

Burrin, Philippe. *France under the Germans: Collaboration and Compromise*. New York: The New Press, 1996.

Busi, Frederick. "La Libre Parole de Drumont et Les Affaires Dreyfus." In *L'Affaire Dreyfus de A à Z*, ed. Michel Drouin. Paris: Flammarion, 1994.

The Pope of Antisemitism: The Career and Legacy of Edouard-Adolphe Drumont. Lanham: University Press of America, 1986.

Calder, Gideon, Phillip Cole, and Jonathan Seglow, eds. *Citizenship Acquisition and National Belonging: Migration, Membership and the Liberal Democratic State*. London: Palgrave Macmillan, 2010.

Callow, Alexander B., ed. *The City Boss in America: An Interpretive Reader*. New York: Oxford University Press, 1976.

Cantier, Jacques. *L'Algérie sous le Régime de Vichy*. Paris: Éditions Odile Jacob, 2002.

Caron, Vicki. "The Antisemitic Revival in France in the 1930s: The Socioeconomic Dimension Reconsidered." *The Journal of Modern History*, Vol. 70 (March 1998): 24–73.

Çelik, Zeynep. *Urban Forms and Colonial Confrontations: Algiers under French Rule.* Berkeley: University of California Press, 1997.

Çelik, Zeynep, Julia Clancy-Smith, and Frances Terpak, eds. *Walls of Algiers: Narratives of the City through Text and Image.* Seattle: University of Washington Press, 2009.

Chafer, Tony and Amanda Sackur, eds. *French Colonial Empire and the Popular Front: Hope and Disillusion.* New York: St. Martin's Press, Inc., 1999.

Chatterjee, Partha. *The Nation and Its Fragments: Colonial and Postcolonial Histories.* Princeton: Princeton University Press, 1993.

Choi, Sung. "Complex Compatriots: Jews in Post-Vichy French Algeria." *The Journal of North African Studies*, Vol. 17, No. 5 (2012): 863–880.

Chouraqui, André N. *Between East and West: A History of the Jews of North Africa.* New York: Temple Books, 1973.

Letter to an Arab Friend. Boston: University of Massachusetts Press, 1972.

Cixous, Hélène. *Portrait of Jacques Derrida as a Young Jewish Saint.* New York: Columbia University Press, 2004.

Clayton, Anthony. "The Sétif Uprising of May 1945." *Small Wars and Insurgencies*, Vol. 3, No. 1 (Spring, 1992): 1–21.

Cohen, David. "Le Comité Juif Algérien d'études sociales dans le débat idéologique pendant la guerre d'Algérie (1954–1961)." *Archives Juives*, Vol. 29, No. 1 (1996): 30–50.

"Les Circonstances de la Fondation du Comité Algérien d'Études Sociales ou la Prise de Conscience d'une Élite Intellectuelle Juive Face Au Phénomène antisémite en Algérie (1915–1921)." *Revue des Études Juives*, Vol. 161, No. (1–2) (janvier-juin 2002): 179–225.

Cohen, Jacques. *Les Israélites de l'Algérie et le Décret Crémieux.* Paris: Libraire nouvelle de Droit et de Jurisprudence, 1900.

Cohen, Mark. "Islam and the Jews: Myth, Counter-Myth, History." In *Jews among Muslims: Communities in the Precolonial Middle East*, ed. Shlomo Deshen and Walter P. Zenner. New York: New York University Press, 1996.

"The *Neo-Lachrymose* Conception of Jewish-Arab History." *Tikkun*, Vol. 6 (May–June 1991): 55–60.

Cohen, William B. "The Colonial Policy of the Popular Front." *French Historical Studies*, Vol. 7, No. 3 (Spring, 1972): 368–393.

Urban Government and the Rise of the French City: Five Municipalities in the Nineteenth Century. New York: St. Martin's Press, 1998.

Cole, Joshua. "Anti-Semitism and the Colonial Situation in Interwar Algeria: The Anti-Jewish Riots in Constantine, August 1934." In *The French Colonial Mind, Volume 2: Violence, Military Encounters, and Colonialism*, ed. Martin Thomas, 77–111. Lincoln: University of Nebraska Press, 2012.

"Constantine before the Riots of August 1934: Civil Status, Anti-Semitism, and the Politics of Assimilation in Interwar French Algeria." *The Journal of North African Studies*, Vol. 17, No. 5 (December 2012): 839–861.

"Massacres and their Historians: Recent Histories of State Violence in France and Algeria in the Twentieth Century." *French Politics, Culture, and Society*, Vol. 28, No. 1 (Spring, 2010): 106–126.

Collot, Claude. *Les Institutions de l'Algérie durant la période coloniale (1830–1962)*. Paris: Édition du CNRS, 1987.

Collot, Claude and Jean-Robert Henry. *Le Mouvement National Algérien, Textes 1912–1954*. Paris: L'Harmattan, 1978.

Comité Algérien d'Études Sociales. *Le Livre d'Or de Judaïsme Algérien*. Algiers: CAES, 1919.

Consistory of Algiers. *Installation de M. Moïse Weil, Grand Rabbin, 16 Avril 1891, 8 nissan 565*. Algiers: Imprimerie Franck et Sodal, 1891.

Cooper, Frederick. *Citizenship between Empire and Nation: Remaking France and French Africa, 1945–1960*. Princeton: Princeton University Press, 2014.

Colonialism in Question: Theory, Knowledge, History. Berkeley: University of California Press, 2005.

Decolonization and African Society: The Labor Question in French and British Africa. Cambridge: Cambridge University Press, 1996.

Cooper, Frederick and Ann Laura Stoler, eds. *Tensions of Empire: Colonial Cultures in a Bourgeois World*. Berkeley: University of California Press, 1997.

Coppa, Frank J. *The Papacy, the Jews, and the Holocaust*. Washington: Catholic University Press, 2006.

Coquery-Vidrovitch, Catherine. "Nationalité et Citoyenneté en Afrique Occidentale Français: Originaires et Citoyens dans le Sénégal Colonial." *The Journal of African History*, Vol. 42 (2001): 285–305.

Crane, Sheila. "Architecture at the Ends of Empire: Urban Reflections between Algiers and Marseille." In *The Spaces of the Modern City: Imaginaries, Politics, and Everyday Life*, ed. Gayan Prakash and Kevin M. Kruse, 99–143. Princeton: Princeton University Press, 2008.

Crémieux, Adolphe. *Refutation de la pétition de M. Du Bouzet*. Paris: Imprimerie Schiller, 1871.

Crespo, Gérard. *Les Italiens en Algérie, 1830–1960: Histoire et Sociologie d'une Migration*. Calvisson: Éditions Jacques Gandini, 1994.

Crowder, Michael, ed. *The Cambridge History of Africa Volume 8: From c.1940 to c.1975*. Cambridge: Cambridge University Press, 1984.

Daughton, James P. "A Colonial Affair?: Dreyfus and the French Empire." *Historical Reflections/Réflexions Historiques*, Vol. 31, No. 3 (2005): 469–483.

Davis, Christian S. *Colonialism, Antisemitism, and Germans of Jewish Descent in Imperial Germany*. Ann Arbor: The University of Michigan Press, 2012.

Davis, Moshe. ed. *Zionism in Transition*. New York: Arno Press, 1980.

Davis, Natalie Zemon. *Fiction in the Archives: Pardon Tales and Their Tellers in Sixteenth-Century France*. Stanford: Stanford University Press, 1987.

Debono, Emmanuel. "Bernard Abraham Lecache, président fondateur de la Ligue internationale contre l'antisémitisme. (Paris (3e), 16 août 1895 – Cannes, 16 août 1968)," *Archives Juives*, Vol. 40, No. 1 (2007): 140–144.

Deldyck, Jean Jacques. *Le Processus d'Acculturation des Juifs d'Algérie*. Paris: L'Harmattan, 2000.

Dermenjian, Geneviève. *La Crise Antijuive Oranaise (1895–1905): L'antisémitisme dans l'Algérie coloniale*. Paris: Éditions L'Harmattan, 1986.

"Le Juif est-il Français? Antisémitisme et l'idée républicaine en Algérie (1830–1939)." In *L'Identité des Juifs d'Algérie: Une expérience originale de la modernité*, ed. Shmuel Trigano. Paris: Éditions du Nadir d'Alliance Israélite Universelle, 2003.

Juifs et Européens d'Algérie: L'Antisémitisme Oranais (1892–1905). Jerusalem: Institut Ben-Zvi, 1983.

Derrida, Jacques. *Monolingualism of the Other, or, the Prosthesis of Origin*. Stanford: Stanford University Press, 1998.

Le monolinguisme de l'autre; ou la prothèse d'origine. Paris: Éditions Galilée, 1996.

des Illiers, Gustave. *Le Juif Algérien et la question antisèmite en Algérie*. Alger: Imprimerie Pascal Crescenzo, 1900.

Donato, Marc. *Elisa La Maltaise: Histoire des Maltais d'Algérie, 1830–1962*. Nice: Éditions Jacques Gandini, 2002.

L'Émigration des Maltais en Algérie au XIXème Siècle. Montpellier: Éditions Africa Nostra, 1985.

le Doussal, Roger. *Commissaire de police en Algérie (1952–1962): Une grenouille dans son puits ne voit qu'un coin du ciel*. Millau: Riveneuve éditions, 2011.

Drumont, Edouard. *La France Juive: Essai d'Histoire Contemporaine*. Vol. 2. Paris: C. Marpon & E. Flammarion, 1886.

Duclert, Vincent and Perrine Simon-Nahum, eds. *L'Affaire Dreyfus: Les événements fondateurs*. Paris: Hachette Book Group, 2009.

Dunwoodie, Peter. *Writing French Algeria*. Oxford: Oxford University Press, 1998.

Echenberg, Myron J. *Colonial Conscripts: The Tirailleurs Sénégalais in French West Africa, 1857–1960*. Portsmouth: Heinemann, 1991.

Eisenbeth, Maurice. *Grand Rabbin d'Alger, Les Juifs de l'Afrique du Nord: Démographie et Onomastique*. Alger: Imprimerie du Lycée, 1936.

Elkins, Caroline and Susan Pederson, eds. *Settler Colonialism in the Twentieth Century: Projects, Practices, and Legacies*. New York: Routledge, 2005.

Ellis, Steven G., Gudmundur Hálfdanarson, and Ann Katherine Isaacs, eds. *Citizenship in Historical Perspective*. Pisa: Pisa University Press, 2006.

Evans, Martin. *Algeria: France's Undeclared War*. Oxford: Oxford University Press, 2011.

Fage, J.D. and Roland Oliver, eds. *The Cambridge History of Africa, Volume 6, 1870–1905*. Cambridge: Cambridge University Press, 1985.

Fahrmeir, Andreas. *Citizenship: The Rise and Fall of a Modern Concept*. New Haven: Yale University Press, 2007.

Favret, Claudine. *Les Tribulations d'une Famille d'Alger*. Saint-Cyr-sur-Loire: Éditions Alan Sutton, 2003.

Fitch, Nancy. "Mass Culture, Mass Parliamentary Politics, and Modern Anti-Semitism: The Dreyfus Affair in Rural France." *The American Historical Review*, Vol. 97, No. 1 (1992): 55–95.

Fogarty, Richard S. *Race and War in France: Colonial Subjects in the French Army, 1914–1918*. Baltimore: The Johns Hopkins University Press, 2008.

Forth, Christopher. *The Dreyfus Affair and the Crisis of French Manhood*. Baltimore: The Johns Hopkins University Press, 2004.

Foucault, Michel. "Governmentality." In *The Foucault Effect: Studies in Governmentality*, ed. Graham Burchell, Colin Gordon, and Peter Miller, 87–104. Chicago: The University of Chicago Press, 1991.

Fresco, Nadine. *Fabrication d'un antisémite*. Paris: Éditions du Seuil, 1999.

Friedman, Elizabeth. *Colonialism and After: An Algerian Jewish Community*. Massachusetts: Bergin and Garvey Publishers, Inc, 1988.

Fromage, Julien. "Innovation politique et mobilisation de masse en 'situation coloniale': un 'printemps algérien' des années 1930? L'expérience de la Fédération des Élus Musulmans du Département de Constantine." *Insaniyat / إنسانيات*, Vol. 57–58 (2012): 167–174.

Funk, Arthur. "Negotiating the 'Deal with Darlan'." *Journal of Contemporary History*, Vol. 8, No. 2 (April 1973): 81–117.

The Politics of Torch: The Allied Landings and the Algiers Putsch, 1942. Lawrence: The University Press of Kansas, 1974.

Gale, George. *Dying on the Vine: How Phylloxera Transformed Wine*. Berkeley: University of California Press, 2011.

Gelb, Norman. *Desperate Venture: The Story of Operation Torch, the Allied Invasion of North Africa*. New York: William Morrow and Company, Inc., 1992.

Goldberg, Harvey. "Jean Jaurès and the Jewish Question: The Evolution of a Position." *Jewish Social Studies*, Vol. 20, No. 2 (April 1958): 372–391.

The Life of Jean Jaurès. Madison: The University of Wisconsin Press, 1962.

Gorman, Daniel. *Imperial Citizenship: Empire and the Question of Belonging*. Manchester: Manchester University Press, 2006.

Gosnell, Jonathan K. *The Politics of Frenchness in Colonial Algeria, 1930–1954*. Rochester: University of Rochester Press, 2002.

Graham, Bruce D. *Choice and Democratic Order: The French Socialist Party, 1937–1950*. Cambridge: Cambridge University Press, 1994.

Gruner, Wolf. "Local Initiatives, Central Coordination: German Municipal Administration and the Holocaust." In *Networks of Nazi Persecution: Bureaucracy, Business and the Organization of the Holocaust*, ed. Gerald D. Feldman and Wolfgang Seibel. New York: Berghahn Books, 2005.

Guénoun, Denis. *Un Sémite*. Clamency: Circé, 2002.

Guignard, Didier. *L'abus de pouvoir dans l'Algérie coloniale (1880–1914). Visibilité et singularité*. Paris: Presses Universitaires de Paris Ouest, 2010.

Harbi, Mohammed and Gilbert Meynier. *Le FLN: Documents et Histoire, 1954–1962*. Paris: Librairie Arthème Fayard, 2004.

Harris, Marvin. "History and Significance of the Emic/Etic Distinction." *Annual Review of Anthropology*, Vol. 5 (1976): 329–350.

Harris, Ruth. *Dreyfus: Politics, Emotion, and the Scandal of the Century*. New York: Macmillan, 2010.

Hebey, Pierre. *Alger 1898: La Grande vague antijuive*. Paris: NiL Éditions, 1996.

Horne, Alistair. *A Savage War of Peace, 1954–1962*. New York: The New York Review of Books, 2006.

Hunt, Lynn. *The French Revolution and Human Rights: A Brief Documentary History*. Boston: Bedford Books/St. Martin's Press, 1996.

Hyman, Paula. *From Dreyfus to Vichy: The Remaking of French Jewry*. New York: Columbia University Press, 1979.

"New Perspectives on the Dreyfus Affair." *Historical Reflections*, Vol. 31, No. 3 (Fall, 2005): 335–349.

Iancu, Carol. "Du Nouveau sur les Troubles Antijuifs en Algérie à la Fin du XIXème Siècle." In *Les Relations entre Juifs et Musulmans en Afrique du Nord, XIXe-XXe Siècles: Actes du colloque international de l'Institut d'Histoire des Pays d'Outre Mer*, ed. Jean-Louis Miege, Paris: Éditions du Centre Nationale de la Recherche Scientifique, 1980.

"The Jews of France and Algeria at the Time of the Dreyfus Affair." *Studia Hebraica*, No. 7 (2007): 51–66.

Jackson, Julian. *The Fall of France: The Nazi Invasion of 1940*. Oxford: Oxford University Press, 2003.

France: The Dark Years: 1940–1944. Oxford: Oxford University Press, 2001.

The Popular Front in France: Defending Democracy, 1934–1938. Cambridge: Cambridge University Press, 1988.

Jean-Baptiste, Rachel. *Conjugal Rights: Marriage, Sexuality, and Urban Life in Colonial Libreville, Gabon*. Athens: Ohio University Press, 2014.

Jennings, Eric T. *Curing the Colonizers: Hydrotherapy, Climatology, and French Colonial Spas*. Durham: Duke University Press, 2006.

Vichy in the Tropics: Pétain's National Revolution in Madagascar, Guadeloupe, and Indochina, 1940–44. Stanford: Stanford University Press, 2001.

Jockusch, Laura. *Collect and Record!: Jewish Holocaust Documentation in Early Postwar Europe*. Oxford: Oxford University Press, 2012.

Johnson, G. Wesley. *The Emergence of Black Politics in Senegal: The Struggle for Power in the Four Communes, 1900–1920*. Stanford: Stanford University Press, 1971.

Joly, Bertrand. "La Ligue antisémitique de Jules Guérin." In *L'Affaire Dreyfus de A à Z*, ed. Michel Drouin. Paris: Flammarion, 1994.

Joly, Laurent and Benn E. Williams. "The Genesis of Vichy's Jewish Statute of October 1940." *Holocaust and Genocide Studies*, Vol. 27, No. 2 (Fall, 2013): 276–298.

Jordi, Jean-Jacques. *Espagnol en Oranie: Histoire d'Une Migration, 1830–1914*. Calvisson: Éditions Jacques Gandini, 1996.

Jousse, Colonel. "La libération de l'Afrique du Nord et la résistance nord-Africaine." *Esprit* Vol. 13, new series (January 1945): 194–208.

Kalman, Julie. *Rethinking Antisemitism in Nineteenth-Century France*. New York: Cambridge University Press, 2010.

Kalman, Samuel. *The Extreme Right in Interwar France: The Faisceau and the Croix de Feu*. Burlington: Ashgate Publishing Company, 2008.

"Fascism and Algérianité: The Croix de Feu and the Indigenous Question in 1930s Algeria." In *The French Colonial Mind, Volume 2: Violence, Military Encounters, and Colonialism*, ed. Martin Thomas, 112–139. Lincoln: University of Nebraska Press, 2012.

French Colonial Fascism: The Extreme Right in Algeria, 1919–1939. New York: Palgrave-Macmillan, 2013.

Katz, Ethan. "Jews and Muslims in the Shadow of Marianne: Conflicting Identities and Republican Culture in France (1914–1975)." PhD Dissertation, University of Wisconsin, 2009.

The Burdens of Brotherhood: Jews and Muslims from North Africa to France. Cambridge, MA: Harvard University Press, 2015.

Katz, Jacob. *Out of the Ghetto: The Social Background of Jewish Emancipation, 1770–1870.* Syracuse: Syracuse University Press, 1998.

Kateb, Kamel. *Européens, "Indigènes" et Juifs en Algérie (1830–1962): Représentations et réalités des populations.* Paris: Éditions de l'Institut National d'Études Démographiques, 2001.

Kennedy, Sean. *Reconciling France against Democracy: The Croix de Feu and the Parti Social Français, 1927–1945.* Montreal: McGill-Queen's University Press, 2007.

Kessler, Amalia D. *A Revolution in Commerce: The Parisian Merchant Court and the Rise of Commercial Society in Eighteenth-Century France.* New Haven: Yale University Press, 2007.

Klier, John Doyle. *Russians, Jews, and the Pogroms of 1881–1882.* Cambridge: Cambridge University Press, 2011.

Krämer, Gudrun. *A History of Palestine: From the Ottoman Conquest to the Founding of the State of Israel.* Princeton: Princeton University Press, 2008.

Krase, Jerome and Charles LaCerra. *Ethnicity and Machine Politics.* Lanham: University Press of America, 1991.

Laloum, Jean. "'En vue d'éliminer toute influence juive dans l'économie algérienne . . .'." *Les cahiers du judaïsme: Spoliations: Nouvelles Recherches,* No. 27 (2009): 104–120.

"Portrait d'un Juif du FLN." *Archives Juives,* Vol. 29, No. 1 (1996): 65–71.

Land-Weber, Ellen. *To Save a Life: Stories of Holocaust Rescue.* Champaign: University of Illinois Press, 2007.

Langmuir, Gavin I. *Toward a Definition of Antisemitism.* Berkeley: University of California Press, 1990.

Laskier, Michael M. *The Alliance Israélite Universelle and the Jewish Communities of Morocco, 1862–1962.* Albany: State University of New York Press, 1983.

"Between Vichy Antisemitism and German Harassment: The Jews of North Africa during the Early 1940s." *Modern Judaism,* Vol. 11, No. 3 (1991): 353–369.

"Israel and Algeria amid French Colonialism and the Arab-Israeli Conflict, 1954–1978." *Israel Studies,* Vol. 6, No. 2 (2001): 1–32.

North African Jewry in the Twentieth Century: The Jews of Morocco, Tunisia, and Algeria. New York: New York University Press, 1994.

Lassner, Phyllis and Lara Trubowitz. *Antisemitism and Philosemitism in the Twentieth and Twenty-first Centuries: Representing Jews, Jewishness, and Jewish Culture.* Newark: University of Delaware Press, 2008.

Lawson, Steven F. *Black Ballots: Voting Rights in the South, 1944–1969.* New York: Columbia University Press, 1976.

Lazeau, Henri. *Max Régis: Mensonges et Vérités.* Issy-les-Moulineaux: Imprimerie Nouvelle, ND.

Lee, Christopher Joon-Hai. "The 'Native' Undefined: Colonial Categories, Anglo-African Status and the Politics of Kinship in British Central Africa, 1929–38." *Journal of African History,* Vol. 46 (2005): 455–478.

Lee, Daniel. *Pétain's Jewish Children: French Jewish Youth and the Vichy Regime, 1940–1942.* Oxford: Oxford University Press, 2014.

Lefeuvre, Daniel. *Chère Algérie: La France et sa colonie, 1930–1962.* Paris: Flammarion, 2005.

Leff, Lisa Moses. *Sacred Bonds of Solidarity: The Rise of Jewish Internationalism in Nineteenth-Century France.* Stanford: Stanford University Press, 2006.

Lévi-Strauss, Claude. *Totemism.* Boston: Beacon Press, 1963.

Liebling, Abbott J. *The Road Back to Paris.* Garden City: Doubleday, Doran and Co., Inc, 1944.

Lorcin, Patricia M.E. "Rome and France in Africa: Recovering Colonial Algeria's Latin Past." *French Historical Studies,* Vol. 25, No. 2 (Spring 2002): 295–329.

Loubere, Leo. *Radicalism in Mediterranean France: Its Rice and Decline, 1848–1914.* Albany: State University of New York Press, 1974.

Lunn, Joe. *Memoires of the Maelstrom: A Senegalese Oral History of the First World War.* Portsmouth: Heinemann, 1999.

Mamdani, Mahmood. *Citizen and Subject: Contemporary Africa and the Legacy of Late Colonialism.* Princeton: Princeton University Press, 1996.

Mann, Gregory. *Native Sons: West African Veterans and France in the Twentieth Century.* Durham: Duke University Press, 2006.

"What Was the Indigénat? The 'Empire of Law' in French West Africa." *The Journal of African History,* Vol. 50 (2009): 331–353.

Marrus, Michael R. *The Politics of Assimilation: A Study of the French Jewish Community at the Time of the Dreyfus Affair.* Oxford: Clarendon Press, 1971.

"The Theory and Practice of Anti-Semitism." *Commentary,* Vol. 74, No. 2 (August 1982): 38–42.

Marrus, Michael R. and Robert O. Paxton. *Vichy France and the Jews.* Stanford: Stanford University Press, 1995.

Masson, E. *Max Régis et son Œuvre.* Paris: Imprimerie de P. Dupont, 1901.

May, Ernest R. *Strange Victory: Hitler's Conquest of France.* New York: Hill and Wang, 2000.

McDonald, Terrence J., ed. *Plunkitt of Tammany Hall.* Boston: St. Martin's, 1994.

McDougall, James. *History and the Culture of Nationalism in Algeria.* Cambridge: Cambridge University Press, 2006.

Memmi, Albert. *The Colonizer and the Colonized.* Boston: Beacon Press, 1967.

Pillar of Salt. Boston: Beacon Press, 1992.

Portrait du Colonisé, Portrait du Colonisateur. Paris: Gallimard, 1985.

Merad, Ali. *Le Réformisme musulman en Algérie de 1925 à 1940.* Paris: Mouton & Co., 1967.

Meynier, Gilbert. *L'Algérie révélée: la guerre de 1914–1918 et le premier quart du XXe siècle.* Geneva: Librairie Droz, 1981.

Moore, Clement Henry. "The Maghrib." In *The Cambridge History of Africa Volume 8: From c.1940 to c.1975,* ed. Michael Crowder, 564–610. Cambridge: Cambridge University Press, 1984.

Morris, Benny. *1948: The First Arab-Israeli War.* New Haven: Yale University Press, 2008.

Mouré, Kenneth. "The Gold Standard Illusion: France and the Gold Standard in an Era of Currency Instability, 1914–1939." In *Crisis and Renewal in France, 1918–1962,* ed. Kenneth Mouré and Martin S. Alexander, 66–87. New York: Berghahn Books, 2002.

Msellati, Henri. *Les Juifs d'Algérie sous le régime de Vichy*. Paris: L'Harmattan, 1999.

Musette. *Cagayous Antijuif*. Alger: Imprimerie Ernest Mallebay, 1898.

Naylor, Phillip C. *France and Algeria: A History of Decolonization and Transformation*. Gainesville: University Press of Florida, 1990.

Nirenberg, David. *Communities of Violence: Persecution of Minorities in the Middle Ages*. Princeton: Princeton University Press, 1996.

Noiriel, Gérard. *The French Melting Pot: Immigration, Citizenship, and National Identity*. Minneapolis: University of Minnesota Press, 1996.

Pappé, Ilan. *A History of Modern Palestine: One Land, Two Peoples*. Cambridge: Cambridge University Press, 2004.

Patterson, Orlando. *Slavery and Social Death: A Comparative Study*. Cambridge: Harvard University Press, 1985.

Paxton, Robert O. *Vichy France: Old Guard and New Order, 1940–1944*. New York: Alfred A. Knopf, 1972.

Peyroulou, Jean-Pierre. *Guelma, 1945: Une subversion française dans l'Algérie coloniale*. Paris: Éditions la Découverte, 2009.

"Les massacres du nord-Constantinois de 1945, un événement polymorphe." In *Histoire de l'Algérie à la période coloniale 1830–1962*, ed. Abderrahmane Bouchène, Jean-Pierre Peyroulou, Ouanassa Siari Tengour, and Sylvie Thénault, 502–507. Paris: Éditions de la Découverte, 2012.

Planche, Jean-Louis. "Les lieux de l'algérianité." In *Alger 1860–1939: Le modèle ambigu du triomphe colonial*, ed. Jean-Jacques Jordi and Jean-Louis Planche, 180–203. Paris: Éditions Autrement, 1999.

"Le Parti communiste d'Algérie et la question nationale au temps du Congrès musulman et du Front populaire." *Cahiers d'histoire de l'Institut de recherches Marxistes*, Vol. 36 (1989): 16–40.

Sétif 1945: Histoire d'un massacre annoncé. Paris: Éditions Perrin, 2006.

Poliakov, Léon. *The History of Antisemitism, Volume Four: Suicidal Europe, 1870–1933*. New York: The Vanguard Press, Inc., 1985.

Prochaska, David. "History as Literature, Literature as History: The Cagayous of Algiers." *The American Historical Review*, Vol. 101, No. 3 (June 1996): 670–711.

Making Algeria French: Colonialism in Bone, 1870–1920. Cambridge: Cambridge University Press, 1990.

"The Political Culture of Settler Colonialism in Algeria: Politics in Bone (1870–1920)." *Revue de l'Occident musulman et de la Méditerranée*, Vol. 48–49 (1988): 293–311.

Pulzer, Peter. *The Rise of Political Anti-Semitism in Germany and Austria*. Cambridge: Harvard University Press, 1988.

Radchenko, Yuri. "Accomplices to Extermination: Municipal Government and the Holocaust in Kharkiv, 1941–1942." *Holocaust and Genocide Studies*, Vol. 27, No. 3 (2013): 443–463.

Rahal, Malika. "Ferhat Abbas, de l'assimilationisme au natioanlisme." In *Histoire de l'Algérie à la période coloniale 1830–1962*, ed. Abderrahmane Bouchène, Jean-Pierre Peyroulou, Ouanassa Siari Tengour, and Sylvie Thénault, 443–446. Paris: Éditions de la Découverte, 2012.

Read, Piers Paul. *The Dreyfus Affair: The Scandal That Tore France in Two.* London: Bloomsbury Publishing, 2012.

Reed-Danahy, Deborah. *Education and Identity in Rural France: The Politics of Schooling.* Cambridge: Cambridge University Press, 1996.

Reggui, Marcel. *Les Massacres de Guelma: Algérie, Mai 1945: Une enquête inédite sur la furie des milices colonials.* Paris: Éditions la Decouverte, 2006.

Roberts, Sophie. "Jews, Vichy, and the Algiers Insurrection." *Holocaust Studies: A Journal of Culture and History,* Vol. 12, No. 3 (Winter, 2006): 63–88.

Robinson, Nehemiah. *Indemnification and Reparations: Jewish Aspects.* New York: Institute of Jewish Affairs of the American Jewish Congress and World Jewish Congress, 1944.

Rodrigue, Aron. *Jews and Muslims: Images of Sephardi and Eastern Jewries in Modern Times.* Seattle: University of Washington Press, 2003.

Rogers, Rebecca. *A Frenchwoman's Imperial Story: Madame Luce in Nineteenth Century Algeria.* Stanford: Stanford University Press, 2013.

Rousso, Henry. *The Vichy Syndrome: History and Memory in France since 1944.* Cambridge: Harvard University Press, 1991.

Rudé, George. *The French Revolution: Its Causes, Its History, and Its Legacy after 200 Years.* New York: Grove Pres, 1998.

Ruedy, John. *Land Policy in Colonial Algeria: The Origins of the Rural Public Domain.* Berkeley: The University of California Press, 1967.

Modern Algeria: The Origins and Development of a Nation. Bloomington: Indiana University Press, 1992.

Ruscio, Alain. "Les communistes et les massacres du Constantinois (Mai-Juin 1945)." *Vingtième Siècle. Revue d'histoire,* Vol. 94, No. 2 (2007): 217–229.

Rush, Gary B. "Status Consistency and Right-Wing Extremism." *American Sociological Review,* Vol. 32, No. 1 (February 1967): 88–92

Ryan, Donna E. *The Holocaust and the Jews of Marseille: The Enforcement of Anti-Semitic Policies in Vichy France.* Urbana: University of Illinois Press, 1996.

Saadoun, Haim. "Le sionisme en Algérie (1898 – 1962): une option marginale." *Archives Juives,* Vol. 45, No. 2 (2012): 68–88.

Sachar, Howard M. *A History of Israel from the Rise of Zionism to Our Time.* New York: Alfred A. Knopf, 2007.

Said, Edward. *Culture and Imperialism.* New York: Alfred A. Knopf, Inc., 1993.

Sainsbury, Keith. *The North Africa Landings, 1942: A Strategic Decision.* Newark: University of Delaware Press, 1976.

Simpson, James. "Cooperation and Conflicts: Institutional Innovation in France's Wine Markets, 1870–1911." *The Business History Review,* Vol. 79, No. 3 (Autumn, 2005): 527–558.

Sarr, Dominque and Richard Roberts. "The Jurisdiction of Muslim Tribunals in Colonial Senegal, 1857–1937." In *Law in Colonial Africa,* ed. Kristin Mann and Richard Roberts, 131–145. Portsmouth: Heinemann Educational Books, 1991.

Sartre, Jean-Paul. *Anti-Semite and Jew.* New York: Grove Press, Inc., 1948.

Schechter, Ronald. *Obstinate Hebrews: Representations of Jews in France, 1715–1815.* Berkeley: University of California Press, 2003.

Schorske, Carl E. *Fin-de-Siècle Vienna: Politics and Culture*. Cambridge: Cambridge University Press, 1981.

Schreier, Joshua. *Arabs of the Jewish Faith: The Civilizing Mission in Colonial Algeria*. Piscataway: Rutgers University Press, 2010.

"'They Swore upon the Tombs Never to Make Peace with Us': Algerian Jews and French Colonialism, 1845–1848." In *Algeria and France, 1800–2000: Identity, Memory, Nostalgia*, ed. Patricia M.E. Lorcin, 101–116. Syracuse: Syracuse University Press, 2006.

Seigman, Joseph. *Jewish Sports Legends*. Dulles: Brassey's Press, 2000.

Sepinwall, Alyssa Goldstein. *The Abbé Grégoire and the French Revolution: The Making of Modern Universalism*. Berkeley: University of California Press, 2005.

Shepard, Todd. *The Invention of Decolonization: The Algerian War and the Remaking of France*. Ithaca: Cornell University Press, 2006.

Siim, Birte and Judith Squires, eds. *Contesting Citizenship*. London: Routledge, 2008.

Simon, Jacques. *Messali Hadj (1898–1974): Chronologie commentée*. Paris: L'Harmattan, 2002.

Le PPA (Le Partie du people algérien), 1937–1947. Paris: L'Harmattan, 2005.

Simon, Reeva Spector, Michael Menachem Laskier, and Sarah Reguer. *The Jews of the Middle East and North Africa in Modern Times*. New York: Columbia University Press, 2003.

Sivan, Emanuel. "Colonialism and Popular Culture in Algeria." *Journal of Contemporary History*, Vol. 14, No. 1 (January, 1979): 21–53.

Communisme et nationalism en Algérie, 1920–1962. Paris: Presses de la Fondation Nationale des Sciences Politiques, 1976.

Slyomovics, Susan. "French Restitution, German Compensation: Algerian Jews and Vichy's Financial Legacy." *The Journal of North African Studies*, Vol. 17, No. 5 (2012): 881–901.

How to Accept German Reparations. Philadelphia: University of Pennsylvania Press, 2014.

Smith, Andrea L. "Citizenship in the Colony: Naturalization Law and Legal Assimilation in the 19th Century Algeria." *PoLAR: Political and Legal Anthropology Review*, Vol. 19, No. 1 (1996): 33–50.

Colonial Memory and Postcolonial Europe: Maltese Settlers in Algeria and France. Bloomington: Indiana University Press, 2006.

Smith, Charles D. *Palestine and the Arab-Israeli Conflict*. Boston: Bedford Press, 2001.

Soustelle, Jacques. *Envers et contre tout: Souvenirs et Documents sur la France libre*, Vol. 2. Paris: Presses R. Laffont, 1950.

Stave, Bruce M. and Sondra Astor Stave, eds. *Urban Bosses, Machines, and Progressive Reformers*. Malabar: Robert E. Krieger Publishing Company, 1984.

Steene, Jean. *Daniel Ulm: Officier Juif et Patriote*. Paris: Henri Fabre et Cie, 1911.

Stein, Sarah A. "Dividing South from North: French Colonialism, Jews, and the Algerian Sahara." *The Journal of North African Studies*, Vol. 17, No. 5 (2012): 773–792.

Plumes: Ostrich Feathers, Jews, and a Lost World of Jewish Commerce. New Haven: Yale University Press, 2008.

Saharan Jews and the Fate of French Algeria. Chicago: The University of Chicago Press, 2014.

Sternhell, Zeev. *Neither Right Nor Left: Fascist Ideology in France.* Translated by David Maisel. Princeton: Princeton University Press, 1986.

"The Roots of Popular Antisemitism in the Third Republic." In *The Jews in Modern France,* ed. Frances Malino and Bernard Wasserstein, 103–134. Hanover: University Press of New England, 1985.

Stillman, Norman A. *Jews of Arab Lands in Modern Times.* Philadelphia: Jewish Publication Society, 2003.

Stoler, Ann Laura. *Along the Archival Grain: Epistemic Anxieties and Colonial Common Sense.* Princeton: Princeton University Press, 2008.

Carnal Knowledge and Imperial Power: Race and the Intimate in Colonial Rule. Berkeley: University of California Press, 2002.

Stora, Benjamin. *Algeria, 1830–2000: A Short History.* Ithaca: Cornell University Press, 2005.

La guerre d'Algérie expliquée à tous. Paris: Éditions du Seuil, 2012.

Messali Hadj: pionnier du nationalism algérien (1898–1974). Paris: Le Sycomore, 1982.

Les Trois Exils: Juifs d'Algérie. Paris: Éditions Stock, 2006.

Stovall, Tyler. *Transnational France: The Modern History of a Universal Nation.* Boulder: Westview Press, 2015.

Sussman, Sarah. *"Changing Lands, Changing Identities. The Migration of Algerian Jewry to France, 1954–1967. "* PhD Dissertation, Stanford University, 2002.

"Jews from Algeria and French Jewish Identity." In *Transnational Spaces and Identities in the Francophone World,* ed. Hafid Gafaïti, Patricia M.E. Lorcin, and David G. Troyansky, 217–242. Lincoln: University of Nebraska Press, 2009.

Szajkowski, Zosa. "Socialists and Radicals in the Development of Antisemitism in Algeria (1884–1900)." *Jewish Social Studies,* Vol. 10, No. 3 (July 1948): 266–270.

Taithe, Bertrand. *Citizenship and Wars: France in Turmoil, 1870–1871.* London: Routledge, 2001.

Taupiac, C. *Les Israélites Indigènes: Réponse a la Pétition de M. Du Bouzet, ancien Préfet d'Oran, Ancien Commissaire extraordinaire de la République par C. Taupiac, Avocat.* Constantine: Chez L. Marle Librairie, 1871.

Tewes, Henning and Jonathan Wright, eds. *Liberalism, Anti-Semitism, and Democracy: Essays in Honour of Peter Pulzer.* Oxford: Oxford University Press, 2001.

Thomas, Martin. "Colonial Minds and Colonial Violence: The Sétif Uprising and the Savage Economics of Colonialism." In *The French Colonial Mind,* Vol. 2, ed. Martin Thomas, 140–176. Lincoln: University of Nebraska Press, 2011.

Tilly, Charles, ed. *Citizenship, Identity and Social History.* Cambridge: Cambridge University Press, 1996.

Trigano, Shmuel, ed. *L'Identité des Juifs d'Algérie: Une Expérience Originale de la Modernité*. Paris: Éditions du Nadir, 2003.

Trigg, Jonathan. *Hitler's Jihadis: Muslim Volunteers of the Waffen-SS*. Gloucestershire: The History Press, 2008.

Trounstine, Jessica. *Political Monopolies in American Cities: The Rise and Fall of Bosses and Reformers*. Chicago: The University of Chicago Press, 2008.

Uchida, Jun. *Brokers of Empire: Japanese Settler Colonialism in Korea, 1876–1945*. Cambridge: Harvard University Press, 2011.

Uran, Steven. "La réception de l'Affaire en Algérie." In *L'Affaire Dreyfus de A à Z*, ed. Michel Drouin. Paris: Flammarion, 1994.

Viollette, Maurice. *L'Algérie Vivra-t-Elle? Notes d'un ancien gouverneur général*. Paris: Librairie Félix Alcan, 1931.

Wardhaugh, Jessica. *In Pursuit of the People: Political Culture in France, 1934–39*. New York: Palgrave MacMillan, 2009.

Weil, Patrick. "The History and Memory of Discrimination in the Domain of French Nationality: The Case of the Jews and Algerian Muslims." *HAGAR, International Social Science Review*, Vol. 6, No. 1 (2005): 49–73.

How to Be French: Nationality in the Making since 1789. Durham: Duke University Press, 2008.

White, Luise. *Speaking with Vampires: Rumor and History in Colonial Africa*. Berkeley: University of California Press, 2000.

Wilson, Stephen. "The Antisemitic Riots of 1898 in France." *The Historical Journal*, Vol. 16, No. 4 (December, 1973): 789–806.

Ideology and Experience: Antisemitism in France at the Time of the Dreyfus Affair. Rutherford: Farleigh Dickinson University Press, 1982.

Winock, Michel. *Nationalism, Anti-Semitism, and Fascism in France*. Stanford: Stanford University Press, 1998.

Wistrich, Robert S. *Antisemitism: The Longest Hatred*. London: Thames Methuen, 1991.

A Lethal Obsession: Antisemitism from Antiquity to the Global Jihad. New York: Random House, 2010.

Younsi, Rochdi Ali. "Caught in a Colonial Triangle: Competing Loyalties within the Jewish Community of Algeria, 1842–1943." Unpublished PhD Dissertation, University of Chicago, 2003.

Zack, Lizabeth. "French and Algerian Identity Formation in 1890s Algiers." *French Colonial History*, Vol. 2, No. 1 (2002): 115–143.

Index